Groups
Process and Practice
SEVENTH EDITION

Marianne Schneider Corey
Private Practice

Gerald Corey

California State University, Fullerton
Diplomate in Counseling Psychology
American Board of Professional Psychology

THOMSON

BROOKS/COLE

Australia • Canada • Mexico • Singapore • Spain
United Kingdom • United States

THOMSON

BROOKS/COLE

Executive Editor: *Lisa Gebo*
Acquisitions Editor: *Marquita Flemming*
Assistant Editor: *Shelley Gesicki*
Editorial Assistant: *Amy Lam/Christine Northup*
Technology Project Manager: *Barry Connolly*
Marketing Manager: *Caroline Concilla*
Marketing Assistant: *Mary Ho*
Advertising Project Manager: *Tami Strang*
Project Manager, Editorial Production: *Katy German*

Art Director: *Vernon Boes*
Print Buyer: *Doreen Suruki*
Permissions Editor: *Joohee Lee*
Production Service: *The Cooper Company*
Designer: *Cheryl Carrington*
Copy Editor: *Kay Mikel*
Cover Image: *Corbis*
Compositor: *Thompson Type*
Printer: *Banta Book Group*

For more information about our products, contact us at

**Thomson Learning Academic Resource Center
1-800-423-0563**

For permission to use material from this text or product, submit a request online at

http://www.thomsonrights.com

Any additional questions about permissions can be submitted by email to

thomsonrights@thomson.com.

Thomson Higher Education
10 Davis Drive
Belmont, CA 94002
USA

Asia
Thomson Learning
5 Shenton Way #01-01
UIC Building
Singapore 068808

Australia/New Zealand
Thomson Learning
102 Dodds Street
Southbank, Victoria 3006
Australia

Canada
Nelson
1120 Birchmount Road
Toronto, Ontario M1K 5G4
Canada

Europe/Middle East/Africa
Thomson Learning
High Holborn House
50/51 Bedford Row
London WC1R 4LR
United Kingdom

Spain/Portugal
Paraninfo
Calle Magallanes, 25
28015 Madrid, Spain

Library of Congress Control Number: 2004107659

Student Edition: 0-534-60795-0

Instructor's Edition: 0-534-60799-3

International Student Edition: 0-495-00573-8

About the Authors

First Edition, 1977   Seventh Edition, 2005

Marianne Schneider Corey is a licensed marriage and family therapist in California and is a National Certified Counselor. She received her master's degree in marriage, family, and child counseling from Chapman College. She is a Fellow of the Association for Specialists in Group Work and was the recipient of this organization's Eminent Career Award in 2001. She also holds memberships in the American Counseling Association; the Association for Specialists in Group Work; the Association for Spiritual, Ethical, and Religious Values in Counseling; and the Western Association for Counselor Education and Supervision.

Marianne is involved in leading groups for different populations, providing training and supervision workshops in group process, facilitating self-exploration groups for graduate students in counseling, and co-facilitating training groups for group counselors and weeklong residential workshops in personal growth. She sees groups as the most effective format in which to work with clients and finds it the most rewarding for her personally. With her husband, Jerry, Marianne has conducted training workshops, continuing education seminars, and personal-growth groups in Germany, Ireland, Belgium, Mexico, China, and Korea, as well as regularly doing these workshops in the United States. In her free time, Marianne enjoys traveling, reading, visiting with friends, and hiking.

Marianne has co-authored several articles in group work, as well as the following books with Thomson Brooks/Cole:

- *I Never Knew I Had a Choice,* Eighth Edition (2006, with Gerald Corey)
- *Group Techniques,* Third Edition (2004, with Gerald Corey, Patrick Callanan, and Michael Russell.
- *Issues and Ethics in the Helping Professions,* Sixth Edition (2003, with Gerald Corey and Patrick Callanan)
- *Becoming a Helper,* Fourth Edition (2003, with Gerald Corey)

Marianne has made several audiovisual programs (with accompanying student workbooks) for Brooks/Cole: *Ethics in Action:* CD-ROM (2003 with Gerald Corey and Robert Haynes); *Ethics in Action* (Institutional Version); and *Groups in Action: Evolution and Challenges, DVD and Workbook* (2006 with Gerald Corey and Robert Haynes).

Marianne and Jerry have been married since 1964. They have two adult daughters, Heidi and Cindy. Marianne grew up in Germany and has kept in close contact with her family there.

Gerald Corey is Professor Emeritus of Human Services at California State University at Fullerton and an Adjunct Professor of Counseling and Family Sciences at Loma Linda University. He received his doctorate in counseling from the University of Southern California. He is a Diplomate in Counseling Psychology, American Board of Professional Psychology; a licensed psychologist; a National Certified Counselor; a Fellow of the American Psychological Association (Counseling Psychology); a Fellow of the American Counseling Association; and a Fellow of the Association for Specialists in Group Work, and was the recipient of the ASGW's Eminent Career Award in 2001. Jerry received the Outstanding Professor of the Year Award from California State University at Fullerton in 1991. He teaches both undergraduate and graduate courses in group counseling, as well as courses in experiential and training groups, the theory and practice of counseling, and ethics in counseling. He is the author or co-author of 15 textbooks in counseling currently in print, along with numerous journal articles. His book, *Theory and Practice of Counseling and Psychotherapy*, has been translated into Arabic, Indonesian, Portuguese, Korean, and Chinese. *Theory and Practice of Group Counseling* has been translated into Chinese, Korean, Spanish, and Russian.

Along with his wife, Marianne Schneider Corey, Jerry often presents workshops in group counseling. In the past 25 years the Coreys have conducted group counseling training workshops for mental health professionals at many universities in the United States as well as in Canada, Mexico, China, Hong Kong, Korea, Germany, Belgium, Scotland, England, and Ireland. In his leisure time, Jerry likes to travel, hike and bicycle in the mountains, and drive his 1931 Model A Ford.

Recent publications by Jerry Corey, all with Thomson Brooks/Cole, include:

- *I Never Knew I Had a Choice*, Eighth Edition (2006, with Marianne Schneider Corey)
- *Theory and Practice of Counseling and Psychotherapy*, Seventh Edition (and *Manual*) (2005)
- *Case Approach to Counseling and Psychotherapy*, Sixth Edition (2005)
- *Theory and Practice of Group Counseling*, Sixth Edition, (and *Manual*) (2004)
- *Group Techniques*, Third Edition (2004, with Marianne Schneider Corey, Patrick Callanan, and J. Michael Russell)
- *Clinical Supervision in the Helping Professions: A Practical Guide* (2003, with Robert Haynes and Patrice Moulton).
- *Issues and Ethics in the Helping Professions*, Sixth Edition (2003, with Marianne Schneider Corey and Patrick Callanan)
- *Becoming a Helper*, Fourth Edition (2003, with Marianne Schneider Corey)
- *The Art of Integrative Counseling* (2001)

Jerry is co-author, with his daughters Cindy Corey and Heidi Jo Corey, of an orientation-to-college book entitled *Living and Learning* (1997), published by Wadsworth. He is also co-author (with Barbara Herlihy) of *Boundary Issues in Counseling: Multiple Roles and Responsibilities* (1997) and *ACA Ethical Standards Casebook*, Fifth Edition (1996), both published by the American Counseling Association.

He has also made three audiovisual programs on various aspects of counseling practice: (1) *CD-ROM for Integrative Counseling* (2005, with Robert Haynes); (2) *Groups in Action: Evolution and Challenges, DVD and Workbook* (2006, with Marianne Schneider Corey and Robert Haynes); and (3) *Ethics in Action: CD-ROM* (2003, with Marianne Schneider Corey and Robert Haynes). All of these programs are available through Thomson Brooks/Cole.

Contents

Chapter 5   *Initial Stage of a Group 131*

Chapter 6   *Transition Stage of a Group* *177*

Chapter 10   *Groups for Adolescents* *327*

Preface

This book outlines the basic issues and key concepts of group process and shows how group leaders can apply these concepts in working with a variety of groups. We hope this book will excite you about the prospect of leading groups and about the value of group work. We are writing primarily for those who want to learn the practical aspects of designing and conducting groups. Based on our teaching of group courses, we are convinced that people learn best about how groups function and how to facilitate them when they become personally and actively involved in the course activities. Your own experience as a group member, prior to taking your first group course, will provide you with a readiness for learning. It is difficult to learn simply by reading about matters that are central to group process such as self-disclosure, working with reluctance, confrontation, giving and receiving feedback nondefensively, and connecting with others. The more you are able to actually *experience* a group, especially from the vantage point of being a participant, the more the concepts presented here will come alive.

In Part 1 we deal with the basic issues in group work. Chapter 1 presents an overview of various types of groups, as well as our perspective on how theory guides practice and a multicultural perspective on group work. Chapter 2 addresses the group counselor as a person and as a professional along with an updated section on the diversity-competent group counselor. This chapter addresses the skills of group leadership and the coleadership model. Chapter 3 has been greatly expanded and now offers updated coverage of ethical and legal aspects of group counseling, and new sections on ethical issues in training group counselors, combining experiential and didactic approaches in teaching group counseling, ethical considerations of addressing cultural diversity in a group, and the ethical issues involved in the use of technology in group work.

In Part 2 separate chapters deal with group process issues for each phase in the evolution of a group. These issues include designing a group and getting one started, working effectively with a coleader at each stage of a group, member roles and leader functions, problems that can occur at different times in a group, and techniques and procedures for facilitating group process. There is updated material summarizing the practical applications of research literature at the various stages of a group. In this edition, we have included a consideration of how diversity influences both the process and outcomes of groups. For example, in Chapter 6 we offer a reconceptualization of resistance and provide a thoroughly revised section on understanding and working with resistance therapeutically. We highlight the necessity of understanding how cultural factors can account for behavioral manifestations that may appear to be problematic behavior. Oftentimes, reluctance and caution on the part of group members can be understood only by appreciating the cultural context of their behavior in groups.

Part 2 includes numerous illustrations of leader interventions in response to the problems often encountered in facilitating various types of groups. In many cases we have provided sample member–leader dialogues to demonstrate our own style of working with group members. Each chapter in this section contains a summary of the characteristics of the particular stage along with member functions and leader functions at each stage of group development. The chapters conclude with several exercises.

In Part 3 we show how the basic concepts examined in Part 2 can be applied to specific types of therapeutic groups. We offer guidelines for group leaders who want to design groups specifically for children, adolescents, adults, and the elderly. We have also updated the discussion of issues in working with these special populations. New to this edition are three group proposals in various settings: groups for children who have been sexually abused, groups for parents who have children diagnosed with depression, and a successful aging group. The 20 group proposals focus on the unique needs of each kind of group and how to meet those needs. New to this edition is additional material on group work in the schools, groups for college students, HIV/AIDS support groups, women's groups, men's groups, group work with domestic violence offenders, group work with healthy aging people, grief work, and research findings with various client populations. Ethical, legal, practical, and professional guidelines for designing and facilitating special age groups are discussed. There is an updated list of references and suggested readings in group work, with approximately 140 new references in this edition.

Groups: Process and Practice is intended for graduate and undergraduate students majoring in psychology, sociology, counseling, social work, marriage and family therapy, education, and human services who are taking courses in group counseling or group leadership. It is also a practical manual for practitioners involved in leading groups and for counselors training to lead various types of groups. Others who may find this book useful in their work are social workers, rehabilitation counselors, school counselors, teachers, pastoral counselors, correctional workers, and marriage and family therapists.

We have developed a self-study student DVD and workbook combination titled *Groups in Action: Evolution and Challenges* that can be used as an integrated learning package with *Groups: Process and Practice*. *Groups in Action* consists of two separate programs. The first program, *Evolution of a Group* (2 hours), depicts central features that illustrate the development of the group process and how the coleaders facilitated that process as the group moved through the various stages: initial, transition, working, and ending. The second program, *Challenges Facing Group Leaders* (90 minutes), demonstrates ways to work therapeutically with a variety of difficult behaviors in groups and approaches to addressing diversity issues in group counseling. The DVD and workbook are sold as a package only, and the workbook, which utilizes an interactive format, requires that students become active learners as they study the group process in action. The *Groups in Action* program is available from Thomson Brooks/Cole.

An *Instructor's Resource Manual* for this seventh edition of *Groups* is now available. It contains multiple-choice test items, essay exam questions, questions for reflection and discussion, additional exercises and activities, guidelines for using the DVD and workbook for *Groups in Action: Evolution and*

Challenges with this book, reading suggestions for instructors in preparing classes, a survey of current practices in the teaching of group counseling courses, transparency masters, and examples of course outlines. We also describe our approach to workshops in training and supervising group leaders, which can be incorporated into many group courses.

Acknowledgments

The reviewers of this seventh edition have been instrumental in making important changes from the earlier editions. Those who reviewed the entire revised manuscript and provided us with many constructive suggestions that found their way into this new edition are Jamie Bludworth, doctoral student, Arizona State University; Patrick Callanan, California State University at Fullerton; Raymond Scott, University of La Verne; Jennifer Smirnoff, University of Toledo; Joy Whitman, DePaul University; and George Williams, The Citadel, Charleston, South Carolina.

The prerevision reviewers provided many suggestions that were incorporated into the new edition. These individuals are Matthew Buckley, Delta State University, Cleveland, Mississippi; Claire Calohan, Florida State University, Panama City Campus; Teresa Christensen, University of New Orleans; Mark Leach, University of Southern Mississippi; Carolyn Magnuson, Lincoln University of Missouri; Brent Richardson, Xavier University, Cincinnati; Brenda Rust O'Beirne, University of Wisconsin at Whitewater; Tracy Stinchfield, Idaho State University; and Margaret Zimmerman, Virginia Wesleyan College.

Special thanks to Sherry Cormier (West Virginia University) who compiled a summary and gave interpretations of survey data for the special groups described in Part 3. Guest contributors provided us with 20 different descriptions of groups they designed, which are found in Part 3. Appreciation goes to the following people for sharing a description of their groups: Jamie Bludworth, Lupe and Randy Alle-Corliss, Sheila Carter, Nancy Ceraso, Teresa Christensen, Elizabeth J. Cracco, Laurie Craigen, Susan Crane, Alan Forrest, Paul Jacobson, Wendy S. Janosik, Deborah Lambert, Stephen Lanzet, Karen Kram Laudenslager, Mo Yee Lee, Michael Nakkula, John Sebold, Jill Thorngren, Adriana Uken, and Ginny Watts. We hope their innovative group proposals and programs inspire those who read this book to think of their own special designs for a group.

Special recognition is due to those individuals with whom we worked closely on the production of this book. These people include Marquita Flemming, editor of counseling and human services, who works closely with us on all our projects; Amy Lam, editorial assistant, who monitored the review process; Katy German, project manager; Cecile Joyner, production editor; and Kay Mikel, the manuscript editor, whose insight and creative editorial skills kept this book reader-friendly. We appreciate the work of Madeleine Clark in compiling the index.

Marianne Schneider Corey
Gerald Corey

Part 1

Introduction
Basic Issues in Group Work

There is a growing interest in using group approaches with a wide variety of populations. When we visit other states for workshops, however, we still hear comments like "My administrator expects me to lead many kinds of groups, yet I don't feel adequately trained." Groups have much to offer, but adequate training in group work is essential to the success of designing and facilitating groups in a variety of settings.

The effort involved in setting up and leading groups is considerable, yet we think that this commitment is essential for successful groups. Groups have immense power to move people in creative and more life-giving directions. But a group hastily thrown together or led by someone without proper training has the potential to be more damaging than beneficial. The purpose of our book is to offer some blueprints for forming and conducting groups in a manner that will release the strivings for health within individuals.

In Part 1 we discuss the fundamentals of group work and provide guidelines for beginning your own work as a group leader. These chapters address the importance of developing a personal style of group leadership and conceptualizing an approach to the practice of group work. We briefly share our own theoretical orientation and describe some aspects that characterize our leadership styles as group practitioners. As leaders, we actively facilitate the group, especially during the beginning and ending phases. Most groups are time limited, and our interventions and structuring are aimed at assisting members to fully use the group process to attain their personal goals. During the initial stage we teach members how to get the most from a group experience. Toward the end of a group we assist members in conceptualizing what they have learned so they can maximize their gains and apply new behaviors to everyday life. ✹

Chapter 1

Introduction to Group Work

3

Focus Questions

*B*efore you read each chapter, we encourage you to assess your current thinking about the concepts or issues that will be addressed. For this chapter, ask yourself these questions: "What experiences have I had with groups?" "How might these experiences influence the attitudes I bring to this group course?" Then, as you read, seek answers to these focus questions:

1. What are the advantages of using both educational and support groups in schools and community agency settings? How do groups address the demand for services in these settings? What kind of group might you be interested in forming and leading?

2. If you were applying for a job leading counseling groups, what theoretical orientation would guide how you design and lead a group? How would you set up a group? How do you view your role as a group facilitator?

3. What are the advantages of practicing within a single theoretical perspective? What are some disadvantages? Do you see value in developing an integrative stance that draws on concepts and techniques from diverse theoretical perspectives? What are the potential difficulties when integrating elements from different theoretical models?

4. Are groups suitable for all client populations? How might you modify the group structure to fit the needs of members of a particular group?

5. If you were setting up a group composed of culturally diverse members, what factors would you consider?

☀ Introduction

In this chapter we discuss our perspective and theory of group work, provide an overview of the various types of groups, and address a multicultural perspective on group work.

Group psychotherapy is as effective as individual therapy in treating a range of psychological problems (Burlingame, Fuhriman, & Johnson, 2004a, 2004b; Fuhriman & Burlingame, 1999; Markus & King, 2003; Piper & Ogrodniczuk, 2004). The benefits of therapeutic groups are increasingly being recognized in mental health settings, and group treatments are more widely used today than they were in the past (Piper, 2001). Piper and Ogrodniczuk (2004) claim that brief group therapy is the treatment of choice for certain types of problems, such as complicated grief, trauma reactions, adjustment problems, and existential concerns. Piper and Ogrodniczuk identify efficacy, applicability, and cost-efficiency as the main benefits of group therapy, and they state: "Given that group therapy is as efficacious as individual therapy and requires less therapist time, it appears to be the more cost-effective treatment" (p. 642).

From our perspective, groups are the treatment of choice, not a second-rate approach to helping people change. Groups are being designed for all kinds of settings today and for many different client groups. Most of these groups are not unstructured personal-growth groups but are short-term groups for specific client populations. These groups are designed to remediate specific problems or to prevent problems.

Counseling groups and psychoeducational groups also fit well in today's managed care scene because they can be designed to be brief, cost-effective treatments. These groups are definitely time limited, however, and they have fairly narrow goals. Many of these groups focus on symptomatic relief, teaching participants problem-solving strategies and interpersonal skills that can accelerate personal changes.

Many of the problems that bring people to counseling are interpersonally rooted and involve difficulties in forming or maintaining intimate relationships. Clients often believe their problems are unique and that they have few options for making significant life changes. They may be at a loss in knowing how to live well with the ones they love. Groups provide a natural laboratory that demonstrates to people that they are not alone and that there is hope for creating a different life. Groups provide a sense of community, which can be an antidote to the impersonal culture in which many clients live. As you will see in the chapters that follow, groups are powerful in part because they allow participants to play out their long-term problems in the group sessions with opportunities to try something different from what they have been doing.

✳ The Theory Behind the Practice

Group Process and Techniques

At the outset we want to differentiate between the concepts of group process and techniques. *Group process* consists of all the elements basic to the unfolding of a group from the time it begins to its termination. Group process pertains to dynamics such as the norms that govern a group, the level of cohesion in the group, how trust is generated, how resistance is manifested, how conflict emerges and is dealt with, the forces that bring about healing, intermember reactions, and the various stages in a group's development.

Techniques are leader interventions aimed at facilitating movement within a group. Virtually anything a group leader does could be viewed as a technique, including being silent, suggesting a new behavior, inviting members to deal with a conflict, offering feedback to members, presenting interpretations, and suggesting homework assignments to be done between group sessions. We generally use the term *technique* to refer to a leader's explicit and directive request of a member for the purpose of focusing on material, augmenting or exaggerating affect, practicing behavior, or solidifying insight. Techniques include conducting initial interviews in which members are asked to focus on their reasons for wanting to join a group, asking a nonproductive group to clarify the direction it wants to take, asking a member to role-play a specific situation, asking a member to practice a new behavior, encouraging a person to repeat certain words or to complete a sentence, helping members summarize what they have learned from a group session, challenging a member's belief system, and working with the cognitions that influence a member's behavior.

We also consider as techniques those procedures aimed at helping group leaders get a sense of the direction they might pursue with a group. In many types of groups, the most useful techniques grow out of the work of the participants and are tailored to situations that evolve in a particular session (Corey, Corey, Callanan, & Russell, 2004).

Our Theoretical Orientation

We are sometimes asked to identify what theory we follow. Neither of us subscribes to any single theory in its totality. Rather, we function within an integrative framework that we continue to develop and modify as we practice. We draw concepts and techniques from most of the contemporary therapeutic models and adapt them to our own unique personalities. Our conceptual framework takes into account the *thinking, feeling,* and *behaving* dimensions of human experience.

Thus, our theoretical orientations and leadership styles are primarily a function of the individuals we are and the experiences we see unfolding in the groups we lead.

An Integrative Approach to Group Practice   We encourage you to look at all the contemporary theories to determine what concepts and techniques you can incorporate in your leadership style. Creating your integrative stance is truly a challenge. It does not mean simply picking bits and pieces from theories in a random and fragmented manner. Each theory represents a different vantage point from which to look at human behavior, but no one theory has "the truth." We make the assumption that there is no one correct or complete theory.

In developing and conceptualizing your integrative approach to counseling, consider your own personality and think about the concepts and techniques that work best with a range of clients. To make effective choices, you need to be well grounded in a number of theories. Remain open to the idea that some aspects of these theories can be unified in some ways, and test your hypotheses to determine how well they are working. It requires knowledge, skill, art, and experience to determine what techniques are suitable for particular problems. It is also an art to know when and how to use a particular therapeutic intervention in a group session.

An integrative approach involves the process of selecting concepts and methods from a variety of systems, and there are multiple pathways to achieving this integration. Two of the most common are technical eclecticism and theoretical integration. *Technical eclecticism* tends to focus on differences, includes aspects from many approaches, and is a collection of techniques. This path combines techniques from different schools without necessarily subscribing to the theoretical positions that spawned them. In contrast, *theoretical integration* refers to a conceptual or theoretical creation beyond a mere blending of techniques. The underlying assumption of this path is that the synthesis of the best of two or more theoretical approaches offers richer possibilities than restricting practice to a single theory.

Although we see many advantages in incorporating a diverse range of techniques from many different theories, we think it is also possible to incorporate some key principles and concepts from various theoretical orientations. Some concepts from the experiential approaches can blend quite well with the cognitive behavioral approaches, for example. For a detailed treatment of developing an integrative approach, see *The Art of Integrative Counseling* (Corey, 2001) and *CD-ROM for Integrative Counseling* (Corey & Haynes, 2005).

A Thinking, Feeling, and Behaving Model   When leading a group, we pay attention to what group members are thinking, feeling, and doing. This entails attending to the cognitive, affective, and behavioral domains. Combining these three domains is the basis for a powerful and comprehensive approach to counseling practice. From our perspective, if any of these dimensions is excluded, the therapeutic approach is incomplete.

We draw from approaches that focus on the *cognitive domain*, which focuses on the *thinking or thought processes* of group members. We typically challenge members to think about early decisions they have made about themselves. We pay attention to members' self-talk: How are members' problems actually caused by the assumptions they make about themselves, about others, and about life? How do members create their own problems by the beliefs they hold? How can they begin to free themselves by critically evaluating the sentences they repeat to themselves? Many of our group techniques are designed to tap members' thinking processes, to help them think about events in their lives and how they have interpreted these events, and to work on a cognitive level to change certain belief systems.

The *affective domain* focuses on the *feelings* of group members. In the groups we lead, we help members identify and express their *feelings*. If members are able to experience the range of their feelings and talk about how certain events have affected them, their healing process is facilitated. If members feel listened to and understood, they are more likely to express feelings they have previously kept to themselves. Many group members can benefit from an emotional catharsis (the release of pent-up feelings), but some cognitive work is also essential if the maximum benefit is to be gained. Thus, we integrate cognitive and affective work in our groups.

The cognitive and affective domains are essential parts of the therapeutic process, but the *behavioral domain* (*acting and doing*) is also central to the change process. Countless hours can be spent gaining insights and ventilating pent-up feelings, but at some point members need to get involved in an action-oriented program of change. Group leaders can ask members useful questions such as these: "What are you doing?" "Does your present behavior have a reasonable chance of getting you what you want now and will it take you in the direction you want to go?" If the focus of group work is on what people are doing, chances are greater that members will also be able to change their thinking and feeling. Bringing feelings and thoughts together by applying them to real-life situations focused on current behavior is emphasized by behavior therapy and reality therapy. These approaches all stress the role of commitment on the members' part to practice new behaviors, to follow through with a realistic plan for change, and to develop practical methods of carrying out this plan in everyday life.

Underlying our integrative emphasis on thinking, feeling, and behaving is our philosophical leaning toward the existential approach, which places primary emphasis on the role of choice and responsibility in the therapeutic process. We challenge people to look at the choices they *do* have, however limited they may be, and to accept responsibility for choosing for themselves. Most of what we do in our groups is based on the assumption that people can exercise their freedom to change situations. Thus, we encourage members to identify and clarify what *they* are thinking, feeling, and doing as opposed to a focus on changing others.

When we facilitate a group, we use a variety of techniques drawn from many theoretical models. Techniques are adapted to the needs of the group participants, and we consider several factors: readiness of members to confront a personal issue, cultural background, value system, and trust in us as leaders. We also consider the level of cohesion and trust among group members when deciding on appropriate interventions. We encourage clients to identify and experience whatever they are feeling, identify the ways their assumptions influence how they feel and behave, and experiment with alternative modes of behaving.

Of necessity this discussion of our theoretical orientation has been brief. For a more elaborate discussion of the various theoretical orientations, see *Theory and Practice of Group Counseling* (G. Corey, 2004), *Case Approach to Counseling and Psychotherapy* (G. Corey, 2005a), and *Theory and Practice of Counseling and Psychotherapy* (G. Corey, 2005b).

Developing Your Own Theory of Group Practice

Leading groups without having an explicit theoretical rationale is like flying a plane without a flight plan. You may eventually get there, but you are equally likely to become confused, waste a lot of time, and become frustrated. Furthermore, if you are unable to draw on theory to support your interventions, your groups may not be productive.

Theory is not a rigid set of structures that prescribes, step by step, what and how you should function as a leader. Rather, theory is a general framework that helps you make sense of the many facets of group process, provides you with a map giving direction to what you do and say in a group, and helps you think about the possible results of your interventions. The "Best Practice Guidelines" (ASGW, 1998) point to the importance of developing a conceptual framework that guides practice and offers a rationale for using techniques. As a part of articulating this general conceptual framework, we encourage you to examine questions such as these:

- How do people change?
- Can people be trusted to determine their own direction in a group, or do they need active leader intervention to keep them moving productively?

- How much responsibility for the group's work lies with the leader? With the members? To what degree should the group be structured by the leader?

- How much personality change is desirable? Should the focus be on attitude change or behavior change?

- What are the considerations for screening or not screening for a group?

- What are the criteria for measuring the success of a group?

A theory can help you to clarify many of these questions.

Ultimately, the most meaningful perspective is one that is an extension of your values and personality. A theory is not something separate from you as a person; it is an integral part of the person you are and an expression of your uniqueness. If you are currently a student in training, developing an integrated, well-defined theoretical model will likely require extensive reading and years of practice leading groups. We encourage you to exchange ideas with other group workers and modify old practices to fit new knowledge, making changes over time.

Throughout this book we stress that your ability to draw on your life experiences and personal characteristics is a powerful therapeutic tool. Particularly important is your willingness to examine how your personality and behavior might either hinder or facilitate your work as a group leader. A thorough understanding of theories applicable to group work, skill acquisition, and supervised experience are not enough to make you an effective leader. You must also be willing to take an honest look at your own life to determine if you are willing to do for yourself what you challenge group members to do.

✳ An Overview of Various Types of Groups

The broad purposes of a *therapeutic group* are to increase members' knowledge of themselves and others, to help members clarify the changes they most want to make in their lives, and to provide members with the tools they need to make these changes. By interacting with others in a trusting and accepting environment, participants are given the opportunity to experiment with novel behavior and to receive honest feedback from others concerning the effects of their behavior. As a result, individuals learn how they appear to others.

Different types of groups require different levels of leader competence, but all group leaders must have some common basic competencies. The Association for Specialists in Group Work (ASGW, 2000) has identified a set of core competencies in general group work. These standards make it clear that mastery of the core competencies does not qualify a group worker to independently practice in any group work specialty. Practitioners must possess advanced competencies relevant to their particular area of group work. The ASGW identifies four areas of advanced practice, referred to as specializations, which we consider next: (a) task groups, (b) psychoeducational groups, (c) counseling groups, and (d) psychotherapy groups. To this list of four groups, we add a description of *brief groups* because of their increasing use in various settings.

Task Groups

Task groups (or task facilitation groups) are common in many organizations and agencies, and they include task forces, committees, planning groups, staff development groups, treatment conferences, community organizations, social action groups, discussion groups, study circles, learning groups, and other similar groups. Task groups are common in community, business, and educational settings. The task group specialist might develop skills in organizational assessment, training, program development, consultation, and program evaluation. The focus of these groups is on the application of group dynamics principles and processes to improve practice and to foster accomplishment of identified work goals. Task groups serve the following main purposes: meeting clients' needs, meeting organizational needs, and meeting community needs (Toseland & Rivas, 2001).

The training for task group leaders involves course work in the broad area of organizational development, consultation, and management. Specialist training in the area of task or work groups requires a minimum of 30 hours (45 hours recommended) of supervised experience in leading or coleading a task or work group.

In *Making Task Groups Work in Your World,* Hulse-Killacky, Killacky, and Donigian (2001) identify the characteristics of effective task groups, which include the following:

- The group has a clear purpose.
- There is a balance of process and content issues.
- A culture exists that recognizes and appreciates differences.
- There is a climate of cooperation, collaboration, and mutual respect.
- If conflict exists, it is addressed.
- Feedback is exchanged in a clear and immediate manner.
- Here-and-now issues in the group are addressed.
- Members are invited to be active resources.
- Members are given time to reflect on their work.

Both leaders and participants in task groups tend to want to get down to business quickly, but focusing exclusively on the task at hand (content) can create problems for the group. A leader's failure to attend to here-and-now factors is likely to result in a group that gets riveted on content concerns and has little appreciation for the role played by process issues in the success of a group. If interpersonal issues within the group are ignored, cooperation and collaboration will not develop, and it is likely that group goals will not be met. It is essential that group leaders recognize that process and relationships are central to getting a job done in this type of group.

It is the leader's role to assist task group participants in understanding how attention to this interpersonal climate directly relates to achieving the purpose and goals of the group (Hulse-Killacky et al., 2001). The balance between content and process in task groups is best achieved by attending to the guiding principles of warm-up, action, and closure. When this is done effectively, task groups are likely to be successful and productive.

Psychoeducational Groups

The psychoeducational group specialist works with group members who are relatively well-functioning individuals but who may have an information deficit in a certain area. Psychoeducational groups focus on developing members' cognitive, affective, and behavioral skills through a structured set of procedures within and across group meetings. The goal is to prevent an array of educational deficits and psychological problems. This group work specialization deals with imparting, discussing, and integrating factual information. New information is incorporated through the use of planned skill-building exercises. An example of a psychoeducational group is a substance abuse prevention group.

Structured groups focus on a particular theme and are often psychoeducational in nature. These groups are increasingly common in agencies, schools, and college counseling centers. Although the specific topic varies according to the interests of the leader and the population of the group, these groups share the aim of providing members with increased awareness of some life problem and the tools to better cope with it. Generally, sessions are about 2 hours each week for 4 to 15 weeks. Some group sessions may be as short as 30 to 45 minutes, especially with children or clients with a short attention span.

At the beginning of a structured group it is common to ask members to complete a questionnaire on how well they are coping with the area of concern. The work of these groups often includes structured exercises, readings, homework assignments, and contracts. When the group comes to an end, another questionnaire is completed to assess members' progress. Psychoeducational groups of this type are useful for a broad range of problems. Here are just a few topic areas for structured groups:

- Managing stress
- Learning assertion training
- Overcoming eating disorders (bulimia and anorexia)
- Supporting women in transition
- Dealing with an alcoholic parent
- Learning anger management skills
- Managing relationships and ending relationships
- Overcoming perfectionism
- Supporting survivors of physical and sexual abuse

Psychoeducational groups can be particularly effective in working with children and adolescents, for this group approach is congruent with the educational experience within a school setting. These groups assist young people in developing behavioral and affective skills necessary to express their emotions appropriately. The emphasis on learning in psychoeducational groups provides members with opportunities to acquire and refine social skills through behavioral rehearsal, skills training, and cognitive exploration. Group leaders in these groups do not necessarily need to possess therapy skills, yet they do need a good grasp of group process and supervised experience in engaging group members in a learning process (Fleckenstein & Horne, 2004).

A variety of short-term structured groups are examined in Part 3 of this book. In addition, the March 2000 special issue of the *Journal for Specialists in Group Work* focuses on psychoeducational group work. Harris, Altekruse, and Engels (2003) describe a psychoeducational group formed to help freshman student athletes adjust to their first semester of college. Some of the topics covered in their 8-session group include time management and study skills, stress management, sexual responsibility, alcohol and drug abuse, career exploration, and life as a student athlete. For other information on psychoeducational groups, see Horne (2003).

Specialist training for psychoeducational group leaders involves course work in the broad area of community psychology, health promotion, marketing, consultation, group training methods, and curriculum design (ASGW, 2000). These specialists should have content knowledge in the topic areas in which they intend to work (such as substance abuse prevention, stress management, parent effectiveness training, assertion training, or living with AIDS). This specialty requires a minimum of 30 hours (45 hours recommended) of additional supervised experience leading or coleading a guidance group in field practice.

Counseling Groups

The group worker who specializes in counseling groups helps participants resolve the usual, yet often difficult, problems of living. Career, education, personal, social, and developmental concerns are frequently addressed. This type of group differs from a psychotherapy group in that it deals with conscious problems, is not aimed at major personality changes, is generally oriented toward the resolution of specific short-term issues, and is not concerned with treatment of the more severe psychological and behavioral disorders. These groups are often found in schools, college and university counseling centers, churches, and community mental health clinics and agencies.

Counseling groups focus on interpersonal process and problem-solving strategies that stress conscious thoughts, feelings, and behavior. A counseling group aims at helping participants resolve problems in living or dealing with developmental concerns. This kind of group also uses interactive feedback and support methods in a here-and-now time frame. The focus of the group is often determined by the members, who are basically well-functioning individuals, and the group is characterized by a growth orientation. Members of a counseling group are guiding in understanding the interpersonal nature of their problems. With an emphasis on discovering inner resources of personal strength and constructively dealing with barriers that are preventing optimal development, members develop interpersonal skills that can equip them to better cope with both current difficulties and future problems. These groups provide the support and the challenge necessary for honest self-exploration. Participants can benefit from the feedback they receive from others by comparing the perceptions they have of themselves with the perceptions others have of them, but ultimately members must decide for themselves what they will do with this information.

Counseling groups range from those with an open structure, in which participants shape the direction of the group, to those characterized by a specific focus. But they all share these goals:

- Helping people develop more positive attitudes and better interpersonal skills
- Using the group process to facilitate behavior change
- Helping members transfer newly acquired skills and behavior learned in the group to everyday life

The counselor's job is to structure the activities of the group, to see that a climate favorable to productive work is maintained, to facilitate members' interactions, to provide information that will help members see alternatives to their modes of behavior, and to encourage members to translate their insights into concrete action plans. To a large extent, counseling group leaders carry out this role by teaching members to focus on the here and now, by modeling appropriate group behavior, and by helping members establish personal goals that will provide direction for the group.

The counseling group becomes a microcosm of society, with a membership that is diverse but that shares common problems. The group process provides a sample of reality, with the struggles that people experience in the group resembling their conflicts in daily life. Participants learn to respect differences in cultures and values and discover that, on a deep level, they are more alike than different. Although participants' individual circumstances may differ, their pain and struggles are universal.

Fairly detailed descriptions of counseling groups for clients of various ages are provided in Part 3 of this book. In Chapter 9 a group program for elementary school children is structured along educational and therapeutic lines, and in Chapter 10 some counseling groups for adolescents are described. There are several examples of group counseling programs for various adult populations in Chapter 11, and Chapter 12 focuses on support groups and counseling groups for the elderly.

Specialist training for group counseling should include at least one course beyond the generalist level. Group counselors should have knowledge in the broad areas of human development, problem identification, and treatment of normal personal and interpersonal problems of living. This specialization requires a minimum of 45 hours (60 hours recommended) of supervised experience in leading or coleading a counseling group (ASGW, 2000).

Psychotherapy Groups

Psychotherapy groups originated in response to a shortage of personnel trained to provide individual therapy during World War II. At first, the group therapist assumed a traditional therapeutic role, frequently working with a small number of clients with a common problem. Gradually, leaders began to experiment with different roles and various approaches. Over time, practitioners discovered that the group setting offered unique therapeutic possibilities. Exchanges among members of a therapy group are viewed as instrumental in bringing about change. This interaction provides a level of support, caring, confrontation, and other qualities not found in individual therapy. Within the group context, members are able to practice new social skills and apply some of their new knowledge.

The group worker who specializes in psychotherapy groups helps individual group members remediate psychological problems. Group members have acute or chronic mental or emotional disorders that evidence marked distress, impairment in functioning, or both. Because the depth and extent of the psychological disturbance is significant, the goal is to aid each individual in reconstructing major personality dimensions. This kind of group explores antecedents to current behavior and connects historical material to the present using interpersonal and intrapersonal assessment, diagnosis, and interpretation.

People generally participate in group therapy in the attempt to alleviate specific symptoms or psychological problems such as depression, sexual difficulties, eating disorders, anxiety, or psychosomatic disorders. A variety of methods are employed in the conduct of therapy groups, including techniques designed to symbolically reexperience earlier experiences and methods to work with unconscious dynamics. The therapist is typically interested in creating a climate that fosters understanding and exploration of a problem area. The process of working through psychological blocks rooted in past experiences often involves exploring dreams, interpreting resistance, dealing with transference that emerges, and helping members develop a new perspective on "unfinished business" with significant others. For a discussion of how to use dreams in group sessions, see Provost (1999) and Ullman (1996).

The specialist training for group psychotherapy focuses on courses in abnormal psychology, psychopathology, and diagnostic assessment to assure capabilities in working with more disturbed populations. This specialization requires a minimum of 45 hours (60 hours recommended) of supervised experience working with psychotherapy groups (ASGW, 2000).

Brief Groups

Brief group therapy (BGT) is a relative term that generally refers to groups that are time limited, structured, last 2 to 3 months, and consist of 8 to 12 weekly sessions. Strictly speaking, brief groups are not a type of group, yet many of the groups described previously are characterized by a time-limited format.

For example, many psychoeducational groups incorporate the characteristics of brief groups into their format.

In the era of managed care, brief interventions and short-term groups have become a necessity. Economic pressures and a shortage of resources have resulted in major changes in the way mental health services are delivered. Managed care has influenced the trend toward developing all forms of briefer treatment, including group treatment.

Rosenberg and Wright (1997) maintain that it is clear that brief group therapy is well suited to the needs of both clients and managed care. Brief groups and managed care both require the group therapist to set clear and realistic treatment goals with the members, to establish a clear focus within the group structure, to maintain an active therapist role, and to work within a limited time frame.

Currently, there is a great deal of interest in the various applications of BGT, largely due to the benefits of this approach to group work. In addition to its cost-effectiveness, one of the advantages of BGT over long-term group approaches is the research evidence pointing to the effectiveness and applicability of brief groups to a wide range of client problems (Piper & Ogrodniczuk, 2004).

What does the research evidence suggest regarding the effectiveness and applicability of brief group therapy? In their review of the group literature, Fuhriman and Burlingame (1994) conclude that group therapy (including BGT) consistently results in positive outcomes with a wide range of client problems. Other reviews of the group literature are consistent in lending a strong endorsement to the efficacy and applicability of BGT (see Burlingame, MacKenzie, & Strauss, 2004; Klein, Brabender, & Fallon, 1994; MacKenzie, 2001; Piper & Joyce, 1996; Piper, McCallum, Joyce, Rosie, & Ogrodniczuk, 2001; Piper and Ogrodniczuk, 2004; Rosenberg & Zimet, 1995; Shapiro, Peltz, & Bernadett-Shapiro, 1998). Among the populations for which BGT shows promising results are cancer patients, those with medical illnesses, personality disorders, trauma reactions, or adjustment problems, and those dealing with grief and bereavement (Piper & Ogrodniczuk, 2004).

In their review of research on brief, time-limited, *outpatient* group therapy, Rosenberg and Zimet (1995) found clear evidence for the effectiveness of time-limited group therapy. Their review also showed that behavioral and cognitive behavioral approaches were particularly well suited to brief group therapy. In addition, long-term psychodynamic approaches could be as useful when adapted to the requirements of brief therapy. Klein, Brabender, and Fallon (1994) report positive results with short-term *inpatient* therapy groups with a variety of client populations and a broad range of problems. Brief interventions and time limitations are especially relevant for a variety of counseling groups, structured groups, and psychoeducational groups. The realistic time constraints in most settings demand that practitioners employ briefer approaches with demonstrated effectiveness.

Although the clinical benefits of brief group therapy are clear, this approach does have some limitations. Piper and Ogrodniczuk (2004) discuss a number of reasons for providing BGT, yet they stress that the benefits of BGT should not be oversold. They emphasize that this approach should not be thought of as a panacea or as a means of producing lasting personality change. For BGT to be effective, it is essential that group leaders have training in both group process and brief therapy because BGT makes unique demands on group practitioners and requires specialized skills.

A Multicultural Perspective on Group Work

The term *culture* encompasses the values, beliefs, and behaviors shared by a group of people. But culture does not just delineate an ethnic or racial heritage; it can also refer to groups identified by age, gender, sexual orientation, religion, or socioeconomic status. Cultural diversity is a fact of life in our contemporary world. You belong to a particular cultural group (or groups), and so do your clients. Culture will influence the behavior of both you and your clients—with or without your awareness. Increasing your awareness of your own cultural values and personal assumptions will help you to work sensitively with culturally diverse clients. This kind of self-awareness is a necessary, but not sufficient, condition for developing competence in multicultural group work. You need knowledge and skills that will enable you to work effectively with a diverse membership.

Asian Americans, African Americans, Latinos, Native Americans, and members of other minority groups terminate counseling significantly earlier than do Euro-American clients. This dropout rate is often related to language difficulties and culture-bound values that hinder formation of a good counseling relationship (Pedersen, 2000; Sue, 1990). Regardless of your ethnic, cultural, and racial background, if you hope to build bridges of understanding between yourself and group members who are different from you, it is essential for you to guard against rigid and stereotyped generalizations about social or cultural groups. In short, you need to acquire a multicultural perspective in your practice.

Pedersen (2000) views multiculturalism as the "fourth force" in the counseling field, along with the psychodynamic, behavioral, and humanistic perspectives. Pedersen makes these basic assumptions about multiculturalism, which have a significant impact on techniques in group work:

- Culture is best defined broadly rather than narrowly so that demographic variables (age, gender, and residence), status variables (social, educational, and economic), and affiliations (formal and informal) are considered as potentially salient cultural features.
- All counseling occurs in a multicultural context given the complexity of every client-therapist relationship.
- Culture includes both the more obvious objective symbols and the more subjective perspectives hidden within individuals.
- Both cultural similarities and differences are equally important in multicultural counseling.

- A multicultural perspective is relevant to all aspects of counseling practice; it is not limited to exotic populations and special interest groups.

- Multiculturalism needs to be understood as a continuous theme in all fields of counseling rather than as an attempt to develop a new and separate field of study.

- Multiculturalism can be the basis for people to disagree without one person being "right" and the other being "wrong."

It is no longer ethically possible for practitioners to ignore their own cultural background or the cultural context of their clients (ASGW, 1999). It is essential that you be open to modifying your strategies to meet the unique needs of the members.

There are advantages and limitations when using group formats with culturally diverse client populations. On the plus side, members can gain much from the power and strength of collective group feedback. They can be supportive of one another in patterns that are familiar. As members see their peers challenging themselves and making desired changes in their lives, it gives them hope that change is possible for them. You can adapt the structure and process of your group to fit the cultural context of the group's members.

DeLucia-Waack and Donigian (2004) point out that the emphasis on the power of group work is based on the Eurocentric assumption of traditional group work, which is that group therapy is more powerful than individual therapy. Although the Western view stresses the importance of group work and acknowledges that groups are a powerful intervention, it is important to realize that groups are not for everyone. Some individuals may be reluctant to disclose personal material or to share family conflicts. They may see it as shameful even to have personal problems and all the more shameful to talk about them in front of strangers. People from some cultures rely on members of the extended family or their clergy for help rather than seeking professional assistance. Some individuals may not feel comfortable in a group or even be willing to be part of a counseling group. Some may be hesitant to join a group because of their unfamiliarity with how groups work. Others may find that what is expected in a group clashes with their cultural values.

Working with culturally diverse client populations requires that group workers possess the awareness, knowledge, and skills to effectively deal with the concerns these clients bring to a group (see Chapter 2). You need to find ways to avoid getting trapped in provincialism, and you need to challenge the degree to which you may be culturally encapsulated (Pedersen, 1997). If you are culturally encapsulated you exhibit monocultural tunnel vision. This involves defining reality according to one set of cultural assumptions. Your cultural tunnel vision traps you in one way of thinking and keeps you from considering alternative perspectives.

Although it is unrealistic to expect you to have an in-depth knowledge of all cultural backgrounds, it is feasible for you to have a comprehensive grasp of the general principles for working successfully amid cultural diversity. What is equally important as having an intellectual understanding about cultural groups is having an attitude that includes an appreciation of the fact that not everyone views the world as you do. Although cognitive learning is important, this learning must be integrated with attitudinal and behavioral shifts. This is a good time to take an inventory of your current level of awareness, knowledge, and skills that have a bearing on your ability to function effectively in multicultural situations. Reflect on these questions:

- Are you familiar with how your own culture influences the way you think, feel, and act?
- How prepared are you to understand and work with clients of different cultural backgrounds?
- Is your academic program providing the awareness, knowledge, and skills you will need to work in groups with diverse client populations?
- To what degree are you now able to accurately compare your own cultural perspective with that of a person from another culture?
- What kinds of life experiences have you had that will better enable you to understand and counsel people who have a different worldview?
- Can you identify any areas of cultural bias that could inhibit your ability to work effectively with people who are different from you? If so, what steps might you take to challenge your biases?

You will need to know much more about diversity if you hope to become an effective multicultural group counselor. We recommend the following sources for educating yourself and acquiring multicultural competence: Atkinson (2004); DeLucia-Waack and Donigian (2004); DeLucia-Waack, Gerrity, Kalodner, and Riva (2004); Ivey, Pedersen, and Ivey (2001); Johnson, Santos Torres, Coleman, and Smith (1995); Merta (1995); Pedersen (2000); Pedersen, Draguns, Lonner, and Trimble (2002); Sue and Sue (2003); Sue, Ivey, and Pedersen (1996); and Yu and Gregg (1993).

We strongly suggest that you now complete the Multicultural Awareness, Knowledge, and Skills Survey (MAKSS) at the end of this chapter. After you score this inventory, look over any items you would like to be able to answer differently. When you finish this book, we encourage you to take time to complete this inventory a second time and compare your results with your initial assessment. Doing this will allow you to determine whether any of your attitudes or beliefs have changed and whether you have acquired new knowledge and skills in multicultural counseling.

✓ Points to Remember

Introduction to Group Work

Here are some key points to remember; many of the following chapters are built on these basic concepts.

✓ Groups have much to offer, but training in both core and specialty competencies is essential to design and facilitate successful groups in a variety of settings.

✓ Groups should be thought of as the treatment of choice rather than as a second-rate approach to helping people change.

✓ It is essential for you to be able to conceptualize what you are attempting to accomplish through the group process.

✓ A general theoretical framework helps you make sense of the many facets of group process, provides you with a map that allows you to intervene in a creative and effective manner, and provides a basis for evaluating the results of your interventions.

✓ An integrative approach incorporates the thinking, feeling, and doing dimensions of human behavior and offers a number of advantages over subscribing to a single theoretical framework.

✓ There are different types of group work, and each of these involves specific training in both core and specialization competencies. The goals of the group, the leader's role, and functions of members vary depending on the type of group work being considered.

✓ Effective delivery of group work involves taking group members' cultures into account. Your challenge will be to modify your strategies to fit the differing needs of the diverse members of your group.

A Challenge to Become an Active Learner

Your ability to function effectively as a group counselor has a lot to do with your beliefs pertaining to groups. If you believe in the therapeutic power and potential of groups, and if you are willing to commit yourself to the disciplined work it takes to learn about groups, you are already taking significant steps toward becoming a competent group leader. If you are suspicious about groups, and if you approach this course with a great deal of hesitation, we challenge you to talk about your reservations and concerns either in the class, if this is appropriate, or with your instructor privately. You will get much more from reading this book and taking a group course or group workshop if you commit yourself to being active, involved, and open to learning about the group process. This is an excellent time to challenge any misconceptions you may have about groups and identify what you need to do to become a productive member of a group. The steps you take now will help you become a vital and creative group leader.

Exercises

The exercises at the end of each chapter can be done on your own or in class in small groups. The goal is to provide you with an opportunity to experience techniques, issues, group processes, and potential problems that can occur at various stages of a group's development. We suggest that you read the exercises at the end of each chapter and focus on those most meaningful to you.

The Multicultural Awareness, Knowledge, and Skills Survey (MAKSS) that follows has been condensed from a 60-item survey designed by Michael D'Andrea, Judy Daniels, and Ronald Heck, all from the University of Hawaii. Respond to all 30 items on the scale, even if you are not working with clients or actively conducting groups. Base your response on what you think at this time. Try to assess yourself as honestly as possible rather than answering in the way you think would be desirable.

The MAKSS is designed as a self-assessment of your multicultural counseling awareness, knowledge, and skills. This shortened form is divided into three sections: Items 1 to 10 provide a measure of multicultural counseling awareness; items 11 to 20 provide a measure of multicultural counseling knowledge; items 21 to 30 provide a measure of multicultural counseling skills.

The Multicultural Awareness, Knowledge, and Skills Survey (MAKSS)*

Multicultural Awareness

1. One of the potential negative consequences about gaining information concerning specific cultures is that students might stereotype members of those cultural groups according to the information they have gained.

   Strongly disagree   **Disagree**   **Agree**   **Strongly agree**

2. At this time in your life, how would you rate yourself in terms of understanding how your cultural background has influenced the way you think and act?

   Very limited   **Limited**   **Fairly aware**   **Very aware**

3. At this point in your life, how would you rate your understanding of the impact of the way you think and act when interacting with persons of different cultural backgrounds?

   Very limited   **Limited**   **Fairly aware**   **Very aware**

4. The human service professions, especially counseling and clinical psychology, have failed to meet the mental health needs of ethnic minorities.

   Strongly disagree   **Disagree**   **Agree**   **Strongly agree**

5. At the present time, how would you generally rate yourself in terms of being able to accurately compare your own cultural perspective with that of a person from another culture?

   Very limited   **Limited**   **Good**   **Very good**

6. The criteria of self-awareness, self-fulfillment, and self-discovery are important measures in most counseling sessions.

   Strongly disagree   **Disagree**   **Agree**   **Strongly agree**

7. Promoting a client's sense of psychological independence is usually a safe goal to strive for in most counseling situations.

Strongly disagree   **Disagree**   **Agree**   **Strongly agree**

8. How would you react to the following statement? In general, counseling services should be directed toward assisting clients to adjust to stressful environmental situations.

Strongly disagree   **Disagree**   **Agree**   **Strongly agree**

9. Psychological problems vary with the culture of the client.

Strongly disagree   **Disagree**   **Agree**   **Strongly agree**

10. There are some basic counseling skills that are applicable to create successful outcomes regardless of the client's cultural background.

Strongly disagree   **Disagree**   **Agree**   **Strongly agree**

Multicultural Knowledge

At the present time, how would you rate your own understanding of the following terms:

11. Culture

Very limited   **Limited**   **Good**   **Very good**

12. Ethnicity

Very limited   **Limited**   **Good**   **Very good**

13. Racism

Very limited   **Limited**   **Good**   **Very good**

14. Prejudice

Very limited   **Limited**   **Good**   **Very good**

15. Multicultural Counseling

Very limited   **Limited**   **Good**   **Very good**

16. Ethnocentrism

Very limited   **Limited**   **Good**   **Very good**

17. Cultural Encapsulation

Very limited   **Limited**   **Good**   **Very good**

18. In counseling, clients from different ethnic/cultural backgrounds should be given the same treatment that white mainstream clients receive.

Strongly disagree   **Disagree**   **Agree**   **Strongly agree**

19. The difficulty with the concept of "integration" is its implicit bias in favor of the dominant culture.

Strongly disagree   **Disagree**   **Agree**   **Strongly agree**

20. Racial and ethnic persons are underrepresented in clinical and counseling psychology.

Strongly disagree   **Disagree**   **Agree**   **Strongly agree**

Multicultural Skills

21. How would you rate your ability to conduct an effective counseling interview with a person from a cultural background significantly different from your own?

Very limited   **Limited**   **Good**   **Very good**

22. How would you rate your ability to effectively assess the mental health needs of a person from a cultural background significantly different from your own?

Very limited   **Limited**   **Good**   **Very good**

23. In general, how would you rate yourself in terms of being able to effectively deal with biases, discrimination, and prejudices directed at you by a client in a counseling setting?

Very limited   **Limited**   **Good**   **Very good**

24. How well would you rate your ability to accurately identify culturally biased assumptions as they relate to your professional training?

Very limited   **Limited**   **Good**   **Very good**

25. In general, how would you rate your skill level in terms of being able to provide appropriate counseling services to culturally different clients?

Very limited   **Limited**   **Good**   **Very good**

26. How would you rate your ability to effectively secure information and resources to better serve culturally different clients?

Very limited   **Limited**   **Good**   **Very good**

27. How would you rate your ability to accurately assess the mental health needs of women?

Very limited   **Limited**   **Good**   **Very good**

28. How would you rate your ability to accurately assess the mental health needs of men?

Very limited   **Limited**   **Good**   **Very good**

29. How well would you rate your ability to accurately assess the mental health needs of older adults?

Very limited   **Limited**   **Good**   **Very good**

30. How well would you rate your ability to accurately assess the mental health needs of persons who come from very poor socioeconomic backgrounds?

Very limited   **Limited**   **Good**   **Very good**

Utilizing This Self-Assessment Inventory as a Pretest and Posttest

Once you have completed the self-assessment inventory, look at the specific items you rated as "very limited" and use them to identify areas that need strengthening. The aim of this survey is to assess where you are now with respect to multicultural awareness, knowledge, and skills. Do you notice any specific strengths or weaknesses among these three areas? In which areas do you have the most strengths? Which areas need the most improvement? Do you have any ideas of how you can increase your multicultural competence in the areas of awareness, knowledge, and skills? Reading in the area of multicultural counseling is one way to begin increasing your ability to work in multicultural situations. Remember to repeat this survey at the end of your course and identify any changes that occur in your multicultural awareness, knowledge, and skills.

---

* The MAKSS has been developed by Michael D'Andrea, Ed.D., Judy Daniels, Ed.D., and Ronald Heck, Ph.D., Department of Counselor Education, University of Hawaii, Manoa, 1776 University Ave., WA2-221, Honolulu, Hawaii 96822; (808) 956-7904. Used by permission.

InfoTrac College Edition

For additional readings, explore InfoTrac College Edition, our online library, at http://www.infotrac.college.com/wadsworth. The following keywords are listed in such a way as to enable the InfoTrac College Edition search engine to locate a wider range of articles. The keywords should be entered exactly as listed, to include asterisks, "w1," "w2," "AND," and other search engine tools.

- work w1 group* AND psych*
- group* w2 couns*
- therapy w2 group* AND psych*
- diversity AND psych* AND group*
- multicult* AND psych* AND group*
- brief group therapy

Chapter 2

The Group Counselor
Person and Professional

Focus Questions

*B*eginning group leaders face a number of concerns when setting up and leading groups. Before you begin reading, ask yourself these questions: "What concerns do I have about leading a group?" "What personal characteristics, skills, and specialized knowledge do I associate with effective group leadership?" As you read this chapter, strive to answer these focus questions:

1. What skills for leading a group do you already possess? What specific skills do you need to acquire or strengthen?

2. To what extent do you think your fear of making mistakes (or perfectionistic standards) might prevent you from being as creative as you would like to be in facilitating a group?

3. When you think about designing and leading groups, what is the major potential problem that you anticipate you will encounter? How might you deal with this challenge?

4. What single personal characteristic do you think is likely to be your main asset in effectively leading groups? What single personal characteristic is most likely to impede your effectiveness as a group leader?

5. In leading a group characterized by many forms of diversity, what do you expect would be your main challenges? To what degree are you confident of your ability to conduct groups characterized by culturally diverse membership?

6. What specific knowledge and skills do you most need to acquire to enhance your effectiveness when working with group members who are culturally different from you? What are a few steps you can take to become culturally competent?

7. How might you modify the techniques you use in a group to suit the specific needs of clients from diverse backgrounds? How can you determine the effectiveness of the techniques you employ in a culturally diverse group?

8. What are some advantages and disadvantages of coleadership of a group, both for the members and for the coleaders? In choosing a coleader, what specific qualities would you most look for?

☀ Introduction

This chapter deals with the influence of the group counselor, both as a person and as a professional, on the direction a group takes. First, we consider the counselor as a person, addressing problems faced by beginning group leaders and the personal qualities of effective leadership. Then, looking at the group counselor as a professional, we consider the specific skills of group leadership, what it means to become an effective multicultural group counselor, and the coleadership model. Finally, we address the notion of developing a research orientation to practice.

✳ The Group Counselor as a Person

The professional practice of leading groups is bound up with who the counselor is as a person. Indeed, the leader's ability to establish solid relationships with others in the group is probably the most important tool he or she has in facilitating group process. As a group leader, you bring your personal qualities, values, and life experiences to every group. The person you are acts as a catalyst for bringing about change in the groups you lead. To promote growth in members' lives, you need to be committed to reflection and growth in your own life.

If you hope to inspire others to get the most out of living, it is imperative that you keep yourself vital. You need to have a purpose for living if you hope to challenge the members of your group to create meaning in their lives. If you are a student, now is a good time to begin this personal quest. How you deal with the stresses and anxieties of a training program have important implications for how you will function as a group counselor in the field (see M. Corey & Corey, 2003).

Problems and Issues Facing Beginning Group Leaders

Those who are just beginning to lead groups typically feel overwhelmed by the problems they face. Those new to group work often ask themselves questions such as these:

- Will I be able to get the group started? How?
- What techniques should I use?
- Should I wait for the group to initiate activity?
- Do I have what it takes to follow through once something has been initiated?
- What if I like some people more than others?
- What if I make mistakes? Can I cause someone serious psychological harm?
- Do I know enough theory? Can I apply whatever I do know in groups?
- Should I share my anxiety with my group?
- What do I do if there is a prolonged silence?
- How much should I participate in or involve myself in a personal way in the groups I lead?
- Will I have the knowledge and skills to work effectively with clients who are culturally different from me?
- What if the entire group attacks me?
- How do I know whether the group is helping people change?
- How can I work with so many people at one time?

Whether you are a beginning group leader or a seasoned one, successful groups cannot be guaranteed. You are sure to make mistakes, and, if you can admit them, you will learn from them. It is important that you not be harshly critical of yourself, imposing standards of perfection. In supervising group leaders, we tell trainees that the fear of making mistakes can stifle their creativity and their ability to remain in the present. For example, when we are processing a group that students have facilitated in class, we ask students to share observations they had during the group work. Oftentimes trainees are very insightful, yet they keep their observations and insights to themselves because of their concern that they might say the "wrong" thing. (For more on how you can learn from your mistakes as a group leader, see Conyne, 1999.)

One problem you will probably face as a beginning group leader is negative reactions from members. You need to learn how to constructively confront those who have these reactions. If you become defensive, the members may, in turn, become increasingly defensive. Allowing an undercurrent of these unresolved issues to continue will sabotage any further work. Later in this section and at different places in this book we suggest ways to deal with these situations.

It takes time to develop leadership skills, and beginning group leaders may feel like quitting after leading only a few sessions. Some people expect to be accomplished leaders without experiencing the self-doubts and fears that may be necessary to their development as leaders. Others feel devastated if they don't receive an abundance of positive feedback. Some struggle with the uncertainty that is a part of learning how to lead well. Nobody expects to perfect any other skill (skiing, playing the guitar, making pottery) in a few introductory lessons, and becoming an accomplished group leader is no different. Those who finally experience success at these endeavors are the ones who have the endurance to progress in increments.

There is probably no better teacher than experience, but unguided experience is often unsatisfactory. We cannot stress enough the importance of supervision by experienced group leaders. Immediate feedback—from a supervisor, from coleaders, or from other students in a training group—enables leaders to profit from their experience. Group supervision of group leaders offers unique opportunities for both cognitive and affective learning because it provides a way to experience group process, to observe models of group leadership, and to receive feedback from many perspectives (DeLucia-Waack & Fauth, 2004).

Personal Characteristics of the Effective Group Leader

In our view who the counselor is as a person is one of the most significant variables influencing the group's success or failure. In discussing the personality characteristics of the effective group practitioner with some of our colleagues, we have found that it is difficult to list all the traits of successful leaders and even more difficult to agree on one particular personality type associated with effective leadership. Following are some aspects of a group leader's personality that we deem to be especially important. As you read about each of these dimensions, reflect on how it applies to you. Consider the degree to which you are at least on the road to acquiring the traits essential for your success as a group leader.

Courage   A critical personal trait of effective group leaders is courage. Courage is demonstrated through your willingness (a) to be vulnerable at times, admitting mistakes and imperfections and taking the same risks you expect group members to take; (b) to confront others but to stay "with" them as you work out conflicts; (c) to act on your beliefs and hunches; (d) to be emotionally affected by others and to draw on your experiences to identify with them; (e) to examine your life; and (f) to be direct and honest with members in a caring and respectful way.

Willingness to Model   One of the best ways to teach desired behaviors is by modeling them in the group. Through your behavior and the attitudes conveyed by it, you can create such group norms as openness, seriousness of purpose, acceptance of others, respect for a diversity of values, and the desirability of taking risks. Remember that you teach largely by example—by doing what you expect members to do. Realize that your role differs from that of the group member, but do not hide behind a professional facade. Engaging in honest, appropriate, and timely self-disclosure can be a way to fulfill the leadership function of modeling.

Presence   The ability to be present with group members is extremely important. Presence involves being touched by others' pain, struggles, and joys. However, it also involves not becoming overwhelmed by a member's pain. Presence implies not being distracted, but being fully attentive to what is going on in the moment. Some members may elicit anger in a group leader, and others may evoke pain, sadness, guilt, or happiness. You become more emotionally involved with others by paying close attention to your own reactions. This does not mean that you will necessarily talk about the situation in your own life that caused you the pain or evoked the anger. It means that you will allow yourself to experience these feelings, even for just a few moments. Fully experiencing emotions gives you the ability to be compassionate and empathic with others. As you are moved by others' experiences, it is equally important to maintain your boundaries and to avoid the trap of overidentifying with your clients' situations.

To increase your ability to be present, spend some time alone before leading a group and block out distractions as much as possible. It is good to prepare yourself by thinking about the people in the group and about how you might increase your involvement with them.

Goodwill, Genuineness, and Caring   A sincere interest in the welfare of others is essential in a group leader. Your main job in the group is to help members get what they are coming for, not to get in their way. Caring involves respecting, trusting, and valuing people. It may be exceedingly difficult for you to care for certain group members, but we hope you will at least want to care. It is vital that you become aware of what kind of people you care for and what kind you find it difficult to care for.

There are various ways of exhibiting a caring attitude. One way is by inviting a client to participate and allowing that person to decide how far to go. Or you can observe discrepancies between a client's words and behavior, and also confront that person in a way that doesn't intensify fear and resistance. Another way to express caring is by giving warmth, concern, and support when, and only when, you genuinely feel it toward a person.

Belief in Group Process   We are convinced that a deep confidence in the value of group process is positively related to constructive outcomes. You need to believe in what you are doing and trust the therapeutic forces in a group. We continue to find that our enthusiasm and convictions are powerful both in attracting a clientele and in providing an incentive to work.

Openness   Openness means that you reveal enough of yourself to give the participants a sense of who you are as a person. It does not mean that you reveal every aspect of your personal life. Your being open can also enhance group process if you appropriately reveal your reactions to the members and to how you are being affected by being with the group. Your openness will foster a corresponding spirit of openness within the group. It will enable members to become more open about their feelings and beliefs, and it will lend a certain fluidity to the group process. Self-revelation is not to be used as a technique; it is best done spontaneously, when it seems appropriate.

Nondefensiveness in Coping With Criticism   Dealing frankly with criticism is related to openness. If you hope to endure as a group leader, you simply cannot afford to have a fragile ego. Group leaders who are easily threatened, who are insecure in their work of leading, who are overly sensitive to negative feedback, and who depend highly on group approval will encounter major problems when carrying out a leadership function. Members may sometimes accuse you of not caring enough, of being selective in your caring, of structuring the sessions too much, or of not providing enough direction. Some of the criticism may be fair—and some of it may be an unfair expression of jealousy, testing authority, or projection onto you of feelings for other people. It is crucial for you to nondefensively explore with the group the feelings behind the criticism.

If members take a risk and confront the leader and are chastised for doing this, they are likely to feel scolded for taking a chance and may withdraw. Furthermore, others in the group may receive the message that openness and honesty are not really valued. Even if someone verbally abuses you as a leader, it is not therapeutic for you to respond in kind. Instead, model an effective and nonaggressive way of expressing your thoughts and feelings. For example, you can tell the person your reactions and let him or her know how you are affected by the confrontation.

Becoming Aware of Your Own Culture   Knowing how your own culture influences your decisions and daily behavior provides a frame of reference for understanding the worldview of those who differ from you. Openness to diversity is the opposite of being entrapped by a narrow existence, which inevitably will restrict your capacity to understand the psychological world of clients who have different values. Cultural encapsulation, or provincialism, affects not only you but your group members as well. Culturally encapsulated counselors make rigid and stereotyped generalizations about individuals within a particular cultural group and impose their own worldview on the members of their groups. This narrowness demonstrates a lack of respect for the complexity of the human struggles that grow out of various cultural backgrounds. If you have a sense of your own culture and of how your values are influenced by your social environment, you have a basis for understanding the world of those who are different from you in a number of respects. If you genuinely respect the differences among the members of your groups and are open to learning from them, you are well on the road to winning their trust.

Willingness to Seek New Experiences   It is important to learn about human struggles by recognizing and wrestling with your own life issues. If you have lived a fairly sheltered life and have known little pain and strife, how can you empathize with clients who have suffered and have made dramatic life choices? If you have never experienced loneliness, joy, anguish, or uncertainty, what basis do you have for tuning in to the pain that your clients experience? Although it is not possible for you to experience directly everything that you encounter in others, you can and should draw on your own emotions in working with group members. It is unrealistic to expect yourself to have experienced the same problems as all of your clients, but the emotions that all of us experience are much the same. We all experience psychological pain, even though the causes of this pain may be different. One basis for empathizing with clients is being open to the sources of pain in your own life without becoming swept up by this pain. It is good to remember that we can only take a client as far on his or her personal journey as the road we have willingly explored ourselves.

Personal Power   Personal power does not entail domination of members or manipulation of them toward the leader's end. Rather, it is the dynamic and vital characteristic of leaders who know who they are and what they want. This power involves a sense of confidence in self. Such leaders' lives are an expression of what they espouse. Instead of merely talking about the importance of being alive, powerful leaders express enthusiastic energy and radiate an aliveness through their actions.

Power and honesty are closely related. In our view people with personal power are the ones who can show themselves. Although they may be frightened by certain qualities within themselves, the fear doesn't keep them from examining these qualities. Powerful people recognize and accept their weaknesses and don't expend energy concealing them from themselves and others.

In contrast, powerless people need very much to defend themselves against self-knowledge. They often act as if they are afraid that their vulnerabilities will be discovered.

Clients sometimes view leaders as perfect. They tend to undercut their own power by giving their leader *all* of the credit for their insights and changes. There is a danger that leaders will become infatuated with clients' perceptions of them as finished products and come to believe this myth. Powerful group leaders recognize the ways in which they have been instrumental in bringing about change, and at the same time they encourage clients to accept their own share of credit for their growth.

Stamina   Group leading can be taxing and draining as well as exciting and energizing. Therefore, you need physical and psychological stamina and the ability to withstand pressure to remain vitalized throughout the course of a group. Some counselors begin a group feeling excited and anticipating each session—until, that is, group members display a range of problematic behaviors, or begin to drop out, or members complain that the group is going nowhere. If you lose most of your stamina at this point, any possibility that the group will be productive may be lost.

Be aware of your own energy level and seek ways to replenish it. It is good to have sources other than your groups for psychological nourishment. If you depend primarily on the success level of your groups for this sustenance, you run a high risk of being undernourished and thus of losing the stamina so vital to your success as a leader. If you work primarily with very challenging groups, this is bound to have an impact on your energy level. Unrealistically high expectations can also affect your stamina. Those leaders who cling to expectations of dramatic change are often disappointed in themselves and in what they perceive as "poor performance" on the part of their groups. Faced with the discrepancy between their vision of what the group *should* be and what actually occurs, these leaders often lose their enthusiasm and begin to needlessly blame both themselves and the group members for what they see as failure.

Self-Awareness   A central characteristic for any therapeutic person is an awareness of self, including one's identity, cultural perspective, goals, motivations, needs, limitations, strengths, values, feelings, and problems. If you have a limited understanding of who you are, you will surely not be able to facilitate this kind of awareness in clients. As we've mentioned, being open to new life experiences is one way to expand your awareness. Involvement in your own personal therapy, both group and individual, is another way for you to become more aware of who you are and whom you might become. It is essential that you become aware of your personal characteristics; unresolved problems may either help or hinder your work as a group counselor. Awareness of why you choose to lead groups is crucial, including knowing what needs you are meeting through your work. How can you encourage others to risk self-discovery if you are hesitant to come to terms with yourself? Reflect on interactions you have had with members of your groups; this is a potentially rich source of information about yourself.

Sense of Humor   Although therapy is serious business, there are many humorous dimensions of the human condition. The ability to laugh at yourself and to see the humor in your human frailties can be extremely useful in helping members keep a balanced perspective and avoid becoming "psychologically heavy." Groups occasionally exhibit a real need for laughter and joking simply to release built-up tension. This release should not be viewed as an escape, for genuine humor can heal. Laughter is good for the soul! If you can enjoy humor and infuse it effectively into the group process, you will have an invaluable asset.

Inventiveness   The capacity to be spontaneously creative, approaching each group with fresh ideas, is a most important characteristic. Freshness may not be easy to maintain, particularly if you lead groups frequently. It is a challenge to avoid becoming trapped in ritualized techniques or a programmed presentation of self that has lost all life. It is important to discover new ways of approaching a group by inventing experiments that emerge from here-and-now interactions rather than using preplanned exercises. Working with interesting coleaders is another source of fresh ideas.

Personal Dedication and Commitment   Being a professional who makes a difference involves having ideals that provide meaning and direction in your life. This kind of dedication has direct application for leading groups. If you believe in the value of group process, and if you have a vision of how groups can empower individuals, you will be better able to ride out difficult times in a group. If you have a guiding vision, you can use it to stay focused and on track with group members when the waters get rough.

Being a dedicated professional also involves humility, which means being open to feedback and ideas and being willing to explore one's self. Humility does not mean being self-effacing. It is the opposite of the arrogance that is implied in convincing ourselves that we have "truly arrived" and that there is nothing more for us to learn. In addition, professional commitment entails staying abreast of changes in the field, reading journals and books, and attending professional seminars.

✳ The Group Counselor as a Professional

Overview of Group Leadership Skills

Although the personality characteristics of the group leader are among the most important determinants of group outcomes, it is a mistake to assume that being a person of goodwill and approaching your group enthusiastically are all you need to lead effectively. Some personality attributes seem positively related to effective leadership, but these characteristics by themselves are not sufficient. Basic counseling skills specific to group situations must be developed. Skill in dealing with diversity is an integral part of becoming a competent group counselor. Later in this chapter, we address in detail the topic of becoming a diversity-competent group counselor. Like most skills, counseling skills can be taught to some degree, but there is also an element of art involved in using these skills in a sensitive and timely way. Learning how and when to use these skills is a function of supervised experience, practice, feedback, and confidence.

Several points about the skills discussed next need to be clarified. First, these skills can best be thought of as existing on a continuum of competence rather than on an all-or-nothing basis. They can be fully mastered and used in a sensitive and appropriate manner, or they can be only minimally developed. Second, these skills can be learned and refined through training and supervised experience. Participating in a group as a member is one good way to determine what a group is about. Leading or coleading a group under supervision is another excellent way to acquire and improve leadership skills. Third, these skills are not discrete entities; they overlap a great deal. Active listening, reflection, and clarification are interdependent. Hence, by developing certain skills, you are bound to automatically improve other skills. Fourth, these skills cannot be divorced from who you are as a person. Fifth, choosing the skills to develop and use are expressions of your personality and your leadership style.

We will now consider some of the skills you will need to acquire and continue to refine as a competent group leader.

Active Listening   It is most important to learn how to pay full attention to others as they communicate, and this process involves more than merely listening to the words. It involves absorbing the content, noting gestures and subtle changes in voice or expression, and sensing underlying messages. Group leaders can improve their listening skills by first recognizing the barriers that interfere with paying attention to others. Some of these roadblocks are not really listening to the other, thinking about what to say next instead of giving full attention to the other, being overly concerned about one's role or about how one will look, and judging and evaluating without putting oneself in the other person's place. Like any other therapeutic skill, active listening exists in degrees. The skilled group leader is sensitive to the congruence (or lack of it) between what a member is saying in words and what he or she is communicating through body posture, gestures, mannerisms, and voice inflections. For instance, a man may be talking about his warm and loving feelings toward his wife, yet his body may be rigid and his fists clenched. A woman recalling a painful situation may both smile and hold back tears.

Reflecting   Reflecting, a skill that is dependent on active listening, is the ability to convey the essence of what a person has communicated so the person can see it. Many inexperienced group leaders find themselves confining most of their interactions to mere reflection. As members continue to talk, these leaders continue to reflect. Carried to its extreme, however, reflection may have little meaning; for example:

> **Member:** *I really didn't want to come to the group today. I'm bored, and I don't think we've gotten anyplace for weeks.*
>
> **Leader:** *You didn't want to come to the group because you're bored and the group isn't getting anywhere.*

There is plenty of rich material here for the leader to respond to in a personal way, with some confrontation, or by asking the person and the other members to examine what is going on in the group. Beginning on a reflective level may have value, but staying on that level produces blandness. The leader might have done better to reply in this way:

> **Leader:** *You sound discouraged about the possibility of getting much from this experience.*

The leader would then have been challenging the member to look at the emotions that lay beneath his words and, in the process, would have been opening up opportunities for meaningful communication.

Clarifying   Clarifying is a skill that can be valuably applied during the initial stages of a group. It involves focusing on key underlying issues and sorting out confusing and conflicting feelings; for example:

> **Member:** *I'm angry with my father, and I wish I didn't have to see him anymore. He hurts me so often. I feel guilty when I feel this way, because I also love him and wish he would appreciate me.*
>
> **Leader:** *You have feelings of love and anger, and somehow having both of these feelings at once doesn't seem OK.*

Clarification can help the client sort out her feelings so that she can eventually experience both love and hate without experiencing guilt. Stronger intervention methods than clarification may have to be used, however, before she can accept this polarity.

Summarizing   The skill of summarizing is particularly useful after an initial check-in at the beginning of a group session. When the group process becomes bogged down or fragmented, summarizing is often helpful in deciding where to go next. For example, after several members have expressed an interest in working on a particular personal problem, the leader might point out common elements that connect these members.

At the end of a session the leader might make some summary statements or ask each member to summarize. For instance, a leader might say, "Before we close, I'd like each of us to make a statement about his or her experience in the group today along with a statement about what is left to think about for future work." It is a good idea for the leader to make the first summary statement, providing members with a model for this behavior.

Facilitating   The group leader can facilitate the group process by (1) assisting members to openly express their fears and expectations, (2) actively working to create a climate of safety and acceptance in which people will trust one another and therefore engage in productive interchanges, (3) providing encouragement and support as members explore highly personal material or as they try new behavior, (4) involving as many members as possible in the group interaction by inviting and sometimes even challenging members to participate, (5) working toward lessening the dependency on the leader by encouraging members to speak directly to one another, (6) encouraging open expression of conflict and controversy, and (7) helping members overcome barriers to direct communication. The aim of most facilitation skills is to help the group members reach their own goals. Essentially, these skills involve opening up clear communication among the members and helping them increase their responsibility for the direction of their group.

Empathizing   An empathic group leader can sense the subjective world of the client. This skill requires the leader to have the characteristics of caring and openness already mentioned. The leader must also have a wide range of experiences to serve as a basis for identifying with others. This is especially important in being able to empathize with a culturally diverse client population. Further, the leader must be able to discern subtle nonverbal messages as well as messages transmitted more directly. It is impossible to fully know what another person is experiencing, but a sensitive group leader can make a good guess. It is also important, however, for the group leader to avoid blurring his or her identity by overidentifying with group members. The core of the skill of empathy lies in being able to openly grasp another's experiencing and at the same time to maintain one's separateness.

Interpreting   Group leaders who are highly directive are likely to make use of interpretation, which entails offering possible explanations for certain behaviors or symptoms. If interpretations are plausible and well timed, they result in a member's moving beyond an impasse. It is not necessary that the leader always make the interpretation for the client; in Gestalt therapy, clients are encouraged to make their own interpretations of their behavior. A group leader can also present an interpretation in the form of a hunch, the truth of which the client can then assess. For instance, an interpretation might be stated as follows: "Harry, when a person in the group talks about something painful, I've noticed that you usually intervene and become reassuring. This tends to stop the person's emotional experience and exploration. What might that say about you?" It is important that the interpretation be presented as a hypothesis rather than as a fact and that the person has a chance to consider the validity of this hunch in the group. It is also essential to consider the cultural context in making an interpretation to avoid mistakenly interpreting a member's behavior. For example, a member's silence may be related to a cultural message rather than being a sign of mistrust or resistance. To interpret the person's silence as a sign of a lack of trust would be a mistake without understanding the cultural aspects of the behavior.

Questioning   Questioning is overused by many group leaders. Interrogation seldom leads to productive outcomes, and more often than not it distracts the person working. If a member happens to be experiencing intense feelings, questioning is one way of reducing the intensity. Asking "Why do you feel that way?" is rarely helpful. However, appropriately timed "what" and "how" questions do serve to intensify experiencing. Examples are questions such as "What is happening with your body now, as you speak about your isolation?" "In what ways do you experience the fear of rejection in this group?" "What are some of the things you imagine happening to you if you reveal your problems to this group?" "How are you coping with your fear that you can't trust some of the members here?" "What would your father's approval do for you?" These open-ended questions direct the person to heighten awareness of the moment. Leaders can develop the skill of asking questions like these and avoiding questions that remove people from themselves. Closed questions that are not helpful include those that search for causes of behavior, probe for information, and the like: "Why do you feel depressed?" "Why don't you leave home?"

Linking   A group leader who has an interactional focus—that is, one who stresses member-to-member rather than leader-to-member communication—makes frequent use of linking. This skill calls on the insightfulness of the leader in finding ways of relating what one person is doing or saying to the concerns of another person. For example, Katherine might be describing her feeling that she won't be loved unless she's perfect. If Pamela has been heard to express a similar feeling, the leader could ask Pamela and Katherine to talk with each other in the group about their fears. By being alert for cues that members have some common concern, the leader can promote member interaction and raise the level of group cohesion. Questions that can promote linking of members include "Does anyone else in the group feel as Katherine?" and "Who else is affected by the interchange between Pamela and Katherine?"

Confronting   Beginning group leaders are often afraid to confront group members for fear of hurting them, of being wrong, or of inviting retaliation. It doesn't take much skill to attack another or to be merely critical. It does take both caring and skill, however, to confront group members when their behavior is disruptive of the group functioning or when there are discrepancies between their verbal messages and their nonverbal messages. In confronting a member, a leader should (1) challenge specifically the behavior to be examined and avoid labeling the person, and (2) share how he or she feels about the person's behavior. For example, Danny has been chastising a group member for being especially quiet in the sessions. The leader might intervene: "Danny, rather than telling her that she should speak up, are you willing to let her know how her silence affects you?"

Supporting   The skill in supportive behavior is knowing when it will be therapeutic and when it will be counterproductive. A common mistake is offering
support before a participant has had an opportunity to fully experience a conflict or some painful feelings. Although the intervention may be done with good
intentions, it may abort certain feelings that the member needs to experience.
Leaders should remember that too much support may send the message that
people are unable to support themselves. Support is appropriate when people
are facing a crisis, when they are venturing into frightening territory, when
they attempt constructive changes and yet feel uncertain about these changes,
and when they are struggling to rid themselves of old patterns that are limiting. For instance, Bing feels very supported when several members sit close to
him and listen intently as he recounts some frightening experiences as a
refugee. Their presence helps him to feel less alone.

Blocking   Group leaders have the responsibility to block certain activities of
group members, such as questioning, probing, gossiping, invading another's
privacy, breaking confidences, and so forth. Blocking helps to establish group
norms and is an important intervention particularly during the group's initial
stages. The skill is to learn to block counterproductive behaviors without attacking the personhood of the perpetrator. This requires both sensitivity and
directness. Here are some examples of behaviors that need to be blocked:

- *Bombarding others with questions.* Members can be asked to make
  direct statements that involve expressing the thoughts and feelings
  that prompted them to ask their questions.
- *Gossiping.* If a member talks *about* another member in the room,
  the leader can ask the person to speak directly *to* the person being
  spoken about.
- *Storytelling.* If lengthy storytelling occurs, a leader can intervene and
  ask the person to say how all this relates to present feelings and events.
- *Breaking confidences.* A member may inadvertently talk about a
  situation that occurred in another group or mention what so-and-so
  did in a prior group. This talk should be stopped by the leader in a
  firm but gentle manner.
- *Invading privacy.* If a person pushes another, probing for personal
  information, this behavior must be blocked by the group leader.

Assessing   Assessment skills involve more than identifying symptoms and
figuring out the cause of behavior. Assessment includes the ability to appraise
certain behavior problems and to choose the appropriate intervention. For example, a leader who determines that a person is angry must consider the safety
and appropriateness of encouraging the member to "let out pent-up rage."
Leaders also need to develop the skill of determining whether a particular
group is indicated or contraindicated for a member, and they need to acquire
the expertise necessary to make appropriate referrals.

Modeling One of the best ways for leaders to teach a desired behavior to members is to model it for them. If group leaders value risk taking, openness, directness, sensitivity, honesty, respect, and enthusiasm, it is essential to demonstrate attitudes and behaviors congruent with these values. Leaders can best foster these qualities in members by demonstrating them in the group. A few specific behaviors leaders can directly model include respect for diversity, appropriate and timely self-disclosure, giving feedback in ways that others can hear and accept nondefensively, receiving feedback from members in a non-defensive manner, involvement in the group process, presence, and challenging others in direct and caring ways. In groups that are cofacilitated, the relationship between the coleaders can set norms for appropriate engagement between members.

Suggesting Leaders can offer suggestions aimed at helping members develop an alternative course of thinking or action. Suggestions can take a number of forms, such as giving information, asking members to consider a specific homework assignment, asking members to create their own experiments, and assisting members in looking at a circumstance from a new vantage point. Leaders can also teach members to offer appropriate suggestions to each other. Although suggestions can facilitate change in members, there is a danger that suggestions can be given too freely and that advice can short-circuit the process of self-exploration. There is a fine line between suggesting and prescribing; the skill is in using suggestions to enhance an individual's movement toward making his or her own decisions.

Initiating When the leader takes an active role in providing direction to members, offers some structure, and takes action when it is needed, the group is aided in staying focused on its task. These leadership skills include using catalysts to get members to focus on their personal goals, assisting members in working through places where they are stuck, helping members identify and resolve conflict, knowing how to use techniques to enhance work, providing links among the various themes in a group, and helping members assume responsibility for directing themselves. Too much leader initiation can stifle the creativity of a group, and too little leader initiation can lead to passivity on the part of the members.

Evaluating A crucial leadership skill is evaluating the ongoing process and dynamics of a group. After each group session it is valuable for the leader to evaluate what happened, both within individual members and among the members, and to think about what interventions might be used next time with the group. Leaders need to get in the habit of asking themselves these questions: "What changes are resulting from the group?" "What are the therapeutic and nontherapeutic forces in the group?"

The leader has the role of teaching participants how to evaluate, so they can appraise the movement and direction of their own group. Once the group has evaluated a session or series of sessions, its members can decide what, if any, changes need to be made. For example, during an evaluation at the close of a session, perhaps the leader and the members agree that the group as a whole has been passive. The leader might say, "I feel the burden of initiating and sense that you're waiting for me to do something to energize you. I'm challenging each of you to examine your behavior and to evaluate to what degree you're willing to take personal responsibility for your experience in this group. Then please think about what, specifically, you're willing to do to change this group."

Terminating   Group leaders must learn when and how to terminate their work with both individuals and groups. They need to develop the ability to tell when a group session should end, when an individual is ready to leave a group, and when a group has completed its work, and they need to learn how to handle each of these types of termination. Of course, at the end of each session it is helpful to create a climate that will encourage members to make contracts to do work between sessions before the next group session. The skill of helping members to bring closure to a particular group experience involves (1) providing members with suggestions for transferring what they have learned in the group to the environment they must return to, (2) preparing people for the psychological problems they may face on leaving a group, (3) arranging for a follow-up group, (4) telling members where they can get additional therapy, and (5) being available for individual consultation at the termination of a group. Follow-up and evaluation activities are particularly important if the leader is to learn the effectiveness of the group as a therapeutic agent.

An Integrated View of Leadership Skills

Some counselor-education programs focus mainly on developing counseling skills and assessing competencies, whereas other programs stress the personal qualities that underlie these skills. Ideally, training programs for group leaders give due weight to both of these aspects. In the following chapter, when professional standards for training group counselors are described, we will go into more detail about the specific areas of knowledge and the skills group workers need.

We want to acknowledge that you are likely to feel somewhat overwhelmed when you consider all the skills that are necessary for effective group leadership. It may help to remember that, as in other areas of life, you will become frustrated if you attempt to focus on all aspects of this field at once. You can expect to gradually refine your leadership style and gain confidence in using these skills effectively.

☀ Becoming a Diversity-Competent Group Counselor

In addition to the group leadership skills already discussed, special knowledge and skills are required when dealing with culturally diverse group members. In this section, we present a conceptual framework that organizes diversity competence into three areas: beliefs and attitudes, knowledge, and skills. As you read, try to become more aware of your own worldview. In Chapter 1 you completed the MAKSS, which assessed your multicultural awareness, knowledge, and skills. As you read and think about the ideas in this section, review your responses to that assessment inventory and make a professional development plan to enhance your diversity competence. Also, at the end of this chapter some activities geared to the DVD program *Groups in Action: Evolution and Challenges* provide concrete illustrations of scenarios in a group that call for multicultural competence as a group leader.

A Starting Place: Understanding Your Own Culture

Effective group counselors must have some level of understanding of their own cultural conditioning, the cultural conditioning of their clients, and an awareness of the sociopolitical system of which they are a part. Pack-Brown, Whittington-Clark, and Parker (1998) maintain that culturally competent group counselors need to be (1) aware of their own personal biases, stereotypes, and prejudices; (2) knowledgeable about the members of their groups; and (3) able to practice skills that are appropriate for the life experiences of their clients.

Competence in the area of diversity includes a deep understanding of your own culture. If you hope to understand the culture of clients who differ from you, it is imperative that you first understand your own culture. If you do not understand how your cultural background influences your thinking and behavior, there is little chance you can work effectively with group members who are culturally different from yourself. It is not necessary for you to have had the same experiences as the client, but it is important to be open to personally reflecting on similar feelings and struggles and that you strive to enter the world of the members of your groups. In your work as a group counselor, it is important for you to transcend your own ethnocentric beliefs and assumptions about the content and process of group counseling. It is also essential to respectfully attend to the needs and perspectives of people who come from cultural backgrounds that are different from your own (D'Andrea, 2004).

The goals and processes of the group should match the cultural values of the members of that group. If you respect the members in your group, you will demonstrate a willingness to learn from them. You will be aware of hesitation on a client's part and will not be too quick to interpret it. Your willingness to put yourself in situations where you can learn about different cultures will be most useful. If you model genuine respect for the differences among members in your groups, all the group members will benefit from this cultural diversity.

DeLucia-Waack and Donigian (2004) suggest ways for group leaders to understand themselves and others as a beginning point in working toward developing and implementing effective interventions in multicultural group work. They propose the following steps that group leaders can take in becoming multiculturally competent counselors:

- Clarify your personal values, beliefs, and how you view people interacting in productive ways.
- Identify the values inherent in your theoretical approach to group work.

- Learn about group interventions shown to be effective with specific cultural groups.
- Identify specific situations where your personal or theoretical values, views, and beliefs might be in conflict with the values of people from diverse backgrounds.
- Avoid imposing your worldview on members of your groups.
- Identify times or situations where you may need to refer a person because of a conflict of personal or cultural values.
- Identify situations when you might need supervision or consultation in working through your biases or views.
- Find a list of sources where you can acquire information about different cultures and potential conflicts related to group work.

DeLucia-Waack and Donigian (2004) emphasize that "you need to constantly think about how your knowledge of culture and cultural values affects how you lead groups, and about how the cultural orientation of group members affects the way they participate in groups" (p. 29).

A Framework for Developing Diversity Competence

Our views about diversity competence have been influenced by the work of a number of writers, including Sue, Arredondo, and McDavis (1992), who have developed a conceptual framework for multicultural counseling competencies and standards. The revised and expanded dimensions of multicultural competency involve three areas: beliefs and attitudes, knowledge, and skill. In addition, Arredondo and colleagues (1996) have developed a comprehensive set of multicultural competency standards, and the ASGW (1999) has adopted "Principles for Diversity-Competent Group Workers." We have condensed the multicultural competencies and standards identified by these sources and adapted them for use by group practitioners.

Beliefs and Attitudes of Diversity-Competent Group Workers   Effective group leaders recognize and understand their own stereotypes and preconceived notions about other racial and ethnic groups. Diversity-competent group workers:

- Do not allow their personal biases, values, or problems to interfere with their ability to work with clients who are culturally different from them.
- Are aware of how their own cultural background and experiences have influenced attitudes, values, and biases about what constitutes psychologically healthy individuals.
- Have moved from being unaware to being increasingly aware of their own race, ethnic and cultural heritage, gender, socioeconomic status, sexual orientation, abilities, spiritual beliefs, and to valuing and respecting differences.

- Seek to examine and understand the world from the vantage point of their clients. They respect clients' religious and spiritual beliefs and values.
- Recognize the sources of their discomfort with differences between themselves and others in terms of race, ethnicity, culture, and beliefs. Because these group leaders welcome diverse value orientations and diverse assumptions about human behavior, they have a basis for sharing the worldview of their clients as opposed to being culturally encapsulated.
- Are able to accept and value cultural diversity rather than insist that their cultural heritage is superior. They are able to identify and understand the central cultural constructs of the members of their groups, and they avoid applying their own cultural constructs inappropriately with these group members.
- Monitor their functioning through consultation, supervision, and further training or education. They realize that group counseling may not be appropriate for all clients or for all problems.

Knowledge of Diversity-Competent Group Workers   Culturally skilled group practitioners possess knowledge about their own racial and cultural heritage and how it affects them in their work. In addition, diversity-competent group workers:

- Understand how oppression, racism, discrimination, and stereotyping affect them personally and professionally. They do not impose their values and expectations on their clients from differing cultural backgrounds, and they avoid stereotyping clients.
- Understand the worldview of their clients, and they learn about their clients' cultural backgrounds. Because they understand the basic values underlying the therapeutic group process, they know how these values may clash with the cultural values of various minority groups.
- Are aware of the institutional barriers that prevent minorities from actively participating or utilizing various types of groups.
- Possess specific knowledge and information about the group members with whom they are working. This includes at least a general knowledge of the values, life experiences, family structures, cultural heritage, and historical background of their culturally different group members.
- Are knowledgeable about the community characteristics and the resources in the community as well as in the family.
- View diversity in a positive light, which allows them to meet and resolve the challenges that arise in their work with a wide range of client populations.
- Know how to help clients make use of indigenous support systems. Where they lack knowledge, they seek resources to assist them. The greater their knowledge of culturally diverse groups, the more likely they are to be effective group leaders.

Skills and Intervention Strategies of Diversity-Competent Group Workers

Diversity-competent group counselors possess a wide range of skills, which they are able to use with diverse client populations. Diversity-competent group workers:

- Familiarize themselves with relevant research and the latest findings regarding mental health issues that affect diverse client populations.

- Actively seek out educational experiences that foster their knowledge and skills for facilitating groups across differences.

- Are able to use methods and strategies and define goals consistent with the life experiences and cultural values of the group members. They are able to modify and adapt their interventions in a group to accommodate cultural differences.

- Are not anchored to one method or approach to group facilitation and recognize that helping styles may be culture bound. They are able to use a variety of culturally appropriate and relevant interventions, which may include consulting with traditional healers and religious and spiritual healers.

- Are able to send and receive both verbal and nonverbal messages accurately and appropriately.

- Are able to become actively involved with minority individuals outside the group setting (community events, celebrations, social and political functions, and neighborhood groups).

- Are committed to understanding themselves as racial and cultural beings and are actively seeking a nonracist identity.

- Take responsibility for educating group members about how groups function, and they use sound ethical practice when facilitating groups with a diverse membership.

Inviting Conversations About Culture With Group Members

One way to actively incorporate a multicultural dimension into your group leadership is to initiate open discussions with the members of your groups about issues of race and ethnicity. Cardemil and Battle (2003) contend that these conversations enhance the therapeutic relationship and also promote better treatment outcomes. We believe their recommendations can be applied to your work as a facilitator of many different kinds of groups.

- Suspend preconceptions about the race or ethnicity of clients or their family members. Avoid making incorrect assumptions about group members that could impede the development of the therapeutic relationship. During the early stage of a group, ask members how they identify their race or ethnicity.

- If you engage group members in conversations about race and ethnicity, there is less chance of stereotyping and making faulty assumptions.
- Be aware that the more comfortable you are with conversations about race and ethnicity, the more easily group members can respond appropriately to others who may be uncomfortable with such discussions.
- Address how racial or ethnic differences between you and the members of your group might affect the process and outcomes of the group. Although it is not possible to identify every between-group difference that could surface during the course of therapy, the critical element is your willingness to consider the relevance of racial or ethnic differences with members.
- Recognize and acknowledge how power, privilege, and racism can affect interactions with clients. Discussing these topics is invaluable in strengthening relationships within the group.
- Be open to ongoing learning about ways that cultural factors affect group work. Although acquiring knowledge about various racial and ethnic groups is important, it is not enough. It is essential that you be willing to identify and examine your own worldview, assumptions, and personal prejudices about other racial and ethnic groups. Know that this skill does not develop quickly or without effort.

To initiate conversations with group members about their cultural identity, you need to have some fundamental understanding about the members' ethnic and cultural backgrounds. However, it is not realistic to expect that you will know everything about the cultural background of all the members in your groups. There is much to be said for letting group members teach you about relevant differences and the meaning these differences hold for them. Ask members to provide you with the information you will need to work effectively with them. In working with culturally diverse individuals within a group, it helps to assess the degree of acculturation and identity development that has taken place. This is especially true for individuals who have had the experience of living in another culture. They often have allegiance to their own home culture but find certain characteristics of their new culture attractive. They may experience conflicts when integrating the values from the two cultures in which they live. These core struggles can be productively explored in an accepting group if the leader and the other members respect this cultural conflict.

Recognizing Your Own Limitations   As a diversity-competent group worker, you are able to recognize the limits of your multicultural competency and expertise when working with group members who are different from you in terms of race, ethnicity, culture, gender, sexual orientation, abilities, religion, or worldview. When necessary, you are willing to refer clients to more qualified individuals or to additional resources.

If you are working with clients from a specific ethnic, racial, and cultural background different from your own, you can benefit from reading books and journal articles addressing group work with diverse client populations. Some resources we recommend, which are found in the Reference and Suggested Reading section, are Arredondo and colleagues (1996), ASGW (1999), DeLucia-Waack, Gerrity, Kalodner, and Riva (2004), DeLucia-Waack and Donigian (2004), Ivey, Pedersen, and Ivey (2001), and Sue and Sue (2003).

✳ The Coleadership Model

The Basis of Coleadership

Many who educate and train group leaders have come to favor the coleadership model of group practice. This model has a number of advantages for all concerned: group members can gain from the perspectives of two leaders; coleaders can confer before and after a group and learn from each other; and supervisors can work closely with coleaders during their training and can provide them with feedback.

We prefer coleadership both for facilitating groups and for training and supervising group leaders, and we usually work as a team. Although each of us has independent professional involvements (including leading groups alone at times), we enjoy coleading and continue to learn from each other as well as from other colleagues we work with. Nevertheless, we do not want to give the impression that coleadership is the only acceptable model; many people facilitate a group alone quite effectively. In conducting training workshops with university students, we continually hear how they value working with a partner, especially if they are leading a group for the first time. As we discussed earlier, group leaders preparing to meet their first group tend to experience self-doubt, anxiety, and downright trepidation! The task seems far less monumental if they meet their new group with a coleader whom they trust and respect.

In training group workers using a coleadership model, we find it is useful to observe the trainees as they colead so we can discuss what they are actually doing as they facilitate a group. Then, as we offer feedback to them, we frequently ask them to talk with each other about how they felt as they were coleading and what they think about the session they have just led. The feedback between these coleaders can be both supportive and challenging. They can make constructive suggestions about each other's style, and the process of exchanging perceptions can enhance their ability to function effectively as coleaders.

The choice of a coleader is a critical variable. If the two leaders are incompatible, their group is bound to be negatively affected. For example, power struggles between coleaders will have the effect of dividing the group. If coleaders are in continual conflict with each other, they are providing a poor model of interpersonal relating, which will influence the group process. Such conflict typically leads to unexpressed reactions within the group, which gets in the way of effective work. We are not suggesting that coleaders will never have conflicts. What is important is that they work out any disputes in a decent and direct manner, for doing so can model ways of coping with interpersonal conflict. If conflict occurs in a group, it should be worked out in the group.

To avoid negatively affecting a group, Riva, Wachtel, and Lasky (2004) point out that coleaders need to share a common view of the basic structural issues of groups and that they need to discuss their working relationship. A key part of their coleadership relationship involves an awareness of their personal issues that could lead to competitiveness, performance anxiety, and power and control struggles between them in the group. They write: "It seems crucial to the health of the group for coleaders to be open, willing to share and listen to different points of view, and to discuss and resolve difficulties that may arise between them" (p. 43).

A major factor in selecting a coleader involves mutual respect. Two or more leaders working together will surely have their differences in leadership style, and they will not always agree or share the same perceptions or interpretations. If there is mutual respect and trust between them, however, they will be able to work cooperatively instead of competitively, and they will be secure enough to be free of the constant need to prove themselves.

It is not essential that you be best friends with your coleader. What you need is a good working relationship, which you can achieve by taking time to talk with each other. Although we take delight in our personal and professional relationship, we are also willing to engage in the hard work necessary to be a successful team. This relationship reflects our belief that it is essential that coleaders get together regularly to discuss any matters that may affect their working as a team. We emphasize discussing how we are feeling in regard to our personal life as well as talking about specific group purposes and making plans for an upcoming group. Further, we tell coleaders in training to arrange to spend time together both before and after each group session to evaluate their leadership and the group's progress, as well as to make plans for future sessions.

Advantages of the Coleadership Model

Having acknowledged our clear preference for coleading groups, here is a summary of the major advantages of using the coleadership method.

1. The chance of burnout can be reduced by working with a coleader. This is especially true if you are working with a draining population, such as the psychologically impaired who often simply get up and leave, who hallucinate during sessions, and who may be withdrawn or be acting out. In such groups one leader can attend to certain problem members while the other attempts to maintain the work going on in the group.

2. If intense emotions are being expressed by one or more members, one leader can pay attention to those members while the other leader scans the

room to note the reactions of other members, who can later be invited to share their feelings. Or, if appropriate, the coleader can find a way to involve members in the work of someone else. Many possibilities exist for linking members, for facilitating interaction between members, and for orchestrating the flow of a group when coleaders are sensitively and harmoniously working as a team.

3. If one leader must be absent because of illness or professional reasons, the group can proceed with the other leader. If one of the coleaders is especially drained on a given day or is temporarily experiencing some emotional pain, the coleader can assume primary leadership, and the leader having problems can feel less burdened with the responsibility to "be there" for the group members.

    In such a case it may be appropriate for the coleader to say to the group that he or she is going through some difficulties personally, without going into great detail. By simply having said this, the leader is likely to feel freer and may be much more present. This admission provides sound modeling for the members, for they can see that group leaders are not beyond dealing with personal problems.

4. Coleader peer supervision is clearly beneficial. If one of the leaders has been strongly affected by a session, he or she can later explore feelings of anger, depression, or the like in some detail with the coleader. The coleader can be used as a sounding board, can check for objectivity, and can offer useful feedback. There is no problem of breaking confidentiality in such instances, for the coleader was also present at the session. However, we do want to emphasize that it is often necessary for leaders to express and deal with such feelings in the session itself, especially if they were aroused in the group setting. For example, if you are aware that you are perpetually annoyed by the behavior of a given member, you might need to deal with your annoyance as a group matter. This is a time when a competent and trusted coleader is especially important.

5. An important advantage of coleading emerges when one of the leaders is affected by a group member to the degree that countertransference is present. Countertransference can distort one's objectivity so that it interferes with leading effectively. For example, your coleader may typically react with annoyance or some other intense feeling to one member who is seen as a problem. Perhaps you are better able to make contact with this member, and so you may be the person who primarily works with him or her. You can be of valuable assistance by helping your coleader talk about, and perhaps even resolve, reactions and attachments toward such a client.

Disadvantages of the Coleadership Model

Even with a coleader you choose, one whom you respect and like, there are likely to be occasional disagreements. This difference of perspective and opinion need not be a disadvantage or a problem. Instead, it can be healthy for both of you because you can keep yourself professionally alert through constructive challenges and differences. Most of the disadvantages in coleading groups have to do with poor selection of a coleader, random assignment to another leader, or failure of the two leaders to meet regularly.

1. Problems can occur if coleaders rarely meet with each other. The results are likely to be a lack of synchronization or even a tendency to work at cross purposes instead of toward a common goal. Leaders need to take time to discuss their differences. For example, we have observed difficulties when one group leader thought all intervention should be positive, supportive, and invitational, whereas the other leader functioned on the assumption that members need to be pushed and directly confronted and that difficult issues should be brought up. The group became fragmented and polarized as a result of these incompatible leadership styles.

2. A related issue is competition and rivalry. For example, one leader may have an exaggerated need to have center stage, to be dominant at all times, and to be perceived as the one in control. Obviously, such a relationship between coleaders is bound to have a negative effect on the group. In some cases members may develop negative reactions toward groups in general, concluding that all that ever goes on in them is conflict and the struggle for power.

3. If coleaders do not have a relationship built on trust and respect or if they do not value each other's competence, they may not trust each other's interventions. Each leader may insist on following his or her own hunches, convinced that the other's are not of value.

4. One leader may side with members against the other leader. For example, assume that Alta confronts a male leader with strong negative reactions and that his coleader (a woman) joins Alta in expressing her reactions and even invites the members to give feedback to the coleader. This practice can divide the group, with members taking sides about who is "right." It is especially a problem if one leader has not previously given negative reactions to the other and uses the situation as a chance to "unload" feelings.

5. Coleaders who are involved in an intimate relationship with each other can get into some problematic situations if they attempt to use time in the session to deal with their own relationship struggles. Although some members may support the coleaders' working on their own issues in the group, most clients are likely to resent these coleaders for abdicating their leadership functions.

We think it is important that the two leaders have some say in deciding to work as a team. Otherwise, there is a potential for harm for both the group members and the coleaders. Careful selection of a coleader and time devoted to meeting together are essential. We encourage those who colead groups to spend some time both *before* and *after* each session discussing their reactions to what is going on in the group as well as their working relationship as coleaders. For another discussion of the coleadership model, see Kottler (2001).

✳ Developing a Research Orientation to Practice

As a group leader, you will be expected to demonstrate the efficacy of your interventions. With the current emphasis on short-term treatments that provide symptom relief or solve clients' problems, familiarity with research in the group work field is becoming an essential part of practice. Along with follow-up group sessions and individual interviews of members of your groups, research can help you come to a better understanding of the specific factors that contributed to the successful outcomes or the failures of your groups. Applied research can help you refine your interventions and identify factors that interfere with group effectiveness. As a practitioner, it is essential that what you do in your groups is supported by research on the process and outcomes of groups. Part of your development as a group leader involves thinking of ways to make evaluation research a basic part of your group practice.

The following sections address the current status of group work research, explain the importance of combining research and practice in group work, identify some of the reasons for the gap between researchers and group practitioners, and describe some attitudes of practitioners toward research.

The Current Status of Group Work Research

Consumers and health care companies are increasingly demanding that practitioners demonstrate the value of their therapeutic strategies. Based on empirical investigations of more than four decades of group work, Dies (1992) writes that the general conclusion is that there is relatively little difference in outcome between individual and group treatments. With the pressures to justify the expense of psychotherapy, Dies suggests that clinicians are likely to face increased challenges to explain why the treatment of choice for most clients is not group therapy. In writing of the future of group therapy, Dies states that research on group interventions is expected to reflect growing efforts to link group process and outcome, provide a more congenial collaboration between practitioners and researchers, and offer a more sophisticated blending of research designs to study group process and outcomes.

Dies (1993) conducted a survey of 156 group psychotherapy researchers representing 29 different countries. Those surveyed agreed that our understanding about the complex interactions that influence treatment outcomes is rather meager. More is known about the general dimensions of group atmosphere, such as cohesion and group climate, than is known about selection of members, group composition, group leader techniques, and underlying group dynamics. Dies believes the trend toward tailoring interventions to address specific diagnostic issues, along with the pressures to design effective, cost-efficient brief interventions, will force researchers to confront these relatively neglected issues in future studies.

Since the early 1980s the focus of group studies has shifted from an emphasis on process research to an examination of outcome studies. There are many unanswered questions related to group process variables, such as matching certain individuals to specific groups, member selection and group composition, style of group leadership, and interventions at various stages of groups (Riva & Smith, 1997).

During the 1990s, research focused on very specific applications of types of group interventions with specific client populations, with much less effort aimed at understanding group dynamics. Research focused on a wide range of problem areas including group treatment of depression, eating disorders, behavioral change programs, couples therapy, support groups for specific disabilities, and bereavement groups for people of different ages (Horne & Rosenthal, 1997). Studies conducted during the 1990s allowed researchers to predict who would do well in which kind of group with which kind of group leader (Barlow, Fuhriman, & Burlingame, 2004).

Burlingame, Fuhriman, and Johnson (2004b) identify four process components that are unique features of the group format: structure, verbal interaction, therapeutic relationship, and therapeutic factors. Based on their review of process findings from the 1990s to the present, Burlingame et al. conclude that "the interactive interpersonal environment of group provides unique and powerful change mechanisms" (p. 54). Burlingame and his colleagues admit that group process and outcome literature has matured over the past decade. However, they want to see more process-outcome studies that link group and theory-specific mechanisms of change.

In their description of the history of research on group work, Horne and Rosenthal (1997) indicate that we have learned much about the complex nature of group work. They state that the efficacy of group treatment appears to have less to do with a specific theoretical orientation than with finding an optimum combination of pregroup training, client characteristics, therapeutic factors, group structure, and stages of group development. In tracing the research trends in group counseling and psychotherapy, Barlow, Fuhriman, and Burlingame (2004) state that empirical research on group counseling has shown that a set of recognizable factors—such as skilled leaders, appropriately referred group members, and defined goals—create positive outcomes in groups. They conclude that group approaches can ameliorate a number of social ills. A survey of more than 40 years of research shows an abundance of evidence that group approaches are associated with clients' improvement in a variety of settings and situations (Barlow et al., 2004; Bednar & Kaul, 1978, 1979, 1994; Bednar & Lawlis, 1971; Burlingame et al., 2004a; Kaul & Bednar, 1978, 1986).

In their discussion of the current status and future directions of group therapy research, Burlingame, Fuhriman, and Johnson (2004a) conclude that the time has never been better for research on group approaches. They add that future challenges facing group researchers include "linking outcome with process, training with practice, practice with research, and facilitating the application of research results by clinicians in the field" (p. 658).

Obstacles to the Advancement of Research on Group Work

Although research on group counseling has improved over the past two decades, many research studies in group work suffer from serious methodological problems. Future group research needs to inform practice and at the same time be guided by the expertise of those who conduct groups (Riva & Kalodner, 1997). A gap exists between research and practice in group counseling, and closing it involves overcoming some major obstacles. Practitioners often view researchers as a "strange breed" preoccupied with trivial issues. Practitioners are likely to dismiss research without weighing its potential contributions. Counseling practitioners (as opposed to counselor educators, consultants, and administrators) are least likely to regularly read group research articles or use published research findings in their work with groups (Robison & Ward, 1990). Furthermore, empirical findings are seldom reported in a way that encourages group leaders to translate research into practice (Dies, 1983b).

As Stockton has observed (as cited in Bednar et al., 1987), the lack of collaboration between researchers and practitioners continues to be a key problem in group work. Researchers often do not really understand what can be learned from clinical experience, and practitioners often perceive research as being irrelevant to clinical practice. Only a small percentage of group practitioners use research findings in any consistent manner or engage in research of their own. If this knowledge gap is to be bridged, practitioners and researchers need to develop an increased mutual respect for what each can offer, and they must learn to work cooperatively, accepting the dual role of practitioner-researcher (Morran & Stockton, 1985).

In their survey of research activities and attitudes among ASGW members, Robison and Ward (1990) found that few respondents conducted research with groups at the time they completed the survey. Research activities, both current and past, were reported most frequently by counselor educators, consultants, and administrators, and reported least by practicing counselors and counseling students. Insufficient time, funds, and employer support were most frequently reported as reasons for not conducting research with groups. Other reasons given for not conducting research on groups included ethical issues or policies prohibiting research with agency clients, lack of interest, research facilities unavailable, lack of training in research methods, and lack of past success in presenting and publishing findings.

The Challenge of Combining Research and Practice

Certainly, the attempt to combine research and practice is challenging. Because of the demands of each role, it is difficult to be both a group practitioner and a researcher. Yalom (1995) admits that few group practitioners will ever have the time, funding, and institutional backing to engage in large-scale research, yet he contends "many can engage in intensive single-patient or single-group research, and *all* clinicians must evaluate published clinical research" (p. 529).

Yalom's (1995) observations suggest a need to consider "doing research" in a different light. Instead of thinking exclusively in terms of rigorous empirical research, practitioners can begin to consider alternatives to traditional scientific methods. For example, systematic observation and assessment can become basic parts of the practice of group work. Another alternative is evaluative research, which is aimed at gathering and assessing data that can be of value in making decisions about programs and in improving the quality of professional services (Dies, 1983a). Pure research in group work should not be seen as the only type of inquiry that has value. Practitioners and researchers can choose to do good field research instead (Morran & Stockton, 1985).

Whether or not group workers actually conduct research with their groups may be less important than their willingness to keep themselves informed about the practical applications of research on group work. At the very least, group counselors need to be up to date with the research implications for practice. Yalom (1995) claims that group trainees need to know more than how to implement techniques in a group—they also need to know how to learn. Faculty should teach and model a basic research orientation characterized by an open, self-critical, inquiring attitude toward clinical and research evidence. He writes that students need to critically evaluate their own work and maintain sufficient flexibility to be responsive to their own observations.

According to Yalom (1995), a research orientation allows group therapists, throughout their career, to remain flexible and responsive to new evidence. Practitioners who lack a research orientation will have no basis to critically evaluate new developments in the field of group work. Without a consistent framework to evaluate evidence of the efficacy of innovations in the field, practitioners run the risk of being unreasonably unreceptive to new approaches. Or, in contrast, they uncritically embrace one fad after another.

In learning how to become a group practitioner, it is necessary to progress from a beginner to a skilled clinician in stages. Likewise, a developmental approach can be useful for understanding the process of teaching students how to get involved in research about groups. Rex Stockton is an advocate for a developmental apprenticeship model. Just as students improve their clinical skills through practice, consultation, supervision, and discussion with mentors and peers, they can become insightful researchers through the same kinds of exposure, practice, consultation, and collaboration with those who are doing research (Stockton & Toth, 1997).

As a group practitioner, whether or not you actually conduct research with your groups is less important than your willingness to keep yourself informed about the practical applications of research on group work. At the very least you need to keep up to date with the research implications for practice. One way to do this is to read professional journal articles that deal with research in the field of group work. Most editions of the *Journal for Specialists in Group Work* have one or more articles pertaining to group research. Reviewing these articles is a good way to gain insight into the direction of group research.

✓ *Points to Remember*

Concepts and Guidelines for Group Practitioners

✓ It is important to have a theoretical rationale to help you make sense of what occurs in a group. Take the time to understand several theoretical orientations, and then select concepts from each to form your own personal style of working.

✓ Personality and character are the most important variables of effective group leaders. Techniques cannot compensate for the shortcomings of leaders who lack self-knowledge, who are not willing to do what they ask group members to do, or who are poorly trained. Think about your personal characteristics and try to decide which will be assets and which liabilities to you as a group leader.

✓ Effective group leaders are knowledgeable about group dynamics and possess leadership skills. Use the self-evaluation inventories at the end of this chapter as a means of thinking about skills you might need to improve and skills you might need to develop.

✓ As a group leader, you need to decide how much responsibility for what goes on in the group belongs to the members and how much to you, how much and what type of structuring is optimal for a group, what kind of self-disclosure is optimal, what role and function you will assume, and how you will integrate both support and confrontation into group practice.

✓ In a therapeutic group, participants can learn more about themselves, explore their conflicts, learn new social skills, get feedback on the impact they have on others, and try out new behaviors. The group becomes a microcosm of society in which members can learn more effective ways of living with others. Depending on the type of group, there are some clear advantages to constituting a group that is diverse with respect to age, gender, sexual orientation, cultural background, race, and philosophical perspectives.

✓ Develop behavioral guidelines and teach them to group members. Some of the behaviors you might stress are keeping the group's activities confidential, respecting the differences that characterize the members, taking responsibility for oneself, working hard in the group, listening, and expressing one's thoughts and feelings.

✓ Pay attention to the diversity that exists within your group, and help members recognize how their diverse backgrounds influence their values and behavior. Highlight cultural themes as they surface during a session.

✓ To become a diversity-competent group worker, you need to possess a range of knowledge and skills competencies. Seek avenues for consultation and supervision as you recognize your limits in understanding diverse groups.

✓ Take some time to think about your therapeutic style and its influence on the process and outcomes of your group. Be able to describe the key features of your style in clear terms.

✓ Look for ways to meaningfully combine a research perspective with your practice when leading groups.

Exercises

We encourage you to complete these exercises before you begin leading and then again toward the end of the semester. The comparison will give you a basis for seeing how your attitudes and ideas may evolve with experience.

Attitude Questionnaire on Group Leadership

Read these statements concerning the role and functions of a group leader. Indicate your position on each statement using the following scale:

1 = strongly agree

2 = slightly agree

3 = slightly disagree

4 = strongly disagree

_____ **1.** It is the leader's job to actively work at shaping group norms.

_____ **2.** Leaders should teach group members how to observe their own group as it unfolds.

_____ **3.** The best way for a leader to function is by becoming a participating member of the group.

_____ **4.** It is generally wise for leaders to reveal their private lives and personal problems in groups they are leading.

_____ **5.** A group leader's primary task is to function as a technical expert.

_____ **6.** It is extremely important for good leaders to have a definite theoretical framework that determines how they function in a group.

_____ **7.** A group leader's function is to draw people out and make sure that silent members participate.

_____ **8.** Group leaders influence group members more through modeling than through the techniques they employ.

_____ **9.** It is generally best for the leader to give some responsibility to the members but also to retain some.

_____ **10.** A major task of a leader is to keep the group focused on the here and now.

_____ **11.** It is unwise to allow members to discuss the past or to discuss events that occurred outside the group.

_____ **12.** It is best to give most of the responsibility for determining the direction of the group to the members.

_____ **13.** It is best for leaders to limit their self-disclosures to matters that have to do with what is going on in the group.

_____ **14.** If group leaders are basically open and disclose themselves, transference by members will not occur.

_____ **15.** A leader who experiences countertransference is not competent to lead groups.

_____ **16.** Group leaders can be expected to develop a personalized theory of leadership based on ideas drawn from many sources.

_____ **17.** To be effective, group leaders need to recognize their reasons for wanting to be leaders.

_____ **18.** Part of the task of group leaders is to determine specific behavioral goals for the participants.

_____ **19.** A leader's theoretical model has little impact on the way people actually interact in a group.

_____ **20.** If group leaders have mastered certain skills and techniques, it is not essential for them to operate from a theoretical framework.

_____ **21.** Leaders who possess personal power generally dominate the group and intimidate the members through this power.

_____ **22.** There is not much place for a sense of humor in conducting groups, because group work is serious business.

_____ **23.** Group leaders should not expect the participants to do anything that they, as leaders, are not willing to do.

_____ **24.** Group leaders have the responsibility for keeping written documentation summarizing group sessions.

_____ **25.** For coleaders to work effectively with each other, it is essential that they share the same style of leadership.

_____ **26.** In selecting a coleader, it is a good idea to consider similarity of values, philosophy of life, and life experiences.

_____ **27.** If coleaders do not respect and trust each other, there is the potential for negative outcomes in the group.

_____ **28.** It is best that those who colead a group be roughly equal in skills, experiences, and status.

_____ **29.** Coleaders should never openly disagree with each other during a session, for this may lead to a division within the group.

_____ **30.** The group is bound to be affected by the type of modeling that the coleaders provide.

After you have completed this self-inventory, we suggest that your class break into small groups to discuss the items.

Self-Assessment of Group Leadership Skills

In this chapter we described a set of skills necessary for effective group leadership. The following self-inventory helps you identify areas of strengths and weaknesses as a group leader. Read the brief description of each skill and then rate yourself on each dimension. Think about the questions listed under each skill. These questions are designed to aid you in assessing your current level of functioning and in identifying specific ways you can improve on each skill.

You can profit from this checklist by reviewing it before and after group sessions. If you are working with a coleader, he or she can provide you with a separate rating. These questions also provide a framework for exploring your level of skill development with fellow students and with your supervisor or instructor.

To what degree do you demonstrate the following? (One space is for you to rate yourself early in the term and the other space for later on.) On each skill, rate yourself using this 3-point scale:

3 = I do this most of the time with a high degree of competence.

2 = I do this some of the time with an adequate degree of competence.

1 = I do this occasionally with a relatively low level of competence.

———— ———— 1. **Active listening.** Hearing and understanding both subtle and direct messages, and communicating that one is doing this.

    a. How well do I listen to members?

    b. How attentive am I to nonverbal language?

    c. Am I able to hear both direct and subtle messages?

    d. Do I teach members how to listen and respond?

———— ———— 2. **Reflecting.** Capturing the underlying meaning of what is said or felt and expressing this without being mechanical.

    a. Can I mirror what another says without being mechanical?

    b. Do my restatements add meaning to what was said by a member?

    c. Do I check with members to determine the accuracy of my reflection?

    d. Am I able to reflect both thoughts and feelings?

———— ———— 3. **Clarifying.** Focusing on the underlying issues and assisting others to get a clearer picture of what they are thinking or feeling.

    a. Do my clarifying remarks help others sort out conflicting feelings?

    b. Am I able to focus on underlying issues and themes?

    c. Do members get a clearer focus on what they are thinking and feeling?

    d. Does my clarification lead to a deeper level of member self-exploration?

———— ———— 4. **Summarizing.** Identifying key elements and common themes and providing a picture of the directional trends of a group session.

    a. Does my summarizing give direction to a session?

    b. Am I able to tie together several themes in a group session?

    c. Do I attend adequately to summarizing at the end of a session?

    d. Do I encourage members to summarize what they heard?

_____ _____ **5. Facilitating.** Helping members to express themselves clearly and to take action in a group.

   a. Am I able to help members work through barriers to communication?

   b. How much do I encourage member interaction?

   c. Am I successful in teaching members to focus on themselves?

   d. Can I steer members into discussing here-and-now reactions?

_____ _____ **6. Empathizing.** Adopting the internal frame of reference of a member.

   a. Are my life experiences diverse enough to provide a basis for understanding members?

   b. Can I maintain my separate identity at the same time as I empathize with others?

   c. Do I communicate to others that I understand their subjective world?

   d. Do I promote expressions of empathy among the members?

_____ _____ **7. Interpreting.** Explaining the meaning of behavior patterns within some theoretical framework.

   a. Are my interpretations accurate and well-timed?

   b. Do I present my interpretations in the form of hunches?

   c. Do I encourage members to provide their own meaning for their behavior?

   d. Do I avoid making dogmatic interpretations?

_____ _____ **8. Questioning.** Using questions to stimulate thought and action but avoiding question/answer patterns of interaction between leader and member.

   a. Do I overuse questioning as a leadership style?

   b. Do I ask "what" and "how" questions instead of "why" questions?

   c. Do I keep myself hidden through asking questions?

   d. Do I use open-ended questions that lead to deeper self-exploration?

_____ _____ **9. Linking.** Promoting member-to-member interaction and facilitating exploration of common themes in a group.

   a. Do my interventions enhance interactions between members?

    b. Do I foster a norm of member-to-member interactions or leader-to-member interactions?

    c. Do I help members find a way to connect with each other?

    d. Am I able to orchestrate interactions so several members can be involved in working at the same time?

_____ _____ **10. Confronting.** Challenging members to look at some aspects of their behavior.

    a. Do I model caring and respectful confrontation?

    b. How do members generally react to my confrontations?

    c. Am I able to confront specific behaviors without being judgmental?

    d. In confronting others, do I let them know how I am affected by their behavior?

_____ _____ **11. Supporting.** Offering some form of positive reinforcement at appropriate times in such a way that it has a facilitating effect.

    a. Do I recognize the progress members make?

    b. Do I build on the strengths and gains made by members?

    c. Do I balance challenge and support?

    d. Does my providing support sometimes get in the way of a member's work?

_____ _____ **12. Blocking.** Intervening to stop counterproductive behaviors in the group or to protect members.

    a. Am I able to intervene when necessary without attacking a member?

    b. Do I block a member's behavior that is disruptive to the group?

    c. Am I aware of when it is necessary for me to protect a member from another member?

    d. Can I effectively block counterproductive behaviors?

_____ _____ **13. Assessing.** Getting a clear sense of members without labeling them.

    a. Can I understand a member's problem without using a label?

    b. Do I help members to assess their own problematic behavior?

    c. Am I able to detect members who may not be appropriate for a group?

    d. Can I create interventions that fit with my assessment?

_____ _____ **14. Modeling.** Demonstrating to members desired behaviors that can be practiced both during and between group sessions.

    a. What kind of behavior do I model during group sessions?

    b. Am I able to model effective self-disclosure?

    c. Can I model caring confrontations?

    d. What is the general effect of my modeling on a group?

_____ _____ **15. Suggesting.** Offering information or possibilities for action that can be used by members in making independent decisions.

    a. Do I differentiate between suggesting and prescribing?

    b. Do my suggestions encourage members to take initiative?

    c. Do I tend to give too many suggestions?

    d. How do I determine when to give suggestions and when to avoid doing so?

_____ _____ **16. Initiating.** Demonstrating an active stance in intervening in a group at appropriate times.

    a. Do I generally get group sessions started in an effective manner?

    b. Do I take active steps to prevent a group from floundering in unproductive ways?

    c. Am I able to initiate new work with others once a member's work comes to an end?

    d. Do I teach members how to initiate their own work in the sessions?

_____ _____ **17. Evaluating.** Appraising the ongoing group process and the individual and group dynamics.

    a. What criteria do I use to assess the progress of my groups?

    b. What kinds of questions do I pose to members to help them evaluate their own gains as well as their contributions to the group?

     c. Do I make a concerted effort to assist members in assessing their progress as a group?

     d. What kind of evaluation instruments do I use in a group?

———— ———— **18. Terminating.** Creating a climate that encourages members to continue working after sessions.

     a. Do I prepare members for termination of a group?

     b. Do I allow adequate time at the end of a session for closure?

     c. Do I help members transfer what they learn in group to daily life?

     d. Do I take steps to help members integrate their learnings in group?

Once you complete this self-assessment, circle the items where you most need improvement (any items that you rated as "1" or "2"). Circle the letter of the questions that are the most meaningful to you, as well as the questions that indicate a need for attention. Think about specific strategies you can design to work on the skills where you see yourself as being most limited. It is a good idea to take this inventory at least twice—once at the beginning of the course and then again later.

Guide to *Groups in Action: Evolution and Challenges* DVD and Workbook

If you are using the *Groups in Action: Evolution and Challenges* DVD and Workbook, you can integrate some of the key ideas in this chapter with the DVD. Refer to a section in this chapter on "Becoming a Diversity-Competent Group Counselor" and review the salient issues discussed. In the *Challenges Facing Group Leaders* DVD, a program segment entitled "Challenges of Addressing Diversity Issues" illustrates various situations that most group leaders would find challenging. The scenarios that are enacted within the group provide an action-oriented picture of the skills needed to effectively address a variety of diversity themes, some of which are listed below.

- What does my culture have to do with my identity?
- I feel different from others in here.
- Sometimes I want to exclude others.
- I struggle with language.
- I resent being stereotyped.
- We are alike and we are different.
- I express myself better in my native language.

- I am color blind.
- I know little about my culture.
- I want more answers from you leaders.

Each of the above themes is enacted in the DVD program and elaborated upon in the workbook. We suggest that you first answer the questions in the workbook dealing with each theme and then use your responses as the basis for discussion in small groups.

InfoTrac College Edition

For additional readings, explore InfoTrac College Edition, our online library, at http://www.infotrac.college.com/wadsworth. The following keywords are listed in such a way as to enable the InfoTrac College Edition search engine to locate a wider range of articles. The keywords should be entered exactly as listed, to include asterisks, "w1," "w2," "AND," and other search engine tools.

- group* w1 couns* AND train*
- group* w1 leader* AND train*
- multicult* AND couns* AND group*
- group* w1 leader* AND skill*
- group* w1 leader* AND therap*

Chapter 3

Ethical and Legal Issues in Group Counseling

Focus Questions

*B*efore reading this chapter, think about what you already know about ethical issues pertaining to group work. What do you consider to be the most important ethical issues involved in facilitating a group? As you read this chapter, consider these focus questions:

1. How can informed consent best be secured from members?

2. What measures would you take to ensure the confidential character of your group? How would you deal with a member who broke confidentiality?

3. Under what circumstances would you feel compelled to breach confidentiality of a member in a counseling group? How would you handle this situation?

4. What special ethical issues may arise when working with a group composed of involuntary members?

5. What psychological risks are associated with group membership? How can these risks be minimized?

6. How do multicultural considerations relate to ethical group practice?

7. What guidelines might you use to determine the ethical use of techniques in group work?

8. What is one value you hold that is likely to influence how you work with individual group members? Which of your values will help or hinder you in gaining the trust of members?

9. What ethical concerns do you have pertaining to the use of technology in group work?

10. What education and training do you think are necessary to be a competent leader? What experience and supervision would you like to receive as part of your program in group leadership?

11. Should membership in a group be a requirement of a group leader's training? What are your thoughts about requiring students to participate in an experiential group as a part of their training in becoming group workers?

12. What legal issues would you consider in setting up a group? Can you think of some legal safeguards to help you avoid a malpractice suit?

✳ Introduction

For those who are preparing to become group leaders, a thorough grounding in ethical issues is as essential as a solid base of psychological knowledge and skills. Our aim in this chapter is to highlight the ethical issues of central significance to group workers. Professionals and student-trainees must be thoroughly familiar with the ethical standards of their professional specialization. They must learn to make ethical decisions, a process that can be taught both in group courses and in supervised practicum experiences.

Group leaders must learn how to apply established ethics codes to a range of dilemmas they will face. As a practitioner, you will have to apply the ethics codes of your profession to the many practical problems you will face. There are no ready-made answers that fit all problems, and the ethics codes of professional organizations typically provide only broad guidelines for responsible practice. Ethical decision making is a never-ending process.

There has been an increased interest in awareness of the ethical, professional, and legal issues relevant to group work in recent years. Malpractice awards to clients who were treated unprofessionally and irresponsibly have increased the anxiety level of many mental health professionals. Becoming an ethical group practitioner involves more than merely avoiding breaking laws or violating ethics codes. Practicing ethically demands a high level of consciousness on your part, both personally and professionally. Personal integrity is a key asset in becoming an ethical practitioner. Examining your own ethical conduct and intentions in your everyday life as well as in your professional life is a good place to start. Being aware of your personal biases and your decision-making style in challenging situations will help you guard against unethical practices in your group work.

Although groups have unique therapeutic power that can be used to empower clients in their life-changing journeys, groups also have the potential to do harm to participants. As a group counselor, your skill, style, personal characteristics, and competence in group work are crucial dimensions that contribute to the quality of the outcomes of a group you might lead. Groups designed around ethically and legally sound principles have a far greater chance of being effective than groups designed without such thought and facilitated inadequately.

Your practice should be guided by established principles that have clear implications for group work. The *codes of ethics* discussed in this chapter constitute the rules professional members must adhere to in their practices. The following are examples of codes of ethics that have some relevance for group practitioners:

- *Code of Ethics and Standards of Practice* (American Counseling Association [ACA], 1995)
- "Ethical Principles of Psychologists and Code of Conduct" (American Psychological Association [APA], 2002)
- *AAMFT Code of Ethics* (American Association for Marriage and Family Therapy [AAMFT], 2000)
- *Code of Ethics* (National Association of Social Workers [NASW], 1999)

These and other professional codes of ethics are available in booklet form and may have been included with your textbook. In addition, the "Best Practice Guidelines" (ASGW, 1998, available online at http://www.asgw.org/best.htm) contains useful ideas for group workers in planning, conducting, and evaluating their groups.

Part of the decision-making process involves learning about the available resources you can draw on when you are struggling with an ethical question.

Although you are ultimately responsible for making ethical decisions, you do not have to do so in a vacuum. You can learn much by consulting with colleagues, by getting continued supervision and training during the early stages of your development as a leader, by keeping up with recent trends, and by attending relevant conventions and workshops.

Some beginning group leaders burden themselves with the expectation that they should always know the "right" thing to do for every possible situation. There is a lot of room for several appropriate responses in most situations. It is our hope that you will gradually refine your position on the issues we raise in this chapter, a process that demands a willingness to remain open and to adopt a questioning yet responsible attitude. We do not think these issues can be resolved once and for all; these complex issues take on new dimensions as you gain experience as a group leader.

※ Ethical Issues in Group Membership

Informed Consent

You have been asked to develop guidelines and information to give students when they first enter a training program. What kind of information would you as a student want prior to enrolling in a group class? What kind of informed consent statement might you develop for students participating in an experientially taught group course? Many group courses entail both a didactic and experiential component. What kind of information do you consider essential to give to students prior to enrolling in a group course?

It is sound policy to provide a professional disclosure statement to group members that includes information on a variety of topics. This can be done at a level that is best comprehended by those who are being considered for a group. The ASGW (1998) "Best Practice Guidelines" suggest providing the following information in writing to potential group members:

- Information on the nature, purposes, and goals of the group
- Confidentiality and exceptions to confidentiality
- Leader's theoretical orientation
- Group services that can be provided
- The role and responsibility of group members and leaders
- The qualifications of the leader to lead a particular group

With this information individuals are in a position to determine whether they want to join a particular group. Other relevant information pertaining to this issue can be found in Chapter 4 (see Guidelines for Announcing a Group and Recruiting Group Members). A more complete discussion of informed consent can be found in Corey, Corey, and Callanan (2003).

Involuntary Membership

You have been told that you are required to participate in a group. What are your immediate reactions? What information would you expect?

Ideally, participation in a group is voluntary, but this is not always the case. Especially when group participation is mandatory, much effort needs to be directed toward clearly and fully informing members of the nature and goals of the group, procedures that will be used, the rights of members to decline certain activities, the limitations of confidentiality, and ways active participation in the group may affect their lives outside the group. On this topic APA (2002) has the following guideline: "When psychological services are court ordered or otherwise mandated, psychologists inform the individual of the nature of the anticipated services, including whether the services are court ordered or mandated and any limits of confidentiality, before proceeding." [3.10c]

For example, in a state mental hospital in which we served as consultants, groups were the basic form of treatment for "those incompetent to stand trial" and for "mentally disordered sex offenders." Further, patients' release from the institution depended in part on their cooperation in treatment and rehabilitation, which included participation in regular group therapy sessions. In cases such as these, getting the *informed consent* of members requires that leaders explore with the members during a screening or orientation session what the group process consists of and that they are careful to ascertain whether the members understand what may be involved. It is also essential to inform sex offenders who are required to have group treatment about the consequences of noncompliance. Members should be informed that if they attend a group but do not participate, this will be documented in their record or clinical file.

Informed consent involves leaders' making members aware of both their rights and responsibilities as group participants. Thus, in mandatory groups or in required groups that emphasize self-disclosure and personal exploration, leaders are advised to take special care in discussing with members what is involved in being part of the group.

In institutions in which the policy is to require group treatment, group members should at least be given the opportunity to express their feelings and thoughts about this requirement. In some mental health facilities, the main therapeutic vehicle is group therapy, and people from all wards may be required to attend these sessions, sometimes several times a week. This situation is somewhat akin to compulsory education—people can be forced to attend but not to learn. Sometimes members are reluctant to become involved because of misinformation or stereotyped views about the nature of therapy. They may not trust the group leaders or the process involved. They may think group therapy is a form of indoctrination. Perhaps they view themselves as healthy and the other members of the group as ill. Most likely, many of them are frightened and have reservations about opening themselves up to others, and they are likely to be very concerned about others' gossiping or maliciously using information against them.

Perceptive leaders will deal with these issues openly. Although group leaders may not be able to give members the option of dropping out of the group, leaders can provide the support necessary to enable members to fully come to grips with their fears and resistances without turning the group into a mere gripe session. Group members can also be given the freedom to decide how to use the session time. Group leaders can reassure members that it is up to them to decide what personal topics they will discuss and what areas they will keep private. In other words, they should be clearly informed that they have the same rights as the members of any group—with the exception of the right not to attend without consequences.

It is crucial that leaders do not start out with the assumption that a mandatory group will automatically be composed of unmotivated clients, for this belief is bound to have a negative effect on group members. Instead, any initial distrust must be treated with respect as this can be the very material for exploration that leads to increased trust. Sometimes people who are mandated to attend groups make significant changes in their lives.

Freedom to Withdraw From a Group

In a group you are leading one member suddenly and unannounced gets up and walks out. How might you be affected? What are you inclined to say or do? How would you react if you were a member of the group rather than the leader?

Leaders should be clear about their policies pertaining to attendance, commitment to remaining in a group for a predetermined number of sessions, and leaving a particular session if they do not like what is going on in the group. Procedures for leaving a group need to be explained to all members during the initial group session. Ideally, both the leader and the member work in a cooperative fashion to determine whether a group experience is productive or counterproductive for each individual. Although members have the right to leave a group, it is important that they inform both the group leader and the members before making their final decision. It is a good policy for a leader to discuss the possible risks involved in leaving the group prematurely. Before leaving a group, members should generally discuss their reasons for wanting to stop attending. It is essential that the group leader intervene if other members use undue pressure to force any member to remain in the group. Adequate preparation and screening can reduce the risk of members leaving a group prematurely. However, when all is said and done, members have a right to quit.

We are not in favor of forcing members to remain in a group regardless of the circumstances, but neither do we emphasize to prospective members that they have the freedom to leave whenever they choose. Instead, during the individual screening interview and the orientation session, we take great care to inform prospective members about the nature of the group. In time-limited, closed groups we also stress to participants the importance of a careful commitment to carrying out their responsibilities. We emphasize how important it is for members to verbalize any doubts or concerns they are having about the group rather than keeping these reactions to themselves. Members need to know that the best way to work through interpersonal conflicts or dissatisfactions with a group is often to stay and talk. If members simply stop coming to a group, it is extremely difficult to develop a working level of trust or to establish group cohesion.

Furthermore, if a person leaves without careful consideration and explanation, the consequences could be negative for the members remaining as well as for the departing member. Some members may feel burdened with guilt and may blame themselves for saying or doing "the wrong thing" and contributing to an individual's decision to quit. And the person who leaves may have unexpressed and unresolved feelings that could have been worked through with some discussion.

With a commitment to discuss the factors related to leaving, there is an opportunity for everyone concerned to express and explore unfinished business.

Psychological Risks for Members

What particular risks would concern you as a member of a group? As a group leader, what potential risks might you explore with potential members during a screening interview?

The forces at work in a therapeutic group are powerful. They can be constructive, bringing about positive change, but their unleashing always entails some risk. It is unrealistic to expect that a group will not involve risk, for all meaningful learning in life involves taking risks. Members of a group may be subjected to scapegoating, group pressure, breaches of confidence, inappropriate reassurance, and aggressive confrontation. However, it is the ethical responsibility of the group leader to ensure that prospective group members are aware of the potential risks and to take every precaution against them and to consider ways of reducing potential risks.

An ACA (1995) ethical standard specifies: "In a group setting, counselors take reasonable precautions to protect clients from physical or psychological trauma" (A.9.b). This includes discussing the impact of potential life changes and helping group members explore their readiness to deal with such changes. A minimal expectation is that group leaders discuss with members the advantages and disadvantages of a given group, that they prepare the members to deal with any problems that might grow out of the group experience, and that they be alert to the fears and reservations members might have.

It is also incumbent on group leaders to have a broad and deep understanding of the forces that operate in groups and how to mobilize those forces for ethical ends. Unless leaders exert caution, members not only may miss the benefits of a group but also could be psychologically harmed by it. Ways of reducing these risks include knowing members' limits, respecting their requests, developing an invitational style as opposed to a pushy or dictatorial style, avoiding assaultive verbal confrontations, describing behavior rather than making judgments, and presenting hunches in a tentative way rather than forcing interpretations on members. These risks should be discussed with the participants during the initial session, and the leader should examine with them how this can be avoided. For example, a leader of a group for women who have been survivors of incest might say, "As you begin to uncover painful memories of your childhood and the abuse that took place, you may feel more depressed and anxious for a time than before you entered this group. It is very important to talk about these feelings in the group, especially if you have thoughts about quitting." Group leaders should also help members explore the concerns they have about transferring what they are learning in the group to their everyday lives.

After an intense group experience, participants may be inclined to make rash decisions that affect not only their own lives but also the lives of members of their families. What the individual sees as the result of newfound spontaneity or decisiveness may be due merely to a burst of energy generated by the group. For example, a woman who has been married for 20 years and who becomes aware of her extreme alienation from her husband may leave the group with a resolve to get a divorce. The group leader should caution her of the danger of making decisions too soon after an intense group session. If this woman has changed in the group, she may be able to relate to her husband differently; if she acts too soon, she may not give this behavioral change a chance to happen. It is not the leader's responsibility to stand in the way of members' decisions, but the leader is responsible for cautioning members against acting prematurely without carefully considering potential consequences. It is also a good practice to caution members who have done significant cathartic work, such as role playing, to refrain from leaving a session and saying in person everything they may have symbolically said to a significant other in a therapeutic context. The group leader can assist members in determining what they most want to communicate and also in finding ways to express their thoughts and feelings in a manner that shows concern and is most likely to lead to a successful encounter.

Sometimes members invent concerns of their own about the group experience and are very fearful. For example, some members may believe that if they allow themselves to feel their pain they will go crazy or sink into a depression so deep they won't be able to climb out of it. Some are convinced that if they give up their self-control they will not be able to function. Others are frightened of letting others know them because they think they will be rejected. Such fears should be explored early so members can determine how realistic they are and how they can best deal with these fears in the group.

Not only do certain risks need to be identified and dealt with in the group, but safeguards against these risks also need to be established. The leader should stress that group members have the right to decide for themselves what to explore and how far to go. Leaders need to be alert to group pressure and block any attempts by members to get others to do something they choose not to do.

We expand our treatment of these issues in Chapter 5, providing guidelines to help participants get the maximum benefit from a group experience. For now, let's look briefly at some possible risks of therapeutic groups.

1. *Self-disclosure* is sometimes misused by group members. The group norm has sometimes been misunderstood to mean the more disclosure that takes place, the better. But privacy can be violated by indiscriminately sharing one's personal life. Self-disclosure is an essential aspect of any working group, but it is a means to the end of fuller self-understanding and should not be glorified in its own right.

2. *Maintaining confidentiality* is a potential risk in every group. Some of the disclosures made during a session may not remain in the group. Group leaders need to continually emphasize the importance of maintaining confidentiality. Even when they do so, however, the possibility remains that some members will talk inappropriately about what was discussed in the group.

3. *Scapegoating* may occur. Occasionally an individual member may be singled out as the scapegoat of the group. Other group members may "gang up" on this person, making him or her the object of hostility or other forms of negativity. Clearly, the group leader can and should take firm steps to eliminate such occurrences.

4. *Confrontation*, a valuable and powerful tool in any group, can be misused, especially when it is employed destructively to attack another. Intrusive interventions, overly confrontive leader tactics, and pushing members beyond their limits often produce negative outcomes. Here, again, leaders (and members as well) must be on guard against behavior that can pose serious psychological risks for group participants. To lessen the risks of nonconstructive confrontation, leaders can model the type of confrontation that focuses on specific behaviors and can avoid making judgments about members. They can teach members how to talk about themselves and the reactions they are having to a certain behavior pattern of a given member.

It is not realistic to expect that all personal risks can be eliminated, and to imply that they can be is to mislead prospective members. But it is essential that members be made aware of the major risks, that they have an opportunity to discuss their willingness and ability to deal with them, and that as many safeguards as possible be built into the structure of the group.

One way to minimize psychological risks in groups is to use a contract, in which the leader specifies his or her responsibilities and the members specify their commitment by stating what they are willing to explore and do in the group. Such a contract reduces the chances that members will be exploited or will leave the group feeling that they have had a negative experience.

✳ Confidentiality

You are a member of a group, and the group leader tells you that "anything said in this group stays in here." Does this satisfy any potential concern you may have regarding confidentiality?

One of the keystone conditions for effective group work is confidentiality. It is especially important because the group leader must not only keep the confidences of members but also get the members to keep one another's confidences. A good practice is to remind participants from time to time of the danger of inadvertently revealing confidences in subtle ways. We find that members rarely gossip maliciously about others in their group, but they may tend to talk more than is appropriate outside the group and can unwittingly offer information about fellow members that should not be revealed. If the maintenance of confidentiality seems to be a matter of concern, the subject should be discussed fully in a group session. Group leaders must express the importance of maintaining confidentiality, consider having members sign contracts agreeing to it, and even impose some form of sanction on those who break it. It is a good practice to have a policy statement on confidentiality. Leaders have a responsibility for taking action if a member breaks confidentiality.

Modeling the importance of maintaining confidentiality is crucial in setting norms for members to follow. If group members sense that the leader takes confidentiality seriously, there is a greater likelihood that they will also be concerned about the matter. Even though it is the leader's role to teach members about confidentiality and to monitor safeguarding of disclosures, the members also have a responsibility in respecting and safeguarding what others share in the group.

The American Counseling Association's *Code of Ethics and Standards of Practice* (ACA, 1995) makes this statement regarding confidentiality in groups:

> In group work, counselors clearly define confidentiality and the parameters for the specific group being entered, explain its importance, and discuss the difficulties related to confidentiality involved in group work. The fact that confidentiality cannot be guaranteed is clearly communicated to group members. (B.2.a)

Group counselors have an ethical and legal responsibility to inform group members of the potential consequences of breaching confidentiality. The leader should explain that legal privilege does not apply to group treatment, unless provided by state statute (ASGW, 1998). In groups in institutions, agencies, and schools, where members know and have frequent contact with one another and with one another's associates outside of the group, confidentiality becomes especially critical and also more difficult to maintain. In an adolescent group in a high school, for example, great care must be exerted to ensure that whatever is discussed in the sessions is not taken out of the group. If some members gossip about things that happened in the group, the group process will come to a halt. People are not going to reveal facts about their personal lives unless they feel quite sure they can trust both the leader and the members to respect their confidences.

We do expect that members will want to talk about their group experiences with significant people in their lives. We caution them, however, about breaking others' confidences in the process. We tell them to be careful not to mention others who were in the group or to talk about what others said and did. Generally, members do not violate confidentiality when they talk about *what they learned in group sessions*. But they are likely to breach confidentiality when they talk about *how* they acquired insights or how they actually interacted in a group. For example, Tarek becomes aware in a session that he invites women to take care of him, only to resent them for treating him like a child. He may want to say to his wife, "I realize I often resent you for the very thing I expect you to do." This is acceptable disclosure, but describing the group exercise involving several women in the group that led him to this insight could break confidentiality guidelines. In addition, in disclosing these details out of context, Tarek runs the risk that his wife may misunderstand him and that he may inappropriately reveal other members' personal work.

Leaders may be tested by some members of the group. For instance, a counselor may tell group participants in a juvenile correctional institution that whatever is discussed will remain in the group. The youths may not believe this and may in many subtle ways test the leader to discover whether in fact he or she will keep this promise. For this reason it is essential that group leaders not promise to keep within the group material they may be required to disclose.

Counselors owe it to their clients to specify at the outset the limits of confidentiality, and in mandatory groups they should inform members of any reporting procedures required of them. Group practitioners should also mention to members any documentation or record-keeping procedures that they may be required to keep.

In general, licensed psychologists, psychiatrists, and licensed clinical social workers are legally entitled to privileged communication. In many states, licensed professional counselors also have privileged communication. This means that these professionals cannot break the confidence of clients unless (1) in their judgment, the clients are likely to do serious harm to themselves, others, and/or physical property; (2) abuse of children or the elderly is suspected; (3) they are ordered by a court to provide information; (4) they are supervisees in a supervisory relationship; or (5) the clients give specific written permission. However, when these professionals are conducting groups, in many states this legal privilege does not apply. In general, confidentiality of interactions among group participants cannot be guaranteed or protected by statute (Rapin, 2004).

A particularly delicate problem is safeguarding the confidentiality of minors in groups. Do parents have a right to information that is disclosed by their children in a group? The answer to that question depends on whether we are looking at it from a legal, ethical, or professional viewpoint. State laws differ regarding counseling minors. It is important for group workers to be aware of the laws related to working with minors in the state where they are practicing as well as local policies for those working in a school setting. Circumstances in which a minor may seek professional help without parental consent, defining an emancipated minor, or the rights of parents (or legal guardians) to have access to the records regarding the professional help received by their minor child vary according to state statutes.

Before any minor enters a group, it is a good practice to obtain written permission from the parents or the guardians. Such a statement might include topics such as a brief description of the purpose of the group, the importance of confidentiality as a prerequisite to accomplishing these purposes, and your intention not to violate any confidences. Although it may be useful to give parents information about their child, this can be done without violating confidences. Parents may inquire about what their child has discussed in a group, and it is the responsibility of the group leader to inform them in advance of the importance of confidentiality. Parents can be told about the purpose of the group, and they can be given some feedback concerning their child, but care must be taken not to reveal specific things the child mentioned. One way to provide feedback to parents is through a session involving one or both parents, the child, and the group leader.

Group leaders have a responsibility in groups that involve children and adolescents to take measures to increase the chances that confidentiality will be kept. It is important to work cooperatively with parents and legal guardians as well as to enlist the trust of the young people. It is also useful to teach minors, using a vocabulary that they are capable of understanding, about the nature, purposes, and limitations of confidentiality. It is helpful to inform and discuss with minors their concerns in advance about confidentiality and how it will be maintained, especially in a school setting. It is critical to teach minors about the limits of confidentiality. Such practices can strengthen the child's trust in the group counselor. It is a good idea for leaders to encourage members to initiate discussions on confidentiality whenever this becomes an issue for them.

A group counselor working with children may be expected to disclose some information to parents if they insist on it, or a leader of a group of parolees may be required to reveal to the members' parole officer any information acquired in the group concerning certain criminal offenses. It is a good policy for leaders to let members know when they may be required to testify against them in court.

Group leaders have some general guidelines for what disclosures they are required to make. Here is the ACA's (1995) standard of practice regarding the confidentiality requirement:

> Counselors must keep information related to counseling services confidential unless disclosure is in the best interests of clients, is required for the welfare of others, or is required by law. When disclosure is required, only information that is essential is revealed and the client is informed of such disclosures. (SP-9)

There are other ramifications of confidentiality that group leaders would do well to consider. Here are some guidelines concerning the issue of confidentiality:

- Confidentiality is crucial to the success of a group, but the leader can do little to guarantee that the policy on confidentiality will be respected by all members. Leaders can only ensure confidentiality on their part, not on the part of others in the group.
- It is essential that group leaders become familiar with the local and state laws that will have an effect on their practice. This is especially

true in cases involving child molestation, neglect or abuse of the elderly and children, or incest.

- Group leaders describe at the outset the roles and responsibilities of all parties and the limits of confidentiality (APA, 2002: Standard 10.03).

- Informing members about the limits of confidentiality helps them determine what (and how much) personal information they will reveal in group sessions.

- In a managed care context, once treatment plans are written and insurance preauthorization is granted, confidentiality is no longer in the control of the leader or the agency. Group members need to be informed that using insurance benefits entails a waiver of confidentiality (Rapin, 2004).

- It is a wise policy to ask participants to sign a contract in which they agree not to discuss or write about what transpires in the sessions or talk about who was present.

It is imperative that the group leader emphasizes at various stages of the group's evolution the importance of maintaining confidentiality. This issue needs to be introduced during the individual screening interview, and it should be clarified at the initial group sessions. At appropriate times during the course of the group, the leader can remind the members not to discuss identities or specific situations. If at any time any member gives indications that confidentiality is not being respected, the leader has the responsibility of exploring this matter with the group as soon as possible.

✳ Uses and Abuses of Group Techniques

During a screening session for potential group members a group leader tells you that she uses a variety of techniques. What, if anything, would you want to know about this?

In Chapter 1 we described how we view and use techniques or interventions. Here we want to add that group leaders have a responsibility to exercise caution in using techniques, especially if these methods are likely to result in the release of intense feelings. It is important that you be equipped to cope with powerful feelings that can be triggered by certain role-playing activities.

Those members who have held in emotions for many years, perhaps out of a fear of negative consequences if they expressed their feelings, would have their fears tragically reinforced if they were to lose control and no one in the group would be able to help and support them. We generally avoid involving the entire group in physical techniques for reasons of safety, and we employ techniques likely to arouse strong emotions only with members with whom we have established a trusting relationship (Corey et al., 2004).

Techniques have a better chance of being used appropriately when there is a rationale underlying their use and when they can be used to foster the client's self-exploration and self-understanding. At their best, techniques are invented in each unique client situation, and they assist the group member in experimenting with some form of new behavior. Generally techniques that are most useful grow out of the work of participants and are tailored to the situations that evolve in a particular group meeting.

It is important to use techniques you have some knowledge about, preferably those you have experienced personally or have received supervision in using. We use the following guidelines in our practice to avoid abusing techniques in a group:

- Techniques are not used to stir up emotions but to work therapeutically with emotional issues members initiate. They can help members experience feelings that are hidden or only beginning to emerge.

- Techniques are not used to cover up the group leader's discomfort or incompetence.

- Techniques are introduced in a sensitive and timely manner.

- Techniques are used with consideration for the member's background.

- Techniques are abandoned if they prove ineffective.

- Members are invited, and not ordered, to participate in certain techniques.

You need to be aware of what a technique might potentially lead to as well as be able to deal with intense emotional outcomes. For example, we have observed student leaders with a reading knowledge of guided fantasy techniques who decided to introduce them in their groups. They were surprised and unprepared to work therapeutically with the emotions released in some members. It would be unrealistic to expect that leaders should always know *exactly* what will result from an intervention, but they should be able to cope with unexpected outcomes. If you are introducing nonverbal exercises, it is especially important to use them appropriately and sensitively. It is also important to intervene if members attempt to coerce or pressure a reluctant member into participating. Participants should have an opportunity to share their reactions to the activities.

GOOD EXP AT INTRO'D NEW TECHNIQUES

In working with culturally diverse client populations, leaders must modify their interventions to suit the member's cultural and ethnic background. For example, if a male group member has been taught not to express his feelings in public, it may be inappropriate to quickly introduce techniques aimed at bringing out his feelings. First, find out if this member is interested in exploring what he has learned from his culture about expressing his feelings. Leaders can respect the cultural values of members and at the same time encourage them to think about how these values and their upbringing have a continuing effect on their behavior. The techniques used by leaders can help such members examine the pros and cons of making changes and the price of doing so. For a more detailed discussion of ethical considerations in using group techniques, see Corey, Corey, Callanan, and Russell (2004, chap. 2).

☀ The Role of the Leader's Values in the Group

As a group leader, what values of group members might you be inclined to challenge, even if members made it clear that they did not want to modify such values?

Your values are a fundamental part of the person you are. Thus, your values will inevitably influence how you lead a therapeutic group. You can increase your effectiveness as a leader by becoming aware of the values you hold and the subtle and direct ways you might influence group members. Your function as a leader is to challenge members to discover what is right for them—not to persuade them to do what you think is right. If members acknowledge that what they are doing is not enabling them to get what they want from life, then a group context is an ideal place for them to modify their attitudes and develop new ways of behaving.

Group members need to clarify their own values and goals, make informed decisions, choose a course of action, and assume responsibility and accountability for the decisions they make. The ACA's (1995) standard here is: "Counselors are aware of their own values, attitudes, beliefs, and behaviors and how these apply in a diverse society, and avoid imposing their values on clients" (A.5.b). Members often bring a number of value-laden issues to a group: religion, spirituality, sexual orientation, abortion, divorce, and family struggles. The purpose of the group is to help members clarify their beliefs and examine options that are most congruent with their own value system. Group counseling is not a forum in which leaders impose their worldview on members.

Values are often conveyed in a subtle way, even without your conscious awareness. For instance, you may be firmly convinced that there are universal values that are good for all, such as autonomy, freedom to make one's own choice, equality in relationships, and independence. But some group members are likely to adhere to a different set of cultural values. The values influencing their behavior might well be interdependence, cooperation, loyalty to family, duty and obligation to parents, and putting the welfare of the family above self-interests. If you assume these members would be far better off by changing their values, you are likely to do them a disservice. Although you may not directly impose your values on them, your interventions could be aimed at getting them to do what you think is best for them.

At times you may be faced with ethical issues over sharp differences between your own values and certain values of your clients. If members ask about your views, it may be appropriate to express them if you are able to do so in a nonjudgmental manner that does not burden members. Expressed values are less likely to interfere with the process in a group than are concealed values. In certain cases it might be necessary to refer clients to someone else because the conflict inhibits your objectivity. However, we would hope that you would not have to refer clients very often because of value conflicts.

We have heard leaders comment that they would not want to make known their personal values concerning religion, abortion, child rearing, and extramarital affairs because of the fear of swaying members to uncritically accept their values, but leaders cannot remain neutral in value-laden areas. Leaders must be clear about their own values and remain objective when working with values that are different from their own. It is also important for group leaders to be aware that extremely needy and dependent members may feel pressure to please the leader at all costs and hence assume the leader's values automatically. This is a useful issue to explore in group sessions.

Consider for a moment the example of a man who is struggling with the decision of whether to file for divorce. He tells the group that he is not sure he is willing to risk the loneliness he fears he will experience as a divorced man, yet he feels stuck in an unsatisfying marriage and sees little hope for things to change for the better. Surely the values you have as a leader will influence how you relate to him. Nevertheless, it is one thing to challenge him to look at all his alternatives before making his decision and to use the group to help him explore these alternatives; it is quite a different matter to persuade him (or to enlist the group to give him advice) to do what you (or they) think he should do. Your own values might include staying with the marriage at all costs, or they might include divorcing if one is unhappy. The key point is that it is not your role as leader to make this man's decision for him, even if he asks you to do so. Your role is to provide a context in which this person can examine his feelings, values, and behavior and eventually arrive at a decision that he will be able to live with.

Many values that pertain to the group process itself can be conveyed by both commission and omission. For example, if you ask group members to focus on their early childhood experiences and bring into the group their past problems, you are conveying the message that the formative years are worth exploration as a way to better understand their adult personality. Alternatively, if you focus mainly on what is going on in the here and now within the group, you are expressing a value of using the group as an interpersonal learning experience. If you make frequent use of homework assignments, this conveys your belief in the benefits for group members of engaging in ways of implementing what they are learning in the group in everyday life situations.

✳ Ethical Issues in Group Work With Diverse Populations

Values and Working With Diversity

The values leaders bring to the group process must consciously acknowledge the reality of human diversity in our society. If leaders ignore some basic differences in people, they can hardly be doing what is in the best interests of their clients. ASGW (1998) guidelines specify that ethical practice requires that leaders become aware of the multicultural context in group work, as can be seen in this recommendation regarding group practice:

> Group Workers practice with broad sensitivity to client differences including, but not limited to ethnic, gender, religious, sexual, psycholog-

ical maturity, economic class, family history, physical characteristics or limitations, and geographic location. Group Workers continuously seek information regarding the cultural issues of the diverse population with whom they are working both by interaction with participants and from using outside resources. (B.8)

Some of the *group norms* generally associated with group participation may not be congruent with the *cultural norms* of some clients. Some group norms that we address in Chapter 5 include staying in the here and now, expressing feelings, asking for what one wants, being direct and honest, sharing personal problems with others, making oneself known to others, being willing to take risks, improving interpersonal communication, giving personal feedback to others, learning to take the initiative in talking, dealing directly with conflict, being willing to confront others, and making decisions for oneself. Some individuals might have difficulty being direct because their culture values an indirect style of communication. Some members may experience difficulty in asking for time in the group, largely because they have learned from their culture that to do so is rude, insensitive, and self-oriented. Some members will not be comfortable making decisions for themselves without considering their extended family. Although some group interventions are designed to assist members in more freely expressing their feelings, certain members will find this offensive. Because of their cultural conditioning, certain individuals are likely to be very slow to express emotions openly or to talk freely about problems within their family. They may have been taught that it is good to withhold their feelings and that it is improper to display emotional reactions publicly.

Cultural diversity affects the issues that members bring to a group and the ways in which they might be either ready or reluctant to explore these issues. As a group counselor, it is of paramount importance that you sensitize yourself to the clues that members often give indicating that they would like to talk about some aspect of how their culture is affecting their participation in the group. It is essential for you to determine with group members what particular behaviors they are interested in changing. Even if you prize being direct and assertive, it is not your place to insist that members embrace your view of desirable behaviors.

Ethics and Standards of Preparation and Practice

The importance of the counselor developing diversity competence is further emphasized by various professional organizations, which have incorporated cultural understanding and competence in codes of ethics and standards for counselor preparation and practice. Being diversity competent is more complex than simply respecting other people. We must also try to understand the differences between people. The ACA (1995) code of ethics puts it this way:

> Counselors will actively attempt to understand the diverse cultural backgrounds of the clients with whom they work. This includes, but is

not limited to, learning how the counselor's own cultural, ethnic, racial identity impacts her/his values and beliefs about the counseling process. (A.2.b)

The ethics codes of most of the professional organizations now emphasize the practitioner's responsibility to have a general understanding of the cultural values of his or her clients, so interventions are congruent with their world-views. The guidelines for competence in diversity issues in group practice that follow have been drawn from a variety of sources, some of which are the ACA (1995), ASGW (1999), APA (1993, 2003), DeLucia-Waack (1996), DeLucia-Waack and Donigian (2004), Arredondo and colleagues (1996), and Sue, Arredondo, and McDavis (1992).

Group counselors:

- Acknowledge that ethnicity and culture influence behavior.
- Understand some ways that issues pertaining to gender and sexual orientation can be productively explored within the group.
- Consider the impact of adverse social, environmental, and political factors in assessing problems and designing interventions.
- Acquire the knowledge and skills necessary to effectively work with the diverse range of members in their groups. They seek consultation, supervision, and further education to fill in any gaps and to keep themselves current.
- Are aware of how their own cultural background, experiences, attitudes, values, beliefs, and biases influence their work. In their practices, they develop sensitivity to issues of oppression, sexism, homophobia, and racism.
- Respect the roles of family and community hierarchies within a client's culture.
- Respect members' religious and spiritual beliefs and values.
- Assist members in determining those instances when their difficulties stem from others' racism or bias, so they do not inappropriately personalize problems.
- Inform members about basic values that are implicit in the group process (such as self-disclosure, reflecting on one's life, and taking risks).

In working with groups characterized by diversity, counselors need to be aware of the assumptions they make about people based on their race, ethnicity, or sexual orientation. It is essential that the goals and processes of the group match the cultural values of the group members. Group workers are challenged to monitor any tendencies to treat people on the basis of stereotypes. To be able to do this, group leaders need to first become aware of their biases based on age, disability, ethnicity, gender, race, religion, or sexual orientation.

Special Issues Pertaining to Sexual Orientation

The ethics codes of the ACA, the APA, and the NASW clearly state that discrimination on the basis of minority status—be it race, ethnicity, gender, or sexual orientation—is unethical and unacceptable.

Working with lesbian, gay, and bisexual individuals often presents a challenge to group counselors who hold traditional values. Counselors who have negative reactions to homosexuality are likely to impose their own values and attitudes on the members of their groups.

Unless group counselors become conscious of their own faulty assumptions and homophobia, they may project their misconceptions and their fears onto those in their groups. Thus, it is essential that group practitioners be willing to critically examine their personal prejudices, myths, fears, and stereotypes regarding sexual orientation.

The American Psychological Association's Division 44 (APA, 2000) has developed a set of guidelines for psychotherapy with lesbian, gay, and bisexual clients. In many respects working with gay, lesbian, and bisexual clients is similar to working with heterosexual clients in groups. However, group counselors need to be prepared to deal with unique issues that are a part of the oppression so often faced by gay and lesbian individuals (Horne & Levitt, 2004). Any therapist who works with lesbian, gay, and bisexual people has a responsibility to understand their special concerns and is ethically obligated to develop the knowledge and skills to competently deliver services to them. Take time to reflect on these guidelines from the Committee on Lesbian, Gay, and Bisexual Concerns Joint Task Force on Guidelines for Psychotherapy with Lesbian, Gay, and Bisexual Clients (APA, 2000). How might you implement them in your practice of group work?

- Psychologists understand that homosexuality and bisexuality are not indicative of mental illness.

- Psychologists strive to understand the ways in which social stigmatization poses risks to the mental health and well-being of lesbian, gay, and bisexual clients.

- Psychologists strive to understand how inaccurate or prejudicial views of homosexuality or bisexuality may affect the client's presentation in treatment and the therapeutic process.

- Psychologists strive to be knowledgeable about and respect the importance of lesbian, gay, and bisexual relationships.

- Psychologists are encouraged to recognize the particular life issues or challenges that are related to multiple and often conflicting cultural norms, values, and beliefs that lesbian, gay, and bisexual members of racial and ethnic minorities face.

- Psychologists strive to understand the special problems and risks that exist for lesbian, gay, and bisexual youth.

- Psychologists make reasonable efforts to familiarize themselves with relevant mental health, educational, and community resources for lesbian, gay, and bisexual people.

These guidelines have relevance to all mental health professionals, not just to psychologists. Which guidelines might be most helpful for you in challenging your beliefs and attitudes regarding sexual orientation? Are there any specific attitudes, beliefs, assumptions, and values you hold that might interfere with your ability to effectively work with lesbian, gay, and bisexual clients in your groups? If you do become aware of some personal limitations at this time, what kinds of changes would you consider making? How might you challenge certain of your attitudes and assumptions pertaining to any of these guidelines?

✳ Ethical Issues in Technology and Group Work

The March 2003 edition of the *Journal for Specialists in Group Work* was devoted to the subject of technology and group work. The articles in this special issue present a variety of applications of technology, and group workers are given the challenge of learning about and engaging in the use of technology in group work. Betsy Page (2003), the editor of this special issue, points out that groups are plentiful on the Internet and that in spite of the fact that many group workers have major concerns about such groups, many people engage in these groups (in one Internet search conducted in June 2002, approximately 214,000 listings were found). Page (2004) states that although research studying online groups is in its infancy, some evidence suggests that online groups are serving a useful function for many people.

In her discussion of ethical issues pertaining to the use of technology in group therapy, Brabender (2002) admits that group practitioners who use technology are venturing into "territory that is relatively uncharted from a legal and ethical perspective" (p. 274). Brabender suggests that group workers who are considering using technology in their group practice should first identify any potential ethical dilemmas and systematically resolve any ethical and legal issues. Chang and Yeh (2003) suggest that practitioners who provide online groups should work together with researchers to formulate, amend, and revise guidelines for developing effective and ethical online groups. They maintain that online groups have a place as an adjunct to face-to-face therapy for individuals who are already in therapy. Chang and Yeh admit that research supporting the effectiveness of online groups is scant:

> Online groups are not, however, equivalent to face-to-face group psychotherapy, and there is no evidence to date that online groups are effective in fostering change. In fact, research examining the effectiveness of online groups in comparison to face-to-face groups has only just begun. (p. 640)

In addition to the question of the effectiveness of online groups, another major ethical concern regarding online groups pertains to problems in safeguarding confidentiality. The limits of confidentiality, including those due to the nature of the technology used, should be made clear to clients and a waiver agreement signed (ACA, 1999). Humphreys, Winzelberg, and Klaw (2000) take the position that online group psychotherapy cannot ethically be conducted over the Internet, except in very limited circumstances. Internet group therapy involves typing, recording, copying, and distributing all the "interactions" that take place online. This makes ensuring clients' privacy and confidentiality a very difficult matter. In addition, individuals cannot be reliably identified over the Internet. A person with access to a client's computer could sign into online group therapy by using the password and the name of the actual client. The implications for lack of confidentiality and privacy are obvious here.

Chang and Yeh (2003) write about online groups as a valuable way to address racial, cultural, and gender issues with Asian American men. They emphasize the importance of group facilitators taking an active role in setting the tone for a group by creating initial ground rules from the outset, especially guidelines for dealing with confidentiality. Chang and Yeh suggest that in closed groups confidentiality can be maximized by instructing participants to avoid disclosing the concerns of other group members to people who are not part of the group. Group members should also be cautioned about not sharing passwords used to access the group with those who are not a part of the group. As the group is beginning, it is essential to address topics such as respectful communication, level of interaction, termination conditions, and opportunities for face-to-face contact.

Dealing with the matter of informed consent pertaining to online groups presents an ethical challenge. In her discussion of the ethical issues involved in online group counseling, Page (2004) states that there is no quick way to easily identify groups led by professionals. She adds that informed consent poses difficulties in online groups because these groups cannot be neatly categorized. She also raises the question, "How can the Internet and possible types of group work be explained to potential consumers, particularly when some consumers have little understanding of computer or Internet functioning" (p. 616)?

Because of the difficulty of ensuring informed consent and maintaining the confidential nature of a group, we are opposed to online groups on both ethical and clinical grounds. Although we take a dim view of providing group services online, we do see value in using some forms of technology in teaching and practicing group work. Indeed, some programs now offer group counseling courses through interactive distance learning online, such as this 8-hour course:

Group Psychotherapy Process: A Developmental Approach
This online course features slides, charts and presentation files, and self-assessment tests after each module as well as an online course evaluation. This course provides participants with information about how to conduct adult group psychotherapy from a developmental perspective. Topics include pre-group screening, building group cohesion,

managing conflict, transference and countertransference, co-leaders, sub-grouping, termination. (Brochure from Alliant International University, Continuing Education, Distance Learning)

Many forms of technology could be used for teaching, training, and supervising group workers (McGlothlin, 2003). Videotape and computer simulation are examples of sophisticated technological applications that have the potential to enhance modeling and behavioral rehearsal in group work practice (Smokowski, 2003).

Because of the growth of the use of technology in counseling, it is important that students be made aware of the ethical considerations involved. Romano and Cikanek (2003) report on the findings of students who completed a group course that made use of computer applications. An evaluation questionnaire completed by students at the conclusion of the course revealed that the majority of students agreed that the class presentation devoted to computer technology in counseling and group work increased their knowledge and awareness of ethical issues related to online group work. All the students believed that discussions of computer technology should be included in future group classes. Furthermore, most students indicated that the technology components of the course increased their awareness of computer applications with groups. Romano and Cikanek emphasize the value of familiarizing students with both the advantages and risks of different types of online groups, as well as the unique ethical issues and considerations that they present.

Humphreys, Winzelberg, and Klaw (2000) state that some kinds of peer groups and self-help groups do utilize Internet technology, but they add that the astonishing growth in the technology has outpaced the development of formal ethical guidelines for practitioners involved in online groups. Humphreys and colleagues write about a therapist's ethical responsibilities in self-help groups, discussion groups, and support groups that operate on the Internet, and they offer practical strategies for avoiding ethical problems.

McGlothlin (2003) maintains that it is necessary for counseling students to be familiar with the legal and ethical issues involved in online counseling and the services provided by the Internet. According to McGlothlin, ASGW needs to become more active in advocating for technology in group settings and that more practical ways of infusing technology into group work need to be developed. McGlothlin asserts that group work practitioners need to be open to the use of technology in group settings and that they would do well to actively seek training in innovative advances in technology. McMinn, Buchanan, Ellens, and Ryan (1999) contend that graduate training and continuing education programs are needed that provide instruction in appropriate technological applications for professional practice.

✳ Competence and Training Issues

As a group leader you must provide only those services and use only those techniques for which you are qualified by training and experience. It is your responsibility as you market your professional services to accurately represent your competence. Although we encourage you to think of creative ways of reaching diverse populations, we also emphasize the need for adequate training and supervision in leading groups with such members. If you lead groups that are clearly beyond the scope of your preparation, this raises ethical issues and also puts you at risk for malpractice.

Because various professions have differing training and educational standards for group work and because specializations call for various skills, we will not try to specify an "ideal" program that would produce competent group leaders. Rather, we will outline several general areas of professional experience that we consider basic in the development of a capable leader.

The Issue of Leader Competence

Competence is one of the major ethical issues in group work. Lacking adequate training or experience, some group leaders hastily gather a group together without taking the time to screen members or to prepare them for a group. It is essential for leaders to recognize the boundaries of their competence and to restrict themselves to working only with those groups for which their training and experience have properly prepared them. Consider these questions:

- Who is qualified to lead groups?
- What are some criteria by which to determine the level of competence of group leaders?
- How can leaders recognize their limits?

Concerning the issue of qualification, several factors must be considered. One is the type of group. Different groups require different leader qualifications. Some professionals who are highly qualified to work with college students are not competent to lead children's groups. Professionals who are trained to lead psychoeducational groups may lack either the training or the experience necessary to administer group therapy to an outpatient population. Group counselors who competently lead face-to-face groups might well lack the training needed to facilitate online groups. So we can restate the basic question: Who is qualified to lead *this type* of group with *this type* of population?

Another issue related to competence is that of licenses, degrees, and credentials. In our judgment the training that leads to attainment of such certification is usually valuable, but degrees alone do not indicate that a person is a qualified leader. During the professional education of counselors who hope to work as group leaders, at least one course in the theory and practice of group counseling is essential. Unfortunately, it is not uncommon to find only one such survey course available to students in a master's degree program in psychology or counseling. A person may hold a PhD in counseling psychology and be licensed to practice psychotherapy yet not be equipped, either by training, experience, or personality, to practice *group* work.

Group leaders need to recognize their limitations. Toward this end, they might well ask themselves these questions:

- What kinds of clients am I capable of dealing with?
- What are my areas of expertise?
- What techniques do I handle well?
- How far can I safely go with clients?
- When should I consult another professional about a client?
- When should I refer a client to someone else?

Professional group workers know their limitations and recognize that they cannot lead all kinds of groups or work with all kinds of clients. They familiarize themselves with referral resources and don't attempt to work with clients who need special help beyond their level of competence. Furthermore, responsible group workers are keenly aware of the importance of continuing their education. Even licensed and experienced professionals attend conventions and workshops, take courses, seek consultation and supervision, and get involved in special training programs from time to time.

Professional competence is not arrived at once and for all. Rather, professional growth is an ongoing developmental process for the duration of your career. The "Best Practice Guidelines" (ASGW, 1998) provide some general suggestions for increasing your level of competence as a group worker:

- Remain current and increase your knowledge and skill competencies through activities such as continuing education, consultation, supervision, and participation in personal and professional development activities.
- Be open to getting professional assistance for your own personal problems or conflicts that may impair your professional judgment or your ability to facilitate a group.
- Utilize consultation and supervision to ensure effective practice when you are working with a group for which you need to acquire more knowledge and skill competencies.

Truly competent group workers have reasons for the activities they suggest in a group. They are able to explain to their clients the theory behind their group work and how it influences their practice. They can tell the members in clear language the goals of a group, and they can state the relationship between the way they lead the group and these goals. Effective group leaders are able to conceptualize the group process and to relate what they do in a group to this model. They continually refine their techniques in light of their model. In short, they possess the knowledge and skills that are described next.

Professional Training Standards for Group Counselors

For proficient group leaders to emerge, a training program must make group work a priority. Unfortunately, in some master's programs in counseling not even one group course is required. In some programs such a course is still an elective. In those programs that do require course work in group counseling, there is typically one course that covers both the didactic and experiential aspects of group process. It is a major undertaking to adequately train group counselors in a single course!

When it comes to training doctoral level psychologists, comprehensive training standards have not been universally or rigorously followed. In a survey of group psychotherapy training during predoctoral psychology internship, Markus and King (2003) found that, much like graduate school programs, predoctoral clinical psychology internships do not routinely provide adequate group therapy training. This survey suggested that there is a lack of depth and breadth of group therapy didactic offerings for psychology interns.

For practitioners to become competent group facilitators, specialized training is essential to obtain proficiency and expertise in group process (Markus & King, 2003). Several professional organizations have outlined the key elements involved in training group leaders. The American Group Psychotherapy Association (AGPA, 2001), the National Registry of Certified Group Psychotherapists (NRCGP, 1993), and the Association for Specialists in Group Work (ASGW, 2000) are in agreement on the essential nature of courses in group work: being involved in experiential group activities, having leadership opportunities, and receiving competent supervision.

The revised *Professional Standards for the Training of Group Workers* (ASGW, 2000) specifies two levels of competencies and related training. A set of core *knowledge* competencies and *skill* competencies provide the foundation on which *specialized* training is built. At a minimum, one group course should be included in a training program, and it should be structured to help students acquire the basic knowledge and skills needed to facilitate a group. These group skills are best mastered through supervised practice, which should include observation and participation in a group experience. Here are the ASGW (2000) recommendations for knowledge, skill, and specialized core competencies:

- *Knowledge Competencies:* Basic areas of knowledge include identifying one's strengths and weaknesses, having clarity of one's values, being able to describe the characteristics associated with the typical stages in a group's development, being able to describe the facilitative and debilitative roles and behaviors that group members may take, knowing the therapeutic factors of a group, understanding the importance of group and member evaluation, and being aware of the ethical issues special to group work. Didactic course work in group counseling is the best route to gaining these knowledge competencies. Other topics recommended for inclusion in group courses include theoretical foundations of group therapy, developmental stages of groups, group leader roles and leadership styles, selection criteria, therapeutic factors operating in groups, termination issues, and ethical issues in group work (AGPA, 2001).

- *Skill Competencies:* Basic skill competencies should be possessed by anyone leading a group. The 18 group leadership skills discussed in

Chapter 2 can be acquired by a combination of both didactic instruction and experiential training in groups. In addition to these generic leadership skills, special skills in effectively addressing diversity issues are a necessary component for competent group leaders.

- *Core Specializations:* Once counselor trainees have mastered these core knowledge and skill domains, they can acquire training in group work specializations in one or more of four areas: (1) task groups, (2) psychoeducational groups, (3) counseling groups, and (4) psychotherapy groups. The AGSW standards detail specific knowledge and skill competencies for these specialties and also specify the recommended number of supervised training hours for each. (Refer to Chapter 1 for a definition of these groups and their specific training requirements.)

The core competencies delineated in the ASGW (2000) training standards are considered the benchmarks for training group workers. The current trend in training group leaders focuses on learning group process by becoming involved in supervised experiences. Both direct participation in planned and supervised small groups and clinical experience in leading various groups under careful supervision are needed to equip leaders with the skills to meet the challenges of group work. Markus and King (2003) maintain that comprehensive training must include intensive supervision by a competent group therapist. Although Markus and King endorse group supervision of group therapy as a powerful cognitive and emotional learning experience, they report that the majority of internships providing supervision of group trainees tend to use the one-to-one model rather than group supervision. Group supervision of multiple group leaders is another alternative that has many advantages in terms of learning about group process as well as getting supervision (DeLucia-Waack & Fauth, 2004).

For a more detailed treatment of suggestions for training and supervising group workers, see ASGW (2000), Conyne (1996), Conyne and Wilson (1998), Conyne, Wilson, and Ward (1997), DeLucia-Waack and Fauth (2004), and Markus and King (2003).

Training and Personal Experience

As is clear from our brief review of the ASGW's professional standards for training, it is essential for prospective group leaders to undergo extensive training appropriate to the general type of group they intend to lead. We highly recommend three types of experience as adjuncts to a training program: personal (private) psychotherapy, group therapy, and participation in a supervised training group.

Personal Psychotherapy for Group Leaders   We encourage trainees to get involved in their own personal counseling, both individual and group. During the course of these sessions, we hope they will come to a greater understanding of their motivation to facilitate groups. They can also explore the biases that might hamper their receptiveness to clients, any unfinished business that might lead to distortions in their perceptions of group members, other needs that might either facilitate or inhibit the group process, current conflicts, and ways they can fully recognize and utilize their strengths. In short, group counselors can be expected to demonstrate the courage to do for themselves what they expect members in their groups to do. Group counselors cannot effectively assist clients to explore conflicts if they do not have the courage to honestly search within themselves and face what they find.

Self-Exploration Groups for Group Leaders   We have discovered that participation in a self-exploration group (or some other type of interactive process-oriented group) is an extremely valuable adjunct to a group leader's internship training experiences. Beginning group leaders typically experience some anxiety regarding their adequacy, and their interactions with group members frequently lead to a surfacing of unresolved past or current problems. It is generally inappropriate for group counselors to use the groups they are responsible for leading to do their own extensive work. At times, there may be a fine line between being a leader and being a member, but leaders who habitually "become members" of their groups would do well to consider joining a therapeutic group as a member and use that group to explore their problems and continue their growth. Besides being of therapeutic value, such a group can be a powerful teaching tool for the trainee. One of the best ways for leaders to learn how to assist members in their struggles is by working themselves as members of a group.

Training Groups for Group Leaders   The training group can lead to insights and awareness without becoming a therapy group. Trainees can learn a great deal about their response to criticism, their competitiveness, their need for approval, their jealousies, their anxieties over being competent, their feelings about certain members of the group they lead, and their power struggles with coleaders or members of their group. Trainees can gain insights into their personal dynamics, such as potential areas of countertransference, which can influence their ability to competently facilitate groups. By identifying areas that can result in countertransference, trainees are in a position to do further work in their own therapy outside of the group.

Leaders who have an exaggerated need for approval may avoid being confrontive, may assume a passive stance, or may become inappropriately supportive in their groups. This need for approval can hamper their potential leadership success by preventing them from effectively encountering others. Another example is the person who is attracted to being a group leader primarily by the power inherent in this position. This person's exaggerated need to control and direct others may lead to the mechanical use of a repertoire of techniques designed to impress the group participants with the therapist's prowess. Styles such as these can be detected and worked with during the session of a training group.

Not only can trainees learn a great deal about their personal dynamics from participating in an experiential process group, but it is an excellent way to learn about group dynamics. Markus and King (2003) assert that it is invaluable for group therapists to have experience as group members. They add that participation in an experiential process group or training group offers a unique way for trainees to learn about group dynamics and gain a real appreciation for how groups work.

Ethical Issues in Training Group Counselors

One controversial ethical issue in the preparation of group leaders involves combining experiential and didactic methods in training. We consider an experiential component to be essential in teaching group counseling courses. Struggling with trusting a group of strangers, risking vulnerability, receiving genuine support from others, developing good working relationships with peers, and being challenged to examine the impact of one's behavior on others are all vital learning experiences for future group leaders. We think group experience for leaders is indispensable, if for no reason other than that it provides an understanding of what clients face.

In their national survey of the training of group counselors, Merta, Wolfgang, and McNeil (1993) found that a large majority of counselor educators continue to use the experiential group in preparing group counselors. In group classes that are taught both experientially and didactically, the first half of the class frequently involves didactic instruction in areas pertaining to group theory, group dynamics, and group process issues. The content of the discussions may be very similar to the material in this textbook. During the second half of the session, many instructors conduct a group in which the students have an opportunity to be members. Sometimes students colead a small group with a peer and are supervised by the instructor. Of course, this arrangement is not without problems. Students may fear that their grades will be influenced by their participation (or lack of it) in the experiential part of the class. This may be the case even if instructors adopt a policy not to grade students on their participation as members.

Although it is common practice to combine the didactic and experiential aspects of learning in group work courses, doing so requires educators to address a number of ethical considerations. Students have a right to be informed of the specific nature of course and program requirements before they enter a program. In experiential training, participants engage in self-exploration and deal with interpersonal issues within the training group as a way of learning how to best facilitate groups. It is our position that the potential risks of experiential methods are offset by the clear benefits to participants who become personally involved in experiential group work as a supplement to didactic approaches to group courses. Many group work educators see a need for an experiential component to assist students in acquiring the skills necessary to function as effective group leaders.

Sample Informed Consent Statement on Experiential Learning   Students can be informed of a program's policy on self-exploration in a variety of ways. Here is one example of a written statement explaining the experiential component to students that I (Jerry) use in one of my group courses:

The faculty members in this program are dedicated to the personal growth and development of their students. We consider personal development to be at least as important as the educational development of the therapist. The helping professions require that the use of self be fully integrated into therapeutic processes; therefore, the personal characteristics of therapists are as critical as the knowledge and skills related to "being" an effective therapist. There will be an emphasis in many of your courses on identifying and exploring personal issues and concerns, especially those that may impede your effectiveness as a therapist. For example, you will have opportunities to identify your family-of-origin issues and explore how these experiences affect your current life and how any unresolved family-of-origin issues can potentially affect your work with clients.

It is not uncommon for people in our profession to feel uncomfortable with a focus on personal development even though, as therapists, we ask others to do that all the time. We believe that is essential to engage in such personal growth. While personal self-disclosures are, therefore, part of your coursework, only you can decide what aspects of your personal life you are willing to share. Creating comfort may not be the desired goal in your courses, yet creating safety is. The faculty is committed to creating a safe environment in which you can address personal concerns. We encourage you as a therapist-in-training to stretch and to risk more with us and your student colleagues than you might normally be prepared to do. In general, self-reflection is worth the discomfort in terms of the growth it can produce for you, and what it adds to your ability to be helpful to others.

Your program includes a course that combines didactic and experiential methods in the training of group counselors and therapists. We expect you to fully participate in the small group experience, both as a group member and as a co-facilitator under direct supervision. These supervised group sessions allow for an integration of learning related group process and the interpersonal styles of student participant-leaders. It is expected that your interactions in these small groups will be real and will be based on personal concerns that are meaningful to you. Special attention is paid to individual vulnerabilities that are likely to evoke unresolved personal issues and affect your work with clients. For example, if you had critical parents, and you are very anxious about making mistakes or are highly self-critical, this will likely impede your ability to make interventions with clients. If you recognize ways that you might engage in critical self-talk, you are in a position to begin to change your self-talk and also to change your behavior.

In the group process course, you will also be expected to give feedback to others as well as listen to and consider feedback that you receive. A focus on here-and-now issues as they emerge within the context of the small groups tends to increase the intensity of the group and follows from those who take the risk of disclosing their fears, concerns, hopes, and personal goals. The group course will provide a context in which you can identify areas for personal growth and will allow for personal exploration of both your concerns and needs. Although the aim is not to resolve personal problems, a desired outcome is that you will have a clearer focus on your struggles that might be productively explored outside of the group in your personal therapy and clinical supervision.

As faculty members, we believe that the most effective way to teach group process is through an integration of knowledge and experience—both as a participant and a leader. And we hope that you will learn from and appreciate the value of this course.

Managing Multiple Roles as an Educator   Group work educators must manage multiple roles and fulfill many responsibilities to their trainees, some of which include facilitator of a group, teacher, evaluator, and supervisor. Faculty who teach group courses cannot realistically be restricted to a singular role in teaching. At various times educators may teach group process concepts, lead a demonstration group in class, set up an exercise to illustrate an intervention in a group situation, and evaluate students' work. Group work educators often have a monitoring function, especially in identifying and intervening when students demonstrate bizarre behavior, are unable to give or receive feedback, or are unable to relate to others in even the most basic manner.

Faculty teaching group courses often assume a supervisory role, observing trainees as they facilitate a group. If an instructor also facilitates a process group, or an interpersonal process-oriented group, this person will at times carry out therapeutic roles and functions with these same students. Although the instructor may avoid becoming a therapist for a student group, he or she might well be called upon to assist participants in identifying personal problems that are likely to interfere with their ability to function effectively in group work.

Educational and therapeutic dimensions are often blended in group courses to enable students to obtain both personal benefits and conceptual knowledge and to acquire leadership skills. However, there are instances where the person teaching a group course may have little formal preparation in group counseling, may never have been a participant in a group, and may not have had any opportunity to gain supervised experience in leading a group. A core ethical issue is the level of competence of the person teaching the group course.

In addition, in cases where group work instructors combine didactic and experiential approaches, the potential for dual role conflicts raises a number of ethical issues. Faculty sometimes function in multiple roles and relationships with students and trainees without establishing and clarifying appropriate boundaries. One example of an ethical issue involves professors who accept students as therapy clients in their private practices. Other problematic areas include professors who reveal personal disclosures of students in a training group to other faculty, those who are unable to establish appropriate professional boundaries, and those who use the training group as a forum for dealing with their own personal problems.

Faculty have sometimes demonstrated poor judgment or misused power, improperly managed multiple roles and relationships, or acted in some other way to bring harm to a student. Some students who have been in a group course have talked about the experience as being anything but a positive learning experience. These students have learned what not to do in their own groups as a result of participating in a group course. For example, in some cases students have not been given any preparation for a group experience, and no attempt has been made to provide for informed consent. In other cases, students are sometimes left alone to form their own process group, which is a required part of the group course, with very little guidance and no supervision from the faculty person teaching the course. Undirected group experiences have the potential for being aimless or even damaging. Conflicts may not be properly addressed, and scapegoating of a particular member may take place. There may also be undue group pressure for members to reveal personal secrets, and hidden agendas can result in the group getting stuck.

Some professional educators have expressed concern about the potential pitfalls of experiential training or about the multiple roles and relationships involved in teaching group work. Although there have been some ethical problems in the attempt to train using experiential approaches, we do not think this warrants the conclusion that experiential approaches are inappropriate or unethical. Overcorrection of a problem of potential abuse does not seem justified to us. Teaching group process by involving students in personal ways is the best way for them to learn how to eventually set up and facilitate groups. We agree with Stockton, Morran, and Krieger (2004) who point out that there is a fine line between offering experiential activities and safeguarding against gaining information that could be used in evaluating students. Faculty who use experiential approaches are often involved in balancing multiple roles, which does require constant monitoring of boundaries. Stockton and colleagues stress that those with the greater power need to exert caution so that they offer training opportunities that will be ethical and efficacious.

Benefits of Experiential Training   Although we admit that there are inherent problems in teaching students how groups function by involving them on an experiential level, we think such difficulties can be resolved. Clear guidelines should be established so students know what their rights and responsibilities are. This arrangement does put a bit more pressure on both the instructor and the students, and it calls for honesty, maturity, and professionalism. The focus of such a group might well be on here-and-now interactions. Even if members choose not to bring up matters such as their childhood, there is plenty to talk about if they deal with how they are affected by the work of other members and their reactions to other people in the group. If members openly and honestly learn to deal with one another, they are making great strides toward learning how to facilitate a group.

No one training model or combination of safeguards is apt to solve the dilemma of protecting students from adverse dual relationships and at the same time providing them with the best possible training (Merta et al., 1993). It is challenging for those who teach group courses to learn ways to differentiate between experiential training workshops and counseling groups. At times it is difficult to draw clear distinctions between training workshops and counseling groups. It is essential that faculty who teach group courses or conduct training workshops for group workers monitor their practices by keeping the purpose of the training workshop clearly in mind. The boundaries between the domains of training workshops and counseling groups can be clarified by discussing relevant issues with colleagues.

It is essential to keep in mind the primary purpose of a group counseling course, which is teaching students leadership skills and providing an understanding of how group process works. Although the main aim of a group course is not to provide personal therapy for students, participating in such a group can and ought to be therapeutic. Students can make a decision about what personal concerns they are willing to share, and they can also determine the depth of their personal disclosures. A group course is not designed to be a substitute for an intensive self-exploration experience, but learning about how groups function can be enhanced through active and personal participation in the group process.

We have found that most students sincerely interested in becoming effective group practitioners are willing to get involved in both the academic training and the self-exploration that lead to becoming the best possible group counselor. Likewise, as educators, it is our challenge to provide the best training available, keeping in mind the safeguards mentioned here. For a useful discussion of the education and training of group therapists, see Sonstegard and Bitter, with Pelonis (2004), and the special issue on teaching group work in the *Journal for Specialists in Group Work* (March 2004) Vol. 29, 1.

✳ Guidelines for Ethical and Legal Practice

Most professional organizations affirm that practitioners should be aware of the prevailing community standards and of the possible impact on their practice of deviation from these standards. Ethical and legal issues are frequently intertwined, which makes it imperative that group practitioners not only follow the codes of ethics of their profession but that they also know their state's laws and their legal boundaries and responsibilities.

Those leaders who work with groups of children, adolescents, and certain involuntary populations are especially advised to learn the laws restricting group work. Issues such as confidentiality, parental consent, informed consent, record keeping, protection of member welfare, and civil rights of institutionalized patients are a few areas in which group workers must be knowledgeable. Because most group workers do not possess detailed legal knowledge, it is a good idea to obtain some legal information concerning group procedures and practices. Awareness of legal rights and responsibilities as they pertain to group work protects not only clients but also those who conduct groups from needless lawsuits arising from negligence or ignorance.

Legal Liability and Malpractice

Group counselors who fail to exercise due care and act in good faith are liable to a civil suit. Professionals leading groups are expected to practice within the code of ethics of their particular profession and to abide by legal standards. Practitioners are subject to civil liability for not doing right or for doing wrong to another. If group members can prove that personal injury or psychological harm is due to a group leader's failure to render proper service, either through negligence or ignorance, then this leader is open to a malpractice suit. Negligence consists of departing from the "standard of care"; that is, breaching the therapist's duty in providing what is determined as commonly accepted practices of others in the profession that leads to injury to the client.

Malpractice suits generally pertain to violations of confidentiality and sexual misconduct. Although these areas have received the greatest attention in the literature as grounds for malpractice suits, several other areas of practice can lead to a legal claim:

- Failure to obtain or document informed consent.
- Inadequate record keeping.
- Abandonment of a client.
- Marked departures from established therapeutic practices.
- Practicing beyond the scope of competency.
- Misdiagnosis.
- Improperly dealing with transference relationships.
- Failure to control a dangerous client.
- Failure to refer a client when it becomes clear that the person needs intervention beyond the worker's level of competence.
- Failure to exercise reasonable care prior to a client's suicide.

Legal Safeguards for Group Practitioners

The key to avoiding a malpractice suit is to maintain reasonable, ordinary, and prudent practices. The group leader guidelines that follow are useful in translating the terms *reasonable, ordinary,* and *prudent* into concrete actions.

1. The best safeguard against legal liability is to practice good client care.
2. Take time and exercise care in screening candidates for a group experience. Many potential problems can be averted by effective screening and referral practices.
3. Give the potential members of your groups enough information to make informed choices about group participation, and do not mystify

the group process. Professional honesty and openness with group members will go a long way toward building a trusting climate.

4. Develop written informed consent procedures at the outset of a group, and make sure that you review this information with the members. Using treatment contracts, signed by both the leader and the members, is an example of an informed consent procedure.

5. Obtain written parental or guardian consent when working with minors. This is generally a good practice even if not required by state law.

6. Keep relevant notes on each group member and each group session, especially if there are any concerns about a particular member.

7. Emphasize the importance of maintaining confidentiality before the group begins and at various times during the course of the group.

8. Inform group members that confidentiality in group counseling may not be protected under the state laws of privileged communication and that it cannot be guaranteed.

9. Be aware of those situations in which you legally *must* break confidentiality. If confidentiality must be breached, discuss it with the group member and obtain a written release.

10. Restrict your scope of practice to client populations for which you are prepared by virtue of your education, training, and experience.

11. Keep lines of communication open with the members of your groups, especially by informing them of your availability outside of the group.

12. Be aware of the state laws and the ethical guidelines of various professional organizations that limit your practice, as well as the policies of the agency for which you work. Practice within the boundaries of these laws and policies. Inform members about these policies and about legal and ethical limitations (such as exceptions to confidentiality and mandatory reporting).

13. Make it a practice to consult with colleagues or clinical supervisors whenever there is a potential ethical or legal concern. Clearly document the nature of the consultation. In addition to consultation, seek sources of ongoing supervision.

14. Have a clear rationale for the techniques you employ in group sessions. Be able to clearly and concisely discuss the theoretical underpinnings of your procedures.

15. Have a clear standard of care that can be applied to your services, and communicate this standard to the members.

16. Contact a group member who does not show up for more than one group session in a row and/or who suddenly terminates the group.

17. Document reasons for a group member's termination and any referrals or recommendations given.

18. Do not promise the members of your group anything you cannot deliver. Help them realize that their degree of effort and commitment will be key factors in determining the outcomes of the group experience.

19. If you work for an agency or institution, have a contract that specifies the employer's legal liability for your professional functioning.

20. Abide by the policies of the institution that employs you. If you disagree with certain policies, first attempt to find out the reasons for them, and then see if it is possible to work within the framework of those policies.

21. Do not become entangled in social relationships with current group members. Be aware of ethical practice regarding former members.

22. Do not engage in sexual relationships with either current or former group members.

23. Promote an atmosphere of respect for diversity within the group context.

24. Make it a practice to assess the general progress of a group, and teach members how to evaluate their individual progress toward their own goals.

25. Develop policies and procedures for suicide assessment and incorporate them into the screening interview.

26. Learn how to assess and intervene in cases in which group participants pose a threat to themselves or others and be sure to document actions taken.

27. Be alert to when it is appropriate to refer a group member for another form of treatment as well as when group counseling might be inadvisable.

28. Remain alert to the ways your personal reactions might inhibit the group process, and monitor your countertransference.

29. Facilitate group sessions in a safe, private location free from distractions or interruptions.

30. Be careful of meeting your own needs at the expense of the members of your group. Avoid using the group as a place where you work through your personal problems.

31. Incorporate established ethical standards in your practice of group work.

32. Take steps to keep up with theoretical and research developments that have a direct application to group work. Update your group leadership skills.

33. Attend risk management workshops periodically with the goal of familiarizing yourself with current standards of practice.

34. Realize that you will never be completely safe from a potential claim or lawsuit, regardless of how competent and ethical you are. However, proactive risk management strategies can lessen the possibility of such claims.

35. Carry malpractice insurance. Students are not protected against malpractice suits.

A useful resource for risk management practices is Kennedy, Vandehey, Norman, and Diekhoff (2003). This article gives recommendations for risk management strategies that can be applied to group work.

This discussion of ethical and legal issues relevant for group work is not intended to increase your anxiety level or make you so careful that you avoid taking any risks. Leading groups is a risky as well as a professionally rewarding venture. You are bound to make mistakes from time to time. Making mistakes is not necessarily fatal: Be willing to acknowledge your mistakes and learn from them. By making full use of supervision, you not only learn from what may seem like mistakes but you also minimize the chances of harming clients. We hope you will not be frozen with anxiety over needing to be all-knowing at all times or afraid to intervene for fear of becoming embroiled in a lawsuit. It is a disservice to treat group members as though they were fragile and, thus, never to challenge them. Perhaps the best way to prevent a malpractice action is by having a sincere interest in doing what is going to benefit your client. We encourage you to remain willing to ask yourself these questions throughout your professional career: *What* am I doing, and *why* am I doing it? And *how* would it be if my colleagues observed my professional behavior? (For a more detailed discussion of ethical and legal issues, see Corey, Corey, and Callanan, 2003.)

✓ *Points to Remember*

Ethical and Legal Issues in Group Counseling

You are challenged to take a position on basic professional issues pertaining to your role as a group practitioner. The guidelines presented here provide a quick reference as you read the remainder of this book. Our aim in presenting these guidelines is to stimulate you to think about a framework that will guide you in making sound decisions as a leader.

✓ Take time to reflect on your personal identity, especially as it is influenced by your professional work. Think about your needs and behavior styles and about the impact of these factors on group participants. It is essential for you to have a clear idea of what your roles and functions are in the group so you can communicate them to members.

✓ Codes of ethics have been established by various professional organizations, and those who belong to such organizations are bound by them. Ethical guidelines governing group practice are not something you decide alone or in a vacuum. Familiarize yourself with these established codes of ethics and with the laws that may affect group practice.

✓ Have a clear idea of the type of group you are designing and why it is the treatment of choice. Be able to express the purpose of the group and the characteristics of the clients who will be admitted. Such a written rationale might include descriptions of the goals of the group, the means that will be used to accomplish these goals, the role of the members, your function and role, and the means that will be used to assess the outcomes.

✓ Be aware of the implications of cultural diversity in designing groups and in orienting members to the group process.

✓ Tell prospective group members what is expected of them, and encourage them to develop a contract that will provide them with the impetus to obtain their personal goals.

✓ Make prospective participants aware of the techniques that will be employed and of the exercises that they may be asked to participate in. Give them the ground rules that will govern group activities.

✓ Make clear from the outset of a group what the focus will be. Will the focus be primarily educational? Will self-understanding be a primary emphasis?

✓ Avoid undertaking a project that is beyond the scope of your training and experience. Make a written statement of your qualifications to conduct a particular group available to the participants.

✓ Point out the risks involved in group participation both before members join and also when it is appropriate throughout the life of the group. It is your responsibility to help members identify and explore their readiness to deal with these potential risks. It is also your job to minimize the risks.

✓ Protect members' rights to decide what to share with the group and what activities to participate in. Be sensitive to any form of group pressure that violates the self-determination of an individual and to any activity, such as scapegoating or stereotyping, that undermines a person's sense of self.

✓ Develop a rationale for using group exercises and be able to verbalize it. Use only techniques you are competent to employ, preferably those you have experienced as a group member.

✓ Relate practice to theory and remain open to integrating multiple approaches in your practice. Keep informed about research findings on group process, and use this information to increase the effectiveness of your practice.

✓ Begin and end group sessions on time.

✓ Be aware of the danger of meeting your needs at the expense of group members' needs.

✓ Emphasize the importance of confidentiality to members before they enter a group, during the group sessions when relevant, and before the group terminates.

✓ Explain to members that legal privilege does not apply to group counseling (unless provided by state statute).

✓ Keep records of group sessions in compliance with codes of ethics and institutional policies.

✓ When it is appropriate, be open with the group about your values but avoid imposing them on members. Recognize the role culture and socialization play in the formulation of members' values. Respect your clients' capacity to think for themselves, and be sure that members give one another the same respect.

✓ Be alert for symptoms of psychological debilitation in group members, which may indicate that participation in the group should be discontinued. Make referral resources available to people who need or desire further psychological assistance.

✓ Encourage participants to discuss their experience in the group and help them evaluate the degree to which they are meeting their personal goals. Set aside some time at the end of each session for members to express their thoughts and feelings about that session.

✓ Do not expect the transfer of learning from the group to daily life to occur automatically. Assist members in applying what they are learning. Prepare them for setbacks they are likely to encounter when they try to transfer their group learning to their daily lives.

✓ Develop some method of evaluation to determine the effectiveness of the procedures you use. Even informal research efforts can help you make informed judgments about how well your leadership style is working.

Exercises

In-Class Activities

1. **Confronting gossiping.** It comes to your attention that certain members have been gossiping about matters that came up in a high school group you are leading. Do you deal with the offenders privately or in the group? What do you say?

2. **Limits of confidentiality.** You are about to begin leading a high school counseling group, and the policy of the school is that any teacher or counselor who becomes aware that a student is using drugs is expected to report the student to the principal. How do you cope with this situation?

3. **Dealing with parents.** You are conducting a self-exploration group with children in a family clinic. The father of one of the children in your group meets with you to find out how his child is doing. What do you tell him? What do you not tell him? Would you be inclined to meet with the father and his child? How might you handle this same situation with a request made by a noncustodial parent where the parents are divorced?

4. **Forming a group.** You are a private practitioner who wants to colead a weekend assertiveness training workshop. How would you announce your workshop? How would you screen potential members? Whom might you exclude from your workshop, and why?

5. **Coping with resistance.** You are employed as a counselor in the adolescent ward of a county mental hospital. As one of your duties you lead a group for the young people, who are required to attend the sessions. You sense resistance on the part of the members. What are the ethical problems involved? How do you deal with the resistance?

6. **Leading an involuntary group.** You are asked to lead a group composed of involuntary clients. Because their participation is mandatory, you want to take steps to clearly and fully inform them of procedures to be used, their rights and responsibilities as members, your expectations of them, and matters such as confidentiality. If you were to write an informed consent document, what would you most want to put in this brief letter?

7. **Confronting an unhappy group member.** A member in a group you are leading comes to you after one of the sessions, saying, "I don't want to come back next week. It doesn't seem as if we're getting anywhere in here,

because all that ever goes on is people putting each other down. I just don't trust anyone in here!" She has not said any of this in the sessions, and the group has been meeting for 5 weeks. What might you say or do? Would you attempt to persuade her to stay in the group? Why or why not?

8. **Leader's values.** Consider some of the following areas in which your values and those of group members might clash. How would you respond in each of these situations that could arise in your group?

   a. A member discloses how excited she is over a current affair and wonders if she should continue staying with her partner.

   b. A woman whose cultural background is different from yours and that of the other members in the group says she is having difficulty expressing what she wants and in behaving assertively (both in the group and at home). She says she has been taught to think of the interests of others and not to be concerned about what she wants.

   c. An adolescent relates that his life feels bland without drugs.

   d. A pregnant 16-year-old is struggling to decide whether to have an abortion or give up her baby to an adoption agency.

   e. A chronically depressed man talks about suicide as his way out of a hopeless situation.

   f. A man says he is very unhappy in his marriage but is unwilling to get a divorce because he is afraid of being alone.

   g. A member who is from a different culture than the other members says he is having difficulty in the group because he is not used to speaking so freely or openly about family problems.

9. **Diversity guidelines.** You are on a committee to formulate guidelines to help counseling students learn how to deal effectively with diversity in their groups. What issues most need to be addressed? What guidelines might you suggest to address these issues? What experiences would help students examine their attitudes and beliefs about diversity? What kind of information do you think students most need, and how might they best acquire this knowledge? What are your recommendations for developing skill in leading culturally diverse groups?

10. **Informed consent.** Create your own informed consent form for a group. What aspects would you want to make sure to include? How would you ascertain whether a member understood the various elements contained in your form?

11. **Experiential work.** In small groups, discuss what you think a university program should inform students of regarding experiential work. Come up with a brief statement about what students can expect regarding experiential aspects of the program. How would you make certain that students had this information prior to enrolling in the program?

12. **Contacting the Association for Specialists in Group Work (ASGW).** For guidelines for training group counselors, for best practice guidelines,

and for guidelines for diversity-competent group work, go to the Web addresses listed here and print out these guidelines. This material can be discussed in class for both Chapters 2 and 3. Information about the Association for Specialists in Group Work (ASGW) is available from the main Web site (http://www.asgw.org).

- "ASGW Professional Standards for the Training of Group Counselors": http://www.asgw.org/training_standards.htm
- "ASGW Best Practice Guidelines": http://www.asgw.org/best.htm
- "ASGW Principles for Diversity-Competent Group Workers": http://www.asgw.org/diversity.htm

13. **Teaching group counseling.** The *Journal for Specialists in Group Work* has a complete volume devoted to teaching group work (see Association for Specialists in Group Work, March 2004). Look up one or more of the following articles pertaining to the teaching of group counseling, and determine the kind of issues being examined: Akos, Goodnough, and Milsom (2004), Barlow (2004), Bemak and Chung (2004), Conyne and Bemak (2004), Davenport (2004), Guth and McDonnell (2004), Killacky and Hulse-Killacky (2004), Kottler (2004), O'Halloran and McCartney (2004), Riva and Korinek (2004), Van Velsor (2004), and Wilson, Rapin, and Haley-Banez (2004).

InfoTrac College Edition

For additional readings, explore InfoTrac College Edition, our online library, at http://www.infotrac.college.com/wadsworth. The following keywords are listed in such a way as to enable the InfoTrac College Edition search engine to locate a wider range of articles. The keywords should be entered exactly as listed, to include asterisks, "w1," "w2," "AND," and other search engine tools.

- group* w2 technique* AND therap*
- multicult* w3 awareness
- group* w2 technique* AND couns*

Part 2

Group Process
Stages of Development

The stages in the life of a group do not generally flow neatly and predictably in the order described in the following chapters. In actuality there is considerable overlap between the stages, and once a group moves to an advanced stage, it is not uncommon for it to stay at a plateau for a time or to temporarily regress to an earlier stage. Similarly, the fact that certain tasks have been accomplished in a group does not mean that new conflicts will not erupt. Groups ebb and flow, and both members and leaders need to pay attention to the factors that affect the direction a group takes.

Understanding the typical patterns during different stages of a group will give you a valuable perspective and help you predict problems and intervene in appropriate and timely ways. Knowledge of the critical turning points in a group can guide you in helping participants mobilize their resources to successfully meet the tasks facing them at each stage. Although we discuss these stages as taking place over the lifetime of the group, it is important to remember that members may work through many of these stages in a single session as well, moving from initial comments to a brief transition, followed by productive work, and ending with reflection on what has been accomplished. The stages of a group include the pregroup, initial, transition, working, and final stages.

The *pregroup stage* consists of all the factors involved in the formation of a group. Careful thought and planning are necessary to lay a solid foundation for any group, including designing a proposal for a group, attracting members, screening and selecting members, and the orientation process. All these practical considerations take a great deal of time, yet attending to this preliminary phase will increase the chances of having a productive group.

The *initial stage* of a group is a time of orientation and exploration, and members tend to present the dimensions of themselves they consider to be socially acceptable. This phase is generally characterized by a certain degree of anxiety and insecurity about the structure of the group. Typically, members bring to the group certain expectations, concerns, and anxieties, and it is vital that they be allowed to express them openly. As members get to know one another and learn how the group functions, they develop the norms that will govern the group, explore fears and expectations pertaining to the group, identify personal goals, clarify personal themes they want to explore, and determine if this group is a safe place. The manner in which the leader deals with the reactions of members determines the degree of trust that develops.

Before group members can interact at the depths they are capable of, the group generally goes through a somewhat challenging *transition stage.* During this stage, the leader's task is to help members learn how to begin working on the concerns that brought them to the group. It is the members' task to monitor their thoughts, feelings, reactions, and actions and to learn to express them verbally. Leaders can help members come to recognize and accept their fear and defensiveness yet, at the same time, challenge them to work through their anxieties and any reluctances they may be experiencing. Group leaders need to understand the impact of apprehension among members and encourage them to explore any reluctance they may have in participating in the group.

The *working stage* is characterized by productiveness, which builds on the effective work done in the initial and transition stages. Mutuality and self-exploration increase, and the group is focused on making behavioral changes. In actual practice the transition stage and the working stage merge with each other. During the working stage, the group may return to earlier themes of trust, conflict, and reluctance to participate. As the group takes on new challenges, deeper levels of trust will be achieved. New conflicts may emerge as the group evolves, and commitment is necessary to do the difficult work of moving forward. All members may not be able to function at the same level of intensity, and some may remain on the periphery, holding back and being more afraid to take risks. Indeed, there are individual differences among members at all of the stages of a group. Productive work occurs at all stages of a group, not just at the working stage, but the quality and depth of the work takes different forms at various developmental phases of the group. Some groups may never reach a working stage, but significant learning often occurs anyway and individuals may still benefit from their group experience.

The *final stage* is a time to further identify what was learned and to decide how this new learning can become part of daily living. Group activities include terminating, summarizing, pulling together loose ends, and integrating and interpreting the group experience. As the group is ending, the focus is on conceptualization and bringing closure to the group experience. During the termination process, the group will deal with feelings of separation, address unfinished business, review the group experience, practice for behavioral change, design action plans, identify strategies for coping with relapse, and build a supportive network. ✳

Chapter 4

Forming a Group

Focus Questions

*B*efore reading this chapter, think about what leaders need to consider in organizing a group. If you have planned for a group in the past, what principles guided your thinking? As you read this chapter, consider these questions:

1. What importance do you place on the planning and formation aspects of a group?

2. How would you draft a written proposal for a group, and how would you "sell" your idea to the agency, school, or institution where you work?

3. How would you announce your group and recruit members? What kind of marketing strategies might you use? What are some practical ways you can think of to get a group started?

4. What criteria would you use to screen and select members for a group? If you decided to exclude someone who had applied, how would you handle this matter?

5. If you were conducting individual interviews to select group participants, what questions would you most want to ask?

6. How would you explain to a potential member the risks and benefits involved in groups? What are some ways of minimizing the psychological risks?

7. What diversity issues would you consider in designing your group and selecting members? How will your group meet the needs of culturally diverse clients?

8. What are some advantages of a preliminary session in which potential members can determine whether a given group is for them? How would you want to make use of this first meeting?

9. What are the major ethical considerations in organizing and forming a group?

10. Do you have different attitudes about forming a voluntary group than you do regarding an involuntary one?

✳ Introduction

We cannot overemphasize the importance of the preparatory period during which a group is organized. Careful attention to forming a group is crucial to its outcome. You will spend time wisely by thinking about what kind of group you want and by getting yourself psychologically ready for your leadership role and functions. The more clearly you can state your expectations, the better you will be able to plan and the more meaningful the experience is likely to be for participants.

A lack of careful thought and planning generally leads to a variety of problems showing up later that result in confusion and floundering among participants. An initial step in planning a group is clarifying the rationale for it, which entails drafting a detailed proposal.

Developing a Proposal for a Group

Many good ideas for groups are never put into practice because they are not developed into a clear and convincing plan. If you are going to create a group under the auspices of an agency, you will probably have to explain your proposed goals and methods. Consider these questions when preparing your proposal:

- What type of group are you forming? Will it be long term or short term?
- For whom is the group intended? Identify the specific population. What do you know about the developmental needs of this population?
- What is the cultural mix of the group, and what are the implications of the cultural mix for forming the group?
- Is the group composed of voluntary or involuntary members? If it is a mandatory group, what special considerations would you address?
- What are the general goals and purposes of this group? That is, what will members gain from participating in it?
- Why is there a need for such a group?
- What are your basic assumptions underlying this project?
- What are your qualifications to lead this group?
- What screening and selection procedures will be used? What is your rationale for these particular procedures?
- How many members will be in the group? Where will the group meet? How often will it meet? How long will each meeting last? Will new people be allowed to join the group once it has started? Will the group be "open" or "closed?"
- How will the members be prepared for the group experience? What ground rules will you establish at the outset?
- What structure will your group have? What techniques will be used? Why are these techniques appropriate? In what ways can you employ your techniques in a flexible manner to meet the needs of culturally diverse client populations?
- How will you handle the fact that people may be taking some risks by participating in the group? What will you do to safeguard members from unnecessary risks? Will you take any special precautions with participants who are minors?
- How will you handle situations such as a member arriving at a group session while under the influence of alcohol or drugs?
- What evaluation procedures do you plan? What follow-up procedures are planned?
- What topics will be explored in this group?

These five general areas form the basis of a sound and practical proposal:

1. **Rationale.** Do you have a clear and convincing rationale for your group? Are you able to answer questions that might be raised?

2. **Objectives.** Are you clear about what you most want to attain and how you will go about doing so? Are your objectives specific, measurable, and attainable within the specified time?

3. **Practical considerations.** Is the membership defined? Are meeting times, frequency of meetings, and duration of the group reasonable?

4. **Procedures.** Have you selected specific procedures to meet the stated objectives? Are these procedures appropriate and realistic for the given population?

5. **Evaluation.** Does your proposal contain strategies for evaluating how well the stated objectives were met? Are your evaluation methods objective, practical, and relevant?

Working Within the System

If you hope to have your proposal accepted both by your supervisors in an agency and by the potential members, you will need to develop the skills necessary to work within a system. To get a group off the ground, you need to negotiate sensitively with the staff of the institution involved. In all clinics, agencies, schools, and hospitals, power issues and political realities play a role. You may become excited about organizing groups only to encounter resistance from your coworkers or your administrators. You may be told, for example, that only psychologists, social workers, and psychiatrists are qualified to lead groups. The rest of the staff may be cynical about the prospects of doing groups in your setting. Or you may be told that classroom academics are more important than having children spend their time in a group dealing with emotional or personal problems. Some of your colleagues may be jealous of your efforts, especially if you have successful groups.

The representatives of institutions need to be educated about the potential value, as well as the realistic limitations, of groups for their clients. It is helpful to be able to predict some of the major concerns that administrators and agency directors are likely to have about the proposal you submit. For example, if you are attempting to organize a group in a public high school, the administrators may be anxious about parental complaints and potential lawsuits. If you are able to appreciate their concerns and speak directly to ethical and legal issues, you stand a better chance of getting your proposal accepted. If you are not clear in your own mind about what you hope to accomplish through group work or how you will conduct the meetings, the chances are slim that a responsible administrator will endorse your program. If you have not thought through some questions you are likely to be asked about your proposal, you are setting yourself up for defeat. Here are a few examples of questions we have been asked as we were presenting a group proposal:

- How will this institution be covered legally in the event of a lawsuit?
- Will the program be voluntary, and will the parents of minors give written consent?

- How will you attend to prospective group members who have special needs, such as those with visual impairments, speech and/or hearing impairments, and those dependent on wheelchairs?
- What will you do if this group proves to be psychologically disruptive for some of the members?
- Are you prepared to deal with confrontations from parents, teachers, or community members?

Regardless of the type of group you wish to form, having a clear and organized written proposal and presenting it personally are key components for translating ideas into action. Twenty sample group proposals are presented in Chapters 9 through 12. As you review these proposals for various groups, think of specific groups that would be appropriate to the population you serve and the setting in which you work. See what aspects you can draw from each of these proposals to fit your needs.

※ Attracting and Screening Members

Assuming that you have been successful in getting a proposal accepted, the next step is to find a practical way to announce your group to prospective participants. How a group is announced influences both the way it will be received by potential members and the kind of people who will join. Although professional standards should prevail over a commercialized approach, we have found that making personal contact with potential members is one of the best methods of recruiting.

Guidelines for Announcing a Group and Recruiting Group Members

Professional issues are involved in publicizing a group and recruiting members. The "Best Practice Guidelines" (ASGW, 1998) state that prospective members should have access to relevant information about the group (preferably in writing), such as the following:

- A professional disclosure statement
- A statement of the goals and purposes of the group
- Policies related to entering and exiting the group
- Expectations for group participation including voluntary and involuntary membership
- Policies and procedures governing mandated groups (where relevant)
- The rights and responsibilities of both group members and the group leader
- Documentation procedures and disclosure of information to others
- Implications of out-of-group contact or involvement among members

- Procedures for consultation between group leader(s) and group member(s)
- Techniques and procedures that may be used
- Education, training, and qualifications of the group leader
- Fees and time parameters
- A realistic statement of what services can and cannot be provided within a particular group structure
- Potential consequences of group participation (personal risks involved in the group)

In writing announcements, it is best to give an accurate picture of the group and to avoid making promises about the outcomes of the group that may raise unrealistic expectations. As we have indicated, making direct contact with the population most likely to benefit from the group is an excellent way to follow up printed announcements. These personal contacts, which can include distributing printed information to those interested, lessen the chance that people will misunderstand the purposes and functioning of the group.

It is also important in announcing and recruiting for a group to inform your agency colleagues. They can then refer clients to you who are appropriate for the particular group. It is possible that they can also do the preliminary screening, including giving written information on the group to potential members with whom they have contact. Involve your coworkers as much as possible in every phase of organizing your group.

Practical Procedures for Announcements and Recruitment

To illustrate how the guidelines for forming a group apply to a school setting, an example of identifying and recruiting a target population is provided by Deborah Lambert and Nancy Ceraso of North Allegheny Senior High School in Pennsylvania. In working with high school students, they had to deal with students' negative perceptions about certain kinds of groups. It was difficult to attract students who could benefit from a group experience because of the pain or stigma associated with a targeted population. One solution to the recruitment difficulty was to promote the group in a positive way. For example, a "Children of Alcoholics" (COA) population can be alternatively served in a "Self-Development Group." This allows school personnel workers to access the desired population, address the skill deficits, and reduce the level of resistance typically encountered. This group offers skill-building opportunities as opposed to addiction education, and a COA student will benefit from participation in either group or from involvement in both groups. Here are some other practical strategies and considerations Lambert and Ceraso find helpful in overcoming student identification and recruitment difficulties:

Classroom Presentations. Presenting the information to individual classrooms or to homerooms is one of the most effective means of announcing and recruiting potential group members. It is also helpful to request the classroom teacher be present while giving your classroom presentation. Films, lectures, and discussions naturally increase knowledge and sensitivity among the student body.

Hallway Posters. Place signs in well-attended areas such as the cafeteria, hallways, and bathrooms. Attractive and eye-catching phrases increase the likelihood of a response. "Tear-off" phone numbers or "take-one" business cards allow for discretion and future reference. Remove the signs after 3 to 4 weeks, but post new ones at regular intervals.

PA Announcements. Public-address announcements have limited effectiveness, given the frequency of students missing them or tuning them out. It is helpful to make announcements at different times in the day or to visually display the announcements' contents at a designated location.

Closed Circuit Cable TV. Facilitators or students can do a 2- or 3-minute segment on specific upcoming groups. Alternatively, general information on the benefits of group participation can be highlighted.

Newspaper Articles. Advertise in the school paper. Include registration information and key phrases to describe the groups. Supply articles written by past or present members or by facilitators.

Student Assistance Web Site. The SAT Web site serves as an excellent vehicle to dispense information about the district's SAT program, advertise upcoming events, and provide updated information on the latest drug and alcohol research, trends, and support groups.

Teacher Contacts. Keep faculty members informed of the groups available. Provide them with a brief description of the types of students you hope to access. Familiarize teachers with the characteristics and behavior that typify the target population. Provide homeroom teachers with an announcement to be read to their classes describing the groups and giving the names of the group facilitators.

Parent Letter or Bulletin. Inform parents of the groups available and the benefits of participating. Include the names and telephone numbers of the facilitators to contact for more information.

Peer Referrals. Friends can be an excellent resource. Follow your school policy on peer referrals. Take steps to screen peer referrals so they are appropriate from a recommendation and motivation standpoint. Offer a "bring a buddy" session in existing groups so that friends can learn about groups.

Discipline Alternatives. When violations of school rules or policies occur, students may be offered group participation as a discipline alternative or consequence. A student may opt to participate in a designated group in lieu of a suspension or to avoid getting a longer suspension. A student may be assigned to a group, or a school staff member may recommend participation in a group instead of suspension.

Student Handbook. Include a description of your program and the various groups that will be held in the student handbook distributed at the beginning of each year.

Counselor Staffing/Child Study Teams. Meet with the counselors, the school nurse, and administrators to let them know about the groups being offered. Interdisciplinary teams are very knowledgeable sources when it comes to identifying potential candidates.

Student Assistance Programs. Some schools have student assistant programs for students experiencing school difficulties that are secondary to drug and alcohol usage, mental health issues, family conflicts, or peer relationships. At-risk students are invited to participate in prevention activities or are offered an intervention opportunity. Faculty members and administrators are trained to become student assistance team members. The facilitation of groups is an integral responsibility of student assistance programs, and in some instances this is the only department offering groups. A partnership with student assistance programs is a valuable resource.

The main point is that Ceraso and Lambert do not wait passively for students to come in and sign up for the groups they offer. Instead, they use multiple approaches to contact students directly (giving talks in the classrooms) and indirectly (meeting with counselors, teachers, and parents). Because of their own enthusiasm for their groups, they are more likely to recruit students who could profit. Chapter 10 includes descriptions of two groups Ceraso and Lambert offer at North Allegheny Senior High School: a group for children of alcoholics and one for students who are recovering from addiction.

Screening and Selection Procedures

After announcing a group and recruiting members, the next crucial step is arranging for screening and selecting the members who will make up the group. The ASGW (1998) "Best Practice Guidelines" state: "Group Workers screen prospective group members if appropriate to the type of group being offered. When selection of group members is appropriate, Group Workers identify group members whose needs and goals are compatible with the goals of the group" (A.7.a). This guideline raises several questions: Should screening be used? If so, what screening method suits the group? How can you determine who would be best suited for the group, who might have a negative impact on the group process, or who might be hurt by the experience? How can you best inform those candidates who, for whatever reason, are not selected for your group?

It is essential to consider including potentially difficult individuals as they may well be the very ones who could most benefit from a group experience. Sometimes leaders screen out individuals due to their own personal dislike or countertransference issues even though these individuals might be appropriate clients for the group. The goal of screening is to prevent potential harm to clients, not to make the leader's job easier by setting up a group of homogeneous members. Indeed, most Adlerians believe that screening potential group members is counterproductive:

> The isolated, noncommunicative, or disruptive can only find real solutions to their problems in a group setting. . . . All of us meet difficult people to varying degrees in everyday life. We cope, or we learn to cope. There is no significant need for group members to be protected from difficult people. . . . When possible, groups work best if (a) no one is compelled to join a group, and (b) no one who wishes to join is turned away. (Sonstegard & Bitter, with Pelonis, 2004, p. 112)

Screening potential group members is contrary to Adlerians' theoretical orientation. They believe "the selection process itself fails to provide an opportunity for those who need it most" (p. 112). Consider whether a selection process is appropriate for your group, and carefully evaluate your screening criteria.

When selecting members of your group, it may be appropriate to consider diversity issues. DeLucia-Waack (1996) suggests that the screening process should take into account balance and diversity, as well as individual characteristics of potential group members. The ideal group should contain a variety of resources, worldviews, and behavioral skills. Consider putting together a group of individuals who share common experiences yet who also are diverse in a number of respects. Through interaction in a diverse group, members often have an opportunity to dispel stereotypes and misconceptions about one another. If member composition is carefully considered and balanced, members have opportunities both to connect with and to learn from each other.

Ultimately, the type of group should determine the kind of members accepted. A person who can work well in a structured, short-term group designed to teach social skills or to cope with stress might not be ready for an intensive therapy type group. Individuals with severe disorders would probably be excluded from a counseling group yet might benefit from a weekly group for outpatients at a mental health center. The question that needs to be considered is: Should *this* particular person be included in *this* particular group at *this* time with *this* group leader?

Preliminary Screening Sessions

We support screening procedures that include a private session between the candidate and the leader. During the individual session, the leader might look for evidence that the group will be beneficial to the candidate. Here are some questions to consider: Is this person motivated to change? Is this a choice of the individual or of someone else? Why this particular type of group? Does this person understand what the purposes of the group are? Are there any indications that group counseling is contraindicated for this person at this time?

Group applicants are to be encouraged, at their private sessions, to interview the group leader. They can be invited to ask questions concerning the procedures, basic purposes, and any other aspect of the group. This questioning is important as a means not only of getting information but also of developing a feeling of confidence in the group leader, which is necessary if productive work is to take place. In other words, we believe screening is best viewed as a two-way process and that potential members be encouraged to form a judgment about the group and the leader. Given enough information about the group, a member can make a more informed decision about whether to join.

In addition to the private screening, a group session for all the candidates is valuable. At a preliminary session the leader can outline the reason for the group and the topics that might be explored. This introduction can be most helpful for people who are uncertain whether they want to invest themselves in this group. Potential members can meet one another and begin to explore the potential of the group.

We submit that screening and selection procedures are subjective and that the intuition and judgment of the leader are crucial. We are concerned that candidates benefit from a group but even more concerned that they might be psychologically hurt by it or might drain the group's energies excessively. Certain members can remain unaffected by a group yet sap its energy for productive work. This is particularly true of hostile people, people who monopolize, extremely aggressive people, and people who act out. The potential gains of including certain of these members must be weighed against the probable losses to the group as a whole. Group counseling is contraindicated for individuals who are suicidal, extremely fragmented or acutely psychotic, sociopathic, facing extreme crises, highly paranoid, or extremely self-centered (Yalom, 1995).

A leader needs to develop a system for assessing the likelihood that a candidate will benefit from a group experience. Factors that must be taken into consideration are the level of training of the leader, the proposed makeup of the group, the setting, and the basic nature of the group. For example, it might be best not to accept a highly defensive individual into an ongoing adolescent group, for several reasons. A group may be too threatening for a person so vulnerable and may lead to increased defensiveness and rigidity, or such a person may have a counterproductive effect on group members who want to do serious work.

In some cases it may not be possible to conduct individual interviews, and alternatives will have to be used. One alternative is group screening sessions. This method saves time and also has the advantage of providing an idea of how each person reacts to a group situation. If you work in a county facility or a state hospital, you may simply be assigned a group and have no opportunity to screen members. The basis for assigning members could be their diagnosis or the ward where they are placed. Even if you are not able to select members for your group, you can make at least brief individual contact to prepare them. You will also have to devote part of the initial sessions to preparation, for many of the members may not have the faintest idea why they are in the group or how the group might be of any value to them. In "open groups," whose membership changes when some clients leave and new ones are added, it is a good practice to meet individually with incoming members so you can orient them.

Assessing and Choosing Members   We are often asked these questions: How do you decide who will best fit into the group, who will most benefit from it, and who is likely to be harmed by the experience? If you decide to exclude a person from the group, how do you handle this in a tactful and therapeutic manner? As a group leader, you are expected to make the ultimate decision to include or exclude certain clients. Because the groups we typically offer are voluntary, one factor we look for during the interview is the degree to which a candidate wants to make changes and is willing to expend the necessary effort. We consider whether a group seems the appropriate method of intervention to accomplish the desired changes. We also weigh heavily how much the candidate seems to want to become a member of this group, especially after he or she is given information about it.

There have been times when we were reluctant to let certain people into a group in spite of their desire to join. As we've mentioned, we do pay attention to our clinical hunches concerning a person, so in the last analysis our screening and selection process is a subjective one. A variety of clinical reasons might lead us to exclude a person, but whatever our reservations are, we discuss them with the prospective member. At times, after we've discussed our concerns, we see matters differently. At other times we simply cannot with a clear conscience admit a person.

If we do not accept people, we tend to stress how the group might not be appropriate for them. We strive to break the news in a manner that is honest, direct, and sensitive and that helps those who are not being accepted to remain open to other options. Ethical practice involves offering those candidates who are not accepted into the group the support they need in dealing with their reactions to not be included in the group, and as well, suggesting alternatives to group participation. For example, we might determine that a highly defensive and extremely anxious person who is very frightened in interpersonal relationships is likely to benefit from a series of individual counseling sessions before being placed in a group situation. We would explain our rationale and encourage the person to consider accepting a referral for an appropriate type of intervention. In other words, we do not close the door on people we exclude from a group with no explanation, nor do we convey that there is something intrinsically wrong with them because they were not included in this particular group.

When we do in-service training workshops for group leaders in various agencies and institutions, many leaders tell us they do not screen people for their groups. They cite any number of reasons: they do not have the time; they do not have much voice in choosing group members because people are simply assigned to a group; they do not really know how to determine who will or will not benefit or will be negatively influenced by a group experience; they cannot see why screening is really important; they do not want to play the role of expert in deciding who will be included or excluded; or they do not want to make a mistake by turning away people who might gain from a group. In those situations where individual screening is not practical, we encourage practitioners to devise alternative strategies. For example, instead of screening people individually, screening and orientation can be done with several potential group members at once. If this is not possible, it is a good idea to at least briefly meet the members of your group prior to the first session. Another alternative is to make the first session of a group the time for orientation and getting a commitment from the members. In any case, we emphasize that we see screening not as a highly objective and scientific process but as a device for getting together the best clientele for a given group.

As we mentioned earlier, our view of screening entails a dialogue with the prospective members. It is an opportunity to give information to them and to orient them to the group, and it is a way to help them share in the decision of whether it is appropriate for them to become involved. This process can be accomplished in many ways.

✳ Practical Considerations in Forming a Group

Group Composition

Whether a group should have a homogeneous membership or a heterogeneous one depends on the group's purpose and goals. In general, for a specific target population with given needs, a group composed entirely of members of that population is more appropriate than a heterogeneous group. Consider a group composed entirely of elderly people. It can focus exclusively on the specific problems that characterize their developmental period, such as loneliness, isolation, lack of meaning, rejection, financial pressures, deterioration of the body, and so forth. This similarity of the members can lead to a great degree of cohesion, which in turn allows for an open and intense exploration of their life crises. Members can express feelings that have been kept private, and their life circumstances can give them a bond with one another.

Examples of other homogeneous groups are Alcoholics Anonymous, Recovery Inc., Parents Without Partners, Divorce Care, and Weight Watchers. It is common, for example, to hear people claim that one cannot fully understand, and thus cannot help with, an alcoholic's unique problems unless one has actually experienced what it is like to be an alcoholic. We do not accept the premise that the group leader must have experienced every problem of the client. It is important only that group leaders be able to identify with the feelings of clients—their loneliness, fear, and anxiety. When a specific problem exists, however, group cohesion can help, and so homogeneity is appropriate.

Sometimes a microcosm of the outside social structure is desired, and in that case diverse membership should be sought. Personal-growth groups, process groups, interpersonal groups, and certain therapy groups tend to be heterogeneous. Members can experiment with new behavior and develop interpersonal skills with the help of feedback from a rich variety of people in an environment that represents everyday reality.

Group Size

What is a desirable size for a group? The answer depends on several factors: age of clients, experience of the leader, type of group, and problems to be explored. For instance, a group composed of elementary school children might be kept to 3 or 4, whereas a group of adolescents might be made up of 6 to 8 people. There may be as many as 20 or 30 children in developmental group guidance classes. For a weekly ongoing group of adults, about 8 people with one leader may be ideal. A group of this size is big enough to give ample opportunity for interaction and small enough for everyone to be involved and to feel a sense of "group."

Frequency and Duration of Meetings

How often should a group meet? For how long? Should a group meet twice weekly for 1-hour sessions? Or is 1½ to 2 hours once a week preferable? With children and adolescents it may be better to meet more frequently and for a shorter period to suit their attention span. If the group is taking place in a school setting, the meeting times can correspond to regularly scheduled class periods. For groups of relatively well-functioning adults, a 2-hour weekly session might be preferable. This 2-hour period is long enough to allow some intensive work yet not so long that fatigue sets in. You can choose any frequency and duration that suit your style of leadership and the type of people in your group. For an inpatient group composed of lower functioning members, it is desirable to meet on a daily basis for 45 minutes. Because of the members' psychological impairment, it may not be possible to hold their attention for a longer period. Even for higher functioning inpatient groups, it is a good practice to meet several times a week, but these groups might be scheduled for 90 minutes. (An excellent description of inpatient therapy groups for both higher level and lower functioning clients is provided by Irvin Yalom in his 1983 book *Inpatient Group Psychotherapy*.)

Length of a Group

What should the duration of a group be? For most groups a termination date can be announced at the outset, so members will have a clear idea of the time limits under which they are working. Our college groups typically run about 15 weeks—the length of a semester. With high school students the same length seems ideal. It is long enough for trust to develop and for work toward behavioral changes to take place.

One of our colleagues has several closed groups in his private practice that last 16 weeks. After a few meetings he schedules an all-day session for these groups, which he finds adds greatly to their cohesion. When the group comes to an end, those who wish to join a new group have that option. The advantages of such an arrangement are that the time span allows for cohesion and productive work and that members can then continue practicing newly acquired interpersonal skills with a new group of people. Perhaps a major value of this type of time-limited group is that members are motivated to realize that they do not have forever to attain their personal goals. At different points in this 16-week group, members are challenged to review their progress, both individually and as a group. If they are dissatisfied with their own participation or with the direction the group is taking, they have the responsibility to do something to change the situation.

Of course, some groups composed of the same members meet for years. Such a time structure allows them to work through issues in some depth and to offer support and challenge in making life changes. These ongoing groups do have the potential for fostering dependency, and thus it is important that both the leader and members be aware of that.

Place for Group Meetings

Where might the group hold its meetings? Many places will do, but privacy is essential. Members must be assured that they will not be overheard by people in adjoining rooms. Groups often fail because of their physical setting. If they are held in a day hall or ward full of distractions, productive group work is not likely to occur. We like a group room that is not cluttered and that allows for a comfortable seating arrangement. We prefer a setting that enables the group to sit in a circle. This arrangement lets all the participants see one another and allows enough freedom of movement that members can spontaneously make physical contact. It is a good idea for coleaders to sit across from each other. In this way the nonverbal language of all members can be observed by one leader or the other and a "we-versus-them" atmosphere can be avoided.

Open Versus Closed Groups

Open groups are characterized by changing membership. As certain members leave, new members are admitted, and the group continues. *Closed groups* typically have some time limitation, with the group meeting for a predetermined number of sessions. Generally, members are expected to remain in the group until it ends, and new members are not added. The question of whether a group should be open or closed depends on a number of variables.

There are some advantages to open groups that incorporate new members as others leave, one of which is an increased opportunity for members to interact with a greater variety of people. This also more accurately reflects people's everyday lives wherein different people enter or exit our relationships. A potential disadvantage of open groups is that rapid changing of members can result in a lack of cohesion, particularly if too many clients leave or too many new ones are introduced at once. Therefore, it may be better to bring in new members one at a time as openings occur. It is a challenge to provide new members of open groups with the orientation they need to learn how to best participate in a group. One way to educate incoming members about group process is by providing a videotape explaining group rules, which can be followed by a face-to-face contact with the group leader. One colleague who coleads open groups in an agency stresses reviewing the ground rules with each incoming member. Rather than taking group time whenever a new person is included, he covers the rules with the new member as part of the intake interview. He also asks other members to teach the new member about a few of the guidelines in an attempt to have them take more responsibility for their own group. If members are dropped and added sensitively, these changes do not necessarily interfere with the cohesiveness of the group.

In some settings, such as mental health wards in state hospitals or certain day-treatment centers, group leaders do not have a choice between an open and a closed group. Because the membership of the group changes almost from week to week, continuity between sessions and cohesion within the group become difficult to achieve. Cohesion is possible, even in cases where members attend only a few times, but a high level of activity is demanded of inpatient group therapists. These leaders must structure and activate the group. They need to call on certain members, they must actively support members, and they need to interact personally with the participants (Yalom, 1983).

If you are forming an open group, it is essential that you have some idea about the rate of turnover of the members. How long a given member can participate in the group may be unpredictable. Therefore, your interventions need to be designed with the idea in mind that many members may attend for only one or two sessions. In conducting an open group, it is good to remind all the members that this may be the only time they have with one another. The interventions that you make need to be tailored to that end. For example, you would not want to facilitate a member's exploration of a painful concern that could not be addressed in that session. You also have a responsibility to facilitate member interactions that can lead to some form of resolution within a given session. This involves leaving enough time to explore with members what they have learned in a session and how they feel about leaving each session.

One of our colleagues regularly conducts several open groups in a community mental health agency. Even though the membership does change somewhat over a period of time, he finds that trust and cohesion do develop in most of these groups because there is a stable core of members. When new members join, they agree to attend for at least six sessions. Also, members who miss two consecutive meetings without a valid excuse are not allowed to continue. These practices increase the chances for continuity and for trust to be developed.

※ The Uses of a Pregroup Meeting

We suggested earlier that a preliminary meeting of all those who were thinking of joining the group was a good follow-up to screening and orientation interviews as well as a useful device when individual interviews were impractical. Such a pregroup session provides an excellent way to prepare members and to get them acquainted with one another. This session also provides the members with more information to help them decide if they are willing to commit themselves to what would be expected of them. If an individual interview or a pregroup session with all members is impractical, the first group meeting can be used to cover the issues we are discussing in this chapter. Our preference is for a separate individual screening and orientation session followed by a pregroup meeting for all participants.

At this initial session, or at the pregroup meeting, the leader explores the members' expectations, clarifies the goals and objectives of the group, imparts some information about group process, and answers members' questions. This is an ideal time to focus on the clients' perceptions, expectations, and concerns. This process does not have to consist of a lecture to the members; it can involve the members and encourage them to interact with one another and the leader from the onset. This interactive model of preparation can reveal interesting information about both the dynamics of the individuals and the "personality of the group." Patterns begin to take shape from the moment a group convenes. Structuring the group, including the specification of procedures and norms, will likely be accomplished early in the group's history. Some of this structuring can be done during the individual intake sessions, but a continuation of it can be the focus of the first group session. Group counselors may either establish ground rules or ask the group to do so. Ideally, group rules are cooperatively developed by the leader and the members as part of the group process.

Clarifying Leader and Member Expectations

The pregroup session is the appropriate time to encourage members to express the expectations they are bringing with them to the group. We typically begin by asking these questions: What are your expectations for this group? What did you have in mind when you signed up? The replies give us a frame of reference for how the members are approaching the group, what they want from it, and what they are willing to give to the group to make it a success.

We also share *our* expectations by giving members an idea of why we designed the group, what we hope will be accomplished, and what we expect of ourselves as leaders and them as members. This is a good time to reemphasize and clarify what you see as your responsibilities to the group and to further discuss the members' rights and responsibilities. You can explain what services you can and cannot realistically provide within the particular structure offered—for example, private consultations or follow-up sessions.

Goals of Pregroup Preparation

In his system of pregroup preparation, Yalom (1995) is guided by the following seven goals:

1. Strive to create an alliance with group members, so they can become collaborators in their own change process. Provide members with a conceptual framework of how group therapy works as a social laboratory.

2. Describe how a therapy group helps members enhance their interpersonal relationships.

3. Give members guidelines about how to get the most from group therapy. Emphasize the importance of members being honest and direct with their feelings in the context of here-and-now group interactions.

4. Anticipate frustrations and disappointments, including predicting stumbling blocks participants are likely to encounter.

5. Give guidelines pertaining to the duration of group therapy.

6. Instill faith in group therapy.

7. Discuss ground rules such as sharing perceptions and reactions about oneself and other members in the group, confidentiality, and subgrouping.

Underlying everything Yalom says about preparing individuals for group therapy is the goal of demystifying the therapeutic process. He emphasizes the collaborative nature of group therapy. If extensive preparation is not possible, even a short preparation is better than none at all.

Attending to Diversity Concerns

If you are forming groups in a community agency setting, it is possible that the members will be culturally diverse. In this case, it is especially important to clarify expectations. Depending on a member's specific cultural heritage, you may need to deal with a variety of expectations of both the group and you as a leader. Some participants may look to you as an authority figure who will direct them, some will view you as an expert, and some may expect you to do most of the talking while they listen.

As a leader, during the screening and pregroup meetings it is incumbent upon you to clarify what needs can or cannot be met within the group. For instance, if you do not view your role as being the expert who provides answers, potential members have a right to know this so that they can determine if this group is what they are seeking. For some groups, it may be both appropriate and useful for you to engage in teaching members the purposes and functions of the group. It is important to invite the members of your groups to verbally state *their* reasons for joining a group, and it is critical that you be willing to explore these expectations during the initial session. It is also useful to encourage members to raise questions about the purpose and goals of the groups, as well as to identify and talk about what they most want from the group and to begin formulating personal goals. You will want to strive for a congruence between members' purposes in attending the group and the overall purpose you had in mind when you designed the group.

In working with culturally diverse groups, it is essential not to make assumptions based on race, ethnicity, or culture without verifying your assumptions with individual members. Never assume that people who give the appearance of being ethnically different are indeed culturally different. If a person with Asian features applies for your group, do not assume that he or she necessarily adheres to Asian cultural values. It is also a mistake to conclude that merely because certain clients have lived in the United States for a period of time they have become acculturated into the mainstream society.

You do not necessarily have to share the culture or the life experience of group members to understand and respect members' experiential world and involve members in their own treatment. A great deal can be done to prevent unnecessary anxiety by allowing members to talk about their reactions to coming to the group and by considering ways the group can lead to their empowerment.

Establishing Basic Ground Rules

The pregroup session is the appropriate place to establish some procedures that will facilitate group process. Some leaders prefer to present their own policies and procedures in a nonauthoritarian manner. Other leaders place the major responsibility on the group members to establish procedures that will assist them in attaining their goals. Whatever approach is taken, some discussion of ground rules is necessary.

In formulating procedures that govern a group, it is important for leaders to protect members by defining clearly what confidentiality means, why it is important, and the difficulties involved in enforcing it. Ideally, confidentiality will be discussed during the individual interview, but it is so important to the functioning of a group that you need to restate it periodically during the life of a group. At the pregroup session, it is a good idea to state that confidentiality is not an absolute and to outline the restrictions. As was mentioned in Chapter 3, leaders cannot guarantee that all member disclosures will be kept within the group. Members have a right to know of the circumstances when leaders must break confidentiality for ethical or legal reasons. In cases of incest and child abuse, elder abuse, and in cases of clients who pose a danger to themselves, others, and/or physical property, confidentiality must be breached. Limitations to confidentiality apply especially to groups with children and adolescents, groups with parolees, groups composed of involuntary populations such as prisoners, and groups of psychiatric patients in a hospital or clinic. These individuals should be told that certain things they say in the group may be recorded in their chart, which might be available for other staff members to read. Furthermore, these individuals need to be informed that if they attend a group session and do not participate, that also will be recorded. It is a good practice to let group members know what kinds of information might be recorded as well as who will have access to it. The members then have a basis for deciding what and how much they will disclose. This kind of honesty about confidentiality will go a long way toward establishing the trust that is essential for a working group. Review Chapter 3 for a further discussion of confidentiality.

Other issues to explore with your group at the first session include policies about showing up for all the group sessions and being on time; drinking and eating during sessions; bringing friends to a session; not being under the influence of alcohol or drugs while attending a group; obtaining written parental permission, in the case of minors; socializing or meeting outside the group with other members; getting involved intimately with other members; and reinforcing member rights and responsibilities. It is important for leaders to be aware of and discuss with members any additional ground rules and policies particular to the setting in which they are working. You will not be able to fully discuss all the policies and procedures you deem essential to the smooth functioning of your group in one or two sessions, but having an established position on these matters will be an asset when particular issues arise at some point in the development of the group.

Approaches to Pregroup Preparation

Research Findings

A good deal of research has examined the value of pretherapy preparation for both individual and group psychotherapy. The overwhelming consensus of this research is that preparation appears to affect early therapeutic processes positively and also seems to be linked to later client improvement (Burlingame et al., 2004b; Fuhriman & Burlingame, 1990). Pregroup preparation (setting expectations, establishing group rules and procedures, role preparation, skill building) is positively associated with cohesion, members' satisfaction, and comfort with the group (Burlingame et al. 2004b). Pregroup orientation is a standard practice for members of short-term therapy groups. A number of factors make such orientation sessions necessary for these clients: the diversity of members in a typical group, the range of personal concerns, the different settings, the time-limited framework, and the unfamiliarity of the group format. The content of this pregroup orientation reflects the perspective of leaders who conduct short-term group therapy. A thorough orientation sets the stage for later development of leader-member and member-member therapeutic relationships. Preparation activities in short-term groups are directed toward facilitating the most effective use of the time that is available (Burlingame & Fuhriman, 1990).

There are many advantages for preparing members for their entrance into a therapeutic group. Group leaders can use the preparation time to address basic information about how groups function prior to the first group session. When a group is made up of members who have had previous group experience with people new to a group, this preparation allows all group members to begin with the same procedural knowledge needed for effective participation (Riva et al., 2004). Practitioners often give positive reports of their particular approach to pregroup preparation, and reviews of the literature are generally favorable about the benefits of advance preparation. Some researchers suggest that members who understand what behaviors are expected of them tend to be more successful. When goals, role requirements, and behavior expectations are understood by members from the outset, therapeutic work proceeds more effectively. Unproductive anxiety can be reduced by informing members about group norms in advance. Preparatory training increases the chances of successful outcomes because it reduces the anxiety participants often experience during the initial sessions and provides a framework for understanding group process (Bednar, Melnick, & Kaul, 1974; Borgers & Tyndall, 1982; Bowman & DeLucia, 1993; Burlingame & Fuhriman, 1990; Burlingame et al., 2004b; Fuhriman & Burlingame, 1990; Meadow, 1988; Piper & Perrault, 1989; Riva et al., 2004; Sklare, Keener, & Mas, 1990; Sklare, Petrosko, & Howell, 1993; Stockton & Morran, 1982; Yalom, 1995).

Based on their review of the literature, Bednar and Kaul (1994) concluded that pregroup training is a potent factor in creating successful therapeutic groups, having a substantial impact on group process and member outcomes. Preparing members for a group through cognitive instructions, behavioral rehearsal, and by watching models all contribute to effective group treatment.

Borgers and Tyndall (1982) and Bowman and DeLucia (1993) describe three ways of preparing members for a group experience: cognitive learning, vicarious experiencing, and behavioral practice. With *cognitive methods*, members acquire information through reading handouts that describe the purpose of the group, member performance expectations, common stumbling blocks, and typical group phenomena. *Vicarious experiencing* includes the use of tape recordings, videotapes, and films to model desired group behavior in a working group. *Behavioral practice* involves members' participating in structured activities such as giving and receiving feedback, confrontation, self-disclosure, and identifying resistance. Borgers and Tyndall (1982) conclude that perhaps the most useful form of pregroup preparation consists of a combination of these approaches. Their conclusions have some research support; studies have consistently shown that groups receiving both instruction and modeling do better than those receiving only one treatment or neither (Stockton & Morran, 1982).

Some practitioners promote the value of lack of leader structuring and view pregroup structuring as counterproductive to the natural evolution of the group (for example, see Rogers, 1970). These practitioners believe that too much advance preparation or teaching members about the process of a group "pollutes" the process and deprives members of the opportunity to create their own structure. We do not endorse this view. As you can see by the emphasis we give to preparation of individuals for group membership, we value pregroup preparation.

The kind of pregroup preparation we advocate assists members in deciding what they want from a group and gives them some tools for attaining their goals. This process is important for groups with different forms, such as inpatient and outpatient groups, open and closed groups, and short- and long-term groups. Although the specific content of pregroup preparation will differ based on the specific kind of group, members stand a better chance of utilizing the group process if they understand how the particular group they will participate in functions and if they know what is expected of them. Some kind of preparation is useful for structured psychoeducational groups and for solution-focused short-term groups as well as for counseling and therapy groups. The basic aim of this preparation is to increase the chances that the group will become a cohesive autonomous unit that will permit individuals to engage in productive work.

Leaders and coleaders must also prepare themselves for the group. Coleaders need to be prepared both individually and as a team. Too often coleaders understand little of each others' philosophy and leadership styles before the group begins. If group leaders are themselves unprepared, it is unlikely that they will be able to effectively prepare members for a meaningful group experience.

Many groups that get stuck at an early developmental stage do so because the foundations were poorly laid. What is labeled "resistance" on the part of group members is often the result of a failure on the leader's part to adequately explain what groups are about, how they function, and how members can become actively involved. In addition to preparing members for a group, it is a good idea for leaders to periodically review with the members some of the guidelines on how they can make the best use of group time. Throughout the life of a group, there are critical times when structuring and teaching can assist members in becoming actively involved in the group process.

In conducting pregroup preparation, we want to caution you against bombarding members with too much information at the preliminary meeting. Many of the topics that relate to participation in the group can be handed out in written form to the members, and clients can be encouraged to raise any questions or concerns they have after they have read this material.

Building Evaluation Into Group Work

If you do group work in a community agency or an institution, you may be required to demonstrate the efficacy of your treatment approach. Federal and state grants typically stipulate measures for accountability. Thus, it is essential in most settings for you to devise procedures to assess the degree to which clients benefit from the group experience. We suggest that you include in your proposals for groups the procedures you intend to use to evaluate both the individual member outcomes and the outcomes of the group as a unit.

There is no need to be intimidated by the idea of incorporating a research spirit in your practice. Nor do you have to think exclusively in terms of rigorous empirical research. Various qualitative methods are appropriate for assessing a group's movement, and these methods may be less intimidating than relying exclusively on quantitative research techniques. One alternative to the traditional scientific method is evaluation research, which provides data that can be useful when making improvements within the structure of a group. *Member-specific measures* are used to assess changes in attitudes and behaviors of individual clients. It is possible to develop your own devices for evaluating the degree to which members attain their goals. *Group-specific measures* assess the changes common to all members of the group, such as increased self-awareness, decreased anxiety, and improved personal relationships. Many of these measures are available in standardized form, or you can adapt them to suit your needs.

The practice of building evaluation into your group programs is a useful procedure for accountability purposes, but it can also help you sharpen your leadership skills, enabling you to see more clearly changes you might want to make in the format for future groups. (The challenges to combining research and practice are addressed in Chapter 2.)

✳ Coleader Issues on Forming a Group

If you are coleading a group, the central issue at this early stage is that you and your coleader have equal responsibility in forming the group and getting it going. Both of you need to be clear about the purpose of the group, what you hope to accomplish with the time you have, and how you will meet your objectives. Cooperation and basic agreement between you and your coleader are essential in getting your group off to a good start.

This cooperative effort might well start with you both meeting to develop a proposal, and ideally both of you will present it to the appropriate authority. This practice ensures that designing and originating the group are not solely one leader's responsibility. This shared responsibility for organizing the group continues throughout the various tasks outlined in this chapter. You and your coleader will be a team when it comes to matters such as announcing and re-cruiting for membership; conducting screening interviews and agreeing on whom to include and exclude; agreeing on basic ground rules, policies, and procedures and presenting them to members; preparing members and orient-ing them to the group process; and sharing in the practical matters that must be handled to form a group.

It may not always be possible to share equally in all the responsibilities. Although it is *ideal* that both leaders interview the applicants, time constraints may make this impractical. Tasks may have to be divided, but both leaders need to be involved as much as possible in making the group a reality. If one leader does a disproportionate share of the work, the other can easily develop a passive role in the leadership of the group once it begins.

If coleaders do not know each other or if they don't have much sense of how the other works professionally, they are likely to get off to a poor start. Simply walking into a group unprepared, without any initial planning or ac-quaintance with your coleader, invites future problems. Just as it is critical that members be prepared for entering a group, the leaders must be psycho-logically prepared and oriented to each other's style. Here are a few sugges-tions coleaders can consider before the initial session:

- Take time to get to know something about each other personally and professionally before you begin leading together.
- Talk about your theoretical orientations and how each of you perceives groups. What kind of group work has each of you experienced? In what ways will your theory and leadership styles influence the direction the group takes?
- Do you have reservations about coleading with each other? What might get in your way in your dealings with each other? How can you use your

separate talents productively as a team? How can your differences in leadership style have a complementary effect and enhance the group?

- Talk with each other about your own strengths and weaknesses. How might this affect your leading together? With this knowledge you may be able to forestall some potential problems.

- For the two of you to work together well as a team, you need to agree on the ethical aspects of group work. Do you share the same viewpoint on what constitutes ethical practice, or are there differences? Discuss the ethical issues touched on both in this chapter and in the preceding two chapters.

Although these suggestions do not represent all the possible areas coleaders can explore in getting to know each other, they do provide a basis for focusing on significant topics.

✓ *Points to Remember*

Member Functions

Group members need to be active in the process of deciding if a group is right for them. To do this, potential members need to possess the knowledge necessary to make an informed decision concerning their participation. Here are some issues that pertain to the role of members at this stage:

✓ Members can expect to have adequate knowledge about the nature of the group and understand the impact the group may have on them.

✓ Members can be encouraged to explore their expectations and concerns with the group leader to determine if *this* group with *this* particular leader is appropriate for them *at this* time.

✓ Members need to be involved in the decision of whether or not they will join the group, and members should not be coerced into joining a group.

✓ Members can prepare themselves for the upcoming group by thinking about what they want from the experience and how they might attain their goals.

✓ Members need to understand their purpose in joining the group. Pretests, either standardized instruments or devices designed by the leader, can be used to assess members' values, perceptions, attitudes, and personal problems.

Leader Functions

Here are the main tasks of group leaders during the formation of a group:

✓ Develop a clearly written proposal for the formation of a group.

✓ Present the proposal to your supervisor and get the idea accepted.

✓ Announce and market the group in such a way as to inform prospective participants.

✓ Conduct pregroup interviews for screening and orientation purposes.

✓ Provide potential members with relevant information necessary for them to make an informed choice about participation.

✓ Make decisions concerning selection of members and composition of the group.

✓ Organize the practical details necessary to launch a successful group.

✓ Get parental permission, if necessary.

✓ Prepare psychologically for leadership tasks, and meet with the coleader, if any.

✓ Arrange a preliminary group session for the purposes of getting acquainted, orientation to ground rules, and preparation of members for a successful group experience.

Exercises

Group Planning

Select a particular type of group (psychoeducational, counseling, or other) and a target population (children, adolescents, adults, or elderly). Answer the following questions for the group you have selected.

1. What is your role in this group?

2. What do you most want to occur in your group? State your purposes simply and concretely.

3. Would you form a contract with your group, and, if so, what would be the essence of the contract? Would you expect each member to develop a contract?

4. List a few ground rules or policies you feel would be essential for your group.

5. How can you determine whether you have the skills necessary to lead this particular type of group?

6. What is the focus of your group?

7. Would you accept only volunteer group members? Why or why not?

8. What characteristics would people need to have to be included? What is the rationale?

9. What procedures and techniques would you use in your group? Are your procedures practical? Are they related to the goals and the population of the group?

10. What evaluation methods might you use to determine the effectiveness of your approaches? Are your evaluation procedures appropriate to the purposes of your group?

Interviewing

1. **Screening Interview.** Ask one person in the class to play the role of a group leader conducting a screening interview for members for a particular type of group. The group leader conducts a 10-minute interview with a potential

member, played by another student. The prospective member then tells the group leader how he or she felt and what impact the group leader made. The group leader shares his or her observations about the prospective group member and tells whether the person would have been accepted in the group, and why or why not. Repeat this exercise with another student/member so the group leader can benefit from the feedback and try some new ideas. Then give other students a chance to experience the roles of interviewer and interviewee. The rest of the class can offer feedback and suggestions for improvement after each interview. This feedback is essential if students are to improve their skills in conducting screening interviews.

2. **Group Member Interview.** We have recommended that prospective group members examine the leader somewhat critically before joining a group. This exercise is just like the preceding one, except that the group member asks questions of the leader, trying to learn things about the leader and the group that will enable the member to make a wise decision about whether to join. After 10 minutes the leader shares observations and reactions, and then the member tells whether he or she would join this leader's group and explains any reservations. Again, the class is invited to make observations.

Group Class

If the group class that you are presently in contains an experiential group component, or if you are required to be in some kind of process group as a part of your group course, observe the parallel processes between what you are learning in the book and what is happening in your experiential group. Your group class is likely to go through the same stages of group formation as those you are studying. For example, the class may begin slowly, with students being anxious and apprehensive. As students begin to develop trust, they will identify and explore some personal issues, work toward specific goals, and finally evaluate the group experience and say good-bye. For each of the chapters that deal with the stages of group development (Chapters 4 through 8), you will be asked to reflect on these parallel processes. At this time, address these questions:

- How well prepared were you for this group class?
- Did you encounter any surprises, and, if so, what were they?
- What kind of information about your group course did you receive, if any, prior to being accepted?

Guide to *Groups in Action: Evolution and Challenges* DVD and Workbook

We have developed the *Groups in Action: Evolution and Challenges* DVD and Workbook (Corey, Corey, & Haynes, 2006) to enhance your study of *Groups: Process and Practice.* At the end of each chapter in Part 2 of the text, we refer you to specific segments in the DVD as examples for each of the stages of a group. Also refer to the corresponding lessons in the workbook, which require you to become an active learner as you study the group process in action.

Before beginning the DVD and workbook program, read the first few pages of the workbook, which contains a synopsis of the DVD program, learning objectives, and how to make the best use of the DVD and workbook.

Questions to Consider

1. If you were a prospective member of this video group, what kind of information would you want before you made a decision to participate?

2. How important would you consider informed consent for this kind of group?

3. How might being a member of this video group for educational purposes affect your participation?

4. How would you deal with issues of confidentiality?

5. What kind of ground rules or policies would be essential in this video group?

InfoTrac College Edition

For additional readings, explore InfoTrac College Edition, our online library, at http://www.infotrac.college.com/wadsworth. The following keywords are listed in such a way as to enable the InfoTrac College Edition search engine to locate a wider range of articles. The keywords should be entered exactly as listed, to include asterisks, "w1," "w2," "AND," and other search engine tools.

- eval* AND group* w1 psych*
- group w1 process
- preparation* AND group* AND therap*
- preparation* AND group* AND psych*
- eval* AND group* w1 couns*

Initial Stage of a Group

Focus Questions

Before reading this chapter, reflect on what you would need to feel trust and safety as a group member. With this in mind, address the following questions pertaining to your tasks during the initial stage as a group leader.

1. What guidelines might you offer to help members get the most from a group experience?

2. How might you assist members in creating trust? What role do you see for yourself in establishing trust during the initial stage of a group?

3. What are some specific ways to help members identify and clarify their goals for group participation?

4. What cultural factors would you consider in assessing a client's readiness to participate in a group?

5. What challenges do you expect to encounter during the first few sessions?

6. What group norms, or standards, would you most want to establish?

7. What are some ways to help a group develop trust at the first few meetings?

8. What are a few things you would attend to in opening each group session?

9. What ideas do you have for effectively bringing each session to a close?

10. How much structuring do you think is helpful for a group to accomplish its tasks? To what degree might you assume the responsibility for providing structure in a group you lead or colead?

✷ Introduction

This chapter contains many examples of teaching members about how groups function. We describe the characteristics of a group in its early stages, discuss the importance of creating trust as the foundation for a group, explore the topic of establishing goals early in the life of a group, discuss formation of group norms and the beginnings of group cohesion, and provide guidelines for helping members get the most from a group. We also suggest some leadership guidelines for opening and closing group meetings.

Imagine what it would be like for you to be a participant in a group. If you have had a group experience or if there is an experiential component to this course, think about how you felt as the group began. What were your thoughts and feelings before joining the group? What information was provided? What information was not given that you would like to have had? As much as possible, we encourage you to study the material in these chapters from a personal perspective. Our hope is that your personal reflections will assist you in better designing and facilitating groups for others.

✳ Group Characteristics at the Initial Stage

The central process during the initial stage of a group is orientation and exploration. Members are getting acquainted, learning how the group functions, developing spoken and unspoken norms that will govern group behavior, exploring their fears and hopes pertaining to the group, clarifying their expectations, identifying personal goals, and determining if this group is safe. This stage is characterized by members expressing fears and hesitations as well as hopes and expectations. The degree of trust that can be established in the group will be determined by how the leader deals with these reactions.

Some Early Concerns

At these early sessions it is common for participants to be tentative and vague about what they hope to get from a group experience. Most members are uncertain about group norms and expected behavior, and there may be moments of silence and awkwardness. Some members may be impatient and ready to work, whereas others may appear hesitant and uninvolved. Still others may be looking for quick solutions to their problems. If your leadership style involves very little structure, the level of anxiety is likely to be high because of the ambiguity of the situation, and there will probably be hesitation and requests from members for direction. Members may ask "What are we supposed to be doing here?" or state "I really don't know what we should be talking about."

When someone does volunteer a problem for discussion, chances are that other members will engage in problem solving. Rather than encouraging the person to fully explore a struggle, some members are likely to offer suggestions and what they consider to be helpful advice. Although this may seem like progress because there is the appearance of group interaction, frequent giving of advice bypasses the necessity for people to explore their problems and discover their own solutions.

During the first few group sessions, members watch the leader's behavior and think about safety in the group. Trust can be lost or gained by how the leader handles conflict or the initial expression of any negative reactions. A member's internal dialogue might go something like this: "I'll take a chance and say what I am thinking, and then I'll see how this leader and others in here respond. If they are willing to listen to what I say bothers me, perhaps I can trust them with some deeper feelings." The group leader's task is to be aware of the tentative nature of discussion in these early sessions and treat negative comments with openness and acceptance.

Initial Hesitation and Cultural Considerations

It is common during the initial phase of a group that members may appear rather hesitant to get involved. Caution on the part of members is to be expected and it makes sense. Participants may feel intimidated by the leader and may view the leader with some degree of suspicion. Others may doubt that counseling groups can be of any real value in helping them solve their problems. Some may not believe they have the freedom to talk about personally significant matters, and may sit back, silently observe, and wait for something to happen.

Cultural factors may also influence clients' readiness to participate in a group. Members may seem to be "holding back" when they are only being true to their cultural heritage. Some members may believe it is distasteful to talk publicly about private matters. Others may feel it is a sign of weakness to disclose personal problems or to express feelings. Those members who have cultural injunctions against talking about their family in a group may be reluctant to engage in role playing involving symbolically talking to their parents. They may not want to reveal certain struggles out of fear that their disclosures would entrench already existing stereotypes and prejudices.

In your role as a group leader you can minimize reluctance on the part of members by inviting a discussion of how they could participate in the group in a way that does not violate their cultural norms. If you are aware of the cultural context of the members of your group, it is possible to both appreciate their cultural values and respectfully encourage them to deal with the concerns that brought them to the group. An important leadership function is assisting members in understanding how some of their initial hesitation to self-disclosure may relate to their cultural conditioning.

Regardless of the type of group, some initial hesitation is normal in the early stage, even if people are eager to join in. This reluctance can be manifested in many different ways. What members do talk about is likely to be less important than what they keep hidden: their real fears about being in this group at this moment. Because cautious behavior often arises from fearful expectations, identifying and discussing these fears now will benefit the whole group. It is not helpful to say to an anxious member "You don't need to be afraid in here. Nobody will hurt you." You cannot honestly make such promises. Some members may very well feel hurt by someone's response to them. What is far more important is that members know that you want them to say when they feel hurt and that you will not abandon them but will help them deal with whatever they are feeling.

Here are some common fears participants identify:

- Will I be accepted or rejected in here?
- Will I be able to express myself so that others can understand me?
- Can I really say what I feel?
- How will this group be any different from my interactions in daily situations?
- I'm afraid of being judged by others, especially if I am different from them.
- I'm concerned that I won't fit into the group.
- If I get scared, I may withdraw.

- Will I feel pressured to disclose deeply personal matters and be pushed to perform?
- What if my teacher or parents ask what I share in my group?
- Will I tell too much about myself?
- I fear being hurt.
- What if the group attacks me?
- What if I'm asked to do something that goes against my cultural values?
- What if I find out things about myself that I can't cope with?
- I'm afraid I'll change and that those I'm close to won't like my changes.

Recognizing that such anxieties exist, we begin by encouraging group members to share and explore them. It sometimes helps in building a trusting atmosphere to ask people to split up into pairs and then to join to make groups of four. In this way members can choose others with whom to share their expectations, get acquainted, and talk about their fears or reservations. Talking with one other person, and then merging with others, is far less threatening to most participants than talking to the entire group. This subgroup approach is an excellent icebreaker, and when the entire group gets together again, there is generally a greater willingness to interact.

Members are testing the waters at the early sessions to see if their concerns are being taken seriously and if the group is a safe place to express what they think and feel. If their reactions, positive or negative, are listened to with respect and acceptance, they have a basis to begin dealing with deeper aspects of themselves. A good way for you to start dealing with members' concerns and hesitations is by listening to their fears and encouraging full expression of them.

Hidden Agendas

A common form of resistance in groups relates to the presence of a hidden agenda—an issue that is not openly acknowledged and discussed. If encouragement to face these issues is lacking, the group process gets bogged down because the norm of being closed, cautious, and defensive replaces the norm of being open. When there are unspoken reactions (by one member, several members, or the entire group), a common set of features emerges: trust is low, interpersonal tensions emerge, people are guarded and unwilling to take risks, the leader seems to be working harder than the members, and there is a vague feeling that something just does not make sense.

In one group a member said, "There's someone in this room I don't like." The entire group was affected by this comment, and several members later disclosed that they had wondered if they were the disliked person. It was not until the member was willing to deal directly with the conflict he was having with another participant that the atmosphere in the room cleared up.

A training workshop we conducted included a number of military personnel as well as civilians. The military trainees held different ranks and included both officers and enlisted personnel. One participant discovered that his wife was working with the wife of another person in the group. The hidden agenda in this group consisted of reactions related to the two men's different ranks and concerns over repercussions of what might be said in the group and how it might be used outside the group. Others wondered if confidentiality would be honored. The concerns that members had were not initially discussed despite our invitations. The polite and hesitant interactions eventually led to a high level of frustration among the participants. Not until one member took the risk of disclosing her real fears did others acknowledge what was really going on.

In another group, the adolescent group members displayed a great unwillingness to talk. The hidden agenda was the concern over rumors that some gossiping was taking place. Members who were concerned about confidentiality were reluctant to express their feelings because of the fear of repercussions.

A hidden agenda emerged in a group that was composed mostly of members from a fundamentalist religious background. Some of the members eventually disclosed that their hesitation to get involved in the group was out of fear that they, as well as their religion, would be unfavorably judged if they revealed any struggles regarding their faith. They were anxious about the reactions of both those members who shared their faith as well as those who did not. Only after addressing their concerns of judgment was the group able to move forward.

In our training and supervision workshops we have sometimes made an erroneous assumption that all the participants are there voluntarily. In several cases in various agencies, resistance was initially high because some members were pressured by their superiors to attend. We encouraged them to express their grievances, after which they were more willing to become involved. Even though we were not able to remove the pressure they felt over having to attend, our willingness to listen to and respect what they had to say did help them overcome their reluctance to participate. If we had not facilitated an exploration of their feelings, little learning would have occurred.

In teaching group counseling courses using a combination of didactic and experiential approaches, we have found that hidden agendas may surface. We typically provide students with opportunities to colead a small group within the class structure. The vast majority of students in these classes state at the end of the course that they appreciate what they learned, not only about facilitating groups but also about their interpersonal style. However, at the beginning of the experience it is not uncommon to hear reservations about self-disclosing and being personal with each other in a small group. Some wonder what their peers might think about them as they get to know them better in this context. Some worry about what and how much to disclose of their personal concerns. Others are hesitant to express here-and-now reactions to others in the sessions for fear of instigating conflict. Most feel some pressure to perform and have concerns about the responsibility for facilitating the group, even though we are directly supervising the small groups. They are anxious about their level of competence and how they might be perceived if they make "mistakes." Any of these concerns has the potential of being a hidden agenda that could impede student involvement if students do not express and explore these concerns.

As a group leader, you cannot burden yourself with knowing all the potential hidden agendas present in a group, but you can anticipate possible hidden agendas that may operate given the nature of a specific group. It is essential that you reflect on the existence of such agendas and find ways to assist members to identify and articulate concerns that are not verbally expressed. Once a hidden agenda is identified, it is less likely to sabotage group process. What is important is that group members acknowledge that some factor is affecting group process. The members can then be challenged to decide how they will deal with that agenda once it has been brought to the surface.

Groups do not move forward unless hidden agendas are uncovered and fully discussed. This process often requires patience from the leader and a willingness to continually check with members to find out if they are saying what they need to say. What bogs groups down is not so much what people *are* saying but what they *are not* saying. Although it is generally not comfortable for leaders to deal with these undercurrents, respectfully, yet firmly, challenging members to express persistent thoughts and feelings about what is emerging in the group is extremely valuable.

Address Conflict Early

Conflict can emerge in any stage of group work, although it is most common during the transition stage. Conflict that arises early in a group must be adequately dealt with, or it is likely that it will inhibit the cohesion of the group. When conflict first occurs, members are keenly aware of and observe the leaders' actions. It is crucial for leaders to respond and facilitate a resolution of the conflict so the group can move forward.

Let's examine a conflict that might surface during the first group session.

> **Leader:** *What are you aware of in the room?*
>
> **Emily** [to Latoya, in an agitated voice]: *I know I'm not going to like you. I think you are critical and judgmental!*
>
> **Latoya:** *That's your problem. I don't like you either!*

The group falls silent, and the tension in the room is obvious to everyone. The leader intervenes.

> **Leader:** *I'm very surprised by the intensity of your reactions toward each other, especially since you just met for the first time in this group today. [The leader is operating on the hunch that there is transference between the two members.] I'm wondering what was on your mind before you made these statements.*

The leader's intention is to ask Emily to examine what led up to her intense reactions to a member she just met. Emily can then be invited to talk about how Latoya's seemingly critical and judgmental qualities affect her.

Given that this intermember conflict arises at the initial meeting, it is critical that the leader teach the norm of appropriate and effective confrontation. If the matter is bypassed, ignored, or smoothed over by the leader's lack of intervention, members are likely to feel cautious and unsafe. This unaddressed conflict can easily become a hidden agenda that impedes the group's progress.

Self-Focus Versus Focus on Others

One characteristic of many members in beginning groups is a tendency to talk about others and to focus on people and situations outside of the group. Participants who engage in storytelling will at times deceive themselves into believing they are really working, when in fact they are avoiding speaking about and dealing with their own feelings. They may talk about life situations, but they have a tendency to focus on what other people are doing to cause them difficulties. Skilled group leaders help such members examine their own reactions to others.

During the initial phase of a group, the leader's primary task is to get group members to focus on themselves. Of course, trust is a prerequisite for this openness. When members focus on others as a way to avoid self-exploration, your leadership task is to steer them back to their own reactions. For example, you might say, "I'm aware that you're talking a lot about several important people in your life. They're not here, and we won't be able to work with them. But we are able to work with your feelings and reactions toward them and how their behavior affects you." An awareness of proper timing is essential. The readiness of a client to accept certain interpretations or observations must be considered. You must be skilled not only in helping people recognize that their focus on others can be defensive but also in encouraging them to talk about their concerns.

Here-and-Now Focus Versus There-and-Then Focus

Some groups have a primary focus on what is occurring right now in the room. The predominant theme these groups explore is present member-member interactions, and the material for discussion emerges from these encounters. Other groups focus largely on outside problems that members bring to the session or deal with specified topics for exploration.

In our groups we have both a here-and-now focus and a there-and-then focus. Members are often not ready to deal with significant issues pertaining to their lives away from the group until they first deal with their reactions to one another in the room. To meaningfully explore personal problems, members must first feel safe and trusting.

During the initial sessions, we ask members to make connections between personal problems they are facing in their world and their experience in the group. If a member discloses that she feels isolated in her life, for instance, we ask her to be aware of how she may be isolating herself in the group setting. If another member shares how he overextends himself in his life and rarely attends to himself because of his concern for others, we would ask him how this might become an issue for him in this group. If a member states that she feels like an outsider, we tend to ask if she often feels this way in her daily life. These members may isolate, overextend themselves, and feel like an outsider in the group sessions, and dealing with these here-and-now occurrences can serve as a springboard for exploring deeper personal concerns.

Focusing on here-and-now interaction is of the utmost value, for the way members behave in the present context of the group is reflective of how they interact with others outside the group. A unique value of groups is the opportunities they provide for interpersonal learning. One of the best ways to learn more about members' interpersonal style is by paying attention to their behavior in the group setting. Members learn a great deal about how they function interpersonally in their world by looking at their patterns in the group sessions.

Interventions that direct members to gain awareness of what they are experiencing in the here and now tend to intensify the emotional quality of interactions. Rather than having members talk about their problems in a reporting fashion, we consistently encourage members to note what it is that they are experiencing presently. If members have a problem in daily life that they want to explore, we typically intervene by helping them bring this concern into the present group context. Although group participants often have a self-protective tendency to avoid the here and now, one of the main tasks of the group facilitator is to consistently challenge them to direct their attention to what they are thinking, feeling, and doing in the moment. The more members are able to immerse themselves in the here and now, the greater chance they have to enhance the quality of their interpersonal relationships in everyday life.

Trust Versus Mistrust

If a basic sense of trust is not established at the outset of a group, serious problems can be predicted. People can be said to be developing trust in one another when they can express any feelings without fear of censure; when they are willing to decide for themselves specific goals and personal areas to explore; when they focus on themselves, not on others; and when they are willing to risk disclosing personal aspects of themselves. Trust involves a sense of safety, but it does not necessarily entail being comfortable.

In contrast, a lack of trust is indicated by an undercurrent of anger and suspicion and an unwillingness to talk about these feelings. Other manifestations of lack of trust are participants' taking refuge in being abstract or overly intellectual and being vague about what they expect from the therapeutic group. Before a climate of trust is established, people tend to wait for the leader to decide for them what they need to examine. Any disclosures that are made tend to be superficial and rehearsed, and risk taking is at a low level.

We emphasize to group members that safety does not necessarily imply comfort. Members often say that they are uncomfortable in a group session. It is important to teach members that they are not apt to feel comfortable if they are talking about matters of significance. We hope they will be willing to endure the anxiety and discomfort associated with taking risks. Members are more likely to push themselves when they perceive the group as being a safe place to challenge themselves. It is through taking risks that safety is formed.

✳ Creating Trust: Leader and Member Roles

The Importance of Modeling

Your success in creating a climate of trust within a group has much to do with how well you have prepared both yourself and the members. If you have given careful thought to why you are organizing the group, what you hope to accomplish, and how you will go about meeting your objectives, the chances are greatly increased that you will inspire confidence. The members will see your willingness to think about the group as a sign that you care about them. Furthermore, if you have done an adequate job with the pregroup issues—informing members of their rights and responsibilities, giving some time to teaching the group process, exploring the congruence between the cultural values of members and what they are expected to do, and preparing the members for a successful experience—the members will realize that you are taking your work seriously and that you are interested in their welfare.

Establishing trust is a central task for the initial stage of a group. It is not possible to overemphasize the significance of the leader's modeling and the attitudes expressed through the leader's behavior in these early sessions. In thinking about your role as a leader, ask yourself these questions:

- Do I feel energetic and enthusiastic about this group?
- Do I trust myself to lead effectively?
- To what degree do I trust the group members to work effectively with one another?
- Am I able to be psychologically present in the sessions, and am I willing to be open about my own reactions to what is going on in the group?

The person you are and, especially, the attitudes about group work and clients that you demonstrate by the way you behave in the sessions are crucial factors in building a trusting community. (Refer to our discussion of the personal characteristics of the effective leader in Chapter 2.) You teach most effectively through your example.

If you trust in the group process and have faith in the members' capacity to make significant changes in themselves, they are likely to see value in their group as a pathway to personal growth. If you listen nondefensively and respectfully and convey that you value members' subjective experience, they are likely to see the power in active listening. If you are genuinely willing to engage in appropriate self-disclosure, you will foster honesty and disclosure among the members. If you are truly able to accept others for who they are and avoid imposing your values on them, your members will learn valuable lessons about accepting people's right to differ and to be themselves. In short, what you model through what you do in the group is one of the most powerful ways of teaching members how to relate to one another constructively.

If you are coleading a group, you and your colleague have ample opportunities to model a behavioral style that will promote trust. If the two of you function harmoniously with a spontaneous give and take, for example, members will feel more trusting in your presence. If your relationship with your coleader is characterized by respect, authenticity, sensitivity, and directness, the members will learn about the value of such attitudes and behaviors. Furthermore, the way the two of you interact with the members contributes to or detracts from the level of trust. If one coleader's typical manner of speaking with members is sharp, short, and sarcastic, for example, members are likely to quickly pick up this leader's lack of respect for them and tend to become closed or defensive. Therefore, it is wise for coleaders to examine each other's style of interacting and to talk about this when they meet privately outside of the group.

It is a mistake to assume that as a leader or a coleader you have sole responsibility for the development and maintenance of trust. The level of trust is engendered by your attitudes and actions, yet it also depends to a large degree on the level of investment of the members. If members want very little for themselves, if they are unwilling to share enough of themselves so that they can be known, if they simply wait passively for you to "make trust happen," and if they are unwilling to take risks in the sessions, trust will be slow to develop. The tone set by your leadership will influence members' willingness to disclose themselves and to begin taking those steps necessary to establish trust.

Attitudes and Actions Leading to Trust

Certain attitudes and actions of leaders enhance the level of trust in a group. Some of these factors include attending and listening, understanding both verbal and nonverbal behavior, empathy, genuineness and self-disclosure, respect, and caring confrontation.

Attending and Listening Careful attending to the verbal and nonverbal messages of others is necessary for trust to occur. If genuine listening and understanding are absent, there is no basis for connection between members. If members feel that they are being heard and deeply understood, they are likely to trust that others care about them.

Both leaders and members may demonstrate a lack of attending in a number of ways. Here are some of the most common ones: (1) not focusing on the speaker but thinking of what to say next, (2) asking many closed questions which probe for irrelevant and detailed information, (3) doing too much talking and not enough listening, (4) giving advice readily instead of encouraging the speaker to explore a struggle, (5) paying attention only to what people say explicitly and thus missing what they express nonverbally, and (6) engaging in selective listening (hearing only what one wants to hear).

Group members do not always possess good listening skills, nor do they always respond effectively to what they perceive. Therefore, teaching basic listening and responding skills is one part of the trust process. Pay attention to the degree of good listening being shown in the group. If members do not feel understood, they are not likely to get very deep or personal. Why should they reveal themselves to those who do not hear them?

Understanding Nonverbal Behavior   Inexperienced group workers frequently make the error of focusing exclusively on what members are saying and miss the more subtle nonverbal messages. People often express themselves more honestly nonverbally than they do through their words. Detecting discrepancies between verbal and nonverbal behavior is an art to be learned. Examples of clients displaying these discrepancies include a member who is talking about a painful experience while smiling; a member who speaks very softly and proclaims that nobody listens to him; a client who is verbally expressing positive feelings yet is very constricted physically; a person who says that she really wants to work and to have group time but consistently waits until the end of a session before bringing up her concerns; a participant who claims that she feels comfortable in the group and really likes the members yet sits with her arms crossed tightly and tends to look at the floor; and a member who displays facial expressions and gestures but denies having any reactions.

What are some guidelines for understanding and dealing with nonverbal behavior? Even though you may think you have a clear idea of what a nonverbal behavior means, it is important not to confront the client with an interpretation. Pointing out discrepancies can be overdone and can result in members becoming annoyed. Instead of too quickly commenting on a member's nonverbal behavior, it is a good idea to file away some of your impressions and draw on them as the group unfolds and as a pattern of behavior becomes manifest. When you do explore nonverbal behavior with a member, it is best to describe the behavior: "I notice that you're smiling, yet you're talking about painful memories, and there are tears in your eyes. Are you aware of that?" After describing what you are seeing, invite the participant to offer the meaning of the nonverbal behavior. At times you may misunderstand nonverbal information and even label it as resistance. The nonverbal behavior may well be a manifestation of a cultural injunction. For example, a leader is role-playing Javier's father and asks Javier to make eye contact with him as he is talking. In spite of many invitations, Javier continues to look at the floor as he talks to his symbolic father. The leader is unaware that Javier would have felt disrespectful if he looked directly at his father or another authority figure. This is something that can be explored if the leader respectfully encourages Javier to do so in the session.

In summary, it is essential that you avoid making assumptions about what members are experiencing and, instead, assist members to recognize and explore the possible meanings of their nonverbal behavior. If you misread or ignore nonverbal messages or if you abrasively confront certain behavior, the level of trust in the group will suffer. Don't be afraid to point out what you are observing, but do so respectfully and nondogmatically.

Empathy   Empathy is the ability to tune in to what others are subjectively experiencing and to see the world through their eyes. When people experience this understanding without critical judgment, they are most likely to reveal their real concerns, for they believe that others are understanding and accepting them as they are. This kind of nonjudgmental understanding is vitally related to trust.

One of your leadership functions is to help members develop greater empathy by pointing out behaviors that block this understanding. Examples of these counterproductive behaviors include responding to others with pat statements, not responding to others at all, questioning inappropriately, telling others how they should be, responding with critical judgments, and being defensive.

Empathy is an avenue of demonstrating support. For example, Judy benefits when others are able to understand her. If she talks about going through an extremely painful divorce, Clyde can let her know the ways in which he identifies with and understands her pain. Though their circumstances are different, he empathizes with her pain and is willing to share with her his feelings of rejection and abandonment when his wife left him. What helps Judy is Clyde's willingness to tell her about his struggles rather than providing her with quick answers. Instead of telling her what he did or someone did, or instead of offering her reassurance, he helps her most by sharing his struggles and pain with her. Our colleague, Patrick Callanan, often says that people learn more from hearing how others are engaged in a struggle than from hearing their solutions to their problems.

Genuineness and Self-Disclosure   Genuineness implies congruence between a person's inner experience and what he or she projects externally. Applied to your role as a leader, genuineness means that you do not pretend to be accepting when internally you are not feeling accepting, you do not rely on behaviors that are aimed at winning approval, and you avoid hiding behind a professional role as a leader. Through your own authenticity, you offer a model to members that inspires them to be real in their interactions.

Consider a couple of examples in which you might be challenged to provide authentic responses rather than expected ones. A member who is new to your group might spontaneously ask you, "What do you think of me?" You could politely respond with, "I think you're a very nice person." A more honest response could be: "I don't know you well enough to have strong reactions to you. I'm sure that as I get to know you better, I'll share my perceptions with you." You might want to ask this person what prompted her question and discover that she is intimidated by your position in the group and needs quick reassurance. By helping her identify the reason for her question, you can help her be more authentic with you. In another case a member says to you in the middle of a conflict with him: "Oh, give me a hug; I don't like this tension between us." Chances are that you don't really feel like hugging him at this moment. It is nevertheless important that you give an honest reply to his request.

You could say, "I'm very much struggling with you right now, and I'm wanting to continue working this through. I'm not willing to hug you now, but that doesn't mean that I won't at some later point."

Related to being real is the matter of self-disclosure. As a leader you can invite members to make themselves known by letting others in the group know you. As we have pointed out before, this openness does not have to entail an indiscriminate sharing of your private life with the participants, but you can reveal your thoughts and feelings related to what is going on within the group. If you are authentic and appropriately self-disclosing and if you avoid hiding, you will encourage the rest of the group to be open about their concerns. Sometimes group participants will challenge you by saying, "We tell you all of our problems, but we don't know any of yours." You could surrender to this pressure to prove that you are "genuine" and end up with a problem. A genuine disclosure is: "Yes, in this group, due to my role, I'm likely to learn more about the nature of your problems than you will learn about my personal concerns, but this doesn't mean that I don't have difficulties in my life. If you and I were members in another group, I expect that you'd learn more about me. While I'm not likely to bring my outside problems into this group, I'm very willing to let you know how I'm being affected in these sessions and also to reveal my reactions to you."

Respect   Respect is shown by what the leader and the members actually do, not simply by what they say. Attitudes and actions that demonstrate respect include avoiding critical judgments, avoiding labeling, looking beyond self-imposed or other-imposed labels, expressing warmth and support that is honestly felt, being genuine and risking, and recognizing the rights of others to be different. For example, if a member discloses his strong sense of filial piety [an accepted norm in his culture], others in the group demonstrate respect when they strive to understand rather than judge his loyalty and need to please his parents. If people receive this type of respect, they are supported in their attempts to talk about themselves in open and meaningful ways.

Nina may express her fear of being judged by others and talk about how she is reluctant to speak because of this fear of criticism. Members are not offering her respect when they too quickly reassure her that they like her just as she is and that they would not judge her. It would be more helpful to encourage her to explore her fear of being judged, both in past situations and in the group. It is important to let her feelings stand and to work with them, rather than discounting them. Most likely her feelings of being judged reside within her and are projected onto others. If the leader allows the members to reassure Nina, she may momentarily feel reassured. As soon as she is away from the group, however, her internal judge will speak up again.

Caring Confrontation   The way in which confrontations are handled can either build or inhibit the development of trust in a group. A confrontation can be an act of caring that takes the form of an invitation for members to examine some discrepancy between what they are saying and what they are doing or between what they are saying and some nonverbal cues they are manifesting. If confrontations are made in an abrasive, "hit-and-run" fashion, or if the leader allows verbal abuse, trust is greatly inhibited. You can teach members directness coupled with sensitivity, which results in their seeing that confrontation can be done in a caring yet honest manner. For example, if Michael says to Ashika in an irritable tone, "Ashika, what you have been saying is ridiculous. You're always in your head!" This is an example of a harsh confrontation. It is judgmental and tells Ashika nothing about how her behavior is affecting Michael. A leader might focus on the fact that Michael is leaving himself out of this interaction and ask Michael to tell Ashika why it is important to him that she change how she is speaking. A useful confrontation involves Michael revealing how Ashika's behavior is getting in his way of being in the group with her. Challenging members is just as important as supporting them, for a timely challenge can inspire them to look at aspects of themselves that they have been avoiding.

Attacking comments or aggressive confrontations close people up by making them defensive, but caring confrontations help members learn to express even negative reactions in a way that respects those they are confronting. For example, Claire is very willing to speak on everything and constantly brings herself in on others' work. An ineffective confrontation by a group leader is this: "I want you to be quiet and let others in here talk." An effective leader confrontation is this: "Claire, I appreciate your willingness to participate and talk about yourself. However, I'm concerned that I have heard very little from several others in the group, and I want to hear from them too."

Maintaining Trust   The attitudes and behaviors described in these sections have an important bearing on the level of trust established within a group. Although trust is the major task to be accomplished at the initial stage of a group's development, it is a mistake to assume that once trust has been established it is ensured for the duration of that group. We want to emphasize that trust ebbs and flows, and new levels of trust must be established as the group progresses toward a deeper level of intimacy. A basic sense of safety is essential for the movement of a group beyond the initial stage, but this trust will be tested time and again and take on new facets in later stages.

✳ Identifying and Clarifying Goals

A major task during the initial stage is for leaders to assist members in identifying and clarifying specific goals that will influence their participation. In the absence of a clear understanding about the purpose of a group and meaningful goals of members, much needless floundering can occur. Members will have real difficulty making progress until they know *why* they are in the group and *how* they can make full use of the group to achieve their goals.

The process of setting goals is important both at the beginning of a new group and at intervals as the group evolves and goals are met. It is essential to establish both group goals and individual goals. Examples of general group goals include creating a climate of trust and acceptance, promoting self-disclosure in significant ways, and encouraging the taking of risks. It is essential that these goals (and norms, which we will discuss later) be explicitly stated, understood, and accepted by the members early in the group. Otherwise, considerable conflict and confusion are certain to occur at a later stage. What follows are some general goals common to most therapeutic groups and some examples of goals for specialized groups.

General Goals for Group Members

Although the members must decide for themselves the specific aims of their group experience, here are some broad goals common to many different types of groups:

- Become aware of one's interpersonal style
- Increase awareness of what prevents intimacy
- Learn how to trust oneself and others
- Become aware of how one's culture affects personal decisions
- Increase self-awareness and thereby increase the possibilities for choice and action
- Challenge and explore certain early decisions (most likely made during childhood) that may no longer be functional
- Recognize that others have similar problems and feelings
- Clarify values and decide whether and how to modify them
- Become both independent and interdependent
- Find better ways to resolve problems
- Become more open and honest with selected others
- Learn a balance between support and challenge
- Learn how to ask others for what one wants
- Become sensitive to the needs and feelings of others
- Provide others with helpful feedback

Once members have narrowed down their list of general goals, group leaders have a responsibility to monitor the group's progress toward attainment of these group goals (ASGW, 1998). In addition, specialized groups often have specific goals for members beyond the broad goals common to most groups. For example:

- **Goals for an incest group** are to assist people in talking about their incest; to discover their feelings of anger, hurt, shame, and guilt; and to work through unfinished business with the perpetrator.
- **Goals for a people with disabilities group** are to express any anger, grief, and resentment they may have about their disability; to learn

to deal with the reduced privacy caused by the disability; to learn to work within the limitations imposed by the handicap; and to establish a support system.

- **Goals for a substance abuse group** are to help the abuser confront difficult issues and learn to cope with life stresses more effectively; to provide a supportive network; and to learn more appropriate social skills.

- **Goals for a group for elderly people** are to review life experiences; to express feelings over losses; to improve members' self-image; and to continue finding meaning in life.

- **Goals for a group for acting-out children** are to accept feelings and at the same time learn ways of constructively expressing them and dealing with them; to develop skills in making friends; and to channel impulses into constructive behavior.

Regardless of the type of therapeutic group, it is important to consider some methods of assisting participants in developing concrete goals that will give them direction. Participants in groups do not automatically formulate clear goals. It is the responsibility of group leaders to use their skills to help members make their goals specific so that others present in the group will understand them.

Helping Members Define Personal Goals

Participants are typically able to state only in broad terms what they expect to get from a group. Too often they come up with unclear goals. When this is the case, the leader's job is to help members translate vague ideas into clear and workable goals. For instance, Ebony, who says she'd like to "relate to others better," needs to specify with whom and under what conditions she encounters difficulties in her interpersonal relationships. She also needs to learn to state concretely what part of her behavior she needs to change. The leader's questions should help her become more specific. With whom is she having difficulties? If the answer is her parents, then what specifically is causing her problems with them? How is she affected by these problems? How does she want to be different with her parents? With all this information the leader has a clearer idea of how to proceed with Ebony.

Here are some examples of how leaders can intervene to help different members make a global goal more specific:

Member A: I want to get in touch with my feelings.

Leader: What kind of feelings are you having difficulty with?

Member B: I want to work on my anger.

Leader: With whom in your life are you angry? What is it about the way you express your anger that you dislike? What do you most want to say to these people you are angry with?

Member C: *I have very low self-esteem.*

Leader: *List some of the ways in which you devalue yourself.*

Member D: *I have trouble with intimacy.*

Leader: *Who in your life are you having trouble getting close to, and what might you be doing to prevent the intimacy you want?*

Member E: *I don't want to feel marginalized.*

Leader: *How do you experience being marginalized? Is feeling marginalized an issue for you in this group?*

The ASGW (1998) guidelines state that it is the responsibility of group leaders to assist members in developing their personal goals in a collaborative fashion. Defining these goals is an ongoing process, not something that is done once and for all. Throughout the course of a group it is important to help members assess the degree to which their personal goals are being met and, if appropriate, to help them revise any of their goals. As members gain more experience, they are in a better position to know what they want from a group, and they also come to recognize additional goals that can guide their participation. Their involvement in the work of other members can act as a catalyst in getting them to think about ways in which they can profit from the group experience.

Establishing a contract is one excellent way for members to clarify and attain their personal goals. Basically, a contract is a statement by participants of what problems they want to explore and what behaviors they are willing to change. In the contract method, group members assume an active and responsible stance. Contracts can be open-ended so that they can be modified or replaced as appropriate. Contracts can be used in most of the groups discussed in this book.

Contracts and homework assignments can be combined fruitfully. In Ebony's case a beginning contract could commit her to observe and write down each time she experiences difficulties with her parents. If she discovers that she usually walks away in times of conflict with them, she might pledge in a follow-up contract to stay in one of these situations rather than avoid the conflict.

As another example, consider a man in an assertiveness training group who decides that he would like to spend more time on activities that interest him. He might make a contract that calls for him to do more of the things he would like to do for himself, and he might assign himself certain activities to be carried out during the group experience. Throughout the group, he would report the results. Partly on the basis of these results, he could decide how much and in what ways he really wants to change.

✳ Group Process Concepts at the Initial Stage

The group process, as we have said, involves the stages groups tend to go through, each characterized by certain feelings and behaviors. Initially, as the members get to know one another, there is a feeling of anxiety. Each typically waits for someone else to begin. Tension and conflict may build up. If things go well, however, the members learn to trust one another and the leader, and they begin to openly express feelings, thoughts, and reactions. Thus, included under the rubric *group process* are activities such as establishing norms and group cohesion, learning to work cooperatively, establishing ways of solving problems, and learning to express conflict openly. We will now discuss in depth two group process concepts that are especially important during the initial stage: group norms and group cohesion.

Group Norms

Group norms are the shared beliefs about expected behaviors aimed at making groups function effectively. Norms and procedures that will help the group attain its goals can be developed during the early stage. If the standards that govern behavior in the group are vague, valuable time will be lost, and tensions will arise over what is appropriate and inappropriate. Norms can be explicitly stated, but many groups also have implicit (or unspoken) norms as well.

Implicit norms may develop because of preconceived ideas about what takes place in a group. Members may assume, for example, that a group is a place where everything must be said, with no room for privacy. Unless the leader calls attention to the possibility that members can be self-disclosing and still retain a measure of privacy, members may misinterpret the norm of openness and honesty as a policy of complete candor, with no secrets. Another example of an implicit norm is pressure to experience catharsis and crying. In most of our intensive therapeutic groups, there is a fair amount of crying and expression of pent-up feelings. However, many individuals engage in significant self-exploration with little, if any, emotional catharsis. Certain members wrongly assume that we judge the quality of their personal work by the volume of tears shed or the intensity of catharsis. Members can learn from cognitive and behavioral exploration as well as from emotional expression and exploration.

Implicit norms may also develop because of modeling by the leader. If a leader uses abrasive language, members are more likely to adopt this pattern of speech in their group interactions, even though the leader has never expressly encouraged people to talk in such a manner. Another example of an implicit norm pertains to changes in members' everyday lives. If an unassertive member reports that she is being perceived as more assertive at work, she may receive applause from the group. Even though behavior change outside of the group is not specifically stated as a norm, this implicit norm can have a powerful effect on shaping the members' responses and behaviors. Implicit norms do affect the group. They are less likely to have an adverse influence if they are made explicit.

Here are some explicit norms, or standards of behavior, that are common in many groups:

- Members are expected to attend regularly and show up on time. When they attend sessions only sporadically, the entire group suffers. Members who regularly attend will resent the lack of commitment of those who miss sessions.

- Members are encouraged to be personal and share meaningful aspects of themselves, communicating directly with others in the group and, in general, being active participants.

- Members are expected to give feedback to one another. They can evaluate the effects of their behavior on others only if the others are willing to say how they have been affected. It is important for members not to withhold their perceptions and reactions but, rather, to let others know what they perceive.

- Members are asked to focus on both thoughts and feelings and express them rather than talking about problems in a detached and intellectual manner.

- Members are encouraged to focus on here-and-now interactions within the group. Members focus on being immediate by expressing and exploring conflicts within the group. Immediacy is called for when there are hidden thoughts and feelings about what is happening in a session, particularly if these reactions will have a detrimental effect on the group process. Thus, one of your leadership functions is to ask questions such as "What is it like to be in this group now?" "With whom do you identify the most in here?" "What are some of the things that you might be rehearsing to yourself silently?" "Whom in this room are you most aware of?" You can also steer members into the here and now by asking them to reveal what they think and feel about what is going on in the group moment by moment.

- Members are expected to bring into the group sessions personal problems and concerns that they are willing to discuss. They can be expected to spend some time before the sessions thinking about the matters they want to work on. This is an area in which unspoken norms frequently function. In some groups, for example, participants may get the idea that they are not good group members unless they bring personal issues from everyday life to work on during the sessions. Members may get the impression that it is not acceptable to focus on here-and-now matters within the group itself and that they should work on outside problems exclusively.

- Members are encouraged to provide therapeutic support. Ideally, this support facilitates both an individual's work and the group process rather than distracting members from self-exploration. But some leaders can implicitly "teach" being overly supportive or, by their modeling, can demonstrate a type of support that has the effect of short-circuiting painful experiences that a member is attempting to work through. Leaders who are uncomfortable with intense emotions (such as anger or the pain associated with past memories) can actually collude with members by fostering a pseudosupportive climate that prevents members from fully experiencing and expressing intense feelings of any kind. Some groups are so supportive that challenge and confrontation are ruled out. A hidden norm in this kind of group results in expressing only positive and favorable reactions. If this practice becomes a pattern, members can get the idea that it is not acceptable to express any challenging feedback.

■ The other side of the norm of support is providing members with challenges to look at themselves. Members need to learn how to confront others without arousing defensiveness. Early in our groups, for example, we establish a norm that it is not acceptable to dismiss another in a judgmental and labeling way, such as by saying "You are too judgmental." Instead, we teach members to directly and sensitively express the anger they are feeling, avoid name-calling, and avoid pronouncing judgments. Members are asked to express the source of their anger, including what led up to their feelings. For example, if Ann says to Rudy, "You're self-centered and uncaring," the leader can ask Ann to let Rudy know how she has been affected by him and by what she perceives as his uncaring behavior. Ann can also be encouraged to express the stored-up reactions that led her to judge him. In contrast, if leaders model harsh confrontations, members soon pick up the unexpressed norm that the appropriate way to relate to others in this group is by attacking them.

■ Groups can operate under either a norm of exploring personal problems or a norm of problem solving. In some groups, for example, as soon as members bring up situations they would like to understand better, they may quickly be given suggestions about how to "solve" these problems. The fact of the matter is that solutions are often not possible, and what members most need is an opportunity to talk. Of course, problem-solving strategies are of use in teaching members new ways of coping with their difficulties. But it is important that clients have an opportunity to explore their concerns before suggested solutions are presented. Ideally, this exploration will enable members to begin to see a range of possibilities open to them and a direction they might pursue in finding their own answers. It is generally more useful for clients to arrive at their own solutions than to follow the advice of others.

■ Members can be taught the norm of listening without thinking of a quick rebuttal and without becoming overly defensive. Although we do not expect people to merely accept all the feedback they receive, we do ask them to really hear what others are saying to them and to seriously consider these messages—particularly ones that are repeated consistently.

Group norms need to be attended throughout the life of a group. Many groups become bogged down because members are unsure of what is expected of them or of the norms of the group. For instance, a member may want to intervene and share her perceptions while a leader is working with another client, but she may be inhibited because she is not sure whether she should interrupt the group leader at work. Another member may feel an inclination to support a fellow group member at the time when that member is experiencing some pain or sadness but may refrain because he is uncertain whether his support will detract from the other's experience. Another member who is bored, session after session, may keep this feeling to herself because she is not sure of the appropriateness of revealing it. Perhaps if she were told that it is useful to express her boredom, she might be more open with her group and, consequently, less bored.

If group norms are clearly presented, and if members see the value of them and cooperatively decide to work with them, norms can be potent forces in shaping the group. Part of the orientation process consists of identifying and discussing norms that are aimed at developing a cohesive and productive group. For a more detailed discussion of therapeutic group norms, see Earley (2000).

Group Cohesion

Group cohesion is a sense of togetherness, or community, within a group. A cohesive group is one in which members have incentives for remaining in the group and share a feeling of belongingness and relatedness. During the early stage of a group, the members do not know one another well enough for a true sense of community to be formed. There is usually some awkwardness as members become acquainted. Though participants talk about themselves, it is likely that they are presenting more of their public selves rather than deeper aspects of their private selves. Genuine cohesion typically comes after groups have struggled with conflict, have shared pain, and have committed themselves to taking significant risks. But the foundations of cohesion can begin to take shape during the initial stage.

Some indicators of this initial degree of cohesion are cooperation among members; a willingness to show up for the meetings and be punctual; an effort to make the group a safe place, including talking about any feelings of lack of trust or fears of trusting; support and caring, as evidenced by being willing to listen to others and accept them for who they are; and a willingness to express reactions to and perceptions of others in the here-and-now context of group interactions. Genuine cohesion is not a fixed condition arrived at automatically. Instead, it is an ongoing process of solidarity that members earn through the risks they take with one another. Group cohesion can be developed, maintained, and increased in a number of ways. Here are some suggestions for enhancing group cohesion.

■ Trust must be developed during the early stage of a group. One of the best ways of building trust is to create a group climate characterized by respect for the opinions and feelings of the members. It is essential that members openly express their feelings concerning the degree of safety they are experiencing. An opportunity can be provided at the outset for members to share their reservations, and this open sharing of concerns will pave the way for productive work.

- If group members share meaningful aspects of themselves, they both learn to take risks and increase group cohesiveness. By modeling—for instance, by sharing their own reactions to what is occurring within the group—leaders can encourage risk-taking behavior. When group members do take risks, they can be reinforced with sincere recognition and support, which will increase their sense of closeness to the others.

- Group goals and individual goals can be jointly determined by the group members and the leader. If a group is without clearly stated goals, animosity can build up that will lead to fragmentation of the group.

- Cohesion can be increased by inviting all members to become active participants. Members who appear to be passive, silent, or withdrawn can be encouraged to express their feelings toward the group. These members may be silent observers for a number of reasons, and these reasons ought to be examined openly in the group.

- Cohesion can be built by sharing the leadership role with the members of the group. In autocratic groups all the decisions are made by the leader. A cooperative group is more likely to develop if members are encouraged to initiate discussion of issues they want to explore. Also, instead of fostering a leader-to-member style of interaction, group leaders can promote member-to-member interactions. This can be done by asking the members to respond to one another, by encouraging feedback and sharing, and by searching for ways to involve as many members as possible in group interactions.

- Conflict is inevitable in groups. It is desirable for group members to recognize sources of conflict and to deal openly with them when they arise. A group can be strengthened by acceptance of conflict and by the honest working through of interpersonal tensions.

- Group attractiveness and cohesion are related. It is generally accepted that the greater the degree of attractiveness of a group to its members, the greater the level of cohesion. If the group deals with matters that interest the members, if the members feel that they are respected, and if the atmosphere is supportive, the chances are good that the group will be perceived as attractive.

- Members can be encouraged to disclose their ideas, feelings, and reactions to what occurs within their group. The expression of both positive and negative reactions should be encouraged. If this is done, an honest exchange can take place, which is essential if a sense of group belongingness is to develop.

❋ Helping Members Get the Most From a Group Experience

Some behaviors and attitudes promote a cohesive and productive group—that is, a group in which meaningful self-exploration takes place and in which honest and appropriate feedback is given and received. We begin orienting and preparing members during the preliminary session, but we typically find that time allows only an introduction to the ways in which clients can get the most from their group experience. Consequently, during the initial phase of the group's evolution, we devote some time to teaching members the basics of group process, especially how they can involve themselves as active participants. We emphasize that they will benefit from the experience in direct proportion to how much they invest of themselves, both in the group and in practicing on the outside what they are learning in the sessions.

We do not present group guidelines as a lecture in one sitting, and we do not overwhelm members with more information than can be assimilated at one time. We begin by giving members written information about their participation in the group. We also allocate time to discuss these topics as they occur naturally within the sessions, which increases the likelihood that members will be receptive to thinking about how they can best participate. We continue to provide information in a timely manner at various points in a group. We encourage you to use these guidelines as a catalyst for thinking about your own approach to preparing members. Reflecting on this material may help you develop an approach that suits your own personality and leadership style and that is appropriate for the groups you lead. The following suggestions are written from the leader's point of view and directed to the members.

Leader Guidelines for Members

Learn to Help Establish Trust   We are convinced that confidentiality is essential if members are to feel a sense of safety in a group. Even if nobody raises questions about the nature and limitations of confidentiality, we still emphasize the importance of respecting the confidential character of the interactions within the group and caution members about how it can be broken. We explain how easy it might be to breach confidentiality without intending to do so. We emphasize to members that it is their responsibility to continually make the room safe by addressing their concerns regarding how their disclosures will be treated. If members feel that others may talk outside the sessions, this uncertainty is bound to hamper their ability to fully participate.

In our groups the members frequently hear from us that it does not make sense to open up quickly without a foundation of safety. One way to create this safe and trusting environment is for the group members to be willing to verbalize their fears, concerns, and here-and-now reactions during the early sessions. It is up to each member to decide what to bring into group and how far to pursue these personal topics. Participants often wait for some other person to take the first risk or to make some gesture of trust. They can challenge this, paradoxically, by revealing their fear of trust. Members can gain from initiating a discussion that will allow genuine trust to develop.

EXAMPLE: Harold was older than most of the other group members, and he was afraid that they would not be able to empathize with him, that they would exclude him from activities, and that they would view him as an outsider—a parent figure. After he disclosed these fears, many members gave Harold praise for his willingness to reveal his mistrust. His disclosure, and the response to it, stimulated others to express some of their concerns. This sharing stimulated trust in the entire group by making it clear that it was appropriate to express fears. Instead of being rejected, Harold was accepted and appreciated because he had been willing to make a significant part of himself known to the rest of the group.

Express Persistent Feelings

Express Persistent Feelings   Sometimes members keep their feelings of boredom, anger, or disappointment a secret from the rest of the group. It is most important that persistent feelings related to the group process be aired. We often make statements to members such as "If you are feeling detached and withdrawn, let it be known" or "If you are experiencing chronic anger or irritation toward others in this group, don't keep these feelings to yourself."

EXAMPLE: In a group of adolescents that met once a week for 10 weeks, Luella waited until the third session to disclose that she did not trust either the members or the leader, that she was angry because she felt pressured to participate, and that she really did not know what was expected of her as a group member. She had experienced reluctance since the initial session but had not verbalized her reactions. The leader let Luella know how important it was for her to reveal these persistent feelings of distrust so they could be explored and resolved.

Beware of Misusing Jargon

Beware of Misusing Jargon   In certain groups people learn a new language that can remove them from their direct experiences. For example, they may learn phrases such as "I can really relate to you," "I want to get closer to my feelings," "I feel connected with you," and "I'd like to stop playing all these games with myself." If terms such as *relate to, get closer to,* and *connected with* are not clearly defined and reserved for certain circumstances, the quality of communication will be poor. We often suggest that members use descriptive language by asking them what they mean by "connected with" or by asking them to clarify what feelings they want to express.

Related to misusing jargon is the way in which members' use of language sometimes distances them from themselves and from others. For example, when people say "I can't" instead of "I won't" or when they use many qualifiers in their speech ("maybe," "perhaps," "but," "I guess"), we ask them to be aware of how they are contributing to their powerlessness by their choice of words. This practice also applies to the use of a generalized "you" or "people" when "I" is what is meant. The more members can assume responsibility for their speech, the more they can reclaim some of the power they have lost through impersonal modes of expression.

EXAMPLE: "People are usually afraid to talk openly in the group," Valerie said. "They feel threatened and scared." The leader intervened by asking Valerie to repeat everything she had just said but to substitute "I" for the general impersonal words "people" and "they." The leader asked her whether using "I" was closer to the truth of what she really wanted to convey. After all, she could speak with authority about her own feelings, but she could not be an expert about others' feelings.

Decide for Yourself How Much to Disclose

Group members are sometimes led to believe that the more they disclose about themselves, the better. Though self-disclosure is an important tool in the group process, it is up to each participant to decide what aspects of his or her life to reveal. This principle cannot be stressed too much, for the idea that members will have to "tell everything" contributes to the resistance of many people to becoming participants in a group.

The most useful kind of disclosure is unrehearsed. It expresses present concern and may entail some risk. As participants open up to a group, they have fears about how other people will receive what they reveal. If a member shares that he is shy, often quiet, and afraid to speak up in the group, the other members will have a frame of reference for more accurately interpreting and reacting to his lack of participation. Had he not spoken up, both the leader and other members would have been more likely to misinterpret his behavior.

Members should be cautioned, however, about the dangers of "paying membership dues" by striving to reveal the biggest secret. Self-disclosure is not a process of "letting everything hang out" and of making oneself psychologically naked. Let members know time and again that they are responsible for deciding what, how much, and when they will share personal conflicts pertaining to their everyday life.

EXAMPLE: In a weekly group, Luis earlier disclosed that he was gay. At work he had not been willing to talk openly about his sexual orientation. Although Luis was willing to share with his group many of his struggles in being a gay Latino, he said he was not ready to talk about the difficulties he was experiencing in his relationship. At this time in his life, Luis felt shame about his sexual orientation, especially with respect to his extended family. Although it was difficult for him to talk about his feelings about being gay in the group, Luis challenged himself to trust others with some of his deepest concerns. One of the cultural values he grew up with was to keep personal concerns private. Although he did not feel comfortable discussing his relationship with his partner, Luis was willing to share with the group many of his doubts, fears, and anxieties over not being accepted for who he was. Luis did not want to go through life living a lie. Other group members respected Luis for his willingness to explore his struggles about being gay, especially his fear of judgment and rejection. Because of this understanding that he felt from other members, Luis was encouraged to share more of his life in the group than he could do with anyone outside of the group.

Be an Active Participant, Not an Observer   A participant might say, "I'm not the talkative type. It's hard for me to formulate my thoughts, and I'm afraid I don't express myself well. So I usually don't say anything in the group. But I listen to what others are saying, and I learn by observing. I really don't think I have to be talking all the time to get something out of these sessions." Although it is true that members can learn by observing interactions and reacting nonverbally, their learning will tend to be limited. If members assume the stance of not contributing, others will never come to know them, and they can easily feel cheated and angry at being the object of others' perhaps flawed observations.

Some members keep themselves passively on the fringe of group activity by continually saying, "I have no real problems in my life at this time, so I don't have much to contribute to the group." Other members remain passive by stating that they see no need to repeat what other members have already expressed because they feel the same way. We attempt to teach these members to share their reactions to their experience in the group as well as to let others know how they are being affected. Members who choose to share little about events outside of the group can actively participate by keeping themselves open to being affected by other members. Leaders can contribute to group cohesion by helping those members who feel that they have nothing to contribute recognize that they can at least share how they are reacting to what others are saying.

> **EXAMPLE:**   When Thelma was asked what she wanted from the group, she replied, "I haven't really given it that much thought. I figured I'd just be spontaneous and wait to see what happens." The leader let Thelma know that sometimes other people's work might indeed evoke some of her own issues and that she might spontaneously react. However, the leader taught her that it was important for her to think about and to bring up the concerns that initially brought her to the group. As the sessions progressed, Thelma did learn to let the other members know what she wanted from them. Instead of being a mere observer without any clear goals who was content to wait for things to happen to her, she began to take the initiative. She showed that she wanted to talk about how lonely she was, how desperate and inadequate she frequently felt, how fearful she was of being weak with men, and how she dreaded facing her world every morning. As she learned to focus on her wants, she found that she could benefit from her weekly sessions.

Expect Some Disruption of Your Life   Participants in therapeutic groups should be given the warning that their involvement may complicate their outside lives for a time. As a result of group experiences, members tend to assume that the people in their lives will be both ready and willing to make significant changes. It can be shocking for members to discover that others thought they were "just fine" the way they were, and the friction that results may make it more difficult than ever to modify familiar patterns. Therefore, it is important for members to be prepared for the fact that not everyone will like or accept some of the changes they want to make.

EXAMPLE: Ricardo came away from his group with the awareness that he was frightened of his wife, that he consistently refrained from expressing his wants to her, and that he related to her as he would to a protective mother. If he asserted himself with her, he feared that she would leave. In the group he not only became tired over his dependent style but also decided that he would treat his wife as an equal and give up his hope of having her become his mother. Ricardo's wife did not cooperate with his valiant efforts to change the nature of their relationship. The more assertive he became, the more disharmony there was in his home. While he was trying to become independent, his wife was struggling to keep their relationship the way it was; she was not willing to respond differently to him.

Expect to Discover Positive Aspects of Yourself   A common fear about therapy is that you will discover how unlovable or how powerless you are. More often than not, though, people in groups begin to realize that they can control more aspects of their lives than they previously thought possible. Members often explore intense feelings of pain in a group. Unrecognized and unexpressed pain is blocking them from living a truly joyous life. It is through releasing and working through these painful experiences that they begin to reclaim a joyful dimension of themselves. For instance, many participants experience an inner strength, discover a real wit and sense of humor, create moving poetry or songs, or dare for the first time to show a creative side of themselves that they have kept hidden from others and from themselves.

EXAMPLE: Francesco expressed the positive side of the group experience rather poetically when he said, "I have learned that there are lots of beautiful rose bushes with pretty flowers, and on those bushes are thorns. I'd never trade the struggle and pain I had to go through to appreciate the joy of smelling and touching those roses. Both the roses and the thorns are a part of life."

Listen Closely and Discriminatingly   Group members can be taught to listen carefully to what the other members say about them, neither accepting it entirely nor rejecting it outright. Members are advised to be as open as possible, yet to also listen discriminatingly, deciding for themselves what does and what does not apply to them. Before they respond, they can be asked to quiet down, to let what is being said to them sink in, and to take note of how it is affecting them. Members are sometimes busy formulating responses while others are still speaking to them. They cannot fully comprehend what is being communicated to them if they are not totally engaged in listening.

EXAMPLE: In an adolescent group, members told Brenden that it was hard for them to listen to his many stories. Although some of his stories were interesting, they gave no clue to the nature of his struggles, which were the reason he was in the group. Other members told him that it was easier to hear what he was saying when he talked about himself. When Brenden became defensive and angry and denied that he had been acting that way, he could have been asked by the leader to think about how he was affected by the feedback and to consider what had been said to him before he so rigorously rejected the feedback.

Pay Attention to Consistent Feedback   Members need to learn that feedback can be a valuable source of information that they can use in assessing what they are doing in the group and how their behavior is affecting others. **Members do well to listen carefully to consistent feedback they receive.** A person may get similar feedback from many people in different groups yet may still dismiss it as invalid. Although it is important to discriminate, it is also important to realize that a message that has been received from a variety of people is likely to have some degree of validity.

> **EXAMPLE:**   In several groups Liam heard people tell him that he did not seem interested in what they had to say and that he appeared distant and detached. Although Liam was physically in the room, he often looked at the ceiling and sighed, moved his chair away from the circle, yawned, and sometimes even took a short nap. Members said they felt that he had no interest in them and that it was difficult for them to get close to him. Liam was surprised by this feedback and insisted that his behavior in the group was very different from his behavior in his outside life—that on the outside he felt close to people and was interested and involved. It seems unlikely that someone could be so different in the two areas, however, and the leader intervened in this way: "You may be different in here than you are on the outside. But would you be willing to monitor how people respond to you away from here and be open to noticing if any of the feedback given to you might be similar?" The leader's response eliminated unnecessary argumentation and debates over who was right.

Do Not Categorize Yourself   During the initial stage of a group, members often present themselves to others in terms of a role—often one they dislike but at the same time appear to cling to. For instance, we have heard people introduce themselves as "the group mother," "the walled-off and impenetrable one," "the fragile person who can't stand conflict," and "the one in this group whom nobody will like." It is important for people not to fatalistically pin labels on themselves, and the group should not fulfill these expectations, thereby further convincing members that they are what they fear. It may be helpful for group leaders to remind themselves and the members of how certain participants can be pegged with labels such as "the monopolist," "the storyteller," "the intellectualizer," "the withdrawn one," "the obsessive-compulsive one," and so on. People may exhibit behaviors that characterize them in one way or another, and it is appropriate to confront them with these actions during the group. But this confronting can be done without cementing people into rigid molds that become very difficult to break.

EXAMPLE: Rosie presented herself to the group as withdrawn and fragile. When she was asked how she would like to be different, she said she would like to speak out more often and more forcefully. She was willing to make a contract that required her to speak out and at least act as if she were strong. In this way she was able to challenge an old image that she had clung to and was able to experiment with a different type of behavior.

Other Suggestions for Group Members   Some additional guidelines that we bring up early in a group, as they seem appropriate, are briefly listed here:

- Be willing to do work both before and after a group. Consider keeping a journal as a supplement to the group experience. Create homework assignments as a way of putting your group learning into practice in everyday living.

- Develop self-evaluation skills as a way of assessing your progress in the group. Ask yourself these questions: "Am I contributing to the group?" "Am I satisfied with what is occurring in the sessions? If not, what am I doing about it?" "Am I using in my life what I'm learning in my group?"

- Spend time clarifying your own goals by reviewing specific issues and themes you want to explore during the sessions. This can best be done by thinking about specific changes you want to make in your life and by deciding what you are willing to do both in and out of the group to bring about these changes.

- Concentrate on making personal and direct statements to others in your group, as opposed to giving advice, making interpretations, and asking impersonal questions. Instead of telling others how they are, let them know how they are affecting you.

- Realize that the real work consists of what you actually do outside of your group. Consider the group as a means to an end, and give some time to thinking about what you will do with what you are learning. Expect some setbacks, and be aware that change may be slow and subtle. Do not expect one group alone to change your entire life.

Avoid Too Much Teaching

Even though we have stressed the value of preparing members for how groups function, be aware that too much emphasis on teaching the group process can have a negative influence. All the spontaneous learning can be taken out of the group experience if members have been told too much of what to expect and have not been allowed to learn for themselves. Moreover, it is possible to foster a dependency on the structure and direction provided by the leader.

Our hope is that members will increasingly be able to function with less intervention from the leader as the group progresses. There is a delicate balance between providing too much structure and failing to give enough structure and information. Especially important, perhaps, is that the leader be aware of factors such as group cohesion, group norms, and group interactions at any given point. With this awareness the leader can decide when it is timely and useful to suggest a discussion of certain behavior that is occurring in the here and now.

The stages in the life of a group are not rigidly defined but are fluid and somewhat overlapping. How we teach members about the group process can have a lot to do with the level to which the group may evolve. Burlingame and Fuhriman (1990) and Yalom (1995) have identified particular therapeutic characteristics that are primarily linked to the various stages of a group. During the beginning phase, the crucial factors are identification, universality, hope, and cohesion. During the middle phase, catharsis, cohesion, interpersonal learning, and insight are essential. As termination approaches, existential factors surface. Understanding these group characteristics will aid you in deciding how much to teach—and when.

Journal Writing as an Adjunct to Group Sessions

Group members can gain more from the group experience by participating in journal writing exercises outside of the group. One way is to ask members to spend even a few minutes each day recording in a journal certain feelings, situations, behaviors, and ideas for courses of action. Alternatively, members can be asked to review certain periods of time in their lives and write about them. For example, they can get out pictures of their childhood years and other reminders of this period and then freely write in a journal whatever comes to mind. Writing in a free-flowing style without censoring can be of great help in getting a focus on feelings.

Members can bring the journals to the group and share a particular experience they had that resulted in problems for them. They can then explore with the group how they might have handled the situation differently. In general, however, these journals help members improve their personal focus for a session, and as such, members can decide what to do with the material they write.

Another way to use journals is as a preparation for encountering others in everyday life. For instance, Jenny is having a great deal of difficulty talking with her husband. She is angry with him much of the time over many of the things he does and does not do. But she sits on this anger, and she feels sad that they do not take time for each other. Jenny typically does not express her sadness to him, nor does she let him know of her resentment toward him for not being involved in their children's lives. To deal with this problem, she can write her husband a detailed and uncensored letter pointing out all the ways she feels angry, hurt, sad, and disappointed and expressing how she would like their life to be different. It is not recommended that she show this letter to her husband. The letter writing is a way for her to clarify what she feels and to prepare herself to work in the group. This work can then help her to be clear about what she wants to say to her husband as well as how she wants to say it. This process works in the following way: In the group Jenny can talk to another member by relating the essence of what she wrote in her letter. This member can role-play Jenny's husband. Others can then express how they experience Jenny and the impact on the way she spoke. Aided by such feedback, she may be able to find a constructive way to express her feelings to her husband.

Still another technique is for members to spontaneously enter in their journals their reactions to themselves in the group, especially during the first few meetings, and to review these thoughts as the group is coming to an end. Answering these questions can help members understand their group experience:

- How do I feel about being in this group?
- How do I see people in the group? How do I see myself in it?
- What are my initial fears or concerns about being in the group?
- How do I most want to use the time in the group sessions?
- What would I like to leave this group having learned or experienced?

If participants write down their reactions, they are more likely to verbalize them during group sessions. If members are afraid to open up in a group because they think others may judge them in a negative way, writing about this in a journal can prepare members for expressing these fears verbally during group sessions.

Writing can be useful as the group progresses as well as during the early stage. At the midpoint of a group, people can take time during the week to write down how they feel about the group at this point, how they view their participation in it so far, what they are doing outside the group to attain their goals, and how they would feel if the group were to end now. By discussing these statements in the group, participants are challenged to reevaluate their level of commitment and are often motivated to increase their participation in the group.

Homework During the Initial Stage

Perhaps one of the best ways to maximize the value of any group experience is to design homework assignments that members can carry out both in and out of the group. Kazantzis and Deane (1999) point out that the use of homework assignments between sessions provides a valuable opportunity to reinforce and extend the benefits of the work done during therapy sessions. They contend that homework assignments facilitate the generalization and maintenance of improvement and produce positive effects in therapy. Kazantzis and Deane offer a number of recommendations for systematic use of homework in therapy. Although they are writing about individual therapy, their recommendations have relevance for group work as well:

- Provide a rationale for homework activity. How will homework help clients attain their therapy goals?
- Provide clients with a choice of homework activities or options in ways they can complete their assignments. Have them decide what tasks are relevant to them.

- Ask clients how confident they are that they will be able to complete the homework assignment.
- At the following session be sure to discuss the extent of homework completion and the outcomes of the assignment.
- Assess and record a client's weekly performance of homework assignments so that progress can be monitored.

In our groups we strongly encourage members to engage in regular journal writing as a part of their homework. Depending on the needs of a group, we might suggest some incomplete sentences for members to spontaneously complete either at the end of a group meeting or as material for journaling at home.

Here are some incomplete sentence assignments that work well in the initial stage of a group:

- What I most want from this group is . . .
- The one thing I most want to be able to say at our final meeting is . . .
- Thinking about being in this group for the next 12 weeks, I . . .
- A fear I have about being a group member is . . .
- One personal concern or problem I would hope to bring up is . . .
- My most dominant reaction to being in the group so far is . . .
- The one aspect I'd most like to change about myself is . . .

The incomplete sentence technique helps members focus on specific aspects of their experience during the early sessions, and several of these questions pertain to member goals. The practice of reflecting on personal goals, and writing about them, is an excellent means of clarifying what it is members want and how they can best obtain what they want. If you are interested in learning more about using homework, we suggest Kazantzis and Deane (1999), Rosenthal (2001), Schulthesis (1998), and Shelton and Levy (1981).

Leader Issues at the Initial Stage

Early in the history of a group it is especially important to think about the balance of responsibility between members and the leader (or coleaders) as well as the degree of structuring that is optimal for the group. If you are working with a coleader, discussing these issues is essential because divergent views are bound to hurt the group. If you assume the majority of the responsibility for keeping the group moving, for example, and your coleader assumes almost no responsibility on the ground that the members must decide for themselves what to do with group time, the members will sense this division and are bound to be confused by it. Similarly, if you function best with a high degree of structure in groups and your coleader believes any structuring should come from the members, this difference of opinion will have a detrimental effect on the group. It is wise to select a coleader who has a philosophy of leadership that is compatible with yours, although this does not mean that both of you need to have the same *style* of leading. Effective coleaders often have differences that complement each other.

Division of Responsibility

A basic issue you will have to consider is responsibility for the direction and outcome of the group. If a group proves to be nonproductive, will this failure stem from your lack of leadership skills, or does the responsibility rest with the group members?

One way of conceptualizing the issue of leader responsibility is to think of it in terms of a continuum. At one end is the leader who assumes a great share of the responsibility for the direction and outcomes of the group. Such leaders tend to have the outlook that the group will flounder if they are not highly directive. These leaders actively intervene to keep the group moving in ways they deem productive. A disadvantage of this form of leadership is that it deprives members of their responsibility for the direction a group takes.

Leaders who assume almost total responsibility not only undermine members' independence but also burden themselves. If people leave unchanged, such leaders tend to see this as their fault. If members remain separate, never forming a cohesive unit, these leaders tend to view this outcome as a reflection of their lack of skill. If the group is disappointed, these leaders feel disappointed and tend to blame themselves, believing that they did not do enough to create a dynamic group. This style of leadership is draining, and leaders who use it may eventually lose the energy required to lead groups.

At the other end of the responsibility continuum is the leader who makes this claim: "I am responsible for me, and you are responsible for you. If you want to leave this group with anything of value, it is strictly up to you. I can't do anything for you—make you feel something or take away any of your defenses—unless you allow me to." This extreme style absolves leaders of any responsibility for what takes place in their groups. To be sure, leaders do have a significant role to play both in the process of a group and in the outcomes. By denying responsibility, leaders do not have to look at what they are doing to establish and maintain a climate that allows productive work to occur in the group.

We tend to be highly active during the initial period in the evolution of a group. We do see it as our responsibility to intervene in very directive ways to establish certain norms within the group. Our intention is not to promote leader dependency but to teach members how they can best attain what they want to accomplish by being a part of this group. We encourage members to take an active role in the process of monitoring what they are thinking, feeling, and doing and to pay attention to the times when they may be engaging in behavior that is not going to help them in this group.

Ideally, you will develop a leadership style that balances responsibility between leader and members. We encourage group leaders to make use of journal writing to clarify how much responsibility they are assuming for the overall functioning of the group. When training group leaders, we ask them to write about themselves and the reactions that are evoked in them as they lead or colead their groups. Rather than describing the dynamics of their members, we suggest that they focus on how specific members affect them personally. Here are some questions we recommend that group leaders address in their journals:

- How did I feel about myself as I was leading or coleading my group?
- How much responsibility did I assume for the outcome of this particular session?
- What did I like best about the group today?
- What most stood out for me during this session?
- How am I being affected personally by each of the members?
- How involved am I in this group? If I am not as involved as I would like to be, what specific steps am I willing to take to change this situation?
- Are any factors getting in the way of my effectively leading this group?

This journal technique for group leaders provides an excellent record of patterns that are shaping up in a group. The practice of writing can also be a useful catalyst for focusing leaders on areas in their own lives that need continued attention.

Degree of Structuring

The issue is not *whether* a group leader should provide structure but, rather, *what degree* of structure should be provided. Like responsibility, structuring exists on a continuum. The leader's theoretical orientation, the type of group, the membership population, and the stage of the group are some of the factors that determine the amount and type of structuring employed.

Balance at the Initial Stage   Providing therapeutic structuring is particularly important during the initial stage of a group when members are typically unclear about what behavior is expected and are therefore anxious. Structure can be both useful and inhibiting in a group's development. Too little structure results in members' becoming unduly anxious, and although some anxiety is productive, too much can inhibit spontaneity. During the early phase of a group, it is useful to encourage members to assume increasing responsibility. Too much structuring and direction can foster leader-dependent attitudes and behavior, with members not taking the initiative to decide what they want from the group. The result tends to be waiting for the leader to "make something happen" instead of acting themselves.

Yalom (1983, 1995) sees the basic task of the group leader as providing enough structure to give a general direction to the members yet avoiding the pitfalls of fostering dependency. His message for leaders is to structure the group in a fashion that facilitates each member's autonomous functioning. An example of fostering dependency on the leader would be encouraging members to speak only when they are invited to do so. Instead, the leader can encourage members to bring themselves into the interactions without being called on.

We do not subscribe to a passive style of group leadership; we do not simply wait and let the group take any direction it happens to go in. Our structuring is aimed at reducing unnecessary floundering and maximizing full participation. We do this by teaching participants a number of ways to derive the maximum benefit from a group. By providing some structure we give group members the opportunity to experiment with new levels of awareness and to build new forms of behavior from this awareness. During the initial stage, our structure is aimed at helping members identify and express their fears, expectations, and personal goals. We often use dyads, go-arounds, and open-ended questions to make it easier for members to talk to one another about current issues in their lives. After talking to several people on a one-to-one basis, members find it easier to talk openly in the entire group. The leadership activity we provide is designed to help members focus on themselves and the issues they most want to explore in the group.

Many short-term psychoeducational groups are structured around a series of topics. In a group for learning effective parenting skills, for example, the sessions are guided by topics such as listening well, setting limits, learning to convey respect, and providing discipline without punishment. Group leaders sometimes rigidly adhere to a structured exercise or a discussion of a topic when another pressing matter demands attention. If there is conflict in the group, it is more important to suspend the topic or exercise until the conflict has been attended to. If the conflict is brushed aside, there is a greater likelihood that discussion of the topic will be superficial. At other times members may spontaneously bring up unrelated concerns, and leaders have difficulty keeping the group focused on the topic in a meaningful way. The leader and members of the group need to explore whether the shift in the topic is due to their discomfort with the issue or to the fact that a more relevant subject has surfaced. If the shift is an avoidance tactic, the facilitator might point out the dynamics of what is occurring.

We often supervise leaders who are facilitating structured interpersonal groups. These groups are focused on different themes for each session. Some of these topics are sex roles, body image, meaning and values, work and leisure, love and sexuality, loneliness, intimacy, and death and dying. We try to teach the group facilitators how to balance a discussion of group process concerns (trust, confrontation, unfinished business, subgrouping) with an exploration of the particular topic. Process issues among members (such as clients' feeling isolated in the group) generally take precedence over dealing with the topic. The art consists of learning how to help members relate topics to themselves in significant ways so that group interaction and group learning can occur.

Research on Structuring   Research indicates the positive value of an initial structure that builds supportive group norms and highlights positive interactions among members. Leaders must carefully monitor this therapeutic structure throughout the life of a group rather than limiting evaluation to the final stage. Structuring that offers a coherent framework for understanding the experiences of individuals and the group process is of the most value. When goals are clear, when appropriate member behaviors are identified, and when the process provides a framework for change, members tend to engage in therapeutic work more quickly (Dies, 1983b). Moreover, leader direction during the early phase of a group tends to facilitate the development of cohesion and the willingness of members to take risks by making themselves known to others and by giving others feedback (Stockton & Morran, 1982). In his review of 51 group studies that dealt with the leader's level of activity during a group session, Dies (1994) reported that group leaders who were more active, directive, and structured had groups with more favorable outcomes in 78% of the studies reviewed.

Research-Based Guidelines for Leaders   Here are some guidelines for providing therapeutic structure in your groups; they underscore many of the major points we have developed in this chapter and the previous one. What follows is an adaptation of some of the conclusions of research on short-term groups as summarized by Dies (1983b):

- Teaching by the group leader tends to facilitate a group's development during the early stages.
- Initial structuring should focus on ways to create supportive group norms and foster the establishment of trust.
- A less directive structure is appropriate during later group stages as members assume increased direction of their group.
- More structured interventions are necessary with clients whose level of personal functioning restricts their capacity to interact in socially competent ways.
- Employ active leadership, but use interventions that encourage members to assume increased responsibility.
- Develop and maintain a task-oriented focus by helping members develop and stick to clear goals.
- Help members understand the value of disclosing themselves, of providing feedback to one another, and of providing a balance between support and confrontation.
- Acknowledge what members do by providing positive concrete feedback that describes specific behavioral characteristics, and teach members to do the same.
- Model directness by speaking *to* members instead of talking *about* them.
- Structure initial sessions in a way that will help members acquire a clear framework for understanding experiences within the group.
- Use interpretations that help members generalize from how they behave in the here and now of the group situation to their problems in everyday living.

■ Discuss with members the value of experimenting with new interpersonal behaviors outside of the group.

Some degree of structuring exists in all groups, even "unstructured" groups, for this itself is a form of structure. The art is to provide structuring that is not so tight that it robs group members of the responsibility for finding their own structure.

Opening and Closing Group Sessions

We discuss opening and closing group sessions here because you need to be aware of this essential aspect of group leadership from the very beginning. These skills are important throughout the group process, and we suggest that you return to this discussion as you read about subsequent stages. The interventions we describe here are not the only "right" ones. There are many effective ways to intervene, depending on your theoretical orientation or leadership style and also on the kind of group you are leading. We have found the following guidelines useful.

Guidelines for Opening Sessions Sometimes leader trainees do not pay enough attention to how they open group sessions. They tend to focus on the person who speaks first and to stay with that person for an undue length of time. Often no attempt is made to link the coming session with the previous session, and the leader does not check with each member to determine how the members want to use the time for this particular session. If a session begins abruptly, it may be difficult to involve many of the members in productive work for that session. Therefore, some kind of warm-up is essential before work on problems begins.

For groups that meet on a regular basis, such as once a week, we suggest some of the following procedures to open each session in an effective way:

■ Ask all members to participate in a check-in process by briefly stating what they want from the session. During the check-in time, our aim is to hear what the members remember from the last session and what they want to say. A quick go-around is all that is needed for members to identify issues they are interested in pursuing; in this way an agenda can be developed that is based on some common concerns. We generally do not stay with one member before we have completed the check-in process because we want all the participants to have a chance to express what they are bringing to this session. The check-in procedure provides a basis for identifying emerging themes present at the beginning of a meeting. If you do not find out what issues the members have brought to a particular session, or if you stay with the first member who speaks, much important material is lost.

■ Give members a brief opportunity to share what they have done in the way of practice outside of the group since the previous session. If members are making use of journal writing and carrying out homework assignments, the beginning of a session is a good time for members to briefly state some of the outcomes of their reflections, writing, and homework. Some may want to talk about problems they are experiencing in transferring their learning from the group into everyday situations. This difficulty can then be the basis for work in that session.

- Ask members if they have any afterthoughts or unresolved feelings about the previous session. If members do not have a chance to mention these concerns, hidden agendas will probably develop and block effective work.

- Begin some sessions by letting the group know what you have been thinking during the week about how the group is progressing. This practice is especially appropriate when you see certain problems emerging or when you think the group is getting stuck. Your self-disclosure can lead the way for members to be open with their reactions to what is or is not going on in the sessions.

- In an open group (in which the membership changes somewhat from week to week), introduce any new members. Rather than putting the spotlight on the incoming member, ask continuing members to briefly reflect on what they have been learning about themselves in the group. Point out that some members may be attending for only a few sessions, and ask them how they expect to get the most from their brief time in the group. We sometimes ask this question: "If this were the only session you had, what would you most want to accomplish?"

Although we do not want to suggest that you memorize certain lines to open a session, we'd like to suggest some comments that convey the spirit of eliciting important material for leading into a session. Let these lines serve as catalysts that can be part of your own leadership style. At different times we've opened a session with remarks such as these:

- How are each of you feeling about being here today?
- Before we begin today's session, I'd like to ask each of you to take a few minutes to silently review your week and think about anything you want to tell us.
- Are you here because you want to be?
- Did anyone have any afterthoughts about last week's session?
- As a way of beginning tonight, let's have a brief go-around. Each of you say what you'd most like to be able to say by the end of this session.
- What are you willing to do to get what you say you want?
- What were you thinking and feeling before coming to the group?
- Whom are you most aware of in this room right now, and why?

Guidelines for Closing Sessions   Just as important as how you open a session is the way in which you bring a meeting to closure. Too often a leader will simply announce that "time is up for today," with no attempt to summarize and integrate and with no encouragement for members to practice certain skills. Our preference for closing each session is to establish a norm of expecting each member to participate in a brief checkout process. Some time, if even only 10 minutes, should be set aside to give participants an opportunity to reflect on what they liked or did not like about the session, to mention what they hope to do outside of the group during the week, and so forth. Attention to closing ensures that consolidation of learning will take place.

For groups that meet weekly, summarize what occurred in that session. At times, it is useful to stop the group halfway through the session and say, "I notice that we have about an hour left today, and I'd like to check out how each of you feels about what you've done so far today. Have you been as involved as you want to be? Are there some issues you'd like to raise before this session ends?" This does not need to be done routinely, but sometimes such an assessment during the session can help members focus their attention on problem areas, especially if you sense that they are not doing and saying what they need to.

In closing a weekly group session, consider these guidelines:

- It is good for clients to leave a session with some unanswered questions. We think it is a mistake to try to ensure that everyone leaves feeling comfortable. If clients leave feeling that everything is nicely closed, they will probably spend very little time during the week reflecting on matters raised in the group.

- Some statement from the members concerning their level of investment of energy is useful. If clients report feeling uninvolved, you can ask them what they are willing to do to increase their investment in the group: "Is your lack of involvement all right, or is this something that you want to change?"

- Ask members to tell the group briefly what they are learning about themselves through their relationships with other members. The participants can briefly indicate some ways they have changed their behavior in response to these insights. If participants find that they would like to change their behavior even more, they can be encouraged to develop specific plans or homework assignments to complete before the next session. This is a good time to identify a few concrete steps that will be taken before the following meeting.

- If members suggest homework that seems unrealistic, the leader or other members can be of assistance in creating realistic homework assignments.

- Ask members whether there are any topics, questions, or problems they would like to explore in the next session. This request creates a link between one session and the next. Prompting the members to think about the upcoming session also indirectly encourages them to stick to their contracts during the week.

■ Have members give one another feedback. Especially helpful are members' positive reactions concerning what they have actually observed. For instance, if Doug's voice is a lot more secure, others may let him know that they perceive this change. Of course, feedback on what members are doing to block their strengths is also very helpful.

■ If your group is one with changing membership, remind members a week before certain participants will be leaving the group. Not only do the terminating members need to talk about what they have learned from the group, but other members are also likely to want to share their feelings. It is essential that time be allotted for any unfinished business.

As we did for opening sessions, we offer some comments for you to consider in closing a session. Of course, not all of them need be asked at any one time.

■ What was it like for you to be in this group today?

■ What affected you the most, and what did you learn?

■ What would each of you be willing to do outside of the group this week to practice some of the new skills you are acquiring?

■ I'd like a quick go-around to have everyone say a few words on how this group is progressing so far and make any suggestions for change.

■ What are you getting or not getting from this group?

■ If you are not satisfied with what is happening in this group, what can you do to change things?

■ Before we close tonight, I'd like to share with you some of my reactions and observations of this session.

By developing skills in opening and closing sessions, you increase the possibility of continuity from meeting to meeting. Such continuity can help members transfer insights and new behaviors from the group into daily life and, along with encouragement and direction from your leadership, can facilitate the participants' ongoing assessment of their level of investment for each session.

If you work with a coleader, the matter of how the sessions are opened and closed should be a topic for discussion. Here are a few questions for exploration: Who typically opens the sessions? Do the two of you agree on when and how to bring a session to a close? With 5 minutes left in the sessions, does one leader want to continue working, whereas the other wants to attempt some summary of the meeting? Do both of you pay attention to unfinished business that might be left toward the end of a session? Although we are not suggesting a mechanical division of time and functions when you begin and end sessions, it is worth noting who tends to assume this responsibility. If one leader typically opens the session, members may be likely to direct their talk to this person. In our groups one of us may open the session while the other elaborates and makes additional remarks. In this way spontaneous give-and-take between coleaders can replace an approach characterized by "Now it's your turn to make a remark."

✓ Points to Remember

Initial Stage Characteristics

The early phase of a group is a time for orientation and determining the structure of the group. At this stage,

✓ Participants test the atmosphere and get acquainted.

✓ Members learn what is expected, how the group functions, and how to participate in a group.

✓ Risk-taking is relatively low, and exploration is tentative.

✓ Group cohesion and trust are gradually established if members are willing to express what they are thinking and feeling.

✓ Members are concerned with whether they are included or excluded, and they are beginning to define their place in the group.

✓ Negative reactions may surface as members test to determine if all feelings are acceptable.

✓ Trust versus mistrust is a central issue.

✓ Periods of silence and awkwardness may occur; members may look for direction and wonder what the group is about.

✓ Members are deciding whom they can trust, how much they will disclose, how safe the group is, whom they like and dislike, and how much to get involved.

✓ Members are learning the basic attitudes of respect, empathy, acceptance, caring, and responding—all attitudes that facilitate building trust.

Member Functions

Early in the course of the group some specific member roles and tasks are critical to shaping the group:

✓ Take active steps to create a trusting climate; distrust and fear will increase members' reluctance to participate.

✓ Learn to express your feelings and thoughts, especially as they pertain to interactions in the group.

✓ Be willing to express fears, hopes, concerns, reservations, and expectations concerning the group.

✓ Be willing to make yourself known to the others in the group; members who remain hidden will not have meaningful interactions with the group.

✓ As much as possible, be involved in the creation of group norms.

✓ Establish personal and specific goals that will govern group participation.

✓ Learn the basics of group process, especially how to be involved in group interactions; problem solving and advice giving interrupt positive group interactions among members.

Leader Functions

The major tasks of group leaders during the orientation and exploration phase of a group are these:

✓ Teach participants some general guidelines and ways to participate actively that will increase their chances of having a productive group.

✓ Develop ground rules and set norms.

✓ Teach the basics of group process.

✓ Assist members in expressing their fears and expectations, and work toward the development of trust.

✓ Model the facilitative dimensions of therapeutic behavior.

✓ Be open with the members and be psychologically present for them.

✓ Clarify the division of responsibility.

✓ Help members establish concrete personal goals.

✓ Deal openly with members' concerns and questions.

✓ Provide a degree of structuring that will neither increase members' dependence nor result in floundering.

✓ Assist members to share what they are thinking and feeling about what is occurring within the group.

✓ Teach members basic interpersonal skills such as active listening and responding.

✓ Assess the needs of the group and lead in such a way that these needs are met.

Exercises

Facilitation of Initial Stage of a Group

1. **Initial Session.** For this exercise 10 students volunteer to assume the roles of group members at an initial group session, and 2 volunteer to take on the roles of coleaders. Have the coleaders begin by giving a brief orientation explaining the group's purpose, the role of the leader, the rights and responsibilities of the members, the ground rules, group process procedures, and any other pertinent information they might actually give in the first session of a group. The members then express their expectations and fears, and the leaders try to deal with them. This lasts for approximately half an hour, and the class members then describe what they saw occurring in the group. The group members describe how they felt during the session and offer suggestions for the coleaders. The coleaders can discuss with each other the nature of their experience and how well they feel they did, either before any of the feedback or afterward.

2. **The Beginning Stage of a Group.** This exercise can be used to get group members acquainted with one another, but you can practice it in class to see how it works. The class breaks into dyads and selects new partners every 10 minutes. Each time you change partners, consider a new question or issue. The main purpose of the exercise is to get members to contact all the other members of the group and to begin to reveal themselves to others.

We encourage you to add your own questions or statements to this list of issues:

- Discuss your reservations about the value of groups.
- What do you fear about groups?
- What do you most want from a group experience?
- Discuss how much trust you have in your group. Do you feel like getting involved? What are some things that contribute to your trust or mistrust?
- Decide which of the two of you is dominant. Does each of you feel satisfied with his or her position?
- Tell your partner how you imagine you would feel if you were to colead a group with him or her.

3. **Meeting With Your Coleader.** Select a person in your class with whom you might like to colead a group. Explore with your partner some of the following dimensions of a group during the initial stage:

- How would both of you assist the members in getting the most from this group? Would you be inclined to discuss any guidelines that would help them be active members?
- How would the two of you attempt to build trust during the initial phase of this group?
- How much structuring would each of you be inclined to do early in a group? Do both of you agree on the degree of structure that would help a group function effectively?
- Whose responsibility is it if the group flounders? What might you do if the group seemed to be lost at the first session?
- What are some specific procedures each of you might use to help members define what they want to get from their group?

4. **Brainstorming About Ways of Creating Trust.** In small groups explore as many ideas and ways you can think of that might facilitate the establishment of trust in your group. What factors do you think are likely to lead to trust? What would it take for *you* to feel a sense of trust in a group? What do you see as the major barriers to the development of trust?

5. **Assessing Your Group.** If there is an experiential group associated with your group class, assess the degree to which the characteristics of your group are similar to the initial stage described in this chapter. What is the atmosphere like in your group? What kind of group participant are you? What is your degree of satisfaction with your group? Are there steps you can take to bring about any changes you may want to see in your group? To what degree is trust being established and what is the safety level in the group? What kinds of norms are being formed at this early stage?

Guide to *Groups in Action: Evolution and Challenges* DVD and Workbook

Here are some suggestions for making the best use of this chapter along with the initial stage segment of the first program, *Evolution of a Group*.

1. **Group Characteristics of the Initial Stage.** Think about how the characteristics described in this chapter are evident in the initial stage of the group depicted in the DVD. What are the members anxious about, and how safe did most of them feel from the very beginning? What early concerns did the members voice? Are there any potential hidden agendas? If so, what might they be? What process is being employed to help the members get acquainted?

2. **Creating Trust: Leader and Member Roles.** Trust issues are never settled once and for all. As you view the first section of the DVD, how would you describe the level of trust during the initial stage in this group? Think about ideas for facilitating trust in groups you will lead. What factors do you think are likely to lead to trust? What would it take for you to feel a sense of trust in a group? What are the major barriers to the development of trust? What are some specific fears members raised, and how were these fears dealt with during this initial session? What did you learn about some ways to create trust in a group by viewing the early phase of this group?

3. **Identifying and Clarifying Goals.** If you were leading this group, would you have a clear sense of what the members wanted to get from the group experience?

4. **Group Process Concepts at the Initial Stage.** Structuring is an important process during the early phase of a group. What kind of structuring did you observe us providing? How might you provide a different kind of structuring if you were leading or cofacilitating this group? How did we deal with the issue of cultural diversity that emerged early in the life of the group? What specific norms are we actively attempting to shape early in this group?

5. **Opening and Closing Group Sessions.** Notice the use of the check-in and the checkout procedures in the DVD. What techniques would you use to open a session in a group you are leading? What did you learn about leader interventions in getting members to check in and state how they would like to use time for a session? What specific techniques for ending a session did you read about and also observe in the DVD? What are some lessons you are learning about the importance of bringing a group session to closure?

6. **Using the Workbook With the DVD.** If you are using the DVD and workbook, refer to Segment 2: Initial Stage of the workbook and complete all the exercises. Reading this section and addressing the questions will help you conceptualize group process by integrating the text with the DVD and the workbook.

InfoTrac College Edition

For additional readings, explore InfoTrac College Edition, our online library, at http://www.infotrac.college.com/wadsworth. The following keywords are listed in such a way as to enable the InfoTrac College Edition search engine to locate a wider range of articles. The keywords should be entered exactly as listed, to include asterisks, "w1," "w2," "AND," and other search engine tools.

- modeling AND psych* AND group*
- group w1 cohesion AND psych*
- group w1 norm* AND psych*
- self w1 focus* AND group*
- group* w2 psych* w4 model*

Chapter *6*

Transition Stage of a Group

Focus Questions

Before reading this chapter, reflect on this question: If your group consisted of members much like yourself, would you like to lead it? As you read this chapter, think about these questions:

1. If you were a participant in a group, in what ways might you be reluctant to participate at times? When you become anxious, how do you deal with this anxiety?

2. What are some kinds of member behaviors that you would identify as problematic? Do you think resistance is a useful concept in explaining these behaviors? Why or why not?

3. Cultural factors sometimes account for lack of participation by a group member. How might you intervene if a member remained silent? What factors might explain the lack of participation by group members?

4. What might you say or do if one of the group members reminds you of someone in your life? How would you deal with this potential counter-transference?

5. How can you challenge members in a caring way without increasing their defensiveness? What cultural dimensions will you need to consider with respect to confrontation?

6. What is the difference between giving advice and giving feedback? When might you give advice to group members?

7. How can you distinguish support that is helpful from support that is a form of defense?

8. How would you react if a member challenged you?

9. What member behavior would you find most difficult or challenging to deal with as a leader? Why? How do you think this member's behavior is likely to affect the way you lead the group?

10. If you have been in a group before, did you experience conflict with anyone else in your group? How was it handled by you, the other members, and the leader?

☀ Introduction

Before groups progress to a level of deeper work, which we refer to as the working stage, they typically go through a transitional phase. During this phase, groups are generally characterized by anxiety, defensiveness, resistance, a range of control issues, intermember conflicts, challenges to or conflicts with the leader, and various patterns of problem behaviors. If group members are not willing to disclose the ways in which they are struggling with both themselves and one another, they are not able to move forward and develop the trust necessary for deeper work. What the members and leaders do during this transitional period often will determine whether a group will develop a cohesive community that allows members to engage in meaningful interpersonal exploration. A group's ability to move forward is dependent on the ability and willingness of both members and leaders to work with whatever is expressed in the here and now.

The transition stage of a group is particularly challenging to group leaders, and it is a difficult time for members as well. During this stage, groups are often described as being "resistive." If you view a group in this light, your interventions are likely to be tainted by your perspective. To avoid entrenching what appears to be uncooperative behavior, shift your attitude and acknowledge that certain behaviors may be the result of members' fear, confusion, and cautiousness. For instance, if you can understand a "resistant" member's behavior as symptomatic of being scared or another member's silence as indicative of his lack of knowledge regarding how to best participate in a group, you will have a way to work with these behaviors. By changing the label "resistant" to more descriptive and nonjudgmental terminology, it is likely that you will change your attitude toward members who appear to be "difficult." As you change the lenses by which you perceive members' behaviors, it will be easier to adopt an understanding attitude and to encourage members to explore ways they are reluctant and self-protective.

In assisting a group to meet the challenges of the transition stage, it is essential that you have a clear understanding of the characteristics and dynamics of a group during this phase of development. Be particularly mindful of your own reactions, especially the tendency to assume total responsibility for whatever is happening in the group—or of putting full responsibility on the members. In this chapter we focus on the typical characteristics of a group during the transition stage and suggest interventions for dealing with transitional group problems.

✳ Characteristics of the Transition Stage

Anxiety underlies much of members' behavior in the transitional phase of a group. To move through this phase members must be able to deal effectively with defensiveness and resistance, confront their fears, and work through conflict and control issues. The goal of this stage is to create a trusting climate that encourages members to take risks by challenging their fears.

Anxiety

During the transition stage, anxiety is high within individuals and within the group itself. For example, Christie's anxiety stems primarily from internal factors: "I'm really afraid to go any further for fear of what I'll find out." But when Sunny says "I'm afraid to speak up in here because several people seem judgmental," her anxiety is due to external factors as well as internal ones. She is inhibited by what others in the group think of her and how they are liable to judge her.

Anxiety also relates to the fear of exposing one's pain, of sounding "not intelligent," of being overcome by intense emotions, of being misunderstood, of being rejected, and of not knowing what is expected. As participants come to more fully trust one another and the leader, they become increasingly able to share their concerns. This openness lessens the anxiety group members have about letting others see them as they are.

Establishing Trust

Establishing trust is a central task of the initial phase in the evolution of a group, but members are still wondering if the group is a safe place for them during the transition phase. Considerable hesitation and observing both the other members and the leader are common. As a climate of trust is gradually created, members can express their reactions without fear of censure or of being judged. Often one member's willingness to take the risk to disclose a concern or fear will lead others to do the same. These disclosures are a turning point in establishing a greater degree of trust.

When trust is high, members are actively involved in the activities in the group: making themselves known to others in personal ways, taking risks both in the group and out of group, focusing on themselves and not on others, actively working in the group on meaningful personal issues, disclosing persistent feelings such as lack of trust, and supporting and challenging others in the group.

By contrast, here are some clear signs that trust is lacking:

- Members will not initiate work.
- Members make excuses for lack of participation due to not feeling well.
- Members are very hesitant to express themselves.
- Members keep their reactions to themselves or express them in indirect ways.
- Members take refuge in storytelling.
- Members are excessively quiet.
- Members put more energy into "helping" others or giving others advice than into sharing their own personal concerns.
- Some members say they have problems the group cannot help them with.
- Others are unwilling to deal openly with conflict or even to acknowledge its existence.

When trust is lacking, members are still checking out what is happening in the room, yet they may be doing so quietly, which makes it difficult to explore what is occurring within the group. Other members may make judgmental statements, which have the effect of inhibiting open participation. We find over and over that problems in a group are not due to the feelings and thoughts people *do* express but to those reactions they *do not* express. Thus, our central task at the transition stage is to continually encourage members to say aloud what they are thinking and feeling pertaining to what is happening within the group.

Defensiveness and Resistance

Group participants will test the leader and other members before the group actually becomes a safe place for transition to the working phase. This testing involves observing the behavior of the leader and other members to determine if they can be trusted. It is essential that the leader encourage members to express their hesitations and anxieties. Participants are torn between wanting to be safe and wanting to risk. It is not unwise for members to proceed with caution. It is unrealistic for a leader to think that members will effortlessly begin intensive work without establishing a climate of safety. Both leader and members must understand the meaning of defensive behavior. It is essential that they be respectful and patient of members' defenses.

From a psychoanalytic perspective, resistance is defined as the individual's reluctance to bring into conscious awareness threatening material that has been previously repressed or denied. It can also be viewed as anything that prevents members from dealing with unconscious material. From a broader perspective, resistance can be viewed as behavior that keeps us from exploring personal conflicts or painful feelings. Resistance can be considered a way we attempt to protect ourselves from anxiety.

Respecting a member's defensiveness means the leader does not chastise a reluctant person but explores the source of the reluctance. Members often have realistic reasons for their reluctance. For example, one woman was typically quiet in group and would speak only when others addressed her. When the group leader pointed this out, she said that she felt embarrassed to speak because of her accent. She was convinced that she did not speak English well enough to be understood; this kept her silent. Although she wanted to bring up this subject, the thought of being the center of attention was so anxiety-provoking for her that she said as little as possible. To dismiss this client as "resistant" shows a lack of respect for her genuine reluctance.

Members often struggle with their fears and rely on defenses they have long used when coping with uncomfortable situations. These problematic behaviors are expressed in many different ways. Resistive behavior is inevitable in groups, and unless it is recognized and explored it will block the progress of the group. Resistance is a normal process and is the very material that can lead to productive exploration in the group. In addition, defensive behaviors reveal important clues about a member's interpersonal style outside of the group. Ormont (1988) associates resistance with a fear of intimacy. The defensive style may take various forms such as conflict, detachment, distrust, or diverting, but the underlying fear is of getting close and the vulnerability this implies. If group leaders demonstrate a willingness to explore and understand resistive behavior, the group is likely to progress.

Although dealing with group members who pose challenges for us is sometimes painful, doing so is often the best way to establish a working relationship with members. By working through the fears associated with intimacy, members become aware of some ways they keep others at a distance. They can move toward greater intimacy in the group. When members develop mature forms of intimacy, as described by Ormont (1988),

- Members make emotional connections with each other.
- Talk is simple and direct.
- Hidden agendas are not present in the group.
- Members openly take risks with one another.
- Feelings are acknowledged and expressed.
- Members are able to experience the present moment as the lingering remnants of their past hurts have been worked through successfully.

The best way for leaders to therapeutically deal with difficult behaviors is to simply describe to members what they are observing and let members know how they are affected by what they see and hear. This approach is an invitation for members to determine if what they are doing is working for them. If leaders do not respect the members' defenses against anxiety, they are really not respecting the members themselves. For example, Melody reveals some painful material and then suddenly stops and says that she doesn't want to go on. In respecting Melody's reluctance, the leader asks her what is stopping her rather than pushing her to continue dealing with her pain. Melody indicates that she is afraid of losing people's respect. The issue now becomes her lack of trust in the group rather than a painful personal problem. If the leader proceeds in this manner, Melody is more likely to eventually talk openly about personal matters. If the leader ignores Melody's initial hesitation by pushing her to open up, she is more likely to close up and not talk. However, if the leader does not inquire about the meaning of her reluctance, she might close off useful avenues of self-exploration.

Sometimes members' unwillingness to cooperate is the result of factors such as an unqualified leader, an aggressive and uncaring leadership style, or a failure to prepare members about how to participate in the group. One of the key tasks of leadership is to accurately appraise whether the source of resistance is the members' fears or ineffective leadership. If you show a willingness to understand the context of the members' behavior, the likelihood of cooperation and risk taking is increased. For an expanded discussion of defenses and resistance, see Earley (2000).

Common Fears Experienced by Members

If group members keep their fears to themselves, all sorts of avoidances are bound to occur. Although members cannot be forced to discuss their fears, you can invite them to recognize that they may be experiencing something that is common to many members. Brief descriptions of common fears manifested during the transition stage are presented next along with possible interventions that might be helpful to members.

The Fear of Appearing Foolish   People sometimes worry about looking foolish if they step out of roles that are familiar to them. Joaquin disclosed that he had held back from saying much because he did not want to look foolish. Therefore, he decided to talk only when he was extremely sure of himself. At other times he found it safer to take the course of censoring and rehearsing his "performances." The leader asked Joaquin, "Next time you become aware of sitting here quietly rehearsing, would you be willing to do so out loud?" The leader was operating on the assumption that Joaquin's internal critic was far harsher on him than others in the room would ever be. As Joaquin rehearsed out loud, others had a better appreciation of the nature of his struggle.

The Fear of Rejection   We often hear participants say that they are reluctant to get involved with others in the group because of their fear of rejection. Stephen repeatedly spoke of his fears that people would not want anything to do with him. He had erected walls to protect himself from the pain of rejection, and he made the assumption that the group would be repulsed if he did show himself. The leader asked, "Are you willing to look around the room and see if indeed you feel that every person in here would surely reject you?" Stephen took some time to look around the room and discovered that out of 10, he was convinced that 4 of them would reject him, and he was not sure of 2 of them. If Stephen agreed to continue working, he could be asked if he was willing to "own" his projections by addressing those whom he had decided might reject him. He could do this by completing the sentence "I'm afraid that you will reject me by. . . ." He could also talk to the people whom he saw as more accepting by letting them know he thought differently of them. When Stephen was finished, others could react to him in a sensitive way. Some in the group might say that they were afraid of him and that they found it difficult to get close to him. Through this exploration, Stephen would learn about his part in creating a sense of rejection. With exercises like these it is important for leaders to intervene when members become defensive and want to respond, thus interrupting the flow of Stephen's work. Once Stephen completes the exercise members can then share whatever reaction they have to what he said to them. It is important that members learn that what Stephen is saying is more about him than about them. The work is about dealing with Stephen's projections and his perception of being rejected rather than establishing, at this moment, whether members are rejecting him or not.

The Fear of Emptiness   Members sometimes fear that if they do get involved and explore issues that they have bottled up, they will discover that they are shallow and empty, that there is nothing in them that anyone would like or value. Adriana expressed this fear, yet she continued in spite of her fears. She realized that even if she did find that she was empty she could begin a process of creating a different kind of existence for herself. She chose not to let her fear prevent her from looking at her life.

The Fear of Losing Control   Marin expressed her fear that she might open up some potentially painful areas and be left even more vulnerable. She was anxious about "opening up Pandora's box," as she put it. She wondered, "Will I be able to stand the pain? Maybe it would be best if things were just left as they are. If I started crying, I might never stop! Even though I might get support in the group, what will I do when I'm on my own?" The leader responded, "I'm sure you've been alone and have found it painful. What do you normally do when this happens?" Marin replied, "I lock myself in the room, I don't talk to anyone, and I just cry by myself and then get depressed." The leader asked Marin to pick two or three people in the room whom she thought would be most able to understand her pain and tell them, while looking at them, about some of the distress in her life. As she did this, she would be likely to discover the difference between isolating herself in pain and sharing it with others and experiencing their support. She could also come to the realization that she was not condemned to dealing with her pain alone, unless she chose to do so. She could be challenged to identify a few people in the group and in her outside life whom she could reach out to in time of need.

The Fear of Self-Disclosure   Members often fear self-disclosure, thinking that they will be pressured to open up before they are ready. It helps to reinforce emphatically to members that they can make themselves known to others and at the same time retain their privacy. Consider this example: "I can't imagine myself talking about my parents in the negative ways that others are doing in here," Nicole said. "If I were to talk this way about my parents, I would be overcome with shame and disloyalty." Because the leader was aware of certain cultural values that Nicole held, he let her know that he respected her decision. He did not push her to do something that she would later regret. But he did encourage her to think of ways she could participate in the group that would be meaningful to her. There is a delicate balance between reluctance because of cultural injunctions and cautiousness in moving into frightening territory. As we explained in Chapter 5, it is the choice of members to determine *what* and *how* much they share. When they recognize that they are responsible for what they tell others about themselves, participants tend to be less fearful of self-disclosure.

Some Other Fears   A variety of other fears are often expressed by members:

- I'm concerned about seeing these people out of group and what they will think of me.
- If I start to cry, I could be overwhelmed.
- I'm afraid I will be talked about outside of group.
- I'm afraid I'll get too dependent on the group and rely too much on others to solve my problems.

- I'm afraid that if I get angry, I'll lose control and hurt somebody.
- I'm uncomfortable with physical contact, and I'm afraid I'll be expected to touch and be touched when I don't want to.
- I'm worried that I'll take too much group time by talking about my problems, that I'll bore people.
- I'm afraid I'll get close to people in here and then never see them again once the group ends.

Though it is not realistic to expect that all these fears can be eliminated, we do think members can be encouraged to face and challenge them by talking about them. Through what you model as a leader, you can help create a trusting climate in which members will feel free enough to test their fears and discriminate between realistic and unrealistic fears. Hopefully, members will be more accepting of their realistic fears and put the unrealistic fears to rest. If members decide to talk about their fears and if this decision is made relatively early in a group, a good foundation of trust is created that will enable them to deal constructively with other personal issues as the group evolves.

Struggles With Control

Maintaining a sense of control is a common theme at the transition stage. Some characteristic group behaviors include discussions about the division of responsibility and decision-making procedures. Participants' main anxieties relate to having too much or too little responsibility. To deal constructively with these issues, members must bring them to the surface and talk about them. If the here-and-now problems are ignored, the group will be inhibited by the hidden agenda. Here are some comments that members might make that illustrate some struggles that are characteristic of the transition stage:

- I don't want to talk. I learn just as much by listening and observing.
- I feel different from others in this group.
- There are several people in here getting all the attention. I'm not one of them.
- I feel weak when I show my feelings.
- I wish the leaders would pay more attention to Arelio. He's been crying several times, and nobody attends to him.
- I get very uncomfortable when people cry, and I want them to feel better.
- I want people, especially the leaders, to draw me out more often.
- The story of my life is that no matter what I say or do, it never seems to be the right thing.

In response to any one of these members' statements, it is imperative that the leader not assume a defensive stance. The leader's task is to help members understand that their struggle to maintain control may be a way of protecting themselves from doing more in-depth work. Assume that Heather says, "No matter what I say or do, it never seems to be the right thing. Why can't I just do it my way?" The leader might respond, "I'm not looking at what you're doing in terms of right or wrong. I'm more concerned that what you do in here will help you achieve the goals you set for yourself. I've noticed that you seem to avoid talking about difficult areas in your life." Another intervention would be to ask Heather, "How would you like to use your time in this group?" Or the leader might say, "Tell me more about what has been helpful to you in this group and what has not."

Conflict

Conflict is a difficult subject for some people to deal with, both in groups and in daily living. There is an assumption that conflict is a sign of something intrinsically wrong and that it should be avoided at all costs. When there are conflicts within a group, the leader and the members sometimes want to avoid them rather than spending the time and effort necessary to work through them. However, conflict is inevitable in all relationships, including groups. It is the avoidance of conflict that makes it problematic.

Conflict may be caused by not attending to the diversity that exists within a group. Some of the areas of diversity in a group that are potential sources of conflict and distrust include differences in age, gender, language, sexual orientation, socioeconomic status, disability, race, ethnicity, and educational attainment. Chen and Rybak (2004) point out that members who come from privileged groups may find it difficult to understand the world of those members who are different from them. For example, a group member who speaks with an accent or who is bicultural may not be understood by those members who have not had to struggle with being discriminated against. If a group member (Maria) talks about her anxiety over peoples' reactions to her accent, and if others in the group are not able to empathize with her concerns, she may be re-wounded in the group as she has been so often in her everyday life. If Maria's concerns are not taken seriously, she is likely to emotionally withdraw from the group because of not feeling understood or safe to explore her feelings. Because her experience is invalidated, Maria is not likely to disclose other significant issues in her life. Instances such as this can result in conflict among the members, and if it is not talked about, this tension can stall a group's progress. Chen and Rybak (2004) put this idea thusly, "Insensitivity to diversity issues, however unintentional it is, can impede the atmosphere of openness and tolerance that the group works hard to build" (p. 198). Any conflict that results from failing to understand and appreciate member differences must be openly addressed and worked through if a trusting climate is to be established. If this conflict is ignored, mistrust is bound to appear.

Unexplored conflict is typically expressed in defensive behavior, indirectness, and a general lack of trust. Groups offer an ideal environment for learning to deal with conflict effectively. During any stage of a group's development, but especially during the early phase, it is crucial that conflict be acknowledged and managed effectively so that the level of trust will increase. Thus, a primary task of leaders is to teach members the value of working through conflicts in a constructive way.

Jennifer expressed a conflict within one group: "Some people in here never say anything." Jeff immediately replied, defensively, "Not everybody has to be as talkative as you." Leticia joined in, sarcastically, "Well, Jennifer, you talk so much you don't give me a chance to participate!" Alejandro's contribution was, "I wish you would stop this arguing. This isn't getting us anywhere."

Ineffective interventions by the leader are: "I agree with you, Alejandro. Why don't we just try to get along? Or "Jennifer, you're right. There are people in here who say very little. I wish they would take as many risks as you do!" Such remarks increase members' defensiveness.

The emerging conflict was dealt with constructively when the leader took the approach of exploring the underlying dynamics of what had been said and what was *not* being said: "I agree with you, Alejandro, that right now we are struggling. But I don't want people to stop talking, because we need to know what all this means." Turning to Jennifer, the leader asked her: "How are you affected by all these reactions? Is there anyone in particular you want to hear from? What does it do to you when people don't say anything?"

Jennifer's original statement was a defensive and chastising remark to the group in general. The group reacted with appropriate defensiveness. The leader focused on Jennifer's difficulty with the group and tried to get her to be more specific about how she was affected by people whom she saw as being silent. The conflict found resolution when she let people know that she was afraid that they were judging her when they said very little and that she was interested in how they perceived her. Chances are that this conflict would not have come about if Jennifer had said something like this to Leticia: "I notice that you're quiet, and I often wonder what you think of me. I'd like to hear from you." Such a statement would have reflected more accurately what was going on with Jennifer than did her punitive remark. It is important for the leader not to cut off the expression of conflict but to facilitate more direct expression of feeling and thinking among the members.

Cohesion within a group typically increases after conflict is recognized and expressed. Stating what is keeping them cautious is one way of testing the freedom and trustworthiness of the group. The participants soon discover whether this group is a safe place in which to disagree openly and whether they will be accepted in spite of the intensity of their feelings. When conflict is constructively discussed, members learn that their relationships are strong enough to withstand an honest level of challenge, which is what many people want to achieve in their outside relationships.

Confrontation

If people want to take a deeper and more honest look at themselves, it is necessary that they be willing to risk expressing what is on their minds, even though doing so may be difficult both to say and to hear. We think people cease being effective catalysts to others' growth if they rarely challenge one another. If confrontations are presented in a caring and respectful manner, these interventions often promote change. It is important for leaders to discuss how confrontation can be useful if this feedback is delivered in a caring manner. It is also essential that group members see that confrontation is often a basic part of the group process.

Leaders have a responsibility to teach members what confrontation is and what it is not and how to challenge others in constructive ways. Confrontation is *not* (1) tearing others down, (2) hitting others with negative feedback and then retreating, (3) being hostile with the aim of hurting others, (4) telling others what is basically wrong with them, or (5) assaulting others' integrity. Ideally, we see confrontation as a form of constructive feedback—an invitation for participants to look at some aspect of their interpersonal style or their lives to determine if they want to make changes. Caring confrontation is designed to help members make an honest assessment of themselves or to speak more about their own reactions rather than talking about others.

In working with culturally diverse clients in groups, even caring confrontations need to be timed well and delivered in such a way that members are more likely to hear the feedback. For example, being indirect may be a cultural value for some group members. If confronted on their indirectness, or if they are expected to change, these group members may perceive such confrontations as signs of rudeness. They may even feel a sense of embarrassment, which could result in their deciding not to return to the group. Respect for a diversity of values and behaviors is crucial; in making confrontations, timing and sensitivity to members' cultural backgrounds are key factors in determining whether confrontations will be effective.

In our work with groups, we provide members with these guidelines for appropriate and responsible confrontation:

- Members or leaders know why they are confronting.
- Confrontations are not dogmatic statements concerning who or what a person is.
- The person being confronted is likely to be less defensive if told what effect he or she has on others rather than simply being labeled or judged.
- Confrontations are more effective if, instead of being global generalizations about a person, they focus on specific, observable behaviors.
- One of the purposes of confrontation is to develop a closer and more genuine relationship with others.
- Sensitivity is an important element of effective confrontation; it is helpful for the person doing the confronting to imagine being the recipient of what is said.
- Confrontation gives others the opportunity to reflect on the feedback they receive before they are expected to respond or to act on this feedback.

- Confrontation is a means to get a client to consider an alternative perspective.
- Those confronting might ask themselves if they are willing to do what they are asking others to do.

The quality of the confrontations that occur in a group is an index of how effective the group is. The more cohesive a group is, the more challenging and daring the members and leaders can be.

To make the issue of confrontation more concrete, let's look at some examples. The first statement in each set illustrates an ineffective confrontation; this is followed by an effective confrontation statement. As you read each of the statements below, imagine that you are the recipient of both the effective and ineffective confrontations. Take note of what it might be like to hear each of these statements. How would you be inclined to respond in each situation?

Ineffective: *You're always judgmental, and you make me feel inadequate.*

Effective: *I feel uncomfortable with you because I'm afraid of what you think of me. Your opinion is important to me. I don't like it that I often feel inadequate when I'm with you.*

Ineffective: *You are dishonest. You're always smiling, and that's not real.*

Effective: *I find it difficult to trust you, because often when you say you're angry, you're smiling. That makes it hard for me to know which to believe.*

Ineffective: *You aren't getting anything from this group. You never talk, you just observe. We're just interesting cases for you.*

Effective: *I'd like to get to know you. I'm interested in what you think and feel, and sometimes I think that you see me as an interesting case. I'd like to change the way I feel around you.*

Ineffective: *If I were your husband, I'd leave you. You're sure to ruin any relationship.*

Effective: *I find it hard to be open with you. Many of the things you say really hurt me, and I want to strike back. For that reason, it would be difficult for me to be involved in an intimate relationship with you.*

Ineffective: *I'm tired of you playing games.*

Effective: *I have trouble believing what you say. It bothers me that I feel this way with you and I would like to talk to you about it.*

In each of the ineffective statements, the people being confronted are being told how they are, and in some way they are being discounted. In the effective statements the members doing the confronting are revealing their perceptions and feelings about the other members and how they are being affected by them. In other words, members own their part in the difficulty or problem instead of blaming others for their struggle.

Challenges to the Group Leader

Although leaders may be challenged throughout a group, they are more often confronted both personally and professionally during the transition stage. For example, several members may complain about not getting the "right" type of leadership, thereby challenging the leader's competence. It is a mistake for leaders to assume that every confrontation is an attack on their integrity. Instead, they need to nondefensively examine what is being said so they can differentiate between a *challenge* and an *attack*. How they respond to members' confrontations has a bearing on how trustingly the participants will approach them in the future.

If Oscar says to the leader "I'm bored in here, and I wish you'd do something to make this a better group," a nontherapeutic reply is "Do you think you could do a better job?" By contrast, therapeutic replies might include: "Tell me more about what you'd like from me or what you'd like me to do differently." "Say more about what's missing for you in this group." "What could you continue to do to make this a more meaningful group for you?" (By saying what he does, Oscar has already taken the first step in changing the situation for himself.) It is not necessary that the leader quickly comply with Oscar's demand to conduct the group differently. What is essential is that she listen nondefensively and promote a full expression of Oscar's dissatisfaction. The leader does not assume total responsibility for his boredom. However, she explores with Oscar their mutual responsibility to make this a meaningful and productive group, and she invites others to express their reactions to what she has said.

Though challenges may never be comfortable to the leader, it is important to recognize that these confrontations are often members' significant first steps toward testing the leader and thus becoming less dependent on the leader's approval. How a leader handles challenges to his or her leadership, at any stage, has a profound impact on the trust level in the group. Leaders can be good role models if they respond openly and avoid becoming defensive. If leaders are overly sensitive to criticism and have fragile egos, they are more likely to take such challenges personally, which limits their effectiveness.

A Critique of the Notion of Resistance

A number of writers in the psychotherapy field have challenged the traditional view of resistance and have reconceptualized the role of resistance in therapy. Erving and Miriam Polster (1973), leading figures in Gestalt therapy, suggest that what often passes for resistance is not simply a barrier to therapy but is a "creative force for managing a difficult world" (p. 52). They assert that the idea of "resistance" is unnecessary and incompatible with Gestalt therapy (Polster & Polster, 1976). The problem associated with labeling a behavior as resistance is the implication that the behavior or trait is "alien" to the person and needs to be eliminated if the person is to function in healthy ways. By not using the term *resistance*, the therapist avoids the assumption that the client is behaving inappropriately. Instead of trying to change a client's behavior or make something happen, the Polsters focus on what is actually happening in the present and explore this with the client.

In writing about resistance in Gestalt therapy, Breshgold (1989) focuses on resistance to awareness and to contact. It is understandable that we may be reluctant to reexperience painful feelings that have become split off from our personality. From the perspective of Gestalt therapy, instead of eliminating resistance, the aim is to reidentify with important aspects of the personality through increased awareness. Breshgold captures the essence of therapy without resistance: "Ultimately, eliminating the concept and use of the word resistance requires a shift in the thinking and approach of the therapist. It requires an ability to be in the present and 'with' the patient rather than assuming the responsibility for moving the patient in a prescribed direction. It means putting aside one's own expectations, beliefs, and biases, and trusting the 'wisdom of the organism'" (p. 99).

Steve de Shazer (1984), one of the pioneers of solution-focused brief therapy, wrote about "The Death of Resistance." He believes the notion of client resistance attributes most of the blame for lack of progress to the client while allowing the practitioner to avoid responsibility for what is happening in therapy. De Shazer assumes that clients are competent in figuring out what they want and need. It is the practitioner's responsibility to assist clients in identifying their competencies and using them to create satisfying lives. If the notion of client competence is accepted, then *client resistance* is better viewed as *practitioner resistance*. According to de Shazer, therapeutic impasses result from the therapist's failure to listen to and understand clients.

Like de Shazer, Bill O'Hanlon (2003) attributes client resistance to misunderstanding and inflexibility on the therapist's part. From O'Hanlon's perspective, what therapists call "resistance" often reflects genuine concerns on the part of clients. O'Hanlon's solution-oriented therapy challenges the basic belief of many therapists who assume that clients do not really want to change and are thus resistant to therapy. O'Hanlon and Weiner-Davis (1989) invite therapists to question their basic assumptions about clients and monitor the ways they use language in therapy. They also caution against self-fulfilling prophecies, stating: "If you are focused on finding resistance, you will almost certainly be able to find something that looks like it" (p. 29).

In writing about resistance in therapy from the perspective of narrative therapy, Winslade, Crocket, and Monk (1997) emphasize the therapeutic relationship. When therapy becomes difficult, they avoid placing the responsibility on the client, for doing so results in blaming him or her for what is happening in the therapeutic relationship. Instead, Winslade and colleagues pay close attention to the conversations with their clients to discover possible reasons for the difficulty in therapy.

In summary, Gestalt therapy, solution-focused therapy, and narrative therapy are therapeutic approaches that question the validity and usefulness of the way resistance is typically used. Each of these therapeutic models reconceptualizes the phenomenon of resistance by encouraging therapists to pay attention to what is transpiring in the present context of the therapeutic relationship. While one of us (Marianne) would like to avoid using the term *resistance* completely, the other (Jerry) is highly resistant to parting with the concept of resistance!

The Leader's Reactions to Defensive Behaviors

Many forms of defensive behaviors emerge during the transition stage. It is essential that you not only learn to recognize and deal with members' defenses, but also that you become aware of your own reactions to the defensive behaviors exhibited by members. Some leaders have a tendency to focus on "problem members" or difficult situations rather than on their own dynamics and how they are affected personally when they encounter a "difficult group." Typically, leaders have a range of feelings: being threatened by what they perceive as a challenge to their leadership role; anger over the members' lack of cooperation and enthusiasm; feelings of inadequacy to the point of wondering if they are qualified to lead groups; resentment toward several of the members, whom they label as some type of problem; and anxiety over the slow pace of the group, with a desire to stir things up so there is some sign of progress.

One of the most powerful ways to intervene when you are experiencing strong feelings over what you perceive as defensiveness is to deal with your own feelings and possible defensive reactions to the situation. If you ignore your reactions, you are leaving yourself out of the interactions that occur in the group. Furthermore, by giving the members your reactions, you are modeling a direct style of dealing with conflict and problematic situations rather than bypassing them. Your own thoughts, feelings, and observations can be the most powerful resource you have in dealing with defensive behavior. When you share what you are feeling and thinking about what is going on in the group—without blaming or criticizing the members for deficiencies—you are letting the members experience an honest and constructive interaction with you.

We hope you will keep these thoughts in mind as you read the next section, which deals with problem behaviors and difficult group members. Although it is understandable that you will want to learn how to handle "problem members" and the disruption they can cause, the emphasis should be on actual *behaviors* rather than on labeling members. It is helpful to consider problem behaviors as manifestations of protecting the self that most participants display at one time or another during the history of a group.

✳ Problem Behaviors and Difficult Group Members

Sometimes members become difficult because of problematic behaviors on the part of group leaders. But, even in groups with the most effective group leader interventions, members have the potential to display problematic behaviors that are a source of difficulty to themselves, other members, and the leader. In establishing norms that minimize problematic behaviors, leaders do well to provide the members with a rationale for not engaging in particular nonproductive behaviors. For example, when members ask why they are discouraged from asking questions, from giving advice, or from telling stories, members deserve a response. It is the leader's task to educate members to involve themselves in productive group behaviors that will maximize the benefits of their group experience. Leaders can assist members in communicating more effectively. Furthermore, in working with problematic behaviors displayed by group members, leaders needs to be mindful of how their interventions can either decrease or escalate these behaviors. Some common denominators characterize appropriate interventions when dealing with difficult behaviors of group members. Effective group leaders:

- Do not dismiss clients.
- Express their difficulty with a member without denigrating the character of the person.
- Avoid responding to a sarcasm with sarcasm.
- Educate the members about how the group works.
- Are honest with members rather than mystifying the process.
- Encourage members to explore their defensiveness rather than demanding they give up their ways of protecting themselves.
- Avoid labeling a member and instead describe the behavior of the member.
- State observations and hunches in a tentative way as opposed to being dogmatic.
- Demonstrate sensitivity to a member's culture and avoid stereotyping the individual.
- Avoid using the leadership role to intimidate members.
- Monitor their own countertransference reactions.
- Challenge members in a caring and respectful way to do things that may be painful and difficult.
- Do not retreat from conflict.
- Provide a balance between support and challenge.
- Do not take member reactions in an overly personal way.
- Facilitate a more focused exploration of the problem rather than offering simple solutions.
- Do not meet their own needs at the expense of their clients.
- Invite group members to state how they are personally affected by problematic behaviors of other members while blocking judgments, evaluations, and criticisms.

In working with difficult group members, we might ask questions such as these: "What am I thinking and feeling as I'm working with this client?" "What am I doing to create or exacerbate the problems?" "Does the client remind me of anyone in my personal life?" These questions help leaders examine and understand how their personal reaction might actually be creating some of the client's defensive behaviors. When working with behaviors that are counterproductive to group functioning, it is useful to understand the meaning these behaviors have for the individual member. People in a group are likely doing the best they know how, even if they become aware that what they are doing is not working well for them. We must remind ourselves that the very reason people seek a group is to assist them in finding more effective ways of expressing themselves and dealing with others.

Silence and Lack of Participation

Silence and lack of participation are two forms of behavior that most group leaders encounter. Even though the verbally silent member may not seem to interfere with a group's functioning, this behavior may constitute a problem for both the member and the group. If quiet members go unnoticed, their pattern of silence may hide a problem that needs to be addressed in the group.

Some silent group members may argue that their lack of verbal participation is not an index of their involvement. They may maintain that they are learning by listening and by identifying with others' problems. These members may say, "I don't feel like talking just to hear myself talk" or "When I have something important to contribute, I will do so." Group leaders need to explore the meaning of silence with the members. We have concerns about members who say that they are uncomfortable verbally participating because we have no way of knowing how they are affected by what is going on during the sessions. They may be triggered by other members' explorations, and if they do not talk about this, then being in the group can actually be counterproductive for them and the group. There are many potential reasons for nonparticipating behavior:

- Showing respect and waiting to be called on by the leader.
- Feeling that one does not have anything worthwhile to say.
- Feeling that one should not talk about oneself or that one should be seen and not heard.
- Uncertainty about how the group process works, such as the fear of not knowing what is appropriate and when to make comments.
- A fear of certain members in the group or of the authority of the group leader.
- Fear of being rejected.
- Lack of trust in the group.
- Fears about confidentiality.

It is important that members not be chastised for their silence but instead be invited to participate. Approach such members by expressing concerns rather than judgments for their silence. Also, group leaders must be careful to avoid consistently calling on a silent person, for in this way the member is relieved of the responsibility of initiating interactions. In addition, it is possible to create dependency if a group member is continuously being drawn out. This can lead to resentment on the part of both the member who is silent and the rest of the group, as well as frustration on the part of the leader.

Members can be invited to explore what their silence means. For example, are they this way outside of the group as well? How does it feel for them to be in this group? Have they any desire to be more verbally active participants? The rest of the group can participate in this discussion, for group members generally do have reactions to silent members. They may feel cheated that they know so little of that person, or they may fear that the person is observing them as they risk and reveal themselves. If there are several participants who rarely talk in a group, the verbally active members may become less revealing because of trust issues.

At times leaders and members may overly rely on active verbal participation and miss the richness of the nonverbal communication clients from various cultural backgrounds may exhibit. Understanding members' cultural norms can shed light on their lack of verbal participation. When leading groups with a diverse population, counselors must recognize and appreciate the various ways in which people make themselves known, both verbally and nonverbally.

The checkout process at the end of a group session is often used to prompt minimal participation from quiet members. This is a less threatening way for members who tend to be quiet to share how they are experiencing the group. It is also important to teach nonparticipating members that others in the group are more likely to project onto them if they say very little during the sessions. The leader may ask members to make a contract to participate at every session, sharing with the group at some point how they responded to the session that day. They can also be asked toward the end of a meeting what it was like for them to be in the group. A leader might ask them if they are getting from the group what they had wanted. If they indicate that there were moments when they wanted to participate, but that time ran out before they got a chance, they can be invited to make a contract to be first on the agenda at the next group meeting.

Monopolistic Behavior

At the other end of the participation continuum is the person who exhibits a high degree of self-centeredness by monopolizing the activities of the group, yet silent and monopolizing behaviors may share common motivations. The member who monopolizes often claims to identify with others but takes others' statements as openings for detailed stories about his or her own life. This person prevents others from getting their share of group time. People sometimes operate under the assumption that a good group member is one who talks a lot. Leaders need to help these members explore the possible dynamics of their behavior. They may be talking excessively out of anxiety, they may be accustomed to being ignored, or they may be attempting to keep control of the group. The end result is that they may talk a lot yet reveal very little about themselves.

During the beginning stage of a group, members as well as some leaders may be relieved that someone else is going first, and no one will intervene to stop the person from taking center stage. As time goes on, however, both leaders and members will become increasingly frustrated. As meetings continue, the group generally becomes less tolerant of the person who monopolizes, and unless these feelings of annoyance are dealt with early, they may be released in an explosive way.

For both ethical and practical reasons it is essential that the monopolizing person be gently challenged to look at the effects of such behavior on the group. Ethical practice dictates that group leaders acquire intervention skills necessary to block rambling. It is desirable that the leader intervene before the members react out of frustration and make a hostile remark. Here are some possible leader interventions:

- "Tanya, you talk often. I notice that you typically identify with many problems that are raised. I have difficulty following you. I'm confused about what you are trying to tell us. In one sentence, what do you most want me to hear?"
- "Tanya, you seem to have a lot to say. I wonder if you're willing to go around the room to different members and finish the following sentence: 'What I most want you to hear about me is . . .'" Other possible incomplete sentences that could lead to fruitful exploration include "If I didn't talk . . ." "If I let others talk . . ." "I have a lot to say because . . ." "When people don't listen to me I feel . . ." "I want you to listen to me because . . ."

Tanya can be asked to make the rounds by addressing each person in the group through the process of completing any one of these sentences. It is important for her not to elaborate or explain but to say the first thing that comes to her mind. It is best to instruct members not to respond during the go-around. Through such exercises we usually discover crucial information that helps everyone get a better sense of the function served by the monopolizing behavior.

Assume that another member, Vance, confronts Tanya in a hostile manner before the leader has said anything about her behavior. Vance asks Tanya: "Why don't you stop talking for a change? Do you think you're the only one who has a right to speak in here?" An appropriate leader intervention could be, "Vance, I'd like you to say more to Tanya. Tell her how her talking affects you. What had you been feeling and thinking before you spoke up?"

We can dismiss Tanya's behavior as simply a nuisance, or we can see it as a defense and encourage her to explore her defenses, as we would any other defense mechanism. Consider that she initially appeared to be a motivated member, yet she seemed to try too hard to fit into the group. She seemed to reveal personal aspects of herself, she readily made suggestions to others, she could identify with most who spoke, and she told detailed stories of her past. Most of her behavior could be an expression of the message "Please notice me and like me." In her own mind she felt that she was doing what was expected of her and viewed herself as an eager participant. One of the issues that she had initially said she wanted to look at was her difficulty in getting close to people. She acknowledged that she had few friends and that people were typically annoyed with her, which she found perplexing. By confronting Tanya in an honest and sensitive manner, the leader can help her learn what she is doing that prevents her from getting close to people. She may discover that during her childhood she was often ignored and not listened to. She may have decided that if she didn't talk a lot, she would be ignored, or if she tried a little harder she would be responded to. The fact is that her familiar behavior is not getting her what she wants, either inside or outside the group. The group experience offers her the possibility of finding ways that can satisfy her wants.

A leader can approach difficult members like Tanya with a sense of interest. The leader's *internal* dialogue might go something like this: "How is it that Tanya is working so hard at getting me to pay attention to her, yet I have no sense of her? How is it that she can get a whole group of people to be angry with her? How is she replicating, in this group, behavior that is problematic on the outside?" You cannot be effective with Tanya if all you feel toward her is annoyance. Instead, explore the context of how her behavior might make sense in her life.

Storytelling

Self-disclosure is frequently misunderstood by some group members to mean a lengthy recitation of their lives, past and present. If they are confronted about the excessive details of their history, they may express resentment, maintaining that they are risking disclosing themselves. In teaching group process, leaders need to differentiate between storytelling, which is merely talking about oneself or about others in endless detail, and disclosure, which is talking about what a person is thinking and feeling now. During the beginning stages of a group the leader may allow some storytelling, for people who are new to groups frequently need to hear facts about others or to share some of their own past. However, if storytelling behavior becomes a familiar style (either for the whole group or for one member), the leader should recognize this problem and deal with it. The following examples illustrate how storytelling can be handled.

Kuan would, almost predictably, bring the group up to date each week on developments in his marriage. He focused on details of his wife's behavior during the week, but he rarely described his own feelings or behavior. Because Kuan was the spouse who was in the group, the leader pointed out that it was him the group was interested in. As Kuan and the group looked more at this behavior, it became obvious to him that this was his way of avoiding talking about himself. He thus made a contract to talk about his reactions and not to talk about his wife in the group each week.

Angelica typically told every detail of her earlier experiences, but even though the group knew a lot about the events in her past, they knew very little about what she thought about or how she felt about what she had experienced. Like Kuan, she felt that she was open in sharing her private life with the group; and, like Kuan's group, her group wanted to know more about how she responded to her life situations. The group leader told her that he was "losing Angelica" in all of the details. He let her know that he was indeed interested in knowing her but that the information she was offering was not helping him do so.

Used as a defense, storytelling can be any form of talking about out-of-group life that is done in a detached manner. Although the member telling the story is giving many details, he or she is unknown. Feedback from the group given directly, without judgment, can assist the person to speak in personal terms and keep the focus on feelings, thoughts, and reactions. However, all storytelling should not be thought of as negative or a sign of resistance. Leaders can assist members in telling their stories in a way that is likely to keep the interest of others. Ultimately, members need to reveal their stories in ways that enable them to reach their personal goals. One way members might enliven their presentation of self is to ask them to write their stories as a homework assignment and then only share in the group what it was like to have done this assignment.

Questioning

Another counterproductive form of behavior in the group is questioning that resembles interrogation. Some members develop a style of relating that involves questioning others, and they intervene at inappropriate times in unhelpful ways. Leaders can teach people who habitually ask questions to see that this behavior generally is not helpful for them or for others. Asking questions of others may be a way of hiding, of remaining safe and unknown in a group. It also directs them toward others, not themselves. It is helpful to teach members that questions tend to direct people toward thinking and away from their feelings. People inundated with questions typically lose the intensity of any emotion they may have been experiencing.

In discouraging the asking of too many questions, it is not enough for leaders to continuously state, "Don't ask questions, but make statements." What is more helpful is to educate members about the function of questions and how asking questions can often be counterproductive. If members see that questions not only intrude on others but also keep the questioner's feelings about others disguised, there is a good chance that they will change. Practice for behavior change might consist of trying to make direct statements. For example, Mirna could be invited to say what had prompted her to ask a question. If she had asked another member why he was so quiet, the leader could encourage her to say what had been going on in her mind before she asked the question. Mirna may tell the leader, "I noticed that Soheil hardly says anything, and I'm interested in him and would like to get to know him." In such a statement Mirna discloses her investment in her question without putting Soheil on the spot. Questions often arouse defensiveness, whereas personal statements are less likely to do so.

Because questions do not tell the entire story, we typically ask members who raise them to fill in the details. We might say: "What prompted you to ask . . . ?" "How come you want to know?" "What are you aware of right now that makes you want to ask that question?" Or "Tell [the person] what led up to your question." Here are some examples of questions and the possible hidden messages they contain:

- "How old are you?" ("I'm much older than you, and I wonder if I'll be able to identify with you.")
- "Why did you make Shirley cry?" ("I don't trust what you did, and I would never open myself up to you the way she did.")
- "Why do you push people so hard?" ("I'm scared, and I don't know how far I want to go.")
- "Why are you laughing?" ("I don't think you take seriously what goes on in this group.")
- "What do you think of me?" ("I like and respect you, and your view of me matters a lot.")
- "Why don't you leave your husband?" ("I care about you and the way you struggle, and I wonder why you stay.")
- "Why do you people always criticize your parents?" ("I'm a parent, and I wonder if my kids are that angry at me.")

Giving Advice

A problem behavior that is related to questioning is giving advice. It is one thing to offer a perception or opinion to other members and quite another to tell people what they should feel or what they should or should not do. We often ask members to share the way in which they struggle with a particular problem rather than give others their suggested solutions to a problem. We think members learn more from one another if they hear how others deal with a problem as opposed to hearing what they "should" do to solve a problem. To be sure, giving advice is not always done directly, such as "I think what you ought to do is. . . ." The advice giving may be subtle: "You shouldn't feel guilty that your parents divorced because that was their decision and not something you made them do." Although this is true, the point is that the young woman does feel guilty and believes her parents might still be married if it had not been for her. It does not serve the best interest of the woman to advise her not to feel guilty. She has to resolve this feeling herself. The man who had a need to tell her that she shouldn't feel guilty could profit from examining his own motives for wanting to remove the guilt. What does it say about him? At this point the focus might be shifted to the advice giver, and the meaning of his giving such advice might be explored.

Advice giving can be less subtle. Nisha has been considering not only leaving her husband but also leaving her two teenage daughters with him. She thinks she wants to live alone, but she feels somewhat guilty. Robin intervenes: "Nisha, you owe it to yourself to do what you want to do. You have been the main caregiver for 9 years. Why not let him have major time with them? Take that job as an investment counselor." This type of behavior raises a lot of questions about Robin. What are her values and possible unresolved problems? Why does she feel a need to so direct Nisha? Could Robin talk about herself instead of deciding what is best for Nisha? The group might now focus on Robin's need to provide others with solutions. Robin might learn about what she is getting from giving advice.

Advice giving has the tendency to interrupt the expression of thoughts and feelings and to increase dependency. If Nisha were given enough time to explore her conflict more fully, she would be better able to make her own decision. In essence, an abundance of advice tells her that she is not capable of finding her own way, and it conditions her to become more dependent on others for direction.

In our opinion, this is not a positive outcome of a therapeutic group. Even if the advice given is helpful and sound, in the long run it does not teach Nisha the process of finding her own solutions to new problems as they occur. Again, Nisha is helped to a greater extent if others refrain from dispensing advice and instead share the ways a similar problem affects them and how they attempt to understand and deal with it.

Both members and leaders need to acquire the skill of assisting others in arriving at their own insights about actions they need to take to bring about the changes they desire. There may be times when advice and suggestions are of value, and certainly leaders can provide information and ideas to members in better coping with difficulties. However, it is always more powerful and creates less dependency if members are first asked about their own thoughts about resolving challenging situations. By doing this they are learning how to solve problems. Members can be asked: "What have you done that has worked or not worked well for you?" "What advice might you give to yourself?"

As a group leader, you must be clear about the goals and purposes of the groups you design and facilitate. Furthermore, it is essential that you inform potential members about the purpose of the group during the screening and orientation meetings. Some psychoeducational groups are designed specifically to provide information and guidance and to teach specific skills. At times, people will join a group with the particular intention of getting advice on solving their problems. These group members may view you as an expert whose job it is to provide them with suggestions and specialized knowledge. Discuss the expectations of members who are seeking advice, and inform them if this is indeed something you will be offering.

Dependency

Group members who are excessively dependent typically look either to the group leader or to the other members to direct them and take care of them. Leaders sometimes foster member dependency. Some leaders have a great desire to be wanted and needed, and they feel a sense of importance when participants rely on them. This is an example of the leader's unmet psychological needs interfering with the therapeutic outcome of a group. Leaders may collude with members to form a dependent alliance for many reasons:

- The leader may need the economic rewards from the members' attendance.
- The group may be filling the leader's unmet needs for a social life.
- Some leaders have a need to be parental in the sense of directing others' lives.
- Leaders may rely on their groups as the sole source of feeling appreciated and recognized.
- Leaders may attempt to work through their own unresolved conflicts by using the group.

These examples show how the personality of the leader cannot be separated from what sometimes appears as problem behavior within the group. The behaviors of the leader and the members have a reciprocal effect on each other.

Dependent behavior is not always problematic. Such behavior needs to be viewed through a cultural lens to determine its function. What may be viewed in one culture as a manifestation of overly dependent behavior might well be viewed by another culture as an appropriate behavioral norm. As is true of seeking and giving advice, the member's cultural background must be considered.

Offering Pseudosupport

Related to the advice-giving style is the style of trying to soothe wounds, lessen pain, and keep people cheerful. This behavior is sometimes manifested by a person who complains of how negative the group is and who wants to focus more on the positive side. Like questioning and giving advice, providing inappropriate support needs to be examined for its meaning to the person who offers it. What this person often fails to realize is the healing power of being able to share a painful experience. Finding it too difficult to witness another's pain, the supportive individual attempts to distract a member who is expressing pain, which is illustrated in the example that follows.

Kange-Tae was finally able to feel his sadness over the distance between his sons and himself, and he cried as he talked about how much he wanted to be a better father. Before Kange-Tae could express what he was feeling, Randy put his hands on Kange-Tae's shoulders and tried to reassure him that he wasn't such a bad father, because at least he lived with his kids. Randy might have wanted to make Kange-Tae feel better so that he himself would feel more comfortable. However, in the process of doing so Kange-Tae was cut off from finally being able to express some of the sadness locked up inside of him.

There is a real difference between offering pseudosupport and behavior that is a genuine expression of care, concern, and empathy. When there is real caring, the interests of the people who are experiencing the pain are given paramount importance. Sometimes it is best to allow them to experience the depths of their pain; ultimately, they may be better off for having done so. They can be supported after they have had the chance to experience the pain.

We want to emphasize that we are not opposed to members' touching others who are experiencing pain. It is the motivation behind the touch that is crucial. Does the person want to communicate "I can't tolerate seeing you in pain, and I want you to stop"? Or is the person saying "I know how hard this is for you, and I want you to know that I support you"? It is surprising to us how often people who are in pain accurately pick up the message of the touch. An important lesson for those who are uncomfortable witnessing or experiencing pain is that the release of pain is often the necessary first step toward healing. This is a lesson that may need to be explicitly stated by the leader.

Hostile Behavior

Hostility is difficult to deal with in a group because the person expressing it often works indirectly. Hostility can take the form of caustic remarks, jokes, sarcasm, and other "hit-and-run" tactics. Members can express their resentment by missing group sessions, coming late, acting obviously bored and detached, leaving the group, being overly polite, or rolling their eyes to express boredom or annoyance. Extremely hostile people are not good candidates for a group because they can have a devastating effect on the group climate. People are not going to make themselves vulnerable if there is a good chance that they will be ridiculed or in some other way devalued.

One way to deal with the person who behaves in a hostile way is to request that he or she listen without responding while the group members tell how they are being affected by that individual. It is important that the members not be allowed to dump their own feelings of hostility, however. Instead, they can describe how they feel in the group with the hostile person and what they would like the person to do differently. Then it should be ascertained what the hostile individual wants from the group. Hostile behavior may be a manifestation of fear of getting intimate or of a limited capacity for vulnerability. If the fears underneath the hostility can be brought to the surface and dealt with, the hostility may decrease.

One notable manifestation of hostility is passive-aggressive behavior. This behavior characteristically involves the element of surprise: The person confronts and then quickly retreats. The confrontation has a sharp and cutting quality, and the person attacking withdraws, leaving the attacked person stunned.

For example, Karl, who has a good relationship in the group with Sana, suddenly calls her a "control freak." Before she has a chance to express her surprise, hurt, and anger, he tells her that he sees his wife in her and that it is not really her he is upset with. Karl has attempted to take back what he said, yet Sana is still stuck with her hurt feelings. On an intellectual level Sana may understand that he is transferring his reactions to her, but on an emotional level she is hurt and has become distrustful of him. Even though it makes sense on an intellectual level, Sana needs some time to recover emotionally. Eventually, Karl acknowledges that he indeed had some negative feelings toward her personally, not just as his symbolic wife. But he wanted to quickly retreat when he saw that she had responded strongly.

Acting Superior

Some group members take on a superior attitude. They may be moralistic and find ways to judge or criticize others for their behavior. These people are unable to identify any pressing problems in their lives. Their attitude and behavior tend to have the same effect on a group as hostility. Participants freeze up, for they are more hesitant to expose their weaknesses to someone who projects an image of being perfect. Take the example of Eliseo, who says, "My problems are nothing compared to yours. I feel sorry that so many of you had such terrible childhoods, and I feel fortunate that my parents really loved me." Eliseo is likely to respond to someone who is sharing a problem with "I used to have your problem, but I don't anymore." He will antagonize others with comments such as "I can identify with you, because at one time I was where you are."

One option is to ask group members to respond to Eliseo by letting him know how his behavior is affecting them. It is important, however, that members speak about themselves and not judge Eliseo. It is also crucial to block a tendency to use Eliseo as a scapegoat and to insist that he needs to have a problem.

You can challenge Eliseo's comments by asking him what he wants from the group. Here is one possible intervention: "You're comparing your problems with those of others in here. What is it that you'd like to get from this group? How is it for you to be here? How are you being affected personally by what you're hearing? How does it feel that people are annoyed with you?" This intervention lessens the chances of pressuring Eliseo to come up with problems that he is likely to deny having. Instead, it gives him some room to talk and respond without having to defend a position of being without problems. Taking an argumentative stance generally leads to a fruitless and frustrating debate. It is more constructive to focus on the reasons Eliseo continues attending this group. If he insists that his primary reason for attending is to observe others and learn about how people function, you may have made a mistake in initially not screening him out. If he shows no willingness to change, you may now be stuck with the difficult task of recommending that he leave. This would be only after you have exhausted all means of engaging him.

Socializing

Out of group socialization must not always be viewed as problematic. Again, it is crucial to keep in mind the goals of the group. In certain groups, member socialization within the group, and even outside the group, is encouraged. When members meet outside of group sessions, group cohesion can be increased. They can extend what they are learning in their group to the informal gatherings. Such meetings can also be useful in challenging members to follow through with their plans and commitments. For some populations, such as an inpatient group for the elderly, this may be the only network of support.

Clearly, there are times when meeting outside the group can be problematic and impede group cohesion. This is especially true when participants form subgroups and talk about group matters but are unwilling to share what they talk about in the group sessions. Other signs that indicate counterproductive socializing include forming cliques and excluding certain members from such gatherings, forming romantic involvements without a willingness to share them in the group, refusing to challenge one another in the group for fear of jeopardizing friendships, and relying on the group exclusively as the source of social life.

When any kind of meetings outside of the sessions hampers group progress, it is essential that the issue be openly examined by the group. You can ask the members if they are genuinely committed to developing the kind of group that will function effectively. You can help them see that forming cliques and making pacts to keep information out of the regular sessions is counterproductive and impedes group development.

Intellectualizing

Some cognitive work is a necessary part of group process, but it should be integrated with members' feelings. When group members discuss, in a very detached way as though out of intellectual interest, topics that for most people are emotionally laden, they can be said to be intellectualizing.

Most of us rely on thinking, and nothing is amiss in using our intellectual faculties. When intellectualizing is used as a defense against experiencing feelings, however, it may become problematic in a person's life and in his or her functioning in a group. People who intellectualize need to be made aware of what they are doing. A question you might raise with members who rely heavily on their intellect is this: "Does what you are doing most of the time get you what you want? Is this something you want to change?" Some experiential techniques (borrowed from Gestalt therapy and psychodrama) can be useful in helping these group members more directly experience the emotions associated with the events they talk about. Clients can be directed to reexperience events in the here and now through role playing.

People who engage in intellectualizing behavior need to decide if this behavioral style is problematic for them. Group leaders do well to avoid making quick judgments about members who do not readily display intense emotions and labeling them as "removed from their feelings" or "detached" or pathologizing their interpersonal style. For many people, operating from a cognitive perspective may be more culturally appropriate than displaying feelings publicly.

Members Becoming Assistant Leaders

Some members may develop an interpersonal style of taking on the role of assistant leaders, asking questions, probing for information, attempting to give advice, and paying attention to the dynamics of individuals and the group. Instead of paying attention to how they may be affected in the group, they shift the focus to others by making interventions and assuming a counselor's role. It is necessary to deal with this problematic behavior because it is likely to be resented by other members and it often impedes the progress of a group. Furthermore, members who take refuge in adopting such a role are deprived of the opportunity to work on the problems that actually brought them to the group in the first place.

Recognizing this behavior as a possible defense, the leader can sensitively block it by pointing out to such members that they are depriving themselves of the maximum benefit from the group by paying more attention to others than to themselves. They joined the group to explore their own concerns, and they can lose sight of this goal if they leave themselves out of the process by constantly assuming leadership functions. Although they may sincerely want to help others, this is done at the expense of helping themselves. It is essential that these members not be chastised or dismissed for their way of interacting; rather, ask them to look at the possible motivations for their behavior. They need to determine if they are pursuing their goals for this group experience.

✳ Dealing With Defensive Behavior Therapeutically

Many interventions can facilitate working *with* challenging group members rather than fighting them. The statements that follow may help members get beyond their reluctance to fully participate. First we give examples of comments that illustrate a particular hesitation or difficulty. These are followed by several simple responses that often help clients move forward. Of course, not all these responses are made simultaneously to each member comment.

Member A: I don't know.

Leader: Pretend you know. And if you did know, what might you say?
What do you know?
What are you aware of as you look at me or others in the room?
Say the first thing that comes to your mind.

Member B [during a role play]: I don't know what to say to my father.

Leader: That's a good place to start. Tell him that.
If this is the last chance you have to speak to him, what do you want to tell him?
If you were your father, what would you want to say? If you were your father, what do you fear you would say?
Tell your father what stops you from talking to him.

Member C: I try so hard to say things the right way.

Leader: Say the first thing that comes to your mind right now.
Rehearse out loud.

Member D: I don't want to be here.

Leader: *Where would you rather be?*
What makes it difficult for you to be here?
Who or what made you come here?
What made you come if you didn't want to be here today?

Member E *[after an intense piece of work]: I feel like withdrawing.*

Leader: *What or whom do you want to get away from?*
Go to a few people and finish the sentence "I want to get away from you because . . ."
Say more about your feeling.

Member F: *I'm afraid to talk more about this.*

Leader: *Can you talk about what's stopping you?*
What do you fear would happen if you said more?
What do you imagine will happen if you don't talk about it?
What would it take for you to feel safer in here?
I hope you'll say more about your fears of talking.

Several Members: *It's far easier to talk in the coffee shop to other group members than it is to express ourselves here.*

Leader: *Form an inner circle. Imagine you're out having coffee. What are you saying to each other?*
Say at least two things to several members about your difficulty in being here. [Some possibilities for incomplete sentences to be completed by a client are "I find it hard to talk in here because . . . ," "I'm afraid to talk because . . . ," and "When I stop myself from talking, I'm most aware of. . . ."]

Member G: *I'm very uncomfortable with the anger in the group.*

Leader: *Tell those whom you see as angry how you're affected by them.*
What happens [happened] when people express [expressed] their anger in your life? [Some possibilities for incomplete sentences to be completed by the client are "I'm afraid to get angry like this because . . . ," "When you're angry with me, I . . . ," "I'm afraid of my anger because . . . ," and "When I witness anger, I want to. . . ."]

Member H *[who typically engages in storytelling]: But you don't understand. I need to tell you all the details so that you'll understand me.*

Leader: *Bear with me. I have a hard time following you when you give so many details. In one sentence, what do you most want me to hear?*
What's it like not to feel understood in here?
What's it like to discover that people don't want to hear your stories?
How does this story relate to the way you're struggling now in your life?
What makes it important that I listen to your story?

Member I: *I feel that my problems are insignificant.*

Leader: *Whose problems in here are more important?*

If you didn't compare your problems with those of others, what could you tell us about yourself?
How are you affected by hearing all these problems?
Tell us about one of your insignificant problems.

Member J *[who has been feeling close to others in the group]: I'm afraid of this closeness, because I'm sure it won't last.*

Leader: *What did you do to get close to people?*
Tell a few people what scares you about remaining close to them.
Tell us how you can get close in here but not in your life.
What would it be like for you if you had people close to you all the time? What is one thing that might keep you from maintaining the closeness you felt?
If nothing changed for you, how might this be? Tell us the advantages of isolating yourself.

Member K *[who is typically silent]: I don't think I need to be talking all the time. I learn a lot by observing.*

Leader: *So, tell us some things you've been observing.*
Are you satisfied with being silent, or would you like to change?
What are some of the things that make it difficult to speak out more?
Would you be willing to select two people you've been observing and tell them how they have affected you?
I'm interested in knowing what you have to say, and I'd like to hear from you.
When you observe me and quietly make assumptions about me, I feel uncomfortable. I'd like to be included in the conclusions you're drawing about me. I hope you are open to that.
When you don't talk about yourself, people are likely to project onto you, and there's a good chance you'll be misunderstood.

Member L *[who tends to give people advice]: I think you should stop criticizing yourself because you're a wonderful person.*

Leader: *For several weeks now you've observed people in this room.*
Give each person an important piece of advice.
When you give advice, do you sound like anyone you know?
How is it for you when others reject your advice?
How are you affected by the person you're about to give advice to?
How do people in your life respond to you when you give them advice?
What advice would you like to give to yourself?

Most of these suggestions for responses by the leader provide encouragement for members to say more rather than stopping at the point of initial resistance. The questions are open-ended and are presented in an invitational manner. The interventions all grow out of clues provided by members, and they are designed to offer directions clients might pursue in becoming unstuck. For another perspective on dealing with difficult group members, see Earley (2000).

✳ Dealing With Avoidance by the Whole Group

We have focused on how to deal therapeutically with the defensive behaviors of individuals, but sometimes an entire group exhibits behavior that makes it almost impossible to achieve a productive level of work. In this section we describe one of our experiences when this was the case. In the interest of maintaining the anonymity of a particular group, we have changed some of the details and included themes that have been characteristic of a number of groups that we have coled. Our main purpose is to demonstrate how we were affected when an entire group made the choice of not working and was unwilling to deal with a number of hidden agendas. We also describe some ways these hidden agendas affect the members as individuals as well as the group as a whole.

At one of our training workshops for group counselors, it was not possible to individually screen candidates. In lieu of screening, we provided all who were interested with a detailed letter describing the workshop and outlining our expectations of participants. We repeated this information at the first session, and participants had an opportunity to raise questions. It was especially crucial to us that they understood that they were to become personally involved and would function both as members and as coleaders during different sessions. The full group was divided into two groups of eight. Each 2-hour period was coled by two different trainees so that they all had an equal opportunity to function both as members and leaders. As supervisors, we changed groups each 2-hour session. This change presented problems for some of the trainees, who said they were inhibited because the same supervisor was not continually in their group.

One of the groups (Group 1) was formed by people who got up and actively chose to be with one another. By contrast, the other group (Group 2) was largely formed by one member who remained seated and said: "I'm staying here. Anyone who wants to join my group can come over here." As the week progressed, some interesting differences arose between the two groups. Group 2 was characterized by an unwillingness to meaningfully interact with one another. Many of them complained that they had not understood that they were to become personally invested in the group process. They said they had expected to learn about groups by observing us do the work rather than by getting actively involved. Although a few of the members disclosed readily, others refused to share and did very little interacting, which eventually led to an increased sense of withholding on the part of all members.

The participants in Group 2 were apparently feeling many things that they had not disclosed. Some of them said that they were enjoying the group time, yet they spoke little and appeared bored. There was considerable subgrouping. During the breaks, members talked about difficulties they were experiencing in the sessions, but they did not bring this information back to their group. Two members ended a session with an unresolved conflict and decided to clear the air during the break, but they did not inform the group of the outcome. Only after some exploration by the supervisor did the members eventually acknowledge that they were preoccupied and concerned about the two people who had had the conflict. The supervisor attempted to teach again how sub-grouping can be deleterious to a group's attaining its purpose.

Several women in Group 2 often confronted one of the male members in a harsh manner. When a supervisor asked how he was affected by the confrontations, he quickly insisted that he was fine. After several sessions, however, he blew up at everyone in the group (including the supervisor) and let them know how angry he was. He declared that he was ready to leave. The group mood was again one of hesitancy, and members interacted very tentatively.

Another pattern that emerged was a tendency of Group 2 to judge itself against the performance of the other group. The members compared themselves unfavorably to those in Group 1 at those times when the two groups joined to discuss the day's progress. At a later point, people in Group 2 revealed the jealousy they had felt over the intensity and closeness that seemed to characterize the other group.

On the next to last day, Group 2's level of trust continued at a low ebb. The members showed great reluctance to be personal and to interact with one another. One of the supervisors (Jerry) told them before the lunch break: "I hope each one of you will spend some time in determining if you are getting what you wanted. This workshop is almost over. If today were the end, how would that be for you? If you aren't satisfied, what do you see that you can do to change the situation?"

The members of Group 2 decided to have lunch together for the first time. The group sessions were scheduled to resume promptly at 1 o'clock. What follows are the comments of the supervisor (Marianne) about what occurred.

"I arrived at the group I was to supervise shortly before 1:00 p.m., and at 1:20 p.m. I was still waiting in a hot and stuffy room with empty chairs. At 1:25 p.m. the group members finally slowly came into the room laughing and joking, telling me what a 'wonderful, intimate lunch' they had had. As they sat down, they let me know that they had felt much more comfortable and cohesive than they did in the group room. Even though I suspected what was occurring with them as a group, I would not have felt very honest if I had not let them know of my annoyance over their being late and not acknowledging this fact.

"Once I had taken care of my feelings with them, I was able to explore the dynamics of what was occurring. I confronted them by saying: 'You say that talking at lunch was very easy and that you felt close to one another. You also say that when you come into this room, you feel stifled. What do you think is different?' Of course, the most obvious variable was the presence of the supervisor. As they began to open up, they initially lashed out at both supervisors. They perceived us as demanding too much, expecting them to be personal and academic at the same time, wanting them to perform, and demanding that they have problems (even if they didn't). They insisted that we had been unclear with them about our expectations. I listened to their grievances, attempting not to be defensive, which was not easy with the degree of hostility that was directed toward me. I did acknowledge that it was a difficult workshop and that indeed much was demanded of them, but I was not apologetic about my standards.

"Finally, as a group, they admitted their envy over the intimacy the other group seemed to have, and they said they had tried to replicate this closeness at lunch. It was then that I challenged them again, as had Jerry before lunch, to reflect and begin to verbalize what they were rehearsing internally and what they were keeping from one another. Furthermore, I told them that I had a difficult time in trusting the sincerity of the intimacy they supposedly had had at lunch if they could not be more direct with one another in the session a few minutes later."

The next session took place the following morning, which also was the last full day of the workshop. At that session the members finally displayed more honesty. They had taken our challenges seriously and had given thought during the evening to their behavior during the workshop. They were willing to take personal responsibility for their actions in the group, and there was no blaming. They accomplished more work in this final session because of their willingness to say what was on their minds. They learned in an experiential way that what they had not expressed during much of the week had kept them from having a productive group. Yet neither they nor we thought that their group had been a failure, because they realized how their behavior had thwarted their progress as a group. Most of them were able to see some of the ways in which their low level of risking had inhibited the flow of their group. Because they were finally willing to talk in honest ways about their involvement in the group, they learned some important lessons about themselves as persons as well as about the group process.

When the two of us conferred privately, we made some comparisons between the two groups. Our comparisons did not focus on labeling one group as a success and the other as a failure. Rather, we were acutely aware of the different dynamics that had characterized each group. Supervising and facilitating each group was demanding work, yet the main difference was Group 1's willingness to at least talk about its difficulties, whereas Group 2 continually withheld important reactions. In the follow-up papers the participants wrote, our hunches were confirmed. Many members of Group 2 wrote about their reactions during the week that they had never mentioned in the sessions. Had they chosen to express them at the time, we are quite certain their experience as a group and their individual experiences would have been very different.

As supervisors, we felt that we had worked diligently with both groups, yet at times we had wondered what the participants in Group 2 were really gaining from the workshop. We experienced how draining it can be to work with a group that has a number of hidden agendas. It was necessary to remind ourselves that this was not the first time we had worked with a difficult group. Our experience has taught us the importance of making a commitment to face what is going on, to bring to the surface the hidden agendas, and to refuse to give up. In spite of our belief in the natural process of a group, our patience was tested. It often seemed that we were doing most of the work. As has been true with other groups, our patience paid off, for the members of this group eventually developed the trust necessary to explore the ways in which they had become stuck and learned what was necessary to move forward. Even though this group did not become cohesive, the members did learn important lessons about what had held them back as individuals and how this impasse at the transition stage had stalled their efforts to become a working group.

✳ Dealing With Transference and Countertransference

As we have emphasized, it is essential when leading groups to recognize how your unresolved personal issues can feed into problematic behaviors in members. This interplay involves transference and countertransference. *Transference* consists of the feelings clients project onto the counselor. These feelings usually have to do with relationships the clients have experienced in the past. When such feelings are attributed to the group counselor, the intensity of the feelings may have more to do with unfinished elements in a member's life than with the current situation. *Countertransference* refers to the feelings aroused in the counselor by clients, feelings that, again, may have more to do with unresolved conflict from other past or present relationships than with any feature of the therapeutic relationship.

A group context has the potential for multiple transferences. Members may project not only onto the leaders but also onto other members in the group. Depending on the kind of group being conducted, members may identify people who elicit feelings in them that are reminiscent of feelings they have for significant people in their lives, past or present. Again, depending on the purpose of the group, these feelings can be productively explored so members become aware of how they are keeping these old patterns functional in present relationships. The group itself provides an ideal place to become aware of certain patterns of psychological vulnerability. Members can gain insight into the ways their unresolved conflicts create certain patterns of dysfunctional behavior. By focusing on what is going on within a group session, the group provides a dynamic understanding of how people function in out-of-group situations.

When group members appear to work very hard at getting the facilitator to push them away, it can be therapeutically useful to explore what potential gains they may be deriving from this self-defeating behavior. The transference reactions members develop toward the group leader and other members can bring out intense feelings in those who are the target of this transference. Handled properly in the therapeutic setting, members can experience and express feelings and reactions toward others in the group and discover how they are projecting outside situations onto the group. When these feelings are productively explored in the group, members often become better able to express their reactions appropriately.

Your own supervision is a central factor in learning how to deal effectively with both transference and countertransference reactions. Your blind spots can easily hamper your ability to deal with various difficult behaviors displayed by members or with your old wounds that surface as you work with the members' pain. Ongoing supervision will enable you to accept responsibility for your reactions and at the same time prevent you from taking full responsibility for directions that specific members take. Meeting with your coleader to talk about how you are affected by certain members is an excellent way to get another's perspective on difficult situations. Self-knowledge is the basic tool in understanding members' transference and in dealing effectively with your own countertransference.

It is essential for group leaders to consider their countertransference as a possible cause of difficulties that develop in a group. Some leaders project their own problems and unfinished business onto "difficult members." If leaders are not willing to deal with their own issues, how can they expect members to take the risks necessary for them to change? As you reflect on ways you may be emotionally triggered in groups you lead, examine your response to members that you perceive as being difficult. Remember, it is generally not useful to assume that your clients merely want to annoy you. Ask yourself these questions:

- How do I respond to the different forms of transference exhibited by members?
- What kind of transference tends to elicit my countertransference?
- Do I take the defensiveness of members in a personal way?
- Do I blame myself for not being skillful enough?
- Do I become combative with clients I view as problematic?
- Does the way in which I respond to problematic behaviors tend to increase or decrease defensiveness on the part of members?

As a group leader, you are faced with the challenge of dealing with the transference reactions members develop toward you, but the solution is often complex and depends on the circumstances under which the relationship develops. Do not quickly discount members' reactions to you as mere transference. Be willing to explore the possibility that members have genuine reactions to the way you have dealt with them. It takes courage on your part to acknowledge that you may have been insensitive to a client and are now receiving warranted reactions. Often, however, members will treat you as if you were a significant figure in their lives, and you get more reactions than you deserve. This is especially likely to be true if members exhibit intense feelings toward you when they have had very little contact with you.

Even if you strongly suspect transference feelings, you would be discounting the person if you said, "You are having a transference reaction toward me. This is not my problem, it's your problem." A less defensive response is, "Tell me more about how I affect you." This intervention elicits additional information about how the group member developed a set of reactions to you. After both you and the individual express your reactions, you could acknowledge that this person does have some real perceptions of your behavior by saying, "I think you have a point. I was preoccupied, and I didn't notice that you wanted to talk to me." Or, if you hardly know the person and he or she reacts right away to you with great intensity, you might say, "I'm surprised at the reactions you're having to me. I wonder if I remind you of someone else in your life?" You probably would not want to make this last statement, however, until you have first explored this member's reactions to you.

When group members identify you as an object of transference, there is the potential for good therapeutic work. You can take on a symbolic role and allow the person to talk to you and work through unfinished business. Additionally, you and the person can engage in role reversal as a way to explore feelings and to gain insight. Assume that a member, Paul, becomes aware that he is behaving around you much as he does with his father. During a role play in which he is talking to you as his father, he says, "I don't feel important in your life. You're too busy and never have time for me. No matter what I do, it's never enough for you. I just don't know how to go about getting your approval." Because you do not know how Paul's father relates to him, you could ask Paul to take on the role of his father by responding as he imagines that his father would respond. After Paul has several interchanges in which he is both himself and his father, you will have a clearer sense of how he struggles with his father. Armed with this information, you can help him work through his unresolved issues with both his father and with you. Through the process of his therapeutic work, Paul may be able to see you as the person you are rather than as the father with whom he is struggling. He might also gain awareness of the ways he talks to his father and how he transfers his feelings toward him to others in everyday life.

These are but a few illustrations of how transference problems can be worked out. The important elements are that (1) the feelings be recognized and expressed and that (2) the feelings then be dealt with therapeutically.

A more delicate issue is how the leader can best deal with feelings toward a group member. Even in the psychoanalytic tradition, which dictates that therapists spend years in analysis to understand and resolve blocked areas, countertransference is a potential problem. So it can be a big problem for the beginning group leader. Some people are attracted to this profession because, on some level, they imagine that as a helper they will be respected, needed, admired, looked to as an expert, and even loved. Perhaps they have never experienced the acceptance and self-confidence in their ordinary lives that they feel while helping others. Such leaders are using groups to fulfill needs that would otherwise go unmet.

The issue of power is germane here. As group members elevate the leader to the level of expert, perfect person, or demanding parent, members give away most of their power. A self-aware therapist who is interested primarily in clients' welfare will not encourage members to remain in an inferior position. The insecure leader who depends on clients' subordinate position for a sense of adequacy and power will tend to keep the group members powerless.

We do not want to convey the impression that it is inappropriate for you to meet some of your needs through your work. Nor are we suggesting that you should not feel powerful. In fact, if you are not meeting your needs through your work, we think you are in danger of losing your enthusiasm. But it is crucial that you do not exploit the members as a way of fulfilling yourself. The problem occurs when you put your own needs first or when you fail to be sensitive to the needs of group members.

Countertransference feelings are likely to develop in the romantic or sexual realm, particularly when an attractive group member indicates an interest in a group leader. Group leaders may never have felt desirable before assuming their professional role. Now that they do, there is the danger that they will depend on group members for this feedback. Through your training, you may have the opportunity to explore with a supervisor your feelings of attraction or repulsion toward certain members. If you are conducting groups independently and become aware of a pattern that indicates possible countertransference problems, you should seek consultation with another therapist or become a member of a group to work through these problems.

When considering possible transference or countertransference, three additional points need to be emphasized:

1. Do not believe uncritically whatever group members tell you, particularly initially. It is easy to become enamored with feedback that tells you how helpful, wise, perceptive, attractive, powerful, and dynamic you are. Avoid being swept away by the unrealistic attributions of group members.

2. Avoid being overly critical and discounting genuine positive feedback. All members who see a leader as helpful or wise are not suffering from "transference disorders." Members can feel genuine affection and respect for group leaders. By the same token, just because participants become angry with you does not mean that they are transferring anger toward their parents onto you. They might well feel genuine anger and have negative reactions toward you personally largely because of certain behaviors you display. In short, all feelings that members direct toward the group leader should not be "analyzed" as transference to be "worked through" for the client's good. A useful guideline that we apply to ourselves is that if we hear a consistent pattern of feedback, then we seriously examine what is being told to us. When we see the validity of this feedback, we are likely to make some changes in our behavior.

3. Recognize that not all of your feelings toward members can be classified as countertransference. You may be operating under the misconception that you should remain objective and care for all members equally. One of your unrealistic beliefs could be your expectation that you should be all things to all members. Countertransference is indicated by exaggerated and persistent feelings that tend to recur with various clients in various groups. You can expect to enjoy some members more than others, yet all the members of your group deserve a chance to be respected and liked by you. It is important that you recognize your own feelings for what they are and that you avoid emotional entanglements that are countertherapeutic.

✳ Effective Leadership: Research Findings

A good deal of research on group process has been focused on the therapeutic relationship, which involves a variety of structural possibilities: member–

member, member–leader, member–group, leader–group, leader–member, and leader–leader relationships (Burlingame et al., 2004b). These alliance relationships are one of the strongest group process variables linked to successful outcomes. In a review of literature on therapeutic relationships in groups, Burlingame, Fuhriman, and Johnson (2002) identified three key constructs that capture the essence of the therapeutic relationship in group treatment: group climate, cohesion, and alliances.

Research has yielded considerable evidence of the importance of a positive therapist–client relationship as a contributing factor to positive change in clients (Burlingame & Fuhriman, 1990). Group leaders play an important role in establishing a positive group climate (Dies, 1994), one that encourages intermember feedback and participation as key group norms. Indeed, such a climate is often viewed as the basic therapeutic factor of group treatment. A high degree of intermember interaction is thought to foster establishment and maintenance of cohesion and group identity, reality testing, and development of coping skills (Burlingame & Fuhriman, 1990).

In addition to facilitating a high level of client interaction, the group leader's relationship with members is also seen as a crucial determinant of the process and outcome of a group. A leader's supportive relationship with members is requisite for client change (Dies, 1994), and the leader's interpersonal skills, genuineness, empathy, and warmth are significant variables in creating the kind of climate that leads to successful outcomes. Some of the literature focuses on the therapist's contributions to the therapeutic enterprise and specifies personality characteristics of successful group leaders. These include empathy, competence, responsiveness and attentiveness, presence, and engagement. The therapist's personal development and awareness of personal style are influential aspects of the therapeutic relationship (Fuhriman & Burlingame, 1990), but awareness of how the therapist's behavior may influence the group is also crucial. Group leaders are responsible for activating the therapeutic factors within the group. Identifying the key therapeutic factors for a particular group is the first step. Riva, Wachtel, and Lasky (2004) sum it up this way: "It is not surprising that group leaders who are warm, supportive, and genuinely interested in individual members, as well as the group as a whole, have group members who make more positive gains" (p. 39).

As we discussed in Chapter 2, however, these relationship variables and other personal characteristics by themselves are not sufficient for effective group outcomes. It is generally accepted that a positive therapeutic relationship is necessary but not sufficient to produce client change. Certainly it is essential that leaders possess the knowledge of how groups best function and that they have the skills to intervene in timely and effective ways. Creating a group climate that fosters interpersonal norms such as openness, directness, respect, and concern for one another will lead to therapeutic interactions among members. Riva, Wachtel, and Lasky (2004) identify the essence of effective leadership in groups: "An essential leader behavior is to foster a group climate that is safe, positive, and supportive, yet strong enough to at times withstand highly charged emotions, challenges, and interactions between members" (p. 41).

Support Versus Confrontation

Forging an effective group requires achieving an appropriate balance between support and challenge. In our opinion, groups having either explicit or implicit norms limiting group interactions to supportive ones do not have the power to help people challenge themselves to take significant risks. We further think that those groups stressing confrontation as a requisite for peeling away the defensive behaviors of members lead to increasingly defensive interactions. The reviews of research that describe negative outcomes in groups consistently cite aggressive confrontation as the leadership style with the highest risks (Yalom, 1995). As group leaders become overly confrontational and actively negative, the odds are that members will be dissatisfied and potentially harmed by the group experience (Dies, 1994).

Dies (1983b) suggests that leaders should not engage in highly confrontational interventions until they have earned that right by building a trusting relationship with the members. Once the foundation of interpersonal trust is established, group members tend to be more open to challenge. Because it takes time to create a supportive atmosphere, Dies suggests that confrontational interactions are probably most appropriate at a later stage of a group's development.

We agree that there are dangers in confronting too soon and that leaders must carefully and sensitively challenge. Attempts to harshly confront defenses can lead to an entrenchment of resistance and may breed resentment and mistrust within the group. But confrontation is appropriate even during the initial stages of a group if it is done with sensitivity and respect. In fact, the foundations of trust are often solidified by caring confrontations on the leader's part. Beginning with the early phase of the group, the leader needs to model ways of providing appropriate support and challenge. To avoid challenging a group in its early phase, when this is what the group needs, is to treat the group members as fragile. How leaders deal with conflict, resistance, anxiety, and defensiveness does much to set the tone of the group. In our view, members have a tendency to follow the leader's manner of confronting.

Guidelines for Creating Therapeutic Relationships With Members

In this section we present further guidelines for group leadership practice based on research summaries done by Bednar and Kaul (1978), Burlingame and Fuhriman (1990), Burlingame, Fuhriman, and Johnson (2002, 2004b), Dies (1983b), Fuhriman and Burlingame (1990), Morran, Stockton, and Whittingham (2004), and Stockton and Morran (1982).

- Strive for positive involvement in the group through genuine, empathic, and caring interactions with members. Impersonal, detached, and judgmental leadership styles can thwart the development of trust and cohesion.
- Develop a reasonably open therapeutic style characterized by appropriate and facilitative self-disclosure, but do not make it a practice to

use the group you lead as a therapy group for yourself. Be willing to share your own reactions and emotional experiences, especially as they relate to events and relationships within the group.

■ Keep in mind that leader self-disclosure can have either a constructive or a detrimental effect on the group process and outcome, depending on specific factors such as the type of group, the stage of its development, and the content and manner of the disclosure.

■ Help members make maximum use of effective role models, especially those members who demonstrate desirable behavior. Members can be encouraged to learn from one another. If you have a coleader, model openness with your partner.

■ Provide an adequate amount of structuring, especially during the early phase of a group, but avoid a controlling style of leadership.

■ Provide opportunities for all members to make maximum use of the resources within the group by teaching them skills of active participation in the group process.

■ Demonstrate your caring by being willing to confront members when that is called for, but do so in a manner that provides members with good modeling of ways to confront sensitively.

■ Set and reinforce clear norms as one way to establish cohesion within the group.

■ When necessary, protect group members and strive to promote a feeling of safety.

■ Intervene when a member is preventing others from using the group's resources by engaging in nonconstructive confrontations, sarcasm, and indirect exchanges. Help members deal with one another in direct and constructive ways.

We want to underscore our belief that you can do much to encourage members to give up some of their defensiveness by reacting to them with directness, honesty, and respect. Members are more likely to develop a stance of openness in a group that they perceive as being safe for them, and your modeling has a lot to do with creating this therapeutic atmosphere.

✳ Coleader Issues at the Transition Stage

As you can see, the transition stage is a critical period in the history of the group. Depending on how conflict and resistance are handled, the group can take a turn for the better or for the worse. If you are working with a coleader, you can efficiently use the time you have for meeting before and after sessions to focus on your own reactions to what is occurring in the group. Here are a few problems that can develop between leaders at this time.

Negative Reactions Toward One Leader   If members direct a challenge or express negative reactions toward a coleader, it is important to avoid either taking sides with your colleague in attacking clients or siding with the members in ganging up against the coleader. Instead, nondefensively (and as objectively as possible) continue your leadership by facilitating a constructive exploration of the situation. You might do this by asking the member who has a reaction to your coleader to speak directly to him or her. You could also invite your coleader to say *what* he or she is hearing and *how* he or she is being affected.

Challenges to Both Leaders   Assume that several members direct criticism to both you and your coleader, saying, "You leaders expect us to be personal in here, but we don't know anything about you that's personal. You should be willing to talk about your problems if that's what you expect us to do." In such a case, difficulties can develop if one of you responds defensively while the other is willing to deal with this confrontation from the members. Ideally, both leaders should talk about the confrontation objectively. If not, this disagreement would surely be a vital topic to discuss in the coleaders' meeting outside of the group or during a supervision session. All such difficulties should not be reserved for a private discussion between coleaders. As much as possible, matters that pertain to what is happening during sessions should be discussed with the entire group. The failure to do so can easily lead to a you-versus-them split within the group.

Dealing With Problem Behaviors   We have discussed a variety of difficult members that you and your coleader may have to confront. We want to caution against the tendency of coleaders to chronically discuss what such members are doing or not doing and never to explore how such behavior affects them as leaders. It is a mistake to dwell almost exclusively on strategies for "curing" problem members while ignoring your own personal reactions to such problematic behaviors.

Dealing With Countertransference   It is not realistic to expect a leader to work equally effectively with every member. At times ineffectiveness results from countertransference reactions on the part of one of the leaders. For example, a male leader could have strong and irrational negative reactions to one of the women in the group. It may be that he is seeing his ex-wife in this member and responding to her in nontherapeutic ways because of his own unresolved issues over the divorce. When this situation occurs, the coleader can be therapeutic for both the member and the leader who is not being helpful. The colleague can intervene during the session itself as well as exploring these countertransference reactions with the other leader outside the session. Coleaders who are willing to be objective and honest with each other can have a positive impact through this process of mutual confrontation.

✓ *Points to Remember*

Transition Stage Characteristics

The transition phase of a group's development is marked by feelings of anxiety and defenses in the form of various behavior patterns.

✓ Members are concerned about what they will think of themselves if they increase their self-awareness and about others' acceptance or rejection of them.

✓ Members test the leader and other members to determine how safe the environment is.

✓ Members struggle between wanting to play it safe and wanting to risk getting involved.

✓ Control and power issues may emerge or some members may experience conflict with others in the group.

✓ Members observe coleaders to determine if they are trustworthy.

✓ Members learn how to express themselves so that others will listen to them.

Member Functions

A central role of members at this time is to recognize and deal with the many forms of resistance.

✓ Members recognize and express any persistent reactions; unexpressed feelings may contribute to a climate of distrust.

✓ Members respect their own defenses but work with them.

✓ Members move from dependence to independence.

✓ Members learn how to confront others in a constructive manner so that they do not retreat into defensive postures.

✓ Members face and deal with reactions toward what is occurring in the group.

✓ Members work through conflicts rather than remaining silent or forming subgroups outside of the sessions.

Leader Functions

The major challenge facing leaders during the transition period is the need to intervene in the group in a sensitive and timely manner. The major task is to provide the encouragement and the challenge necessary for members to face and resolve conflicts and negative reactions that exist within the group and certain behaviors that stem from their defenses against anxiety. To meet this challenge, leaders have the following tasks:

✓ Teach members the value of recognizing and dealing fully with conflict situations.

✓ Assist members to recognize their own patterns of defensiveness.

✓ Teach members to respect anxiety and defensive behavior and to work constructively with attempts at self-protection.

✓ Provide a model for members by dealing directly and tactfully with any challenges, either personal or professional.

✓ Avoid labeling members, but learn how to understand certain problematic behaviors.

✓ Assist members to become interdependent and independent.

✓ Encourage members to express reactions that pertain to here-and-now happenings in the sessions.

Exercises

Self-Assessment Scale

Use this self-assessment scale to determine your strengths and weaknesses as a group member. Rate yourself as you see yourself at this time. If you have not had some type of group experience, rate yourself in terms of your behavior in the class you are now in. This exercise can help you determine the degree to which you may be either a resistive or a productive group member. If you identify specific problem areas, you can decide to work on them in your group.

After everyone has completed the inventory, the class should break into small groups, each person trying to join the people he or she knows best. Members of the groups should then assess one another's self-ratings.

Rate yourself from 1 to 5 on each of the following self-descriptions, using these extremes:

5 = This is almost always true of me.

4 = This is frequently true of me.

3 = This is sometimes true of me.

2 = This is rarely true of me.

1 = This is never true of me.

_____ **1.** I am readily able to trust others in a group.

_____ **2.** Others tend to trust me in a group situation.

_____ **3.** I disclose personal and meaningful material.

_____ **4.** I am willing to formulate specific goals and contracts.

_____ **5.** I am generally an active participant as opposed to an observer.

_____ **6.** I am willing to openly express my feelings about and reactions to what is occurring within a group.

_____ **7.** I listen attentively to what others are saying, and I am able to discern more than the mere content of what is said.

_____ **8.** I do not give in to group pressure by doing or saying things that do not seem right to me.

_____ **9.** I am able to give direct and honest feedback to others, and I am open to receiving feedback about my behavior from others.

_____ **10.** I prepare myself for a given group by thinking of what I want from that experience and what I am willing to do to achieve my goals.

_____ **11.** I avoid monopolizing the group time.

_____ **12.** I avoid storytelling by describing what I am experiencing now.

_____ **13.** I avoid questioning others; instead I make direct statements to them.

_____ **14.** I am able to be supportive of others when it is appropriate without giving pseudosupport.

_____ **15.** I am able to confront others in a direct and caring manner by letting them know how I am affected by them.

Questions for Exploration

Many of the following exercises are ideally suited for small group interaction and discussion. Explore these questions from the vantage point of a group leader.

1. **Working With Members' Fears.** Assume that various members make these statements:

   - "I'm afraid of looking like a fool in the group."
   - "My greatest fear is that the other members will reject me."
   - "I'm afraid to look at myself, because if I do, I might discover that I'm empty."
   - "I'm reluctant to let others know who I really am, because I've never done it before."

   With each of these statements, what might you say or do? Can you think of ways to work with members who express these fears?

2. **Moving Beyond Playing It Safe.** Imagine that you are leading a group that does not seem to want to get beyond the stage of "playing it safe." Members' disclosures are superficial, their risk-taking is minimal, and they display a variety of resistances. What might you do in such a situation? How do you imagine you would feel if you were leading such a group?

3. **Confronting Conflicts.** Assume that there is a good deal of conflict in a group you are leading. When you point this discord out to members and encourage them to deal with it, most of them tell you that they do not see any point in talking about the conflicts because "things won't change." What might be your response? How would you deal with a group that seemed to want to avoid facing and working with conflicts?

4. **Challenging the Leader.** In a group you are coleading, several members challenge your competence. In essence, they give you the message that you are not working professionally and that they favor the other leader. How do you imagine you would feel in such a situation? What do you think you would do or say?

5. **Intervening With a Silent Member.** Betty is a group member who rarely speaks, even if encouraged to do so. What are your reactions to the following leader interventions?

   a. Ignore her.

   b. Ask others in the group how they react to her silence.

   c. Remind her of her contract detailing her responsibility to participate.

   d. Ask her what is keeping her from contributing.

   e. Frequently attempt to draw her out.

   What interventions would you be likely to make?

6. **Redirecting a Questioner.** Larry has a style of asking many questions of fellow group members. You notice that his questioning has the effect of

distracting members and interfering with their expression of feelings. What are some things you might say to him?

7. **Confronting a Member Who Is Storytelling.** Jessica has a habit of going into great detail in telling stories when she speaks. She typically focuses on details about others in her life, saying little about how she is affected by them. Eventually, another member says to her, "I'm really having trouble staying with you. I get bored and impatient with you when you go into such detail about others. I want to hear more about you and less about others." Jessica responds, "That really upsets me. I feel I've been risking a lot by telling you about problems in my life. Now I feel like not saying any more!" What interventions would you make at this point?

8. **Identifying Countertransference.** From what you know of yourself, in what areas are you most likely to experience countertransference? If you found your objectivity seriously hampered in a group because of your own personal issues, what might you do?

9. **Assessing Your Experiential Group.** If you are involved in an experiential group as part of your group class, this would be a good time to assess any characteristics in your group that are typical of the transition stage. Assess your own level of participation in the group. What changes, if any, would you like to make as a member of your group? As a group, spend some time exploring these questions: How is resistance being dealt with in the group? How trusting is the climate? If conflict is present, how is it being dealt with and how does this influence the group process? Are any hidden agendas present? What are you learning about what makes groups function effectively or what gets in the way of effective group interaction?

Guide to *Groups in Action: Evolution and Challenges* DVD and Workbook

Evolution of a Group

Here are some suggestions for making effective use of this chapter along with the transition stage segment of *Evolution of a Group*, the first program in *Groups in Action*.

1. **Characteristics of the Transition Stage.** In this chapter we identify some key characteristic of groups in transition. As you view the DVD, what characteristics do you observe unfolding in the group during the transition stage?

2. **Common Fears of Members.** Some common fears are typical during the transition stage. On the DVD members articulate some of their fears. What kind of fears might you have if you were in this type of group?

3. **Dealing With Conflict and Confrontation.** Although conflict often occurs during the transition stage, it can surface during the initial group session. On the DVD conflict occurs during both the initial and the ending stages. Did you learn anything about how to deal with conflict, regardless of when

it occurs, from viewing the sessions? What are the possible consequences of ignoring conflict or dealing with it ineffectively? What guidelines would you want to teach members of your group about how to confront effectively?

4. **Using the Workbook.** If you are using the DVD and workbook, refer to Segment 3: Transition Stage of the workbook and complete all the exercises. Take the self-inventory and review the Coreys' commentary.

Challenges Facing Group Leaders

Here are some suggestions for making effective use of this chapter along with the first segment of *Challenges Facing Group Leaders,* the second program in *Groups in Action.*

1. **Characteristics of the Transition Stage.** As you view this second program, what characteristics do you observe in this group that are typical of the transition stage?

2. **Challenges During the Transition Stage.** As coleaders, we see our task as intervening in a way that makes the room safe and provides a climate whereby members can talk about their hesitations. What is the importance of carefully working with whatever members bring to a group regarding their fears, concerns, or reservations? How is this transitional work essential if you hope to help a group move to a deeper level of interpersonal interaction? From reading this chapter and viewing the DVD, what are you learning about the leader's task during the transition stage in a group?

3. **Problem Behaviors and Difficult Group Members.** As you watch and study Segment 1, notice signs of problematic behaviors on the part of members. Also notice signs of defensiveness and reluctance and how members express and work with their resistance. The themes that are enacted in segment one of the DVD are illustrative of challenges that group leaders typically encounter in many different groups. These themes include the following:

- Checking in: What was it like to return to group?
- The leaders let me down.
- I'm not feeling safe in here.
- I didn't want to come back to group.
- I'm in this group against my will.
- Emotions make me uncomfortable.
- I'm self-conscious about my accent.
- I want the leaders to disclose more.
- I learn a lot by being quiet.
- Silence serves a function.
- I feel pressured to disclose.
- What's wrong with helping others?

- Can't we stop all this conflict?
- I feel weak when I show feelings.
- Checking out: What are each of you taking from this session?

In small groups, explore these questions: What kind of difficult group member would present the greatest challenge to you? Do you have any ideas about why a certain problematic member might "trigger" you more than others? What do you see the coleaders doing when members display behaviors that could be seen as problematic? What lessons are you learning about how to work therapeutically with resistance of group members? How can you apply the discussion of reframing resistance in this chapter to better understand what is going on in the DVD?

4. **Challenging Members and Creating Linkages.** Establishing trust is especially important as members identify some of the ways they typically protect themselves and express how they are holding back. What are you learning about the critical balance between support and confrontation? As you watch the first segment, how are members being challenged? How do they respond? As coleaders, we are consistently asking members to say more about what they are thinking and feeling as it pertains to being in the group. We also look for opportunities for members to establish linkages with one another and to talk to each other directly in the group. What are you learning about how to encourage members to express themselves more fully?

5. **Using the Workbook.** If you are using the DVD and workbook, refer to Segment 3: Challenges of Dealing With Difficult Behaviors in Group of the workbook and write your comments in the "Reflection and Responses" section. Review the Coreys' reflections on the session and their commentary.

InfoTrac College Edition

For additional readings, explore InfoTrac College Edition, our online library, at http://www.infotrac.college.com/wadsworth. The following keywords are listed in such a way as to enable the InfoTrac College Edition search engine to locate a wider range of articles. The keywords should be entered exactly as listed, to include asterisks, "w1," "w2," "AND," and other search engine tools.

- group* w1 psych* AND control
- group* w1 couns* AND intervention*
- anxiety AND group* w1 psych*
- group* w1 couns* AND support*
- conflict AND group* w1 psych*

Chapter 7

Working Stage of a Group

Focus Questions

Before reading this chapter, ask yourself what questions are on your mind about the working stage. As you read, think about these questions:

1. What are the major differences between a working and a nonworking group? Between a working and a nonworking member?

2. How can a client who has gained insight into the reasons for a problem be helped to act on this awareness?

3. What are the values and limitations of catharsis in groups?

4. What can you do to assist participants in making constructive choices about their behavior in the group?

5. Would you use exercises to facilitate communication and interaction? Why or why not?

6. What is your view of the "ideal" group member?

7. What are three major therapeutic factors that you think bring about change in clients?

8. What specific guidelines would you follow to determine whether self-disclosure would be appropriate and facilitative for you as a leader?

9. What would you want to teach members during the working stage about giving and receiving feedback?

10. What prevents a group from reaching a working stage?

※ Introduction

The working stage is characterized by the commitment of members to explore significant problems they bring to the sessions and by their attention to the dynamics within the group. At this time in a group's evolution, we find that less structuring and intervention is required than during the initial and transition stages. By the working stage participants have learned how to involve themselves in group interactions without waiting to be invited into an interaction.

As members assume greater responsibility for the work that occurs, they play a key role in the direction a group takes. This does not mean that the members become coleaders, but members do initiate work more readily, bring themselves into the work of others without waiting for the leader to call on them, and spontaneously offer personal feedback to others.

There are no arbitrary dividing lines between the phases of a group. In actual practice there is considerable overlapping of stages, and this is especially true of movement from the transition stage to the working stage. For example, assume that Vance says, "There is something I want to talk about, but I'm afraid that some people might make fun of me." If Vance stops with this comment and declines an invitation to say more, his behavior would be transitional. However, if he decides to go further, he may discover that the very people he feared would make fun of him actually support him. With that decision and Vance's willingness to express what is on his mind, he may be able to move to a deeper level of work. As you can see, this shift from transition to deeper work can happen within a very short period of time.

Many groups never evolve to a true working level, but significant work takes place at every stage of a group, not just during the working stage. Even when groups are stuck, embroiled in conflict, or when members are extremely anxious and hesitant, many lessons can be learned. Some groups may not reach the working stage because members do not develop trust, cohesion, and continuity. Group participants who are unwilling to deal with hidden agendas, or who refuse to work with conflicts that are obvious, or who are stopped by their anxieties and fears, are unable to create the climate and cohesion within the group that allows for more productive work. Factors such as time limits and shifting of membership from session to session may also contribute to a group not reaching a working stage. For a group to reach the working stage, it is essential that members make a commitment to face and work through barriers that interfere with the group's progress.

Being in a working stage as a group does not imply that all members function optimally. All members are not at the same level of readiness. Indeed, some members may be on the fringe, some may not yet be ready for in-depth exploration, and some may not feel they are an integral part of the group. Conversely, a very difficult group might well have one or more members who are very willing to engage in productive work. Some may be more motivated than others, and some may be less willing to take risks. Individual differences among members are characteristic of all group stages.

In this chapter we examine these questions:

- What are the characteristics of the working stage of groups?
- How does a leader facilitate a group's movement from the transition stage to the working stage?
- What are some of the therapeutic factors that operate in the working stage?
- What are some of the factors that influence change within an individual and a group, and how do these changes come about?
- How does cohesion foster a spirit of productivity among group members?
- How are leader and member self-disclosures particularly important during the working stage?
- What kind of feedback is especially valuable to members during a working stage? What are some guidelines for giving and receiving feedback?
- What are some potential coleader issues to consider at this stage?

✳ Progressing to the Working Stage

In Chapter 6 we described the characteristics of a group in its transition stage. With a few examples, we now show how a leader's intervention can assist a group in transition to become a working group.

> **EXAMPLE 1:**   Frank and Judy complain that not enough is happening in the group and that they are getting impatient. They are likely to back off if the leader responds defensively. Therapeutic interventions could be any of the following:

- What would you like to see happening?
- I suggest that you tell each person one thing you would like him or her to do to improve this group.
- You might have some reactions to the way I'm leading. Is there anything you need to say to me?

These interventions can help Frank and Judy go beyond complaining, explore the source of their dissatisfaction, and express what they would like to see happen.

When Vince, another member, makes a sarcastic remark ("If you don't like it, leave the group."), the leader can ask Vince to make some direct statements to Frank and Judy instead of dismissing them. As Vince talks about his own reactions to Judy and Frank, he might well identify and get involved in his own issues in a more personal way, bringing into the group some unresolved business he has with others in his life. If the leader does not address Vince's sarcastic remarks, they most likely will have a negative impact on the group.

> **EXAMPLE 2:**   Sunny says that she is afraid of talking about herself in the group because she fears others will judge her. This can be another opportunity for productive work. A good place to begin is with her admission that she feels judged. The leader can further Sunny's work by intervening in any of these ways:

- Would you be willing to talk to one person in here who you think would judge you the most harshly? Tell that person all the things you imagine he or she would think about you?
- Go around the group and finish this sentence: "If I let you know me, I'm afraid you would judge me by . . ."
- Would you be willing to close your eyes and imagine all the judgments people in here could possibly make about you? Don't verbalize what you imagine, but do let yourself feel what it is like to be judged by everyone in the group.

Each of these interventions has the potential for leading to greater exploration, which can assist Sunny in learning how she allows herself to be inhibited by her fear of others' judgments. If she follows any of these leader suggestions, she has a basis for actually working through her fears.

She will probably discover that she makes many unfounded assumptions about people.

EXAMPLE 3:   Jennifer says that she never gets any attention in the group and that the leader seems more attentive to other members. The leader does not convey to her that she is indeed a valued member; rather, he just listens to her and does little with it. He then asks her to talk directly to the members whom she sees as getting more of his attention. After some time, she talks about her feelings about being pushed aside. The leader intervenes with: "I wonder if the feelings you are having in this group are familiar to you in your life outside of group?" This intervention can encourage Jennifer to work in greater depth on connecting her past and present outside life with reactions she is having in the here-and-now context of her group.

If Jennifer acknowledges that she often feels ignored and pushed aside in her family of origin, especially by her father, the leader can give her an opportunity to continue her work by helping her explore some of the ways she might be identifying the leader with her father. Once Jennifer recognizes that she is mixing feelings toward the leader with feelings she has toward her father, she is free to work on her issues with her father. She may find out that she is often overly sensitive to the ways older male authority figures interact with her. She has read into these interactions much more than is warranted.

Jennifer's declaration that she does not get proper attention in the group is a typical reaction during the transition stage. As the leader works with this feeling, Jennifer ends up having new insight regarding how she is making the group leader (and others) into her father. Jennifer's insights and behavior changes are indicative of productive activity in the working stage. The leader's intervention resulted in some significant work on her part. In addition, she might well experience intense emotions over her feelings about her father, and she is likely to express and explore such painful feelings in the group. As a result of her work in the group, Jennifer now pays attention to how she feels when she is with her father and tries out new ways of responding to him. Because she is aware of her tendency to attribute certain qualities to men in authority, she is now in a position to react differently toward them.

✳ Leader Interventions in Working With a Member's Fear

Members may become more aware of their apprehensions as they experience the group process. As the group (and individuals) move through the stages, the leader's relationship with individual members will become deeper, and the leader's interventions will likely be different. To illustrate this progression, let's examine how one member's fear would be addressed at each group stage. Cirecie, a member of an ongoing group, says, "I'm afraid people in here will be critical. I rehearse endlessly before I speak because I want to express myself clearly so others won't think I'm not together." Cirecie is aware that she wants to appear intelligent. She states that her fears get in the way of freely participating in the group. We find that group members often express a range of apprehensions similar to those disclosed by Cirecie, fearing that others will see them as stupid, incoherent, weird, selfish, and the like. The techniques we describe in working with Cirecie's particular fear of being judged can easily be applied to these other fears. The way we work with her differs according to the depth of the relationship we have established with her.

Interventions at the Initial Stage

During the initial stage, our interventions are aimed at providing encouragement for Cirecie to say more about her fear of being judged and to talk about how this fear is affecting what she is doing in the group. We facilitate a deeper exploration of her concern in any of the following ways:

- We encourage other members to talk about any fears they have, especially their concerns over how others perceive them. If Susan also says that she fears others' reactions, we can ask her to talk directly to Cirecie about her fears. (Here we are teaching member-to-member interaction.)
- After the exchange between Susan and Cirecie we ask, "Do any of the rest of you have similar feelings?" (Our aim is to involve others in this interaction by stating ways in which they identify with Susan and Cirecie.)
- Members who have fears that they would like to explore are invited to share their fears with Cirecie. We leave the structure open-ended, so they can talk about whatever fears they are experiencing. (In a nonthreatening way we link Cirecie's work with that of others, and both trust and cohesion are being established.)

Interventions at the Transition Stage

If during the transition stage Cirecie makes the statement "I'm afraid people in here will be critical," we are likely to encourage her to identify ways in which she has already inhibited herself because of her fear of judgment. She can be asked to say *how* she experiences her particular fear in this group. Such an intervention demands more of her than our interventions at the initial stage. We ask her questions such as these:

- When you have that fear, whom in this room are you the most aware of?
- What are your fears about?
- How have your fears stopped you in this group?
- What are some of the things you have been thinking and feeling but have not expressed?

Cirecie eventually indicates she is concerned about how three group members in particular will think about her and about how they might judge her. We suggest to Cirecie that she speak to the people whom she feels would most likely judge her and tell them what she imagines they are thinking and feeling about her. In this way we get her to acknowledge her possible projections and to learn how to check out her assumptions. We are also gathering data that can be useful for exploration later in the group.

We can bring group members into this interaction by inviting them to give their reactions to what Cirecie has just said. The interchange between her and other members can lead to further exploration. She has probably created some distance between herself and others in the group by avoiding them out of fear of their negative reactions. By talking about her reactions to others, she is taking responsibility for the distance she has partially created. She can work out a new stance with those whom she has been avoiding.

The work that we have just described could be done during any stage. What makes this scenario characteristic of the transition stage is the fact that members are beginning to express reactions and perceptions that they have been aware of but have kept to themselves.

Interventions at the Working Stage

If Cirecie discloses her fear during the working stage, we look for ways to involve the entire group in her work. Members may acknowledge how they feel put off by her, how they feel judged by her, or how they really do not know her. Of course, members' reactions such as this would need to be dealt with in an effective way. By expressing feelings that they have kept to themselves, they are moving out of the transition stage and into the working stage. They acknowledge reactions and perceptions, clear up projections and misunderstandings, and work through any possible conflict. The group can get stuck in the transition stage if people do not go further and express reactions that have undermined their level of trust. What moves the group into the working stage is the members' commitment to work through an impasse.

We can use other techniques to help Cirecie attain a deeper level of self-exploration. One is to ask her to identify people in her life whom she feels have judged her, enabling her to connect her past struggles to her present ones. We may then ask her to tell some members how she has felt toward significant people in her life. She may even let others in the group "become" these significant figures and may say things to them that she has kept to herself. Of course, doing this may well serve as a catalyst for getting others to talk about their unfinished business with important figures in their lives.

Here are some other strategies we might use:

- Cirecie can be invited to simply talk more about what it is like for her to be in this group with these fears: "What have you wanted to say or do that you were afraid to say or do? If you didn't have the fear of being judged, how might you be different in this group?"

- Cirecie can role-play with a member who reminds her of her mother, who often cautioned her about thinking before she speaks.
- Cirecie can write an uncensored letter to her mother, which she does not mail.
- By using role reversal, Cirecie can "become" her mother and go around to each person in the room, telling them how they should behave.
- She can monitor her own behavior between group sessions, taking special note of those situations in daily life in which she stops herself because of her fear of being judged.
- Using cognitive procedures, Cirecie can pay more attention to her self-talk and eventually learn to give herself new messages. Instead of accepting self-defeating messages, she can begin to say constructive things to herself. She can change her negative beliefs and expectancies to positive ones.
- She can make decisions to try new behavior during the group, giving herself full permission to think out loud instead of rehearsing silently as she typically does.
- Both in the group and in daily life, Cirecie can make a contract to forge ahead with what she wants to say or do despite her fears.

As can be seen, our interventions in working with Cirecie's fear are geared to the level of trust that has been established in the group, the quality of our relationship with her, and the stage of the group's development. We hope Cirecie has learned the value of checking out her assumptions about others. We challenge her to continue acting in new ways, even if this means putting herself in places where she runs the risk of being judged for some of her thoughts, feelings, and actions. By now Cirecie may have developed the personal strength to challenge her fears rather than allowing herself to be controlled by them. She realizes that it is not necessary for her to think through everything she wants to say. Instead, she can be spontaneous in expressing her thoughts and feelings without expecting judgment. In the final stage of the group, we emphasize the importance for Cirecie to review what she has learned, to understand how she acquired these insights, and to continue to translate her insights into behavioral changes outside of the group.

✳ Tasks of the Working Stage

Even if the group reaches a high level of productivity during the working stage, the group may not remain at that level. The group may stay on a plateau for a time and then regress to an earlier developmental phase characterized by issues faced during the initial and transition stages. Periods of stagnation can be expected, but if they are recognized, they can be challenged. Because groups are not static entities, both the leader and the members have the task of accurately assessing a group's ever-changing character, as well as its effectiveness.

Group Norms and Behavior

During the working stage, group norms that were formed in earlier stages are further developed and solidified. Members are more aware of facilitative behaviors, and unspoken norms become more explicit. At this time the following group behaviors tend to be manifested:

- Members are provided with both support and challenge; they are reinforced for making behavioral changes both inside and outside of the sessions.

- The leader employs a variety of therapeutic interventions designed for further self-exploration and that lead to experimentation with new behavior.

- Members increasingly interact with one another in more direct ways; there is less dependence on the leader for direction and less eye contact directed toward the leader as members talk.

- If interpersonal conflicts emerge within the group, they become the basis of discussion and tend to be worked through. Members discover how they deal with conflict in everyday situations by paying attention to how they interact with one another in the group.

- A healing capacity develops within the group as members increasingly experience acceptance of who they are. There is less need to put up facades as members learn that they are respected for showing deeper facets of themselves.

Group cohesion, a primary characteristic of a well-functioning group, actually fosters action-oriented behaviors such as self-disclosure, giving and receiving feedback, discussion of here-and-now interactions, constructive confrontation, and translating insight into action. Though cohesion is necessary for effective group work, it is not sufficient. Some groups make an implicit decision to stop at the level of comfort and security and do not push ahead to new levels. Groups can reach an impasse unless members are willing to have meaningful interactions with one another. In an effective group the cohesion that has developed marks the beginning of a lengthy working process.

In the next section we discuss the factors that differentiate a working group from a nonworking one.

Contrasts Between a Working Group and a Nonworking Group

The following lists represent our view of some basic differences between working and nonworking groups. As you study these characteristics, think of any other factors you could add. If you are or have been in a group, think about how these characteristics apply to your group experience.

Working Group

Members trust other members and the leaders, or at least they openly express any lack of trust. There is a willingness to take risks by sharing meaningful here-and-now reactions.

Goals are clear and specific and are determined jointly by the members and the leader. There is a willingness to direct group behavior toward realizing these goals.

Most members feel a sense of inclusion, and excluded members are invited to become more active. Communication among most members is open and involves accurate expression of what is being experienced.

There is a focus on the here and now, and participants talk directly to one another about what they are experiencing.

People feel free to bring themselves into the work of others. They do not wait for permission from the leader.

There is a willingness to risk disclosing threatening material; people become known.

Cohesion is high; there is a close emotional bond among members based on sharing universal human experiences. Members identify with one another and are willing to risk experimental behavior because of the closeness and support for new ways of being.

Conflict among members or with the leader is recognized, discussed, and often resolved.

Members accept the responsibility for deciding what action they will take to solve their problems.

Feedback is given freely and accepted without defensiveness. There is a willingness to seriously reflect on the accuracy of the feedback.

Members feel hopeful; they feel that constructive change is possible—that people can become what they want to become.

Nonworking Group

Mistrust is evidenced by an undercurrent of unexpressed hostility. Members withhold themselves, refusing to express feelings and thoughts.

Goals are fuzzy, abstract, and general. Members have unclear personal goals or no goals at all.

Many members feel excluded or cannot identify with other members. Cliques are formed that tend to lead to fragmentation. There is fear of expressing feelings of being left out.

People tend to focus on others and not on themselves, and storytelling is typical. There is a resistance to dealing with reactions to one another.

Members lean on the leaders for all direction. There are power conflicts among members as well as between members and the leader.

Participants hold back, and disclosure is at a minimum.

Fragmentation exists; members feel distant from one another. There is a lack of caring or empathy. Members do not encourage one another to engage in new and risky behavior, so familiar ways of being are rigidly maintained.

Conflicts or negative reactions are ignored, denied, or avoided.

Members blame others for their personal difficulties and are not willing to take action to change.

What little feedback is given is rejected defensively. Feedback is given without care or compassion.

Members feel despairing, helpless, trapped, and victimized.

Working Group

Confrontation occurs in such a way that the confronter shares his or her reactions to the person being confronted. Confrontation is accepted as a challenge to examine one's behavior and not as an uncaring attack.

Communication is clear and direct.

Group members use one another as a resource and show interest in one another.

Members feel good about themselves and others. They feel a sense of power with one another.

There is an awareness of group process, and members know what makes the group function effectively.

Diversity is encouraged, and there is a respect for individual and cultural differences.

Group norms are developed cooperatively by the members and the leader. Norms are clear and are designed to help the members attain their goals.

There is an emphasis on combining the feeling and thinking functions. Catharsis and expression of feeling occur, but so does thinking about the meaning of various emotional experiences.

Group members use out-of-group time to work on problems raised in the group.

Nonworking Group

Confrontation is done in a hostile, attacking way; the confronted one feels judged and rejected. At times the members gang up on a member, using this person as a scapegoat.

Communication is unclear and indirect.

Members are interested only in themselves.

Members do not like themselves or others.

There is an indifference or lack of awareness of what is going on within the group, and group dynamics are rarely discussed.

Conformity is prized, and individual and cultural differences are devalued. Members are disrespectful to those who are different from themselves.

Norms are imposed by the leader without the input of members. These norms may not be clear.

The group reinforces the expression of feelings, but with little emphasis on integrating insights with emotional expression.

Group members think about group activity very little when they are outside the group.

Deepening Trust During the Working Stage

Safety within a group can become an issue even at a later stage of its development, and trust may need to be reestablished. Some members may close off and withdraw because intensive work threatens them, they have doubts about the validity of what they have experienced, they have second thoughts about how involved they want to remain, they are frightened by the display of conflict between members or the expression of painful experiences, or they are anticipating the eventual ending of the group and are prematurely winding down.

The reality of the changing character of trust within a group is illustrated in this example of an adolescent group. Members had done some productive work, both with individuals outside of the group and with one another during the sessions. At one previous meeting, several members experienced intense emotional catharsis. Felix, who had initially identified his worst fear as "breaking down and crying in front of everyone," did cry and released some repressed pain over being denied his father's acceptance. In role playing with his "father," Felix became angry and told him how hurt he felt because of his seeming indifference. Later in this scenario, he cried and told his "father" that he really loved him. Before he left the session, Felix said that he felt relieved.

The particular session just described was characterized by a high level of trust, risk-taking, caring, and cohesion. At the next session, however, the group leader was surprised at how difficult it was to draw people out. Members were hesitant to speak. Felix said very little. The leader described what she saw in the room and asked the members what made it so hard to talk, especially in light of the fact that the previous session had gone so well. Several members expressed annoyance, making comments such as these: "Do we always have to bring up problems in here?" "Do we need to cry to show that we're good members?" "I think you're pushing people too hard." Felix finally admitted that he had felt very embarrassed over "breaking down" and that during the week he had convinced himself that others saw him as weak and foolish. He added that in his culture men never show their tears in public. Some others admitted that although they saw value in what Felix had done they would not want to go through what he had out of fear of what others might think of them. Again, the task of this group was to deal with the lack of trust that members had in one another ("I'm afraid of what others will think of me"). Several of the members' statements implied a lack of trust in the leader, which made it imperative that she encourage the members to discuss this dynamic.

In retrospect, what could the leader have done differently? It is possible that Felix might have felt less embarrassed had the leader remembered his original fear and dealt with it, and also checked out some possible cultural injunctions against public display of emotions. She might have said: "Felix, I remember that one of your fears was crying in the presence of others. You just did. How was it for you to have done this?" She could also have invited others to tell him how they had been affected by his work. Assume that Felix had said: "I feel good, and I got a lot from what I did." Then the leader might have replied: "Imagine two days from now, when you think about what you did this morning. Might you regret what you've done or might you be critical of yourself?" If Felix had replied with a smile, saying: "You may be right," she could have suggested that if he caught himself discounting his work it would be helpful to remember the support he had felt from everyone in the room and how they had acknowledged his courage.

On the other hand, assume that Felix had responded to the leader's inquiry by saying "I feel embarrassed" and looking down at the floor. She might have replied: "I know how hard it was for you to express yourself in this way. I really hope you won't run away. Would you be willing to look at different people in this room, especially the ones whom you feel most embarrassed with? What do you imagine they're saying about you right now?" After Felix told others what he imagined they were thinking of him, they could be invited to give their honest reactions. Typically, members do not make disparaging remarks after someone has done significant work. As this example shows, it is not uncommon for the issue of trust to resurface in an intense and productive session. After times like this, members may be frightened and may have a tendency to retreat. Leaders who are aware of this tendency can take some preventive measures, as we have described. When a group does appear to regress, the most critical intervention is for the leader to describe what is happening and to get members to express what they are thinking and feeling.

Choices to Be Made During the Working Stage

In discussing the initial stages of a group's evolution, we described several critical issues, such as trust versus mistrust, the struggle for power, and self-focus versus focus on others. During the more intense working period of a group, certain other key issues are at stake, and again the group as a whole must resolve the issues for better or worse. These themes include disclosure versus anonymity, honesty versus superficiality, spontaneity versus control, acceptance versus rejection, and cohesion versus fragmentation. A group's identity is shaped by the way its members resolve these critical issues.

Disclosure Versus Anonymity   Members can decide to disclose themselves in a significant and appropriate way, or they can choose to remain hidden out of fear. People may protect themselves through anonymity, yet the very reason many become involved in a therapeutic group is because they want to make themselves known to others and to come to know others and themselves in a deeper way. If the group process is to work effectively, members must be willing to share meaningful dimensions of themselves, for it is through self-disclosure that others come to know them.

Honesty Versus Superficiality   To survive in the real world, some people believe they must sacrifice their honesty and substitute deceit or remain on the surface. They may say that to get ahead they have to suppress what they really think and feel, figure out what others expect from them, and then meet those expectations.

It is fundamental to the success of a therapeutic group that honesty prevails and that members do not have to be dishonest to win acceptance. If these conditions hold, participants can both be themselves and learn to accept the true selves of others. If they do not, what goes on in a group is characterized by superficial interaction. Real intimacy is not possible when people remain unknown or when they remain on a superficial level. Indeed, relationships both within the group and in daily life are enhanced with caring honesty rather than by hiding behind masks. Honesty, however, does not mean saying anything and everything to another person (or about oneself). Saying "I hate the sight of you" is not honest—it is cruel and judgmental. As one of our colleagues says, "Honesty without caring is cruelty."

Spontaneity Versus Control   We hope that group participants will make the choice to relinquish some of their controlled and rehearsed ways and allow themselves to respond more spontaneously to events of the moment. We encourage members to "rehearse out loud" so that both they and others get a glimpse of their internal processing. Spontaneity can be fostered indirectly, by making clients feel that it is all right to say and do many of the things they have been preventing themselves from saying or doing. This does not mean that members "do their own thing" at the expense of others. Members sometimes stifle themselves by endlessly rehearsing everything they say. As a result, they often sit quietly and rehearse internally. We generally make contracts with clients like this, asking them to agree to rehearse out loud and to speak more freely, even at the risk of not making sense. We encourage them to try out unrehearsed behavior in the group setting, and then they can decide which aspects of their behavior they may want to change away from the group.

Acceptance Versus Rejection   Throughout the course of a group the members frequently deal with the acceptance–rejection polarity. We sometimes hear a member say "I'd like to be myself, yet I'm afraid that if I'm me in here, I'll not be accepted. I worry about this, because I often feel that I really don't fit into the group." The basis of this fear can be explored, which most often results in challenging unrealistic fears. Members are likely to find that they reject themselves more often than others reject them. These members may also discover that they are frightened about the prospects of being accepted as well as of being rejected. Although they do not enjoy rejection, it has often become a familiar feeling, and feelings of acceptance can be unsettling: "If you accept me or love me or care for me, I won't know how to respond."

The group setting offers people opportunities to learn some of these ways in which they are setting themselves up to be rejected by behaving in certain ways. We hope group members will recognize their own role and responsibility in the creation of an accepting climate and come to understand that by contributing to a climate either of acceptance or of rejection they can help determine whether they as individuals will be accepted or rejected.

Cohesion Versus Fragmentation   Cohesion is largely the result of the group's choice to work actively at developing unifying bonds. Members do this mainly by choosing to make themselves known to others, by sharing their pain, by allowing caring to develop, by initiating meaningful work, and by giving honest feedback to others.

If a group chooses to remain comfortable or to stick with superficial interactions, there will be little group togetherness. There are times when members choose not to express their fears, suspicions, disappointments, and doubts. When they do conceal their reactions, fragmentation and lack of trust typically result. Cohesion comes from working with meaningful, painful problems as well as from intimately sharing humorous and joyous moments.

Homework During the Working Stage

The group is not an end in itself; rather, it is a place where people can learn new behaviors, acquire a range of skills in living, and practice these skills and behaviors both during the group session and outside of the group. Homework maximizes what is learned in the group and is a means of translating this learning to many different situations in daily life. Members can be encouraged to devise their own homework assignments, ideally at each of the group sessions. If members are willing to create homework and follow through with it, this increases their motivation and the overall level of cohesion in the group.

Although we often suggest to members an activity for them to consider doing outside of the group, we avoid being prescriptive and telling members what they should do for homework. Our suggestions are presented in the spirit of assisting members in increasing the chances of them getting what they say they want from the group experience. As much as possible, homework is designed collaboratively with group members. Frequently we will ask, "What can you do between today and the next session to practice what you are learning in here?" Or we may say, "You are getting clearer about what you want with others in your life. What specific tasks are you willing to set for yourself during the week that will move you closer to what you want?"

We encourage group members to keep a journal, and these writings can be a catalyst to encourage members to engage in new behavior within the group. For example, Phil indicates that he tends to hang back, even though he wants to ask for time and would like to participate more. Typically, at the end of a group session he thinks of what he wished he had said earlier. We are likely to challenge Phil to write in his journal about what goes on with him as he waits and what it is like for him when he leaves the group each time. Then, we invite Phil to make a commitment to state that he will share what he wrote in his journal at the beginning of the group meeting. Making a commitment a week in advance may help Phil to push himself to speak up at the next session.

Oftentimes members do some very intense exploration within the group about significant relationships. Although talking about a relationship can be very therapeutic and members may gain insights into the dynamics of the relationship, this is only the beginning of change. Members then need to decide if they are interested in talking differently to this person in their life. For example, Rosa decides on the following homework. She wants to approach her mother in a different manner than she typically does—without arguing and getting defensive. First she practices in the group what she wants to express to her mother. She receives feedback and support from other members regarding her symbolic interaction with her mother in this way. When Rosa is clear about what she wants with her mother based on her behavioral rehearsal in the group, she will be better prepared to behave differently with her mother. Group practice and homework can often be combined in this way to help members make important changes in their everyday lives.

☀ Therapeutic Factors That Operate in a Group

The therapeutic factors discussed in this section operate to differing degrees in all stages of a group, but they are most often manifested during the working stage. These factors play a key role in producing constructive changes.

A variety of forces within groups can be healing, or therapeutic, and these forces are interrelated. The therapeutic factors discussed here reflect our own experiences in leading groups and the reports of hundreds of people who have participated in our groups. (We ask participants in our groups to write follow-up reaction papers describing what factors they think were related to their changes in attitudes and behavior.) We are particularly indebted to Irvin Yalom (1995) for his pioneering work in identifying therapeutic factors in therapy groups. Additional discussion of therapeutic factors in groups can be found in Chen and Rybak (2004, chap. 1) and Kivlighan and Holmes (2004).

Self-Disclosure and the Group Member

The willingness to make oneself known to others is part of each stage of a group, but at the working stage self-disclosure is more frequent and more personal. Since members are expected to self-disclose in a group, the leader needs to teach and facilitate how to best engage in making oneself known to others. Although disclosure is not an end in itself, it is the means by which open communication occurs within the group. The purpose of the group, the stage of a group's development, the timing, and the depth of disclosures all need to be considered in determining the usefulness of members' self-disclosure.

Group members are able to deepen their self-knowledge through disclosing themselves to others. They develop a richer and more integrated picture of who they are, and they are better able to recognize the impact they have on others. Through this process, the participants experience a healing force and gain new insights that often lead to desired life changes. If disclosures are limited to safe topics, the group does not progress beyond a superficial level.

We tell the members of our therapeutic groups that it is essential to let others know about them, especially as it pertains to their experience of being in the group. Otherwise, they are likely to be misunderstood because people tend to project their own feelings onto members who keep themselves unknown. For example, Andrea thinks that Walfred is very critical of her. When Walfred finally talks, he discloses that he is both attracted to and fearful of Andrea. Walfred can be asked to share what it was like for him to say what he did to Andrea. Self-disclosure entails revealing current struggles with unresolved personal issues; goals and aspirations; fears and expectations; hopes, pains, and joys; strengths and weaknesses; and personal experiences. If members keep themselves anonymous and say little about themselves that is personal, it is difficult for others to care for them. Genuine concern comes from knowledge of the person. As you can see, this disclosure is not limited simply to revealing personal concerns; it is equally important to disclose ongoing persistent reactions toward other members and the leader.

In leading groups, you cannot apply the same criteria in assessing the value of self-disclosure for all members equally. Differences exist among people due to variables such as cultural background, sexual orientation, and age. For example, an older woman who has never publicly talked about some personal aspects of her marriage may be taking large steps in even approaching this subject. Respect the risks she is taking, and avoid comparing her with members who self-disclose freely. A lesbian who discloses difficulties she is having with her partner may wonder if others in the group accept her feelings. A man who discloses that he is gay may experience self-doubts due to internalized homophobia. If this is the first time he has disclosed that he is gay, the leader will most likely want to ask what it was like for him to make this disclosure. The leader needs to be attentive to any possible afterthoughts or regrets the member may have for sharing.

The cultural context also needs to be considered in what you might expect in terms of self-disclosure from some members. For example, it may be overwhelming and frightening if you were to ask a recent Japanese immigrant to participate in an exercise in which members are exploring conflicts with their parents. He may consider any discussion pertaining to his family as shaming or betraying them. In all of these examples, it is important to explore how the members can meaningfully participate in a way that enables them to reach their goals in this group.

What Disclosure Is Not   We have found that group participants frequently misunderstand what it means to self-disclose, equating disclosure with keeping nothing private and saying too much. By displaying hidden secrets to the group, members may feel that they are disclosing useful information, which is often not the case. Those who participate in a group need to learn the difference between appropriate and inappropriate (or useful and nonhelpful) self-disclosure. Here are some observations on what self-disclosure is *not:*

- Self-disclosure is not merely telling stories about one's past in a rehearsed and mechanical manner. It is not a mere reporting of there-and-then events. A client needs to ask the question, "How is what I reveal related to my present conflicts?"
- In the name of being open and honest and as a result of the pressure of other group members, people often say more than is necessary for others to understand them. They confuse being self-disclosing with being open to the extent that nothing remains private. As a result, they may feel exposed in front of others.
- Expressing every fleeting feeling or reaction to others is not to be confused with self-disclosure. Judgment is needed in deciding how appropriate it is to share certain reactions. Persistent reactions are generally best shared, but people can be honest without being tactless and insensitive.

Guidelines for Appropriate Member Self-Disclosure   In our groups we suggest the following guidelines as a way of assisting participants in determining *what* to disclose and *when* self-disclosure is both appropriate and facilitative.

- Disclosure should be related to the purposes and goals of the group.
- If members have persistent reactions to certain people in the group, members should be encouraged to bring them out into the open, especially when these reactions are inhibiting their level of participation.

- Members must determine *what* and *how much* they want others to know about them. They also have to decide what they are willing to risk and how far they are willing to go.

- Reasonable risks can be expected to accompany self-disclosure. If groups are limited by overly safe disclosures, the interactions become fairly meaningless.

- The stage of group development has some bearing on the appropriateness of self-disclosure. Certain disclosures may be too deep for an initial session but quite appropriate during the working stage.

Related to the issue of member self-disclosure is the role of self-disclosures by the leader. We now turn to some guidelines designed to assist leaders in thinking about what disclosures can have a facilitative effect on a group.

Self-Disclosure and the Group Leader

The key question is not whether leaders should disclose themselves to the group but, rather, *how much* and *when*. What are the effects of leaders' disclosures on the group? What are the effects on the leader?

Some group leaders keep themselves mysterious. They are careful not to make themselves personally known to the group, and they strive to keep their personal involvement in the group to a minimum. Some do this because of a theoretical preference. They view their role as one of a "transference figure" on whom their group members can project feelings that they have experienced toward parents and other significant people in their lives. By remaining anonymous, the leader limits the reactions of group members to projections. Through this re-creation of an earlier relationship, unresolved conflicts can be exposed and worked through.

Other reasons group leaders may not reveal themselves personally are that they do not want to incur the risk of losing their "professional" image. Leaders may also operate on the assumption that personal disclosure would contaminate the therapeutic relationship. Some leaders disclose very little about how they feel in the group or how they feel toward members. Instead of sharing these reactions, they intervene, making interpretations and suggestions, clarifying issues, acting as a moderator or coordinator, evaluating, and using structured exercises to keep the group moving.

What about the leaders at the other end of the continuum, whose attitude is the more disclosure, the better? Inexperienced group leaders tend to make the mistake of trying too hard to prove that they are just as human as the members. They freely disclose details of their personal lives and explore their current problems in the groups they lead. These leaders may have submitted to group pressure to stop acting like a leader and become more of a group member. They may also feel that it is unfair to expect members to disclose and risk unless they are also willing to do so. Although this reasoning has merit, it is important that group leaders not fall into the trap of pretending that there are no differences between the roles and functions of leaders and members.

Even though group leaders can function as participants at times, their primary role in the group is to initiate, facilitate, direct, and evaluate the process of interaction among members. If leaders are uncomfortable in this role, perhaps this is an indication that they should be participating in a group (other than the one they are leading) as a full-fledged member.

Consider the following four guidelines in determining your own position on the issue of leader self-disclosure:

1. If you determine that you have problems you wish to explore, consider finding your own therapeutic group. This would allow you to be a fully participating member without the concern of how your personal work would affect the group. You have a demanding job and should not make it even more difficult by confusing your role with that of the participants.

2. Ask yourself why you are disclosing certain personal material. Is it to be seen as a "regular person," no different from the members? Is it to model disclosing behavior for others? Is it because you genuinely want to show private dimensions to the members? It may be therapeutic for group members to know you and your struggles, but they do not need to know them in elaborate detail. For instance, if a member is exploring her fear of not being loved unless she is perfect, you might reveal in a few words that you also wrestle with this fear, if indeed you do. Your sharing makes it possible for your client to feel a sense of identification with you. At another time it may be appropriate for you to talk briefly about how this fear is manifested in the way you lead groups, particularly if it is revealed in your feeling pressured to be a good group leader. Again, the timing and considering the population of your group are crucial in doing what is compatible with your personal therapeutic style. Although this disclosure may be appropriate in the advanced stages of a group, sharing it initially may burden the participants with the feeling that they should help you or should take your pain away. It is important to realize that some group members may respond with embarrassment and discomfort over a leader's self-disclosure, especially if they view the leader as an expert. Certain leader self-disclosure, such as sharing performance anxiety, could diminish members' perceptions about a leader's competence and thus impede establishing trust. Once again, timing is crucial.

3. Disclosure that is related to what is going on in the group is the most productive. For instance, any persistent feelings you have about a member or about what is happening (or not happening) are generally best revealed. If you are being affected by a member's behavior, it is usually advisable to let the member know your reaction. If you sense a general reluctance in the group, it is best to talk openly about the cautiousness and about how it feels to experience it. Disclosure related to how you feel in the group is generally more appropriate than disclosure of personal material that is not relevant to the ongoing interaction of the group.

4. Ask yourself how much you want to reveal about your private life to the many people with whom you will come into contact. In our workshops,

other groups, and classes we want to feel the freedom to function openly as people, but at the same time we want to preserve a measure of our privacy. Moreover, if we always gave detailed accounts about ourselves, we would lose spontaneity. It is impossible to maintain a fresh and unrehearsed style with such repetition.

Later in this chapter we take another look at what research shows regarding the role of self-disclosure in groups.

Confrontation

As was discussed in Chapters 5 and 6, constructive confrontation is a basic part of a productive group. A lack of confrontation can result in stagnation. It is through acts of caring confrontation that members are invited to examine discrepancies between what they say and do, to become aware of potentials that are dormant, and to find ways of putting their insights into action. Sensitive confrontation by others helps members develop the capacity for the self-confrontation, a skill they will need in applying what they have learned to the problems they face in their daily lives. Effective confrontations can result in sustained behavior change.

> **EXAMPLE:**   Alexander complained of feeling tired and drained. He asserted that everyone in his life was demanding. In the group his style of interacting involved being a helper. He was attentive to what others needed, yet he rarely asked anything for himself. In one session he finally admitted that he was not getting what he wanted from the group and that he did not feel like returning again. The leader confronted Alexander: "I have seen you do many times in this group what you say you typically do with people in your life. I see you as being very helpful, yet you rarely ask for anything for yourself. I'm not surprised about your reluctance over coming back to the group. You've created the same environment in here as the one at home. I'm glad you're seeing this. Is this something you are willing to work on?"

Feedback

One of the most important ways learning takes place in a group is through a combination of self-disclosure and feedback. This often leads to deeper levels of intimacy in the group. Interpersonal feedback is a process that influences the development of many therapeutic factors. Through the use of a variety of feedback interventions, group leaders can facilitate growth among group members (Morran, Stockton, Cline, & Teed, 1998).

If feedback is given honestly and with sensitivity, members are able to understand the impact they have on others and decide what, if anything, they want to change about their interpersonal style. The process of interpersonal feedback encourages members to accept responsibility for the outcomes of a group and for changing the style in which they relate to others.

Like self-disclosure, group leaders need to teach the participants how to give and receive feedback. Although feedback as a process in groups is given further consideration in Chapter 8, we want to discuss some guidelines for effective feedback during the working stage. The ideas presented here are modified from Rothke's (1986) article on the role of interpersonal feedback in group psychotherapy and also contain some of the key points we emphasize in teaching members how to give and receive feedback:

- Concise feedback given in a clear and straightforward manner is more helpful than statements with qualifiers. For instance, Lilia is being quite clear and direct with Brian when she tells him: "I feel uncomfortable when I'm sharing very personal things about myself and I see you smiling. It makes me wonder if you're taking me seriously."

- Give others feedback throughout the course of a group. In doing so, share with them how they affect you rather than giving them advice or making an assessment of them. In the preceding example, Lilia is speaking about her own discomfort and how she is affected by Brian's smiling, rather than telling Brian how he is.

- Avoid giving global feedback, for it is of little value. Feedback that relates to specific behavior exhibited in the group provides members with helpful information that they can consider using. Feedback that is particularly helpful deals with immediate events in the group. With this kind of here-and-now feedback, others in the group can confirm the message that is being sent, or they can offer a different perception. Lilia's comments to Brian meet all of these characteristics of specific feedback.

- Feedback must be timed well and be given in a nonjudgmental way; otherwise the person receiving it is likely to become defensive and reject it. In Lilia's case, her feedback to Brian is focused on her feelings, and it represents a risky self-disclosure. She is not judging Brian, which increases the chance that he will be able to consider what she is telling him.

- The most meaningful kind of feedback deals with the relationship between the sender and the receiver. For instance, in giving feedback to Brian, Lilia might add: "I really do want your acceptance, and I'd like to feel closer to you. But I'm aware that I'm careful what I say when I'm around you, because I don't know what you are thinking. When you look away and either smile or frown when I talk, I'm left wondering how what I'm saying affects you. I'd like not to feel so cautious around you, and this is why I'm telling you this." With this kind of statement, Lilia is talking about her feelings of fear and uncertainty, but she is also letting Brian know that she would like a different kind of relationship with him.

- In giving feedback, concentrate on what you like about a person and on the person's strengths, not just on the difficulties you are experiencing with this person. It is a good idea to focus on strengths and how people might be blocking them. One of our colleagues, George Williams, endorses "sandwich feedback." This involves a first slice of bread with some positive statement, followed by the "meaty difficulty," which is then followed by another slice of bread with another positive acknowledgment. For example, a leader might say to a member who is getting lost in the details of her story: "I'm glad you spoke up. I did have some difficulty in following your story and staying focused with you, since you were talking more about others than about yourself. However, I do have a better understanding of your struggle, and I hope you strive to keep focused on your own experience."

EXAMPLE: Members sometimes make a sweeping declaration such as Florian's comment: "I'd like to know what you think of me, and I'd like some feedback!" His spontaneous request puts people in the group on the spot. He has hit the ball into their court. If we were to hear this, we would probably say to the group "Before anyone gives you feedback Florian, we'd like you to say more about what prompted you to ask for these reactions." This intervention puts the ball back into Florian's court, for he will be making significant disclosures about himself rather than insisting that others disclose themselves to him first. Members are more likely to respond to him when they know more about his needs for their feedback. Behind his question may well be any of these statements: "I'm afraid, and I don't know if I'm liked." "I'm afraid people are judging me." "I don't have many friends in my life, and it's important that these people like me."

If Florian has said very little about himself, it is difficult to give him many reactions. To find out how others perceive him, it is necessary that he let himself be known. After he has explored his need for feedback, the group leader can ask members if they want to react to him. However, the leader should not pressure everyone in the group to give him their comments. When people do offer their reactions, the leader can ask Florian to listen nondefensively, to hear what others have to say to him, and to consider what, if anything, he may want to do with this information.

As the group progresses to a working stage, we typically see a willingness of members to freely give one another their reactions. Feedback is at its best when members spontaneously let others know how they are affected by them and their work. The norm of asking for, receiving, and giving feedback is one that needs to be established early in a group. Furthermore, it is the leader's task to teach members how to give useful feedback. Here is an example of this:

EXAMPLE: Ferming joined a group because he found himself isolated from people. Soon he found that he felt isolated in the group also. He was sarcastic in his group, a trait that quickly alienated others. Because the members were willing to tell him in a caring way that they felt put off and distanced by his sarcastic style, he was able to examine and eventually assume responsibility for creating the distance and lack of intimacy he typically experienced. With the encouragement of his group, he sought out his son, toward whom he felt much anger. When he let go of his sarcasm and talked honestly with his son, he found that his son was willing to listen, and they felt closer to each other.

Later in this chapter we look at what researchers have discovered about the role of feedback exchange in groups.

Cohesion and Universality

A central characteristic of the working stage is group cohesion, which results from members' willingness to let others know them in meaningful ways. If members dealt effectively with the various tasks of the earlier stages, this deepens the level of trust, which allows for increased cohesion.

At the working stage members are able to see commonalities, and they are often struck by the universality of their life issues. For example, our therapeutic groups are composed of a very wide mixture of people. The members come from all walks of life, and they differ in many respects: age, sexual orientation, social and cultural backgrounds, career paths, and level of education. Although in the earlier stages members are likely to be aware of their differences and at times feel separated, as the group achieves increased cohesion, these differences recede into the background. Members comment more on how they are alike than on how they are different. A woman in her early 50s discovers that she is still striving for parental approval, just as is a man in his early 20s. A man learns that his struggles with masculinity are not that different from a woman's concern about her femininity. A woman in a heterosexual relationship discovers that she can relate to a lesbian's fear of intimacy in her relationship. Both women are able to connect with each other as they explore their fear of rejection in their relationships.

The circumstances leading to hurt and disappointment may be very different from person to person or from culture to culture, but the resulting emotions have a universal quality. Although we may not speak the same language or come from the same society, we are connected through our feelings of joy and pain. It is when group members no longer get lost in the details of daily experiences and instead share their deeper struggles with these universal human themes that a group is most cohesive. The leader can help the group achieve this level of cohesion by focusing on the underlying issues, feelings, and needs that the members seem to share.

This bonding provides the group with the impetus to move forward, for participants gain courage by discovering that they are not alone in their feelings. A woman experiences a great sense of relief when she discovers, through statements by other women, that she is not strange for feeling resentment over the many demands her family makes on her. Men find that they can share their tears and affection with other men without being robbed of their masculinity. Other common themes evolving in this stage that lead to increased cohesion and trust are members' fears of rejection, feelings of loneliness and abandonment, feelings of inferiority and failure to live up to others' expectations, painful memories, guilt and remorse over what they have and have not done, discovery that their worst enemy lives within them, need for and fear of intimacy, feelings about sexual identity and sexual performance, and unfinished business with their parents. This list is not exhaustive but merely a sample of the universal human issues that participants recognize and explore with one another as the group progresses, regardless of their sometimes obvious differences. Earlier we discussed group cohesion as an achievement of the initial stage of a group. The cohesion that is characteristic of the working stage is a deeper intimacy that develops with time and commitment. This bonding is a form of affection and genuine caring that often results from sharing the expression of painful experiences.

> **EXAMPLE:**   A couple of women, both of whom immigrated to this country, express the pain they feel over having left their own countries. Until this time, they had felt rather isolated from other group members. Sharing their struggle touched just about everyone in the group. Members could identify with their pain and loss even though they did not share the same experiences. The work of these two women was productive for them, but it also stimulated other members to talk about times in their lives when they felt deep loss. During closure of the session, as members made comments about how they were affected by the meeting, they talked about how close they felt and the bond of trust that had developed. Despite having different backgrounds, these group members were brought together by a deeply personal sharing of common themes and feelings.

Hope

Hope is the belief that change is possible. Some people approach a group convinced that they have absolutely no control of external circumstances. Members who are mandated to attend group may feel extremely hopeless and be convinced that nothing will really change. In the group, however, they may encounter others who have struggled and found ways to assume effective control over their lives. Seeing and being associated with such people can inspire a new sense of optimism that their lives can be different. Hope is therapeutic in itself, because it gives members confidence that they have the power to choose to be different.

People are sometimes so discouraged that they are unable to see any signs of being able to change a life situation. Group leaders need to be cautious so as not to get drawn into the hopelessness of such members. It is imperative that leaders approach their groups with a conviction that change and a better outcome are possible—and leaders need to have knowledge of resources that can be useful for members.

> **EXAMPLE:**   Anthony was left paralyzed as a result of a motorcycle accident, and he spent most of his energy thinking about all that he could

no longer do. With the encouragement of his physician, Anthony joined a rehabilitation group where he met several people who had at one time felt as he was feeling. By listening to their struggles and how they had effectively coped with their disabilities, Anthony found hope that he, too, could discover more effective ways of living his life.

Willingness to Risk and to Trust

Risking involves opening oneself to others, being vulnerable, and actively doing in a group what is necessary for change. Taking risks requires moving past what is known and secure toward more uncertain terrain. If members are primarily motivated to remain comfortable, or if they are unwilling to risk challenging themselves and others, they stand to gain very little from the group. Members' willingness to reveal themselves is largely a function of how much they trust the other group members and the leader. The higher the level of trust in a group, the more likely members are to push themselves beyond their own comfort level. From the outset, members can be invited to risk by talking about their feelings of being in the group. As a few members engage in even minor risk-taking, others will follow suit. By taking risks in disclosing here-and-now observations and reactions, members are actively creating trust and making it possible to engage in deeper self-exploration. Trust is a healing agent—it allows people to show the many facets of themselves, encourages experimental behavior, and allows people to look at themselves in new ways.

> **EXAMPLE:**   Carmen expressed considerable resentment to the men in her group. Eventually, she took the risk of disclosing that as a child she had been sexually abused by her stepfather. As she explored ways in which she had generalized her distrust of getting close to men in everyday life and in her group, she began to see how she was keeping men at a distance so they would never again have the chance to hurt her. Finally, she made a new decision that all men would not necessarily want to hurt her and if they did she could take care of herself. Had she been unwilling to risk making the disclosure in her group, it is unlikely that she would have made this attitudinal and behavioral change.

Caring and Acceptance

Caring is demonstrated by listening and by involvement. It can be expressed by tenderness, compassion, support, and even confrontation. One way caring is demonstrated is by staying present with someone who has received some feedback that was difficult to hear. If members sense a lack of caring, either from other members or from the leader, their willingness to make themselves known to others will be limited. Members are able to risk being vulnerable if they sense that their concerns are important to others and that they are valued as people.

Caring implies acceptance, a genuine support from others that says, in effect: "We will accept all of your feelings. You do count here. It is acceptable to be yourself—you do not have to strive to please everyone." Acceptance involves affirming each person's right to have and express feelings and values.

Caring and acceptance develop into empathy, a deep understanding of another's struggles. Commonalities emerge in groups that unite the members. The realization that certain problems are universal—loneliness, the need for acceptance, the fear of rejection, the fear of intimacy, hurt over past experiences—lessens the feelings that we are alone. Moreover, through identification with others we are able to see ourselves more clearly.

> **EXAMPLE:**   Bobby, who was in a group for children of divorce, finally began to talk about his sadness over not having his father at home anymore. Other children were very attentive. When Bobby said that he was embarrassed by his crying, two other boys told him that they also cried. This sharing of loneliness and hurt bonded the children, who learned that what they were feeling was normal.

Power

A feeling of power emerges from the recognition that one has untapped internal reserves of spontaneity, creativity, courage, and strength. This strength is not a power over others; rather, it is the sense that one has the resources necessary to direct the course of one's own life. In groups personal power can be experienced in ways that were formerly denied, and people can discover how they are blocking their strengths. Some people enter groups feeling that they are powerless. They become empowered when they realize they can take certain steps in their current situation to make life more rewarding. However, it is crucial for leaders to understand and appreciate the context surrounding the lack of power that some members may experience. It is not safe for some individuals to assert newly founded power in every life situation. For example, Alfonso's father may never speak to him again if Alfonso asserts himself by confronting his father. Leaders need to assist members in assessing the potential consequences, as well as when and where it may not be safe to express themselves fully. Here is an example of a member reclaiming a sense of power.

> **EXAMPLE:**   As a child, Ethyl was often hit by her parents if she made herself visible. She made an early decision to keep a low profile to avoid being abused physically and psychologically. Through her participation in a group, she discovered that she was still behaving as if everyone was out to get her, and that her defensive ways were no longer warranted. Because she chose not to make her presence known in her group, people saw her as distant, cold, and aloof. Ethyl gradually discovered that she was no longer a helpless child who could not protect herself in a cruel adult world. By challenging her assumptions and by taking risks with people in her group, Ethyl also assumed more power over how she felt about herself and how she allowed herself to be treated by others.

Catharsis

Released energy that has been tied up in withholding threatening feelings can be therapeutic. Unexpressed feelings often result in physical symptoms such as chronic headaches, stomach pains, muscle tension, and high blood pressure. At times we hear group members say that they do not want to remember painful feelings, not understanding that the body can be carrying the pain and giving expression to it with various physical symptoms. When people finally do express their stored-up pain and other unexpressed feelings, they typically report a tremendous physical and emotional release. For instance, Cheryl reported that all of her chronic neck pains were gone after she expressed some very painful feelings.

Although members often report that their cathartic experiences feel good, it is unrealistic to encourage people to give vent to their pent-up emotions in everyday life. If these emotions are expressed when they have been submerged, they can be overwhelming to both the recipient and the giver. It is critical to help members learn how to monitor their emotions and express them in ways that are appropriate to the context of their encounters.

Emotional release plays an important part in many kinds of groups, and the expression of feeling can facilitate trust and cohesion. But it is not true that only experiencing catharsis implies "real work." Members who do not have an emotional release may become convinced that they are not really getting involved. Although it is often healing, catharsis by itself may be limited in terms of producing long-lasting changes. Members need to learn how to make sense of their emotional experiences, and one way of doing so is by putting words to their intense emotions and attempting to understand them.

Often the best route to assisting members in examining their thought patterns and behaviors is by encouraging them to identify, express, and deal with what they are feeling. It can be tempting to emphasize catharsis and view the release of emotions as an end in itself, but this is not the final aim of a group experience. After the release of feeling it is essential to work with a member's insights associated with an emotional situation and the cognitions underlying these emotional patterns. Ideally, group leaders will help members link emotional exploration to cognitive and behavioral work.

In their review of the literature on the role of catharsis in group psychotherapy, Bemak and Young (1998) contend that there is therapeutic value in catharsis if effective interventions are made in a timely way. The use of catharsis is not limited to any particular theoretical orientation and is used in both brief and long-term group psychotherapy. Bemak and Young point out that group therapists can help clients face intense feelings and at the same time also encourage them to translate insights into positive action within the group setting.

EXAMPLE: Selene learned that she could experience both love and anger toward her mother. For years she had buried her resentment over what she saw as her mother's continual attempts to control her life. In one session Selene allowed herself to feel and to fully express her resentment to her mother in a symbolic way. Through a role play the group leader assisted Selene in telling her mother many of the things that had contributed to her feelings of resentment. She felt a great sense of relief after having expressed these pent-up emotions. The leader cautioned her about the dangers of repeating in real life everything that she had just said in the therapy session. It would not be necessary to harshly confront her mother and to expose the full range of her pain and anger. Instead, Selene learned that it was important to understand how her resentment toward her mother was continuing to affect her now, both in her present dealings with her mother and in her relationship to others. The issue of control was a problem to Selene in all her relationships. By releasing her feelings she became more aware that everyone does not control her. It was essential that Selene become clear about what she really wanted with her mother and what was still keeping her from getting closer to her. Selene can choose what she wants to tell her mother, and she can also deal with her in more direct and honest ways than she has in the past.

The Cognitive Component

Members who *experience* feelings often have difficulty integrating what they learn from these experiences. After catharsis has occurred, it is extremely important to work through the feelings that emerged, to gain some understanding of the meaning of the experience, and also to formulate new decisions based on their understanding. Some conceptualization of the meaning of the intense feelings associated with certain experiences is essential to further deeper exploration of one's struggles. The cognitive component includes explaining, clarifying, interpreting, formulating ideas, and providing the cognitive framework for creating a new perspective on problems. Yalom (1995) cites substantial research evidence demonstrating that to profit from a group experience the members require a cognitive framework that will enable them to put their here-and-now experiencing into perspective.

> **EXAMPLE:**   Felix, the adolescent who expressed pent-up hurt, initially felt better after an outburst of crying, but he soon discounted the experience. Felix needed to put into words the meaning of his emotional interchange. He may have learned any of the following: that he was storing up feelings of anger toward his father, that he had a mixture of resentment and love for his father, that he had made a decision that his father would never change, that there were many things he could say to his father, or that there were numerous ways that he could act differently with his father. It was therapeutically important for him to release his bottled-up emotions. It was also essential that he clarify his insights and discover ways to use them to improve his relationship with his father.

Commitment to Change

The commitment to change involves members' being willing to make use of the tools offered by group process to explore ways of modifying their behavior. Participants need to formulate action plans and strategies to employ in their day-to-day existence to implement change. The group affords them the opportunity to plan realistically and responsibly and offers members the opportunity to evaluate the effectiveness of their actions. It is crucial for members to commit themselves to following through on their plans, and the group itself can help members develop the motivation to follow through with their commitments. If members find that carrying out some of their plans is difficult or if they do not do what they had planned, it is essential that they talk about their difficulties in group sessions.

> **EXAMPLE:** Pearl discovered her tendency to wait until the session was almost over to bring up her concerns. She described many situations in her life when she did not get what she wanted. She insisted that she wanted to make some changes and behave differently. The leader issued the following challenge: "Pearl, would you be willing to be the first to speak at the next group session? I'd like you to also think of at least one situation this week in which your needs are not being met because you are holding yourself back. What could you do to bring about a more positive outcome for yourself?" Thus, the leader provided Pearl with alternatives for taking the initiative to try new ways of acting, both in real life and in the group sessions. If she continued to sabotage meeting her needs by not doing what she said she would do, the leader and members might confront her by sharing their observations.

Freedom to Experiment

The group situation provides a safe place for experimentation with new behavior. Members are able to show facets of themselves that they often keep hidden in everyday situations. In the accepting environment of a group, a shy member can exhibit spontaneous behavior and be outgoing. A person who typically is very quiet may experiment with being more verbal. After trying new behaviors, members can gauge how much they want to change their existing behavior.

> **EXAMPLE:** Myrtle said she was tired of being so shy all the time and would like to let people know her better. The leader responded "Myrtle, would you be willing to pick out a person in this group who is the opposite of you?" Myrtle identified Patti. After getting Patti's approval, the leader suggested to Myrtle: "Go around to each person in the room, and act in a way that you have seen Patti behave. Assume her body posture, her gestures, and her tone of voice. Then, tell each person something that you would want them to know about you." As a variation, Myrtle could have been asked to share with all of the members her observations and reactions to them. Yet another variation would have

included asking Patti to be Myrtle's coach and assist her in carrying out this task. It can be surprising how outgoing members are when they pretend to be in someone else's skin. What Myrtle gained from this experiment was the recognition that she did possess the capacity to be outgoing and that she could practice being different by being herself.

Humor

Humor can help group members get insight or a new perspective on their problems, and it can be a source of healing. But humor should never be used to embarrass a group member. Effective feedback can sometimes be given in a humorous way. Laughing at oneself and *with* others can be extremely therapeutic. As a matter of fact, much has been written about the healing effects of humor, and some workshops focus on the therapeutic aspects of humor.

Humor requires seeing one's problems in a new perspective. Laughter and humor can draw everyone in the group closer. Humor often puts problems in a new light, and it sets a tone in a group indicating that work can occur in a context of fun. The power of humor as a therapeutic tool is often underrated. Vergeer (1995) suggests that humor can assist in coping with stress, promote honesty by facilitating self-disclosure, and provide an outlet for frustration and anger. Vergeer states that humor can be useful in both the assessment and the treatment process. It often balances the relationship between members and leaders, it can empower members, and it establishes an environment that is maximally therapeutic to members. Humor is a coping strategy that enables group members to find the absurd or ironic aspects in their situations. It also has a transformational character in that it enables members to gain a sense of perspective and control over situations not under their direct control.

Spontaneity seems to be the key to using humor effectively, for "planned humor" can certainly fall flat. A level of trust must be established before taking too many liberties with humor. This brand of humor is not laughing *at* people but laughing *with* them out of a sense of affection and caring.

> **EXAMPLE:**   Abe was a serious person who tended to sit back quietly and observe others in the group. When the leader challenged Abe on his observational stance, he said that he could write a comedy about this group. The leader knew that he was a creative writer and, hoping to get him involved in verbal ways, asked him to write in his journal a comical account of what he saw taking place in the group. When he later read parts of what he had written in his journal about this group, just about everyone in the group laughed. In the process Abe also shared many of his own reactions to others in the group through his humor. Clearly he was not laughing at them, yet he was able to capture some of the humorous dimensions of what was taking place. By getting active through humor he was able to give a number of members some very insightful feedback, which they would have been denied had he continued sitting silently and observing others. In his account he

was able to capture some very funny sides of his own behavior, which gave others a completely different picture of him.

✳ Research Implications for the Working Stage

In their comparative analysis of research into individual and group psychotherapy, Fuhriman and Burlingame (1990) conclude that these two forms of treatment share many therapeutic factors. Some of the common factors they identify are insight, catharsis, reality testing, hope for change, disclosure, and identification.

Insight is unanimously thought to be a central therapeutic factor in fostering clients' improvement in both individual and group treatment.

Catharsis, or emotional ventilation, is valued as a therapeutic process of both individual and group therapy from a conceptual perspective. However, empirical reviews of individual therapy do not show a consensus supporting the relationship between catharsis and clients' improvement.

Reality testing is provided in a group by both the leader and the members through feedback. There is a great deal of conceptual support for the importance of this therapeutic factor for both individual and group therapy.

Hope for change, or the expectation of improvement, has both conceptual and empirical support in both individual and group therapy and has been shown to be related to clients' improvement.

Disclosure can be divided into two categories: therapist self-disclosure and client self-disclosure. In group therapy there is a considerable amount of evidence suggesting that client disclosure facilitates the development of other therapeutic factors.

Identification is the process by which a client can relate to others. The group therapy literature suggests that clients who identify with both the therapist and with other group members tend to improve more than those who do not. The group process affords opportunities for members to form multiple identifications.

In addition to these therapeutic factors, three group process variables—cohesion, self-disclosure, and feedback—have a central role in determining group productivity.

Research Into Cohesion

Perhaps no other construct in group counseling has received as much extensive and intensive study as has cohesion. Nevertheless, it is difficult to demonstrate a clear relationship between cohesion and the outcomes of a group because cohesion is a multidimensional, interactive construct that can be studied from various perspectives (Fuhriman & Burlingame, 1990). Although cohesion has been defined in a variety of ways, phrases commonly used include a climate of support, bonding, attractiveness, sharing of experiences, mutuality within a group, the togetherness that unites members, a sense of belonging, warmth and closeness, and caring and acceptance. A group characterized by a high degree of cohesion provides a climate in which members feel free enough to do meaningful work. Cohesiveness seems to be a critical factor in the successful outcomes of a group, with members more likely to express what they feel and think, engage in significant self-exploration, and relate more deeply to others (Bednar & Kaul, 1978).

Yalom (1995) maintains that research shows cohesion to be a strong determinant of positive group outcome. Highly cohesive groups tend to be characterized by better attendance and less turnover. The evidence indicates that this stability increases cohesiveness and leads to increased self-disclosure, risk-taking, and the constructive expression of conflicts in the group. Furthermore, group cohesiveness has consequences for other factors contributing to the success of a group. Cohesion operates as a therapeutic factor at first by enhancing group support and acceptance, and later it plays a crucial role in interpersonal learning. Yalom (1995) points out that members of a cohesive group, in contrast to members of a noncohesive group, have these characteristics:

- Members are more interested in influencing other group members.
- Members are more open to influence from others in the group.
- Members are more willing to listen to others and be accepting of others.
- Members experience more safety within the group.
- Members participate more freely and actively in sessions.
- Members self-disclose to a greater extent.
- Members protect group norms and exert more pressure on members who are not supporting these norms.
- Members are less susceptible to disruption as a group when a member terminates membership.

Members of a cohesive group show greater acceptance, intimacy, and understanding, and Yalom (1995) claims that cohesion also helps members recognize and work through conflicts. Members feel free to express anger and deal with conflict if they feel a sense of commitment to the group and if they perceive the group as a safe place.

How, then, is group cohesion developed? If a group is to be cohesive, its members must perceive it as a means to helping them achieve their personal goals. According to Yalom (1983, 1995), groups with a here-and-now focus are almost invariably vital and cohesive. By contrast, groups in which members engage in much "talking about," with a there-and-then focus, rarely develop much cohesiveness.

Cohesion is thought to be one of the crucial factors related to positive group process and outcomes, but despite the vast amount of research on it the literature provides some conflicting conclusions. Rather than being a stable factor, group cohesion is a complex process, and systematic research is needed (Bednar & Kaul, 1994; Kaul & Bednar, 1986; Stockton & Hulse, 1981). Bednar and Kaul (1994) contend that there is no consensus about the definition or composition of the cohesion construct. They compare cohesion to the concept of dignity—everyone is able to recognize it, but no one is able to describe or measure it accurately.

Research Into Self-Disclosure

Like cohesion, self-disclosure cannot be studied and discussed in a simple way. The empirical base for self-disclosure in group counseling is somewhat limited, but it suggests a complex, multidimensional interaction between frequency of disclosure and other factors such as type of group and population, level of disclosure, and timing (Morran, 1982; Stockton & Morran, 1982).

Robison, Stockton, and Morran (1990) found that providing more structure during the early phase of a group increased the frequency of intermember communications such as self-disclosure, feedback, and confrontation. However, members who are not inclined to take risks in a group tend to remain concerned about the undesired consequences of engaging in self-disclosure and giving feedback. When members are provided with an opportunity to discuss and evaluate their concerns about the undesired consequences associated with self-disclosure, their negative attitudes about disclosure tend to be reduced, and they disclose more readily.

Research and clinical evidence clearly point toward the desirability of encouraging the norm of member self-disclosure, but these findings do not demonstrate that more disclosure is always better. There is a curvilinear relationship between self-disclosure and optimal group functioning, and both too much and too little disclosure are counterproductive. Although self-disclosure should be encouraged, a balance must be maintained so that a single member does not lead the others by too great a gap in terms of frequency and depth of disclosure (Yalom, 1995).

After surveying the literature, Dies (1983b) suggests that leader self-disclosure may have either a constructive or a detrimental effect on group process and outcome, depending on specific factors such as the type of group, the stage of group development, and the content of disclosure. Dies concludes that therapist self-disclosure is less appropriate with client populations that are psychologically impaired. Group leaders who are willing to be open about their own reactions to what is going on within the group are more likely to foster development of positive interpersonal relationships. But Dies adds the cautionary note that clients tend to expect the group leader to possess confidence and competence and to provide some initial structuring and direction. Group members may not want leaders to be too revealing of their feelings, experiences, or conflicts early in the course of a group.

Knox, Hess, Petersen, and Hill (1997) conducted a qualitative analysis of client perceptions of the effects of helpful therapist self-disclosure. Their study involved long-term individual psychotherapy, but there may be implications of this study for group leader self-disclosure. Knox and her colleagues found that therapist self-disclosures resulted in positive consequences for clients that included insight or a new perspective from which to make changes, an improved therapeutic relationship, normalization of experiences, and reassurance. Their study revealed that therapist self-disclosures resulted in both positive and negative consequences, yet there were more positive than negative consequences. Here are a few positive consequences of appropriate and helpful therapist self-disclosures:

- Clients perceived the therapist as more human, and they seemed to appreciate the realness of their therapists.
- This increased realness did not appear to result in any loss of status for the therapist.
- The disclosures appeared to equalize the power balance in the therapeutic relationship.
- Therapist self-disclosures resulted in client insights or new perspectives.
- Clients were encouraged to rethink old assumptions about themselves or about others, were able to see solutions to their problems, and acquired a better sense of a developmental process with which they were struggling.
- Clients tended to feel reassured that their feelings and experiences were normal, which increased a sense of universality.
- Clients used therapists as models to make changes in themselves. Therapists' disclosures served as a guide for clients' own thoughts, feelings, and behaviors, both inside and outside of the therapy setting.

The critical aspect is that the group therapist's self-disclosures should be appropriate, timely, helpful, and done for the good of the group members. As a group leader, ask yourself, "How will what I'm about to say be therapeutic or useful to the group members?" Morran, Stockton, and Whittingham (2004) caution that "leaders should avoid self-disclosures that are designed only to impress members, gain sympathy, or unburden personal problems" (p. 99). Group leaders need to accurately assess their own motivations for engaging in self-disclosure and also assess the impact on both individual group members and the consequences on the group as a whole.

Leaders can facilitate interaction within the group by disclosing some of their personal reactions related to the here and now, because this type of information generally pertains directly to member opportunities for interpersonal learning (Morran, 1982). But leaders who disclose to meet their own needs rather than the needs of the members may cause members to question their leaders' capabilities.

Yalom (1983, 1995) stresses that leader self-disclosure must be instrumental in helping the *members* attain their goals. He calls for selective therapist disclosure that provides members with acceptance, support, and encouragement.

For Yalom, group leaders who disclose here-and-now reactions rather than detailed personal events from their past facilitate the movement of the group.

Research Into Feedback

Interpersonal feedback, which occurs when group participants or leaders share their observations, insights, and personal reactions regarding the behavior, thoughts, or feelings of another, is one of the major therapeutic factors in group therapy. The exchange of feedback among group members is widely considered to be a key element in promoting both interpersonal learning and group development (Morran, Stockton, & Bond, 1991; Morran et al., 1998; Morran et al., 2004). Group leaders need to have knowledge about the role of feedback exchange as an underlying therapeutic factor if done properly (Stockton et al., 2004). For members (or for leaders) to benefit from feedback, it is critical that they be willing to listen to the reactions others offer. Members are more likely to consider feedback that may be difficult to hear if there is a balance between "positive" and "corrective" feedback (sometimes referred to as "negative" feedback). With respect to labeling the quality of feedback, we prefer the terms "supportive" and "challenging" as opposed to "positive" and "negative." Furthermore, we believe members can benefit from both supportive and challenging feedback, especially if the feedback is given in a clear, caring, and personal manner.

Kaul and Bednar (1986) suggest that feedback can be considered along a number of dimensions, including its *valence* (the positive or negative nature of the message), *content* (either behavioral, which describes another member's behavior, or emotional, which describes the feelings of the person giving the feedback), *source* (public or anonymous), *form of delivery* (written or spoken), and *time reference* (here and now or there and then). Here are some research findings on these specific dimensions of feedback:

1. Feedback messages are likely to be most effective when they are focused on observable and specific behaviors (Morran et al., 1998).

2. Positive feedback is almost invariably rated as being more desirable, more credible, having greater impact, and leading to greater intention to change than corrective (or negative) feedback (Dies, 1983b; Morran, Robison, & Stockton, 1985; Morran & Stockton, 1980; Morran et al., 1998).

3. Positive feedback is accepted more readily and should be emphasized during the early stage of group (Riva et al., 2004). Positive feedback tends to be useful as a way to reinforce appropriate behaviors at any stage of a group (Morran et al., 2004).

4. Group members tend to be more accepting of positive feedback than of corrective (or difficult-to-hear) feedback, especially during the early stage of a group. Positive and corrective feedback should be balanced during the middle and later stages (Morran et al., 1998; Morran ct al., 2004).

5. Corrective feedback seems to be more credible, useful, and becomes increasingly more accepted by members if it comes during the working and ending stages of the group, but it may also be useful during the transition stage to help the group identify blocks that impede progress (Morran et al., 1998; Morran et al., 2004).

6. Positive comments should be given before negative ones. Corrective feedback is more readily accepted when it follows, rather than precedes, the exchange of positive feedback (Riva et al., 2004; Stockton, Morran, & Harris, 1991; Morran et al., 1998; Morran et al., 2004).

7. Careful consideration and sensitivity should be given to the readiness and openness of a group member before delivering corrective feedback messages (Morran et al., 1998).

8. Group members are more reluctant to give corrective feedback than positive feedback, which may be due to fears of rejection for engaging in therapeutic confrontations and fear of harming the recipient. Group leaders can guide members toward exploring these fears and teach them how to give and receive feedback (Morran et al., 1991).

9. Leader feedback is generally of higher quality than member feedback, but it is not more readily accepted (Morran et al., 1985).

10. Feedback tends to be of higher quality and to be more accepted in later sessions than in earlier ones (Morran et al., 1985).

11. The feedback leaders give may elicit strong reactions from group members. Thus, leaders should carefully evaluate a member's readiness before giving feedback and allow adequate time to process corrective feedback (Stockton et al., 1991).

12. Leaders do well to model effective delivery of feedback and to encourage members to engage in thoughtful feedback exchange (Morran et al., 1998; Stockton et al., 2004).

13. The feedback offered by both members and the leader is useful in reality testing. A group offers opportunities for members to check out some of their assumptions underlying their behavior, and feedback can add realistic and objective perspectives (Fuhriman & Burlingame, 1990). Through a process of feedback exchange members have opportunities to view their interpersonal style from new perspectives and are able to make meaningful changes in their behavior (Stockton et al., 2004).

14. One of the main goals of feedback is to provide individuals with information to correct their distortions and past errors. When reality testing is considered in this light, research shows a relationship between feedback and other therapeutic factors in groups, such as cohesion (Kaul & Bednar, 1986; Morran et al., 1998).

15. In small groups structured feedback contributes to helping members attain their goals (Rohde & Stockton, 1992).

16. To prepare for structured feedback exercises, group leaders can discuss the risks and benefits of feedback exchange and how feedback can be most effectively used within the group (Morran et al., 1998).

17. The impact of the feedback being offered in a group is a reflection of the progress the group has made (Rothke, 1986). If the feedback being given is honest, personal, risky, and deals with interpersonal relationships within the group, this in itself is a sign that cohesion and trust have been established. Feedback that may be difficult to hear must be presented in a timely way and given in a nonjudgmental manner. Otherwise, the person receiving it will probably become defensive and reject it. The quality of feedback exchanged is one of the indicators that the group is moving toward a working stage.

The beneficial outcomes of feedback have been well documented in the group research literature. Feedback has been associated with increased motivation for change, greater insight into how one's behavior affects others, increased willingness to take risks, and group members evaluating their group experience more positively (Morran et al., 2004). In summarizing the research findings, Morran, Robison, and Stockton (1985) identify conditions associated with effective feedback. Feedback is most readily accepted when it is unqualified, refers to specific and concrete situations, is delivered after trust has developed, and describes the giver's reactions rather than being evaluative or judgmental. One of the most powerful tools for encouraging feedback among group members is for the group leader to consistently model effective ways to both give and receive feedback (Morran et al., 1998).

✳ Coleader Issues During the Working Stage

When we colead groups or intensive workshops, we become energized if the group is motivated to work. In effective groups the members do the bulk of the work, for they bring up subjects they want to talk about and demonstrate a willingness to be known. Between group sessions we devote time to discussing our reactions to group members, to thinking of ways of involving the various members in transactions with one another, and to exploring possible ways of helping participants understand their behavior in the group and resolve some of their conflicts. We also look critically at what we are doing as leaders and examine the impact of our behavior on the group. Toward this end we reflect on the patterns of feedback we have received from the members about how our behavior has affected them. We also talk about the process and dynamics of the group. If we find that we have differing perceptions of the group process, we discuss our differences.

We cannot overemphasize the importance of meeting with one's coleader throughout the duration of the group. Many suggestions in earlier chapters for issues for discussion at these meetings also apply to the working stage. Here are a few other issues that are particularly relevant to the working stage.

Ongoing Evaluation of the Group   Coleaders can make it a practice to devote some time to appraising the direction the group is taking and its level of productivity. If the group is a closed one with a predetermined termination date (say, 20 weeks), coleaders would do well to evaluate the group's progress around the 10th week. This evaluation can be a topic of discussion both privately and in the group itself. If both leaders agree that the group seems to be bogging down and that members are losing interest, for example, leaders should surely bring these perceptions into the group so that the members can look at their degree of satisfaction with their direction and progress.

Discussion of Techniques   It is useful to discuss techniques and leadership styles with a coleader. One of the leaders might be hesitant to try any technique because of a fear of making a mistake, because of not knowing where to go next, or because of passively waiting for permission from the coleader to introduce techniques. Such issues, along with any stylistic differences between leaders, are topics for exploration.

Theoretical Orientations   As we have mentioned earlier, it is not essential that coleaders share the same theory of group work, for sometimes differing theoretical preferences can blend nicely. You can learn a lot from discussing theory as it applies to practice. Therefore, we encourage you to read, attend workshops and special seminars, and discuss what you are learning with your coleader. Doing so can result in bringing to the group sessions some new and interesting variations.

Self-Disclosure Issues   Coleaders should explore their sense of appropriate and therapeutic self-disclosure. For example, if you are willing to share with members your reactions that pertain to group issues yet are reserved in disclosing personal outside issues, whereas your coleader freely and fully talks about her marital situation, members may perceive you as holding back. This issue, too, can be discussed both in the group and privately with your coleader.

Confrontation Issues   What we have just said about self-disclosure also applies to confrontation. You can imagine the problems that could ensue from your coleader's practice of harsh and unrelenting confrontations to get members to open up if you believe in providing support to the exclusion of any confrontation. You might easily be labeled as the "good guy" and your coleader as the "bad guy." If such differences in style exist, the two of you surely need to talk about them at length if the group is not to suffer.

✓ *Points to Remember*

Working Stage Characteristics

When a group reaches the working stage, its central characteristics include the following:

✓ The level of trust and cohesion is high.

✓ Communication within the group is open and involves an accurate expression of what is being experienced.

✓ Members interact with one another freely and directly.

✓ There is a willingness to take risks and to make oneself known to others; members bring to the group personal topics they want to explore and understand better.

✓ Conflict among members, if it exists, is recognized and dealt with directly and effectively.

✓ Feedback is given freely and accepted and considered nondefensively.

✓ Confrontation occurs in a way in which those doing the challenging avoid using judgmental labels.

✓ Members are willing to work outside the group to achieve behavioral changes.

✓ Participants feel supported in their attempts to change and are willing to risk new behavior.

✓ Members feel hopeful that they can change if they are willing to take action; they do not feel helpless.

Member Functions

The working stage is characterized by the exploration of personally meaningful material. To reach this stage, members will have to fulfill these tasks and roles:

✓ Bring into group sessions issues they are willing to discuss.

✓ Offer feedback and remain open to feedback from others even though this may increase anxiety for some members.

✓ Be willing to practice new skills and behaviors in daily life and bring the results to the sessions; insight alone will not produce change.

✓ Offer both challenge and support to others and engage in self-confrontation; the work of the group will stop if members become too relaxed and comfortable.

✓ Continually assess their level of satisfaction with the group and actively take steps to change their level of involvement in the sessions if necessary.

Leader Functions

Leaders address these central leadership functions at the working stage:

✓ Continue to model appropriate behavior, especially caring confrontation, and disclose ongoing reactions to the group.

✓ Provide a balance between support and confrontation.

✓ Support the members' willingness to take risks and assist them in carrying this into their daily living.

✓ Interpret the meaning of behavior patterns at appropriate times so that members will be able to engage in a deeper level of self-exploration and consider alternative behaviors.

✓ Explore common themes that provide for some universality, and link one or more members' work with that of others in the group.

✓ Focus on the importance of translating insight into action; encourage members to practice new skills.

✓ Promote those behaviors that will increase the level of cohesion.

Exercises

Assessment of the Working Stage

1. **Key Indicators.** What signs do you look for to determine whether a group has attained the working stage? Identify specific characteristics you see as especially related to this stage. To what degree has your group class evolved to the working stage? To what degree are you accomplishing your personal goals in the group?

2. **Changing Membership in Open Groups.** Assume that you are leading a group with a changing membership. Although there is a core of members who attend consistently, clients eventually terminate, and new members join the group. What obstacles will the members have to deal with if this group is to reach a working stage? How would you work to increase cohesion in this type of group? How would you handle the reality of members' terminating and new members' being assimilated into the group?

3. **Guidelines for Self-Disclosure.** What guidelines would you offer to members on appropriate self-disclosure? How might you respond to this statement made by a member, Carol? "I don't see why there is so much emphasis on telling others what I think and feel. I've always been a private person, and all this personal talk makes me feel uncomfortable." How might you deal with Carol if she were in a voluntary group? An involuntary group?

4. **Effective Confrontation.** There are important differences between effective and ineffective confrontation. How would you explain this difference to group members? Think about how you might respond to a person who had been in your group for some time and who said "I don't see why we focus so much on problems and on confronting people with negative feelings. All this makes me want to retreat. I'm afraid to say much because I'd rather hear positive feedback."

Guide to *Groups in Action: Evolution and Challenges* DVD and Workbook

Here are some suggestions for making use of this chapter along with the working stage segment of *Evolution of a Group*, the first program in *Groups in Action.*

1. **Characteristics of the Working Stage.** In a concise way, identify the key characteristics of a group in a working stage. On the DVD, how does the

group seem different during the working stage than it did during the initial and transition stages? Review the section in this chapter on the contrasts between a working group and a nonworking group. How do these points apply to this group?

2. **Therapeutic Factors That Operate in Groups.** As you view the DVD, look for specific illustrations of members' work unfolding in that group. See the workbook for a few of the scenarios that are played out during the working stage by various members. What can you learn about the value of role playing, encouraging the group members to work in the here and now, and sharing reactions to one another? What is the value of allowing members to express their feelings over painful issues? What is the value of linking members together with common themes and pursuing work with several members at the same time? How does role playing influence the process of the group? On the DVD can you identify one member's work that acted as a catalyst to bring others into the interactions? Both the text and the DVD illustrate examples of symbolically speaking to a parent in one's primary language through role playing. What are you learning about techniques to facilitate self-exploration through symbolically dealing with a parent in a group? How does staying in the here and now enhance the depth of self-exploration?

3. **Working With Metaphors.** The DVD demonstrates ways we, as coleaders, can follow a client's lead by paying attention to his or her metaphors. What can you learn about the value of working with metaphors from this piece of work?

4. **Applying the DVD Group to Yourself.** As you view the working segment, ask yourself "Which member (or members) most stands out for me in this segment, and why? What leader functions do I see being illustrated?"

5. **Using the Workbook.** Refer to Segment 4: Working Stage in the workbook and complete all the inventories and exercises.

☞ InfoTrac College Edition

For additional readings, explore InfoTrac College Edition, our online library, at http://www.infotrac.college.com/wadsworth. The following keywords are listed in such a way as to enable the InfoTrac College Edition search engine to locate a wider range of articles. The keywords should be entered exactly as listed, to include asterisks, "w1," "w2," "AND," and other search engine tools.

- group w1 process
- group* w1 psych* AND cognit*
- group* w1 psych* AND experiment*
- group* w1 psych* AND change*
- group* AND self w1 disclosure

Chapter 8

Final Stage of a Group

Focus Questions

Before reading this chapter, reflect on your own experiences at the termination of a group in which you participated. How did you feel about the ending of your group? What are the leader's responsibilities when bringing a group to an end? As you read this chapter, consider these questions:

1. If a member wants to leave a closed group before its termination, how might the leader best handle the situation?

2. What activities are most important during the closing phase of a group? What are some of the obstacles to effective termination?

3. What questions might you ask members to determine how the group had affected them?

4. How might you deal with members' requests to continue a time-limited group that is approaching termination?

5. How important do you think it is to hold some type of follow-up session? What would you want the group to discuss at such a session?

6. How might you handle an individual's leaving an open group? How would you work a new member into the group?

7. What personal characteristics of yours could get in the way of helping members in your groups deal with separation and termination issues?

8. What specific methods and procedures would you use to help members review the group experience and make plans for using what they had learned that they want to apply to everyday life?

9. What assessment techniques might you use at both the beginning and the end of a group? How can you build evaluation research into your group design? Do you see any value in combining research and practice in group work?

10. What issues would you think of exploring with your coleader after a group terminates?

☀ Introduction

The initial phase of a group's development is crucial—participants are getting acquainted, basic trust is being established, norms are being determined that will govern later intensive work, and a unique group identity is taking shape. The final stages of group evolution are equally vital, for members have an opportunity to clarify the meaning of their experiences in the group, consolidate the gains they have made, and decide what newly acquired behaviors they are committed to bringing to their everyday lives.

In this chapter we discuss ways of bringing the group experience to an end. We show how you can help those who participate in your groups evaluate the meaning of their behavior in the group. We explore these questions:

- What are the main tasks to be accomplished during the final stages of a group?
- What are some techniques that are appropriate during the final stages of a group? What interventions will assist members in consolidating their learning?
- How can members be encouraged to evaluate their satisfaction with each session?
- How does a group complete its unfinished business?
- How can members best be prepared for leaving the group and continuing to carry their learning into everyday living?
- What are the difficulties in saying good-bye, and how can they best be dealt with?
- How can you help members prepare to deal with their tendencies to regress to old ways or to discount the meaning of their experiences in the face of outside pressures and skepticism?
- Are follow-ups necessary? If so, how should they be designed?
- How can leaders get participants to actively prepare themselves for a follow-up session?
- How can members and leaders evaluate the overall group experience?

Several tasks need to be accomplished in the final stage of a group's history, but it is difficult to offer one general guideline that covers all kinds of groups. Many variables must be considered in deciding how much time to allow for ending. For example, the number of sessions devoted to reviewing and integrating the group experience is dependent on how long the group has been in existence and whether the group is an open or closed group. Whatever the type of group, adequate time should be set aside for integrating and evaluating the experience. Several sessions before the last meeting may be required to complete the tasks of the final phase. There is a danger of attempting to cover too much in one final meeting, which can have the effect of fragmenting the group instead of leading to transferable learning.

✳ Tasks of the Final Stage of a Group: Consolidation of Learning

The final phase in the life of a group is the time for members to consolidate their learning and develop strategies for transferring what they learned in the group to daily life. At this time members need to be able to express what the group experience has meant to them and to state where they intend to go from here. For many group members endings are difficult because they realize that time is limited in their group. Members need to face the reality of termination and learn how to say good-bye. If the group has been truly therapeutic, members will be able to extend their learning outside, even though they may well experience a sense of sadness and loss.

As a leader, your task is to assist members in learning to put what has occurred in the group into a meaningful perspective. One of the purposes of a group is to implement in-group learning in the daily life of members. The potential for learning permanent lessons is likely to be lost if the leader does not provide a structure that helps members review and integrate what they have learned. When termination is not dealt with, the group misses an opportunity to explore concerns that will affect many members, and the clients' therapy is jeopardized.

In a *closed* group the task of leaders is to help members review their individual work and the evolving patterns from the first to the final session. Of particular value is having members give one another feedback on specific changes they have made.

An *open* group has different challenges from a closed group because members leave the group and new members are incorporated into the group at various times. Here are some tasks to be accomplished with a person who is terminating membership in an open group:

- It is a useful policy to educate members in an open group to give adequate notice when they decide it is time to terminate. This policy will ensure that members have time to address any unfinished business with themselves or others in the group.

- Allow time for the person who will be leaving to prepare emotionally for termination.

- Give an opportunity to others to say good-bye and to share their own reactions and give feedback. Remaining group members often have feelings about the loss of a member, and it is essential that they have an opportunity to express their feelings.

- Sometimes members will terminate without any prior notice. If it is at all possible, group leaders can encourage such members to explore their motivations for terminating and to remain in the group long enough to address possible reasons for termination.

- Assist the member who is leaving to review what has been learned in the group and, specifically, what to do with this learning.

- Make referrals, when appropriate.

This discussion on the consolidation and termination phase applies to both closed groups (those with the same membership for the group's history) and open groups (those with a turnover of members).

✳ Termination of the Group Experience

Dealing With Feelings of Separation

In discussing the initial phase of a group, we commented on the importance of encouraging members to express their fears and expectations so that trust would not be inhibited. As members approach the ending of the group, it is equally essential that they be encouraged to express their reactions. They may have fears or concerns about separating. For some, leaving the group may be as anxiety producing as entering it. Certain members are likely to be convinced that the trust they now feel in the group will not be replicated outside. A central task of the leader at this time is to remind members that the cohesion they now have is the result of active steps they took. Members need to be reminded that close relationships do not happen by accident; rather, they are the product of considerable struggle and commitment to work through interpersonal conflicts.

Even if the participants realize that they can create meaningful relationships and build a support system outside the group, they still may experience a sense of loss and sadness over the ending of this particular community. To facilitate members' expressions of their feelings over separation, it is important for you, as the facilitator, to recognize and deal with your own feelings about the ending of the group.

At times leaders find it difficult to end a group because of their own discomfort with endings or unresolved issues about separation. They may be too enamored with the accolades they receive from group members who are too quick to ascribe most of the credit of a successful experience to what they did. Although leaders can take partial credit for group outcomes, it is essential that they assist members in identifying what they did to create a successful group. In our experience, when members want to give us more credit than we think we deserve, we may reply with: "There is no magic here. The group was successful because all of us worked hard. If you can remember what you specifically did in here that resulted in desired changes, then you are more likely to be able to create a context for similar changes in your everyday life once this group ends."

Comparing Early and Later Perceptions in the Group

In many of the groups we lead, we typically ask members at the first session to spend a few minutes looking around the room quietly. We say: "As you are looking at different people, be aware of your reactions. Are you already drawn to certain people more than others? Are there some in here whom you already feel intimidated by? Are you catching yourself making judgments about people?" After a few minutes of this silent scanning of the room, we ask members to refrain from sharing anything that they have just thought or felt. Generally, we let the members know that we will ask them to repeat this exercise at the final group session. When this time arrives, we tell them: "Check out the room again, being aware of each person in here. Do you remember the reactions you had at that first meeting? How have your reactions changed toward group members, if at all? How does it feel to be in here now compared with what it was like for you when the group began?" A main task for members during the final session is to put into words what has transpired from the first to the final session and what they have learned about others and themselves. If the group appears different at this final meeting, we ask members to reflect on what they did, both individually and as a group, to bring about these changes.

Dealing With Unfinished Business

During the final phase of a group, time needs to be allotted for expressing and working through any unfinished business relating to transactions between members or to the group process and goals. Some members may not get their issues fully resolved, but they should be encouraged to discuss them. For example, Glen may have unfinished business with another member (or members) or with the leader. It may well be his responsibility for having waited too long to bring up such matters, and he can be assisted in looking at some of the ways in which he got into the situation. Members like Glen may need help in bringing some closure to deeply personal issues they have raised and explored.

It is not realistic to assume that all the issues that were explored will have been worked through. If members are given this reminder a few sessions before the final meeting, they can be motivated to use the remaining time to complete their own personal agenda. We often ask this question: "If this were the last session of this group, how would you feel about what you have done, and what would you wish you had done differently?" In addition, the group may point out many areas on which people could productively focus once they leave the group.

Reviewing the Group Experience

At the final stage of a group we again review *what* members have learned throughout the sessions and *how* they learned these lessons. For example, Adam learned that denying his anger had contributed to his feelings of depression and to many psychosomatic ailments. In the sessions he practiced expressing his anger instead of smiling and denying those feelings, and as a result he acquired important skills. It is helpful for Adam to recall what he actually did to get others to take him seriously, for he could easily forget these hard-learned lessons.

Part of our practice for ending groups involves setting aside time for all the participants to discuss matters such as what they have learned in the group, turning points for them, what they liked and what was difficult about the group, ways that the sessions could have had a greater impact, and the entire history of the group as seen in some perspective. To make this evaluation meaningful, we encourage participants to be concrete. When members make global statements such as "This group has been fantastic, and I grew a lot from it" or "I don't think I'll ever forget all the things I learned in here," we assist them in being more specific. We might ask some of these questions:

- How has this group been important for you?
- In what specific ways has it been fantastic?
- What are a few of the things you've learned that you'd most want to remember?
- What are some of the "snapshots" of the group experience for you?
- When you say that you've grown a lot, what are some of the changes you've seen in yourself?

By asking members to pinpoint what they learned about themselves in the group, they are in a better position to determine what they are willing to do with this increased knowledge. We frequently emphasize to members the importance of putting what they have learned into specific language and stating the ways in which they have translated their insights into action. If they can put what they have learned into concrete, descriptive terms, they are more likely to be able to translate what they learned to daily situations.

Practice for Behavioral Change

In groups that meet weekly there are many opportunities for practicing new behaviors during each group session. It is good to encourage members to think of how they can continue such work between sessions. Members can carry out homework assignments and give a report in the next session on how well they succeeded with trying new ways of behaving in various situations. In this way the transfer of learning is maximized. During the final stage of a group, we reemphasize the value of such actual practice (both in group situations and in outside life) as a way of solidifying and consolidating their learning. We rely heavily on role-playing situations and behavioral rehearsals for anticipated interactions, teaching members specific skills that will help them make their desired behavioral changes. We encourage members to continue to take action and to try out new behavioral patterns with selected others outside the group.

We ask members to look at themselves and the ways in which they want to continue changing, rather than considering how they can change others. If Luke would like his wife to show more interest in the family and be more accepting of his changes, we encourage him to tell his wife about *his* changes and about himself. We caution him about the temptation of demanding that his wife be different. In rehearsals and role-playing situations we typically ask members to state briefly the essence of what they want to say to the significant people in their lives so that they do not lose the message they most want to convey.

Carrying Learning Further

One of the tasks of the final phase of a group is to develop a specific plan of action for ways to continue applying changes to situations outside of the group. Assisting members to carry their learning into action is one of the most important functions of leaders. It is our practice to routinely discuss with participants various ways in which they can use what they have learned in the group in other situations. For many members a group is merely the beginning of personal change. At the end of a member's first group experience she might say, "One of the most valuable things I'm taking from this group is that I need to do more work on how I tend to invite people to dominate and intimidate me. I wasn't aware of how passive I was. I let myself listen to what others in the group were telling me, and I saw how I was backing away from any possible conflict."

If a group has been successful, members now have some new directions to follow in dealing with problems as they arise. Furthermore, members acquire some needed tools and resources for continuing the process of personal growth. For this reason, discussing available programs and making referrals is especially timely as a group is ending.

One strategy for assisting members to conceptualize some long-term directions is asking them to project themselves into the future. The leader can ask members to think of the changes they would most like to have made six months hence or one year hence. Members can then imagine that the entire group is meeting at one of these designated times and can say what they'd most want to say to each other at that time. They can also describe what they will have to do to accomplish these long-term goals.

The technique of future projection, often used in psychodrama, is designed to help group members express and clarify concerns they have about their future. Rather than merely talking about what they would like in their lives at some future time, members are invited to create this future in the here and now. For example, they might role-play with another group member a conversation they hope to have with a loved one. By enacting this future time and place with selected people and by bringing this event into the present, they are able get a new perspective on how best to get what they want.

Giving and Receiving Feedback

Feedback from others in the group is especially helpful to members who identify and discuss changes they expect to make in their everyday lives. This preparation for dealing with others outside the group is essential if members are to maximize the effects of what they have learned. Members benefit by practicing new interpersonal skills, by getting feedback, by discussing this feedback, and by modifying certain behaviors so that they are more likely to bring about desired changes once they leave the group.

Throughout the history of a group the members have been giving and receiving feedback, which has helped them assess the impact they are having on others. During the closing sessions, however, we like to emphasize a more focused type of feedback for each person. We generally begin by asking members for a brief report on how they have perceived themselves in the group, how the group has affected them, what conflicts have become clearer, and what (if any) decisions they have contemplated. Then the rest of the members give feedback concerning how they have perceived and been affected by that person.

A potential problem as a group is ending is that members have a tendency to give global feedback, which will not be remembered nor be very helpful. We caution against expressing sentiments such as "I really like you." "I feel close to you." "You are a super person." or "I will always remember you." In addition, we provide guidelines on how to give meaningful feedback, suggesting that members begin with one of these ideas:

- My greatest fear for you is . . .
- My hope for you is . . .
- I hope that you will consider . . .

- I see you denying your strengths by . . .
- Some things I hope you will do for yourself are . . .
- Some ways I hope you will be different with others are . . .

Here are some examples of specific comments that members are likely to remember after a group ends:

- I want you to remember that the reason you and I felt distant from each other is that we were scared of each other. What brought us closer is that we talked about those fears and assumptions.
- I like your ability to be direct and honest in giving feedback while at the same time treating people with dignity.
- I remember that I liked you much better when you stopped being sarcastic.
- The times you gave advice, people tended to reject it. They responded more favorably to you when you shared your own struggles rather than giving them solutions.
- I would like you to remember how easy it was for me to respond to you when you stopped bombarding me with questions and instead started to tell me about yourself.
- My fear for you is that you will forget that you are judging yourself more harshly than others do.
- Remember that your isolation not only keeps others away from you but also keeps you lonely.
- My hope for you is that when you criticize yourself and tell yourself that you are not enough you will listen to the other voice that tells you differently.

Feedback in the later stages of a group needs to focus on integration and synthesis of learning. As the group nears termination, constructive feedback is stated in such a manner that the individual is given an opportunity for closure. It is not the time for members to unload stored-up negative reactions, for the member being confronted does not have a real opportunity to work through this feedback.

During this feedback session, we emphasize that participants can make some specific contracts to explore further areas after the group ends. We suggest some type of group follow-up session at a later date, which gives the members added incentive to think about ways to keep their new decisions alive.

The Use of a Contract and Homework

One useful way to assist members in continuing the new beginnings established during the group is to devote time during one of the final sessions to writing contracts. These contracts outline steps the members agree to take to increase their chances of successfully meeting their goals when the group ends. It is essential that the members themselves develop their own contracts and that the plan is not so ambitious that they are setting themselves up for failure.

If the participants choose to, they can read their contracts aloud so others can give specific helpful feedback. It is also of value to ask members to select at least one person in the group to whom they can report on their progress toward their goals, especially now when they are about to lose the support of their weekly group. This arrangement is useful not only for encouraging accountability but also for teaching people the value of establishing a support system as a way to help them bring about desired changes. Here are a few illustrations of contracts members have made during final group sessions:

- Josh has worked on speaking up more frequently in his classes. He contracts to continue his verbal participation in class and to call at least two members at the end of the semester to let them know about his progress.

- Miriam contracts to call Berrin when she feels misunderstood by her husband and wants to shut him out.

Triangulation?

- Roland has explored his tendency to isolate himself from people and has made some gains in reaching out to others, both in and out of group. He says that he feels better about himself, and he contracts with Venetia and Mayra to call them once a month to simply talk to them.

- Jason became aware of his bias against people who think and act differently from him. In his group he has challenged himself to approach members that he might shy away from because of such differences, which resulted in favorable outcomes. Jason wants to continue this new behavior when he leaves the group. He contracts to call several of the group members that he initially backed away from to inform them of his progress.

We have recommended using homework during all the stages of a group. As a group is approaching its ending phase, however, homework of a different nature must be crafted. Homework can be included in the contracts members formulate, and measures can be discussed that will help members when the assignments they have given themselves do not materialize as they had expected.

Dealing With Setbacks

Even with hard work and commitment, members will not always get what they expected from their encounters. During the final stages of a group, it is helpful to reinforce members so that they can cope with realistic setbacks and avoid getting discouraged and giving up. Assisting members in creating a support system is a good way to help them deal with setbacks and keep focused on what they need to do to accomplish their goals.

It is very important to have a discussion about regressions and how to cope with unexpected outcomes. The chances of disappointing outcomes are lessened if members have given themselves homework that is manageable. It is essential to tailor homework to each member's contract and to caution members about overambitious plans. If there is a follow-up meeting after the group terminates, this is an excellent time to reevaluate contracts and evaluate the degree to which members' homework is effective. (We consider follow-up meetings later in this chapter.) We always stress to members how important it is that they attend the follow-up meeting, especially if they have not done all that they had agreed to do after the termination of the group. The follow-up session is another opportunity to evaluate each member's plan for future action.

Guidelines for Applying Group Learning to Life

Certain behaviors and attitudes increase the chances that meaningful self-exploration will occur in a group. At this time we suggest that you refer to the section in Chapter 5 that deals with guidelines on getting the most from a group experience. As members enter a group during the early phase, we teach them how to actively involve themselves. This teaching continues throughout the life of the group. At the final phase we reinforce some teaching points to help members consolidate what they have learned and to apply their learning to daily life. Toward the end of a group, the participants are likely to be receptive to considering how they can implement what they have learned.

Realize That the Group Is a Means to an End   We do not consider a group experience an end in itself. Although feeling close may be pleasant, the purpose of a group is to enable participants to make decisions about how they will change their lives in the real world. Groups that are therapeutic encourage people to look at themselves, to decide whether they like what they see, and if they so desire, to make plans for change.

As a group approaches termination, it is your task to help members reflect on *what* they have learned, *how* they have learned it, and *what* they intend to continue doing with their insights. Members are then in a position to decide what they are willing to do about what they have learned.

Realize That Change May Be Slow and Subtle   People sometimes expect change to come about automatically, and once they do make changes, they may expect them to be permanent. This expectation can lead to discouragement when temporary setbacks occur. Ideally, members will bring these setbacks back to their group. This realization that the process of change can be slow makes useful material for exploration in a group.

Do Not Expect One Group Alone to Change Your Life   Those who seek a therapeutic group sometimes cling to unrealistic expectations. They expect rapid, dramatic change. Members need to be reminded that a single therapeutic experience, as potent as it may be in itself as a catalyst for significant change, is rarely sufficient to sustain these decisions. People spend many years creating a unique personality with its masks and defenses. It takes time to establish constructive alternatives. People do not easily relinquish familiar defenses, for even though the defenses may entail some pain, they do work. In some ways, the change process is just that—a process, not a final state.

Decide What to Do With What You Have Learned   At its best a group will provide moments of truth during which clients can see who they are and how they present themselves to others. Ultimately, it is up to the members to do something with the glimpses of truth they gain. Many people seek therapy because they have lost the ability to live their lives meaningfully and have become dependent on others to direct their lives and take responsibility for their decisions. They expect the group to decide for them, or they are sensitively attuned to being what the group expects them to be. If groups are truly useful, members will learn to make decisions about how they want to be different in everyday life.

Some Final Considerations

As our groups are coming to an end, we take the opportunity to remind participants of a few concerns, especially about maintaining confidentiality once the group ends and how to lessen the chance of forgetting the lessons they have learned.

At the final session we again comment on the importance of keeping confidentiality, even after the group has ended. We caution that confidences are often divulged unintentionally by members enthusiastically wanting to share with others the details of their group experience. We provide examples of how they can talk about the group without breaking confidences. A suggestion we offer is that members can tell others *what* they learned but should be careful about describing the details of *how* they learned something. It is when members discuss the "how" of their experience that they are inclined to inappropriately refer to other members. Also, we encourage participants to talk about themselves and not about the problems of other participants.

We have observed that even enthusiastic group members are not beyond forgetting and discounting what they have learned soon after the termination of their group. This is especially true if they leave a supportive group and go out into an environment that is not supportive or speaks disparagingly about the changes they are making. For example, Dennis learned the value of being open and direct with people in the group. Later he tried this same approach with certain people at work, only to meet with negative reactions. Before the group ends, we ask members such as Dennis to imagine how they might discount the value of the lessons they have learned when they are faced with people who do not appreciate their changes. In the case of Dennis we might have said: "So talk out loud now about how honesty doesn't really work in everyday life. How might you convince yourself that the only place you can be direct and honest with people is in this group?" If people are able to foresee how they might minimize what they learned from their group experience, they are less likely to do so.

✳ Evaluation of the Group Experience

Evaluation is a basic aspect of any group experience, and it can benefit both members and the leader. Some type of rating scale can be devised to give the leader a good sense of how each member experienced and evaluated the group. Standardized instruments can also tap individual changes in attitudes and values. Such practical evaluation instruments can help members make a personal assessment of the group and can also help the leader know what interventions were more, or less, helpful. A willingness to build evaluation into the structure of the group is bound to result in improving the design of future groups.

After a group ends, we have at times sent out a questionnaire to the members. It is quite possible for members to have different perceptions about the group once they have had some distance from it. Asking members to address in writing some of our questions encourages them to again reflect and one more time put into words the meaning of their experience in the group. By writing about their perceptions of the group experience, they are able to evaluate how effective the group has been for them. The responses we receive from the members tell us whether we succeeded in our therapeutic efforts and how we might modify our approach for future groups.

Here is a sample questionnaire:

1. What general effect has your group experience had on your life?

2. What were some specific things you became aware of about your lifestyle, attitudes, and relationships with others? What are some changes you have made in your life that you can attribute at least partially to your group experience?

3. What problems did you encounter on leaving the group and following up on your decisions to change?

4. What effects do you think your participation in the group had on the significant people in your life?

5. Have there been any crises in your life since the termination of the group? How did you handle them?

6. How might your life be different now had you not experienced the group?

7. Do you have anything else to say about yourself and your experience either during or since the group?

We use the following measures to evaluate the effectiveness of our groups:

- We conduct individual follow-up interviews with members or keep in contact with members; letters and telephone conversations have been substituted when person-to-person interviews were not feasible.

- We hold one or more postgroup meetings, which will be described in a later section.

- We ask members to complete brief questionnaires, such as the one included here, to assess what they found most and least valuable in their group experience.

- We ask or require (depending on the type of group) that members keep process notes in a journal. On the basis of their journal notes, which are private, members write several reaction papers describing their subjective experience in the group as well as what they are doing outside the group. These reaction papers are given to us both during the life of the group and after the group has terminated.

Members have continued to report to us that they found the writing they did both during and after the group extremely valuable to them in maintaining their commitment to change. By writing members are able to focus on relevant trends and the key things they are discovering about themselves. Through the use of journals, they have a chance to privately clarify what they are experiencing and to rehearse what they want to say to significant people. Their writing also gives them a chance to recall turning points in the group for them, helps them evaluate the impact of the group in retrospect, and gives them a basis for putting this experience into meaningful perspective.

✳ Coleader Issues as the Group Ends

It is critical that coleaders agree on termination. They need to be in tune with each other about not bringing up new material that cannot be dealt with adequately before the end of the group. Members sometimes save up topics until the very end, almost hoping that there will be no time to explore them. It could be tempting to one of the coleaders to initiate new work with such a member; the other coleader may be ready to bring the group to an end.

Here are some specific topics that you can discuss with your coleader during the final stage to ensure that you are working together:

- Are either of you concerned about any members? Are there any things you might want to say to certain members?

- Do you or your coleader have perceptions and reactions about the group that would be useful to share with the members before the final session?

- Are both of you able to deal with your own feelings of separation and ending? If not, you may collude with the members by avoiding talking about feelings pertaining to the termination of the group.

- Have both of you given thought to how you can best help members review what they have learned from the group and translate this learning to everyday situations?

- Do you have some plan to help members evaluate the group experience before the end of the group or at a follow-up session?

Once the group ends, we encourage coleaders to meet to discuss their experience in leading with each other and to put the entire history of the group in perspective. This practice is consistent with the ASGW (1998) "Best Practice Guidelines," which encourage leaders to process the workings of the group with themselves, group members, supervisors, or other colleagues. The guideline is: "Processing may occur both within sessions and before or after each session, at time of termination, and later follow-up, as appropriate" (C.1). Here are some ideas that you might want to process with your coleader as a way to integrate your experiences and learning:

- Discuss the balance of responsibility between the coleaders. Did one coleader assume primary responsibility for directing while the other followed? Did one leader overshadow the other?

- Was one coleader overly supportive and the other overly confrontational?

- How did your styles of leadership blend, and what effect did this have on the group?

- Did you agree on basic matters such as evaluation of the group's direction and what was needed to keep the group progressing?

- Talk about what you liked and what was challenging about leading with each other. You can benefit by a frank discussion of what each of you learned from the other personally and professionally, including weaknesses and strengths, skills, and styles of leading.

- Evaluate each other in addition to evaluating yourself. Comparing your self-evaluation as a leader with your coleader's evaluation of you can be of great value. Look for areas needing further work; in this way each of you can grow in your capacity to lead effectively.

- You both can learn much from reviewing the turning points in the group. How did the group begin? How did it end? What happened in the group to account for its success or failure? This type of overall assessment helps in understanding the group process, which can be essential information in leading future groups.

It is a good policy for group leaders to write an assessment of the group as a whole and to also make summary comments about individual members, if appropriate. Keeping good notes, especially about the progress of a group, is particularly helpful in terms of making changes in future groups.

✳ Follow-Up

Postgroup Sessions

A follow-up group session scheduled sometime after the termination of a group can be an invaluable accountability measure. Such evaluation and follow-up is recommended by the ASGW (1998) "Best Practice Guidelines": "Group Workers conduct follow-up contact with group members, as appropriate, to assess outcomes or when requested by a group member(s)" (C.3).

Because members know that they will come together to evaluate their progress toward their stated goals, they are likely to be motivated to take steps to make changes. Participants can develop contracts at the final sessions that involve action between the termination and the follow-up session. Members often use one another as a support system. If they experience difficulties in following through on their commitments after the group, they can discuss these difficulties. It is a matter not so much of relying on one another for advice as of using the resources of the group for support.

At follow-up sessions the participants can share difficulties they have encountered since leaving the group, talk about specific steps they have taken to keep themselves open for change, and remember some of the most positive experiences during the group itself. Follow-ups also give members a chance to express and possibly work through any afterthoughts or feelings connected with the group experience. When a group has been cohesive at the end, there may be a temptation for members to dismiss any feelings of regrets about their role in a group. However, as they gain distance from a group experience, they may identify certain regrets or afterthoughts. A follow-up meeting provides an avenue to express such thoughts and feelings about their group experience after the passage of some time. This reduces the risks involved in a group.

In our groups, we make sure that group members know about the goals for a follow-up session. It is not geared to doing new work; rather, this session is for finding out what people did with their experience in the group in their daily living. The members are asked to report on whether and how they are using their expanded self-awareness in their relationships in the outside world. The follow-up group session is a means of accountability for both the leader and the members. We ask members at the follow-up session whether they are continuing to reach out for what they want. What changes are they making, if any? Are they taking more risks? If they are trying out new behavior, what results are they getting? These are a few topics that we explore during this session. For additional topics and questions, refer to the questionnaire described earlier that we use as a basis for evaluation.

A follow-up session offers us one more opportunity to remind people that they are responsible for what they become and the necessity of taking risks in order to change. The follow-up session provides a timely opportunity to encourage and to discuss once more other avenues for continuing the work they did in group.

If you administered any pretests to assess beliefs, values, attitudes, and levels of personal adjustment, the postgroup meeting is an ideal time to administer some of these same instruments for comparison purposes. We support the practice of developing an assessment instrument that can be given before members join a group (or at the initial session), again at one of the last sessions, and finally at some time after termination. If you meet with the members on an individual basis to review how well they have accomplished their personal goals, these assessment devices can be of value in discussing specific changes in attitudes and behaviors.

Of course, follow-up group sessions are not always practical or possible. Alternatives can be developed, such as sending a brief questionnaire, which we described earlier, to assess members' perceptions about the group and its impact on their lives. Members can also be contacted for individual follow-up sessions. Note that it is important to have advanced informed consent about how to contact members to avoid potential invasion of privacy or breach of confidentiality.

Individual Follow-Up Interviews

If group follow-up sessions are impractical, an alternative is one-to-one sessions with as many members as possible. Though ideally it is a good practice to meet with each member, even if the session lasts only 15 minutes, we realize the practical problems in arranging these sessions. If you are working in private practice, in a school setting, or in an institution and see the members on a fairly regular basis, then such follow-up interviews may be realistic. In other cases the members may never be seen again.

The individual screening interview as a part of the formation of a group aims at ascertaining why people would like to join a group, helping them identify some personal goals, and discussing their expectations. The postgroup interview can be used to determine the degree to which members have accomplished their stated goals and met their expectations. Participants can also discuss what the group meant to them in retrospect. In addition, this one-on-one interview provides an ideal opportunity to discuss referral resources, should they be indicated. In our opinion this practice is one of the best ways for a leader to evaluate the effectiveness of a group.

The individual follow-up sessions can be very informal, or they can be structured with a common set of questions the leader asks of each member. Of course, members should be given latitude to say whatever they want and not merely answer questions. The questionnaire to evaluate a group experience that we presented earlier can be used for individual follow-up meetings as well. You can adapt your questions to the population of your group. The data from these individual sessions, especially when combined with a follow-up group session, provide valuable information for improving future groups.

In open groups it is not feasible to arrange for group follow-up sessions because the membership changes over a period of time. However, it is an excellent practice to schedule an individual follow-up session about a month after a member terminates. This gives both the member and the leader an opportunity to review significant turning points in the group as well as the ways in which the group experience has influenced the member's behavior.

√ *Points to Remember*

Final Stage Characteristics

During the final phase of a group these characteristics are typically evident:

✓ There may be some sadness and anxiety over the reality of separation.

✓ Members are likely to pull back and participate in less intense ways in anticipation of the ending of the group.

✓ Members are deciding what courses of action they are likely to take.

✓ There may be some fears of separation as well as fears about being able to carry over into daily life some of what was experienced in the group.

✓ Members may express their fears, hopes, and concerns for one another.

✓ Group sessions may be devoted partly to preparing members to meet significant others in everyday life. Role playing and behavioral rehearsal for relating to others more effectively are common.

✓ Members will hopefully be involved in evaluation of the group experience.

✓ There may be some talk about follow-up meetings or some plan for accountability so that members will be encouraged to carry out their plans for change.

Member Functions

The major task facing members during the final stage of a group is consolidating their learning and transferring it to the outside environment. This is the time for them to review and put into some cognitive framework the meaning of the group experience. Here are some tasks for members at this time:

✓ Deal with feelings about separation and termination so members do not distance themselves from the group.

✓ Prepare to generalize learning to everyday life so members do not get discouraged and discount the value of the group work.

✓ Complete any unfinished business, either issues brought into the group or issues that pertain to people in the group.

✓ Evaluate the impact of the group and remember that change takes time, effort, and practice.

✓ Make decisions and plans concerning changes members want to make and how they will go about making them.

After their group ends, the members' main functions are applying in-group learning to an action program in their daily lives, evaluating the group, and attending some type of follow-up session (if practical). Here are some key tasks for members:

✓ Find ways to reinforce themselves without the support of the group.

✓ Find ways to continue new behaviors through some kind of self-directed program for change without the supportive environment of the group.

Leader Functions

The group leader's central goals in the consolidation phase are to provide a structure that enables participants to clarify the meaning of their experiences in the group and to assist members in generalizing their learning from the group to everyday life. Here are some group leader tasks at this stage:

✓ Assist members in dealing with any feelings they might have about termination.

✓ Provide members with an opportunity to express and deal with any unfinished business within the group.

✓ Reinforce changes members have made and ensure that members have information about resources to enable them to make further progress.

✓ Assist members in determining how they will apply specific skills in a variety of situations in daily life.

✓ Work with members to develop specific contracts and homework assignments as practical ways of making changes.

✓ Assist participants in developing a conceptual framework that will help them understand, integrate, consolidate, and remember what they have learned in the group.

✓ Provide opportunities for members to give one another constructive feedback.

✓ Reemphasize the importance of maintaining confidentiality after the group is over.

After the termination of a group, leaders have these tasks:

✓ Offer private consultations if any member should need this service, at least on a limited basis, to discuss members' reactions to the group experience.

✓ If applicable, provide for a follow-up group session or follow-up individual interviews to assess the impact of the group.

✓ Provide specific referral resources for members who want or need further consultation.

✓ Encourage members to find some avenues of continued support and challenge so that

the ending of the group can lead to new directions.

✓ If applicable, meet with the coleader to assess the overall effectiveness of the group.

✓ Administer some type of end-of-group assessment instrument to evaluate the nature of individual changes and the strengths and weaknesses of the group.

✓ Document a summary report of the group and file your records in a confidential location.

Exercises

Final Stage of a Group

Here are a few exercises appropriate to the final stage of a group. Again, most of the exercises we suggest are suitable both for a classroom and for a counseling group.

1. **Discounting.** When Sophia left her group, she felt close to many people and decided that it was worth it to risk getting close. She tried this at work, was rebuffed, and began telling herself that what she had experienced in the group was not real. Discounting the group experience or allowing old

patterns to block establishment of new behaviors are common reactions after a group ends. For this exercise imagine all the things you might say to yourself to sabotage your plans for change. The idea is to openly acknowledge tendencies you have that will interfere with establishing new behavior.

2. **Group Termination.** Students take turns pretending that they are leaders and that the class is a group about to terminate. Consider how to prepare members for leaving a group.

3. **Termination Interview.** A person in the class volunteers to become a group leader and to conduct an interview with a group member (also a volunteer) as though they had just completed a group experience together. For about 10 minutes the group leader interviews the client regarding the nature of his or her group experience. After the exercise the client reacts to the interview.

4. **Future Projection.** During the last session, members can be asked to imagine that it is 1 year (or 5 years or 10 years) in the future, and the group is meeting for a reunion. What would they most hope to be able to say to the group about their lives, the changes they have made, and the influence the group had on them? What fears might they have concerning this reunion?

5. **Remembering.** It is helpful to simply share memories and turning points during the group's history. Members could be given the task of recalling events and happenings that most stand out for them.

6. **Working on Specific Contracts.** During the final sessions, members might formulate contracts that state specific actions they are willing to take to enhance the changes they have begun. These contracts can be written down and then read to the group. Others can give each member feedback and alternative ways of completing the contract.

7. **Reviewing the Class and Group Experience.** Form small groups and discuss what you have learned about yourself up to this point that you think would either contribute to or detract from your effectiveness as a group leader. How willing have you been to take risks in this class? What have you learned about how groups best function (or what gets in the way of an effective group) through your experience in your class and your group experience? To what degree did you accomplish your personal goals in your group? How did your group deal with the tasks of termination? What were significant turning points in your group? As a group, how would you evaluate the level of interaction and the cohesion attained?

Guide to *Groups in Action: Evolution and Challenges* DVD and Workbook

Here are some suggestions for making use of this chapter along with the final stage segment of *Evolution of a Group*.

1. **Tasks of the Final Stage.** Review the tasks that need to be accomplished during the final stage of the group that are presented in this chapter. As you

study the ending stage of the DVD group, how do you see these tasks being accomplished?

2. **Termination of the Group Experience.** How are the group members prepared for the termination of a group? How do the members conceptualize their learnings? How does the group seem different at this stage than during the early phase of its development?

3. **Using the Workbook.** Refer to Segment 5: Ending Stage in the workbook and complete all the exercises. Reading this section and addressing the questions will help you conceptualize group process by integrating the text with the DVD and the workbook.

InfoTrac College Edition

For additional readings, explore InfoTrac College Edition, our online library, at http://www.infotrac.college.com/wadsworth. The following keywords are listed in such a way as to enable the InfoTrac College Edition search engine to locate a wider range of articles. The keywords should be entered exactly as listed, to include asterisks, "w1," "w2," "AND," and other search engine tools.

- group* w1 psych* AND evaluation
- group* w1 psych* AND follow w1 up
- group* w1 psych* AND review NOT book

Application of Group Process to Specific Groups

Part 3 illustrates how group process concepts and practices are used in groups geared to the needs of particular client populations. Group leaders who work with children, adolescents, adults, and the elderly each have special responsibilities. Guest contributors help us describe how to set up these specialized groups and share approaches that may be useful as you design your own groups. In setting up and leading any of these special types of groups, leaders must have the necessary competence to facilitate them. In addition to skills and knowledge about group process, group leaders must be familiar with the particular needs of the target population for a group.

Students in counseling and related programs must often complete an internship involving work with a variety of people—children or adolescents, the elderly, clients with substance abuse problems, hospital patients, or outpatients in a community agency. As a mental health worker, you may be asked to set up and lead a variety of groups. Of course, not all of these specialized groups can be described in this book, but a sample of programs can give you ideas to apply in creating a group that is suitable for your personal style, your clients, and the setting in which you work.

The concepts described in the sample group proposals can be applied to many different populations. These examples illustrate how various practitioners have designed groups to meet a need in the setting in which they work. There are many ways to present an idea to an administrator of an agency, and we hope that these examples will stimulate you to think creatively about how to design groups to effectively meet the needs of your diverse client populations.

Regardless of the kind of group you design, you will be concerned with factors such as securing informed consent, creating trust, dealing with a possible hidden agenda, balancing group process with content, and facilitating members through the various stages of a group, to mention a few. You are also responsible for documenting the process and outcomes of your groups, and the kind of group you are leading, the setting in which you work, and your client population will influence your decision about the kind of notes you may need to keep.

After you have read the various group proposals presented in Chapters 9 through 12, we suggest that you look for common denominators among these groups. Most of the group proposals have the following components: organizing the group, group goals, group format, and group outcomes. As you think about designing your own group, consider these elements. We recommend that you write down some key points for each of these general areas and then begin to think about designing a proposal you may someday implement. To read more about groups designed for various populations with a range of special concerns, we recommend Capuzzi (2003), DeLucia-Waack et al. (2004), and Gladding (2003).

The proposals you will read in Part 3 were developed by group practitioners who followed their passions and interests. We encourage you to discover your passion and begin to investigate ways to implement a group that interests you. ✳

Chapter 9

Groups for Children

Focus Questions

*B*efore reading this chapter, ask yourself what kinds of experiences and training you think you would need to facilitate a group with children. What questions do you have about designing a group for children? As you read this chapter, consider these questions:

1. What do you consider to be the most important guidelines for group work with children and adolescents?

2. What are some of the personal and professional qualifications needed to effectively conduct groups for children?

3. If you were designing a group for young schoolchildren, what steps might you take to involve parents or guardians of the children? How might you involve teachers and the principal?

4. What are some of the advantages of using both educational and support groups for children in schools? If you were working in a school setting, what steps would you take to assess the need for a variety of groups? What kinds of groups do you think might be most useful?

5. There has been increased attention given to violence in elementary schools. If you were asked to develop a group program aimed at helping children learn to deal with anger and conflict, what would be the key features of your program?

✳ Introduction

In this chapter we describe children's groups that were led by one of us (Marianne) or by colleagues. The general group format described here can be applied in various other settings, including private practice and public and private clinics. You can also use many of the ideas in this chapter for groups dealing with a variety of special needs, including those of abused children, children of alcoholic families, and children with learning and behavioral disorders. Creating groups to meet the needs of these children is challenging. Here are a few of the problems for which children are sent to group counseling:

- Low self-esteem
- Inability to get along with peers
- Excessive fighting
- Feelings of failure
- Loss and grief
- Physical and sexual abuse
- Feeling isolated and lonely
- Struggling with living between two cultures
- Hurting other children frequently
- Violation of school rules

- Poor attitude toward school
- Depression and anxiety
- Violent or angry outbursts at home or school
- Children without a home
- Excessive truancy
- Substance abuse
- Dealing with divorce
- Experiencing a crisis situation

This chapter alone will not provide you with enough information to conduct your own groups with children. We hope, however, that it will stimulate you to do further reading, attend specialized workshops, and arrange for supervised field experience. See Smead (1995) and Smead Morganett (1994) for more on group work with children and adolescents.

✳ Guidelines for Group Work With Children and Adolescents

This section contains practical guidelines for counselors who are considering setting up groups for minors. These guidelines apply to children's groups and to groups for adolescents, which we consider in Chapter 10.

Developing a Sound Proposal

We discussed group proposals in detail in Chapter 4, and the same principles apply here to planning groups for children. As you develop your group proposal, keep these steps in mind:

- Describe your goals and purposes clearly.
- Develop a clearly stated rationale for your proposed group.
- State your aims, the procedures to be used, the evaluation process you will use, and the reasons a group approach has particular merit.
- Indicate what form of documentation you will use.

One reason groups fail to materialize is that the leader impulsively decides to lead a group but puts little serious thought into planning an effective design. You can prevent such failures by thinking through your group proposal and designing it for success.

The support of administrators in both schools and agencies is essential. If your design for a group is well organized, you will probably receive support and constructive suggestions from them. It may be necessary to make certain compromises in your proposal, so keep an open mind. Remember that the school principal or the agency head—not you—will probably be the target of criticism if your counseling group is ineffectively run or compromises the integrity of the institution. If you have overlooked the need to get parental permission (where required), it is the administrator who will field the calls from parents who want to know what right the school has to probe into the personal lives of their children.

One practitioner reported that she had encountered resistance from her school principal when she suggested forming a "divorce group" for children. She then renamed it the "loss group," which she thought would be more descriptive, but this new title confused the children. They reported to the office saying, "We're the *lost* group; we're here to be found."

Legal Considerations

Be aware of your state's laws regarding children. Know the rules and regulations as they specifically apply to your agency or institution, as well as the ethical principles specific to counseling children. For example, do not tell children that you can keep everything they discuss confidential and then be put in the position of having to disclose information about them to your agency or school administrator. Know the policies and procedures of the school district or agency where you work. Be clear about what you can and cannot promise in the way of privacy. Be aware of your legal responsibility to report abuse or suspected abuse of minors. In this situation confidentiality *must* be broken; the law requires you to take action by notifying the appropriate authorities. For other ethical considerations in setting up groups for minors, review the discussion of such standards in Chapters 3 and 4.

For some groups written parental permission may not be a legal requirement, but it is a good idea to secure the written consent of parents or guardians of any person under 18 who wishes to participate in group counseling. Doing so also tends to enhance the working relationship and gain the cooperation of legal guardians.

Practical Considerations

The size and duration of a group depend on the age of the members. As a general rule, the younger the children, the smaller the group and the shorter the duration of the sessions. Take into account the fact that the attention span of a child age 4 to 6 is quite different from that of a child who is 10 or 12. Another consideration in forming a group is the severity of the children's problems. For example, a group of acting-out 12-year-olds might have to be as small as a group of preschoolers. It might also be important to find out whether a child in your group is currently taking any medications. For example, a child who has been diagnosed with ADHD might be on medication. You must also consider your own attention span and tolerance for dealing with children who will test your limits. Resist getting impatient at each session, thus becoming more of a disciplinarian than a counselor. As is the case with adult clients, children can evoke your own countertransference. If you are aware of this, there is less chance that your feelings and reactions will interfere with your ability to work with children.

The Setting   Consider the meeting place in terms of its effectiveness for the work you want to do with your young clients. Will they be able to roam around freely and not have to be continually asked to talk softly so as not to disturb others in an adjacent room? Will the site for group meetings provide privacy and freedom from interruptions? Is there anything in the room that could easily be damaged by the children or that is obviously unsafe for them?

Communicate Your Expectations   Be able to tell the children or adolescents in their language about the purpose of your group, what you expect of them, and what they can expect from you. Make sure that they understand the basic, nonnegotiable ground rules and, as much as is realistic, attempt to involve them in the establishment and reinforcement of the rules that will govern their group. Once rules are set, it is essential to follow through with firmness, yet without an autocratic tone and style.

Preparation   Prepare adequately for each session. In fact, you may need to structure sessions even more carefully than you would for some adult groups. However, be flexible enough to adjust your format and topics for a given session to respond to spontaneous situations. Avoid insisting on "covering your agenda" no matter what; be creative, but not careless.

Involve Parents   Parents (or legal guardians) and counselors are partners with a common goal, which is helping children to become all they are capable of becoming. Be respectful of the rights of parents to know what is happening with their children at school. As with the young people, explain to their parents your expectations and purposes in such a way that they can understand and not become suspicious. You reduce the chances of encountering resistant and defensive parents by approaching them with an attitude of "How can you help me in my work with your child, and how can we work as a team for a common purpose?" You might spend an evening presenting your program in a group meeting of parents, or you might send them a letter briefly describing your groups. This letter can be sent with the parental consent form.

Strategies in the Group

Self-Disclosure   Consider the purposes and goals of your group in deciding how much to encourage self-disclosure, especially in matters relating to family life. It is difficult to say what is the right degree of disclosure. Some personal topics may be beyond the scope of the group's purpose and more appropriate for individual therapy. Use judgment as to the appropriateness of letting a child go into detail about personal matters in a group. For example, in a group in an elementary school, you may not want to let a child go into detail about a parental fight. An important intervention is directing this child to express how he or she was affected by the incident.

Emphasize Confidentiality   It is more difficult to maintain confidentiality in a school setting than in private practice. In schools children spend much time together outside of the group, where confidentiality leaks are more possible. As with adults, it is helpful to teach students how to talk about the group experience in a way that they do not betray confidentiality. The counselor needs to communicate the importance of confidentiality by using language that is developmentally tailored for the age level. It is helpful to teach and to practice with the children how to talk about the group in appropriate ways and to give specific guidelines on what to say if someone probes them for information. Parental support can also be solicited by encouraging parents to avoid asking questions that could result in their child breaching confidentiality.

Maintain Neutrality   Avoid siding with children or adolescents against their parents or a particular institution. They may like and admire you for your patience and understanding and complain about missing these traits in parents or teachers. Deal with this complaint realistically, keeping in mind that you are spending an hour each week with them as opposed to living with them every day. Help the young people to understand the other side.

Use Appropriate Exercises and Techniques   If you use interaction exercises, you can explain their purpose in a general way without diminishing their impact. Children should not be pressured into participating in certain activities if they are uncomfortable doing so. Although their unwillingness to take part in exercises often stems from a lack of understanding, children or adolescents will sometimes be reluctant to participate because they may wonder about the purpose of such exercises.

Listen and Remain Open   A skillful counselor will listen to behavior as well as words. Young people can teach us a great deal. Encourage young people to express themselves in their own words. Let them lead the way, and follow their clues. Listen to their words, and also pay attention to the possible meanings of their behavior. For example, if a child is acting out, is she telling you "Please stop me, because I can't stop myself"? If a child is continually screaming, he might be saying "Notice me! Nobody else does." Remaining open to what children are trying to tell us about themselves is essential if we are going to help them. Be aware of preconceived labels and diagnoses that may subtly influence your interactions. The children you work with are often categorized and labeled. Be careful not to limit the ability of children to change by responding to them as if they are their labels.

Prepare for Termination   Children are quick to form attachments with adults who display a concerned and caring attitude toward them. Well before your group ends—for example, 3 sessions before the end of a 12-session group— you must let the children know that the termination point is not far off. This notice enables the children to express their sadness, and it enables you to share your sadness with them. Avoid promising them that you will keep in contact with them, if that is not possible. If you do not deal with these issues, they may see you as running out on them and consider you as one more adult they cannot trust. (At this point it is a good idea to review the guidelines for the final stage of a group, described in Chapter 8.)

Personal and Professional Qualifications

It is essential to recognize the impact that conducting groups can have on you personally. For example, in working with youngsters who are abused and neglected, you might find it difficult to separate yourself from their life situations. If you are consistently preoccupied with their problems, you may discover that this is affecting your life and your relationships negatively. It is a personal matter for you to discover how much you are capable of giving, as well as how much and what you need to do to replenish yourself to stay excited and creative in your work.

Some of the *personal characteristics* that we see as important in working with children are patience, caring, playfulness, a good sense of humor, the ability to tune in to and remember one's own childhood and adolescent experiences, firmness without punitiveness, flexibility, the ability to express anger without sarcasm, great concern for and interest in children, and the other characteristics of group leaders that were described in Chapter 2.

We believe five *professional qualifications* are especially important for those leading groups with children:

- A thorough understanding of the developmental tasks and stages of the particular age group
- A good understanding of counseling skills, especially as they pertain to group work
- Knowledge and skills necessary to work effectively with children from culturally diverse populations
- Supervised training in working with children in groups before leading a group alone
- Knowledge of the literature and significant research pertaining to counseling children and adolescents. In addition to these qualifications, other specific competencies and skills are essential to effectively lead groups of children or adolescents. For a listing, refer to Chapter 2 and review the *Professional Standards for the Training of Group Workers* (ASGW, 2000).

✳ Group Counseling in the School Setting

Counseling groups in the schools consist of a wide array of topics and formats. These groups are a mainstay of the psychological services offered by the schools. According to Hoag and Burlingame (1997), more than 70% of all counseling groups for children are found in the school setting. Such groups are generally brief, structured, problem focused, homogeneous in membership, and have a cognitive behavioral orientation. Most of the research that has been conducted on groups for children and adolescents has also been done in the schools. This research tends to be clustered in the areas of social competence problems, adjustment to parent divorce, behavior problems, and learning disabilities. Riva and Haub (2004) report that groups for children and adolescents occupy a major place in the counseling services provided in the schools because of their efficacy in delivering information and treatment. The effectiveness of groups for both prevention and remediation has gathered considerable empirical support. Riva and Haub conclude that "the real benefit of school-based treatment is that it can potentially reach many students before they need remedial counseling for more serious mental health problems" (p. 318).

One of the problems that many school counselors face in designing and facilitating groups is lack of training, because they generally receive very little training that specifically targets children and adolescents in group formats. The training they receive with adults tends not to generalize well to children in groups (Riva & Haub, 2004). Being able to do successful group work with children implies that certain topics are addressed in group courses. Van Velsor (2004) identifies the following topical areas as especially important in working with children: selecting children for groups, working with children at different developmental levels, facilitating children's groups at different stages, evaluating individual and group progress, and protecting children's confidentiality in groups. In their discussion of preparing school counselors for group work, Akos, Goodnough, and Milsom (2004) make a number of recommendations to group work educators as a way to maximize training in group work for school counselors. Some of these recommendations are to

- strive to infuse group concepts throughout the curriculum and discuss the group process involved in group supervision and cooperative learning.
- utilize role-play activities to practice group skills needed to work with children.
- sequence program course work and the group course itself to emphasize a developmental, skill-based preparation appropriate to school counseling.
- select practicum and internship sites that provide opportunities to students to participate in group work.

It is easy to overextend yourself when working with children and adolescents whose problems are pressing and severe. Be realistic and realize that you cannot work effectively with every child or provide all the needed services. If you are doing group work in the schools, it is essential that you know the boundaries of your competence and the scope of your job description. Know how to differentiate between therapy groups and group with a developmental, preventive, and educational focus. Counseling groups for children and adolescents in the schools typically focus on preventive and developmental issues. These groups are ideally suited for primary prevention because both concepts and methods of prevention can be appropriately integrated (Kulic, Dagley, & Horne, 2001). Treatment of more severe problems is generally not within the scope of counseling services offered in a school setting. Treating these problems is in the province of outside agencies. Because not all children are ready for group participation, it is important to know how to suggest alternative helping approaches. Make it a practice to know referral resources and be willing to make use of these resources when it is in the child's best interest.

A School Counseling Group
for 6- to 11-Year-Olds

This section is written from the perspective of Marianne Schneider Corey. ■

I designed a group for children ranging in age from 6 to 11 at an elementary school. My caseload included 10 to 15 children, and I was to see each child once a week for about an hour for a total of 24 visits. The children were referred to me by the principal, the teacher, or the school nurse. These children had a host of problems similar to those listed in the introduction to this chapter. It was up to me to design a group that would improve the children's behavior in school.

Organizing the Group

Contact With School Personnel

Being aware that outsiders are sometimes mistrusted in schools, my first goal was to earn the trust of the teachers and administrators. I met with them to determine what they hoped the project would accomplish. I told them that I wanted to work closely with them, providing feedback about the children, making specific recommendations, and getting their suggestions. I let them know that I intended to work with the children individually and in groups and to involve the parents in the treatment process as much as possible.

Accordingly, I developed a program in which I was in continuous contact with the children's teachers, principal, and parents. The teachers and the principal were very cooperative about meeting with me. I also spoke frequently with the school psychologist, and the school secretaries about particular children, gathering as much information as I could. This information turned out to be most helpful.

The Setting

The setting for my work with the children was not ideal. The school was short on space (a new school was being built), and I was continually looking for a place to meet with the children.

When the weather allowed, we often met on the school lawn. I needed a place where they could explore, touch, talk loudly, shout if they were angry, or give vent to any other emotions they were experiencing. If I took them off campus or did anything special with them, I first obtained written permission from the parents and the school authorities. Although I never had an ideal place to work, this did not keep me from working effectively with the children, as we often improvised together. The children were very adaptive, and I too had to learn to adapt to less than ideal situations.

Due to the setting, I had to pick up the children from their classrooms, something that concerned me. How would the children react to being singled out? Would my special attention to them amid their peers affect them negatively? Fortunately, I found the contrary to be true. The children responded very positively to my coming to pick them up and were always ready to come with me, even during recess time.

Initial Contact With the Parents

After meeting with the school staff, who identified which children I would be working with, I contacted the parents of each child and attempted to arrange for an individual meeting with the parents. They knew before I visited them about my intended involvement with their child because I had asked the principal and the child's teacher to contact them. During my initial contact, I explained that their child had been referred to me by the teacher, who had become concerned about the student's behavior in class. This interview gave the parents a chance to get to know me and to ask questions, and it gave me the chance to get the parents' permission to work with their child. At this time I gathered information regarding any difficulties the parents were having with the child and collected the data I needed to complete numerous forms. If parents became anxious over my probing or over the fact that *their* child had been singled out for counseling, I explained to them that because teachers have to deal with so many children they cannot always provide all the attention a child needs. It would be my job, I said, to provide this extra attention.

Although the school's policy stipulated obtaining parental permission for children to become participants in a group, this is not a required policy in all school districts. State laws regarding parental permission to counsel minors also vary. As a general rule, I think it is best to get the parents' permission and to work with them as allies rather than risk their disapproval by counseling their children without their knowledge and consent. There are exceptions, however. When counselors are not legally required to secure the consent of parents and when notifying them could be detrimental to the minor client, the welfare of these children always takes priority.

For the most part parents were willing to cooperate and gave their consent. In response to my question about any difficulties they might be experiencing with their child at home, which I asked to get clues to the child's behavior in school, the parents were guarded at first. They became much more open with time and frequent contacts. My aim was not to communicate in any way that they were "bad" parents, as this would certainly have aroused their defensiveness. Their children were experiencing difficulties, and I wanted to solicit their help in assisting the students to work through these problems. By going into the child's home, I was able to get information relating to the problems the child was exhibiting that would otherwise have been difficult, if not impossible, to obtain.

I told the parents that their children would be discussing with me problems related to school, home, and peers. I explained that I wished to keep as confidential as possible what the child and I would be exploring in our sessions. Therefore, I explained, I would let them know in a general way how I was proceeding with the child but would not reveal any of the specifics, unless I was required to do so by law.

I also told them that I hoped to see them sometimes together with their children. It was difficult to see some parents again after my initial contact, however, because every one of them was employed. I was able to make at least some additional contact with most parents, and I spoke with others on the telephone.

Special Problems Requiring Out-of-Group Attention

Like the parents, the teachers provided me with ongoing information regarding the children's progress. I was able to use this information in deciding how long to see a particular child or what problem area to focus on. In addition, the teachers prepared written evaluations for the program director, and they shared these evaluations with me. I kept documentation of my work with each child in the group, my observation of the child, my recommendations for teachers, and as well, I kept notes regarding my contacts with teachers and parents.

In doing these groups I learned that children have a multitude of developmental issues with which they must cope. There are many avenues of help for these problems. In working effectively with children, counselors do well to involve as many resources and people as possible. There is room for creativity in developing groups to meet the diverse needs and the diverse cultural backgrounds of children. It is important to let the parents or legal guardians know about these programs and resources so that they, too, are involved in the helping process.

The children referred to me were, almost without exception, identified as having learning problems. Often these learning disabilities were a reflection of their emotional conflicts.

Because I was unable to provide the necessary tutorial assistance, I contacted a nearby university and recruited five graduate students to tutor the children for credit in their child psychology course. In addition to providing tutorial services, they gave the children additional positive individual attention. This tutoring proved very successful for both the children and the university students.

When I detected health problems, I referred the child to the school nurse. When I suspected neglect or abuse, I took the appropriate action. As counselors who work with minors, we need to be aware of the reporting laws for suspected abuse in our state as well as our work setting. We must know the specific steps to be taken in making the required reports. In a school setting the first step may be to report a situation to the principal. It is always helpful to communicate with Child Protective Services (or the Department of Social Services) to obtain information on assessing and reporting suspected child abuse.

Many children are undernourished, inappropriately clothed, and in need of medical assistance, recreational opportunities, or supervision after school. Counseling is more likely to have an effect if the child's basic needs are being met. I found it necessary to do much of the legwork required to obtain food, clothing, money, or special services for the children and their families. Essentially, I had a lot of case management responsibilities. Some families resisted turning to outside agencies because of pride or fear that strings would be attached or simply out of ignorance about where to go for help. When a family did want help with emotional, economic, or medical problems, I referred them to one of the appropriate agencies, but I often also made the contacts with the agencies and did the paperwork they required. More often than not counselors do not have time to make the contacts I have described, but they can be creative in finding ways to delegate these tasks to others.

Group Format

Initial Contact With the Children

The children were reluctant to initiate a conversation, being accustomed only to answering questions. They needed some structure and some guidelines for expressing themselves and an acknowledgment that it was difficult for them. I introduced myself to them, saying that I was a special type of teacher called a counselor. I explained that their teacher was concerned about their behavior in class and that they would be talking with me several times a week—individually, as a group, and in their homes. I told them that we would be discussing problems they had in school, at home, or with fellow students.

Because of my belief that children's rights to privacy are often ignored and violated,

I let them know that I would be talking about them with their parents and teachers. I explained that I would tell them when I made such contacts. Although I said I did consider much of what we would talk about in the group to be confidential, I told them I would discuss with their parents and teachers anything that would be important in helping them work through any of their difficulties. At this time I also let them know that they were not to talk to others about what fellow group members revealed. This was one of the rules we discussed again in the group sessions. I told them that they could talk about matters that concerned them, including their fears and their hurts. Additionally, I let them know that I could not keep everything confidential, especially if it concerned their safety. In language that they could understand, I explained the purpose of confidentiality and its limitations. They were also informed that they would not be allowed to hurt other children, either physically or verbally, or to destroy any property. Other rules were established, and I made the children aware of their responsibility. To be part of the group, they had to agree to follow these rules.

Working With the Children in a Group

My goal was to pinpoint some of the children's maladaptive behaviors, teach them how to express emotions without hurting themselves or others, and provide a climate in which they would feel free to express a range of feelings. I wanted to convey to the youngsters that feelings such as anger did not get them into trouble; rather, it is certain ways of acting on these feelings that can lead to problems. In an effort to teach them ways of safely expressing the full gambit of their feelings, I involved them in a variety of activities, including role playing, play therapy, acting out special situations, painting, finishing stories that I began, putting on puppet shows, playing music, movement, and dancing.

The groups that were easiest to work with and most productive were composed of 3 to 5 children of the same age and gender. In larger groups I found myself (1) unable to relate intensely to individuals, (2) slipping into the role of disciplinarian to counteract the increased distractions, (3) feeling frustrated at the number of children competing for my attention, and (4) not having enough time left over to pay attention to the underlying dynamics. In addition, children between the ages of 6 and 11 tend to become impatient if they have to wait very long for their turn to speak.

I took care to combine withdrawn children with more outgoing ones, but I also felt that it was important for the children to be with others who were experiencing similar conflicts. For example, I put in the same group two boys who felt much anger, hurt, grief, and frustration over their parents' divorces and subsequent remarriages. They slowly learned how to express their feelings about not having much contact with the parent they didn't live with. At first the boys could only express their feelings symbolically, through play; later they learned to put words to their emotions and to talk about their feelings.

As I had planned, I provided some time for each child during which he or she could have my attention alone. I noticed that in the group all the children became less jealous of one another about me and trusted me more once I had begun to provide this individual time.

Alone, the children were more cooperative and less competitive. They felt less need to seek attention in undesirable ways. Having an adult spend time with them individually gave them a sense of importance. With the teacher's consent I frequently visited the children who were in my group in their class-rooms and on the playground, sometimes just observing and sometimes making a brief contact through touch or words. Although this was time consuming, it proved to be productive in the long run.

Our scheduled group and individual sessions took place twice a week and lasted from half an hour to an hour. It would have been a mistake for me to insist that sessions always last a certain length of time because the children's patience varied from session to session.

When they wanted to leave a group session, I would say in a friendly manner that they were free to leave, but I wished they would stay until the session was over. They usually elected to stay. If they chose to leave, I would not have them come back to that session. Most of the time the children enjoyed the sessions. It was a good practice to let them know in advance that a session was coming to an end and then to be firm about having them leave and not give in to their demands that the group continue.

My groups were open, in that new members could join. The children already in the group handled this situation very well. They knew the newcomer from school and did not meet the child with any negative reactions or resistance. During the sessions, I let the children lead the way and listened to what they had to say, directly or through various symbolic means. Playing with puppets turned out to be an excellent means of revealing a variety of emotions and dramatizing situations that produce conflict. I made puppets available to the first- and second-grade children but found that even the fourth- and fifth-grade students were able to use them to vent their pent-up emotions.

The groups offered the children the opportunity to act out situations that aroused conflicting feelings. Sometimes I would suggest a problem situation, and at other times the children would select a problem to act out. The children would take the role of teacher, friend, principal, parent, brother, sister, or whoever else was involved. In this way they were able to release their emotions without hurting others.

Several sessions might pass before a child would speak freely. I sat on the floor close to the children during the sessions, often maintaining physical contact, which seemed to have a calming effect by itself. I listened to them attentively and often reflected for them what they were saying. More important, however, I communicated to them, usually nonverbally, that I was with them, that what they were saying was important, and that I cared about what they had to say. I insisted that other members in the group listen, and I reassured all of them that each would have a time to speak. This is a very difficult concept to get across, especially to a 6- or 7-year-old who is still learning to share.

After a session that I thought had been unproductive, I was sometimes surprised to hear a teacher comment on a child's changed behavior. After one such session, a boy who had previously been very destructive and disobedient became cooperative and able to relate to his peers. Pounding a lump of clay, which could be interpreted as nonproductive, turned out to have been very important to him. It had relieved much of his anger and so reduced his need to strike out at others.

At times I questioned whether my work with the children was doing any good. Changes in their behavior were slow in coming and sometimes temporary. Some children gave the appearance of improving one week, yet the next week their behavior would again be very negative. My firm belief that a child can change if afforded the opportunity to change was challenged again and again. However, most children did make definite changes, as observed by the teacher, the principal, the parents, and me. Truants began to come to school more regularly. A boy who was in the habit of stealing and giving his loot to other children so they would like him learned that his behavior was one of the reasons others disliked him in the first place, and he began to get their attention through more positive actions. A girl who had been conditioned not to trust learned to make friends and to reach out first, doing what at one time she had most feared.

These changes, though encouraging, needed to be reinforced at home. Although most parents welcomed many of their child's new behaviors, some found the new behavior threatening. For instance, one girl caused her mother some anxiety by beginning to ask probing questions about her absent father. I encouraged this mother—and other parents facing similar problems—to try to listen to the child nondefensively.

It was disconcerting to know that some of the children frequently faced difficult circumstances at home, and yet I realized that I did not have control over that domain. Rather than allowing myself to get too discouraged over the fact that I could not change their situation at home, I had to remind myself that I could provide them with a positive experience at school that would have a constructive impact on them. As counselors, we need to remind ourselves to focus on what we can do and not become overwhelmed by all that we cannot do.

Termination of the Group

When I began to work with the children, I told them that the sessions would go on for only a limited time during the school year. Several sessions before termination, I reminded them that the group and individual sessions would be ending soon, and we discussed the imminent termination of our meetings.

Although I had been affectionate with the children during our time together, I had not deceived them by becoming a substitute mother or by establishing myself as a permanent fixture who would totally satisfy all their needs. I was aware of establishing appropriate boundaries in carrying out the primary purpose of the group experience. By being realistic about the limits of my job from the beginning, I was able to prevent termination from being a catastrophic experience for the children.

Teacher Evaluation of the Counseling Program

Like the parents, the teachers provided me with ongoing information regarding the children's progress. I was able to use this information in deciding how long to see a particular child or what problem area to focus on. In addition, the teachers completed written evaluations for the program director, and they shared these evaluations with me.

A Group for Elementary School Children
of Divorce and Changing Families

The material in this section is written from the perspective of Karen Kram Laudenslager, a school counselor. For more information on these groups, you can contact Karen at Allentown School District, 31 S. Penn Street, Box 328, Allentown, PA 18105; telephone (484) 765-4055, or by e-mail at Klaudenslager@aol.com. ■

It is not uncommon for many children in any elementary school to come from divorced homes. These pupils face a number of personal and social problems, which include being lonely, feeling responsible for the divorce, experiencing divided loyalties, not knowing how to deal with parental conflicts, and facing the loss of family stability. Schools and community agencies are addressing the needs of these children by offering groups structured around these themes. This proposal describes counseling groups designed for children from divorced and changing families.

Organizing the Group

Before actually getting a group going, a great deal of careful preliminary work needs to be done. This preparation includes conducting a needs survey, announcing the group to children and teachers, obtaining parental permission, orienting the children to the rules for participating in a group, and presenting my goals in a clear way to the children, parents, teachers, and administrators. If adequate attention is not given to these preliminary details, the group may never materialize.

Survey the Children's Needs

It is very helpful to assess the needs of children before deciding on a program. I do this by making an initial classroom visit to discuss with both the teachers and the children how small group counseling can be beneficial. I explain the topical focus of these groups or, as I later refer to them, "clubs." The family club is geared for grades 2 through 5. I explain that a specific day and time have been scheduled for club meetings at each grade level and that all clubs run for 30 minutes once a week for six sessions.

The needs survey is then handed out, and I ask all students to think about the issues and react truthfully. I explain that these surveys are private and will be read only by the classroom teacher and me. The selection of students is based on comments by both students and teachers.

Obtain Parental Permission

A letter is sent home with every child who has agreed to participate in the group. The letter outlines the issues and topics to be discussed, requests parental permission, and encourages parental support and involvement. I am convinced of the value of involving both parents whenever possible. I encourage each child to discuss the group with his or her parents.

Group Rules

All students voluntarily agree to be members of the club. I encourage children who are shy or slightly reluctant to give it a try. Anyone who wishes to leave the group is free to do so.

Children always have the right to remain silent. I reinforce the importance of listening and learning from one another. Some students feel more comfortable knowing that they will never be forced to share or discuss any issue that they feel is private. Other rules include (1) anyone who wants to may have a turn, (2) everyone is listened to, (3) no laughing or making fun of what anyone says, (4) honesty is required, and (5) confidentiality is respected.

The students, with my guidance, make up the rules during the first session. They usually come up with all of the above on their own. If the group does not identify some critical norms, I will add them to our list of rules. I explain the reasons for the rules, which increases the chances that the children will abide by them. Finally, we all sign our names, making a commitment and agreement to follow the rules. These rules are posted and reviewed before each session.

Group Goals

What Children Need to Know

Through my research, reading, and direct contact with children, I have discovered some important messages children need to hear. I continually discuss, explain, and reinforce these statements throughout the 6-week sessions:

✓ You are special.

✓ You can get through this difficult time.

✓ You have people who care about you.

✓ It [the divorce or separation] is not your fault.

✓ You are not to blame.

✓ It is not your divorce, and no one is divorcing you. Mom and Dad are divorcing each other.

✓ You did not cause the problems between your parents, and you cannot fix them.

✓ You can help each other.

What I Hope to Accomplish

Some objectives of the groups are:

✓ Give support when needed

✓ Let children know they are not alone

✓ Teach coping skills

✓ Reinforce students' need to talk and deal with feelings

✓ Help children deal with emotional and behavioral concerns so they can concentrate on learning and work to reach their potential

✓ Offer resources to students and parents such as bibliotherapy and outside private counseling when needed

✓ Help children open lines of communication with other students, teachers, and parents

Group Format

The focus of these clubs is developmental rather than therapeutic. The groups are designed to provide support, teach coping skills, and help children of changing families explore ways to express and deal with their feelings. When more involved counseling is needed, the parents are always contacted and an outside referral is made.

Any counselor who works in an elementary school can testify to the importance of getting feedback and support from teachers and parents. I have found that it is critical to involve parents, teachers, and administrators in these group programs so that they become allies of the children and the counselor. Their support of the program goes a long way toward ensuring its success; their resistance can thwart its progress.

Teachers' feedback is critical because they see the student daily and can monitor changes in behavior. I make an effort to talk with each classroom teacher as often as possible. Teachers can tell counselors about pupils' self-esteem, self-confidence, interaction with their peers, and homework completion. They can also share comments and reactions that students make in class, both orally and in their written work. All of this information helps me monitor the students' emotional and social progress.

Sessions of 30 minutes each, once a week for 6 weeks, work well. This schedule gives me time to run more groups and see more children. With so many students experiencing family changes, I try to help as many as possible. This time structure interferes only minimally with classroom learning. I try to be sensitive to the reactions of both students and teachers to interrupting the learning process. Too much time out of class for extended periods can cause additional stress, and we are all concerned with supporting and enhancing the learning process, not disrupting it. At times these clubs meet at lunch.

The Initial Meeting

The first session is clearly structured by focusing on a discussion of the purpose of the club, on my role as a group facilitator, and on helping the children identify why they are in the group. We play a "name game" in which the children introduce themselves by selecting an adjective describing them that starts with the first letter of their first name (such as Wonderful Wanda or Nice Nick). The only guideline is that the adjective must be a positive one. We define *family,* and each child introduces him- or herself by answering the question "Who am I, and who lives at my house?" I ask younger children to draw pictures of who lives in different houses. We discuss how many different places we live and

with whom. I encourage them to describe how it is for them to be in their family. At this session the ground rules are established and written on chart paper for use as a reminder at all subsequent sessions. My goal for this first meeting is to help the children find out that they are not alone in their situation. If time allows, I encourage them to see similarities and differences in their family situations. I may ask "Who would like to share how your family is the same as or different from others in this group?"

The Next Four Sessions

I have found that my groups differ somewhat, depending on the themes brought out at the initial session. I use selected exercises as a focus for interaction. The middle four sessions are structured in accordance with the needs of those who are in the group. Here are a few of the activities that are often part of these sessions:

✓ We play the "feeling game." Students brainstorm feelings, and we write them down. The children then select three feelings that describe how they feel about their family situation, and we discuss them.

✓ The children identify three wishes they have for their family. One overwhelming wish that generally emerges is that their mother and father will get back together. They also wish to spend more time with the noncustodial parent. These children often express how difficult it is for them to be placed in the middle of a struggle, and they wish for peace. They would like this harmony at any cost, and they are willing to do anything to bring it about.

✓ We go around the table taking turns to "check in," sharing on a scale from 1 to 10 how we are feeling and why.

✓ The children decide "what I want each of my parents to know." (Stepparents and stepbrothers and stepsisters may also be included, if appropriate.) I often find that children are hesitant to reveal some differences they might have with their new stepmother or stepfather. They frequently want their parents to understand their feelings about being in a new family. Sometimes children feel forced to make an adjustment before they are ready, and they often have uncomfortable feelings that have not been discussed.

✓ We discuss what children can control and what they cannot. For example, they can control their own behavior. We also talk about ways they can control certain feelings. However, they cannot control the decisions that their parents make about the divorce or current living situations. I also talk with the children about the fact that this is not *their* divorce. In other words, Mom and Dad are divorcing each other, not the children. What I hope to get across to the group members is that they did not cause the divorce and cannot "fix" the situation. Much of the group time is devoted to exploring and brainstorming alternatives for the children to change themselves in their situations at home.

✓ We discuss the issue of change. The children identify what they consider to be positive and negative changes in their lives as a result of the new family situation.

✓ A question box is available during all sessions. Students can anonymously write questions or concerns that they might not feel comfortable sharing in group and drop them in the question box. These issues are discussed at the next session.

✓ We read and discuss the following books, depending on relevance and interest: *Dinosaurs Divorce: A Guide for Changing Families* (Brown & Brown, 1986), *Now I*

Have a Step Parent and It's Kind of Confusing (Stenson, 1979), *Divorce Is a Grown-Up Problem* (Sinberg, 1978), *The Divorce Workbook: A Guide for Kids and Families* (Ives, Fassler, & Lash, 1985), *I Survived the Divorce Monster* (Williamson, 1990), and *Stepping Back From Anger: Protecting Your Children During Divorce* (American Academy of Matrimonial Lawyers, 1998).

The Last Session

As is true of the initial session, the final meeting is also fairly structured, this time around the tasks of termination. The children typically discuss feelings about the club ending and identify what they have learned from these sessions. There is also some time for a special celebration with cupcake or popcorn treats. Each student receives a recognition certificate, which says: *The Counselor Said I Am Special!*

Group Outcomes

Student Perceptions

Students report feeling more comfortable with themselves and with their family situations when they belong to the club and realize that they are not alone. They need to identify with other children who are experiencing similar concerns and feelings. Together, group members can begin to understand the stages that everyone goes through and can learn skills to help themselves feel better. Through the group process, they help one another let go of what they cannot control and take responsibility for what they can control.

Parent Perceptions

Parents report that their children enjoy the club meetings and often come home and share what was discussed. Their children gain a better understanding of divorce by learning how others adjust. Parents are often in so much pain and conflict themselves during the separation or divorce that they are relieved and happy that someone else is there supporting their children.

Parents show an interest in what their children are doing in the group, and parents often read some of the recommended books with their children. Many parents have expressed a need for more information on how they can help their children. I have offered evening workshops and parenting classes. I would like to develop an ongoing parent support group to meet the needs of adults. I have also thought it might be helpful to facilitate one or two sessions with both parents and children together.

Follow-Up

My follow-up consists of checking with teachers on the students' progress and checking with the students themselves by classroom visits, by seeing them individually, and by encouraging self-referrals. I also hold club "reunions" the following year to see how things have been going.

Personal Sources of Frustration

The biggest frustration for me is ending the clubs. The children always resist terminating and bargain or plead to continue with more sessions. I find it extremely difficult to end when I know how much these children need to talk and learn. I am unable to directly solve some of the children's problems, and that adds to my level of frustration. Here are some of the complex problems these children face:

✓ Infrequent visitations with a parent as a result of the parent's emotional problems

✓ Dislocations because a child is "interfering" with a parent's relationships

✓ Frequent court testimony in sexual abuse cases

✓ Violence in the family

✓ Parental neglect

✓ Conflicts over being asked by parents to choose sides

✓ Parents' extramarital affairs

✓ Alcohol and drug abuse

✓ Spousal abuse

✓ Physical or emotional abuse

✓ Custody battles

✓ Financial concerns

Another source of frustration is time. There never seems to be enough time to see all the students who need help. Nor is there enough time to meet with all the parents to discuss the progress of each child. I do, however, refer families for outside counseling if during the club sessions I see a need for more in-depth therapy.

Concluding Comments

I have found the group experience to be very effective and instrumental in supporting students with changes and family issues. Students are able to connect with each other and offer support, encouragement, suggestions, and hope. In the group they can help each other to understand feelings and learn how to handle difficult situations in a safe place. It has been my experience that this small group structure is extremely beneficial. I strongly recommend that counselors provide this kind of counseling service for students.

※ The Challenge of Helping Children Deal With Anger and Conflict

As counselors, we know that metal detectors and increased law enforcement presence will not solve the dilemma schools face in light of the increase in the frequency and intensity of violence. Helping children learn to be aware of and manage anger and conflict will help prevent violent actions. Conflict management groups and groups designed to teach children appropriate ways to express and deal with their anger are excellent means of prevention, and these groups can be most useful in the school environment. These groups are aimed at learning effective ways to deal with anger through interpersonal skills development, problem solving, and learning self-talk. A review of the literature indicates that anger management groups are effective for bringing about changes in children, adolescents, and adults (Fleckenstein & Horne, 2004).

Typically, school counselors have an unrealistically large caseload. Regardless of how talented the counselor might be, there are limitations on what can be done to bring about significant behavior change. The counselor's time is often spent reacting to the immediate needs of children rather than on developing prevention programs. Given adequate resources and increased numbers of competent counselors, we would like to see school guidance programs include group counseling on the elementary, middle, and secondary levels. Group counseling would be aimed at cultivating caring and compassionate individuals. Group counseling can be an ideal forum for creating what Adlerians term "social interest." In the context of a group, priority could be given to helping children deal with feelings of rejection, anger, alienation, and isolation. The group is also a place where children can learn the meaning of belonging and contributing to society. For an interesting discussion of the Adlerian approach to counseling children in groups, see Sonstegard and Bitter, with Pelonis (2004).

A particularly useful resource for counselors who work with children in groups is *The Handbook of Group Play Therapy* (Sweeney & Homeyer, 1999). Group play therapy can be designed to help children manage their anger, and this format has many applications in working with a range of problems in other kinds of children's groups as well. Sweeney and Homeyer maintain that group play therapy is a blend of play therapy and group process that is a natural and intuitive response to the need of emotionally hurting children. Children benefit from the relationships and interactions with other children in the context of a group play therapy setting. Group play therapy provides a context for children that encourages them to learn about themselves and others. Sweeney and Homeyer's edited book has a variety of chapters on many facets of utilizing play therapy approaches in groups. This book features a number of different theoretical approaches to group play therapy with children, such as the client-centered approach, Adlerian play therapy, Jungian group play therapy, and Gestalt therapy. Other chapters in this book include play group therapy for younger children, art in group play therapy, group puppetry, multicultural considerations in group play therapy, and play groups in elementary school.

Children's Elementary School Anger Management and Conflict Resolution Group

The material in this section is written from the perspective of Karen Kram Laudenslager, a school counselor. For more information on these groups, you can contact Karen at Allentown School District, 31 S. Penn Street, Box 328, Allentown, PA 18105; telephone (484) 765-4055 or by e-mail at Klaudenslager@aol.com. ■

Schools today are faced with increasing incidents of violence and aggression. Programs to help protect our children and teach them the skills to deal effectively with conflicts are becoming a shared responsibility among home, school, and community. In the Allentown School District, school counselors are facilitating anger management and conflict resolution groups in the elementary, middle, and secondary schools. What follows is an overview of an elementary school "peacemaker club," and with some modifications similar groups can be formed with adolescent students. It is recommended that parental permission be obtained for all group experiences.

Organizing the Group

Many children have difficulty dealing with their anger and resolving conflicts without aggression. The selection of children for this type of group needs to be done carefully. I recommend 6 to 8 students grouped by grade level. It is important to select children with varying abilities in problem solving and anger management. I strive to create a group of students who can both learn from and help each other develop and strengthen these peacemaking skills. The overall goal of the group centers on acquiring the ability to recognize, effectively express, and manage anger in a host of conflict situations. To select the most troubled and angry children will set up an extremely unmanageable situation for both students and facilitator. Some children who carry a great deal of unresolved anger might need to be seen individually or referred for outside counseling.

Group Goals

A number of life skills need to be developed, including skills in communication, listening, decision making, problem solving, and compromising. Some specific goals for the group are listed here:

✓ Provide information and explain attitudes related to conflict management.

✓ Increase skills in recognizing and managing anger.

✓ Increase awareness of diversity issues.

✓ Increase ability to identify feelings.

✓ Introduce effective ways to resolve conflicts.

What Children Need to Know

I find that a number of basic ideas are important for children to know. These groups focus on themes around learning how to recognize, express, and manage a host of feelings and behaviors pertaining to conflict and anger.

Concepts such as the following are integrated and discussed throughout the group process:

✓ Everyone gets angry. What is important is learning how to express anger appropriately.

✓ It is okay to feel angry, but it is not okay to hurt someone, to hurt yourself, or to destroy property.

✓ Conflict is a natural part of everyday life.

✓ Conflicts happen because people have different opinions, feelings, needs, and beliefs.

✓ There are many ways of viewing a problem or conflict situation, and a range of acceptable solutions.

✓ Conflicts can be resolved with "win-win" outcomes, so that both sides are satisfied.

Group Format

The Initial Meeting

The first session (out of 6 meetings) is spent getting to know each other, establishing group rules, and revealing expectations. The term "conflict" is defined, and ways to handle conflicts are discussed. We go over the topics for the remaining sessions. I also explain the group's purpose and the skills the children will learn and practice.

The Next Four Meetings

It is important to empower children to be peacemakers and to help them gain confidence and skill in dealing with difficult situations without resorting to violence and aggression. During group meetings, I have found the following activities to be effective in promoting understanding and effective resolution of conflict situations:

✓ The children create a "conflict web" and a "peace web" by brainstorming words and feelings associated with both. We

discuss the differences and implications for each.

✓ The children make a list of "what makes me angry." Using a "thermometer" visual, they discuss the "degrees" they feel for each situation ranging from a low level of anger all the way up to a boiling point. They realize that the same problem can be perceived differently and can elicit different reactions from everyone. We then discuss "ways to cool down," and the children develop a list of what works for them to calm down when they are angry and before they lose control.

✓ The difference between listening and hearing is explored, and the children practice effective listening skills such as maintaining eye contact, not interrupting, and reflecting back what they hear another person saying. This reflective listening skill is practiced by dividing the group into pairs and having everyone take turns talking. Each child in the pair then listens and reflects back what he or she hears. This is essential in conveying what each child is perceiving and feeling, and helps the other child get a sense of the degree to which he or she is understood. Time is devoted to learning and practice sending "I messages."

✓ A "toolbox" activity is used to help the children identify a variety of tools and skills that they have for solving problems. Examples of such tools are sharing, taking turns, flipping a coin, talking it out, apologizing, using humor, and compromising. The children can actually create their own personal toolbox of ideas to keep with them.

✓ We watch the video *Songs for Peacemakers*. Following this we discuss the role that each of us plays in taking responsibility for our behavior, for solving problems peacefully, and for promoting safe schools, homes, and communities.

The Final Meeting

The last session is a wrap-up and review of everything the children have learned. Each child makes a commitment to being a peacemaker, signs a peacemaking pledge, and receives a peacemaker certificate. The children are encouraged to use the mediation program as needed for additional help in resolving conflicts.

Group Outcomes

I continue to find that children respond extremely well to a group situation where they are able to openly share their personal concerns and problems. They are also very interested in learning how to take responsibility for safety issues and overall violence prevention. It is important for the children to see themselves as part of the problem-solving process and to realize that even though adults still need to intervene and help out at times there are many situations they can work out for themselves. The frustration is in not being able to reach all the children who could use this help and in continuing to look for ways to get parents involved in applying some of these techniques at home. This quote from Ghandi sums up the challenge counselors face in our schools: "If we are to reach real peace in this world, we shall have to begin with the children."

If you would like to explore some resources for peacemaking clubs, I recommend the record *Songs for Peacemakers* by Marcia Nass and Max Nass (1991). Further information is also available through the Association for Supervision and Curriculum Development (1250 N. Pitt Street, Alexandria, VA 22314) and the Peace Education Foundation (P.O. Box 191153, Miami, FL 33132). Other useful books and workbooks include those by Johnson and Johnson (1995), Schmidt and Friedman (1991), Freeman (1995), and Boulden and Boulden (1994, 1995).

A Group for Children Who Have Been Abused

For further information contact Dr. Teresa M. Christensen at University of New Orleans, Department of Counselor Education, New Orleans, LA 70148; telephone (504) 280-7434; e-mail tchriste@uno.edu. ■

Introduction

The effects of child abuse are pervasive and often multifaceted. Aside from the obvious physical injury sustained from any number of abusive violations, children who are abused often experience a range of feelings and thoughts related to anger and hostility, fear and anxiety, vulnerability and powerlessness, sadness and loss, shame, and guilt. These children struggle with trust issues, self-blame, depression, isolation, poor self-image, and many other interpersonal relationship issues. Counselors continually yearn for new ideas about how to work with children affected by abuse. Many experts contend that effective interventions focus on the appropriate expression of emotions, a positive self-image, interpersonal relationship skills, and rebuilding trust in a variety of social situations. Group counseling provides a nonjudgmental and safe climate in which children are encouraged to address a multitude of issues and in which they have the opportunity to establish relationships with their peers who have similar experiences. I have found group counseling based on the model that follows to be quite helpful for children affected by abuse. This model has emerged from my experiences as a group counselor with children affected by varying forms of abuse.

Group Goals

The main goal of this group is to foster a therapeutic relationship in which children who have been abused feel safe enough to risk trusting other children and another adult. The group is designed to establish a safe environment, empower children, and enhance their sense of self. In addition, children discover that they are not alone in their experiences and feelings and that others understand and care. This is accomplished by providing an environment in which children have an opportunity to act out the intrusive and abusive experiences. By assisting children to express the full range of mixed and confusing emotions felt toward the perpetrator, children experience a sense of control and mastery, which is another goal of this group. By the end of the group, it is hoped that all children have learned to express their feelings appropriately, acknowledge their personal strengths, and develop skills about how to have healthy interpersonal interactions and relationships.

Setting Up the Group

Screening

Screening is crucial when counseling children who have been abused, and good timing is essential in choosing group members. Children must be ready and willing to interact with other children in a therapeutic setting as evidenced by their desire to play games, talk, and generally spend time with others. All children involved in my groups have completed or are concurrently involved in individual and family counseling, and I utilize these case notes and clinical impressions to assist in the screening process. When I believe a child is ready, I invite the child to participate in group counseling. I emphasize that he or she can decline, thus empowering the child to make choices.

Group counseling is contraindicated if (1) the abuse happened recently, (2) if the abuse is still highly traumatizing to the child, (3) if the child has serious psychiatric disturbances such as suicidal behavior, self-mutilation, or severe mood or thought disturbances, or (4) if the child was abused by more than one person at a time.

The functioning and climate of the group is dependent on the behavioral patterns of prospective members. Accordingly, it is essential to balance the group with members similar in age, physical size, and gender. Likewise, the type and severity of the abuse must also be considered when composing the group so that children are not retraumatized by other children's stories. When children are deemed ready for group counseling, I seek consent from the legal guardian.

Parent or Legal Guardian Consent

In most cases, I converse with parents or legal guardians in person, but sometimes I send a letter of consent. The letter outlines

---

Dear Parent/Legal Guardian:

As you are well aware, children who have been abused often struggle with trust issues, self-blame, depression, isolation, poor self-image, and many other interpersonal relationship issues. These problems are currently or have been addressed with your child in individual and/or family counseling, but I believe group counseling can also be highly therapeutic and beneficial to your child's well-being.

My experience as a counselor and play therapist has shown me that many children affected by abuse struggle with relationships, especially peer relationships. Research indicates, and I firmly believe, that group counseling can assist many children in (1) learning how to trust others, (2) understanding that they aren't alone in their experiences, (3) developing healthy interpersonal relationship skills, and (4) increasing their sense of control and mastery in social situations. By interacting with others who have similar feelings, experiences, and concerns, children learn how to accept and cope with their emotions and thoughts more effectively.

Based on clinical observations and my professional judgment, I believe that your child is ready and prepared for a group counseling experience. Accordingly, I am requesting that you grant permission for _____ (child's name) to take part in a 10-week group that will include 5 to 7 other children who have similar concerns and are compatible in terms of age, size, and gender.

Group sessions will include an array of structured and nonstructured conversations and activities related to abuse and other mental health issues. All children and parents will be informed about the need for confidentiality, but I cannot control what children say or do outside of the session. I will, however, make every effort to enforce confidentiality and ensure the physical and emotional safety of your child. Should you have any questions or concerns about the group, please contact me at _____.

By signing this form, you acknowledge and support your child's participation in this group counseling experience and hereby provide written consent.

_____   _____
Parent's/Guardian's Signature   Date

_____   _____
Witness's Signature   Date

_____   _____
Teresa M. Christensen, PhD   Date

issues of confidentiality, therapeutic factors, and topics to be discussed in the group, and it includes a description of the process and provides a rationale for group counseling with children affected by abuse (see letter). I emphasize that group does not take the place of individual counseling but is a supplement to the current treatment plan.

Written consent is obtained from the legal guardian prior to informing the child about the group. (It is important to attain proof of legal guardianship, particularly when children have been abused.) Legal guardians may be foster or adoptive parents, grandparents, or other members of the extended family.

Group Composition and Characteristics

This type of group works most efficiently with children of similar ages (only 2 to 3 years apart) who have suffered the same type of abuse. Adolescents can also benefit from such a group, but the activities described here pertain to a group for children ages 7 to 12 who have been sexually abused. Because developmental and gender issues need to be considered, each group is structured a bit differently depending on the specific needs of the members. Due to factors such as trust, power and control, group cohesion, and boundary issues, this is a closed group. The group consists of four to six members and meets for 45 to 60 minutes once a week for 10 consecutive sessions.

Setting

Because of my experience as a play therapist, I prefer to facilitate groups with children ages 4 to 12 in the playroom. This space allows for a variety of structured activities that incorporate free play with therapeutic toys, art supplies, sand, and other creative materials.

Group Format

I use a combination of directive and nondirective techniques, and development and process issues are addressed by dividing each group session into three basic segments (warm-up, work, and wrap-up). The structure and topic for each session varies depending on the issues and needs of the individual members and the group as a whole. Aside from the initial session (Orientation) and the last session (Celebration), weekly sessions alternate between structured and nonstructured activities. Sessions 1, 2, 4, 6, 8, and 10 are highly structured through one or more activities focused on topics related to abuse. I use a variety of activities and games in the structured sessions, which are derived from my clinical experience and other resources. Sessions 3, 5, 7, and 9 are process oriented and begin with nonstructured time in the playroom with a variety of games, toys, art supplies, and activities that group members are free to choose from. The group begins with 5 to 10 minutes for warm-up which includes (a) a check-in with each member about how he or she is feeling today, (b) time to reflect on and talk about what happened in the last session, and (c) dialogue about what this group session will be like. The next 25 to 35 minutes of the group is the work phase and includes either a structured activity or free play. The final 10 to 15 minutes of each session is reserved for wrap-up, also known as T&T (Treat and Talk Time). During T&T, group members process their reactions to the session, discuss what they have learned, and establish generalizations about how their experiences in the group might affect them outside of group. The following outline includes examples of topics and activities for each of the structured sessions.

Session 1: Orientation

The initial session includes discussions about confidentiality, the purpose and structure of the group, and rules (policies). I usually begin by thanking members for choosing to be a part of this group. I also state that everyone in the group has been abused but that this is not the only reason members were selected for this experience. I explain that this group is about getting to know others and themselves and then transition into a go-around activity to break the ice. To help children get acquainted with one another, I often use an exercise in which they say their name and share their favorite animal.

During the last half of the group, I use the term *group policies* to introduce a discussion of group rules and enlist the help of group members in making a list of rules for this group. This sets the tone for empowering the children to co-construct the group experience. I record this information on a poster titled our "Group Declaration Banner" and provide a variety of art materials and encourage children to sign their names and decorate the Group Banner, which will be displayed during each group session and referred to whenever necessary to set limits. I closely monitor what policies members choose to adopt and make certain that we include rules to protect physical and emotional safety. I make certain that our declaration gives children the freedom to remain silent or pass on go-around activities, and I also emphasize boundary issues such as confidentiality and physical touch. In most cases, group members come up with policies that far surpass the rules or limits that I would enforce. Accordingly, I monitor the group to make certain that they don't make too many policies, or that the policies aren't too rigid.

Session 2: Awareness Activity

Session 2 includes a relationship-building activity intended to promote member interaction. Each member of the group creates an "identity collage," choosing four or five magazine images or words that describe how the member sees him- or herself. Once members

have had the opportunity to share their collages, they are encouraged to reflect on how they have changed since the abuse. Group members are then encouraged to select at least one more item that represents how they believe they have changed as a result of the abuse and how they feel about this change. These items are used to alter the existing collage, and group members are again given the opportunity to share their collages.

This activity gives group members an opportunity for self-reflection and self-exploration on how the abuse has affected them. When processing this activity, it is important to discuss the multitude of feelings children associate with the abuse as well as the changes they have encountered. For example, the following remarks were shared in groups I facilitated with children who had been molested: "I am sad that I don't live with my mom and dad anymore." "I hate being a boy! My body does strange and dirty things." "I don't know if I will ever find a husband, because no boy will want me after they learn about what happened with my dad."

Session 4: Trust Activity

During the fourth session, I focus on activities pertaining to trust. Examples might include doing a trust walk and then having members create a list of people that they can trust in their lives and tell why. This session also includes an activity specific to appropriate touching and secrets, which is intended to help children learn how to set physical boundaries and how to distinguish between safe and unsafe secrets. For example, I explain that "A safe secret is not telling someone about a birthday present, whereas an unsafe secret is knowing that something hurtful or dangerous is happening to someone or you and keeping it a secret by not telling anyone." As a group activity, members are then encouraged to come up with lists of appropriate and inappropriate forms of touching and safe and unsafe secrets. This activity ends with members developing a plan about how to handle touching and secrets in a healthy manner in the future.

Session 6: Interpersonal Interaction Activity

At this point in the process, it is important to help members address relationship issues, and we cover a variety of topics related to communication including using "I" messages, how to show respect for emotional and physical boundaries, and ways to appropriately express feelings. A number of games and structured activities are specifically designed to address these topics, including The "talking, feeling, doing" game, role plays, puppet shows, family drawings, blowing bubbles (to represent physical boundaries), and the game telephone. We also might read from books that address issues related to abuse.

At the end of this session I remind members that we only have three more sessions until our last meeting, and I ask members to begin to think about how other groups in their lives have ended. I give examples of endings by talking about what it might be like when clubs or teams don't meet anymore or the end of the school year. In particular we discuss how members have learned to say good-bye to others, we talk about "good-bye rituals" that members have experienced in their families and communities, and we begin to prepare for the end of our group.

Session 8: Resilience Activity

The goal of this session is to assist members in developing a positive self-image. The focus is on helping children identify personal strengths and learn how to use their strengths to make healthy choices in the future. At the beginning of the session, I clarify what a strength is and encourage members to take a few moments to construct a list of at least four strengths they recognize in themselves. Examples have included "I am a good listener." "I am a good friend." "I have learned how to show my anger without hitting someone or something." and "I know how to say NO." Because self-esteem can be damaged by child abuse, the group counselor's assistance is especially important here. As a group we decide what we can do to creatively exhibit our strengths. Sometimes members use art and construction materials to build kites, personal or family shields, personalized license plates, or T-shirts. Then members list their wants and needs in life, and we brainstorm ideas about how they can use their strengths to get their needs met and satisfy their desires in a healthy manner. I emphasize that they still have a choice about many aspects of their lives regardless of what people have said or done to them in the past. We talk about how their strengths can help them make healthy choices, about how to get their needs met in the future, and how to express their feelings and thoughts.

At the end of this session we discuss the upcoming celebration session. We brainstorm ideas about what they want to do (activities, games, art, talk, sing, dance). I inform group members that I will provide some sort of drink (usually juice) and one treat (usually fruit or popcorn) and tell members that they are welcome to bring something but are not required to do so. This takes pressure off children who are anxious about bringing something or whose parents/guardians don't have the resources or aren't actively involved in this process.

Session 10: Celebration

The last session is a celebration and a time to reminisce about the group experience, which includes members talking about what they have learned about themselves and others. The intent of this session is to achieve some sense of closure, and because group members have a hand in planning this session the structure often varies. Final sessions have included, but are not limited to, the following. Younger children may want to create good-bye pictures that everyone in the group signs, create and act out a skit or role play, or play a game together. Older children and adolescents are more likely to provide free time in which members of the group reminisce about previous sessions and engage in dialogue about their experiences in the group. On many occasions, the children in my groups brought refreshments to the last session and created personal journals out of art materials, which were then autographed or decorated by every member in the group as a memory of this experience. Regardless of the format, I request that all members share the following information: (a) what they have learned about their individual strengths and talents, (b) their plan about how to continue building healthy relationships outside of group, and (c) their individual plans about how to take care of themselves.

Expected Group Outcomes

Children who have been abused deserve opportunities to express their feelings and reactions in a safe and constructive environment. Group provides such an environment while also creating an experiential atmosphere in which children are able to break down the barriers of isolation, express their inner most struggles, clarify misplaced blame, and generally feel more comfortable about interacting with others. This is where healing happens with children who have been affected by abuse, and changes I have observed include enhanced interpersonal relationship skills and increased confidence, independence, and increased self-assurance. The struggle to assist children in healing from intrusive and abusive experiences can be complicated and sensitive, but I encourage group counselors to continue pursuing unique and creative ways to incorporate the therapeutic factors of group work in their interventions with children affected by abuse.

Resources that I found useful in designing this group include Hindman (1993), Kleven (1997), Rohnke (1984), and Spinal-Robinson and Wickham (1992a, 1992b, 1993).

Group Proposal

A Group for Parents Living With a Depressed Child

This group proposal had not been implemented at the time of this writing, but we include it here because it illustrates challenges group workers may face in putting groups they design into action. Often the best way to bring about change in children is to work in collaboration with the parents and, ideally, to do this in a group context. This proposal is written from the perspective of Laurie Craigen, a doctoral student at the College of William and Mary. For further information on this group, contact her by e-mail at lmcrai@wm.edu. ∎

Over the last 20 years, there has been a major shift in our nation's treatment of the mentally ill from a hospital-centered to a community-centered approach. This trend, known as deinstitutionalization, has placed an overwhelming burden on families for the care for their loved ones, with little help from the mental health treatment system.

Organizing the Group

Through my experiences in a family counseling practicum for families in which a child was diagnosed with depression, I discovered that many parents felt alone, were uninformed about their child's condition of depression, and were not aware of sources of support within the community. It became evident to me that these parents needed something in addition to family counseling. Based on my belief in the therapeutic power of working systemically and indirectly with children through the parents, I designed a com-

bined psychoeducational and support group for parents living with a depressed child.

This group has not yet been implemented due to a number of obstacles. First of all, it has been quite difficult to find a place to conduct the group. I learned that because I was not affiliated with a community agency or a clinic I could not use their resources. Universities often have limited space at inconvenient times for group meetings, and they also have policies and procedures that make it difficult to implement this kind of group. Furthermore, running the group at a public school poses problems because the schools are closed after hours. These difficulties demonstrate the importance of forming an alliance with community agencies and educating public schools about the necessity and importance of running counseling groups on their grounds.

Let me share some other issues I have confronted in my attempts to implement this group. It was important for me to decide where I would recruit the potential participants for the group. If I targeted schools, then I would need to contact school counselors and school psychologists. If I decided to target the community as the setting, then meeting with local physicians and community and agency mental health professionals was in order. Before deciding on my target population, I needed to consider the advantages and disadvantages of recruiting participants from each location.

The next challenge was to decide if (and how) I would screen potential group members. As a part of the screening and orientation process, I decided to use a pretest to assess the parents' level of knowledge about depression and the support they believed was available to them. This test can also be used as a posttest to measure any shifts in the parents' attitudes and knowledge of depression. I decided that informal interviews with the parents would be a useful part of the screening process because I wanted to get a sense of parents' motivations and expectations about the group. One important consideration was evaluating whether the participants I interviewed would constitute a well-balanced group.

Group Goals

I identified a number of key goals that would assist in structuring the group. For example, I hoped participation in this group would help parents do the following:

✓ Begin to understand the role that a child's depression plays within their family

✓ Gain support in understanding and dealing with depression

✓ Become more aware of the resources available to them in the community

✓ Come to a better understanding of the physiological factors associated with depression

✓ Learn better and more effective communication strategies with their child

Group Format

The group is designed to meet for 90 minutes once a week for eight sessions, and the group is limited to 8 to 10 parents. Restricting the size of the group provides opportunities to develop cohesion and trust, which will promote communication and interaction among group members.

Before the initial group meeting, it is important for me to have some understanding of the knowledge and attitudes that the parents may be bringing with them to the group. Families are sometimes reluctant to change and strive to preserve a sense of stability. For me, it has been important to consider the entire family system in understanding how a child's depression may be serving some functions in a family.

Although parents may want help in understanding their child, it is not uncommon for them to have some reluctance in recognizing and accepting the role that depression is playing in their family life. Parents may enter the group at different stages of knowledge and with a diverse range of emotional reactions to their child's condition. For example, some parents may feel confused, angry, or depressed whereas others may be experiencing grief and concern for what their child is experiencing. Some parents may enter the group with a great deal of knowledge about depression and others may know very little. I think it is essential that group leaders understand something about the participants' background and how to work effectively with them.

The format and specific structure of the group depends on the needs of the participants. The group may range from a structured one to a more open discussion or support group, depending on the knowledge base and background of the members. Generally, sessions involve some teaching of content and also exploration of the interactions within the group. Some sessions are psychoeducationally oriented, and others more process oriented. Flexibility in the range of topics and the structure of the group are important considerations in implementing a successful group.

The following descriptions are illustrative of how this 8-week group is generally structured.

Session 1: Orientation Session

In the initial session it is important to allow members to introduce themselves, to state and explore their expectations, and to give a brief sense of how they are affected by having a child with depression. In addition to having each member share his or her reason for being in the group, it is important to form personal goals at this time. The first session is also a time for providing an orientation to how the group process works and the main purposes of the group. This includes identifying and discussing some basic ground rules, such as confidentiality, attendance, ways to get involved in the group sessions, and procedures for effectively meeting the intent of the group.

Sessions 2 and 3: Common Difficulties and Strategies

Two sessions are anticipated for this discussion because it is expected that many parents will be in need of support and education in this area. Parents are encouraged to talk about specific frustrations, problems, and behaviors they are dealing with pertaining to their child's situation. It may be important for parents to hear that they are not alone in the situation they are facing. Group members are encouraged to explore specific strategies they have employed in dealing with their child. Especially important are strategies that they felt actually helped the situation. In this way members can learn from one another and build on their strengths and the resources they may already possess. In addition, strategies such as using humor, setting and maintaining boundaries, and parental self-care are taught. During these sessions, members have the opportunity to role-play specific strategies.

Session 4: Explanation/Definition of Depression

A brief explanation of the potential causes of depression is given. This is presented in an unbiased, neutral way, addressing both the biological and environmental theories. Be-

fore the presentation, parents may be asked the following questions: What do you believe is the cause of your child's depression? What messages does society give to parents about the causes of depression? After the presentation, parents may be asked, what was most surprising about the presentation? What do you now believe contributed to your child's depression? Have your thoughts changed as a result of this presentation?

Session 5: Therapy Options

During the first part of this session, group members are taught ways of seeking out mental health professionals. Attention is given to demystifying the psychotherapy process and to showing how it can be a useful resource. Various theories of counseling are addressed, qualifications of the mental health professional are explained, and specific questions to ask a mental health professional are provided to parents. Group members will have time to discuss their reactions to this information. As part of an open discussion, members are encouraged to talk about their present concerns or to ask questions that are relevant to the group.

Session 6: Medication Options

During the first part of the session, parents are given information about the range of different medications available for treating depression. It is important to make family members aware of these options and to educate them about the medication their child is taking. It can also be useful to talk about the validity of using medication in treating depression. Some theorists believe that depression can be treated with psychotherapy alone. As is the case with all group sessions, members have time to discuss their reactions to the information they receive and are given the opportunity to raise questions about their concerns.

Session 7: Awareness/Education of Outside Resources

The role that the educational, medical, insurance, and criminal justice systems play in providing assistance in understanding and dealing with depression is a key topic. Certain professionals in each arena are invited to speak to the group, and the participants can direct questions to these professionals. During the latter portion of the group session, members are encouraged to reflect, process, and react to the speakers' presentations.

Session 8: Ending the Group

It is important to remind the members prior to the final group session that the group will be ending so that they can prepare themselves for closure of the experience. At the last group session members review their group experience, take the posttest discussed previously, and reflect on questions such as these:

✓ What have you learned about yourself and your child as a result of participating in this group?

✓ Have you discovered new ways of coping with your child's depression?

✓ What was most valuable about this group?

✓ What specific information was most helpful to you?

✓ What did you learn about yourself?

✓ Who in the group was most instrumental/helpful to you?

✓ To what extent do you intend to stay in touch with any of the group members?

✓ How will you continue to find support and education for yourself now that this group is coming to an end? [Members are encouraged to do something for themselves in this 90-minute time period each week after the end of the group.)

Before the group ends, plans are made for follow-up meetings to check on members' progress.

Group Outcomes

The effectiveness of the group can be measured informally by monitoring participants' behavior in the group, attendance, and completion of homework assignments, or more formally through pre- and posttests, which are useful for determining any shifts in the thinking of parents.

In addition, follow-up interviews conducted with both the parents and their children provide important outcome measures. These interviews are scheduled for one month, six months, and one year after the conclusion of the group and include questions asked at the final group session as well as issues addressed in the posttest evaluation. Results from the evaluations and the follow-up meetings are critical resources in determining what changes to make in future groups.

Resources

I would like to acknowledge Laura Hoffman, Dr. Sandra Ward, and Dr. Tammi Milliken for their insight and assistance on this project. In designing this proposal I found these sources especially useful for information on support groups for family members living with children with depression: Adamec (1996), Papolos (1997), and Sheffield (1998). Other sources that provided useful research information include Biegel and Schulz (1999), Marsh (1998), Thompson and Doll (1982), and Whisman and Bruce (1999).

The following organizations offer information about depression, including addresses of local and state chapters and support groups:

✓ National Alliance for the Mentally Ill
  1(800) 950-NAMI

✓ National Foundation for Depressive Illness 1(800) 248-4344

✓ National Mental Health Association 1(800) 969-6642

Useful information about depression for family members and professionals can be found at these Web sites:

✓ Anne Sheffield (for information about the effects of caring for a loved one with depression): www.depressionfallout.com

✓ Families for Depression Awareness (raising awareness of depression and reducing associated stigma): www.familyaware.org/

✓ *Points to Remember*

Groups for Children

Here are some key points in designing and conducting a group for children:

✓ In designing a group in schools or agencies, strive to develop collaborative relationships with agency directors, principals, and colleagues.

✓ It is essential to understand the laws of your state regarding children and the policies of the agency where you work.

✓ It is a good practice to obtain written permission of parents or guardians for group members who are under the age of 18.

✓ Confidentiality is particularly important in groups with children. Communicate with children about the importance of keeping confidences.

✓ Remember that ethical practice demands that you have the training and supervision required to facilitate a group with children.

✓ Not all children are ready for group participation. You need to have clear criteria regarding who can benefit from involvement in a group.

✓ Having some structure is particularly important in groups with children.

✓ If you practice group work with children, give thought to helpful methods of evaluating the outcomes of your groups.

Exercises

In-Class Activities

1. **Designing Groups for Children.** In small groups work collaboratively to design different kinds of groups for children. In developing your proposal, consider factors such as type of group, goals and purposes, strategies for recruiting members, format and structure of the group, and methods for evaluating outcomes.

2. **Critiquing Group Proposals.** In small groups critique the group proposals presented in this chapter. How creative are the proposals? What aspects of each proposal would you want to incorporate in one of your group proposals? What are some of the advantages of using a group format for the kinds of problems explored in each group?

3. **Guest Speaker.** Invite a therapist who conducts groups with children to your class to discuss how he or she sets up such a group. The speaker could share both the challenges in doing group work with children and the unique benefits for children.

4. **Reporting on Children's Groups.** Some class members can make a visit to a school or a community agency where groups are available for children. Find out what types of groups are offered, the structure of these groups, and the reactions of children who are in the groups. Present what you find to your class.

InfoTrac College Edition

For additional readings, explore InfoTrac College Edition, our online library, at http://www.infotrac.college.com/wadsworth. The following keywords are listed in such a way as to enable the InfoTrac College Edition search engine to locate a wider range of articles. The keywords should be entered exactly as listed, to include asterisks, "w1," "w2," "AND," and other search engine tools.

- group* w1 psych* AND children
- group* w1 psych* AND school

Chapter 10

Groups for Adolescents

Focus Questions

*B*efore reading this chapter, ask yourself what kinds of experiences and training you would need to facilitate a group with adolescents. What questions do you have about designing a group for adolescents? As you read this chapter, consider these questions:

1. If you were going to organize a group experience for adolescents in either a school or a community setting, what specific steps would you take? What would be some of the basic aspects of your written proposal?

2. If you were facilitating an adolescent group, how would you get the members to actively participate? How might you deal with reluctance on the part of members?

3. If you were asked to colead a multiple family therapy group, what challenges might you face? What kinds of issues would you most want to explore with your coleader before you began such a group?

4. If you were working in a community mental health agency and asked to do outreach work with adolescents, what kind of group skills would be especially important to you? What kinds of groups would be particularly useful as part of a prevention program with at-risk adolescents?

5. After reading the various proposals for groups with adolescents in this chapter, which specific proposal most captures your interest? What are you learning about designing a particular group from studying these proposals?

❋ Introduction

A detailed description of the unique needs and problems of adolescents is beyond the scope of this book. For group leaders who work with adolescents, good courses in the psychology of adolescents are essential. Reading and reflecting on one's own adolescent experiences and perhaps reliving some of these experiences are also valuable means of preparing to counsel adolescents.

The adolescent period is a time of searching for an identity and clarifying a system of values that will influence the course of one's life. One of the most important needs of this period is to experience successes that will lead to a sense of individuality and connectedness, which in turn lead to self-confidence and self-respect regarding their uniqueness and their sameness. Adolescents need opportunities to explore and understand the wide range of their feelings and to learn how to communicate with significant others in such a way that they can make their wants, feelings, thoughts, and beliefs known.

The adolescent years can be extremely lonely ones; it is not unusual for adolescents to feel that they are alone in their conflicts and self-doubt. It is a period of life when people feel a need for universal approval yet must learn to distinguish between living for others' approval and earning their own. During these years, the dependence–independence struggle becomes central. Although teenagers yearn for independence from their parents, they also long for security.

Adolescents often experience stressors associated with pubertal changes, demands for and engagement in sexual activity, and fears of early, unwanted pregnancy (Rose, 1998). Sexual conflicts are also part of the adolescent period; adolescents not only need to establish a meaningful guide for their sexual behavior but also must wrestle with the problem of their gender-role identification. Teenagers often have difficulty clarifying what it means to be a man or a woman and what kind of man or woman they want to become.

Adolescents are pressured to succeed; they are expected to perform, frequently up to others' standards. There are pressures to succeed in school and to be thinking about what they want to do for a career. They need to be trusted and given the freedom to make some significant decisions, and they need the faith and support of caring adults. But they also need guidelines and limits.

Adolescence is a time for continually testing limits, for this period is characterized by an urge to break away from control or dependent ties that restrict freedom. Although adolescents are often frightened of the freedom they do experience, they tend to mask their fears with rebellion and cover up their dependency needs by exaggerating their newly felt autonomy. They are often moody, negativistic, and rebellious. The rebellion of adolescents can be understood as an attempt to determine the course of their own lives and to assert that they are who and what they want to be—rather than what others expect of them.

A central part of the adolescent experience is peer group pressure, a potent force that pulls at the person to conform to the standards of friends. Because of adolescents' exaggerated need for approval, there is a danger that they will increasingly look to others to tell them who and what they should be. The need for acceptance by one's peer group is often stronger than the need for self-respect. This can lead to a range of behaviors that cause problems for adolescents such as dependence on drugs or alcohol in order to feel anything or to escape from painful feelings.

Adolescents tend to be more aware of what the world does to them than of what they do to the world. Thus, they can be highly critical and fault finding. At times they may want to drop out of society, yet at other times they may idealistically strive to reform society. Adolescents confront dilemmas similar to those faced by the elderly in our society: finding meaning in life and wrestling with feelings of uselessness. Adolescents are continually preparing for the future, which is often marked by uncertainty.

In sum, for most people adolescence is a difficult period characterized by paradoxes: they strive for closeness, yet they also fear intimacy and often avoid it; they rebel against control, yet they want direction and structure; although they push and test limits imposed on them, they see some limits as a sign of caring; they are not given complete autonomy, yet they are often expected to act as though they were mature adults; they are typically highly self-centered, self-conscious, and preoccupied with their own world, yet they are expected to cope with societal demands to go outside themselves by expanding their horizons; they are asked to face and accept reality, and at the same time they are tempted by many avenues of escape; and they are exhorted to think of the future, yet they have strong urges to live for the moment and to enjoy life. With all these polarities it is easy to understand that adolescence is typically a turbulent and fast-moving time, one that can accentuate loneliness and isolation. Group experiences can be very useful in helping teenagers deal with these feelings of isolation and make constructive choices for a satisfying life.

※ Developmental Group Counseling With Adolescents

This brief sketch of the main currents of adolescent life highlights the need for developmental counseling in this population. The group leader needs to understand the development needs of children and adolescents. Generally, adolescents are more concerned with friendship issues than are younger children, and adolescents struggle with separation from parents and self-identity issues. These different needs influence the group structure, group process, topics for discussions, and the interventions that will be used (Shechtman, 2004).

Because the peer group is an important source of support for adolescents, groups are the treatment of choice (Shechtman, 2004). Based on various literature reviews, it is clear that group counseling is effective for children and adolescents (Gazda, Ginter, & Horne, 2001; Hoag & Burlingame, 1997). Group therapy has been shown to be as effective as individual therapy and there is the advantage of cost-effectiveness of groups. With the prevalence of mental health problems among children and adolescents, group counseling has become an appropriate response (Rose, 1998).

Group counseling is especially suitable because adolescents can identify and experience their conflicting feelings, discover that they are not unique in their struggles, openly question those values they decide to modify, learn to communicate with peers and adults, learn from the modeling provided by the leader, and learn how to accept what others offer and to give of themselves in return. Adolescents often need to learn to label and verbalize their feelings. Groups provide a place where they can safely experiment with reality and test their limits. A unique value of group counseling is that it lets adolescents be instrumental in one another's growth; group members help one another in the struggle for self-understanding. Most important, a group gives adolescents a chance to express themselves and to be heard and to interact with their peers.

Groups for adolescents can combine personal themes with psychoeducational goals. In working with adolescents it is a good practice to have clearly defined goals, relevant themes, and a structure that will enable members to develop trust in the group. Aronson and Scheidlinger (1994) state that adolescents tend to function best in homogeneous groups with explicit limits and clear ground rules. They address the importance of considering the age of members in structuring an adolescent group, making these points:

- Between the ages of 10 and 14, young people are prone to denial and externalization, tend to be more concrete in their thinking, are more self-conscious, and may not show great interest in the process of self-awareness. They function better in either all-male or all-female groups.

- Between the ages of 15 and 18, adolescents are generally able to tolerate more anxiety, and it is critical that older adolescents learn how to interact in a group with both sexes.

Time-limited groups are growing in popularity in schools, clinics, and community agencies. The number of specialized groups has increased, including groups for sexually abused adolescents, teenagers from alcoholic families, and youths with chronic medical conditions (Aronson & Scheidlinger, 1994). Not all adolescents belong in a group or benefit from one. For instance, individual counseling may be more appropriate for adolescents who are acting out their hostility. Riva and Haub (2004) stress that group treatment is not suitable for all children and adolescents. They indicate that students who are highly anxious or extremely shy might find a counseling group too stressful.

Agencies and schools are cautioned not to put young people into a group primarily because it is cost-effective or because there are not enough counselors to meet the demand for services. Adolescents should be carefully selected for a particular group. Inadequate screening procedures can defeat the potential effectiveness of the group process. Even though many adolescents can benefit from participation in a group, individual and family interventions are also of value and can supplement group work (Rose, 1998).

✳ Issues and Challenges in Leading Adolescent Groups

Motivating the adolescent to become an active group participant can be challenging. Group leaders need to clearly state the guidelines for conduct during sessions and gain members' acceptance. Creativity may be required to keep meetings moving in a meaningful direction. Additional challenges include creating trust, dealing with resistance, facilitating action, using role playing, sustaining the interest of the group, and involving as many members as possible.

✳ Establishing Trust

At a point early in an adolescent group's history, we might say something like this: "We hope you will eventually feel free enough to say in the group what you think and feel, especially if it is a persistent reaction. It is especially important that you talk about any fears you are having about being in this group. What do you imagine it would be like for you to talk about personal struggles with the people in this room? We hope this will become a place where you can reveal personal concerns and find, with the help of others, a way of recognizing, understanding, and perhaps resolving certain problems. Our aim is to create a climate in which you can feel that what you say is important and that you're respected for who you are. The value of the sessions depends on your level of commitment. If you merely show up and listen, you are likely to leave disappointed. We'd like you to think about what you want from each session. These sessions are aimed at exploring any topics that you bring to the group. There may be times when you will be uncomfortable in here, and we encourage you to take the risk of talking about your discomfort. You are likely to discover that the atmosphere in this group differs from many other social settings. It is our expectation that you will be honest with yourself and with others in this group."

As part of the discussion in an initial session, it is essential to cover issues such as confidentiality, group norms, ground rules, establishing boundaries to clarify appropriate and facilitative ways of interacting within the group, giving and receiving feedback, and suggestions for applications outside of the group. (For other topics that we typically explore during the early phase of a group as a way of generating trust, refer to the discussion in Chapter 5 on the initial stage.)

Knowing Your Comfort Zone With Self-Disclosure

Adolescents often test group leaders to determine whether they mean what they have told them about the group. For example, adolescents will frequently ask the group leader questions such as "Have you ever experimented with drugs?" or "Have you ever been divorced?" or "What are your thoughts about casual sex?" How leaders respond to questions such as these tells the members how much they can trust them as group leaders. If this testing by adolescents is accepted in a nonjudgmental and nondefensive way, trust is enhanced and reluctance to participate in the group is reduced. Adolescents are quick to detect both authenticity and inauthenticity. A key leader task is to model congruence between what is said and what is actually done.

Working With Involuntary and Reluctant Adolescent Group Members

In working with adolescents who are involuntary members and are reluctant to participate, we have found some of the following interventions helpful. Consider how these ideas could be applied to some groups you may lead or colead.

First of all, much of the negative reaction of adolescents to involuntary participation in a group can be effectively explored by first meeting with them individually. At this meeting you can discuss their reservations, give them specific information about the group, and in a nondefensive way explore their attitudes and provide them with an opportunity to express their reactions to being "forced" into the group. You can also point out to them that they *did* make a choice to come to the group. They could have refused and taken the consequences of not complying with the directive. During the individual pregroup meeting, it is helpful to explore any of the adolescent's past experiences with therapy. You can do a lot to demystify the process by providing accurate information about the goals of the group, your role as a group leader, and other considerations that we discussed in Chapters 2, 3, and 4.

Another way to work with uncooperative adolescents is to respect their reservations, rather than fighting *against* them, and to attempt to work out alternatives to a group. One example of such an option is to continue seeing these adolescents individually for a number of sessions to establish a relationship with them before putting them in a group. You might also invite them to join the group for three sessions and to make a sincere effort to participate. Then if they are still reluctant to participate in the group, consider allowing them to leave. The rationale for this strategy is that these adolescents will have some basis for a decision after they have been to a few group sessions. Even though they were directed to "get counseling," this is one way to provide some increased element of choice. Because forced therapy would only entrench negative attitudes, the leader may genuinely be able to help them find another solution.

Another alternative is to invite a skeptical adolescent to attend the group for a session or so without any pressure to participate. It is important to let the other members know that this person is an observer, there to determine if he or she wants to continue. Group members will then be less likely to resent the nonparticipant, and they can let this person know whether they themselves have overcome their reluctance to actively participating in the group.

Adolescents who attend a session involuntarily often show their reluctance through sarcasm and silence. It is important to respond not with defensiveness but with honesty, firmness, and caring confrontations. Assume that Dwight says "I don't want to be here!" Examples of unhelpful responses are: "Look, I don't want to be here either." "Well, if you don't like being here, leave." "I don't care what you want. You're here, and I expect you to participate." "Life is tough. We don't always get what we want." Obviously, these leader responses are very defensive and do not encourage member participation. The following dialogue presents a more effective intervention.

> **Leader** [in a nondefensive tone]: *Tell me more about not wanting to be here.*
>
> **Dwight:** *They sent me, and I don't need this group.*
>
> **Leader:** *I know it's difficult doing something you don't want to do. I don't like it when people tell me what to do either. So tell me a bit more about what it's like for you to be here.*

Rather than responding too quickly in a defensive manner, the leader asks for more information in order to understand Dwight's behavior. Instead of getting into a debate over whether he needs the group, the leader accepts his immediate feelings and makes them the focus of discussion. There are many appropriate responses to his reluctance. Here are a few suggestions:

- How about if you come to the group twice to see what this is about and then decide if you want to continue?
- A lot of the members in the group felt the same way you do. Maybe they could tell you what it was like for them.
- Do you know anything about counseling? Have you ever participated in a group before?
- Why do you think you were sent here?
- I understand that you don't want to be here. Are there consequences if you choose not to attend?

It is essential to follow the adolescent's lead. At times you may feel personally rejected, but it is essential not to get bogged down in feeling ineffective and unappreciated. You cannot afford to feel highly vulnerable to rejection. Taking as a personal affront all the abrasiveness and defensiveness that some adolescents display is a quick route to burnout.

We are not suggesting that you give adolescents with negative attitudes permission to verbally abuse you. It is possible to stand up for yourself in a direct and nondefensive way. If an involuntary client taunts you with "You're a phony, and you're only in it for the money," it is not helpful to lash out and then proceed to defend yourself. Doing this can easily lead to becoming entangled in countertransference. An alternative response could be: "I don't like being called a phony by you. We've just met, and you don't have enough information about me to make that judgment. I'd like to have a chance with you before you dismiss me." This is an example of speaking for yourself and keeping the lines of communication open.

One of our colleagues, Paul Jacobson, works with imprisoned young gang members who are ordered into counseling by the court. Paul has conducted a variety of groups for this involuntary population, including emancipation groups, groups for youthful sex offenders, drug education groups, groups for teenage fathers, groups for those who chronically fail to conform to the rules of the residential facility, and groups for both perpetrators and victims of abuse. He finds that his clients lack both insight and sophistication in expressing their thoughts and feelings. His involuntary clients typically approach counseling with skepticism, doubt, lack of motivation, and hostility. They do not believe what occurs in a group can be applied to themselves and their life situation. In working with this difficult population, Paul has formulated some useful suggestions:

- *Modify your expectations.* Understand the client's world, which may be foreign to your life experience.
- *Learn to accept subtle* behavioral *changes.*
- Do not be blocked or put off by the client's abrasive language, especially if the client is cooperating behaviorally.
- Be aware of setting limits and establishing boundaries that may differ from individual to individual.
- Earn trust by being honest and direct in your reactions to clients personally.
- Find ways of supporting the expression of clients' feelings without necessarily approving of destructive actions.
- Be aware of your own motivations for choosing to work with a difficult population.
- *Realize that the rewards may not be dramatic* and that you *may not* often have the satisfaction of knowing that you have made a difference in a person's life.

In working with extremely challenging adolescents, Paul continually re-evaluates his goals and reflects on these issues. He knows that it is essential to pay attention to the impact that his work has on him personally and to take preventive measures against the ever-present threat of burnout.

The Influence of the Leader's Personality

Adolescents tend to respond well to leaders who share themselves with the group, displaying a caring attitude, enthusiasm and vitality, openness, and directness. Adolescents will generally relate well to you as a leader if you appropriately reveal your personal experiences or concerns. If you genuinely respect and enjoy adolescents, you will typically be rewarded with a reciprocal respect.

Adolescents will also be aware if you have never fully experienced your adolescence or if you have some major unfinished business from those years that gets in your way as a leader. For example, an adult who has never faced or resolved certain adolescent fears related to sexuality or lovability may find these fears resurfacing as he or she leads an adolescent group. It is crucial that you be willing and courageous enough to explore much of your own adolescent experience so you do not become enmeshed in countertransference.

We think it is wise to avoid trying to become like adolescents by imitating their slang and manner of speaking. By trying too hard to be accepted, you may lose adolescents' trust and respect. You would do well to remember that you hold a different position from theirs and that they usually expect you to act differently.

Keeping the Sessions Moving

It is not an easy task to challenge participants in an adolescent group to focus on themselves in the here and now. Especially in the beginning, members have a tendency to tell elaborate stories. It is sometimes useful to say to a member after a long story, "If you had only one sentence to express what you have just said, what would it be?" A detailed story could be simply stated as "I sometimes resent my girlfriend for the way she treats me!" Our task is to teach members to express themselves in personal and concrete ways and to steer them away from telling irrelevant stories. This requires active intervention on the leader's part.

We favor active intervention and structuring for adolescent groups, particularly during the initial stage. Some structuring can provide the direction needed to keep the sessions moving. Specifying a theme or topic related to the interests and needs of the adolescents is one way to provide structure to the discussion. Avoid adult themes such as "How can you improve your study habits?" or "How can you learn to respect your teachers?" as the group may well have little interest in these topics and the sessions are bound to bog down.

Our preference is to request that members say how they are affected by a situation rather than how other people act toward them. For instance, Yesenia began by talking about how she felt misunderstood by her mother. She started to tell stories about her mother, blaming her for her unhappiness, and focused on her mother's feelings. The leader might intervene in this way: "You seem to be talking more about your mother right now than about yourself. Tell us about *you*."

Another dynamic that commonly keeps a group from reaching a productive level is one member bombarding another with questions instead of making a personal statement. When such questioning occurs, it is appropriate for the group leader to make a comment such as "Marco, instead of questioning Charlene, tell her what it was that provoked you to ask the question." Unless the questioning is stopped in this way, the intensity of Charlene's experience may soon be dissipated. The leader can try to prevent this from happening by stressing that it is far better for members to say how they are affected by someone's experience and in what ways they are identifying with the person than to distract the member with questions.

Teaching members how to share themselves through statements rather than questioning is more effective when it is done in a timely, appropriate, and sensitive manner as certain behaviors or interactions are occurring in the session. For example, instead of asking "Why are you so quiet?" a leader can intervene with "Would you be willing to let her know how you're being affected by her silence?"

Action-Oriented Techniques of Role Playing

Role playing is an excellent way to keep the interest level high, to involve a lot of the members, and to give a here-and-now flavor to the work being done. Role playing fosters creative problem solving, encourages spontaneity, usually intensifies feelings, and gets people to identify with others. By role playing, participants can learn how to express themselves more effectively, test reality, and practice new behavior.

If members are well prepared for action-oriented techniques, role-playing methods can bring vitality to the sessions. For instance, if Scott is complaining about how his girlfriend, Dawn, treats him, someone can role-play his girl friend and symbolically Scott can let her know how he is affected by the way she treats him. If appropriate, still another member might "become Dawn" and tell everyone in the group what she thinks of Scott; this could be useful in helping him stand in her shoes. Through such action-oriented techniques, more feelings are elicited, and de-energizing stories are minimized. Members also get a chance to say out loud things that they have kept inside. Through role reversal, they can gain empathy for others in their lives.

We find that members become comfortable with role playing more quickly if we engage with them in role-playing a situation. For instance, if a female participant has been describing how she views her parents and how frustrated she feels when she tries to talk with them, we might take the part of her mother and father. That will enable her to deal directly, albeit symbolically, with her parents and feel her frustration intensely. We can then stop the action and ask her: "What are you experiencing now? What would you most like to do now? If you could reach us, make us really hear you, what would you most want to say?" The role playing may be brief. When it is over, the person should discuss the experience and plan how to handle this situation when it arises in the future.

Adolescents are often self-conscious about getting involved in role playing. It is useful to provide a general orientation to the techniques you employ, which could be done at a pregroup session. Both the timing and manner of introducing techniques are directly related to whether adolescents are likely to cooperate. When an adolescent says he or she would feel silly in role playing, you might respond with "I know it seems silly and a bit awkward, but how about trying it anyway to see what you might learn about yourself?" Generally, if we approach role playing in this light and gentle way, the self-consciousness dissipates, and before the participant knows it, he or she is playing a role with gusto. We check frequently to see whether a person wants to explore a particular problem and is willing to use role playing to do so. One of us might say: "You seem to be unclear about how your mother really affects you and how you should deal with her. Are you willing to try something?"

There are many variations of role-playing techniques. To illustrate, we will use the example of Sally, who discloses that she feels she can never please her father and that this hurts her. She says that she and her father are not close and that she would like to change that. She is afraid of her father. She sees him as critical of her, and she feels that unless she is perfect she cannot win his approval. Several role-playing situations are possible; for example:

- **Sally can play her father,** to provide a picture of how she perceives him, and give a lecture telling Sally all the things she must become before she is worthwhile in his eyes. Speaking as her father, Sally might say something like this: "I know you have a lot more ability than you show. Why didn't you get all A's? Yes, I'm proud of you for getting five A's, but I must confess I'm let down by that one B. If you really put your mind to it, I know you could do better." We would encourage Sally to stay in her father's role for a time and say things that she imagines he is thinking but not expressing.
- A group member who identifies with Sally can play her while Sally continues playing her father. From the dialogue that ensues, Sally can get an idea of how her father feels with her. A group member with a similar conflict can benefit from involvement in the situation.
- A member who feels that he or she can identify with the father can play that role. If nobody in the group jumps at this opportunity, the leader can take the parent role. This situation enables Sally to intensify her feelings and to demonstrate how she deals with her father. As the role playing continues, she may achieve insight into herself that will help her make some changes.
- **Sally can play both herself and her father.** She can be directed to say (as her father) what she wishes he would say to her. This is a future projection, and it taps the person's hopes.
- Sally can present a soliloquy, talking aloud as her father, saying what she imagines her father might say about her. She can also use the

soliloquy approach when she is in her own role, after she finishes an exchange with her father. She can express many of the thoughts and feelings she generally keeps locked within herself when she talks with her father.

- Several other group members can sit in for Sally and show how they would deal with her father. This may suggest to her options she had not considered.

- Other members who role-played Sally's father can provide helpful feedback to her by telling her what they felt as they were listening to her. She may be less defensive in hearing from her peers about how they were put off by her abrasive style than if an adult provided feedback.

- If Sally decides she wants to talk to her father in real life, it is important to caution her to avoid a blaming stance toward her father. Instead, Sally can be helped to deliver her message to him in a way that he is more likely willing to hear.

Because it is important for members to process these dramas, the leader should ask them to think about the implications of what they observed in themselves in the role-playing situations. At this time feedback from other members and interpretations from the leader can enable the members to see with more clarity their own part in their conflicts with others and what they can do to make life better for themselves. If you are interested in a more in-depth discussion of role-playing techniques in groups, refer to Chapter 8 ("Psychodrama") and Chapter 11 ("Gestalt Therapy") in G. Corey (2004).

Getting Group Members to Participate and Initiate

During the sessions we look for ways to bring uninvolved group members into the interactions. After Sally's role playing, for example, we might encourage other members to tell what they experienced as she was working with her father. We might ask: "Can any of you give Sally feedback? What did you see her doing? Did she spark any feelings in you?" Adolescents are usually most eager to become personally involved when other members touch vulnerable spots in them. As we have mentioned, one real advantage of group counseling is that the members can be of service to their peers by giving their perceptions, revealing similar problems, suggesting alternatives, supporting them in times of despair, reflecting what they hear them saying, and confronting their inconsistencies. Therefore, we try to involve as many members as possible in the group process.

In addition, we try to shape the group so that we will be less and less required to give direction. One of the signs of an effective group is that members gradually assume an increasing share of the leadership functions. For instance, if a group that usually functions effectively begins to stray aimlessly, a member will probably point this out. If a group member gets bogged down in story-telling and intellectualizing, we expect members to react. In short, one of our aims is to teach adolescents to monitor themselves in their group and become less dependent on us for direction.

Multiple Family Group Therapy

For further information contact Dr. Jill Thorngren at Montana State University, Department of Health and Human Development, 318 Herrick Hall, Bozeman, MT 59717-3540; telephone (406) 994-3299; fax (406) 994-2013; e-mail jillt@montana.edu. ■

Organizing the Group

Adolescence can be a turbulent period for both the individual and his or her family members. The inherent search for an identity coupled with the influences of societal, parental, and peer pressure can lead to upheaval in any adolescent's life. Although a great many adolescents and their families cope quite well with this developmental stage, some do not. The search for individual identity and increased autonomy and, at the same time, acceptance may be undertaken by experimenting with illegal activities, abusing substances, or becoming involved with "gang" activities. At this point the juvenile justice system may become involved in the lives of these adolescents and their families.

Oftentimes, family counseling is mandated as part of a juvenile probation order. The challenges for the counselor are then multiplied. Not only are the typical power struggles between parents and adolescents at play, but there often ensues a power struggle between the family and the court system. One method that I have found especially useful for working with these complex interrelationships is multiple family group therapy (MFGT), which my colleagues and I have written about elsewhere (see Thorngren, Christensen, and Kleist, 1998; Thorngren and Kleist, 2002).

The Advantages of MFGT

Multiple family group therapy (MFGT) is a planned, psychosocial approach to treatment that involves two or more families. This approach combines elements of education and group process to harness the strengths of individual families and their members to bring about greater problem-solving abilities and enhanced functioning for the group as a whole. MFGT originated within large mental hospitals in the late 1950s, and it has been recognized as a viable treatment method in residential group homes, outpatient hospital settings, and community agencies. MFGT offers an exciting combination of family systems and group theories that enable therapists and family members to explore the dynamics of multiple subsystems and the stages of group development.

Inherent in **MFGT** is a rich sampling of subsystems and boundary issues. Parental subsystems, children subsystems, and sibling subsystems are readily visible within individual families and across the group as a whole. Types of boundaries that surround each subsystem can be delineated and discussed. There is plenty of room to explore interactional patterns within individual families and between various families. One of the most rewarding aspects of MFGT is the cross-generational support of subsystems that is engendered. Oftentimes, adolescents from one family admonish adolescents from another family to respect and listen to their parents. Concurrently, parents in one family may encourage parents in another family to recognize the strengths that are apparent in that family's adolescent. Families can confront and illuminate one another's dynamics very effectively. Families may "hear" one another easier than they "hear" the therapist.

Multiple family group therapy brings together families who are often experiencing severe stress and feelings of isolation. As families engage in risk-taking and self-disclosure to share their stories, trust is built, and it becomes apparent that they are not alone in their struggles. Difficulties may be slightly different, but each family has dealt with critical blows to its intactness. Often, one family has just gone through a stage that another family is beginning. These similarities and differences enable families to connect and impart hope. Each family has particular strengths that become apparent to other members. Members can provide effective confrontation and feedback from a place of experience. Families can impart information about what has worked for them and what has not been successful. Not only is the content of information beneficial, the processes of socializing and learning through interpersonal interaction are invaluable for all members.

Multiple family group therapy utilizes theories of family and group therapy in ways that can be beneficial to many kinds of families. Most families can benefit from interaction with others and from the experiences that each has to share. The MFGT program described here serves families that have an adolescent who has been identified as the "problem" or targeted client. The adolescent may have been involved in substance abuse, probation violation, school-related problems, or any number of "delinquent" behaviors.

Practical Considerations

In multiple family group therapy each subgroup of parents and children should be coled by two facilitators. One of these facili-

tators should be designated the leader to take charge in facilitating whole group activities with help from the others. Leaders must be able to tolerate ambiguity and be flexible in their leadership.

Composition of multiple family groups is likely to be varied, with ages ranging from 5 years to 70-plus years if grandparents are part of the family structure. It is important to keep in mind that families exist in varied compositions and that the group can learn to exist with and learn from variation. The group described here was designed to reflect the experiences of families in their everyday lives. Other proponents of MFGT have designed groups that include only the identified patient and the parental figures.

Group leaders are left with deciding who to include in their MFGT programs, as well as how to divide the children into groups. Activities are designed to reflect the developmental and emotional needs of each group. Using a sense of humor with all participants is strongly encouraged.

As with all types of therapy, confidentiality is of utmost importance when conducting MFGT. Parents and children may be reluctant to share their family concerns, and leaders should acknowledge the difficulty inherent in this process. Leaders must model and promote open communication within and between families and work hard to ensure a safe atmosphere in which participants are able to share their unique perspectives. Basic rules such as no put-downs and one person speaking at a time may be implemented as necessary.

Other practical considerations include room, time, meals, and day care. The structure of this MFGT demanded ample room for subgroup meetings and experiential activities. The time scheduled for MFGT is typically during evening hours. A concern for many families is the interruption of their dinner hour, and funding was available to provide snacks or a light meal to participating families. This was named as a positive aspect by all participating members, and social skills around eating were incorporated in the group activities.

Funding was also available to provide day care for infants and toddlers. This, too, enabled many families to attend.

Contraindications to Participation in MFGT

Multiple family group therapy has been utilized quite successfully with court-ordered and "resistant" families. However, leaders should be aware of the additional dynamics that animosity toward forced attendance may create. I have dealt with angry families by validating their anger and giving them room to vent. This typically alleviates the need to dismiss certain members from the group. There are some basic ground rules around attendance, however. Members are asked to leave should they attend under the influence of drugs and alcohol. They are invited to attend the next session sober. It is also made clear in the beginning of the group that though expression of feelings is highly encouraged, no violence will be tolerated. Establishing norms and rules with the group members that are comfortable and provide safety for all who are involved typically decreases hurtful or inappropriate group behavior.

Group Goals

The overall goal of this group is to improve individual and family functioning for all involved. This includes improving communication, conflict resolution, and social skills, as well as fostering insight and understanding of members' individual contributions to their families through a combination of experiential and insight-based activities. Family

systems and group development theories are combined and utilized in a collaborative manner between families and leaders. Social constructionist ideas, which emphasize egalitarian relationships, multiple viewpoints, and groups of people cocreating new possibilities, are part of the underpinnings of this group. Interpersonal development theories, which emphasize people's collective influence on one another and the influence of past experiences on current behaviors, are also used to form the theoretical base of this program.

Care is taken to elicit each family member's perspective on the family. Present interactions are highlighted, and the influences of past experiences are also illuminated. Old family stories are told, and new family stories are created through the punctuation of new events and insights.

Each group takes on a life of its own that is reflective of the individual members and the styles of the leaders. Elements of both psychoeducation and group process become intertwined, depending on the needs of group members and the developmental stage of the group.

Group Format

This group is designed for up to six families. As few as two families have participated, and more families could be included depending on the number of therapists and the size of the families. All family members who are ages 5 or older are encouraged to attend.

The group meets for 2 hours per week over an 8-week period. Each week begins with a brief meeting of the entire group. Parents and children are then typically separated into groups, although families sometimes meet as a joint group for the entire evening. Depending on the makeup of the group, the children may be divided into groups of adolescents (12 and older) and groups of younger children (5–11). Discussion or activities in each group focus on a topic relevant to family functioning. Following the individual groups, members are reconvened to participate in either whole group interactions or individual family activities. The meeting ends with the entire group processing the evening's events.

Session 1: Introduction

Families and leaders introduce themselves through various icebreaking activities. For example, members may be asked to take several pieces of candy. For each piece that was taken, they are asked to say something about their family. After initial introductions and icebreaking, the primary activity is having each family describe its "story" complete with title, plot, and key characters as reflective of their current experience. This sets the theme for reauthoring family stories that are not productive, or cocreating new possibilities. Each week, families will be asked to update the group on additions or revisions to their stories.

After this activity, leaders present an overview of topics to be discussed and invite all group members to give feedback regarding what they want to discuss or accomplish in the group. All suggestions are incorporated into the discussion topics. The overview of each week is recorded on a flip chart and includes the additional topics suggested by the families.

Session 2: Communication of Feelings

In separate groups parents and children discuss aspects of communication with a key emphasis on recognizing and expressing emotion. The joint group activity is a game that includes children and parents guessing one another's emotions about certain family situations. Group members are asked to volunteer scenarios that arouse emotions. After the scenario is described, other members are asked to guess what types of emotions may go with the situation.

Session 3: Developmental Needs

Parents are given information regarding the developmental needs of children and encouraged to discuss their own needs. Discussion with the children focuses on individual identity and the particular challenges faced by each age group. A joint group activity highlights the concept of empathy during which children and parents identify the needs and feelings of one another. Parents and children are divided into separate teams. Each team is asked to identify the top 10 needs of the other team. Each team also presents scenarios reflecting challenges of their developmental stages and asks the other team to identify feelings that accompany those challenges.

Session 4: Expectations and Experiences

Parent group discussion focuses on parenting roles and styles. Specific family-of-origin experiences regarding parenting are pinpointed. Children's groups focus on identifying roles and responsibilities within each family. The families are then asked to meet in individual units to discuss and define family roles and responsibilities and to complete a family map depicting these roles. Maps are shared as part of the final group process.

Session 5: Trust Building

This week's session consists of a joint meeting of all families to discuss and define trust from each member's perspective. After a definition of trust has been agreed on, all members participate in adventure-based trust-building activities designed and led by an experienced coordinator. These activities conclude with a debriefing and meaning attachment discussion centered on trust issues within and between the families.

Session 6: Family Values

After the joint check-in families meet in individual units to discuss their family values. Parents are asked to share what values they have regarding family life and to examine the origination of those values. Children are encouraged to share what they perceive to be their family's values. In a joint group activity, families share their values with other families, and a game is played that assesses the importance of particular values to each family. Values such as trust, loyalty, and communication are named, and the family on the "hot seat" ranks on a scale of 1 to 10 how much their family values that particular construct. Other families attempt to guess the value that was given based on their observations and interactions with that family in the group.

Session 7: Conflict Resolution and Special Topics

After the initial joint group meeting and check-in, parents and children are separated to discuss their perspectives on conflicts that are most prevalent in their family. Individuals are asked to consider what they could contribute to solving the conflicts. After a short break the group is reconvened to participate in a conflict resolution activity.

Members discuss a short conflict resolution plan that includes the following steps: (a) identifying the specific conflict, (b) assessing who is involved in the conflict, (c) identifying the needs and feelings of those involved, (d) identifying viable options, (e) describing consequences of each option, (f) noting what each involved person can contribute to resolution, and (g) asking other involved people for necessary help. Active listening and communicating skills (for example, "I" messages) are also reviewed.

After this presentation and review each family is asked to determine a "hot topic" in their family. Topics such as money, substance abuse, sexual behaviors, and curfews have all been named for discussion. As each family presents their conflict around an identified topic, other families help them toward resolution using the conflict resolution plan. Group members are encouraged to coach one another in using effective communication skills.

Session 8: Celebration and Wrap-Up

The final session consists of a joint group meeting for the entire time. Each family is asked to tell a new story that incorporates the changes each of their members has made. The evening concludes with a potluck dinner and program evaluation.

Group Outcomes

Members who participate in MFGT generally report positive outcomes, with the number one benefit of attendance being increased social support. This typically breaks down into support from same generation peers as well as support across generations. Families tend to feel less isolated socially and more connected individually.

Though this group may form around the "identified patient" concept, the goal is to focus on all family interactions and contributions. Care is taken to focus on the strengths of individual families and members and to punctuate changes. Leaders encourage all members to take interpersonal risks in disclosing their needs, wants, feelings, and reactions. Though members are hesitant initially, much growth has occurred through this process. Parents and teens may have new experiences of being truly honest with one another. Adolescents report discovering their parents are "human," and parents report an increased ability to treat their adolescents humanely. Increased understanding occurs for all when feelings behind behaviors are unmasked. Members have reported a sense of empowerment and the ability to view their family more positively after participating in the group.

If you are interested in further reading on multiple family group therapy, we recommend Thorngren, Christensen, and Kleist (1998); Thorngren and Kleist (2002); McKay, Gonzales, Stone, Ryland, and Kohner (1995); Meezan, O'Keefe, and Zariani (1997); and O'Shea and Phelps (1985).

Group Proposal

Teens Making a Change (T-MAC): A Group Addressing Teen Delinquency in an Apartment Complex

A more comprehensive look at T-MAC is provided in the guidebook Combating Teen Delinquency in an Apartment Setting Through Village Building *(Carter, 1998), or contact Director Sheila D. Carter, Psy.D. (drsheila_2000 @yahoo.com), The South Central Training Consortium, Inc., 1672 W. Avenue J., Suite 207, Lancaster, CA 93534; (661) 951-4662, or (661) 789-0857.* ■

Grassroots community-based groups for troubled youth can be considered the wave of the future. Based on a community psychology perspective, this group is designed as a preventive and intervention measure to help youth that live in an apartment complex. This setting is primarily composed of low socioeconomic status working-class African American and Latino families. The group serves as an additional support to families raising adolescents who may be susceptible to delinquent behaviors due to social and environmental factors. The group addresses traditional delinquent behaviors as well as teen dating, gangs, and racial differences and similarities. This is accomplished by incorporating several different components to increase awareness, promote dialogue, and instill pride and a sense of belonging.

Organizing the Group

The group is housed in an apartment complex where the youth live with their families, and it involves neighbors as well as community leaders, business professionals, and politicians. Group members range in ages from 12 to 19 and are self-referred. The group is composed of several different components to help youth become more productive in their community, school, and family. The group has adopted the motto "Hood life isn't the only life," and the group focuses on outings to areas outside their immediate living environment. The group meets weekly for 60 minutes with a group facilitator and parent/neighbor volunteer. Typically, the group is open-ended and ongoing; however, there may be a summer break to accommodate youth who go on summer vacation with their families.

The group agrees on rules for group behavior, consequences, and leadership. Confidentiality and safety issues are also discussed and honored. The facilitator also explains the importance of parental involvement and the limits of confidentiality when it concerns serious threats of harm to self or others. The group addresses delinquent behaviors through open discussions. The structure includes viewing videotapes, interacting with guest speakers, and role plays. Several components have proved beneficial to the success of the group.

✓ *Discussion Groups.* Today's teens are still searching for a caring ear and a way to express themselves in a healthy way. They are mostly concerned with and interested in subjects such as dating, sex, peer and family relations, careers, gangs, and fashion. Many inner-city youth do not have a forum in which to openly express their concerns in these areas, especially with a concerned and caring adult. Group members should be encouraged to present topics of interest.

✓ *Activities and Outings.* Outings play an important part for this group in that they help actualize opportunity. Teens from the neighborhood already know how to survive the social and environmental ills surrounding them. For many this way of life is all they know. Showing youth that the world is large and filled with great opportunities enhances their confidence and gives them a chance to explore new avenues. T-MAC outings have included a trip to the state capitol in Sacramento, hiking, going to museums and amusement parks, taking a trip to the snow in the mountains, going to stage plays, and a host of other outings and activities. Members also have participated in cleaning up graffiti and marching with political figures to protest crime and violence in the neighborhood.

✓ *Fund-Raising.* T-MAC is a grassroots group. To fund outings and group activities, fundraising events are employed. Group members present fund-raising ideas, which include bake sales and car washes, to help realize the group's mission and motto. In addition, donations and sponsorships are also sought from various sources.

✓ *Guest Speakers.* Guest speakers on topics of gangs, building self-esteem, teen dating, violence, college, and career choices have played important roles in providing members with alternative perspectives and motivation.

✓ *Parental Involvement.* Parents have contributed by providing transportation, food preparation, and chaperoning.

✓ *Community Involvement.* Local business owners, community leaders, and politicians have contributed by providing donations, supplies, sponsorships, and other resources.

Group Goals

The primary goal is to end delinquent behaviors by providing alternative ways of dealing with urban stressors such as gangs, drugs, peer pressure, crime and violence, and poverty. In addition, we hope to expand the worldview and the opportunities for success for these teens. To that end, this program focuses on these goals:

✓ Learning positive behaviors

✓ Increasing social skills

✓ Increasing positive attitudes about self and others

✓ Increasing school functioning

✓ Increasing community productiveness

✓ Alleviating neighborhood vandalism

✓ Building a sense of community belongingness

✓ Including as many influential and caring adults as possible to provide positive role modeling

✓ Providing community resources to aid families

Group Format

T-MAC was designed to meet the needs of a particular population. In keeping with the community psychology perspective, group members and the apartment complex community at large are directly involved in determining the topics and components of the group. The 15 weekly sessions outlined here address gangs and gang involvement. Each session begins by introducing the particular topic and ends by reviewing and incorporating new knowledge. These sessions can be adapted to fit a variety of groups or populations.

Session 1: Group Introduction

✓ The facilitator describes the purpose and focus of the group and reviews safety and confidentiality.

✓ Members introduce themselves, create group rules (such as one person talks at a time, respect toward other members, no use of profanity), and develop topics for group discussion.

Sessions 2 and 3: History of Gangs

✓ The facilitator provides a history of gangs from assorted readings.

✓ Members discuss the readings and relate this information to their own knowledge about gangs.

✓ Members pair up in dyads and discuss the readings.

✓ Dyads discuss their perceptions with the group.

Sessions 4, 5, and 6: Personal Experience With Gangs

✓ Members discuss which identifiable gangs are in their neighborhood and what colors are not safe to wear.

✓ Members discuss personal experiences with gang involvement or near involvement.

✓ Members discuss their worries and fears.

✓ Members discuss how gangs affect the neighborhood and the apartment complex.

✓ Members discuss personal affiliations with family members or friends.

✓ One member gives a presentation to the larger group about his or her experiences with gang members.

✓ Members answer questions from the larger group.

Sessions 7 and 8: Videotape Presentation

✓ Members view and discuss contents of videotapes of *Scared Straight* and *Menace to Society*.

✓ Facilitator summarizes the videotapes.

✓ Facilitator identifies alternatives to gang involvement.

Session 9: Making Connections

✓ Facilitator engages group members in discussing how the videotapes relate to what is happening in the neighborhood or in their own lives.

✓ Members discuss alternatives and write different endings for each videotape character.

✓ Members share and discuss the new characters with the group. For instance, they may be asked "How is the new character's behavior different and how does this difference influence the story?"

Sessions 10 and 11: Making Changes

✓ Facilitator engages group members in discussing how their neighborhood or apartment complex would change if there were no gang members.

✓ Members answer questions such as "What positive alternatives for youth could replace gangs?" and "How could gangs change to promote a positive image?"

✓ Members map out and visualize their neighborhood without gangs.

Session 12: Role Plays to Help Avoid Involvement

✓ Facilitator provides scenarios for role plays.

✓ Members create role plays for what they can do if they are approached by gang members.

✓ Members alternate between providing scenarios and participating in role plays.

✓ Members pair up to write about their experiences and share them with group members.

Sessions 13, 14, and 15: Alternatives

✓ Guest speaker presents personal experience with gangs and how he or she overcame gang life.

✓ Facilitator engages group in discussing and summarizing topics about gangs.

✓ Facilitator helps to identify new knowledge and ways to implement alternative coping strategies to deal with gangs.

✓ Members discuss new knowledge and alternatives to gang involvement.

✓ Members discuss their learning and where to go from here.

✓ Members continue implementing plans for change.

Group Outcomes

Although there are no formal outcome measures for this group, the participants benefit from having a safe place to share normal adolescent developmental issues and acquire adaptive coping skills to deal with social and environmental ills plaguing their neighborhood.

As part of the group process, members are encouraged to describe what they are learning and how the group is affecting them. As termination of the group approaches, the members are asked to write about the personal benefits of the experience. One 12-year-old African American boy writes, "The benefits of being in the T-MAC club is having fun, solving problems, and doing lots of activities." According to a 16-year-old Latina, "The benefits of being in T-MAC is that we have experiences that make us think about what we are seeing and doing. It helps me see where I want to go. I also enjoy being in the club because of the activities. Instead of drugs and violence, we go places." These subjective accounts indicate generally positive experiences of group members. The apartment complex management is also in favor of T-MAC due to a decrease in repairs related to vandalism. Loitering is also reduced.

Developing and facilitating T-MAC has proven to be challenging as well as rewarding. Providing youth with opportunities for discovering new experiences and helping them face and work through difficult personal issues are among the benefits of facilitating this group. I have learned many valuable lessons regarding the adolescent world, intervention strategies for preventing delinquency, how to access community resources, and how to interact effectively with business, political, and community leaders. Moreover, the ideology of apartment-based prevention and intervention to combat teen delinquency is an innovative concept. A future study measuring the effectiveness of such a group would be beneficial to the advancement of apartment-based prevention and community psychology.

Group Proposal

A High School Group for Children of Alcoholics

This proposal is written from the perspective of Deborah Lambert and Nancy Ceraso. For further information contact them at North Allegheny High School, 10375 Perry Highway, Wexford, PA 15090. COA group curriculum is copyrighted. N. English © July 1991.∎

Children raised in alcoholic families enter adolescence with strategies for survival that worked to some degree in their childhood years. As these teens approach adulthood, however, these coping strategies may be costly in terms of psychological health and well-being. Over the years children of alcoholics refine certain behaviors, such as being super responsible, adjusting, placating, not talking, not trusting, and not feeling. When they grow up, most adult children of alcoholics (sometimes referred to as ACOAs) continue to struggle with problems related to trust, dependency, control, identification, and expression of feelings. Counselors who intend to work with children of alcoholics should be well versed in the literature and issues pertaining to substance abuse.

This counseling group was designed for high school students living with a family member who has a problem with alcohol or other drugs. Deborah Lambert is the coordinator of a student assistance program at North Allegheny Senior High School in Pennsylvania. She works with Nancy Ceraso, school social worker with expertise in chemical dependency, to provide school-based support and consultation to students experiencing academic, behavioral, and emotional conflict related to drug/alcohol situations and relationships.

Organizing the Group

The groups are offered to students in high school. The length of the weekly sessions is one class period, typically 40 minutes. Two facilitators work together to provide a blend of academic and prevention expertise. The coleaders explain that although the groups follow an education-based curriculum therapeutic gains can occur. Students are encouraged to attend 12-step community groups, and the meeting lists for Al-Anon, Alateen, Alcoholics Anonymous (AA), and Narcotics Anonymous (NA) are available. These community resources provide tools for recovery, promote positive relationships, and offer hope.

The ground rules for confidentiality are established by the facilitators and clarified during the group's introduction. Exceptions to confidentiality are carefully explained to the members. Rather than promise them "total confidentiality," students are informed of school policy guidelines regarding safety situations such as child abuse, dating violence, and harm to self and others.

As school professionals, facilitators have a dual responsibility to students and parents. Letters are sent home to inform parents of the group's purpose and to obtain their consent. This positive partnership can decrease parental resistance, increase opportunities for open and ongoing communication, and replace the unhealthy cycle of secrecy and shame with understanding and trust. Students are informed that parental consent is necessary. Before letters go home, students have the opportunity to share their concerns about parental involvement and obtaining consent.

Group Goals

This group has the following goals:

✓ To identify how chemical dependency affects *all* family members/loved ones

✓ To provide alternatives to chemical usage

✓ To validate feelings and differentiate healthy versus unhealthy ways of expressing them

✓ To share similar experiences with others

✓ To create an emotionally safe environment

✓ To identify codependent behaviors

✓ To define the addiction process

✓ To offer information on community resources

Group Format

The description of each session provided here is typical for meeting these goals in this group.

Session 1: Group Introduction

✓ Members introduce themselves and participate in establishing group rules. For example, everyone is expected to participate, students are expected to make up missed class work and assignments, it is good to speak for oneself, and be honest about thoughts and feelings. Confidentiality and its exceptions are defined.

✓ Members review the purpose of the group.

✓ An icebreaker activity is provided that encourages members to share personal information in a playful, nonthreatening way.

Session 2: The Impact of Addiction on the Family

✓ Members identify the problem of addiction.

✓ Members share how a family member's or friend's addiction has affected their lives.

✓ Members list all potential consequences and situations associated with addiction.

Session 3: Introducing Addiction

✓ Facilitators discuss the progressive nature of addiction. Each stage is defined in terms of consumption, consequences, relationship casualties, and loss of control.

✓ Members draw a picture of a time when they were sick.

✓ As members share their pictures, discussion focuses on how their experience with illness parallels or differs from addiction.

Session 4: "My Feelings About Addiction"

✓ Members provide two examples of how they have been affected by another person's usage.

✓ Members think up as many "feeling words" as they can, and a facilitator writes them on the board.

✓ Members are asked to connect or relate their feelings to the examples they shared earlier.

✓ Facilitators highlight how emotions can be conflicting or competing in nature and intensity.

Session 5: The Addicted Parent

✓ Members describe typical behaviors that accompany each stage of addiction.

✓ Members draw a picture of the worst thing that has happened because of a loved one's addiction.

✓ Facilitators point out the universal aspects of addiction.

Session 6: Continuing with the Addicted Parent

✓ Members watch a video depicting an addicted person.

✓ At various points the video is turned off to allow for discussion.

✓ Members discuss the video's relevance to their situation.

Session 7: The Recovering Parent

✓ Facilitators explain the process of recovery and the dynamics of relapse.

✓ Members are given information on emotional, behavioral, and situational triggers contributing to relapse.

Session 8: Codependency

✓ Facilitators define and illustrate codependency.

✓ Members identify codependent behaviors.

✓ Members identify key features of healthy relationships (for example, balance, reciprocity, intimacy, trust, nurturing, boundaries, and self-worth).

Session 9: Roles

✓ Facilitators discuss the roles that typically characterize children of alcoholics.

✓ Members fill out handouts explaining how they have assumed these roles at different times in their lives.

Session 10: Coping and Hoping

✓ Members select a card from a special deck, the "Problem Pack," and either talk about

or role-play how they would feel and what they would do in each difficult situation. Examples are: (1) It is very late and your parents are out drinking. (2) You need to talk about a major problem and your parent says, "Sorry, I have to go to an AA meeting." (3) Your friend is drunk and he is driving.

✓ Each member receives an updated listing of community resources and a schedule of support group meetings in the area.

✓ Students are encouraged to attend Alateen or Al-Anon meetings before the next session.

Session 11: Affirmations

✓ Facilitators introduce the purpose and power of affirmations.

✓ Students share examples of negative self-talk and criticism.

✓ Facilitators teach reframing techniques.

✓ Members reframe one of their own negative messages.

✓ Members write an affirmation to practice saying daily.

Session 12: Good Thoughts, Good Feelings, and Good-Byes

✓ Members talk about the value of their group experience.

✓ Members receive positive feedback on their contributions to the group.

✓ Members have an opportunity to exchange phone numbers.

✓ Members complete a group evaluation form.

Group Outcomes

Written and verbal responses from members consistently reflect positive feelings, attitudes, and experiences. Members consistently cite these group benefits: personal growth, peer support, acceptance and validation, and practical guidance. The number one suggestion for improvement is additional group time.

School-based groups have the opportunity to succeed if the faculty and administration are aware of the purpose of the group and all the components involved in the group process. Teachers appreciate notification of student participation, documentation of attendance at group, and rotation of class periods when scheduling group sessions. Teachers are requested to provide updates on members' academic progress. This two-way system of communication contributes to a successful outcome.

The rewards for facilitators include:

✓ Participating in students' personal growth

✓ Observing members gain insight into their codependent behaviors

✓ Fostering the process of recovery

✓ Helping members establish personal supports

✓ Restoring balance and playfulness in members' lives

Some of the frustrations facilitators have experienced include:

✓ Members' hesitancy to utilize available community supports

✓ Witnessing the tragic consequences of high-risk behavior

✓ Difficulty confronting the powerful nature of denial

✓ Increasing demands on professional time given the immediacy of student needs and paperwork deadlines

Group Proposal

Insight and Aftercare Groups for Students Involved in Drug and Alcohol Usage

In addition to the group just described, Deborah Lambert and Nancy Ceraso offer support groups for students involved in drug usage or at any stage of recovery. This section, too, is written from the perspective of Nancy Ceraso and Deborah Lambert. ■

Overview of the Drug Problem in Schools

As student assistance team members working with adolescents, our experiences parallel those who work in community mental health centers or in the area of drugs and alcohol. Today, the changes in adolescent attitudes and behavior regarding the use of drugs is alarming. We find that many adolescents who have substance abuse problems also have a range of psychological problems that may have predated their drug use. Teens are using "harder" drugs and faster-addicting drugs. Drug consumption is more excessive with onset of usage occurring at younger ages. Indeed, substance abuse is a problem at the elementary, middle, and secondary school levels. Students can go to extraordinary lengths to get "high." Even household products and over-the-counter medications are misused with the aim of getting intoxicated. Poly-substance abuse is a phenomenon that we are increasingly seeing in the schools. Young people are knowledgeable about drugs and their availability, and when the drug of choice is not available, they often substitute something else. Other times, various drugs are simultaneously combined to "enhance the high."

The earlier onset of usage increasingly makes drug involvement a school issue that teachers, administrators, and counselors must address. Prevention efforts often include a wide spectrum of activities such as teaching about drugs in the school curriculum, refusal skills training, after-school programs, parent education programs, urine testing, drug-trained dogs, and police presence in the building. Although all of these efforts have individual merit, none provide a guarantee.

Despite the outstanding and ongoing drug education awareness efforts, it is extremely difficult to counter the mind-set and naiveté of adolescents. Children and adolescents inherently possess a sense of omnipotence. Intellectually, they *know* drugs are "bad," yet they may believe they can be more "careful" about usage and avoid its casualties. Some believe their "privileged" status offers immunity from drug-related consequences. When a tragedy occurs, it's attributed to "bad luck" or a "freak accident." Some teens believe that using drugs is okay, but getting "caught" is what should be avoided.

Pro drug endorsements have infiltrated all areas of the adolescent's world. Parents can be active drug users or have a history of earlier usage themselves. Older siblings often introduce younger ones to drugs. Sports and extracurricular activities, once considered drug-free havens, are now drug exposed as well.

Those personnel who facilitate groups in schools need to continually update their knowledge and skills to be able to offer effective strategies and accurate education. Credibility and trust are earned commodities and are essential to successful intervention. Networking with community and law enforcement agencies mobilizes resources, coordinates efforts, and makes for positive partnerships.

Organizing the Group

The primary distinction between insight groups and aftercare groups is the level of commitment to recovery. *Insight groups* offer education on usage and addiction. Members usually have no history of rehabilitation efforts or have demonstrated a lack of readiness to commit to recovery. *Aftercare groups* are designed for students who desire recovery and demonstrate behavior toward that goal. Both populations experience relapse and setbacks. Sometimes the frequency and severity of relapse makes for a very toxic group population. Facilitators are challenged to continually monitor and address the health or toxicity of the group membership.

Based on the assumption that recovery is a life-long process, ongoing weekly sessions in an open-group format allow students to be referred to groups throughout the school year. Although the majority of students learn about the group by word of mouth, facilitators also advertise via PA announcements, posters, flyers, and the school cable channel. (Refer to Chapter 4 for a description of the procedures we use to identify and recruit group members.) Students are strongly encouraged to continue with their AA and NA 12-step meetings, individual therapy, and community-based aftercare groups.

Group Goals

The goals for both insight and aftercare groups are identical. What varies is the amount of time and information spent on the individual goals. One must match the level of intervention and the group activities to the existing population. In an insight group, the majority of effort might address getting members to accurately assess the consequences of their usage. In an aftercare group, more attention is given to obstacles to recovery. What follows are illustrative group goals for both groups:

✓ Define chemical dependency, relapse, and recovery.

✓ Accurately report progression of usage and its consequences.

✓ Increase awareness of the widespread infiltration of usage into our culture/community.

✓ Educate on the drug trafficking industry to reduce teens' vulnerability.

✓ Deglamorize and debunk the "myths" about usage.

✓ Address school-related issues to usage.

✓ Target the challenges and successes associated with recovery.

✓ Identify healthy alternatives to chemical usage.

✓ Practice refusal skills.

✓ Assess and monitor mental health issues.

✓ Network with drug-free students and community resources that support recovery.

✓ Celebrate the gifts of recovery.

Group Format

The groups are available once a week throughout the school year. Here are descriptions of some of the sessions.

Session 1: Group Introduction

✓ Facilitators explain the purpose of the group.

✓ Members introduce themselves and share referral circumstances (for example, "What got me to group?").

✓ Rules are established, and confidentiality guidelines are reviewed.

✓ Facilitators provide an icebreaker activity that encourages students to share personal information in a playful, non-threatening way.

Session 2: Addiction and Me

✓ Members provide a chronology of their chemical history.

✓ Students volunteer their understanding of addiction.

✓ Facilitators review stages of addiction.

Session 3: Safeguards for School Events and Holidays

✓ Facilitators discuss recovery challenges associated with school-sponsored dances, athletic events, and holidays.

✓ Group generates a list of common relapse behaviors.

✓ Members identify their "relapse triggers."

✓ Facilitators highlight potential dangers associated with recreational activities attractive to youth, such as raves, sleepovers, concerts, online activity, and isolation.

Session 5: Recovery Updates

✓ Students provide academic updates (grades, attendance, discipline record, and staff relations).

✓ Students share their recovery efforts including sobriety status, 12-step attendance, and identification of "relapse triggers."

✓ Students discuss their feelings regarding the challenges of recovery.

Session 6: Challenge by Choice

✓ Facilitators provide an opportunity to practice trust and team building.

✓ Members participate in a "ropes course" activity. Ropes courses are typically available at treatment facilities. They offer students an opportunity to challenge themselves as individuals and as team members. Completion of the course can take 2 to 6 hours depending on the group goals and the number of elements and activities selected. In a practical and memorable way, the course reinforces the intrinsic value of groups: respect for individual ideas and choices, group support for individual accomplishments, and the opportunity to move beyond self-imposed boundaries with the support of the group.

Session 10: Relapse

✓ Facilitators remind members that relapse monitoring is an integral part of recovery.

✓ Students are encouraged to report episodes of relapse.

✓ Relapse experiences become opportunities for all members to talk about denial, vulnerability, and sobriety safeguards.

Session 30: Final Group

✓ Facilitators provide an activity that celebrates sobriety. Some examples are having a picnic in the park, a young person in recovery speaking to the group, or gratitude gift bags being exchanged in which members thank one another for their personal gifts and group contributions.

✓ Members evaluate the group experience.

✓ Facilitators discuss summer safeties to protect sobriety.

Group Outcomes

Based on years of experience in designing and facilitating aftercare groups, we have found these ideas to be useful in designing a program with successful outcomes for the participants:

✓ Have a designated room, and post a schedule of session dates and times.

✓ Rotate the time periods when group meets to minimize class absenteeism in any particular subject area.

✓ Have an established curriculum that is flexible and can accommodate crisis situations and special concerns of members.

✓ Prepare members for upcoming school functions and holidays by providing sobriety safeguards and practicing refusal skills.

✓ Have members give brief weekly updates on abstinence, attendance at AA and NA meetings, and relapse indicators.

✓ Secure releases of information to maintain a collaborative partnership with treatment resources.

✓ Implement a written or verbal communication system with staff so observations and concerns are routinely available. This enables earlier intervention in conflicts and ongoing reinforcement of accomplishments.

Sex Offender Treatment Group for Boys

For additional information about adolescent offender groups, you may contact Ginny Watts at the Belgrade Counseling Clinic, 103 W. Jefferson, Suite A, Belgrade, MT 59714; telephone (406) 388-1607; e-mail ginnywatts @earthlink.net. You can also contact Susan Crane at e-mail susan.crane@unco.edu. ∎

The first comprehensive evaluation and treatment program for adolescent sex offenders in the United States started in 1975 at the University of Washington (Knopp, 1982). Since that time, numerous treatment models and programs have developed across the country. The following is a description of our open, ongoing, long-term treatment group serving preadolescent and adolescent boys in a rural community. Ours is the first adolescent treatment program in our geographic area. We began our group in October 1997.

Organizing the Group

To meet the needs for outpatient adolescent sex offender treatment in a rural environment, the group structure is heterogeneous on several levels. This group consisted of eight members who varied in age from 11 to 18 years old and who came from five neighboring communities ranging in population from 1,000 to 30,000 people. This heterogeneous mix of group members has both challenges and advantages. Some members are participating in treatment whereas others in the group are participating in aftercare. Because the membership contains a combination of different family histories, offending histories, developmental levels, and treat-

ment experiences, the group setting does not constantly meet any one person's needs. Some members may "check out" when they do not feel connected to the topic of discussion, and group cohesion is often threatened. This challenge can also be an advantage because it presents the opportunity for group members to serve as mentors/leaders in the area in which they have greater experience and expertise.

Group Goals

This group has a number of important goals:

✓ To protect the community

✓ To prevent reoffenses

✓ To ensure complete disclosures of all offending and deviant sexual behaviors and all nonsexual offending/illegal behaviors

✓ To understand healthy/unhealthy power and develop behaviors based in healthy power

✓ To develop empathy for the victim

✓ To develop affective skills and demonstrate appropriate management of emotions including anger management and conflict resolution

✓ To understand and confront thinking errors and defense mechanisms and practice responsible choices and behaviors

✓ To understand and develop legal, social, and personal boundaries

✓ To understand and develop relationship skills (including age-appropriate knowledge about human sexuality)

✓ To understand and work through their own victimization (if applicable)

✓ To develop and practice a relapse prevention plan and plan for healthy living

These goals are best met through a combination of cognitive behavioral, experiential, confrontive, and humanistic techniques.

As coleaders, we conduct the group sessions together and divide responsibility for individual and family sessions and case management for individual members, each leader being responsible for approximately half of the total group members. We meet before and after each session to plan and evaluate the group sessions. We also meet together when a member is in crisis or to provide additional planning for special sessions.

Screening

Screening and orientation are critical to the success of any adolescent group, and this process can be particularly helpful for any involuntary adolescent clients. The first step is to determine that the client's needs match the goals of the group. Individuals must have participated in a psychosexual evaluation and been recommended for outpatient therapy or intensive outpatient therapy or completed a treatment program. Therapists often send a summary of treatment or speak directly to one of us regarding clients, and case managers or probation officers facilitate the process for an individual coming from another treatment setting. To be accepted into our group, a prospective member must be deemed a low to moderate risk for reoffense, must have adequate family support, comprehensive supervision, and must admit to at least a portion of his offenses. Individuals who are not accepted into our program are given referrals to more intensive treatment options.

Group Contract

Prior to entering the group, the new member meets with one of the coleaders (who will be his individual and family therapist throughout treatment) to discuss the group process and sign necessary documents, including the group contract. The contract includes specific guidelines for appropriate group behavior. Reviewing this contract provides an orientation to appropriate group behavior and a preliminary shaping of group norms. If possible, the group contract is reviewed with the prospective member's guardian as well. An adolescent's success in treatment is often strongly influenced by his family's attitudes.

The contract also includes specific guidelines for appropriate group behavior. Reviewing this contract provides an orientation to the group and begins the process of shaping group norms.

Group Format

This group combines educational and therapeutic components. Because the membership changes periodically and treatment and aftercare are combined into one group, the content of sessions is flexible to meet the needs of the particular members. However, an overall structure is maintained for each session. At each session a member volunteers to keep the time of each segment of the session to ensure that the group does not bog down and fail to complete necessary work. Sessions begin with a check-in that permits each member to be immediately involved in the group before the focus of the session settles on a particular member. The check-in is a brief statement of the most prominent feeling the member is experiencing at the beginning of group (this helps members focus on affect and on the here and now), one positive experience the member has had over the intervening time since the last group, and one challenging experience the member has had since the last group (this helps members focus on how their lives outside the group relate to work being done in group sessions).

Check-in is followed by urgent issues. Members are given time to discuss events in their lives that relate to their treatment. Topics include loss of freedom, family conflict, dating and intimacy, disclosing past offenses, conflict with peers and authority figures, peer pressure, academic struggles, and issues resulting from public knowledge of their offending history. The group then offers feedback, relates similar experiences, or assists in role plays, brainstorming, or other activities. The focus on urgent issues enables therapeutic interventions within the group format.

Homework is presented next. Homework assignments are drawn from various workbooks and from the content of individual, family, and group sessions. All members are expected to be prepared to present chapter summaries or particular assignments although not every member has the opportunity to present at every session. Group members provide feedback regarding the quality of the work, additions or corrections that need to be made, and any improvements or regressions in the quality of the individual's work. Presenting to the group encourages members to recognize the group as a source for accountability, enables members to learn from each other about group norms and expectations, and gives members a structure within which to learn about accepting and giving feedback.

The final portion of the session includes a closure exercise and a review of how well members complied with group ground rules. The closure exercise relates the content of a particular group session to the overall goals of the group. For example, members may be asked to state one emotion that they hid or minimized in the session. These two final activities help to give closure to each session.

Given the nature of the population participating in an offender group, members may be removed from a placement to inpatient treatment or incarceration at any time. As a result, it is important to provide some sense of closure to each session to help members adjust if someone is removed from treatment and does not return to group.

Special Concerns

Measures of Progress in Treatment

Members' progress is measured from several different perspectives. Completion of assignments is a concrete milestone for progress. Changes in behavior, both in the group and outside of the group, are also important measures of the progress in assimilating the information and skills taught in group.

Advantages of a Coleadership Model

We have found that coleading adolescent sexual offender groups is definitely preferable, if not essential, and is advantageous for any involuntary adolescent group. This is intense work with a high therapist burnout rate. We help each other by breaking the isolation, keeping each other healthier, and improving our therapeutic effectiveness. Working together provides us with the opportunity to process, vent, conceptualize, reduce the workload, offer and receive feedback and support, and brainstorm.

Group members also benefit from two leaders. At different times members are observed connecting more to one leader or the other. Because this therapy has a strong confrontive and accountability element, we take turns offering challenges or support to various members. Two leaders also offer more opportunity for projection and transference. As this is occurring with one of us, the other can observe the process and more easily make therapeutic interventions. Coleading is also ideal for modeling healthy communication in the group. We openly share feelings and reactions in group sessions, as well as share our thoughts pertaining to the group process as it unfolds.

Challenges

Obtaining the training necessary for work with offenders is a considerable challenge. We are licensed clinical professional counselors who are also members of the Montana Sex Offender Treatment Association (MSOTA). In addition to state licensure, evaluation samples, letters of reference, and successful completion of the clinical examination, qualifying for clinical membership in MSOTA requires 2,000 hours of face-to-face work with offenders supervised by a clinical member of MSOTA. Work with offenders in Montana cannot be conducted without MSOTA or equivalent qualifications, and the standards are stringent. Sex offender treatment is a high-risk, specialized field that should not be attempted without proper credentials. Therapists should not attempt to replicate this adolescent therapy group without proper supervision and training. To begin this work, therapists are advised to join the national Association for the Treatment of Sexual Abusers (ATSA) and their state organizations to determine how to obtain the training necessary to practice locally.

As with any open group, subgroups of members are at different stages in group development. Members receive benefits and experience challenges within this heterogeneous format. We have to stay alert not only to overall group development and cohesion but also to the individual and subgroup processes. As a result, we often spend additional time processing these dynamics and doing group activities that address the particular needs of members. For example, we have periodically used experiential "ropes course" activities, in part, to help new members assimilate into the group. This technique is particularly appropriate to pre-adolescent and adolescent boys who often join by doing. The members find it easier to process the concrete events of experiential activities and then use these examples as metaphors for how they function in more abstract ways.

We have chosen to work with offenders due to professional and personal experiences with the traumatic effects of sexual abuse, and a primary motivation for us is prevention of further sexual assaults. The top challenge of this work is the enormous sense of responsibility and knowing that mediocre effectiveness in this field can result in more incidents of sexual victimization, which can result in potential legal battles, professional liability, and even worse, emotional devastation. We often struggle with the extent and limits of our abilities and our responsibilities. At times we terminate members and recommend more intensive treatment only to find that family or probation does not follow through in moving the youth into more appropriate treatment.

Another issue that creates challenges is the involuntary nature of the group. This is dealt with as therapeutically as possible, but resistance often slows the treatment process. Even more challenging for us is that we are often the focus of members' anger, rebellion, and personal attacks. Youths who offend are often masters at arguing, manipulating, and "pushing buttons." In addition, family members may demonstrate similar skills as a natural part of the family dynamics. As co-leaders, in and out of group, we operate as one another's reality check. We find the following responses helpful when dealing with resistant adolescents and their families:

✓ Explore the resistance rather than attempting to shut it down.

✓ Encourage clients to develop goals of their own that are compatible with treatment.

✓ Challenge clients to consider how defensive behaviors may affect the achievement of their goals.

✓ Coordinate with other service providers to prevent confusion, splitting and mixed messages, and present a united front in dealing with treatment.

✓ Establish firm guidelines at the start and hold clients to them.

✓ Work to join with adolescents and their families, acknowledging their fears, frustrations, points of view, discouragement, successes and hopes.

Sex offender treatment groups cannot stand alone. Members must also participate in individual and family therapy, and we need to coordinate services with a great number of agencies that typically serve each youth. These agencies can provide support, but they also may present conflicting opinions, create miscommunications, and require a great deal of extra time and energy. Additionally, in dealing with agencies, the public, and families regarding such an upsetting topic, we often encounter an unusual amount of resistance. These reactions often seem to be unconscious, which adds to the challenge of working through the issue with those people who are not in therapy but whose resistance affects the treatment of the abusive youth. Therapists' awareness of this dynamic is helpful in developing patience and trying different approaches with adjunct professionals.

Finally, due to the challenges related to sexual assault work, burnout is a significant professional issue. As mentioned previously, working with a coleader is one of the best prevention agents against burnout. Consultation with other professionals in the field is also key. Meaningful outside interests and a sense of humor cannot be overestimated in maintaining perspective. Despite these challenges, treatment of adolescents who have sexually offended is gratifying and vital work.

If you are interested in a more detailed discussion of the topics pertaining to this kind of group, we recommend Cunningham and MacFarlane (1997), Knopp (1982), Ryan and Lane (1997), Schwartz and Cellini (1995), and Wyatt and Powell (1988).

✓ *Points to Remember*

Groups for Adolescents

✓ Group work is especially suited for adolescents if they are adequately prepared for the group experience. Groups help adolescents clarify a sense of individuality and also provide opportunities to discover shared developmental themes.

✓ Groups for adolescents can combine personal themes with psychoeducational goals.

✓ Time-limited groups are growing in popularity in schools, clinics, and community agencies. The range of groups for adolescents is limited only by the imagination of those who are in charge of designing such groups.

✓ As with most kinds of groups, it is wise to conduct a needs assessment in the setting in which you work to identify a particular kind of group that will be most useful.

✓ In working with reluctant behaviors of adolescents who are required to attend a group, it is critical to understand and respect resistance. Leaders must refrain from becoming defensive or sarcastic at those times when they encounter challenging behavior.

✓ Role-playing techniques can often be used creatively in adolescent groups. Understand the purpose that a specific role-playing intervention can serve, and consider timing in introducing these techniques.

✓ Multiple family group therapy is a unique treatment modality that combines elements of education and group process to assist families in dealing with a range of problems.

✓ As is the case in working with children, it is recommended that ways be found to involve parents in group work with adolescents.

✓ Groups have been successfully organized to deal with a range of adolescent problems. A few kinds of adolescent groups include groups for students on drug rehabilitation, teen delinquency prevention groups, and sex offender treatment groups.

✓ Coleadership models are especially useful in facilitating adolescent groups.

Exercises

In-Class Activities

1. **Design a Group.** Break up into small groups in the classroom and work collaboratively to design different kinds of groups for adolescents. Each of the subgroups can work on a different kind of group. Identify the specific type of group you would be interested in forming, and brainstorm possible steps for establishing this group. What does your group consider to be essential in organizing and implementing your proposal?

2. **Examine MFGT.** Review the description of the multiple family group therapy proposal in this chapter. What do you think of the rationale and assumptions underlying this particular group? Based on the proposal, to what degree would you be interested in coleading this group?

3. **Review the T-MAC Group Concept.** Review the teens making a change group (T-MAC). If you were the director of an agency, what kind of response would you have toward funding this group as a community project?

4. **Challenge Yourself.** Review the sex offenders treatment group for boys described in this chapter. Would you be interested in coleading a group like this? Why or why not? What challenges might you face if you were to work with this population in a group?

5. **Evaluate the Group Proposals.** In small groups critique the other group proposals presented in this chapter. What aspects of each proposal would you want to incorporate in one of your group proposals? What are some of the advantages of using a group format for the kinds of problems explored in each group? Of all the proposals presented in this chapter, which proposal did you find to be the most unusual and why?

6. **Guest Speaker.** Invite a guest speaker who has experience in group work with adolescents. Ask the speaker how to organize and conduct a specific kind of adolescent group.

7. **Community Programs.** Some class members can make a visit to a school or a community agency where groups are available for adolescents. Find out what types of groups are offered, the structure of these groups, and the reactions of the members. Present what you find to your class.

InfoTrac College Edition

For additional readings, explore InfoTrac College Edition, our online library, at http://www.infotrac.college.com/wadsworth. The following keywords are listed in such a way as to enable the InfoTrac College Edition search engine to locate a wider range of articles. The keywords should be entered exactly as listed, to include asterisks, "w1," "w2," "AND," and other search engine tools.

- group* w1 psych* AND peer
- group* w1 psych* AND adolescent*
- group* w1 psych* AND parent*
- group* w1 psych* AND alcohol*
- group* w1 psych* AND teenage*

Chapter 11

Groups for Adults

Focus Questions

*B*efore reading this chapter, reflect on one kind of group with adults that you would be most interested in organizing and facilitating. What kinds of experiences and training do you think you would need to facilitate such a group? What questions do you have about designing this kind of group? As you read this chapter, consider these questions:

1. If you and your coleader were designing a group to treat compulsive eating, what elements would you want to include in a written proposal? What ideas do you have for recruiting, screening, and orienting members for this specific group?

2. What are some ways to combine educational and therapeutic goals in an HIV/AIDS support group? What are some advantages of using a psychoeducational approach in this type of group?

3. If you worked in a community agency and were asked to organize a group for either women or men, what steps would you take in designing your group? Assume that you were expected to form a psychoeducational group. What topics would you build into your group?

4. After reading the various proposals for groups with adults in this chapter, which specific proposal most captures your interest? What are you learning about designing a particular group from studying these proposals? What other proposals for groups with adults would be worthwhile developing?

5. What are some key ethical issues to consider in conducting a group for a given population?

6. If you were leading any one of the adult groups described in this chapter, how would you deal with diversity issues?

7. What thoughts do you have regarding evaluation of a group?

☀ Introduction

This chapter presents a variety of special interest groups for adults. We try to be as practical as possible so you will be able to incorporate our suggestions in your practice. We begin with some observations on a theme-oriented approach to adult groups. We describe several special interest groups for college students that can be formed in public and private agencies as well as in college counseling centers. Also described are groups for the treatment of compulsive eating, HIV/AIDS support groups, a women's group in a college counseling center, a women's support group for survivors of incest, a men's group, and a domestic violence group.

☀ Topic-Oriented Groups

Topic-oriented groups have many advantages for adults. If topics reflect the life issues of the participants, they can be powerful catalysts. Several factors must be considered if you decide to structure your groups around topics, but perhaps the most important is to think about the common developmental life concerns characteristic of the group membership. The topics selected also reflect the main goals of the group. For example, if the group is made up of middle-aged participants, leaders might consider structuring the group around such themes as coping with the pressure of time, adjusting to children's growing up and leaving home, marital crises, spirituality, changing roles of women and men, coping with aging, the death of one's parents, divorce and separation, stagnation in work, changing one's occupation or career, finding meaning in life apart from rearing a family, creatively coping with stress, and facing loneliness.

In many of our groups we have used topics as catalysts for promoting personal reflection and interaction within the group. In *I Never Knew I Had a Choice* (Corey & Corey, 2006), we discuss topics such as reviewing your childhood and adolescence, adulthood and autonomy, gender roles, work and leisure, your body, wellness and life choices, managing stress, love, relationships, sexuality, loneliness and solitude, death and loss, meaning and values, and pathways for continued growth. Members make use of readings and personal reflection as a way to prepare themselves to become actively involved in the group experience.

Who decides on the topics for a group? This depends on many factors, including your leadership style and the level of sophistication of your group. You and the members can cooperatively develop topics that will provide direction for the sessions, but consider the readiness of members to fully explore these themes. Death, loneliness and isolation, anger, depression, and other potentially intense topics can trigger feelings that have been repressed for many years, and both the leader and the members must be able to handle the emotional intensity generated. If members have a role in selecting the topics, there is a greater chance that they will be able to face the issues explored in the group.

✳ Groups for College Students

A common complaint we hear is that it is easy to feel isolated on a university campus. With the emphasis on intellectual development, students often feel that relatively little attention is paid to their personal development. From our work in counseling centers at universities, we have come to realize that many students seek counseling services not only because of serious problems but also because they want to develop aspects of their personalities in addition to their thinking abilities. A diversity of special needs on the college campus can be explored through a group experience. In a group setting students can formulate goals, explore areas of themselves they have kept hidden that are causing them difficulties in interpersonal relating, and identify the internal blocks impeding the full utilization of their capabilities. By dealing with their personal problems, students free themselves of certain emotional blocks to learning and become far better students, approaching their studies with a sense of enthusiasm and commitment.

Common Topics in College Groups

Time-limited groups with structured topics or themes are most commonly offered in university counseling centers. This makes sense because counselors frequently say they have difficulty promoting open-ended process groups. Instead, groups are most often formed by an emerging need or client populations with specific concerns. On any college campus a number of students are likely to be victims of violence, rape, sexual abuse, sexual harassment, racism, or discrimination. The themes that emerge from a group often reflect the unique composition of that group. A good place to begin designing a group is to conduct a needs survey on the college campus.

A variety of both psychoeducational and counseling groups are frequently offered at college and university counseling centers: support groups for adult children of alcoholics, anxiety-management groups, veterans' groups, family issues groups, living under the influence groups, eating disorder groups, stress-management groups, grief groups, cultural identity groups, nontraditional age student groups, groups for those with relationship concerns, gay and lesbian support groups, self-esteem groups, groups for survivors of childhood sexual abuse, and personal identity groups. These groups are typically short term, lasting from 4 to 16 weeks, and are aimed at meeting a variety of special needs by combining a therapeutic focus with an educational one. The scope of the topics for structured groups is limited only by the needs of the population, the creativity of the counselor, and the effort it takes to promote the group. Many of the groups described in this chapter (groups for weight control, HIV/AIDS support groups, women's groups, and men's groups) are popular at college and university counseling centers. College and university counseling centers must address the academic and personal/social concerns of students, and with few resources. Therapeutic groups in counseling centers are a cost-effective approach to meeting these needs of a diverse range of students (Kincade & Kalodner, 2004).

Cornish and Benton (2001) describe a model of an eight-session group in a university counseling center that addresses themes pertaining to "getting started in healthier relationships." They developed their group counseling model due to demands for shorter, more focused treatment. In their model, the principles of brief dynamic therapy, interpersonal theory, and solution-focused brief therapy are combined to provide the maximum benefit from a group experience. This integrated group counseling model can be applied to various themes that are relevant to the developmental levels of college students.

✳ Groups for Weight Control

Although weight control and body image are concerns regardless of gender, women especially feel pressured to have an "ideal body," because there is a strong social bias against "overweight" women in our society. Women especially tend to internalize societal messages to be unrealistically thin, and if they are not, there are psychological and social prices to pay. Many overweight women experience chronic depression and low self-esteem.

University counseling centers are increasingly offering groups for people with eating disorders. These groups are often designed for women who are bulimic or anorexic or are compulsive eaters. There is growing recognition that individuals with eating disorders can benefit from group psychotherapy (Brisman & Siegel, 1985; Fettes & Peters, 1992; Hendren, Atkins, Sumner, & Barber, 1987; Rosenvige, 1990; Roth & Ross, 1988). Key benefits of groups for people with eating disorders are that groups can alleviate shame and isolation and increase hope. This is extremely important for people with eating disorders, which is one of the reasons group work is so potent with this population (see Garner & Garfinkel, 1997).

Groups are a useful therapeutic approach for people who struggle with weight problems. The following group proposal describes a group approach for treating compulsive eating.

A Group for Treating Compulsive Eating

For additional information about this group, contact Susan C. M. Crane at susan.crane @unco.edu. ■

Organizing the Group

Eating problems are particularly troublesome for the female population. Although a great number of women suffer from compulsive eating, they are largely overlooked because their concerns are not perceived to be as serious as eating disorders such as anorexia and bulimia. (For the purposes of this treatment group, compulsive eating is defined as "thinking about food and eating food—in the absence of physical hunger—to a degree that feels troublesome to the individual.") Dancing Without Diets therapy groups have been developed to address compulsive eating in a more meaningful and healthy manner than dieting permits.

To date, eight Dancing Without Diets groups have been conducted. Five of these groups have been structured, theme-centered groups, and three of the groups have been follow-up, nonstructured support groups. These groups are based on a mixture of cognitive, behavioral, feminist, and humanistic theory and use a combination of educational, experiential, and interactional methods to work toward the resolution of compulsive eaters' painful issues.

Probably the most unique (and sometimes controversial) aspect of the groups is the tenet that compulsive eaters can develop a natural, healthy relationship with food. In the pursuit of improved body image, a second principle of treatment emphasizes that all body sizes and shapes are to be accepted and celebrated. Therefore, weight loss is neither a goal nor a measure of success for these groups. These groups assist motivated members in developing a healthy relationship with food and in strengthening their positive feelings about themselves. The specific goals of the group are listed here:

✓ Explore individuals' history with compulsive eating and body image issues.

✓ Educate about some of the origins of women's food and body issues.

✓ Lessen the negative impact of individual and societal messages regarding women's bodies.

✓ Foster greater body acceptance.

✓ Establish demand eating.

✓ Improve self-esteem.

✓ Identify and begin to deal with possible issues underlying compulsive eating behaviors.

Participants are initially identified by their telephone call to the group leader. They may have learned about the group from their therapists or from the publicity for the group. Publicity for the groups has included posters, newspaper interviews with the group leader, flyers and letters sent to all the therapists in town, and announcements to college classes.

Once a potential member responds, a screening interview is scheduled. This interview is extensive and provides potential members with a detailed description of the group expectations, goals, approach, logistics, selection procedures, and time line; informs participants about the possible benefits and risks of group therapy; and addresses any of the individual's questions and concerns.

Women are not selected for the group if they are currently experiencing anorexia or bulimia, if their goals are incompatible with those of the group, or if there appears to be any reason that their participation could be detrimental to themselves or to the group. (Although there is some overlap with the compulsive eater's binging and bulimia, these groups are not designed to treat women who are currently suffering from these eating disorders.) The groups are composed of six to eight women ranging in age from 18 to 62 years old. This approach seems to appeal more to women beyond traditional college age, with most of the participants falling in the 30- to 50-year-old age range.

Group Format

Dancing Without Diets groups are time limited, typically meeting for twelve 2-hour sessions. Some of the groups have also included two 3-hour experiential "ropes course" sessions. Group members are expected to attend all sessions and are encouraged to do the weekly assigned readings (usually about 25 pages), listen to 60 to 90 minutes of audiotaped lecture and mental exercises, and complete worksheets and journal entries between the sessions.

Each group meeting begins with a review of the written agenda. The agenda includes reminders, group ground rules review, overview of the meeting (with any changes made), brief check-in, presentation of educational information, discussion of information and homework, free interaction, homework reminders, and closure (which includes a feelings check). In each 2-hour group meeting, the first 30–45 minutes are spent on the presentation and discussion of selected topics. During the next 15–30 minutes of the session, the group members explore their own issues and reactions to these topics through activities such as guided imageries and journal writing. The second hour of the group provides an opportunity for members to share their reactions, feelings, and experiences related to the topic. There is also a focus placed on processing how the topic and individuals' experiences affect the way members relate to each other in the group. The time allocations and structure of the agenda are flexible, depending on the events and needs of the group.

Susan Kano's (1989) book, *Making Peace With Food,* is used extensively in the group.

Typically, members read one of the chapters from Kano's book each week. Photographs, poetry, and magazine and journal articles are also used by the group, and videotapes are shown during group sessions. Many topics and activities are addressed in the course of the treatment, including those listed here:

✓ Introductions and acquaintanceship activities, including work in dyads

✓ Communication skills instruction and practice for more effective group participation

✓ Experiential "ropes course" sessions that use metaphors about eating, body image, and self-care and process group members' roles and interaction styles

✓ Cultural pressures on women to be thin

✓ The physical and psychological hazards of diets and deprivation

✓ Natural weight set-points, family weight and body types, and realistic physical expectations

✓ Demand feeding, including carrying "food bags" to eat in response to physical hunger in any location and at any time

✓ Exercises for increasing pleasurable eating experiences and reducing shame around physical needs

✓ Self-esteem and body image activities

✓ Exploring pleasurable physical activity and movement

✓ Assertiveness, including expressing rights and needs in all areas of life

✓ Healthier options for dealing with emotions

✓ Values clarification, including achievement, competition, conflict, femininity, sex roles, relationships, career, family, marriage, control, and time allotment

✓ Underlying issues that are sometimes numbed or masked by compulsive eating

✓ Closure activities

✓ Anonymous evaluations that include rating scales and comment for the program materials each meeting, overall suggestions and reactions to the treatment, evaluation of the facilitator's performance, and a self-evaluation section

✓ Exit interviews with each member

Group Outcomes

Dancing Without Diets group evaluations evoke a rich variety of responses from the participants. Overall, the comments are highly enthusiastic but vary in what aspects of the treatment members find to be the most beneficial. Many members rank the group time as being the most helpful, and others state that the textbook and journaling have the greatest impact for them. This type of feedback encourages the continued use of mixed materials, media, and means for inviting change.

Group members often comment that they appreciate the leader's willingness to share personal reactions and struggles with body image. The leader's self-disclosure assists members in feeling greater safety and hope in the group and serves to model appropriate communication. However, it is important to maintain a balance of appropriate sharing without shifting the focus to the leader's therapeutic needs. This balance is achieved through supervision, consultation, and personal therapy.

Many members indicate that the treatment has resulted in a significant reduction of compulsive eating behaviors. Improving body image is the area in which the majority of members note that they feel they still have the most work to do.

Body image issues are deeply rooted, and participation in a nonstructured group after the structured experience is strongly encouraged. This group combination seems to provide the optimal opportunity to incorporate the educational pieces from the therapy group into everyday living.

To overcome the social dynamics that lead to compulsive eating and body hatred, education in the community at large is a long-term goal. We have begun this process by educating therapists at state and national conferences. Additionally, the leader and a coworker are providing the opportunity for therapists to do their own work in this area during intensive body image weekend retreats in Montana.

✳ The AIDS Crisis as a Challenge for Group Workers

Acquired immune deficiency syndrome (AIDS) has become a critical health problem facing contemporary society. AIDS and HIV already affect a wide population and have certainly become an increasing problem. It has been called an "equal opportunity disease" that strikes at diverse populations. As a counselor, you will inevitably come in contact with people who have AIDS, with people who have tested positive and are carriers of the human immunodeficiency virus (HIV), or with people who are close to them. You will not be able to educate those with whom you come in contact unless you learn about the problem yourself. We encourage you to explore your own attitudes, values, and fears about working with people living with AIDS or those who are HIV-positive, and with those who have been affected by the AIDS epidemic.

How Groups Can Help

Both those who have AIDS and those who discover that they have the HIV virus within them struggle with the stigma attached to this disease. People who are HIV-positive live with the anxiety of wondering whether they will come down with this potentially incurable disease. They also live in fear of discovery and rejection by society in general and by significant persons in their life.

People affected by HIV/AIDS often stigmatize themselves and perpetuate beliefs such as "I feel guilty and ashamed," "I feel that God is punishing me," "I am a horrible person, and therefore I deserve to suffer," and "I am to blame for getting this disease." Indeed, they often accept what they have heard from others: "You got what you deserved." Because of this stigma, support groups for people with HIV/AIDS differ from groups for other diseases. The opportunity for people to share similar concerns can be educational, empowering, and can result in activism (Horne & Levitt, 2004).

Many of the social fears felt by people with HIV or AIDS are realistic. Some family members actually disown the person with AIDS out of fear. This type of treatment naturally inspires anger, depression, and feelings of hopelessness in the person who has been rejected. He or she may express this anger by asking, over and over: "What did I do to deserve this? Why me?" This anger is sometimes directed at God for letting this happen, and then the person may feel guilty for having reacted this way. Anger is also directed toward others, especially those who are likely to have transmitted the virus.

A support group can provide a safe place for participants to deal with the impact of this social stigma and vent their anger and other feelings, enabling them to form a new perspective on their situation. In the supportive climate of a group, these people can openly talk about the burdens of carrying the stigma and can begin to challenge self-destructive beliefs. Instead of blaming themselves, they can begin to forgive themselves and decide how to make the most of the time they do have.

Participants in an HIV/AIDS support group find some measure of hope by sharing their fears and realizing that they are not completely alone in facing an uncertain future. The fact that others are waging a common struggle brings about a high level of cohesiveness in this kind of support group. The participants have many physical, psychological, and spiritual challenges to meet, and a group can be of major help. Gushue and Brazaitis (2003) note that there are common denominators in groups for people diagnosed with HIV/AIDS as there are in many support groups for people living with a chronic or terminal illness. Some of these issues include concerns over deteriorating health, feelings of helplessness in coping with advancing disease, confusion over diagnoses and treatments, and dealing with loss, death, and grief. Gushue and Brazaitis identify the following topics that are commonly explored in HIV/AIDS support groups: stigma and shame attached to their diagnosis, guilt over not practicing safe sex or using intravenous drugs, and coping with loss of family or friends to AIDS. Stewart and Gregory (1996) address the value of group treatment for people with HIV/AIDS. They pay particular attention to six content themes that emerged in a long-term support group for people living with AIDS: marginality, making choices, coping with the emotional roller coaster phenomenon, premature confrontation of life issues, living with chronic illness versus dying with a terminal disease, and death and dying. Dealing with shame, guilt, anger, loss, and coping with physical decline and facing death are issues that are frequently identified and explored in an HIV/AIDS support group (Stewart & Gregory, 1996).

An Educational Focus in HIV/AIDS Groups

The supportive environment of a group provides an ideal means for reinforcing and maintaining behavior change. This kind of group can be aimed at helping members translate what they know into specific actions. But there must be a plan to include information in a meaningful way. In HIV/AIDS support groups it is important that there be an educational component as well as a therapeutic focus. People in these groups, as well as their friends and family members, often labor under a host of myths and misconceptions about both HIV and AIDS.

As a responsible practitioner, you must dispel these misconceptions and help people acquire realistic knowledge and attitudes. For example, a major misconception is that HIV/AIDS affects only the gay population and that if you are not gay you have no need to worry about being infected. In fact, heterosexuals have become infected through blood transfusions, through needle sharing by illicit drug users, and through sexual contact with people who themselves are carriers of the virus. The truth of the matter is that the AIDS epidemic does affect many of us, either directly or indirectly.

Education of various target groups is key in preventing sharp rises in the number of people who become infected. To be able to educate members of your groups, you need to have current information. This certainly includes an awareness of the values, mores, and cultural background of the various clients you serve. In attempting to change the habits of racial, cultural, and religious groups, you are likely to run up against considerable resistance unless you are able to "speak their language." Furthermore, in educating the general public, it is important to realize that people living with HIV/AIDS can easily become scapegoats of people's projections of their unconscious fears and hatred.

Both support and psychoeducational groups for people with HIV/AIDS offer valuable therapeutic and educational functions. Members in these groups can learn the truth about the facts surrounding their disease, and they can acquire a range of cognitive and behavioral strategies for enhancing the quality of life. The acceptance and caring within the group can foster an increased sense of hope and can facilitate development of their inner resources to create a meaningful existence. Excellent articles that deal with the value of support groups for people with HIV/AIDS include Gushue and Brazaitis (2003) and Stewart and Gregory (1996).

In the group proposal presented here one counselor tells how he began organizing HIV/AIDS support groups. His personal account applies many of the principles of group work outlined in this book and describes some unique challenges in conducting counseling groups with this population.

Group Proposal

An HIV/AIDS Support Group

Steven I. Lanzet is a licensed clinical professional counselor and a licensed marriage and family therapist and was the HIV testing and counseling program director at Planned Parenthood of Idaho. He has provided assistance to the Idaho AIDS Foundation and other HIV service providers in the Northwest. The discussion that follows is written from the perspective of Steven I. Lanzet. For further information on this topic, contact: Steven I. Lanzet, Life Works Community Ltd., The Grange, Old Woking, High Street, Old Woking, Surrey GU 22 8LB, United Kingdom, E-mail: slanzet@mac.com, Website: http://lifeworkscommunity.com ■

Organizing the Group

In 1987 I decided to take an HIV test. Later I received word that I had tested negative. I experienced a great deal of emotional turmoil while waiting for the results, and I suspected that others went through a similar experience. Being a group counselor and believing in the power of the group process, I decided to begin a support group for people who were dealing with HIV/AIDS. Although most people thought the group was a good idea, they felt it was highly unlikely that anyone from this very conservative community would come to the group. It did not take long for me to realize that there were two epidemics: one called AIDS and the other called AFRAIDS.

I met a nurse epidemiologist at the local health department who was administering the HIV tests, Linda Poulsen, and discovered that many people were testing positive. We thought an AIDS support group would be helpful and together we planned our ideal

group. We were very surprised that eight people showed up for what turned out to be a powerful first group session. Most of these people had many things in common, which is best captured by the statement "I felt as if I was the only one who was going through this."

As we started to reach out, we realized that, unfortunately for us (in 1987 in Boise, Idaho), there was not a lot of support from the medical community. In designing the group, Linda was able to answer the questions of group participants about the physiological aspects of HIV/AIDS. The health department is often a good place to look for help and for a coleader when you decide to start a group. These people have direct knowledge and experience in dealing with the virus. In addition to the health department, our major source of support was the Idaho AIDS Foundation. To find out what help is available in your community, call the National AIDS Hotline at (800) 342-AIDS.

One of our first tasks was to find a suitable location. Even though churches are abundant in our community and available for this kind of purpose, gay people are often not welcomed in the mainline denominations. We also ruled out the use of the health department. Many people had found that they were HIV-positive there, and we thought they would have negative associations to it. We wanted a space that was comfortable, relaxed, and as noninstitutional as possible. Eventually, we decided to use the YWCA. It was very flexible and had a reputation of being open to new ideas.

Another source of support was the local gay community. The Gay Community Center put us in touch with various gay organizations, and we were able to put out the word that we were starting the group. After a few months we sent a flier to health care providers, psychologists, counselors, and social workers about the services we could offer. I quickly discovered that if we showed some flexibility many people in the community were willing to work with us and to share their knowledge. We invited guest speakers to every other group session.

Group Format

From the outset I decided that it would be best to use trained group leaders rather than to rely on volunteers. Professionals expressed interest in working with people with HIV/AIDS, and I provided ongoing coordination.

The format for these groups was the result of trial and error. When we began, we decided on an open support group that included a variety of people with AIDS, people who had tested HIV-positive, friends, family, parents, and those who were worried about being infected. In addition, health professionals and volunteers could attend. Although it is possible to have an open, heterogeneous group as we did, an increasing number of organizations are moving toward more homogeneous groups such as these:

✓ Family and friends

✓ Those who have not tested HIV-positive but who are affected by the disease in other ways ("the worried well")

✓ Women only

✓ HIV-positive youth group

✓ Caregivers

✓ Substance abusers

✓ Gay only

✓ Nongay only

✓ Groups for various minority groups conducted in language of origin

✓ Newly diagnosed clients

✓ HIV-positive without symptoms

✓ HIV-positive with symptoms

✓ Terminal-stage AIDS

✓ Long-term survivors

I quickly found out we were better off with a heterogeneous approach as groups build up a genuine cohesiveness and are very resistant to making a switch. I recommend that you assess your situation and decide what works best for you and your group members.

At our first and second meetings we asked people to brainstorm with us what topics would be most interesting and relevant to deal with in the group. We did this exercise a number of times in different groups and combined the needs assessment lists. They became the foundation for the guest speakers we asked to our groups. Here are some of the topics we explored:

✓ The grief and loss process

✓ Assertiveness training (dealing with doctors and other professionals)

✓ Family issues

✓ Spirituality

✓ Medication and other health care concerns

✓ Nutrition and exercise

✓ Learning about how to be sexually safer

✓ Coping with homophobia and other forms of discrimination

✓ Living wills and other legal issues

✓ Coping with depression and other mental health concerns

✓ The hope of the new medications and dealing with living longer than expected

Group sessions typically begin with a quick go-around. The importance of confidentiality is emphasized at the beginning of each session. If the members care to, they talk about what has brought them to the meeting that night. Often they go into their history, how they came to be HIV-positive, and what their experience has been before and after that time. As early as possible in each group meeting, the group leaders help members identify common concerns and link the work of members. Before people come to these groups, their overwhelming feeling is that "I am all alone with this issue." It is difficult to maintain this defense when they see other people dealing with similar concerns.

Later in the session we invite questions and comments from the participants. We also bring in outside resources and guests to lead the group on a particular question raised by members. These guests have been well received, and this practice also introduces members to the resources available in the community.

At each meeting we encourage members to bring up personal concerns they want to explore. Here are some typical concerns of group members:

✓ I told my mother about my health.

✓ My lover left me.

✓ I have a hard time adjusting to my medications, and I don't know what to do.

✓ I've been in jail since I last saw you.

✓ I'm feeling good (I'm feeling bad).

The role of the coleaders at this time is to help people express themselves and to encourage people to speak to one another in the group rather than through the leaders. People are allowed to respond to what others say, but we ask them to be nonjudgmental, to use "I" language, and to speak directly to the other person.

The group ends with some sort of ritual. One of our early rituals was standing in a circle and giving a mutual shoulder rub. I assumed that many of the participants in our group had stopped getting touched after they were diagnosed and that if they came to the group they could be guaranteed a little bit of nonsexual body contact such as a couple of hugs. We encourage people to give and get hugs if they so desire. At some groups participants have asked if people would be willing to share names and phone numbers so they can develop a network outside of the group.

Group Outcomes

Over the years that I have led these groups, a number of issues resurface time and again, one of which is confidentiality. We continually need to redefine confidentiality, answer any questions about it, discuss it fully, and get everybody to agree to abide by this practice. Sometimes we have spent as much as half of a meeting discussing confidentiality and trust.

When an individual has knowingly broken confidentiality, the members tell the person that he or she is no longer welcome at the group. The group has been consistent with this norm. I stress that no one can confirm an individual's HIV status except that person. Nevertheless, group members remain afraid of disclosure and have faced serious consequences when their status was disclosed.

Dealing in the group with people who are ill is a matter that must be addressed. Our members have depressed immune systems, and we ask those who are contagious not to come to the group that evening. We have had people come to the group when they were very ill yet noncontagious. Certain other members have had a variety of reactions, which need to be dealt with in an open fashion.

When a new member enters the group, we encourage returning members to share more about their stories before asking the new client to participate. In telling their stories, returning members often relate what their life was like before they were HIV-positive, what it was like to test positive, and what their subsequent experience has been. They also tend to talk about what the group has meant to them. By the time we come around to the new individuals, it is much easier for them to express themselves. We then say, "You probably have some questions that you would like answered, and this would be a good time to do it." Typical questions are "I'm feeling very depressed too. Tell me about that and what you have done about it." or "I haven't told my parents, and you said you haven't told your parents. I'm curious who has told their parents." This practice helps the new member get involved with the group and feel connected.

There is a lot of humor in our groups. People new to the group may be somewhat put off by the laughing initially, but eventually most of them learn the value of humor in putting concerns into perspective. The leaders must remember to accentuate the feelings that go along with the laughter and to look for the pain as well as the humor.

Dealing with grief and loss is a recurring theme. We are constantly reminding people about the grief cycle. Probably the most common reaction we get in the group is members experiencing an emotion and feeling as if they are going crazy or are out of control. It is essential to teach people to identify where in the grief cycle they are. Then, when their anger erupts, they see it as a natural and necessary process. Almost always there is someone else in the group who has experienced the same kind of feeling and can speak to this issue.

When a member of the group either becomes very ill or dies, it is essential to explore the feelings evoked in other members. We spend some time at the meeting following the member's death in remembering him or her and talking about things that we liked about that person. Of course, along with this process comes dealing with the members' feelings about dying and grief. Usually there is talk about the funeral, which sometimes leads to a discussion about what others hope their memorial service will be like. We encourage this kind of talk because it helps to reveal some of the members' own issues and helps them to discuss their own mortality.

The issues surrounding HIV have changed dramatically in the last few years. HIV disease is no longer a "death sentence" but a treatable condition. Although it still may be fatal over time, the protease inhibitor "cocktails," a powerful combination of medicines, have helped people live their lives with little evidence of disease.

Staying alive with HIV disease has raised other issues. Some people who had been very ill suddenly became healthy, and we talk about how their life picture has changed. If a client is sure his or her time is limited and then learns he or she can live a longer life, important adjustments must be made. Clients also deal with a myriad of other issues:

✓ Intimacy as an HIV-positive person

✓ Spirituality issues, compounded because of rejection by many religious organizations

✓ Dislike of a medication regimen while staying committed to it

✓ An ironic appreciation of HIV disease and of life itself

✓ A second "coming out" process concerning HIV status

Personal Concerns

As a result of leading these groups, I have learned to cope with anger directed at me. The first time someone in the group got mad at me, I did not know how to respond. I eventually understood that anger was sometimes directed at me because the clients felt more comfortable with me than with other people. One of the doctors in our area who deals with people with HIV/AIDS told me he had many patients who were angry with him. As we talked, I began to realize that there is a great deal of anger associated with AIDS, but people have few places to vent their anger. Clients know that I am a safe and nonrejecting target, and I try to help clients redirect their anger and find ways to work through it.

Perhaps the greatest anxiety I experienced was feeling that the time I have to work in the HIV/AIDS area is limited. I realize that burnout is always tapping at my shoulder. The toll of running a group like this and losing so many group members to this disease has been high. I find that the best way to deal with my personal reactions is to meet outside the sessions to talk about feelings with colleagues. This kind of support is imperative.

I ran the HIV support group for 4 years. This was possible because I took periodic breaks from facilitating groups and reduced the frequency of the groups that I led. Having a cofacilitator is very helpful and highly recommended. Also, it is important to help other counselors become involved so you can take short or extended breaks. The support groups I have developed with other counselors who do not deal primarily with AIDS continue to be a key way to prevent burnout. I currently work with HIV/AIDS clients individually.

Looking Ahead

Although the issues have changed over time, HIV disease is still a harsh reality. The incidence of HIV continues to grow in young people, drug users, women, ethnic minorities, and poor people. The youthful sense of invulnerability provides a special challenge. We will need to address these new populations as we design our groups. I urge any trained group facilitator to learn more about HIV/AIDS to help meet urgent community needs and to consider starting or helping with an HIV/AIDS support group. It is both very demanding and very rewarding. I learned more about myself in those years and faced many of my own issues.

✳ Group Work With Women

In her article on the evolution of women's groups, Horne (1999) points out that women's groups have been central in the development of contemporary group work. Historically, one of the key contributions is the initiation of consciousness-raising groups in the 1960s. A more recent contribution to group work is the advent of member-led international action groups in the 1990s. Horne contends that the reciprocal interaction between personal empowerment and systemic change is one of the main strengths of women's groups, which is having an effect worldwide. Horne provides an overview of the types of women's groups that have developed over the years, documents the important historical processes in group work with women, and explores the current and future directions of women's group work.

In identifying practice trends in women's groups, Kees and Leech (2004) state that diversity is a characteristic of women's groups. Although these groups are as diverse as the women who comprise them, they share a common denominator emphasizing support for the experience of women. The literature reveals that women join these groups to realize that they are not alone and to gain validation for their experience. Through their group participation, women learn that their individual experiences are frequently rooted in problems within the system. In conjunction with the group members, the group leader's job is to design a group that leads to both individual and systemic change (Kees & Leech, 2004). A useful resource on diversity in group work with women is *Images of Me: A Guide to Group Work With African-American Women* (Pack-Brown, Whittington-Clark, & Parker, 1998). This book describes an Afrocentric approach to group counseling and provides a set of therapeutic tools and culturally appropriate knowledge that is essential to working effectively with African American women in groups.

The next two group proposals describe two different kinds of support groups for women.

A Relational Women's Support Group: A Power Source for Women's Voices

This group proposal is written from the perspective of Elizabeth J. Cracco and Wendy S. Janosik. For more information contact Wendy Janosik, CICSW, PhD, at University of Wisconsin Counseling and Consultation Services, 905 University Avenue, 4th Floor, University of Wisconsin–Madison, Madison, WI 53715-1005; e-mail schmidtJ@facstaff.wisc. edu. Or contact Elizabeth J. Cracco, PhD, at the College of the Holy Cross, Counseling Center, P.O. Box D, Worcester, MA 01610; e-mail ecracco@holycross.edu. ∎

Organizing the Group

Some years ago we discovered a book by Jean Baker Miller titled *Toward a New Psychology of Women* (1976). Miller proposed the critical role of connection to women's growth. Her power to name women's experience resonated with our own private and professional struggles with invisibility and isolation.

Although 80 to 90% of our caseloads were female, we found little professional dialogue concerning women's particular therapeutic and developmental needs. As a result of our conversations with each other, we realized that we were feeling enlivened and more able to take action. It seemed intuitive that other women would benefit from a similar process, and we decided to apply our newfound energy to doing women's groups together. Ultimately, we hoped to create an atmosphere within a group context that would allow college women, who often feel isolated and deenergized, to validate each other's experience and find power in that connection.

The Relational Paradox

To understand how the relationships fostered in a group therapy context are unique, powerful, and curative, it is important to understand a basic principle of relational theory known as the "relational paradox." Individuals who have experienced violation or injury in relationships will employ self-protective strategies such as silencing, emotional disengagement, or role playing both to protect the self and to preserve or protect the relationship in times of conflict or difficulty (Miller & Stiver, 1991, 1997). Miller and Stiver suggested that although individuals yearn for connection with others, they also keep large parts of themselves out of connection. As a result, truly authentic connection is rendered impossible, and the self is sacrificed, ostensibly in the hope of maintaining the relationships. By understanding the paradox, group leaders are able to explore individual and group strategies for disconnection. Through their compassion and empathy, group leaders are able to guide group members in establishing authentic connection. Helping women move toward optimum mental health necessarily means helping women find authenticity and voice *within connection.*

Screening

When we screen potential members for this women's group, we concentrate on these goals and tasks:

✓ Set a tone of participation in group

✓ Introduce basic principles of the relational model

✓ Evaluate client's capacity to tolerate the responsibility of mutual empathy

Mutuality in the therapeutic setting refers to an involvement and openness on behalf of all participants that leads to a sense of shared purpose. From the outset we attempt to foster this dynamic of participation and engagement. Most clearly related to this objective, we communicate the expectation of regular attendance. The group meets weekly for 90 minutes over the duration of the semester

(approximately 13 weeks). We also suggest alerting clients to the focus on connection and the hope that they will attend to the here-and-now relationships with the other women within group. Therefore, participants should be evaluated in terms of their ability to participate in connection with others, even if they currently struggle with relationships. We suggest to clients who are acutely suicidal, are experiencing extreme vegetative symptoms of depression, or whose first and primary presentation is acute trauma or grief, that they would be better served through an initial course of individual therapy.

Group Goals

These goals of relational group practice provide a focus for our group work:

✓ To call attention to the sources and repercussions of silence in participants' lives

✓ To create a corrective experience through relationship by building empathy for self (self-empathy) and with others (mutual empathy)

✓ To create an increased capacity to engage in mutually empowering relationships outside of the group

When planning groups based on this template, leaders should carefully consider the unique contextual and demographic factors that might influence each stage in the process. The groups we refer to in this group proposal are White, middle- to upper-middle-class, heterosexual college women 18 to 22 years of age. The texture and structure of our groups are very much a product of the cultural context and the worldview that traditionally accompany those social locations. The core healing component of connection can transcend a number of different groups, but greater diversity among members will likely present heightened challenges and rewards in creating "empathy across difference."

Group Format

Opening Phase: Creating Safety by Offering Control and Connections

Establishing safety is the cardinal goal during the beginning stages of any group's life. In a relational group this is achieved through two important pathways: by offering clients a sense of control over the group and by witnessing and responding to their experiences.

During the opening phases of group we can draw attention to the theme of relationships in a context of safety by providing structure. When offering alternative exercises, we make several efforts to respect shared control of the group by allowing the group to elect or reject the activity. A useful opening exercise is to have members explore the relational aspects of "naming" and "being named." For example, we ask participants to share the story of their names, highlighting connections to family that might emerge and validating their own feelings about this inheritance. We also invite participants to "name themselves" within the group, introducing the idea that choices about self-expression are possible. Having participants draw representations of each of these selves and discussing their drawings with the group further enhances this exercise. The presence of crayons is often a great tension reducer, enabling visually and kinesthetically oriented members to flourish.

In our groups we consciously avoid what we have metaphorically referred to as the "Wizard of Oz phenomenon," whereby the power to "heal" in the group is controlled by the facilitators from behind a curtain. Our intention in drawing back this curtain is to communicate empathy and, most important, to model mutuality for participants. We want to invest ourselves in connection with the group,

with each of its members, and with each other. First, we strive to convey an openness to personal investment in the therapeutic encounter. As women, we also have experienced invisibility and lack of information in obtaining health services for ourselves. Tapping our own experiences in service to client concerns enlarges our capacity for empathic attunement and response. Second, we openly express different reflections about what has transpired within the group. For example, Wendy might say, "It seems as if people are feeling confused." If Elizabeth has a different perception, there is no hesitation in saying to the group and to Wendy, "I was sensing more disappointment in the room. What are others feeling?" Within these differences we continually note and honor each other's perspectives and strengths. Elizabeth may note for the group her admiration for Wendy's ability to really connect with individuals about the heart of their struggle. She, in turn, may thank Elizabeth for her strength in summarizing a complex interaction for the group. This models for group members the possibility that connection does not always require agreement or acquiescence.

Participants bring to group not only the pain of injurious relationships but also the despair of having that pain ignored or discounted. During the initial phases of group, we bear witness to the pain of being invisible that is often unseen by the participants themselves. We work hard at making the invisible visible. As clients begin to talk of hurtful relationships, we figuratively hold up a mirror by repeating the story back to the participant and commenting on what we see as the emotional cost or impact. When the empathic response of another group member comes close to the core of the participant's experience, the reaction is often nonverbal and may include tearing, a flushed face, averting of gaze, or fidgeting. Now a part of the self previously protected and hidden is being seen and honored by others, and a new, deeper level of connection is possible.

These vulnerable moments must be facilitated with care and respect. Participants may respond in a number of ways. Often there is a flood of tears and a great sense of relief at finally having one's pain witnessed. Others, especially during the initial phase, comment that this new way of being in relation feels uncomfortable or strange. For many women invisibility is so normative that being recognized in any way, even emotionally, elicits a shame response, followed by attempts to move back toward anonymity. These countermoves may include denying feelings, literally shrinking physically, or deflecting the topic of conversation to another subject or object. During these moments, it is especially critical that the therapists create an environment of challenge and support that honors these longstanding strategies of disconnection as important protective devices.

Building Bridges: The Working Phase

The major objective of the working phase is for group members to find connection within difference, bringing more authentic parts of themselves to their relationships within the group. During the initial phase of the group, bonds often form around a central, socially acceptable issue. Quite typically these discussions focus on romantic relationships. Although this strategy may be successful in creating some form of common ground, it may also demand that participants remain in old roles or scripts that keep them disconnected and isolated, and it fails to tap the power of within-group relationships.

Among college women one script is so ubiquitous it has earned its own slang within our groups—that is, the "nice girl" script. Although these young women have met all of the external benchmarks of success—they are excellent students, athletes, popular, fashion-

able, thin, and "fun-loving"—eventually the push toward authenticity that is part of group experience comes into conflict with the "nice girl" role. A profound example of this tension unfolded just after the spring break when a group member reported her disappointment over not having as much fun as she had hoped. She was upset by the way that she saw women being objectified at the beaches and clubs. In the past she had been able to "party" and enjoy this scene with the rest of her friends, but now she felt a disconcerting sadness and chastised herself for being "negative." In the context of the group relational space, the other members responded with empathy and provided a place for both her anger and her sadness. Moreover, her disclosure allowed other women to come forward and reveal that they often did not enjoy the college "party scene" for similar reasons.

An extended conversation about the many costs of the "nice girl" script ensued throughout the life of this group, and here-and-now interactions emerged that mirrored the outside-of-group predicament. As members realized that they played "nice girl" within the group as well, they began to see how this taxed their ability to maintain authentic connections. Eventually members learned to have a deep sense of appreciation for their ability to maintain support through both their similarities and their differences.

Group Outcomes

Jean Baker Miller (1976) defined power as "the capacity to move or produce change," and relational groups can serve as a power source for women's development. One client reported during our closing ritual that through the group she had learned how to be a "real girl" instead of a "nice girl." Through mutual empathy and self-empathy, clients are able to change in many ways.

Miller and Stiver (1991) describe "five good things" that result from mutually empowering relationships: (1) increased ability to act or take action within relationships, (2) greater knowledge of self and other, (3) greater sense of self-worth, (4) a desire for more connection, and (5) a greater sense of zest or vitality. These five things serve as excellent outcomes by which to mark the effectiveness of a relational group, and all of them have been evidenced among participants in the women's groups we have facilitated. We are continually amazed and honored to witness such profound power and movement. In the concluding sessions of group, participants have made life-changing decisions—to leave or continue relationships, to travel around the world, to pursue new career paths, to open new dialogues with parents, or to attend AA, to name only a few. The rela-

tional model provides a unique and effective approach that honors women's strength in connection and exposes participants to the tranformative power within each of us—the power of empathy in relationship. The relational model allows for creation of mutuality and safety that supports participants in bringing more authentic dimensions of themselves into both the group and into relationships in everyday life (Comstock, Duffey, & St. George, 2002).

To learn more about the relational model, and the role of voice in women's development, we recommend Brown and Gilligan (1992); Comstock, Duffey, and St. George (2002); Jack (1991); Jordan (1997); Jordan, Kaplan, Miller, Stiver, and Surrey (1991); Kees & Leech (2004); McManus, Redford, and Hughes (1997); Miller (1976); Miller and Stiver (1991, 1997); and Surrey (1997).

Group Proposal

A Women's Support Group for Survivors of Incest

The following description, written from the perspective of Lupe Alle-Corliss, highlights key features of the many groups she has conducted. For further information about this group, contact Lupe Alle-Corliss, LCSW, at her private practice: telephone (909) 920-1850, or by e-mail: LupeLCSW@aol.com. ■

Sexual abuse of children by family members continues to come to the attention of mental health professionals. A sexual encounter with a trusted family member not only typically results in a major psychological trauma itself but also frequently leads to emotional prob-

lems for the survivor later in life. Some of the common problems include impaired self-esteem, negative identity formation, difficulty in intimate relationships, sexual dysfunction, and repeated victimization (Herman, 1992; Meiselman, 1978, 1990).

Various types of groups are being used in treating survivors of childhood sexual abuse including support groups, psychoeducational groups, time-limited groups, long-term or open-ended groups, and retreats (Courtois, 1996). This group proposal describes a time-limited therapy group designed to enable women to begin the process of working through unresolved issues related to their incestuous past. Today, with the rapidly changing state of mental health care, being able to conduct time-limited groups is even more advantageous because it is cost-effective, efficient, and fits the demands for short-term treatment.

Organizing the Group

A combination of group and individual therapy is generally considered to be the treatment of choice for survivors of incest. Briere (1996) recommends concurrent group and individual therapy due to the stress resulting from clients' own memories and from hearing the stories of other group members. Structure is an important dimension in group treatment because it provides safety and allows the group members to observe consistent and clear boundaries in the therapeutic process (Gerrity & Peterson, 2004). In providing a safe and therapeutic environment for incest survivors, the main goal is to empower these women by helping them get past the molestation and the "victimization" role. Other objectives are to help women share their secret and recognize that they are not alone, understand the current impact of this experience, begin to work through and resolve feelings associated with their trauma, and make changes. In a group situation women find a commonality and a basis for identification, and a new type of family can emerge, one that is different from the client's original family, which may have been dysfunctional.

I recruit potential members by publicizing my groups within my own agency by way of memos, announcements, and personal contact with colleagues. In considering membership, I seek clients who display a readiness to deal openly with the trauma of incest.

Typically, these women are in individual therapy. For women who are involved with another therapist, I ask for a release form so I can consult and coordinate with the individual therapist.

I meet regularly with each potential member to assess their readiness and the appropriateness of a group experience and to orient them to the group process and goals. Through screening I also determine how well they are likely to fit with other potential group members. Some prospective members verbalize their eagerness to be part of the group, yet they may not actually be ready. They might be extremely uncomfortable with certain questions regarding the incest that are sure to come up in the group. Others may have been referred, and it is important to assess their true motivation because they may not be completely ready to involve themselves in this type of intense group. They may be acting on the basis of pressure or the need to please others. Also, based on the emerging composition of the group, it might become clear that a particular client may not be a compatible member in a specific group.

Clients are asked about their interest in such a group, and an attempt is made to determine how ready the individual is to talk in a group setting about the incest and its impact. Other screening questions include the following: "If you have had any previous group experience, what was this like for you?" "Were you, or are you now, involved in individual therapy, and what was this experience like?" "What are your personal goals for the group?" "What are your expectations, hopes, and fears about participating in the group?" Applicants are also encouraged to ask me questions about the group and my therapeutic style.

It is critical that members possess the ego strength to deal with the material that will be explored during the sessions. Members need to have adequate interpersonal skills to deal with others in a group situation. People with suicidal and extremely self-destructive tendencies and people who do not have adequate contact with reality are screened out. Also, clients with recent drug addictions may be at a vulnerable place in their recovery process and therefore may not be ready to enter into such an emotionally demanding group. Care is taken not to include family members or friends in the same group. Also excluded are those who are not ready or willing to talk openly about their experiences. Women who have been molested by non–family members may not fit in as well.

Group Format

The group is closed and meets weekly for 75 minutes during a 12-week period. This time limitation is designed to facilitate bonding and to produce a reasonable degree of pressure necessary to work through the members' resistances. Although each group has its own process, these groups generally go through the phases described here.

Initial Phase

The initial phase involves getting to know one another, establishing ground rules, and identifying personal goals. This stage is crucial in the development of trust and rapport and in giving members permission for catharsis and ventilation. A signed contract is used to encourage commitment and to help the clients feel that their participation is valued and important.

At the first group meeting I emphasize the importance of regular attendance, being prompt, confidentiality, the limitations of time, and bringing any unresolved issues back to the group rather than dealing with them outside of the group. A date for the postgroup meeting, which is typically about

3 months after termination, is established at the first session. In the early phase of the group, members express empathy with one another over the difficulty of sharing the incest issue. The following guideline questions are provided to help them deal directly with the impact of incest on them: "How did the molestation happen?" "Who molested you?" "How old were you?" "How long did it go on?" "How did you deal with it?" "How did you feel toward the people who were in a position to protect you from the molestation but failed to do so?" "What impact does this experience have on you today?"

Much of the initial phase is focused on identifying and discussing personal goals, which enables all in the group to know of each person's goals and provides a direction for the sessions. The goals for my group are similar to those identified by Thompson and Renninger (1995) in their short-term therapy groups with survivors of sexual abuse:

✓ Provide education, validation, and support via other survivors of sexual abuse

✓ Explore past sexual abuse and its effects on current life functioning and behavior

✓ Decrease isolation and increase self-esteem

✓ Increase ability to trust oneself and others

✓ Instill a sense of empowerment

✓ Decrease secrecy, shame, and stigmatization associated with the abuse

Members generally feel much anxiety and apprehension at first. A member often feels that she is the only one with such a terrible burden, and she may feel that she would be an outcast if others knew about her secret. As members realize that they have a common experience, they begin to open up and find the support available in the group useful. By sharing the incest experience, members free themselves to look at how it continues to have an impact on them. The focus of the sessions is not merely on reporting the details of the specific acts but also on exploring their feelings, beliefs, and perceptions about what happened. Although it is important for these women to share their past history, it is essential that they deal with the effects the incest continues to have on their lives. They need to acquire present coping skills that will empower them and enable them to move forward.

Middle Phase

During the middle phase, the focus is on accomplishing the goals of individual members. Connections are made between a woman's past behavior and her present behavior. In this way she begins to see patterns and to understand her own dynamics. For instance, a woman might have chosen men who dominated her, abused her, or in some way took advantage of her. She sees with greater clarity her own part in allowing this type of treatment to continue. A group is a good way to help such a woman become aware of and challenge her faulty belief systems. Through the group process, these women can rid themselves of destructive beliefs and can learn to create functional self-statements.

As well as gaining insight into her own dynamics, a woman learns that she can be of help to others through her disclosures. By expressing intense emotions and personal sharing, a safe climate is created that facilitates further explorations of common themes such as isolation, secrecy, shame, powerlessness, hurt, and anger. This mutual sharing tends to increase cohesion within the group.

As the group evolves, other themes in an individual's life are typically identified. A number of therapeutic strategies can promote change in feelings, attitudes, and behaviors. Some specific techniques include providing reassurance for women that they

behaved normally in an abnormal situation; reading books in a personal way; keeping a diary or journal that includes thoughts, feelings, and behaviors in certain situations; writing letters that are not sent; talking to other family members; and recording and sharing dreams.

A very useful way of helping these women express their emotions is through artwork. By asking them to draw the abused child within them, insights unfold surrounding their ordeal. Participating in art often enables them to face the total impact of their molestation. There is some support in the literature for the therapeutic value of these expressive techniques. According to Thompson and Renninger (1995), art and drawing assist clients in arriving at an emotional understanding of their past experiences. Along with cognitive behavioral techniques, visual exercises facilitate positive change.

Members are encouraged to continue to work on recovering memories and dealing with flashbacks, which may seem very real and are a common occurrence for the incest survivor. It is important to remind these women that they are no longer little children and that these flashbacks are only a memory of the past. Much needed support and validation is provided, and clients are assisted in recognizing maladaptive defense patterns and in developing healthier coping styles.

Final Phase

Toward the end of the group the women are reminded of the upcoming termination. I assist members in reviewing what happened in the group as a whole as well as what they individually learned and how they can now continue to apply their insights and newly acquired behaviors to situations outside of the group. Role playing helps in this consolidation process. I give a structured questionnaire to help members pull together and assess their learning. The members evaluate their progress and determine future plans, including what work they still need to do. They give feedback to one another, and they identify certain people in the group that can serve as a support system. Although the women cognitively know that the group will be ending, it is a common reaction for them to not want to terminate.

Members celebrate the ending of the group by sharing food as well as participating in a "Personal Poster" in which each member can give individual support and constructive feedback to every group member. The rationale for this exercise is that each member is able to take with her some constructive feedback or supportive comments and can use this experience for support and encouragement. This serves as a reminder of their gains through the group experience. I also encourage the women in my groups to remain open to further therapeutic work if they are not already concurrently in individual or group therapy.

Group Outcomes

Building follow-up procedures into the group design provides a basis for understanding the longer-term value of the group experience as well as improving the design for future groups. In the short-term groups reported on by Herman and Schatzow (1984), the results of a 6-month follow-up survey of 28 women supported their assumption that this therapeutic approach was particularly effective in resolving the issues of shame, secrecy, and stigmatization associated with incest. Outcomes included improved self-esteem, increased safety, and decreased shame, guilt, and isolation. The single most helpful factor was the contact with other survivors. The literature reveals that group therapy for survivors of childhood sexual abuse is effective (see Gerrity & Peterson, 2004).

I schedule several follow-up meetings to help group members make the transition from the weekly groups to being on their own and relying on the support networks they have developed. Part of the purpose of this follow-up is to reinforce what was learned and to provide renewed support. Follow-up sessions are scheduled 6 to 12 weeks after the end of the group. During these sessions, clients are asked these questions:

✓ What did you like best about the group?

✓ What did you like least about the group?

✓ How do you feel that you have changed as a result of being in this group?

Group members are also asked to rate themselves as "better," "worse," or "the same" in regard to the following areas: work, friendships, relationships with family members, intimate relationships, feelings about sex, feelings about oneself, and the ability to protect and take care of oneself.

Based on many follow-up group meetings with the members of my groups, it is clear that a well-developed group format with proper screening can result in a therapeutic group experience. Overall, I continue to find that carefully planned groups greatly enhance the treatment of incest survivors because they can be seen on a regular basis and can be provided with continuity and the support they need for healing. The women in these groups are able to develop a strong support network that provides them with the strength and courage to begin to resolve past issues, overcome negative patterns, and set healthy goals for their future. Perhaps the greatest message they receive is that they "deserve" to feel good about themselves and lead more productive lives. Through the years, group members have felt safe to return for brief treatment if they feel a need for further consultation.

If you are interested in learning more about designing groups with women with a history of incest, there are many excellent articles and books on the subject. You might begin by reading the articles by Herman and Schatzow (1984) and by Thompson and Renninger (1995). Other useful resources include Briere (1996), Courtois (1996), Gerrity and Peterson (2004), Herman (1981, 1992), Marotta and Asner (1999), McBride and Emerson (1989), and Meiselman (1978, 1990).

✳ Group Work With Men

Traditional forms of individual therapy may not be the best way to reach male clients. Groups for men offer some unique advantages in assisting men in clarifying their gender roles and helping them cope with life's struggles. In writing about group therapy for traditional men, Brooks (1998) states: "Traditional men hate psychotherapy and will do almost anything to avoid a therapist's office" (p. 84). Group work is a viable alternative for men to receive help with their problems without having to experience many of the factors that restrict their participation in therapy (Andronico, 1996). In a men's group, members learn a great deal about themselves by sharing their experiences. Brooks (1998) sums up the unique therapeutic value of group work with men: "With skillful leadership, the male group can nurture and encourage men in a manner not possible in any other therapy format" (p. 95).

In general, the stereotypical view of a traditional male is one who is cool, detached, objective, rational, worldly, competitive, and strong. Men in our society often hear messages that dictate ways they should think, feel, and act. Corey and Corey (2006) identify the following traits that are often associated with the traditional male role: emotional unavailability, independence, power and aggressiveness, denial of fears, protection of inner self, invulnerability, lack of bodily self-awareness, remoteness with other men, drive to succeed, denial of "feminine" qualities, avoidance of physical contact, rigid perceptions, devotion to work, loss of male spirit, and experience of depression. Andronico and Horne (2004) contend that "while many traditional roles have changed, most men still feel the pressure of fulfilling the three P's: Provider, Protector, and Procreator" (457).

In our book, *I Never Knew I Had a Choice*, we describe the price men pay for remaining in traditional roles. A man often loses a sense of himself because of his concern with being the way he thinks he should be as a male. A man often hides his feelings, largely due to the fear that someone might discover what lies beneath the image he projects.

Rabinowitz and Cochran (2002) describe how men's groups are able to deepen a man's experiences. In such a group, men are given the opportunity to face and express their disappointments and losses. Rather than denying their psychic pain and wounding, men are provided with a context where they can bring all of their feelings into the open and where they can be healed by the support of others in the group. Some of the themes and issues that Rabinowitz and Cochran observe in their group work with men include trust, vulnerability, fear, shame, strength, weakness, male-male relationships, competition, family of origin issues, sexuality, friendship, dominance, submissiveness, love, hatred, dreams, grief, obsessions, work, and death. According to Rabinowitz and Cochran, men's groups provide an interpersonally inviting atmosphere by modeling how to be intimate and how to trust others and oneself. Most men's groups contain both a psychoeducational component and an interpersonal, process-oriented dimension. Psychoeducational groups, which tend to be theme and task oriented, may have more appeal to men than feeling-oriented groups (Andronico, 1996). The group proposal that follows describes one such group.

If you are interested in some resources pertaining to working with men in groups, we recommend Andronico (1996), Andronico and Horne (2004), Brooks (1998), Brooks and Good (2001a, 2001b), Pollack and Levant (1998), Rabinowitz (2001), and Rabinowitz and Cochran (2002).

Group Proposal

A Men's Group in a Community Agency

Randy Alle-Corliss, a clinical social worker in a department of psychiatry in a large health maintenance organization (HMO), designed and coleads a men's group in the agency where he works with Abran Esquibel, a clinical social worker. The following discussion is written from the perspective of Randy Alle-Corliss. For further information about this men's group, contact Randy Alle-Corliss, LCSW, at telephone (909) 920-1850, or by e-mail at: RandyLCSW@aol.com. ■

This proposal describes a group aimed at helping men explore ways they experience and express their gender roles. It contains both a psychoeducational component and an interpersonal, process-oriented dimension. The purpose of this group is to provide men coming to a psychiatric counseling center with an opportunity to work together on common issues such as depression, stress, marital and relationship difficulties, parenting concerns, work-related issues, loneliness, and isolation.

Organizing the Group

Although no men's groups were being offered in our area, my coleader and I believed that men could profit from talking about life struggles in a safe and supportive group. We assumed that exploring deeply personal concerns would lead to a reduction of isolation and increase the bonding among men. Many of our male clients did not have significant male friendships; if they had friends, they were often distant from them. We felt personally challenged to begin a group for men, which we did more than 13 years ago. To date we have conducted about 30 of these groups.

Because we were working for a large HMO, we knew the number of group sessions would be limited. The group format, whereby more clients could be seen in a shorter amount of time, at a greater frequency, could serve the needs of the clients and at the same time serve the needs of the organization. And we were convinced that the group would have other therapeutic benefits in addition to the cost-effectiveness factor. We assumed that the group would offer a place for men to discover universal themes, to ventilate feelings they had stored up, and to practice skills they could carry outside of the group and apply in various settings in everyday life.

We began by writing a proposal and presenting it to the administration. We developed a memorandum describing the purpose of the group and sent it to other clinicians, asking them to recommend appropriate candidates for this type of group. We excluded from the group candidates who were psychotic or suicidal, in extreme crisis, and those who lacked the psychological strength required for sustained group interaction.

Group Format

The group meets for 90 minutes each week for a total of 16 weeks. In addition, the co-leaders meet regularly for 15 minutes before each session and 15 minutes afterward. The group is topically oriented, educationally and therapeutically focused, and combines a variety of techniques. At times it takes longer than one session to cover a particular topic.

The Initial Session

We start the group with general introductions from each member and ourselves. We also cover the basic ground rules in the first meeting, including confidentiality, attendance, and basic HMO policies. During this first meeting, we explore gender-related issues such as what it means to be a man, the messages the men received in growing up, and how these messages affect them today. We typically discuss

a number of norms pertaining to being a man. The members are invited to share their reactions to adhering to or breaking these norms and how these norms influence their daily behavior. Typical topics discussed at other sessions are described next.

Relationships With Father and Mother

We examine relationships with parents, particularly with fathers, because this seems to be a central influence in the lives of most men. Many of the men are disappointed by their father's absence or are angry about the excessive force and aggression their fathers used to discipline them. We also explore their relationships with their mothers, especially as it relates to how they handled their feelings around them. We typically invite members to write letters to their parents, which they share in the group.

Relationships With Significant Others

It is clear to us that the men in our groups often experience difficulty simply recognizing, let alone expressing, their feelings. One reason some men join the group is because they have trouble expressing feelings and behaving assertively. Members have opportunities to talk about their relationships with significant others, especially with women. Some of them may be going through a divorce or having marital difficulties. We broadened our description of relationships to include gay relationships. Our experience in working with some gay men in these groups has taught us the importance of using language that is free of bias with respect to sexual orientation. Regardless of one's sexual orientation, the men in our groups discover that they have a great deal in common.

Developing and Maintaining Friendships

We include discussion about friendships with other men and women, for we continue to find that men receive conflicting messages about appropriate gender roles. We also find that men have difficulty initiating friendships and maintaining intimacy. They tend to be quite isolated from other men, and one purpose of the group is to provide them with rich sources of support. We encourage the men in the group to get together outside of the group and to develop other sources of support, especially with other men. However, we caution the members about subgrouping in a way that could detract from group cohesion.

Relationships With Children

We typically examine relationships with children, as many of the men enter the group with concerns about being an effective parent. We discuss the importance of men's relationships with their children. We teach assertiveness skills to assist the men in setting limits and following through on consequences with their children. We often have the men write letters to their children, which they read in group, to help them express and explore unrecognized feelings.

Relationship to Work

Those members who have lost a job often struggle with feeling devastated over not working. The members talk about how work affects their lives at home, especially with their partners and children. Men often struggle with working too much, setting limits, and frustration on the job. Many men report feeling overly responsible and stressed when assuming the role of provider. By talking about the importance of work, many of the men learn that there is more to life than simply providing and working and come to realize the importance of a balance between work and play.

Sexuality

Most of the men have a host of concerns regarding sexuality, but they tend to be reluc-

tant to discuss such concerns openly. We have small handouts to spur the men's thinking on particular topics, such as sexual performance, feelings of attraction to other people, impotence, differences in sexual appetites, and aging. Due to the commonalities among the members, men can explore fears regarding their sexuality and sexual practices in ways that enable them to gain a deeper understanding of their sexuality.

Closing the Group

We end the group with good-byes and reminiscing among members and leaders. Valuable feedback is given, and the members evaluate their experience. We reinforce any gains the members have made and give them tangible items to take with them to remind them of their participation in the group. We have given out certificates of attendance with the statement: "It is okay to be a man." We encourage the members to continue their new behaviors. We also point out to them potential pitfalls they are likely to encounter in applying what they learned in the group to everyday living.

Group Outcomes

It is critical to assist the members in evaluating the impact of the group experience. Toward this end, we arrange for a postsession group, which we call the "reunion group." Between the ending of a 16-week group and the beginning of a new group, we have the members from the previous group meet again. Reminders are sent to all the members urging them to attend. The reunion group gives members a chance to take another look at what the group meant to them. We place special emphasis on how they have been applying their learning in their everyday lives. The men have an opportunity to discuss any problems they have encountered in implementing a new style of behavior. In addition to providing support, we also challenge the members to take further risks where it seems appropriate. The follow-up group gives these men a way to establish a plan for putting their new goals into action now that the group has ended.

The members' evaluations of their experience at the follow-up session are typically positive and constructive. Many of the men say they had been looking for this kind of group for years. They often report that they greatly valued the opportunity to discuss personally significant topics in a group setting. They report feeling less depressed, less isolated, and being more able to recognize and communicate their feelings. Some men re-

turn to the group later when their benefits allow them the opportunity for continuing their treatment.

Men report that the group has helped them to manage their anger more effectively, to develop more male friends, and to become more assertive. Many of the men are able to use the feedback they receive in immediate ways by becoming more aware of their feelings and more communicative in their relationships. They begin to think of themselves and other men more positively. In general, they say that they feel more content with themselves, they feel a wider range of emotions, and they are able to laugh and have more fun.

☀ Group Treatment of Domestic Violence Offenders

The problem of domestic violence is pervasive. It is estimated that every 15 seconds someone commits a crime of domestic violence in the United States. Many states have a mandatory treatment program for those convicted of the crime of domestic violence, and professional licensure renewals in some states now require a one-day continuing education course on domestic violence.

In *Solution-Focused Treatment of Domestic Violence Offenders: Accountability for Change,* Lee, Sebold, and Uken (2003) describe a cutting-edge treatment that seems to create effective, positive change in domestic violence offenders. This approach has a recidivism rate of 16.7% and a completion rate of 92.9%. More traditional approaches typically generate recidivism rates between 40 and 60% and completion rates of less than 50% (Lee et al., 2003). The approach focuses on holding offenders accountable and responsible for building solutions rather than emphasizing their problems and deficits, which is dramatically different from the traditional approach to this problem. This approach is time limited and is brief when measured against traditional program standards, consisting of only 8 sessions over a 10- to 12-week period.

The solution-focused approach strongly emphasizes formation of concrete, achievable, behavior-specific goals that each participant must establish by the third session and must continue to consistently work on throughout the treatment process. The group facilitators use changes associated with each group member's goal to assist him in redefining who he is as an individual, a family member, and a community member.

If you are interested in designing a group for domestic violence offenders, we recommend Lee, Sebold, and Uken's (2003) book, which outlines this approach to group treatment in detail, or contact the authors directly: Mo Yee Lee, e-mail lee.355@osu.edu; John Sebold, e-mail jsebold@kingsview.org.

The following group proposal, designed and facilitated by Paul Jacobson, describes another treatment approach with domestic violence offenders.

Group Proposal

A Domestic Violence Group

This group proposal is presented from the perspective of Paul Jacobson, a licensed marriage and family therapist, who designed and conducted a group for men with a history of domestic violence. For further information on this group, contact Paul Jacobson, P. O. Box 1935, Idyllwild, CA 92549; telephone (909) 652-5466; e-mail: PaulJ@pe.net. ■

Organizing the Group

Most group counseling is aimed toward people seeking help, but the domestic violence group I describe here was for a specialized involuntary population. The men who came to this group were ordered into treatment by court judges or probation officers. Most of these group members typically arrived with attitudes of resentment, blaming others, and operating under the conviction that they did not need counseling. The techniques and strategies for working with this type of resistance differ somewhat from those used with a voluntary population.

Resistance to Group Work

An individual assessment interview was conducted for all members prior to attending any group meetings. This was deemed essential to both reduce their potential for disruptive hostility and to ease them into the more stressful group situation. During this time, an attempt was made to support the individual, explore the circumstances of the abusive behavior and his arrest, challenge his defenses in a moderate manner, and gain his cooperation through suggestions of therapeutic need.

The assessment interview was also essential to begin developing a therapeutic relationship. The importance of establishing an honest relationship between the member and the facilitator cannot be overestimated. Without this, self-disclosure in a group of guarded strangers would be very unlikely. The design of this group was based on the assumption that, when given the opportunity, participants would willingly apply personal information to themselves, even without initially accepting responsibility for their actions.

I agree with Edleson and Tolman (1994), who contend that men who are prone to violence must accept responsibility for their actions if a treatment approach is to succeed. In my own groups for men who are violent, I have observed the same dynamics that Edleson and Tolman describe. Men who batter often begin group counseling in a state of denial. They typically externalize the source of their problems, and they rarely attribute their problems to their violent behavior. For change to occur, these men need to understand their own dynamics and take responsibility for their behavior. If they do not eventually recognize and accept their own problematic behavior, it is unlikely they will change. Nor will they understand the impact of their behavior on their partners, their relationships, and themselves.

A Case Illustration

To give a concrete idea of how this resistance influences a member's participation in a group, let me use Jerome as an example. Jerome arrived for this meeting 20 minutes late, complaining that he had totally forgotten the appointment he made 2 days prior. Jerome, like all the group members, had been ordered into the program following plea bargaining in which he agreed to attend counseling rather than spend 45 days in jail. His charges had been reduced from felony spousal abuse to a misdemeanor.

Although Jerome had chosen the group alternative, he insisted that he did not need counseling and preferred the quicker remedy of jail. He blamed the public defender for getting him into this program rather than pursuing his choice. As we talked, his initial agitation diminished somewhat. But when he described the situation of abuse with his wife, he again became loud, animated, and emotional. Jerome told about coming home late one night after having a few beers and getting angry because his wife had not made him dinner. When he ordered her to do so, she responded with "Make it yourself." With this he apparently lost control and claimed he was not aware of what he was doing, but he insisted he never hit her with a closed fist. Jerome was adamant that if she had only made dinner none of this would have happened. Thus, it was her fault. He further blamed her friends for putting "uppity" ideas into her head.

In exploring other anger experiences, Jerome admitted that it bothered him a little when he became violent, and he wanted to control himself better. This statement was one of the first signs of a more personal stake for participating in the group. Further questioning found Jerome glad to be working again after several months of unemployment, and he admitted that his drinking had increased a little while he was unemployed. Jerome was clearly removed from his emotions, unaware of his own stress level, and unaware of his dependency on alcohol. Furthermore, he did not take responsibility for his actions or his feelings.

Suggestions for Leading a Domestic Violence Group

✓ Know your motivation for organizing and facilitating a domestic violence group.

✓ Be aware of your own stress level and reactions.

✓ Try to maintain equanimity and respond rationally.

✓ Learn to verbalize theoretical ideas in common everyday language.

✓ Remember that commonly accepted therapeutic concepts are not universally understood or accepted.

✓ Discover your own similar issues with group members.

✓ Expect resistance and avoid taking it personally. Respect resistance and work with it therapeutically by encouraging clients to explore any hesitation or cautions about participating in the group.

✓ Use any medium at your disposal to teach and intervene (such as art, video, and handouts).

✓ Learn to recognize small incremental changes as progress toward discrete, obtainable therapeutic goals.

✓ Develop a good support system for yourself.

Group Goals

Because the group members had each been arrested for violence against their partners, goals were developed to assist in more optimal relational functioning. Some goals were agreed on during the assessment interview, but most were selected by the leader for individual treatment plans. Here is a list of some group goals:

✓ Develop behavioral alternatives to physical violence.

✓ Learn cognitive techniques for anger management.

✓ Discuss abusive events and behavioral alternatives.

✓ Gain an overview of relationship dynamics, expectations, and the development of physical abuse.

✓ Learn about physiological reactions as correlates of stress and stress reduction methods.

✓ Develop a recognition of feelings and emotional processing.

✓ Increase self-disclosures, personal discussion, and assertive communications.

✓ Increase personal responsibility.

✓ Increase empathy and understanding of significant others.

✓ Stop or decrease alcohol/drug use and recognize use patterns.

Group Format

Each group session began with a didactic presentation. The group was designed to address both educational and therapeutic goals. Following the didactic segment of the initial session, members were given a written multiple-choice questionnaire. This allowed individual responses without the pressures inherent with group verbalization. Then a go-around was used to stimulate discussion.

Jerome became more involved at this point and actively verbalized his answers, interacted with other members, and demonstrated an understanding of the concepts. Verbal participation was one of the facilitator's main goals for each group member.

The 15-week program was conducted using an open group format, and participants were added intermittently throughout the group's duration. The major advantage of an open group was to maintain an adequate number of members in the face of high drop-out rates. The main disadvantage was difficulty developing group cohesion and trust.

Some Ground Rules

A few group members appeared extremely impulsive and easily frustrated or angered. Several individuals were excluded from the group due to alcohol/drug problems, and many used these substances. During the initial interview members were told of the group rule of abstinence from drugs prior to meetings. If someone arrived intoxicated, they were not allowed into the group. Two such occurrences meant termination. The only other requirement was attendance, and several individuals were terminated for missing more than the allowable three sessions.

Developing Topics for Group Interaction

Meetings were structured around topics deemed relevant to group goals. The topics themselves were arrived at through several trials of alternatives and might have evolved differently with other geographic and socioeconomic populations. Topic discussions were designed to educate, gain involvement, convey information, and confront issues relevant to this population. For instance, Jerome gained valuable insight through the topics of stress and substance abuse. He realized that his own unemployment had led to a high unconscious stress level, which, in turn, aggravated his alcohol use. Unfortunately, now that Jerome was employed, he believed he no longer needed to worry about stress. If Jerome faces a similar situation in the future, we hope he will remember the stress reduction techniques he was taught.

The topics presented to the groups were loosely divided into areas of interpersonal and intrapersonal experience. Intrapersonal topics included education concerning human physiology and endocrine systems functioning, cognitive techniques for emotional processing, relaxation methods, drug and alcohol effects, stress and stress reduction, and anger. As many members appeared to have underlying issues about personal adequacy, other topics included meaning in life and the benefits of goal accomplishment. These issues are covered in depth by Wexler (2000) in his book, *Domestic Violence: Group Leader's Manual.* The interpersonal topics involving relationships included communication theories, problem-solving techniques, sex roles, relational expectations, human needs and differences, values, and family experiences.

The topics overlapped considerably, which afforded members an opportunity to explore interpersonal issues in several ways. For example, most communication issues were mentioned under the topics of transactional analysis, assertion training, and problem solving. In many of these groups, written worksheets, scripted role playing, or other activities were used to encourage member participation. If personal experiences were forthcoming, these were also used to explore and demonstrate relevant issues.

In one group Jerome and other members practiced rewording their communications into assertive statements. If members could learn the ideas and concepts through practice in relatively anxiety-free situations, it was believed they could more easily apply them to the conflict-laden areas in everyday life. After Jerome practiced role playing as a coworker and relating assertively to an imagined checkout clerk, he was able to discuss his assertive attempts with his wife. At this point he was not only applying the concepts to his own life but also reporting his attempts in the group. This progress not only demonstrated his greatly increased trust and openness but also enabled him to receive the support and feedback usually necessary for behavior change.

Group Outcomes

Some of the group goals were broad and more suited for long-term treatment, yet many members showed observable progress. Others continued to blame their partners for their situation throughout the group. For me, working with this population was difficult, trying, frustrating, and yet also rewarding. To remain personally invested, it became necessary to notice small incremental changes and regard these as signs of success and progress. One source of reinforcement was through observing improvement and through a few individuals who expressed their gratitude. I was continually forced to evaluate my statements, style, countertransference, and motivations. I discovered related issues of my own and made significant insights into the functioning of this population in general. The development of this program challenged my theoretical beliefs and therapeutic skills, thus motivating me to seek new information and education. This, in itself, has been rewarding. Although perhaps toward an extreme, these issues are relevant within the modern-day "men's movement," and thus apply somewhat to all of us.

For more information on this topic, useful resources are Edleson and Tolman (1994), Lee, Sebold, and Uken (2003), Schwartz and Waldo (2004), and Wexler (2000). Wexler's (2001) book, *Domestic Violence: Group Lead-* *er's Manual,* provides a description of a well-researched program for domestic violence treatment. The manual contains worksheets, exercises, and theoretical background for group leaders.

√ *Points to Remember*

Groups for Adults

✓ Theme-oriented groups with a psycho-educational emphasis are quite popular, and short-term structured groups meet the needs of a variety of adult populations.

✓ Time-limited groups with structured topics are frequently offered in college counseling centers. These groups typically meet a variety of special needs by combining a therapeutic and an educational focus.

✓ University counseling centers are increasingly offering specialized groups such as groups for people with eating disorders, women's groups, and men's groups.

✓ Support groups have special advantages for people who are HIV-positive or people with AIDS. There has been considerable writing on the topic of how groups can help and how best to design such a group.

✓ One kind of group that appears to be gaining prominence is a domestic violence group. Conducting such a group demands a great deal of patience and competence in dealing with difficult clients.

✓ In any kind of group for adults it is essential to be sensitive to diversity. Techniques should be appropriate for the life experiences of the members and should not be forced on members.

Exercises

In-Class Activities

1. **Critique Group Proposals.** Form small discussion groups in class to analyze and critique the special types of groups for adults that are described in this chapter. As you look at each group proposal, discuss what features you find to be the most innovative and useful. If you were going to design a similar group, what changes might you want to make from the proposal?

2. **College Groups.** Assume you are doing an internship or working in a college counseling center. What kinds of groups would you most want to have available for the students?

3. **Design a Weight-Control Group.** If you were going to design a group for weight control, what topics would you be inclined to use as a way to struc-

ture your group? What are your thoughts about the group proposal for treating compulsive eating?

4. **Evaluate the HIV/AIDS Support Group.** Examine the HIV/AIDS support group described in this chapter. If you were an administrator of an agency, would you be supportive of this type of group based on the proposal?

5. **A Group for Women.** Review the relational women's support group described in this chapter. Based on this proposal, would you be inclined to join this group if you are a woman? Why or why not?

6. **A Group for Men.** Review the men's group in a community agency. If you are a man, would you be inclined to join this group? Why or why not?

7. **Choose a Proposal to Evaluate.** As you review each of the group proposals in this chapter, which one interests you the most? What aspects of this particular proposal would you be inclined to use in a group you might design?

InfoTrac College Edition

For additional readings, explore InfoTrac College Edition, our online library, at http://www.infotrac.college.com/wadsworth. The following keywords are listed in such a way as to enable the InfoTrac College Edition search engine to locate a wider range of articles. The keywords should be entered exactly as listed, to include asterisks, "w1," "w2," "AND," and other search engine tools.

- group* w1 psych* AND women*
- group* w1 psych* AND abuse*
- group* w1 psych* AND men*
- group* w1 psych* AND violence*
- group* w1 psych* AND aids*

Chapter 12

Groups for the Elderly*

*This chapter is written from the perspective of Marianne Schneider Corey.

Focus Questions

*B*efore reading this chapter, ask yourself what kinds of experiences and training you think you would need to facilitate a group for the elderly. What questions do you have about designing a group for the elderly? As you read this chapter, consider these questions:

1. What are the most important practical and professional considerations for group work with the elderly?

2. What special considerations and guidelines would you take into account in designing a group program for institutionalized elderly people?

3. If you were asked to form a group for healthy aging people in a community center, what steps would you take to organize this group and to get members? What are some things you would want to tell potential members about this particular group?

4. How ready do you think you are to colead a group for the elderly? What kinds of personal issues might either help or hinder you in being able to effectively facilitate such a group?

5. What are some of the advantages of bereavement groups for the elderly? If you were designing such a group, what topics might you include for exploration in group sessions? What challenges do you expect to face in conducting this kind of group?

✳ Introduction

When I first started working with the elderly in the 1970s, there was little interest in addressing their needs. People, even old people, asked me "Why would a young person want to work with old people?" But the graduate students of today are unlikely to get this reaction. In the 30 years since the first edition of this book, several trends have emerged:

- There are a lot more elderly in this country.
- There is an increased interest in working with the elderly.
- Many innovative groups are being designed to meet the needs of the elderly.
- Many graduate students in the helping professions are interested in specializing in gerontology.
- Older people think of themselves as younger and stay active longer.
- Americans are beginning to perceive old people as vital members of society and to treat them with more respect.

The elderly have special needs, problems, and potentials that should not be ignored by any helping professional. Older people have a range of life experiences and personal strengths that are often overlooked. Group work with the elderly is one way to promote the positive aspects of aging as well as helping participants cope with the challenges of aging. The interpersonal nature of groups can be therapeutic for older persons, especially those who are isolated and lonely (Henderson & Gladding, 2004).

Counselors need to develop special programs for the elderly and to continue their efforts to find the means to reach this clientele. Group workers of the future will increasingly be held accountable for developing programs to help the elderly find meaning in their lives and be productive after retirement. As mental health professionals become involved with the elderly, their challenge is to do more than add years to a person's life—they must help individuals lead fuller and better lives.

The extraordinary growth of the older population worldwide offers both opportunities and challenges. As reported by the U.S. Bureau of the Census (1996), adults 65 years of age or older comprise about 13% of the total population, and it is expected that this percentage will rise by 20% by the year 2020. The overall outlook for the elderly is positive. Older adults often have a positive outlook on life and seek to engage in challenges that will maintain their well-being. In fact, general life satisfaction among the elderly is as good as that of any other age group (APA Working Group on the Older Adult, 1998). The Administration on Aging (2000) observes that 43 million Americans (one in six) are now over age 60, and Social Security, Medicare and pension plans, and better health care have increased the life span for many. Most Americans now enjoy almost 14 years of retirement with a high degree of independence and economic security. At the same time there are still some vulnerable older Americans:

- The 3 million Americans who are 85 or older
- Elders living alone without a caregiver
- Elders who are members of minority groups
- Older persons with physical or mental impairments
- Low-income older persons
- Older persons who are abused, neglected, or exploited

Villa (1999) points out that an examination of socioeconomic status among the elderly population reveals both diversity and vulnerability. She adds that as we move further into the new century there will be an increase in diversity of the total U.S. population, and we will witness an aging of minority populations. Projections of the U.S. Bureau of the Census (1996) indicate that, by 2050, 8.4 million older persons will be Black, 6.7 million will be races other than White, and 12.5 million will be Hispanic. Although there have been gains in social and economic status among the older population, some groups continue to experience both economic uncertainty and health vulnerabilities (Villa, 1999). As more people live longer, there are also higher survival rates for persons having severe physical disabilities and an increase in the occurrence of milder disabilities, prompting new challenges to provide a full range of human services. With biomedical advances, persons with developmental disabilities are much more likely to outlive their parents, raising new social policy and family issues (Ansello, 1988).

Much of this chapter is based on a description of my (Marianne's) group work with the elderly in institutions. Mental health professionals often encounter obstacles when organizing and conducting groups for the elderly. Some of the barriers are due to the unique characteristics of this population, but other obstacles are found within the system or the institutions themselves—for example, lack of interest in therapeutic work for the elderly, lack of administrative support for group work, lack of cooperation from staff workers, and lack of proper training in working with the elderly for graduate students.

※ Unique Characteristics of the Elderly

A liking for old people does not alone make a good counselor. This unique population requires special skills and knowledge. Leaders forming their first groups for the elderly will find some definite differences from their work with other age groups, and counselors need to be aware of the particular life issues faced by older people. In referring to the elderly we are speaking of people who are beyond 65 years of age. Although I (Marianne) am 63 and Jerry is 67, neither of us view ourselves as "elderly," and we both thought age 75 would usher in the elderly years! I have made the following observations over the years as a result of my personal and professional contact with the elderly:

1. The attention span of some elderly people may be short because of physical or psychological difficulties. Consequently, the pace of the group needs to be slower.

2. The elderly often are taking medications that interfere with their ability to be fully present.

3. With some who are in advanced stages of senility, reality orientation becomes a problem. Sometimes they simply forget to come to sessions.

4. Regular attendance at group sessions can be problematic because of physical ailments, transportation difficulties, costs, interruptions in the schedules of institutions, and conflicting appointments with doctors, social workers, and other professionals.

5. Older people often need support and encouragement more than they need confrontation. Therefore, group work is oriented less toward radical personality reconstruction and more toward making life in the present more meaningful and enjoyable. However, never to challenge older people could be seen as patronizing and may be based on the distorted belief that they are psychologically fragile and cannot change.

6. The elderly have a great need to be listened to and understood. Respect is shown by accepting them through hearing their underlying messages and not treating them in a condescending way. The elderly often suffer from "conversation deprivation." To be encouraged to share and relate with others has therapeutic value in itself (Burnside, 1984).

7. Some older people are more difficult to reach. They may be distrustful and skeptical about the effectiveness of counseling, and it may take more time

to establish trust. It is very important to carefully consider the titles you use in describing your services for the elderly, because older people are more sensitive to feeling stigmatized when they seek out a mental health professional.

8. Themes more prevalent with the elderly than with other age groups include loss; loneliness and social isolation; poverty; feelings of rejection; the struggle to find meaning in life; dependency; feelings of uselessness, hopelessness, and despair; fears of death and dying; grief over others' deaths; sadness over physical and mental deterioration; and regrets over past events.

9. Older people become increasingly aware that they have a limited time left to live. They realize that the joys associated with old age, such as wisdom and integrity, are limited in a way unknown in earlier years (Henderson & Gladding, 2004).

10. Loss is probably the central theme of growing old. People in their 60s, 70s, 80s, and beyond are more likely to experience negative life events than are middle-aged adults. The elderly are challenged in dealing with a variety of cognitive and physiological changes—such as memory loss, sensory impairments, and decreased physical strength (Molinari et al., 2003). We live most of our adult years with an internal locus of control. As we age, we have to adjust to an increasingly external locus of control when confronted with losses over which we have little control.

11. Normal aging does not necessarily equate with illness and frailty. Chronic diseases and disabilities increase with age, but as Hazzard, Larson, and Perls (1998) point out, disease and disability can be deferred or mitigated with interventions such as proper nutrition and exercise. Nor is disability necessarily a one-way street for the elderly. Resnick (1998) points out the effectiveness of interventions to improve motivation in helping older adults recover from disabling events. This is not to deny frailty among the elderly population, but the quality of life of our elders can be improved by encouraging them to increase their functional abilities.

✳ Practical and Professional Considerations for Group Work With the Elderly

Guidelines for the Group Process

The issues addressed in Part 2 of this book pertaining to stages in the development of a group have some applicability to designing and conducting groups for the elderly. This section provides brief examples of practical issues for you to think about in forming specialized groups for older people.

The Group Proposal It is especially important to develop a sound proposal because you may encounter resistance from agencies dealing with the elderly. Refer to Chapter 4 for the elements that might be included in a proposal for groups for the elderly.

Screening and Selection Issues   The needs of the elderly are diverse. Carefully consider the purposes of the group in determining who will or will not benefit from the experience. The decision to include or exclude members must be made appropriately and sensitively. For example, to mix regressed patients (such as people with Alzheimer's disease) with relatively well-functioning older people is to invite fragmentation. There may be a rationale for excluding people who are highly agitated, are delusional, have severe physical problems that could inhibit their benefiting from the group, or display other behaviors that are likely to be counterproductive to the group as a whole.

Purpose of the Group   Elderly people generally need a clear, organized explanation of the specific purposes of a group and why they can benefit from it. It is important to present a positive approach to potential group members. The anxiety level may be high among an elderly group, which calls for a clear structure and repetition of the goals and procedures of the group.

Practical Issues   Practical considerations regarding the size, duration, setting, and techniques to be used depend on the level of functioning of a particular group. For example, more members could be included in a well-functioning group than in an organic brain syndrome group. The attention span of a group of outpatients would be longer than that of patients who are out of contact with reality. It is essential for you to have a good understanding of the members' mental and physical capabilities. In designing a group, avoid anything that could result in unnecessary frustration of the members.

Confidentiality   Institutional life is often not conducive to privacy. Elderly group members may be suspicious when they are asked to talk about themselves, and they may fear some sort of retaliation by the staff or fellow members. Exert care in defining the boundaries of confidentiality to ensure that confidences will not be broken and to provide a safe and nonthreatening environment.

Labeling and Prejudging Group Members   Institutions are quick to diagnose and categorize people, and they are slow to remove such labels when they no longer fit. In working with the elderly, be careful not to be rigidly influenced by what you hear or read about a given member. Remain open to forming your own impressions and be willing to challenge any limiting labels imposed on your elderly clients.

Visitors to Groups   As is often the case in institutions, visitors and other staff members may wish to attend a particular group session. A good practice with even severely regressed patients of any age (who may not be aware of another's presence) is to announce visitors in advance of their attending a session and again at the beginning of the session. In addition, the purpose of their visit can be mentioned to lessen suspicion.

Value Differences   A good understanding of the social and cultural background of your members will enable you to work with their concerns in a sensitive way. As was true in my case, you may be younger than the members, and this age difference may signal significant value differences. For example, a group leader in her early 20s might consider living together as an unmarried couple an acceptable norm, whereas a member in her mid-70s might suffer guilt and shame for doing so. This leader needs to take this member's anxiety seriously and not simply reassure her that she has no need to feel guilty. You are likely to assume that there is therapeutic value in discussing personal problems and conflicts openly. However, revealing personal matters may be extremely difficult for some elderly people because of their cultural conditioning. Respect members' decisions to proceed at their own pace in revealing themselves.

The Issue of Touching   Aging people often have a special need to be touched. Many older people live alone, and you and others in their group may be their only source of touching. Your own comfort level with touching will be a vital factor in determining how free members feel to exchange touches. It is also critical that you not misinterpret an older person's touching.

The need for touching among the elderly was vividly expressed during my visit to the respected home for the elderly in China. I observed an elderly woman lying on her bed, mumbling to herself, and looking extremely withdrawn. As I stood near her bed, I struggled with myself over the appropriateness of touching her, not knowing if it would be accepted in a different cultural setting. I gave in to my urge to hold the woman's hand, and she reciprocated immediately by pressing my hand and turning toward me. She slowly began to talk, and I asked our tour guide to translate. He introduced my daughters and me to her, and she showed great interest in where we were from and what we were doing. She kept repeating how lucky I was to have two daughters. She touched my daughters and me again and again. Within a short time this woman sat up on her bed and began laughing and talking. She had been an artist, and my daughters and I shared our interest in art with her. The young tour guide, who had never been in a home such as this, told me how surprised he was by her intellectual sharpness. When he initially saw her lying on her bed, he thought that she might be dying. The attending nurse mentioned that this woman had indeed been very withdrawn and depressed, and the nurse was surprised by the woman's excitement and interest in us. Within a span of 20 minutes she had become completely animated. This episode reminded me again of how much we can communicate with a touch or a smile.

My own intuitions about the therapeutic value of touch in working with elderly persons are supported by the literature. In their review of the literature on groups for older persons, Myers, Poidevant, and Dean (1991) encourage counselors to provide physical contact including hugging and touching, but only when this contact is deemed acceptable by older clients. In their discussion of group work with the very old, Hern and Weis (1991) found the use of touch to be one of the most effective forms of positive reinforcement. Even a pat on the hand or the joining of hands appeared to increase feelings of belonging. This being said, it needs to be added that cultural diversity must be respected. Muok and DuBray (1998) recommend caution with people from

Southeast Asian cultures, where elaborate rules apply to the use and interpretation of physical touch.

Difficult Group Members   You may encounter many types of difficult members in this age group. Some may refuse to speak or make any contact, some may never stop talking or interrupting, and some may be highly agitated and hostile. Learn to set firm limits, and deal with these members nondefensively. Members who display problematic behaviors are not to be labeled and categorized. The challenge is to understand the broader meaning of the behaviors that these members are manifesting in the group rather than simply labeling them "resisters."

Some Cautions   Here are some *do's* and *don'ts* in your practice of group work with the elderly:

- Do not treat people as if they are frail when they are not.
- Avoid keeping members busy with meaningless activities.
- Affirm the dignity, intelligence, and pride of elderly group members.
- Do not assume that every elderly person likes being called by his or her first name or "honey" or "sweetie."
- Make use of humor appropriately. Avoid laughing at your members for failing to accomplish tasks, but laugh with them when, for instance, they have created a funny poem.
- Avoid talking to them as if they were small children, no matter how severely impaired they may be.
- Allow your members to complain, even if there is nothing you can do about their complaints. Do not burden yourself with the feeling that you should do something about all of their grievances; sometimes venting can be sufficient.
- Avoid probing for the release of strong emotions that neither you nor they can handle effectively in the group sessions.
- Determine how much you can do without feeling depleted, and find avenues for staying vital and enthusiastic.

Attitudes, Knowledge, and Skills of Leaders

Just as specialized knowledge is required for therapists who work with children and adolescents, so too is specialized knowledge required to treat the unique problems that people face in the latter half of life (Molinari et al., 2003). The rapid population growth among the elderly has resulted in a greater demand for mental health practitioners able to provide adequate psychological services to this group. To meet the rapidly increasing need for mental health professionals who can effectively address the mental and behavioral needs of the elderly, two kinds of training need to be increased: (a) formal training in internships and (b) continuing education programs for experienced practitioners (Qualls, Segal, Norman, Niederehe, & Gallagher-Thompson, 2002).

It is critical to be aware of how your own feelings and attitudes may affect your work with the elderly. Your range of life experiences, as well as your basic personality characteristics, can either help or hinder you in your work. (This would be a good time to review the personal characteristics of effective group leaders discussed in Chapter 2.) I consider the following to be important assets for group work with the elderly:

- Genuine respect for older people
- Positive experiences with older people
- A deep sense of caring for the elderly
- Respect for the elderly person's cultural values
- An understanding of how the individual's cultural background continues to influence present attitudes and behaviors
- An ability and desire to learn from older people
- The conviction that the last years of life can be both challenging and rewarding
- Patience, especially with repetition of stories
- Knowledge of the special physiological, psychological, spiritual, and social needs of the aged
- Sensitivity to the burdens and anxieties of older people
- The ability to get older people to challenge many of the myths about old age
- A willingness to touch or be touched, if doing so is culturally appropriate
- A healthy attitude regarding one's own aging
- A background in the pathology of aging
- The ability to deal with extreme feelings of loss, depression, isolation, hopelessness, grief, hostility, and despair
- A working knowledge of the special skills needed for group work with the elderly
- Knowledge about AARP (American Association for Retired Persons)

Mental health practitioners need to know more about working with older adults because the number and proportion of elderly people in the United States is increasing, and clinicians are faced with the challenge of providing effective psychological services to this age group. Both individual and group therapy seem to be effective in treating the psychological problems of older adults. However, as with younger people, differences in culture, race, gender, sexual orientation, and social class need to be understood in making interventions with elderly people (APA Working Group on the Older Adult, 1998).

Preparing Yourself to Work With the Elderly

If you are interested in working with the elderly, you can gain valuable experience by becoming involved with older people and their families. It is important that you explore your feelings about responsibilities toward older family members, which can help you understand the struggles of the members of the groups you lead. Here are a number of other steps you can take to better prepare yourself to work with the elderly:

- Take courses dealing with the problems of the aged.
- Get involved in fieldwork and internship experiences working with the elderly.
- Visit agencies for the care of the elderly, both in your own country and on any trips you take abroad.
- Attend conventions on gerontology, a mushrooming field.
- Investigate institutes and special workshops that provide training in leading groups for the elderly.
- Explore your feelings toward your own aging and toward older people in your life.
- Visit some homes for the elderly that represent a particular cultural or religious group, which will give you some insight into how the elderly are perceived and treated by different groups.
- Create a list of what you would like to see for yourself when you are elderly. How would you like to be viewed? How would you like to be attended to? How do you hope you could perceive yourself? If you can identify a list of traits and qualities you hope you will have as an elderly person, you may get some idea of the needs of the elderly people in your groups.
- You can learn a lot by talking with elderly people about their experiences. Based on your discussions with them, create a needs assessment as a basis for a group that you may be interested in formulating.

One practical way to expand your knowledge base is to read the literature in group work with the elderly. A few useful resources that can help you increase your understanding of older people include the APA Working Group on the Older Adult (1998), Bengston and Schaie (1999), Birren and Schaie (1996), Henderson and Gladding (2004), and Molinari et al. (2003).

☀ Special Groups for the Elderly

Not all people can be placed in the same type of group, and this is true for the elderly as well. Leaders must take into account the special needs of potential group members. Some groups that are commonly offered include those with an emphasis on reminiscing, physical fitness, body awareness, grief work, occupational therapy, reality orientation, music and art therapy, combined dance and movement, preretirement and postretirement issues, remotivation, preplacement (preparing people to move from an institutional to a community setting), organic brain syndrome, education, poetry, health-related issues, family therapy, and assertion training. This is certainly not a complete list, and leaders can invent ways to bring their particular talents to a group setting to promote interaction among elderly members. One example in this chapter is a group composed of adolescents and the elderly. Leaders who have artistic hobbies can have members do something with their hands. In the process of creating products, the members often talk about themselves in spontaneous ways.

Reminiscence and Life Review Groups

Reminiscence therapy, which encourages members to recall and reexperience the past, is a useful kind of group for the elderly. In reminiscence groups the participants share memories, increase their personal integration, and gain insights into the lives of others and themselves (Henderson & Gladding, 2004). This therapy approach can help the elderly build bridges and bring vitality into their present existence. Reminiscence was once viewed as an unproductive escape into the past, but it is now considered to be a useful therapeutic strategy in promoting psychological integration for individuals in the later stages of life.

Most agencies that work with the elderly offer reminiscence and life review groups. According to Lewis and Butler (1984), the life review is seen as a universal psychological process associated with increased awareness of one's finiteness. The myth of immortality gives way to an acceptance of one's death. The life review involves a progressive return to consciousness of earlier experiences, a resurgence of unresolved past conflicts, and bringing up memories that have been deeply buried in the unconscious. Although some older people are aware of a need to put their entire life in a meaningful perspective, others avoid this type of review as a protection against painful memories.

Singer, Tracz, and Dworkin (1991) point out that a reminiscence group provides elderly participants with an opportunity to communicate with others who share similar concerns and experiences. Because depression over loss and change is such a central theme in the lives of elderly people, a group offers a safe place for them to express their feelings of loneliness and hopelessness. Clearly, reminiscence groups facilitate socialization, which is a crucial ingredient in overcoming isolation.

Creanza and McWhirter (1994) make use of life themes as a way to stimulate participants in recalling and reliving past experiences. They designed a pregroup screening and orientation method using life themes such as childhood memories, working life, psychological stress, and gender issues. They found that inviting seniors to reminisce about their past was an ideal way to structure the pregroup interview. Doing so gave members a comfortable way of getting to know one another, it provided common themes for exploration in future sessions, and it enhanced the attractiveness of the group.

According to Molinari (1994), a therapeutic life review group can be beneficial by assisting elderly clients in the process of putting life events into a new perspective. Molinari designed a six-session life review group structured this way:

Introduction. How can the use of reminiscence reveal who you are and how you feel about yourself?

Family history. Describe the family members who have influenced you the most.

Developmental stages. Make an outline of your life, dividing it into significant periods.

Life crises. Describe some of the major crises in your life, how they have affected you, and how you have coped with them.

Experiences with death. Share examples of personal encounters with death and your present concerns about dying.

Meaning of life. Discuss the evolution of your life goals from past to present. To what degree do your goals provide you with meaning in your life today?

Molinari contends that groups can help elderly clients integrate current life changes into an overall developmental perspective. In a group, elderly members are encouraged to reflect on who they are, where they have been, and to identify future goals. The group provides an ideal forum for socialization, allowing members to share their concerns over aging in a supportive context with their peers.

Groups for People With Aging Relatives

In addition to groups for the elderly, there is a pressing need for therapy groups for people who have aged relatives in an institution. Very often a family's feelings of guilt, anger, failure, and hopelessness will keep them away from a relative who is institutionalized, thus depriving him or her of the joy of visits. Or the family members may visit but transmit their negative feelings to the older person. In either case, everyone suffers from the loss of true contact. By enabling families to share their concerns with other families, groups can relieve much of the tension that normally results from the responsibility of caring for a loved one who is old. For example, in the group for institutionalized elders described next, my coleader and I held several sessions with one member and his entire family. The family members talked about the shame they felt over having one of their relatives committed to a mental institution, and the patient expressed the anger he felt over being ignored by his family. After expressing their feelings, the family members made the decision to visit the institutionalized member more often.

Group Proposal

A Program for Institutionalized Elderly People

This proposal is written from the perspective of Marianne Schneider Corey. ■

Many different types of groups are suitable for elderly people. The number and types of groups possible is limited only by the imagination of the counselor and the counselor's willingness to create groups to meet the special needs of elderly clients. The group described here is a preplacement group in a psychiatric hospital.

Organizing the Group

The preplacement group consisted of individuals in an institutional setting who were going to be released into community settings—either returning home or going to board-and-care residential facilities. As with other group populations, it is necessary to give careful consideration to the selection of members. A group is not likely to function well if severely disturbed and hallucinating members are mixed with clients who are psychologically intact. It is a good practice, however, to combine talkative and quiet people, depressed and ebullient types, excitable with calmer clients, suspicious with more trusting individuals, and people with different backgrounds. The size of the group is determined by the level of psychological and social functioning of the participants. A group of 10 relatively well-functioning people is much easier to manage than even a smaller number of regressed clients.

The preplacement group that my coleader and I formed consisted of three men and four women—a good balance of the sexes

and a workable number for two leaders. Before the first meeting I contacted the members individually and gave them a basic orientation to the group. I told them the purpose of the group, what the activities might be, and where, when, and for how long the group would meet. I let each person know that membership was voluntary. When people seemed hesitant to attend, I suggested that they come to the initial session and then decide whether they wanted to continue.

Group Goals and Group Format

Before the first session my coleader and I decided on a few general goals for the group. Our primary goal would be to provide an atmosphere in which common concerns could be freely discussed and in which members could interact with one another. We wanted to provide an opportunity for members to voice complaints and to be included in a decision-making process. We felt strongly that these people could make changes and that the group process could stimulate them to do so.

The group met once a week for an hour in the visitors' room. Before each group session I contacted all the members, reminded them that the group would meet shortly, invited them to attend, and accompanied them to the group room. I learned that it was difficult for them to remember the time of the meetings, so individual assistance would be important in ensuring regular attendance. Those who were absent were either ill or involved in an activity that could not be rescheduled, such as physical therapy. The group was an open one: Members would occasionally be discharged, and we encouraged newly admitted patients to join. This did not seem to bother the members, and it did not affect the cohesion of the group. As leaders, we also attempted to make entrance into the group as easy as possible.

We always allowed some time for the new members to be introduced and to say anything they wanted to about being new to the group, and we asked current group members to welcome them.

The Initial Stage

During the initial sessions, members showed a tendency to direct all of their statements to the two leaders. In the hope that we could break the shell that isolated each person in a private and detached world, my coleader and I immediately began to encourage the members to talk to one another, not to us. When members talked about a member, we asked them to speak directly to that member. When members discussed a particular problem or concern, we encouraged others to share similar difficulties.

In the beginning members resisted talking about themselves, voicing complaints, or discussing what they expected after their release from the institution. Their usual comment reflected their hopelessness: "What good will it do? No one will listen to us anyway." Our task was to teach them to listen to one another.

The Importance of Listening and Acting

My coleader and I felt that one way of teaching these people to listen would be by modeling—by demonstrating that we were really listening to them. Thus, when members spoke of problems related to life on the ward, my coleader and I became actively involved with them in solving some of these conflicts. For example, one member complained that one of the patients in his room shouted for much of the night. We were able to get the unhappy member placed in another room. When some members shared their fears about the board-and-care homes they were to be released to, we arranged to take them to several such homes so that they could make an informed choice of placement. One woman complained that her husband did not visit her enough and that, when he did take her home, he was uncaring and uninterested in her sexually. On several occasions my coleader and I held private sessions with the couple.

Some men complained that there was nothing to do, so we arranged for them to get involved in planting a garden. Another group member shared the fact that she was an artist, so we asked her to lead some people in the group and on the ward in art projects. She reacted enthusiastically and succeeded in involving several other members.

Our philosophy was to encourage the members to again become active, even in a small way, in making decisions about their lives. We learned *not* to do two things: (1) encourage a patient to participate in an activity that would be frustrating and thereby further erode an already poor self-image or (2) make promises we could not keep.

Listening to Reminiscences

In addition to dealing with the day-to-day problems of the members, we spent much time listening as they reminisced about sadness and guilt they had experienced, their many losses, the places they had lived and visited, the mistakes they had made, and so on. By remembering and actively reconstructing their past, older people can work to resolve the conflicts affecting them and decide how to use the time left to them. In addition, members enjoy remembering happy times when they were more productive and powerful than they are now. I believe this life review, which was discussed earlier in this chapter, is an important and healthy process and that older people need to experience it.

The Use of Exercises

My role as a leader of this group differed from the roles I had played in other types of groups. I found that I was more directive, that I was much less confrontive and much more supportive, and that I spent a lot of time teaching the members how to express themselves and listen to others. My coleader and I designed a variety of exercises to catalyze member interaction. We used these exercises as simple means of getting group interaction going. We always began by showing how an exercise could be done. Here are some exercises we used in this group:

✓ Go on an imaginary trip, and pick a couple of the other group members to accompany you. (Although you may have to deal with feelings of rejection expressed by those not chosen, this exercise is very helpful for people who are reluctant to reach out to one another and make friends.)

✓ If you could do anything you wanted, what would it be?

✓ Bring a picture of you and your family, and talk about your family.

✓ Describe some of the memories that are important to you.

✓ Tell what your favorite holiday is and what you enjoy doing on that day.

Another exercise that helps the elderly focus and contributes to member interaction is the sentence-completion method for low-level clients (Yalom, 1983). Incomplete sentences can be structured around a variety of themes. Here are a few examples:

✓ Self-disclosure (One thing about me that people would be surprised to know is . . .)

✓ Separation (The hardest separation that I have ever had is . . .)

✓ Anger (One thing that really irritates me is . . .)

✓ Isolation (The time in my life when I felt most alone was . . .)

✓ Ward events (The fight on the ward last night made me feel . . .)

✓ Empathy (I feel touched by others when . . .)

✓ Here-and-now interactions (The person whom I am most like in this room is . . .)

✓ Personal change (Something I want to change about myself is . . .)

✓ Stress (I experience tension when . . .)

Working with incomplete sentences can trigger intense emotions, and the group leader needs to be skilled in dealing with these feelings.

By encouraging the members to express themselves, these exercises led to their getting to know one another, which led in turn to a lessening of the "what's the use" feeling that was universal in the beginning.

Debunking Myths

My coleader and I explored some myths and attitudes that prevail regarding the aged to challenge the members' acceptance of these myths. Here are some of the beliefs we considered:

✓ Old people cannot change; it is a waste of time and effort to try to help them with counseling or therapy.

✓ All people who retire become depressed.

✓ It is disgraceful for an old person to remarry.

✓ Most old people are set in their ways and unable to change.

✓ It is almost impossible for old people to learn new things.

✓ Most old people are very much alike.

✓ Young people are never forgetful; old people always are.

✓ Forgetfulness is a sign of senility.

✓ Old people cannot contribute to society.

✓ Most young people want to neglect the elderly members of their family.

✓ Old people are always emotional and are financial burdens, whether their children take them into their home or not.

✓ People should retire at 65.

✓ Old people are not creative.

✓ An elderly person will die soon after his or her mate dies.

✓ Becoming old always means having a number of serious physical problems.

✓ Most elderly people are barely able to cope with the inevitable declines associated with aging.

✓ Old people do not understand the problems of younger people.

✓ Old people are no longer beautiful.

✓ Old people are dependent and need to be taken care of.

✓ Most old people are generally lonely.

✓ Old people are no longer interested in sex.

✓ Old people have little fear of dying.

✓ Most old people become senile and are not suitable candidates for psychotherapy.

✓ Treatment of emotional problems in the elderly is not effective.

Anyone working with elderly people needs to differentiate between myths and facts surrounding what it means to grow old. Many healthy older people have difficulty with being labeled and categorized because of the incongruity of how they view themselves and how society often views them (Henderson & Gladding, 2004). According to Molinari (1994),

both professionals and lay people alike harbor a host of misconceptions about the elderly. The facts are that the elderly can and do learn and change. Creative and informed professionals can do much to enhance the lives of their elderly clients, thereby helping to dispel the myths that have acted as a barrier to providing quality services for the elderly.

Termination

I was to be coleader of this group for only 3 months, and I prepared the members for my departure several weeks in advance. After I left, my coleader continued the group by himself. On occasion I visited the group, and I was remembered and felt very welcome.

Group Outcomes

To work successfully with the elderly, one must take into account the basic limitations in their resources for change yet not adopt a fatalistic attitude that will only reinforce their sense of hopelessness. Had my coleader and I expected to bring about dramatic personality changes, we would soon have been frustrated. The changes that occurred were small and came slowly. Instead, we expected to have only a modest impact, and so the subtle changes that took place were enough to give us the incentive and energy to continue. Here are some of the outcomes we observed:

✓ Members realized that they were not alone in experiencing problems.

✓ The participants learned from one another's feedback.

✓ People in the group felt an acceptance of their feelings and realized that they had a right to express them.

✓ Members said that they liked coming to the meetings, and they told this to patients who were not members.

✓ The group atmosphere became one of trust, caring, and friendliness.

✓ The members continued the socializing that had begun in the group outside group sessions.

✓ The members learned one another's names, which contributed to increased interaction on the ward.

✓ Participants engaged in activities that stimulated them rather than merely waiting for their release.

✓ The members began to talk more personally about their sorrows, losses, hopes, joys, memories, fears, regrets, and so on, saying that it felt good to be listened to and to talk.

✓ The enthusiasm of the members and the staff led to the formation of another group for ward members.

✓ The nurses reported seeing a change in the patients and expressed a desire to learn the skills needed to facilitate such groups.

✓ Staff members noticed positive changes, such as elevated spirits, in some of the members.

✓ Staff members became involved in thinking of appropriate activities for different members and helped the members carry them out.

My coleader and I also encountered some frustrating circumstances during the course of the group. For instance, the members occasionally seemed very lethargic. We later discovered that this occurred when the participants had received medication just before the group session. Still, it was difficult to discern whether a member's condition was due to the medication or to psychological factors. It was not uncommon to find a member functioning well one week and feeling good about herself and then to discover, the next week,

that she had had a psychotic episode and was unable to respond to anyone.

Some small changes that occurred in the group sessions were undone by the routine of ward life. Some of the members resisted making their life on the ward more pleasant for fear of giving the impression that their stay would be a long one. It was as though they were saying "If I communicate that I like it here, you might not let me go." Other members resigned themselves to institutional life and saw the ward as their home, expressing very directly that they did not want to leave.

Working with the elderly can be very rewarding, but it also can be draining and demanding. Sometimes I felt depressed, hopeless, and angry. These feelings were seldom directly connected with my activities with the patients; the smallest changes I observed in them were rewarding and gave me an incentive to go on. I felt annoyed when I saw student psychiatric technicians or other staff members show disrespect for the patients. These students often called an elderly person by his or her first name yet insisted that they themselves be addressed by their surname. Occasionally, an agitated patient would be restrained physically or with medication without ever being asked what had made him or her so upset in the first place. Another upsetting sight was a patient in a wheelchair being pushed around and not being told where he or she was going.

Sometimes patient behavior was treated as crazy when in reality there was a good reason for it that could have been discovered if anybody had tried. One day a student brought a blind person to the meeting, and the blind man proceeded to take off his shoes. The student shouted at him to put them back on. I approached Mr. W. and kneeled in front of him. "Mr. W., you are taking your shoes off in our group session," I said. "How come?" He apologized, saying he thought he was being taken to the physical therapy room.

In another case, a 75-year-old patient kept taking his shoes off all day long, always gathering up newspaper to put around his feet. Everyone considered this behavior bizarre. I remembered that during my childhood in Germany I was often told in the winter to put newspaper into my shoes to keep my feet warm. After spending some time with this man, I found that this "strange" behavior was based on the same experience. I learned to be careful not to judge a patient as bizarre or delusional too quickly but rather to take the time to find out whether there was a logical reason for a peculiar behavior.

Patients were sometimes discouraged or made to feel shameful when they physically expressed affection for another ward member. Sensuality was perceived by the staff as bad because of "what it could lead to." I had several very good discussions with staff members about our attitudes toward the sexuality of the aged. By dealing with our own attitudes, misperceptions, and fears, we were able to be more understanding and helpful to the patients.

✳ Guidelines for Working With Healthy Aging People in Groups

The preceding section focused on group programs for institutionalized elderly people, but it is a mistake to assume that groups have value only to the frail or ill elderly. Groups are a most effective approach in addressing developmental issues of aging and the challenges of finding meaning in later life. In working with the *well* elderly, the social support mechanisms of a group help members understand the universality of their struggles. Many elderly people who are not institutionalized have problems coping with the aging process. These people have to deal with the many losses associated with old age in addition to the pressures and conflicts that the younger generation experiences, and they can profit from personal-growth groups that serve people of all ages. Here are a few suggestions for helping healthy, well-functioning elderly people:

- Combine a group of people over 65 with a group of adolescents and have them explore their common struggles—their feelings of uselessness, difference, and isolation from the rest of society.

- Aging people can be employed or asked to volunteer as teacher aides in elementary and secondary schools.

- High school or college students learning to speak a foreign language can visit homes for the aged that include people who speak the language the student is learning. In addition to helping the student, this provides some badly needed stimulation for the elderly person.

- Groups can be formed to explore themes such as love, sex, marriage, meaning in life, death, failing health, and body images. Many of the myths surrounding these issues for elderly people can be examined in depth.

- Teachers can invite elderly people to be guest speakers in their classes and ask them to discuss historical events they experienced that are being studied by the students.

- People in senior citizen centers can be asked to teach young people arts and crafts and other skills.

A Successful Aging Group

For further information contact Jamie Blud-worth, M.Ed., by e-mail at Jamieblud@ hotmail.com. ■

Organizing the Group

During my time as an intern (and later as a staff member) at a large hospital, I facilitated many groups for older adults: arthritis support groups, Parkinson's support groups, dementia caregivers' support groups, bereavement groups, and a reminiscence group. These groups seemed to focus on what was "wrong" in members' lives. In addition, when group members were frustrated about setbacks in their lives, they often attributed their difficulties solely to the fact that they were aging, without considering other possible intervening factors.

It seemed to me that many of the elderly people with whom I worked had bought into various negative myths and stereotypes about what it means to get older and that these beliefs were preventing them from leading more satisfying and socially engaged lives. I also encountered group members who did not appear to believe the stereotypes and myths about growing older and who were active and thoroughly engaged in their commu-

nities. They were an inspiration to the groups in which they participated, and they were a touchstone for me in the creation of a group for older adults focused solely on debunking the commonly held myths about aging while encouraging healthy lifestyle changes. I developed a group around the concept of successful aging, which was offered at the local senior center. This group became very popular among the guests of the center and was effective in meeting many of its stated goals.

Basic Components of the Group

Type of Group   The Successful Aging Group was a psychoeducational group with a developmental focus on the issues that older adults must confront in the challenging task of maintaining physical and mental strength as they move further along the continuum of aging. The group was held at the local senior center. Publicity for the group was in the form of flyers posted on the premises as well as advertisements in the senior center newsletter.

Population   Although the group was designed primarily for older adults (ages 65 and up), persons of any age were encouraged to participate. Group members were especially encouraged to bring family members to the group, as the information provided could be of great benefit toward a deeper understanding of aging among and between family members.

Rationale   Traditionally, older adults have been portrayed in a stereotypical manner by the American media. Examples of the doddering old grandfather, or the memory lapsed, hearing impaired grandmother have been the butt of countless jokes in commercials and situational comedies. Conversely, there are rare examples of the 80-year-old woman who is preternaturally agile and able to hurdle park benches or chase down purse-snatchers with ease. These images are but a miniscule sample of the misconceptions and overly simplified views that many people hold about older adults.

Basic Assumptions   In my relatively brief experience working with older adults in groups at the local senior center, I found that a preponderance of them believed that it was inevitable that they would experience increasingly deteriorating health, both physical and mental. Worse, they also believed nothing could be done to counter their "inescapable fate." In short, it was clear to me that many of the older adults who attended groups at the senior center bought into the myths and stereotypes about aging, which likely contributed to them leading increasingly constricted and unsatisfying lives.

Although my personal experience with the elderly members of my groups was very informative, it was important for me to consult the research literature to gain a more thorough understanding of what might have been occurring. Moreover, having empirical support for the rationale of the proposed group served to lend credibility to my argument that a successful aging group would be beneficial for the clients served by the hospi-

tal. Rowe and Kahn (1998) found the following to be true for older adults:

✓ Age-related stereotypes exist, and older people as well as younger people are susceptible to them.

✓ Older adults who are exposed to negative, ageist stereotypes show significant declines in their task performance.

✓ Older adults who are exposed to positive messages about aging show improvements in task performance.

Resources and Methods   The primary resource for this group was *Successful Aging* (Rowe & Kahn, 1998). This book chronicles the MacArthur Foundation longitudinal study on aging begun in 1984, which consisted of several research projects in the domains of general medicine, psychology, neurobiology, sociology, and several other disciplines to create a "new gerontology." The MacArthur study represents the latest scientific knowledge in the realm of human aging. In the opening session I suggested that group members purchase a copy of *Successful Aging* to facilitate discussion and to encourage them to remain in the successful aging conversation outside of group. Supplemental literature, such as magazine, newspaper, and journal articles was also utilized.

Group Goals

I set out to design a group that not only challenged members' belief systems regarding aging but also presented them with alternative information that was accurate, based in science, and of a positive and encouraging nature. I hoped that educational intervention, presented in an interactional group format, would affect a shift in group members' schemas regarding aging. I believed that if a shift in this domain could occur, then group members would be more likely to make changes in their lifestyle choices that could not only "add years to their lives but also add life to their years." The goals of the group were as follows:

✓ To foster an increased awareness of the existence of stereotypes and myths regarding older adults among group members.

✓ For group members to gain an understanding of the ways in which belief in stereotypes or limiting thoughts have a discernable negative effect on their lives.

✓ To increase members' knowledge in the domains of physical, intellectual, and emotional health.

✓ For members to utilize knowledge acquired in the group to challenge and debunk the myths and stereotypes of aging.

✓ To create a social support network among members.

✓ For members to make informed lifestyle choices that would reduce the risks of age-related disease and disability while fostering greater engagement with life.

Group Format

The first half of each session was utilized primarily for a psychoeducational presentation. The second half was more interactional in nature with group members sharing their personal reactions and experiences regarding the session topic. Although this group was limited to 12 sessions, it was open for new members throughout its duration. At the end of 12 sessions there was a break of 2 weeks and then the sessions resumed, recycling back to session one.

Session 1: Introduction

✓ Introduce the goals and nature of the group. Obtain informed consent.

✓ Introduce the concept of myths and stereotypes about aging. This can be done by asking group members to respond to the question: "What comes to your mind in response to the following words: elderly, aged, or older adult." The responses can be written on the board.

✓ Choose a few of these salient, popular myths and refute them with evidence. Engage members in discussion about the beliefs and attitudes they hold about the elderly and about the attitudes they believe others hold about them.

Session 2: Usual Aging Versus Successful Aging

✓ "Usual aging" describes older adults who are relatively high functioning but are also at a significant risk for disease or disability. Provide details and examples such as "syndrome X."

✓ "Successful aging" describes older adults who have the ability to maintain the following key behaviors: (a) low risk of diseases and concomitant disabilities, (b) high levels of physical and mental functioning, and (c) active engagement with life or social vitality.

✓ Explore any myths or stereotypes about these topics.

Session 3: Environment Versus Genetics

✓ Present evidence that explains how lifestyle choices are the key to successful aging and how many chronic illnesses may be prevented or treated through lifestyle changes. Some examples are smoking cessation, diet, and exercise.

✓ This session provides a foundation for the basic premise of the group, which states that lifestyle choices have a greater effect on one's experience of aging than do genetics.

✓ It is important to explain that lifestyle change is not an easy process.

Session 4: Detection, Treatment, and Prevention of Disease

✓ Develop strategies for the early detection of disease and encourage a self-monitoring process.

✓ Make the distinction between diseases that are primarily due to lifestyle (for example, hypertension, diabetes, lung cancer, and heart disease) and other kinds of genetically linked diseases such as Parkinson's and rheumatoid arthritis.

✓ Provide evidence (both empirical and anecdotal) for the importance of early detection in most diseases.

✓ Discuss the commonly recommended strategies for the prevention of disease (diet, exercise, and social engagement).

Session 5: Exercise and Nutrition

✓ Present the latest findings on this topic and its relationship to healthy aging.

✓ Discuss community resources tailored to the nutritional and exercise regimens for the elderly such as walking clubs, aquatic programs, and strength and balance programs.

✓ Provide a guest speaker who has knowledge of and can demonstrate appropriate exercise regimens for the elderly.

✓ Make it clear that group members should consult their physicians before embarking on any lifestyle changes.

Session 6: Aging and Memory

✓ Present and discuss the latest information about the aging process and normal memory function.

✓ Provide detailed information about dementia and Alzheimer's disease with community resources such as the National Alzheimer's Association. Also provide information regarding the latest methods of treating dementia.

✓ Educate members about effects of the interactions of multiple medications and the implications for negative side effects in cognitive functioning.

✓ Present strategies for maintaining and enhancing memory and mental functioning such as mnemonics, appointment books, and calendars.

✓ It is important to normalize members' experience of minor memory loss (forgetting where their keys are, having brief difficulty remembering where the car is parked when shopping).

Session 7: Mental Health

✓ Present and discuss the topics of depression, anxiety, and possible mental health concerns with which group members might be faced.

✓ Many elderly people have negative attitudes about mental health issues and see depression or anxiety as a sign of weakness. It is important to provide education about such issues that presents a more balanced view.

✓ Discuss the environmental and developmental factors involved in mental health issues of the elderly (death of loved ones, coping with disease or disability, and interactions of multiple medications).

✓ Provide a comprehensive list of community resources and be prepared to make referrals for members when appropriate.

Session 8: Relationships

✓ Discuss the connection between social engagement and overall health in later life. Research findings suggest that social support is a key element in successful aging, which is often overlooked.

✓ Describe the various kinds of social support. It is especially important to mention the health monitoring function of a social support network, wherein friends encourage an individual to seek medical attention when that individual may not otherwise do so.

✓ Link this topic with any relationships that may be developing in the group.

Sessions 9–11: Consolidation of Learning and Preparation for Termination

Typically, consolidation occurs through a review of material presented in earlier sessions. For example, in session 9 we reviewed information presented in sessions 1–3; session 10 reviewed sessions 4–6; and in session 11 a review of sessions 7 and 8 was the focus.

It is important to note, however, that the review sessions should not simply consist of the facilitator reciting information in a lecture type format. One exercise I used to make the consolidation sessions more interactive was "Successful Aging Jeopardy." In this exercise, I generated questions of varying difficulty that corresponded to the topics to be reviewed. For example, in session 10 the categories were disease prevention, exercise and nutrition, and aging and memory. I then organized the questions within each category based on the difficulty of the question (difficult questions were worth more points, much like the television game show). The group was divided into two teams, with each team having an equal opportunity to answer a question.

At first, members appeared to be reluctant to play this game. Nevertheless, after encouragement from me, and a little bit of coaxing by some of the more outgoing group members, they reluctantly engaged in the exercise. It took only a few minutes before a friendly competition developed and the group as a whole became thoroughly enthusiastic. This exercise provided an opening wherein group members could review information while simultaneously engaging in spirited interaction regarding the session topics and associated myths about aging.

It is essential that the facilitator of this exercise provide clear ground rules as to how the game will be played. Most of the ground rules that I insisted upon were interpersonal in nature. For example, members were not allowed to criticize a person if he or she could not answer a question correctly. The "Successful Aging Jeopardy" sessions tended to be the most energy infused of all the meetings. Although the game can be fun for the group, it is vital that the facilitator maintains the topical focus and continues to intervene in ways that encourage the deepening of group members' knowledge and awareness.

The topic of termination was introduced in session 9 and briefly revisited in session 10 and 11 with statements like the following: "Our meetings will be coming to an end in three sessions. It is important for each of you to take a look at how you would best like to use the time that we have remaining."

Session 12: Termination

Session 12 was devoted solely to termination. In this session, each member was encouraged to share what he or she experienced over the course of the 12 weeks spent together. Additionally, members were encouraged to discuss any changes they had made in their lifestyles and to brainstorm with each other about ways in which they might maintain such changes. Because of the epidemic proportions of isolation among the elderly, I placed great emphasis on fostering social interaction and support outside of the group, prevailing upon members to continue their interpersonal connections after termination.

Special Considerations

Group facilitators must be vigilant not to practice outside their area of expertise. Group members will often ask for medical advice. *Always* refer them to their physician for such advice. Beyond that, each group should end with a disclaimer that says something to this effect: This group is designed to provide the latest information about aging. The group is not intended to provide medical or other professional advice. Always consult your physician or other medical professional before making any changes in your health-related behaviors.

The age of the facilitator can also be a factor in the development of trust and credibility with older adult group members. The difference in ages between the group members and myself was quite obvious. By addressing this issue in the first session in a nondefensive manner, group members were able to trust me, and my credibility with them increased. I told them that I had no idea what it's like to be 70 and that I hoped that we could learn from each other. It was also important for me to mention my qualifications to facilitate such a group. Moreover, I explained my interest in working with older adults in an open and honest manner, mentioning the importance of my grandparents in my life and my struggle to understand and cope with the declining health of my beloved grandmother. Group members seemed to accept my role as facilitator of the group even though I was less than half their ages in many cases. I believe my genuine respect for them and honesty and openness about my motivation to lead the group created the space for this to occur.

Many group members had significant physical limitations, and it was vitally important to accommodate these limitations. For example, members who had hearing loss were seated closer to me so that they could hear what was being said. Other group members were encouraged to speak loudly so that everyone could hear. Space was made to accommodate people in wheelchairs. When I wrote on the board, I used large letters to assist those members who had visual difficulties. It was essential to be flexible in facilitating the safety and comfort of members with special needs.

Group Outcomes

Several members of this group made significant lifestyle changes. One woman in her late 70s took up swimming again. She had been a competitive swimmer for many years but had stopped when she "got old." After several weeks of swimming at the YWCA she was invited to compete on a masters swim team. When she told the group, she was clearly very proud, and it appeared that she had a newfound confidence. Later, several of the group members went to cheer her on in her first competition in more than 40 years!

In similar fashion, a 92-year-old man had always wanted to write a book. Somehow he had never done it. Through the distinctions he gained in the group (and some good old cajoling by group members) he started writing his memoirs. He often gave the group updates about how many pages he had written. Toward the end of the group he read a passage aloud and was very moved by the experience, as was the rest of the group.

One woman in her 70s started a monthly outing group, organizing trips to museums, a flea market, a wine tasting, or other such events. The group chartered a small bus and took photographs of their adventures that they would later share with the rest of the group. This motivated other group members to join them. Many people in the monthly outing group reported that it had been years since they had been out with a group of people and that they felt more vital and alive from doing something that they simply had "let slip."

Many members of the group made new social connections in which they were able to provide support for each other outside of the group. In one instance, members of the group noticed something different about another member and encouraged her to see a doctor. This led to an early detection of a potentially life-threatening disease that was treated before it became unmanageable.

Finally, the elderly group members were not the only beneficiaries of the successful aging group. I was deeply moved and inspired by many of the members. I saw firsthand the resiliency and dignity of older women and men who often were overlooked by society and their families alike. I learned that a sense of humor goes a long way when things get tough. Most of all, I learned the value of true mutual respect. Some of the members of those first successful aging groups have since died. Although I have been saddened by their deaths, I have also taken great solace from knowing that they were known and cared for by the members of their group and that in some cases they had taken the opportunity to reclaim something that they had lost.

In designing this group, I found the following references to be helpful: Erber, Szuchman, and Rothberg (1990, 1991); Levy (1996); and Rowe and Kahn (1998).

Group Proposal

A Combined Group for the Elderly and Adolescents

For more detailed information about the group discussed here, contact Michael Nakkula, Ed.D., Harvard University, Graduate School of Education, 505 Larsen Hall, Appian Way, Cambridge, Massachusetts 02138; telephone (617) 496-2607; e-mail Michael_Nakkula @Harvard.edu. ■

Organizing the Group

I (Michael Nakkula) conducted an innovative group combining older people with adolescents. This group, originally designed as a master's thesis project, was aimed at assessing members' changes in attitude as a result of their experiences in eight group sessions (see Nakkula, 1984).

Basic Assumptions

This study was based on a review of the literature, my personal observations on the developmental tasks of the young and the old, and my experience as a group leader for the elderly and for adolescents separately. Here are some of the key assumptions in designing this group:

✓ Part of maintaining health in the elderly is staying in contact with all age groups. The old need to have an opportunity to pass on their wisdom to the younger generation.

✓ The young need exposure to the elderly to gain wisdom.

✓ The elderly can become a "living history book" to young people.

✓ There is a need to bring these two age groups together to exchange elderly wisdom and youthful vitality.

✓ Older people benefit from the knowledge that their investment in society can live on beyond their own lives.

✓ Adolescents need role models for their developing value systems.

✓ The benefit of interaction between the young and the old is based not only on what they can learn from their differences but also on what they can learn from their similarities.

✓ Contact between the two age groups can lead to less fear and more realistic attitudes about the aging process among adolescents.

✓ The two age groups display a striking resemblance in their struggle to understand the purpose of their lives.

✓ Both groups suffer from apparent alienation within our social structure.

✓ The elderly are stifled in their attempt to realize their full potential; adolescents are stifled by their limited power and control and lack experience in using the power they do have.

Based on these assumptions, I hypothesized that combining the two age groups would result in positive changes in attitude toward members of the other age group due to increased knowledge and understanding. I also hypothesized that the group experience would lead to an increase of self-esteem in the elderly.

Implications and Commentary

Through my work in Harvard University's Risk and Prevention Program, I thought of the elderly–adolescent group in terms of risk and protective factors. *Risk factors* increase the likelihood of negative life outcomes. *Protective factors* bolster the individual in the face of life's difficulties. Surviving or thriving through difficult experiences builds strength or resiliency, which in turn serves as one of life's essential protective factors. The elderly–adolescent group can serve as a protective factor for both the old and the young.

For the elderly, the groups can serve as protection against depression, which often stems from loneliness, isolation, and feelings of worthlessness. Many elderly people experience multiple losses over short periods of time, including the loss of a spouse, of friends, of their health, and, in the case of those living in senior citizens' centers, of their homes. This array of losses places the elderly at high risk for depression and apathy, which depletes them of the energy required to remain physically and emotionally healthy. Involvement in a discussion group or related activity with children or early adolescents gives the elderly something to look forward to, and it gives them an important role in a society where many young people are in desperate need of guidance and mentoring. This role is a vital protective factor against the risks of loss and isolation.

For the adolescents, the groups can help to build character, a primary form of resiliency. The opportunity to make a meaningful contribution to the well-being of another person is missing for many youth. When the adolescents begin to feel their value in the lives of their new elderly friends, it can fill them with a sense of pride and importance. For some, this experience is an initiation into the world of community involvement and human responsibility. Such an experience serves as protection against feelings of alienation, which are common when the adolescent search for meaning in life goes unfulfilled.

Group Format

Participants were divided into two groups, each consisting of five junior high school students, aged 12 and 13, and five elderly people who lived in a nursing home. The groups met for eight sessions.

Session 1

The purpose of the group was explained. The members were asked to interview one another and later to introduce one another to the rest of the group.

Session 2

The objective was to help members look at their similarities and differences. Classical music was played, and members were asked to think about the most critical task in their life. The differences and similarities of these tasks were then discussed in the group.

Session 3

The goal was to discuss what factors would lead to personal strength and, in turn, to personal happiness. Members were asked to think about their assets and how they thought their strengths contributed to their happiness. Then they were asked to choose a strength from the other age group that they would like to possess.

Session 4

The purpose was to assist the elderly in putting their life experiences in perspective and to teach adolescents that life is an ongoing process that demands work. Members brought to the session photographs of themselves at different points in their lives. They talked about their favorite picture, explaining why it was associated with special meaning.

Session 5

The aim was to examine how the young and the old were represented in the media. Members shared and discussed news articles, identifying adjectives used by the media in describing the young and the old.

Session 6

The purpose was to examine the messages found in music and to compare yesterday's with today's music, as well as to look for common themes. After listening to selected pieces of music, members discussed the feelings that were aroused and the people and situations they associated with each piece. They also talked about what was happening in the world at the time these songs were written. All the members sang a song known to everyone.

Session 7

The elderly were given an opportunity to share the significance of their heritage with the young, and the young had an opportunity to realize the importance of the elderly in connecting them with their roots. The members discussed their ethnic backgrounds. Adolescents discussed what they knew about their heritage. The elderly talked about how their families had come to the United States and what it had been like for them, their parents, and their grandparents from the beginning.

Session 8

The purpose was to say good-bye and to leave one another having earned mutual respect. The members divided into pairs and talked about what they had learned from and enjoyed about each other. They also identified at least one misconception they had had about the other age group and how it had been clarified. They exchanged names and addresses so that they might stay in touch.

Group Outcomes

This study used a pretest and posttest design with treatment and comparison groups to assess adolescent attitudes toward the elderly and to assess the degree to which the elderly felt useful in society. The young people who participated in the discussion group changed many of their attitudes or biases toward the elderly from pretest to posttest, whereas those in the nonparticipant comparison group did not. Changes included an increase in the perception of elderly people as wise and a decrease in the perception of them as senile; an increase in the perception of them as interesting and a decrease in the perception of them as boring; and an increase in the belief that the elderly are an attribute rather than a burden to society. The elderly who participated in the study showed a general increase in self-esteem, whereas those in the comparison group did not. Connected with the change in self-esteem was the chance to socialize with curious and enthusiastic youngsters who seemed to genuinely enjoy listening to their reminiscing about these experiences.

Groups combining old and young people provide an economical response to the mental health needs of the increasing elderly population while also creating a vehicle through which young people can contribute something valuable to the community. They target precisely what lies at the core of distress and despair for many old and young people alike: loneliness.

An example of having older people live with younger people is Advent Christian Village, a retirement, nursing, and child care community in Dowling Park, Florida. The elderly attended to the needs of the younger residents and in many cases became substitute parents. The younger residents were able to offer meaningful companionship to the elderly residents. It is remarkable that the village, which was founded in 1913 as a home for orphans and retired preachers, has managed to keep pace with the ever-changing concerns of contemporary society. It provides professional care for neglected youths, a serene and secure environment for active retirees, and competent care for impaired and frail elderly residents.

There are many possibilities for designing programs that combine the elderly and the young. It is up to the creativity of the group practitioner to come up with variations. For more information on day care centers in which the aged are involved, write to the National Council on the Aging, Department Y, 600 Maryland Avenue, SW, Washington, DC 20024.

✳ The Therapeutic Value of Grief Work

Grief is a necessary and natural process after a significant loss. However, many forces in our society make it difficult for people to completely experience grief. Social norms demand a "quick cure," and other people often cannot understand why it is taking "such a long time" for a grieving person to "get back to normal." As is the case with any emotion that is not expressed, unresolved grief lingers in the background and prevents people from letting go of losses and forming new relationships.

Hospice centers help the terminally ill deal with their impending death and also help survivors who have lost a loved one feel their full range of emotions during bereavement. Hospices typically offer closed groups, time-limited groups, and short-term groups with changing membership. Many survivors need the reassurance that they are not "going crazy."

Kübler-Ross (1969) made a significant contribution in describing the stages a dying person tends to go through, from denial to acceptance. But, as she emphasized, all people who are dying do not conform to sequential stages in a neat and tidy way. Likewise, people who are working through a loss also grieve in their own way, and they do not necessarily proceed from denial to acceptance of their losses. Some are never able to accept the death of a child or a spouse. They may get stuck by denying their feelings and by not facing and working through the pain over the loss. Those therapists who work with grieving clients know full well the therapeutic value of fully experiencing the pain. At some point in the grief process, people may feel numb, as if they were functioning on automatic pilot. Once this numbness wears off, the pain seems to intensify. People who are going through this pain need to understand that they may well get worse before they feel better. To put to rest unresolved issues and unexpressed feelings, people need to express their anger, regrets, guilt, and frustrations. When they attempt to deny their pain, they inevitably wind up being stuck, for this unexpressed pain tends to eat away at them both physically and psychologically.

Unresolved grief accounts for many of the referrals for counseling and psychotherapy. This grief may be over many types of losses besides a death, such as the breakup of a relationship, the loss of one's career, or children leaving home. Groups can be instrumental in helping people feel less isolated as they move at their own pace in their own way in working through their pain and grief. The group process can be used to therapeutic advantage by individuals who are struggling to adjust to many of the changes that confront them because of their loss. Although addressing issues such as loss and pain in grief groups is important, MacNair-Semands (2004) points out that this is not sufficient without also addressing growth and new relationships. She states: "Rather than overemphasizing the components of loss and pain, a group focus on new social and intimate relationships can help grief group members expand personal identity, address existential issues about death, and discover new personal resources and strengths" (p. 528).

Bereavement is a particularly critical developmental task for older people, not only because of the loss of others who are close to them but also because of the loss of some of their capacities. Although death strikes at children as well as the elderly, facing one's own death and the death of significant others takes on special significance with aging. If people who are experiencing bereavement are able to express the full range of their thoughts and feelings, they stand a better chance of adjusting to a new environment. Indeed, part of the grief process involves making basic life changes and experiencing new growth. If people have gone through the necessary cycle of bereavement, they are better equipped to take on a new purpose and a new reason for living. Group counseling can be especially helpful to people at this time. For a group proposal on "Grieving Our Losses," see Bethune (2003), and for an expanded discussion on grief and loss, see Freeman (2005).

Group Proposal

An Elderly Bereavement Group

This group was designed and conducted by Alan Forrest, a professor of counseling at Radford University. For further information contact Alan Forrest, Ed.D., Department of Counselor Education, P.O. Box 6994, Radford University, Radford, VA 24142; telephone (540) 831-5214; e-mail aforrest @radford.edu. ∎

Introduction

Before I (Alan Forrest) began facilitating loss and bereavement groups I was filled with enthusiasm, excitement, and altruism, tempered somewhat by numerous fears, anxieties, and insecurities. What could I give to those who were experiencing intense emotional pain and psychic distress? Would I have the "right" answers? Would I be good enough? How could I provide relief from the suffering of a spouse who lost her husband of 50 years?

I discovered that I did not need to have all the answers and that if I trusted the group process I would never be disappointed. At times no words can express the intensity of feelings in the group; that is how I learned the value of therapeutic silence and how one's presence can be healing. To hear and truly feel another person's pain is not without effort, and knowing you cannot take away that pain can be frustrating and depressing. The first group session is usually the most difficult because each group member relates the circumstance of his or her loss. The hurt, suffering, and pain can be overwhelming, but there is also comfort in knowing that one does not have to be alone.

Organizing the Group

One of the primary goals of a bereavement group is to educate the mourner to the reality that grief is a process that is measured in years, not months. It does not proceed the same for everyone; as one widow stated, "You never really get over the loss, but the challenge is learning how to live with it." The following guidelines are suggested for beginning a group and making it work effectively.

Be clear about the purpose and structure of the group. A bereavement group for the elderly should have a psychoeducational focus, including elements of education, emotional support, and encouragement for social interaction. The group can serve as a catalyst for meeting the members' emotional needs, for dispelling myths and misconceptions of loss responses, and for enhancing the ability to develop new relationships outside the group. This has the tendency to assist the grief process and nurture self-esteem. To achieve a high level of group cohesion and trust, I have designed a closed, time-limited group. The group meets for 8 to 10 sessions, each lasting for 2 hours, and is limited to no more than eight members.

Screening

The screening and selection process is an essential variable contributing to the success of the group. It is essential to have a clear sense of who will likely benefit from a group in making the determination of whom to include. One consideration is recency of the loss. I did not include people whose loss had occurred less than 12 weeks ago. This early into their bereavement, most people are not ready for a group experience. It is essential to rule out candidates who exhibit serious pathology as they are likely to impede the group process and take precious time from the other group members.

Counselor Self-Awareness

To function successfully as a grief counselor requires an awareness of self and one's own experiences of loss. The issues that encompass grief and loss are very emotional and touch our deepest fears as human beings. As a counselor, one has a desire to be helpful to other people, yet the anguish and pain the counselor witnesses cannot be removed from the grieving individual. This may result in discomfort and frustration on the part of the counselor. If the counselor is not aware of personal loss issues, the grief work with clients experiencing loss will be seriously affected and compromised.

The experience of bereavement necessitates that the counselor examine, at least minimally, three personal areas. First, working with the bereaved increases one's awareness of one's own losses. Examining personal issues (past and present) surrounding loss and bereavement is a difficult task, filled with profound sentiments. What is important is not that counselors have completely resolved all the loss issues they have experienced but rather that they be aware and actively involved in working on them. If a client is experiencing a loss similar to that of a recent loss in the life of the counselor, it may be difficult to therapeutically help the client.

Second, grief may interfere in working with clients with regard to a counselor's own feared losses. Although all counselors have experienced losses in the past, there may be apprehension over future losses. Counselors may encounter personal anxiety when thoughts of losing their own children, partners, or parents enter into their work with clients. This is usually not problematic unless the loss a client presents is similar to the one we fear most. For example, if the counselor has an elderly parent, he or she may have difficulty facilitating an elderly bereavement group.

A third area involves the counselor's existential anxiety and personal death awareness. Death is a part of the cycle of life, and working with bereaved individuals is a constant reminder of the inevitability of one's own life and the lives of those we care for deeply. Most of us think about our own mortality and, in varying degrees, experience anxiety about it. However, it is possible to acknowledge this reality and not allow it to impede our work with clients. How we choose to respond to the losses in our own lives will determine how effective we are in providing comfort and growth experiences in the lives of others.

Leadership Issues

Leadership style and the activity level of the leader are important considerations for a bereavement group. A high degree of leader involvement is effective during the early stages of group. But as the group evolves into a cohesive unit, I tend to become less active. I recommend a coleader format. One coleader can concentrate on helping an individual express and work through a painful experience while the other coleader pays attention to members reacting to this pain.

Disruptive behaviors can impede the group process. It is important to address disruptive behavior as soon as it occurs. For example, it is not unusual for a group member to express the attitude that "my loss is greater than your loss." I handled this by saying, "We are not here to compare losses. Everyone's loss is unique. We are here because of losing someone, and everyone's loss is important in this group." Other disruptive behaviors to be aware of include the person who habitually gives advice but rarely engages in personal sharing; the person who gives moralistic advice and uses "shoulds," "musts," and "have tos"; the member who usually observes but seldom participates in personal sharing; the person who makes irrelevant comments; and the person who continually interrupts other group members when they are working on their loss issues.

Group Format

Norms and Expectations

During the initial session of the group, I discuss group norms and expectations, including beginning and ending on time and socializing outside of the group. I also address members' questions about how the group functions. Ending sessions on time can be difficult, because it is hard to accurately gauge the length of time it takes for the expression of the intense emotions that are elicited.

Socializing outside of group is generally discouraged because subgroups may form, which can have a negative effect on the cohesion and process of the group. However, I do not adhere to this norm when leading bereavement groups for the elderly. There are advantages to outside contact among members, such as helping them deal with the loneliness and social isolation that are a part of the bereavement experience.

Participant Introductions

At the first group meeting I ask participants to introduce themselves and share something personal about themselves. I monitor these disclosures so that each member has approximately equal time to share. The introductions provide each member with the opportunity to be the focal point of the group and also facilitate the universality of the feelings and expression of grief. Introductions are generally limited to name, circumstances of the loss, fears and anxieties participants have, and anything else they want others to know about them. One useful technique is to have group members share what they were thinking and feeling while they were on their way to this first meeting. The commonalities are noted, which begins a linking process. Due to the excessive anxiety many individuals experience, it is sometimes necessary to do this exercise in dyads prior to introductions to the entire group.

Sharing Personal Loss and Bereavement Experiences

At some point in the first group session each participant is given the opportunity to discuss in detail his or her loss and bereavement experiences up to this point in life. Introductions allow for some of this to occur, and as group members become more comfortable with one another, they are more receptive to discussing their losses in greater detail and in more personal ways.

Learning About the Grief Process

Perhaps the single most important gift counselors can give to bereaved individuals is an accurate understanding of the grief process so individuals no longer believe their grieving is abnormal or that they are "going crazy." Areas typically discussed are descriptions of the grief process, possible reactions such as physical symptoms, suicidal ideation, increased dependence on medication, depression, typical behaviors, and the reactions of others to one's loss.

Topical Issues

Topics generally addressed in the group include guilt, loneliness, a changing identity, fear of letting go of the deceased, changed social and interpersonal roles, important dates issues, rituals, the influence of family members on the grieving process, nutrition and physical exercise, and termination of the group itself, which is another loss that participants will need to address. Although the group facilitator may bring any of these themes up for discussion, it is also important to be open to topics group members want to explore.

Photographs and Memories

In an effort to make the deceased real and concrete to the other group members, I encourage members to bring in and share photographs.

Additionally, each group member is given the opportunity to tell the group about that person. This exercise assists group members to feel a deeper sense of each other's loss and gives each mourner the chance to share a memory, thereby reaffirming his or her relationship with the deceased. Each photograph is passed around, and group participants can be encouraged to ask questions or share their observations of the person in the photograph.

Addressing Secondary Losses

Secondary losses are frequently ignored in the bereavement process despite the fact that they can be as powerful as the loss itself. A secondary loss—a loss that occurs as a consequence of a death—may take many forms and can affect a group in dramatic fashion. For example, one widow, whose husband had died very suddenly and unexpectedly shortly after taking early retirement, was struggling not only with him physically being gone but also with the loss of all the hopes, plans, and dreams they had shared. It was difficult for her to discuss moving on with her life because her future plans were so intertwined with those of her husband. It was not until she examined her secondary losses that she could open up, engage in the group, and re-

ceive group support. Clients need to identify and anticipate secondary losses so they can be prepared for and grieved.

Emotional Intensity

A bereavement group contains a high level of emotional intensity, but many clients are unable or ill prepared to deal with the breadth and depth of emotions they will encounter in themselves or in others. A degree of vulnerability accompanies the expression of emotions, and many participants may not be ready for it. Others may perceive this vulnerability as a sign of weakness. Therefore, these concerns must be addressed repeatedly throughout the group experience. Some group members will weep from the start to the end of each group session, which clearly communicates how difficult the group is for them. This emotion is acknowledged, but it may not be immediately addressed. Members may require time to process their emotions before feeling comfortable in verbally expressing them. These individuals receive support from the group by others respecting their need, for a period of time, to maintain some emotional distance.

Confidence and Skill Building

Many of the bereaved elderly, particularly widows, had been very dependent on their spouses. It is possible that some of this dependency may be transferred to their adult children. Although these individuals are grieving and are in emotional pain, they have the capacity to develop new skills. Doing so can bring increased confidence and self-esteem. One group participant whose husband died shared, with much embarrassment, that she was having difficulty balancing her checkbook because her husband had always attended to family financial matters. When others in the group shared similar situations of being dependent on their spouses, she was encouraged and went to her bank to learn how to balance the checkbook. This particular woman gained so much confidence in herself that by the final group session she shared that she had bought a new car, something that her husband had always done for her. It is important to remember that confidence and self-esteem are just as essential for the elderly as for anyone else.

Multiple Losses

When a group member appears to be stuck and not moving through the grieving process, it can be an indication that the current loss has stimulated previously unresolved loss issues. With age comes an increased number of losses: friends, family, and other losses such as retirement, declining health, home, and for some, mental and cognitive functioning. All of these life transitions, in addition to losses through death, need to be grieved and are areas to be addressed. In the context of the group, the universality gained from discussing these issues is invaluable.

The Use of Touch

Many of the elderly, particularly those who have lost a spouse, have a strong need to be touched. Without a spouse, it is difficult to get this need met. If a counselor is comfortable with the use of therapeutic touching, it is a way to meet the need of being touched on the part of the client and also a way for the counselor, or other group member, to physically make contact with another. It is paramount that the counselor be clear as to the appropriateness of the touching and whether or not the client is willing to be touched. A word of caution in using touch with a grieving individual: The touch may be countertherapeutic if it is used to communicate or is interpreted as "Don't cry, everything's going to be all right." Crying is part of the healing process, so group facilitators need to carefully attend to the participants and take their lead from them.

Termination

I have had some group members who terminated prematurely and suddenly after two or three sessions. Follow-up interviews indicated a number of reasons for leaving, some of which include members' perceptions that the group is too emotionally threatening, too intimate, too sad, or that they "should" be able to cope with their loss on their own. It is important to be cognizant of generational, cultural, and gender differences when working with an elderly population. Separately, or together, each will have an effect on whether or not one chooses to remain in the group.

What are some lessons that can be learned from the termination of the group as a whole? Termination of the bereavement group provides participants with another opportunity to learn how to deal with loss in a healthy manner. Members are encouraged to address any unfinished business toward the deceased or toward other group members or the facilitators. The members can anticipate how it will be to no longer have a group, explore what the group experience has meant to them, and examine their plans for continued support.

Rituals can be used effectively throughout the group experience and can be powerful tools to increase self-awareness, especially during the termination process. One technique that has proven to be a powerful group ending experience is to have each participant light a candle that represents the deceased. Participants share with the group any thoughts about what they learned or about their deceased or what the group has meant to them. This exercise engages the group in a final shared experience, provides an ending ritual, uses light as a metaphor for insight and illumination, and leaves each participant with something concrete (the candle) to take home. Group members have found this to be a highly emotional and healing experience.

Group Outcomes

How effective are elderly bereavement groups? Although no empirical outcome studies have been done on the elderly bereavement groups I have facilitated, there is some interesting anecdotal information that supports the value of these groups.

A primary goal of an elderly bereavement group is to reduce the isolation and loneliness that may be the result of a loss, particularly when someone has lost their spouse of many years. At the conclusion of one of the groups, all the participants exchanged phone numbers and would periodically meet informally for emotional and social support. Another group contracted with me to meet once a month, for 3 months, in what we referred to as an "aftercare group" following formal termination of the group. In each of these groups all members had been strangers at the beginning of the group.

What have I learned from facilitating these groups? I have shared tears, and I have shared laughter working with bereaved elderly groups. It may seem paradoxical, but I have learned more about the process of living than about dying and grieving from facilitating these groups. Facilitating an elderly bereavement group is life affirming and personally enriching. I have learned to celebrate each day as a precious gift and to deeply value my personal relationships. Wisdom, courage, and strength of character cannot be taught in graduate school, but I have profited from some wise, courageous, and strong individuals—my clients.

If you would like to learn more about designing and conducting bereavement groups with the elderly, I recommend Brok (1997); Capuzzi (2003); Fitzgerald (1994); Folken (1991); James and Friedman (1998); Lund, Diamond, and Juretich (1985); MacLennan (1988); Tedeschi and Calhoun (1993); Worden (2002); Yalom and Vinogradov (1988); and Zimpfer (1991).

✓ *Points to Remember*

Groups for the Elderly

✓ Group workers will increasingly be challenged to develop programs to help the elderly find meaning in their lives and be productive after retirement.

✓ Group counselors often encounter obstacles in their attempts to organize and conduct groups for the elderly. Some of the barriers are due to the unique characteristics of this population, yet other obstacles are found within the system that does not support group work for the elderly.

✓ Groups offer unique advantages for the elderly who have a great need to be listened to and understood. The group process encourages sharing and relating, which has a therapeutic value for the elderly person. The group provides an ideal forum for socialization that enables members to share their concerns over aging in a supportive context with their peers.

✓ Groups can help elderly people integrate current life changes into an overall developmental perspective. In such a group the members can be encouraged to reflect on who they are, where they have been, and to identify future goals.

✓ Some themes are more prevalent with the elderly than with other age groups, including loss; loneliness and social isolation; poverty; feelings of rejection; the struggle to find meaning in life; dependency; feelings of uselessness, hopelessness, and despair; fears of death and dying; grief over others' deaths; sadness over physical and mental deterioration; and regrets over past events.

✓ Loss is probably the central theme of growing old. Anxiety, low self-esteem, and somatic complaints are typical responses to the losses faced by elderly persons. Group interaction can focus on how older group members can realistically deal with loss.

✓ In designing a group for the elderly, leaders must take into account the special needs of potential group members. Some groups commonly offered include those with an emphasis on reminiscing, physical fitness, body awareness, grief work, occupational therapy, reality orientation, music and art therapy, combined dance and movement, preretirement and postretirement issues, remotivation, organic brain syndrome,

education, poetry, health-related issues, family therapy, and assertion training.

✓ Elderly people generally need a clear, organized explanation of the specific purposes of a group and why they can benefit from it. It is important to present a positive approach to the members.

✓ Elderly group members in an institution may be suspicious when they are asked to talk about themselves and fear some sort of retaliation by the staff or fellow members. It is crucial to define the boundaries of confidentiality to ensure that confidences will not be broken and to provide a safe and supportive environment.

✓ Revealing personal matters may be extremely difficult for some elderly people because of their cultural conditioning. Respect members' decisions to proceed at their own pace in revealing themselves.

✓ A good understanding of the social, cultural, and spiritual backgrounds of your members will enable you to work with their concerns in a sensitive way.

✓ In working with the elderly, be careful to avoid being influenced by what you hear or read about a given group member. Remain open to forming your own impressions and be willing to challenge any limiting labels imposed on your elderly clients.

Exercises

In-Class Activities

1. **Critiquing the Group Proposals.** Form small groups in class to analyze and discuss the special types of groups for the elderly that are described in this chapter. What aspects of each proposal do you find most helpful? What specific ideas did you discover that might help you if you were going to design a group for this population?

2. **Institutional Groups.** Assume you are working in an institution for the elderly and are asked to design a variety of groups. Where would you begin? What contacts would you want to make? What specific groups would you be most interested in forming?

3. **Leadership Characteristics.** What guidelines are important when establishing groups for elderly people? What personal characteristics of a leader are important? What attitudes and skills do you consider essential?

4. **Community Groups for Older People.** Assume you are doing an internship or are employed in a community mental health center and have been asked to develop strategies for reaching and serving the needs of older people in the community. What steps would you take in assessing community needs and developing appropriate group programs?

5. **Techniques for Institutional Groups.** Review the group proposal for institutionalized elderly people described in this chapter. What specific techniques and exercises do you think are most useful with this particular group?

6. **Mixed Age Groups.** In the combined group for the elderly and adolescents, what is the rationale for mixing these different populations in the same group? What do you think of this proposal? What other kind of group can you think of that would combine populations?

7. **Organizing a Group for Healthy Older People.** Review the description given of the successful aging group. What did you learn from reading this proposal? What are some challenges you might face in organizing this kind of group? What are some benefits of a group for successful aging?

8. **Organizing a Bereavement Group.** Review the description given of a bereavement group. What are the main elements that account for the therapeutic value of grief work? What are some advantages of using a group format for dealing with loss with the elderly? If you were to form a similar group, what changes might you make in organizing and conducting such a group?

9. **Contacting Professional Resources in Working With the Elderly.** As a class project, divide the resources listed here among groups of students. Contact each of the organizations for information that can be brought to the entire class.

American Psychological Association—Affiliated Groups and Divisions

APA Office on Aging
Public Interest Directorate
American Psychological Association
750 First Street, NE
Washington, DC: 20002-4242
Phone: (202) 336-6135
Fax: (202) 336-6040
E-mail: ddiGilio@apa.org
Web site: http://www.apa.org/pi/aging

Division 20 (Adult Development and Aging)
[For excellent resources and links, see the Web site]
Web site: http://aging.ufl.edu/apadiv20/apadiv20.htm

Division 12, Section II (Clinical Geropsychology)
Lynn G. Peterson, Administrative Officer
P. O. Box 1082
Niwot, CO 80544
Phone: (303) 652-3126
Fax: (303) 652-2723
E-mail: lpete@gowebway.com
Web site: http://bama.ua.edu/~appgero/apa12_2

Other Societies and Organizations

American Society on Aging
Mental Health and Aging Network
833 Market Street, Suite 511
San Francisco, CA 94103-1824
Phone: (415) 974-9600
Web site: www.asaging.org

Gerontological Society of America
Mental Health Practice and Aging Interest Group
1030 15th Street, NW, Suite 250
Washington, DC 20005
Phone: (202) 842-1275
E-mail: geron@geron.org
Web site: www.geron.org

InfoTrac College Edition

For additional readings, explore InfoTrac College Edition, our online library, at http://www.infotrac.college.com/wadsworth. The following keywords are listed in such a way as to enable the InfoTrac College Edition search engine to locate a wider range of articles. The keywords should be entered exactly as listed, to include asterisks, "w1," "w2," "AND," and other search engine tools.

- group* w1 psych* AND elderly*
- group* w1 psych* AND bereave*

Appendix

Web Site Resources

Professional Organizations of Interest to Group Workers

It is a good idea to begin your identification with state, regional, and national professional associations while you are a student, and the major national professional organizations are listed here. Although not all of these organizations have special divisions devoted to group work, they are all at least indirectly relevant to the work of group practitioners. In addition, each has its own code of ethics, which can be obtained by contacting the particular organization. It is essential that you know the basic content of the codes of your profession and how they apply to you as a group worker.

Links to Web sites for these organizations are available at http://counseling.wadsworth.com/corey/groups7e, and many of the codes of ethics and guidelines for practice are available in the booklet *Codes of Ethics for the Helping Professions* (2nd ed., 2004, Thomson Brooks/Cole), which is sold at a nominal price when packaged with this textbook.

American Counseling Association (ACA)

Student memberships are available to both undergraduate and graduate students enrolled at least half time or more at the college level. ACA membership provides many benefits, including a subscription to the *Journal of Counseling and Development* and also a monthly newspaper titled *Counseling Today,* eligibility for professional liability insurance programs, legal defense services, and professional development through workshops and conventions.

ACA puts out a resource catalog that provides information on the various aspects of the counseling profession along with detailed information about membership, journals, books, home-study programs, videotapes, audiotapes, and liability insurance. For further information, contact:

American Counseling Association
5999 Stevenson Avenue
Alexandria, VA 22304-3300
Telephone: (703) 823-9800 or (800) 347-6647
Fax: (703) 823-0252

American Psychological Association (APA)

The APA has a Student Affiliates category rather than student membership. Journals and subscriptions are extra. Each year in August the APA holds a national convention. Membership includes a monthly subscription to the journal *American Psychologist* and to the magazine *Monitor on Psychology.* For further information, contact:

American Psychological Association
750 First Street, NE Washington, DC
20002-4242

Telephone: (202) 336-5500 or (800) 374-2721
Fax: (202) 336-5568

National Association of Social Workers (NASW)

NASW membership is open to all professional social workers, and there is a student membership category. The NASW Press produces *Social Work* and the *NASW News* as membership benefits, as well as providing a number of pamphlets, and is a major service in professional development. For further information, contact:

National Association of Social Workers
750 First Street, NE, Suite 700
Washington, DC 20002-4241
Telephone: (202) 408-8600 or (800) 638-8799
Fax: (202) 336-8310

American Association for Marriage and Family Therapy (AAMFT)

The AAMFT has a student membership category. Members receive the *Journal of Marital and Family Therapy*, which is published four times a year, and a subscription to six issues yearly of *The Family Therapy Magazine*. For a copy of the AAMFT Code of Ethics, membership applications, and further information, contact:

American Association for Marriage and
Family Therapy
112 South Alfred Street
Alexandria, VA 22314
Telephone: (703) 838-9808
Fax: (703) 838-9805

National Organization for Human Service Education (NOHSE)

The National Organization for Human Service Education (NOHSE) is made up of members from diverse disciplines—mental health, child care, social services, gerontology, recreation, corrections, and developmental disabilities. Membership is open to human-service educators, students, fieldwork supervisors, and direct-care professionals.

Student membership is $28 per year, which includes a subscription to the newsletter (the *Link*), the yearly journal, *Human Services Educa-*

tion, and a discount price for the yearly conference (held in October). For further information, contact:

Chrisanne Christensen
Sul Ross State University
Rio Grande College
Rt. 3, Box 1200
Eagle Pass, TX 78852
Telephone: (830) 758-5112
Fax: (830) 758-5001

Organizations Devoted Specifically to Group Work

Association for Specialists in Group Work (ASGW)

ASGW, a member organization of the American Counseling Association, is one of the most important professional organizations devoted to the promotion of group work. Both regular and student members receive *The Journal for Specialists in Group Work*, which is published in March, May, September, and November; they also receive the ASGW newsletter, *The Group Worker*, which is published three times a year. The journal and newsletter are excellent sources for staying current in the field of group work. ASGW often holds a convention in late January. For information about joining ASGW, contact ACA:

American Counseling Association
5999 Stevenson Avenue
Alexandria, VA 22304-3300
Telephone: (703) 823-9800 or (800) 347-6647
Fax: (703) 823-0252

The ASGW Web page was established to provide a resource base for teachers, students, and practitioners of group work. It includes both organizational information and professional resources (ASGW products, ASGW institutes, and links to other Web pages of interest to group workers. *The Professional Standards for the Training of Group Workers* is available on the ASGW Web site.

American Group Psychotherapy Association (AGPA)

AGPA is an interdisciplinary community that has been enhancing theory, practice, and research of group therapy since 1942. Both student and regular memberships are available. Membership includes a subscription to an excellent journal, the *International Journal of Group Psychotherapy,* which is published four times a year. The journal contains a variety of articles dealing with theory and practice of group therapy. Each year in February the AGPA sponsors a 5-day annual meeting that features a variety of institutes, seminars, open sessions, and workshops. For further information, journal subscriptions, and membership requirements, contact:

American Group Psychotherapy Association, Inc. (AGPA)
25 East 21st Street, 6th Floor
New York, NY 10010
Telephone: (212) 477-2677
Fax: (212) 979-6627

The AGPA Web site provides information about group psychotherapy and ethical guidelines for group therapists.

American Society of Group Psychotherapy and Psychodrama (ASGPP)

ASGPP is an interdisciplinary society with members from all of the helping fields. The goals of the organization are to establish standards for specialists in group therapy and psychodrama and to support the exploration of new areas of endeavors in research, practice, teaching, and training. The ASGPP holds national and regional conferences, provides a national journal, the *Journal of Group Psychotherapy, Psychodrama and Sociometry,* and offers a number of membership benefits. For further information, contact:

American Society of Group Psychotherapy and Psychodrama
301 N. Harrison Street, Suite 508
Princeton, NJ 08540
Telephone: (609) 452-1339
Fax: (609) 936-1695

Group Psychology and Group Psychotherapy, Division 49 of APA

Division 49 of the American Psychological Association provides a forum for psychologists interested in research, teaching, and practice in group psychology and group psychotherapy. Current projects include developing national guidelines for doctoral and postdoctoral training in group psychotherapy.

The division's quarterly journal, *Group Dynamics: Theory, Research and Practice,* and its newsletter, *The Group Psychologist,* are sent to all members and affiliates. For additional information, contact:

Thomas V. Sayger, Ph.D.
Counseling Psychology, Room 100
Ball Education Building
University of Memphis
Memphis, TN 38152
Telephone: (901) 678-3418
E-mail: sayger.tom@coe.memphis.edu

References and Suggested Readings*

Adamec, C. (1996). *How to live with a mentally ill person: A handbook of day-to-day strategies.* New York: Wiley.

The Administration on Aging. (2000). Online at http://www.aoa.dhhs.gov/aoa/.

Akos, P., Goodnough, G. E., & Milsom, A. S. (2004). Preparing school counselors for group work. *Journal for Specialists in Group Work, 29*(1), 127–136.

American Academy of Matrimonial Lawyers. (1998). *Stepping back from anger: Protecting your children during divorce.* Chicago, IL: Author.

American Association for Marriage and Family Therapy. (2000). *AAMFT code of ethics.* Washington, DC: Author.

American Counseling Association. (1995). *Code of ethics and standards of practice.* Alexandria, VA: Author.

American Counseling Association. (1999). *Ethical standards for Internet on-line counseling.* Alexandria, VA: Author.

American Group Psychotherapy Association. (2001). *Principles of group psychotherapy: Faculty core course manual.* New York: Author.

American Psychological Association. (1993). Guidelines for providers of psychological services to ethnic, linguistic, and culturally diverse populations. *American Psychologist, 48*(1), 45–48.

American Psychological Association. (2002). Ethical principles of psychologists and code of conduct. *American Psychologist, 57*(12), 1060–1073.

American Psychological Association. (2003). Guidelines on multicultural education, training, research, practice, and organizational change for psychologists. *American Psychologist, 58*(5), 377–402.

American Psychological Association. Division 44. (2000). Guidelines for psychotherapy with lesbian, gay, and bisexual clients. *American Psychologist, 55*(12), 1440–1451.

APA Working Group on the Older Adult. (1998). What practitioners should know about working with older adults. *Professional Psychology: Research and Practice, 29,* 413–427.

Andronico, M. P. (1996). *Men in groups: Insights, interventions, and psychoeducational work.* Washington, DC: American Psychological Association.

Andronico, M. P., & Horne, A. M. (2004). Counseling men in groups: The role of myths, therapeutic factors, leadership, and rituals. In

*This list contains both references cited in the text and suggestions for further reading.

J. L. DeLucia-Waack, D. Gerrity, C. R. Kalodner, & M. T. Riva (Eds.), *Handbook of group counseling and psychotherapy* (pp. 456–468). Thousand Oaks, CA: Sage.

Ansello, E. F. (1988). Intersecting of aging and disabilities. *Educational Gerontology, 14,* 351–363.

Aronson, S., & Scheidlinger, S. (1994). Group therapy for adolescents. *Directions in Mental Health Counseling, 4*(2), 3–11.

Arredondo, P., Toporek, R., Brown, S. P., Jones, J., Locke, D. C., Sanchez, J., & Stadler, H. (1996). Operationalization of the multicultural counseling competencies. *Journal of Multicultural Counseling and Development, 24*(1), 42–78.

Association for Specialists in Group Work. (1998). Best practice guidelines. *Journal for Specialists in Group Work, 23*(3), 237–244. Available online: http://www.asgw.org/best.htm.

Association for Specialists in Group Work. (1999). Principles for diversity-competent group workers. *Journal for Specialists in Group Work, 24*(1), 7–14. Available online: http://www.asgw. org/diversity.htm.

Association for Specialists in Group Work. (2000). Professional standards for the training of group workers. *Group Worker, 29*(3), 1–10. Available online: http://www.asgw.org/ training_standards.htm.

Association for Specialists in Group Work. (March, 2004). Special Issue on Teaching Group Work. *Journal for Specialists in Group Work.* Volume 29, Number 1.

Barlow, S. H. (2004). A strategic three-year plan to teach beginning, intermediate, and advanced group skills. *Journal for Specialists in Group Work, 29*(1), 113–126.

Barlow, S. H., Fuhriman, A. J., & Burlingame, G. M. (2004). The history of group counseling and psychotherapy. In J. L. DeLucia-Waack, D. Gerrity, C. R. Kalodner, & M. T. Riva (Eds.), *Handbook of group counseling and psychotherapy* (pp. 3–22). Thousand Oaks, CA: Sage.

Bednar, R. L., Corey, G., Evans, N. J., Gazda, G. M., Pistole, M. C., Stockton, R., & Robison, F. F. (1987). Overcoming obstacles to the future development of research on group work. *Journal for Specialists in Group Work, 12*(3), 98–111.

Bednar, R. L., & Kaul, T. J. (1978). Experiential group research: Current perspectives. In S. L. Garfield & A. E. Bergin (Eds.), *Handbook of psychotherapy and behavior changes: An empirical analysis* (2nd ed., pp. 769–815). New York: Wiley.

Bednar, R. L., & Kaul, T. J. (1979). Experiential group research: What never happened. *Journal of Applied Behavioral Science, 11,* 311–319.

Bednar, R. L., & Kaul, T. J. (1994). Experiential group research: Can the cannon fire? In A. E. Bergin & S. L. Garfield (Eds.), *Handbook of psychotherapy and behavior change* (pp. 631–663). New York: Wiley.

Bednar, R. L., & Lawlis, F. (1971). Empirical research in group psychotherapy. In A. E. Bergin & S. L. Garfield (Eds.), *Handbook for psychotherapy and behavior change* (pp. 812–838). New York: Wiley.

Bednar, R. L., Melnick, J., & Kaul, T. J. (1974). Risk, responsibility, and structure: A conceptual framework for initiating group counseling and psychotherapy. *Journal of Counseling Psychology, 21,* 31–37.

Bemak, F., & Chung, R. C-Y. (2004). Teaching multicultural group counseling: Perspectives for a new era. *Journal for Specialists in Group Work, 29*(1), 31–41.

Bemak, F., & Young, M. E. (1998). Role of catharsis in group psychotherapy. *International Journal of Action Methods: Psychodrama, Skill Training, and Role Playing, 50*(4), 166–184.

Bengston, V. L., & Schaie, K. W. (Eds.). (1999). *Handbook of theories of aging.* New York: Springer.

Berg, R. C., Landreth, G. L., & Fall, K. A. (1998). *Group counseling: Concepts and procedures* (3rd ed.). Philadelphia, PA: Accelerated Development (Taylor & Francis).

Berube, L. (1999). Dream work: Demystifying dreams using a small group for personal growth. *Journal for Specialists in Group Work, 24*(1), 88–101.

Bethune, A. S. (2003). Grieving our losses. In D. Capuzzi (Ed.), *Approaches to group work: A handbook for group practitioners* (pp. 127–134). Upper Saddle River, NJ: Merrill/Prentice-Hall.

Biegel, D. E., & Schulz, R. (1999). Caregiving and caregiver interventions in aging and mental illness. *Family Relations, 48,* 345–354.

Birren, J. E., & Schaie, K. W. (Eds.). (1996). *Handbook of the psychology of aging* (4th ed.). San Diego, CA: Academic Press.

Borgers, S. B., & Tyndall, L. W. (1982). Setting expectations for groups. *Journal for Specialists in Group Work, 7*(2), 109–111.

Boulden, J., & Boulden, J. (1994). *Push & shove: The bully and victim activity book.* Weaver, CA: Boulden Publishing.

Boulden, J., & Boulden, J. (1995). *Give and take: A conflict resolution activity book.* Weaverville, CA: Boulden Publishing.

Bowman, V. E., & DeLucia, J. L. (1993). Preparation for group therapy: The effects of preparer and modality on group process and individual functioning. *Journal for Specialists in Group Work, 18*(2), 67–79.

Brabender, V. (2002). *Introduction to group therapy.* New York: Wiley.

Breshgold, E. (1989). Resistance in Gestalt therapy: An historical theoretical perspective. *The Gestalt Journal, 12*(2), 73–102.

Briere, J. (1996). *Therapy for adults molested as children: Beyond survival.* New York: Springer.

Brisman, J., & Siegel, M. (1985). The bulimia workshop: A unique integration of group treatment approaches. *International Journal of Group Psychotherapy, 35*(4), 585–601.

Brok, A. J. (1997). A modified cognitive-behavioral approach to group therapy with the elderly. *Group, 21*(2),115.

Brooks, G. R. (1998). Group therapy for traditional men. In W. S. Pollack & R. F. Levant (Eds.), *New psychotherapy for men* (pp. 83–96). New York: Wiley.

Brooks, G. R., & Good, G. E. (Eds.). (2001a). *The new handbook of psychotherapy and counseling with men: A comprehensive guide to settings, problems, and treatment approaches* (Vol. 1). San Francisco: Jossey-Bass.

Brooks, G. R., & Good, G. E. (Eds.). (2001b). *The new handbook of psychotherapy and counseling with men: A comprehensive guide to settings,* *problems, and treatment approaches* (Vol. 2). San Francisco: Jossey-Bass.

Brown, L. K., & Brown, M. (1986). *Dinosaurs divorce: A guide for changing families.* Boston: Little, Brown.

Burlingame, G. M., & Fuhriman, A. (1990). Time-limited group therapy. *Counseling Psychologist, 18*(1), 93–118.

Burlingame, G. M., Fuhriman, A. J., & Johnson, J. (2002). Cohesion in group psychotherapy. In J. C. Norcross (Ed.), *A guide to psychotherapy relationships that work.* Oxford, England: Oxford University Press.

Burlingame, G. M., Fuhriman, A. J., & Johnson, J. (2004a). Current status and future directions of group therapy research. In J. L. DeLucia-Waack, D. Gerrity, C. R. Kalodner, & M. T. Riva (Eds.), *Handbook of group counseling and psychotherapy* (pp. 651–660). Thousand Oaks, CA: Sage.

Burlingame, G. M., Fuhriman, A. J., & Johnson, J. (2004b). Process and outcome in group counseling and psychotherapy: A perspective. In J. L. DeLucia-Waack, D. Gerrity, C. R. Kalodner, & M. T. Riva (Eds.), *Handbook of group counseling and psychotherapy* (pp. 49–61). Thousand Oaks, CA: Sage.

Burlingame, G. M., MacKenzie, K. R., & Strauss, B. (2004). Small group treatment: Evidence for effectiveness and mechanisms of change. In M. Lambert (Ed.), *Handbook of psychotherapy and behavior change* (5th ed., pp. 647–696). New York: Wiley.

Burnside, I. (Ed.). (1984). *Working with the elderly: Group process and techniques* (2nd ed.). Belmont, CA: Wadsworth.

Capuzzi, D. (2003). *Approaches to group work: A handbook for group practitioners.* Upper Saddle River, NJ: Merrill/Prentice-Hall.

Cardemil, E. V., & Battle, C. L. (2003). Guess who's coming to therapy? Getting comfortable with conversations about race and ethnicity in psychotherapy. *Professional Psychology: Research and Practice, 34*(3), 278–286.

Carter, S. (1998). *Combating teen delinquency in an apartment setting through village building.* Los Angeles: South Central Training Consortium, Inc.

Chang, T., & Yeh, C. J. (2003). Using online groups to provide support to Asian American men: Racial, cultural, gender, and treatment issues. *Professional Psychology: Research and Practice, 34*(6), 634–643.

Chen, M., & Rybak, C. J. (2004). *Group leadership skills: Interpersonal process in group counseling and therapy.* Belmont, CA: Brooks/Cole.

Comstock, D. L., Duffey, T., & St. George, H. (2002). The relational-cultural model: A framework for group process. *Journal for Specialists in Group Work, 27*(3), 254–272.

Conyne, R. K. (1996). The Association for Specialists in Group Work Training Standards: Some considerations and suggestions for training. *Journal for Specialists in Group Work, 21*(3), 155–162.

Conyne, R. K. (1999). *Failures in group work: How we can learn from our mistakes.* Thousand Oaks, CA: Sage.

Conyne, R. K., & Bemak, F. (2004). Teaching group work from an ecological perspective. *Journal for Specialists in Group Work, 29*(1), 7–18.

Conyne, R. K., & Wilson, R. F. (1998). Toward a standards-based classification of group work offerings. *Journal for Specialists in Group Work, 23*(2), 177–184.

Conyne, R. K., Wilson, F. R., & Ward, D. E. (1997). *Comprehensive group work: What it means and how to teach it.* Alexandria, VA: American Counseling Association.

Corey, G. (2001). *The art of integrative counseling.* Belmont, CA: Thomson Brooks/Cole.

Corey, G. (2004). *Theory and practice of group counseling* (6th ed.) and *Manual.* Belmont, CA: Thomson Brooks/Cole.

Corey, G. (2005a). *Case approach to counseling and psychotherapy* (6th ed.). Belmont, CA: Thomson Brooks/Cole.

Corey, G. (2005b). *Theory and practice of counseling and psychotherapy* (7th ed.) and *Manual.* Belmont, CA: Thomson Brooks/Cole.

Corey, G., & Corey, M. (2006). *I never knew I had a choice* (8th ed.). Belmont, CA: Thomson Brooks/Cole.

Corey, G., Corey, M., & Callanan, P. (2003). *Issues and ethics in the helping professions* (6th ed.). Belmont, CA: Thomson Brooks/Cole.

Corey, G., Corey, M., Callanan, P., & Russell, J. M. (2004). *Group techniques* (3rd ed.). Belmont, CA: Thomson Brooks/Cole.

Corey, G., Corey, M. S., & Haynes, R. (2006). *Groups in action: Evolution and challenges, DVD and workbook.* Belmont, CA: Thomson Brooks/Cole.

Corey, G., & Haynes, R. (2005). *CD-ROM for integrative counseling.* Belmont, CA: Thomson Brooks/Cole.

Corey, M., & Corey, G. (2003). *Becoming a helper* (4th ed.). Belmont, CA: Thomson Brooks/Cole.

Corey, M., & Corey, G. (2004). Reframing resistance. *The Group Worker: Association for Specialists in Group Work, 32*(2), 5–8.

Cornish, P. A., & Benton, D. (2001). Getting started in healthier relationships. Brief integrated dynamic group counseling in a university counseling setting. *Journal for Specialists in Group Work, 26*(2), 129–143.

Courtois, C. A. (1996). *Healing the incest wound: Adult survivors in therapy.* New York: Norton.

Creanza, A. L., & McWhirter, J. J. (1994). Reminiscence: A strategy for getting to know you. *Journal for Specialists in Group Work, 19*(4), 232–237.

Cunningham, C., & MacFarlane, K. (1997). *When children abuse: Group treatment strategies for children with impulse control problems.* Brandon, VT: The Safer Society Press.

D'Andrea, M. (2004). The impact of racial-cultural identity of group leaders and members: Theory and recommendations. In J. L. DeLucia-Waack, D. Gerrity, C. R. Kalodner, & M. T. Riva (Eds.), *Handbook of group counseling and psychotherapy* (pp. 265–282). Thousand Oaks, CA: Sage.

Davenport, D. S. (2004). Ethical issues in the teaching of group counseling. *Journal for Specialists in Group Work, 29*(1), 43–49.

DeLucia-Waack, J. L. (1996). Multicultural group counseling: Addressing diversity to facilitate universality and self-understanding. In J. L.

DeLucia-Waack (Ed.), *Multicultural counseling competencies: Implications for training and practice* (pp. 157–195). Alexandria, VA: Association for Counselor Education and Supervision.

DeLucia-Waack, J. L., & Donigian, J. (2004). *The practice of multicultural group work: Visions and perspectives from the field.* Belmont, CA: Brooks/Cole-Thomson Learning.

DeLucia-Waack, J. L., & Fauth, J. (2004). Effective supervision of group leaders: Current theory, research, and implications for practice. In J. L. DeLucia-Waack, D. Gerrity, C. R. Kalodner, & M. T. Riva (Eds.), *Handbook of group counseling and psychotherapy* (pp. 136–150). Thousand Oaks, CA: Sage.

DeLucia-Waack, J. L., Gerrity, D., Kalodner, C. R., & Riva, M. T. (Eds.). (2004). *Handbook of group counseling and psychotherapy.* Thousand Oaks, CA: Sage.

de Shazer, S. (1984). The death of resistance. *Family Process, 23,* 79–93.

Dies, R. R. (1983a). Bridging the gap between research and practice in group psychotherapy. In R. R. Dies & R. MacKenzie (Eds.), *Advances in group psychotherapy: Integrating research and practice* (American Group Psychotherapy Association Monograph Series, pp. 1–26). New York: International Universities Press.

Dies, R. R. (1983b). Clinical implications of research on leadership in short-term group psychotherapy. In R. R. Dies & R. MacKenzie (Eds.), *Advances in group psychotherapy: Integrating research and practice* (American Group Psychotherapy Association Monograph Series, pp. 27–28). New York: International Universities Press.

Dies, R. R. (1992). The future of group therapy. *Psychotherapy, 29*(1), 58–64.

Dies, R. R. (1993). Research on group psychotherapy: Overview and clinical applications. In A. Alonso & H. I. Swiller (Eds.), *Group therapy in clinical practice* (pp. 473–518). Washington, DC: American Psychiatric Press.

Dies, R. R. (1994). Therapist variable in group psychotherapy research. In A. Fuhriman & G. M. Burlingame (Eds.), *Handbook of group psychotherapy: An empirical and clinical synthesis* (pp. 114–154). New York: Wiley.

Donigian, J., & Hulse-Killacky, D. (1999). *Critical incidents in group therapy* (2nd ed.). Pacific Grove, CA: Brooks/Cole.

Earley, J. (2000). *Interactive group therapy: Integrating interpersonal, action-oriented, and psychodynamic approaches.* Philadelphia, PA: Brunner/Mazel (Taylor & Francis Group).

Edleson, J. L., & Tolman, R. M. (1994). Group intervention strategies for men who batter. *Directions in Mental Health Counseling, 4*(7), 3–16.

Erber, J., Szuchman, L. T., & Rothberg, S. T. (1990). Everyday memory failure: Age differences in appraisal and attribution. *Psychology and Aging, 5*(2), 236–241.

Erber, J., Szuchman, L. T., & Rothberg, S. T. (1991). Age, gender, and individual differences in memory failure appraisal. *Psychology and Aging, 5*(4), 600–603.

Fettes, P. A., & Peters, J. M. (1992). A meta-analysis of group treatments for bulimia nervosa. *International Journal of Eating Disorders, 11,* 97–110.

Fitzgerald, H. (1994). *The mourning handbook.* New York: Simon & Schuster.

Fleckenstein, L. B., & Horne, A. M. (2004). Anger management groups. In J. L. DeLucia-Waack, D. Gerrity, C. R. Kalodner, & M. T. Riva (Eds.), *Handbook of group counseling and psychotherapy* (pp. 547–562). Thousand Oaks, CA: Sage.

Folken, M. H. (1991). The importance of group support for widowed persons. *Journal for Specialists in Group Work, 16*(3), 172–177.

Freeman, S. J. (2005). *Grief and loss: Understanding the journey.* Belmont, CA: Thomson Brooks/Cole.

Freeman, S. M. (1995). *Developing group skills* (5th ed.). Waconia, MN: F.I.G. Publications.

Fuhriman, A., & Burlingame, G. M. (1990). Consistency of matter: A comparative analysis of individual and group process variables. *Counseling Psychologist, 18*(1), 6–63.

Fuhriman, A., & Burlingame, G. M. (1994). Group psychotherapy: Research and practice. In A. Fuhriman & G. M. Burlingame (Eds.), *Handbook of group psychotherapy: An empirical and clinical synthesis* (pp. 3–40). New York: Wiley.

Fuhriman, A., & Burlingame, G. M. (1999). Does group psychotherapy work? In J. R. Price, D. R. Hescheles, & A. R. Price (Eds.), *A guide to starting psychotherapy groups* (pp. 81–98). San Diego, CA: Academic Press.

Fuhriman, A., & Burlingame, G. M. (2001). Group psychotherapy training and effectiveness. *International Journal of Group Psychotherapy, 51,* 399–416.

Garner, D. M., & Garfinkel, P. E. (1997). *Handbook of treatment for eating disorders* (2nd ed.). New York: Guilford.

Gazda, G. M., Ginter, E. J., & Horne, A. M. (2001). *Group counseling and group psychotherapy: Theory and application.* Boston, MA: Allyn & Bacon.

Gerrity, D. A., & Peterson, T. L. (2004). Groups for survivors of childhood sexual abuse. In J. L. DeLucia-Waack, D. Gerrity, C. R. Kalodner, & M. T. Riva (Eds.), *Handbook of group counseling and psychotherapy* (pp. 497–517). Thousand Oaks, CA: Sage.

Gladding, S. (2003). *Group work: A counseling specialty* (4th ed.). Upper Saddle River, NJ: Merrill/Prentice-Hall.

Gushue, G. V., & Brazaitis, S. J. (2003). Lazarus and group psychotherapy: AIDS in the era of protease inhibitors. *The Counseling Psychologist, 31*(3), 314–342.

Guth, L. J., & McDonnell, K. A. (2004). Designing class activities to meet specific core training competencies: A developmental approach. *Journal for Specialists in Group Work, 29*(1), 97–107.

Harris, H. L., Altekruse, M. K., & Engels, D. W. (2003). Helping freshman student athletes adjust to college life using psychoeducational groups. *Journal for Specialists in Group Work, 28*(1), 64–81.

Hazzard, W. R., Larson, E. B., & Perls, T. T. (1998). Preventive gerontology: Strategies for optimal aging. *Patient Care, 32,* 198–211.

Henderson, D. A., & Gladding, S. T. (2004). Group counseling with older adults. In J. L. DeLucia-Waack, D. Gerrity, C. R. Kalodner, & M. T. Riva (Eds.), *Handbook of group counseling and psychotherapy* (pp. 469–478). Thousand Oaks, CA: Sage.

Hendren, R. L., Atkins, D. M., Sumner, C. R., & Barber, J. K. (1987). Model for the group treatment of eating disorders. *International Journal of Group Psychotherapy, 37*(4), 589–602.

Herlihy, B., & Corey, G. (1996). *ACA ethical standards casebook* (5th ed.). Alexandria, VA: American Counseling Association.

Herlihy, B., & Corey, G. (1997). *Boundary issues in counseling: Multiple roles and responsibilities.* Alexandria, VA: American Counseling Association.

Herman, J. (1981). *Father-daughter incest.* Cambridge, MA: Harvard University Press.

Herman, J. (1992). *Trauma and recovery.* New York: Basic Books.

Herman, J., & Schatzow, E. (1984). Time-limited group therapy for women with a history of incest. *International Journal of Group Psychotherapy, 35*(4), 605–616.

Hern, B. G., & Weis, D. M. (1991). A group counseling experience with the very old. *Journal for Specialists in Group Work, 16*(3), 143–151.

Hindman, J. (1993). *A touching book: . . . for little people and for big people.* Ontario, OR: AlexAndria Assoc.

Hoag, M. J., & Burlingame, G. M. (1997). Evaluating the effectiveness of child and adolescent group treatment: A meta-analysis review. *Journal of Clinical Child Psychology, 26,* 234–246.

Horne, A. M. (2003). Setting up for success with psychoeducational groups. *Group Worker, 31*(2), 10–13.

Horne, A. M., & Rosenthal, R. (1997). Research in group work: How did we get where we are? *Journal for Specialists in Group Work, 22*(4), 228–240.

Horne, S. (1999). From coping to creating change: The evolution of women's groups. *Journal for Specialists in Group Work, 24*(3), 231–245.

Horne, S. G., & Levitt, H. M. (2004). Psychoeducational and counseling groups with gay, lesbian, bisexual, and transgendered clients. In J. L. DeLucia-Waack, D. Gerrity, C. R. Kalodner, & M. T. Riva (Eds.), *Handbook of group counseling and psychotherapy* (pp. 224–238). Thousand Oaks, CA: Sage.

Hulse-Killacky, D., Killacky, J., & Donigian, J. (2001). *Making task groups work in your world.* Upper Saddle River, NJ: Merrill/Prentice-Hall.

Humphreys, K., Winzelberg, A., & Klaw, E. (2000). Psychologists' ethical responsibilities in Internet-based groups: Issues, strategies, and a call for dialogue. *Professional Psychology: Research and Practice, 31*(5), 493–496.

Ivey, A. E., Pedersen, P. B., & Ivey, M. B. (2001). *Intentional group counseling: A microskills approach.* Pacific Grove, CA: Brooks/Cole.

Jack, D. C. (1991). *Silencing the self: Women and depression.* New York: HarperPerennial.

James, J. W., & Friedman, R. (1998). *The grief recovery handbook.* New York: HarperCollins.

Johnson, D. W., & Johnson, T. R. (1995). *Reducing school violence through conflict resolution.* Alexandria, VA: Association for Supervision and Curriculum Department.

Johnson, I. H., Santos Torres, J., Coleman, V. D., & Smith, M. C. (1995). Issues and strategies in leading culturally diverse counseling groups. *Journal for Specialists in Group Work, 20*(3), 143–150.

Jordan, J. V. (Ed.). (1997). *Women's growth in diversity: More writings from the Stone Center.* New York: Guilford.

Jordan, J. V., Kaplan, A. G., Miller, J. B., Stiver, I. P., & Surrey, J. L. (Eds.). (1991). *Women's growth in connection.* New York: Guilford.

Kano, S. (1989). *Making peace with food: Freeing yourself from the diet/weight obsession.* New York: Harper & Row.

Kaul, T. J., & Bednar, R. L. (1978). Conceptualizing group research: A preliminary analysis. *Small Group Behavior, 9,* 173–191.

Kaul, T. J., & Bednar, R. L. (1986). Experiential group research: Results, questions, and suggestions. In S. L. Garfield & A. E. Bergin (Eds.), *Handbook for psychotherapy and behavior change* (3rd ed., pp. 671–714). New York: Wiley.

Kazantzis, N., & Deane, F. P. (1999). Psychologists' use of homework assignments in clinical practice. *Professional Psychology: Research and Practice, 30*(6), 581–585.

Kees, N., & Leech, N. (2004). Practice trends in women's groups: An inclusive view. In J. L. DeLucia-Waack, D. Gerrity, C. R. Kalodner, & M. T. Riva (Eds.), *Handbook of group counseling and psychotherapy* (pp. 445–455). Thousand Oaks, CA: Sage.

Kennedy, P. F., Vandehey, M., Norman, W. B., & Diekhoff, G. M. (2003). Recommendations for risk-management practices. *Professional Psychology: Research and Practice, 34*(3), 309–311.

Killacky, J., & Hulse-Killacky, D. (2004). Group work is not just for the group class anymore: Teaching generic group competency skills across the counselor education curriculum. *Journal for Specialists in Group Work, 29*(1), 87–96.

Kincade, E. A., & Kalodner, C. R. (2004). The use of groups in college and university counseling centers. In J. L. DeLucia-Waack, D. Gerrity, C. R. Kalodner, & M. T. Riva (Eds.), *Handbook of group counseling and psychotherapy* (pp. 366–377). Thousand Oaks, CA: Sage.

Kivlighan, D. M., & Holmes, S. E. (2004). The importance of therapeutic factors: A typology of therapeutic factors studies. In J. L. DeLucia-Waack, D. Gerrity, C. R. Kalodner, & M. T. Riva (Eds.), *Handbook of group counseling and psychotherapy* (pp. 23–36). Thousand Oaks, CA: Sage.

Klein, R., Brabender, V., & Fallon, A. (1994). Inpatient group therapy. In A. Fuhriman & G. Burlingame (Eds.), *Handbook of group psychotherapy: An empirical and clinical synthesis* (pp. 370–415). New York: Wiley.

Kleven, S. (1997). *The right touch: A read-aloud story to help prevent child abuse.* Bellevue, WA: Illumination Arts.

Kline, W. B. (2003). *Interactive group counseling and therapy.* Upper Saddle River, NJ: Merrill/Prentice-Hall.

Knopp, F. (1982). *Remedial intervention in adolescent sex offenses: Nine program descriptions.* Syracuse: Safety Society Program.

Knox, S., Hess, S. A., Petersen, D. A., & Hill, C. E. (1997). A qualitative analysis of client perceptions of the effects of helpful therapist self-disclosure in long-term therapy. *Journal of Counseling Psychology, 44*(3), 274–283.

Kottler, J. A. (1994). *Advanced group leadership.* Pacific Grove, CA: Brooks/Cole.

Kottler, J. A. (2001). *Learning group leadership: An experiential approach.* Boston: Allyn & Bacon.

Kottler, J. A. (2004). Realities of teaching group counseling. *Journal for Specialists in Group Work, 29*(1), 51–53.

Kübler-Ross, E. (1969). *On death and dying.* New York: Macmillan.

Kulic, K. R., Dagley, J. C., & Horne, A. M. (2001). Prevention groups with children and adolescents. *Journal for Specialists in Group Work, 26*(3), 211–218.

Lee, M. Y., Sebold, J., & Uken, A. (2003). *Solution-focused treatment of domestic violence offenders: Accountability for change.* New York: Oxford University Press.

Levy, B. (1996). Improving memory in old age through implicit self-stereotyping. *Journal of Personality and Social Psychology, 71*(6), 1092–1107.

Lewis, M. I., & Butler, R. N. (1984). Life-review therapy: Putting memories to work. In I. Burnside (Ed.), *Working with the elderly: Group process and techniques* (2nd ed., pp. 50–59). Belmont, CA: Wadsworth.

Lund, D. A., Diamond, M. F., & Juretich, M. (1985). Bereavement support groups for the elderly: Characteristics of potential participants. *Death Studies, 9,* 309–321.

MacKenzie, K. R. (2001). Group psychotherapy. In W. J. Livesley (Ed.), *Handbook of personality disorders* (pp. 497–526). New York: Guilford.

MacLennan, B. W. (1988). Discussion of "bereavement groups." *International Journal of Group Psychotherapy, 38*(4), 453–458.

MacNair-Semands, R. R. (2004). Theory, practice, and research of grief groups. In J. L. DeLucia-Waack, D. Gerrity, C. R. Kalodner, & M. T. Riva (Eds.), *Handbook of group counseling and psychotherapy* (pp. 518–531). Thousand Oaks, CA: Sage.

Markus, H. E., & King, D. A. (2003). A survey of group psychotherapy training during predoctoral psychology internship. *Professional Psychology: Research and Practice, 34*(2), 203–209.

Marotta, S. A., & Asner, K. K. (1999). Group psychotherapy for women with a history of incest: The research base. *Journal of Counseling and Development, 77*(3), 315–323.

Marsh, D. T. (1998). *Serious mental illness and the family: A practitioner's guide.* New York: Wiley.

McBride, M. C., & Emerson, S. (1989). Group work with women who were molested as children. *Journal for Specialists in Group Work, 14*(1), 25–33.

McGlothlin, J. M. (2003). Response to the mini special issue on technology and group work. *Journal for Specialists in Group Work, 28*(1), 42–47.

McKay, M. M., Gonzalez, J. J., Stone, S., Ryland, D., & Kohner, K. (1995). Multiple family therapy groups: A responsive intervention model for inner-city families. *Social Work With Groups, 18,* 41–56.

McManus, P. W., Redford, J. L., & Hughes, R. B. (1997). Connecting to self and others: A structured group for women. *Journal for Specialists in Group Work, 22*(1), 22–30.

McMinn, M. R., Buchanan, T., Ellens, B. M., & Ryan, M. K. (1999). Technology, professional practice, and ethics: Survey findings and implications. *Professional Psychology: Research and Practice, 30*(2), 165–172.

Meadow, D. (1988). Preparation of individuals for participation in a treatment group: Development and empirical testing of a model. *International Journal of Group Psychotherapy, 38*(3), 367–385.

Meezan, W., O'Keefe, M., & Zariani, M. (1997). A model of multi-family group therapy for abusive and neglectful parents and their children. *Social Work With Groups, 20*(2), 71–88.

Meiselman, K. (1978). *Incest: A psychological study of cause and effects with treatment recommendations.* San Francisco: Jossey-Bass.

Meiselman, K. (1990). *Resolving the trauma of incest: Reintegration therapy with survivors.* San Francisco: Jossey-Bass.

Merta, R. J. (1995). Group work: Multicultural perspectives. In J. G. Ponterotto, J. M. Casas, L. A. Suzuki, & C. M. Alexander (Eds.), *Handbook of multicultural counseling* (pp. 567–585). Newbury Park, CA: Sage.

Merta, R. J., Wolfgang, L., & McNeil, K. (1993). Five models for using the experiential group in the preparation of group counselors. *Journal for Specialists in Group Work, 18*(4), 200–207.

Miller, J. B. (1976). *Toward a new psychology of women.* Boston: Beacon.

Miller, J. B., & Stiver, I. P. (1991). *A relational reframing of therapy. Work in Progress, No. 52, Stone Center.* Wellesley, MA: Stone Center.

Miller, J. B., & Stiver, I. P. (1997). *The healing connection: How women form relationships in therapy and in life.* Boston: Beacon.

Molinari, V. (1994). Current approaches to psychotherapy with elderly adults. *Directions in Mental Health Counseling, 4*(3), 3–13.

Molinari, V., Karel, M., Jones, S., Zeiss, A., Cooley, S. G., Wray, L., Brown, E., & Gallagher-Thompson, D. (2003). Recommendations about the knowledge and skills required of psychologists working with older adults. *Professional Psychology: Research and Practice, 34*(4), 435–443.

Morganett, R. S. (1990). *Skills for living: Group counseling activities for young adolescents.* Champaign, IL: Research Press.

Morran, D. K. (1982). Leader and member self-disclosing behavior in counseling groups. *Journal for Specialists in Group Work, 7*(4), 218–223.

Morran, D. K., Robison, F. F., & Stockton, R. (1985). Feedback exchange in counseling groups: An analysis of message content and receiver acceptance as a function of leader versus member delivery, session, and valence. *Journal of Counseling Psychology, 32*, 57–67.

Morran, D. K., & Stockton, R. (1980). Effect of self concept on group member reception of positive and negative feedback. *Journal of Counseling Psychology, 27*, 260–267.

Morran, D. K., & Stockton, R. (1985). Perspectives on group research programs. *Journal for Specialists in Group Work, 10*(4), 186–191.

Morran, D. K., Stockton, R., & Bond, L. (1991). Delivery of positive and corrective feedback in counseling groups. *Journal of Counseling Psychology, 38*(4), 410–415.

Morran, D. K., Stockton, R., Cline, R. J., & Teed, C. (1998). Facilitating feedback exchange in groups: Leader interventions. *Journal for Specialists in Group Work, 23*(3), 257–268.

Morran, D. K., Stockton, R., & Whittingham, M. H. (2004). Effective leader interventions for counseling and psychotherapy groups. In J. L. DeLucia-Waack, D. Gerrity, C. R. Kalodner, & M. T. Riva (Eds.), *Handbook of group counseling and psychotherapy* (pp. 91–103). Thousand Oaks, CA: Sage.

Muok, C., & DuBray, W. (1998). Southeast Asian refugees. In W. DuBray (Ed.) and associates, *Mental health interventions with people of color* (2nd ed., pp. 119–130). Cincinnati, OH: Thomson Learning Custom Publishing, a Division of Thomson Learning, Inc.

Myers, J. E., Poidevant, J. M., & Dean, L. A. (1991). Groups for older persons and their caregivers: A review of the literature. *Journal for Specialists in Group Work, 16*(3), 197–205.

Nakkula, M. J. (1984). *Elderly and adolescence: A group approach to integrating the isolated.* Unpublished master's project, University of Minnesota, Duluth.

Napier, R. W., & Gershenfeld, M. K. (2004). *Groups: Theory and experience* (7th ed.). Boston: Houghton Mifflin.

Nass, M., & Nass, M. (1991). *Songs for peacemakers* [record]. Freeport, NY: Activity Records, Inc.

National Association of Social Workers. (1999). *Code of ethics.* Washington, DC: Author.

National Registry of Certified Group Psychotherapists. (1993). *Certified group psychotherapists: A professional certification program.* New York: Author.

O'Halloran, T. M., & McCartney, T. J. (2004). An evaluation of the use of technology as a tool to meet group training standards. *Journal for Specialists in Group Work, 29*(1), 65–74.

O'Hanlon, B. (2003). *A guide to inclusive therapy: 26 methods of respectful, resistance-dissolving therapy.* New York: Norton.

O'Hanlon W. H., & Weiner-Davis, M. (1989). *In search of solutions: A new direction in psychotherapy.* New York: Norton.

Ormont, L. R. (1988). The leader's role in resolving resistances to intimacy in the group setting. *International Journal of Group Psychotherapy, 38*(1), 29–46.

O'Shea, M., & Phelps, R. (1985). Multiple family therapy: Current status and critical appraisal. *Family Process, 24,* 555–582.

Pack-Brown, S. P., Whittington-Clark, L. E., & Parker, W. M. (1998). *Images of me: A guide to group work with African-American women.* Boston: Allyn & Bacon.

Page, B. J. (2003). Introduction to using technology in group work. *Journal for Specialists in Group Work, 28*(1), 7–8.

Page, B. J. (2004). Online group counseling. In J. L. DeLucia-Waack, D. Gerrity, C. R. Kalodner, & M. T. Riva (Eds.), *Handbook of group counseling and psychotherapy* (pp. 609–620). Thousand Oaks, CA: Sage.

Papolos, D. F. (1997). *Overcoming depression: The definitive resource for patients and families who live with depression and manic depression.* New York: Harper Trade.

Parr, G., Haberstroh, S., & Kottler, J. (2000). Interactive journal writing as an adjunct in group work. *Journal for Specialists in Group Work, 25*(3), 229–242.

Pedersen, P. (1997). The cultural context of the American Counseling Association code of ethics. *Journal of Counseling and Development, 76*(1), 23–28.

Pedersen, P. (2000). *A handbook for developing multicultural awareness* (3rd ed.). Alexandria, VA: American Counseling Association.

Pedersen, P., Draguns, J., Lonner, W., & Trimble, J. (Eds.). (2002). *Counseling across cultures* (5th ed.). Thousand Oaks, CA: Sage.

Piper, W. E. (2001). Commentary on my editorship (1993–2001). *International Journal of Group Psychotherapy, 51,* 165–168.

Piper, W. E., & Joyce, A. S. (1996). A consideration of factors influencing the utilization of time-limited, short-term group therapy. *International Journal of Group Psychotherapy, 46,* 311–328.

Piper, W. E., McCallum, M., Joyce, A. S., Rosie, J. S., & Ogrodniczuk, J. S. (2001). Patient personality and time-limited psychotherapy for complicated grief. *International Journal of Group Psychotherapy, 51,* 525–552.

Piper, W. E., & Ogrodniczuk, J. S. (2004). Brief group therapy. In J. L. DeLucia-Waack, D. Gerrity, C. R. Kalodner, & M. T. Riva (Eds.), *Handbook of group counseling and psychotherapy* (pp. 641–650). Thousand Oaks, CA: Sage.

Piper, W. E., & Perrault, E. L. (1989). Pretherapy preparation for group members. *International Journal of Group Psychotherapy, 39*(1), 17–34.

Pollack, W. S., & Levant, R. F. (Eds.). (1998). *New psychotherapy for men.* New York: Wiley.

Polster, E., & Polster, M. (1973). *Gestalt therapy integrated.* New York: Brunner/Mazel.

Polster, E., & Polster, M. (1976). Therapy without resistance: Gestalt therapy. In A. Burton (Ed.), *What makes behavior change possible?* New York: Brunner/Mazel.

Provost, J. A. (1999). A dream focus for short-term growth groups. *Journal for Specialists in Group Work, 24*(1), 74–87.

Qualls, S. H., Segal, D. L., Norman, S., Niederehe, G., & Gallagher-Thompson, D. (2002). Psychologists in practice with older adults: Current patterns, sources of training, and need for continuing education. *Professional Psychology: Research and Practice, 33*(5), 435–442.

Rabinowitz, F. E. (2001). Group therapy for men. In G. R. Brooks & G. E. Good (Eds.), *The new handbook of psychotherapy and counseling with men* (Vol. 2, pp. 603–621). San Francisco: Jossey-Bass.

Rabinowitz, F. E., & Cochran, S. V. (2002). *Deepening psychotherapy with men.* Washington, DC: American Psychological Association.

Rapin, L. S. (2004). Guidelines for ethical and legal practice in counseling and psychotherapy groups. In J. L. DeLucia-Waack, D. Gerrity, C. R. Kalodner, & M. T. Riva (Eds.), *Handbook of group counseling and psychotherapy* (pp. 151–165). Thousand Oaks, CA: Sage.

Resnick, B. (1998). Motivating older adults to perform functional activities. *Journal of Gerontological Nursing, 24,* 23–30.

Riva, M. T., & Haub, A. L. (2004). Group counseling in the schools. In J. L. DeLucia-Waack, D. Gerrity, C. R. Kalodner, & M. T. Riva (Eds.), *Handbook of group counseling and psychotherapy* (pp. 309–321). Thousand Oaks, CA: Sage.

Riva, M. T., & Kalodner, C. R. (1997). Group research: Encouraging a collaboration between practitioners and researchers. *Journal for Specialists in Group Work, 22*(4), 226–227.

Riva, M. T., & Korinek, L. (2004). Teaching group work: Modeling group leader and member behaviors in the classroom to demonstrate group theory. *Journal for Specialists in Group Work, 29*(1), 55–63.

Riva, M. T., & Smith, R. D. (1997). Looking into the future of group research: Where do we go from here? *Journal for Specialists in Group Work, 22*(4), 266–276.

Riva, M. T., Wachtel, M., & Lasky, G. B. (2004). Effective leadership in group counseling and psychotherapy: Research and practice. In J. L. DeLucia-Waack, D. Gerrity, C. R. Kalodner, & M. T. Riva (Eds.), *Handbook of group counseling and psychotherapy* (pp. 37–48). Thousand Oaks, CA: Sage.

Robison, F. F., Stockton, R., & Morran, D. K. (1990). Anticipated consequences of self-disclosure during early therapeutic group development. *Journal of Group Psychotherapy, Psychodrama, and Sociometry, 43*(1), 3–18.

Robison, F. F., & Ward, D. (1990). Research activities and attitudes among ASGW members. *Journal for Specialists in Group Work, 19*(4), 215–224.

Rohde, R., & Stockton, R. (1992). The effect of structured feedback on goal attainment, attraction to the group, and satisfaction with the group in small group counseling. *Journal of Group Psychotherapy, Psychodrama, and Sociometry, 44*(4), 172–180.

Rohnke, K. (1984). *Silver bullets: A guide to initiative problems, adventure games, and trust activities.* Dubuque, IA: Kendall/Hunt.

Romano, J. L., & Cikanek, K. L. (2003). Group work and computer applications: Instructional components for graduate students. *Journal for Specialists in Group Work, 28*(1), 23–34.

Rose, S. D. (1989). *Working with adults in groups: Integrating cognitive-behavioral and small group strategies.* San Francisco: Jossey-Bass.

Rose, S. D. (1998). *Group therapy with troubled youth: A cognitive-behavioral interactive approach.* Thousand Oaks, CA: Sage.

Rose, S. D., & Edleson, J. L. (1987). *Working with children and adolescents in groups: A multimethod approach.* San Francisco: Jossey-Bass.

Rose, S. R. (1998). *Group work with children and adolescents: Prevention and intervention in school and community systems.* Thousand Oaks, CA: Sage.

Rosenberg, S., & Wright, P. (1997). Brief group psychotherapy and managed mental health care. In R. M. Alperin & D. G. Phillips (Eds.), *The impact of managed care on the practice of psychotherapy: Innovation, implementation, and controversy* (pp. 105–119). New York: Brunner/Mazel.

Rosenberg, S., & Zimet, C. (1995). Brief group treatment and managed mental health care. *International Journal of Group Psychotherapy, 45,* 367–379.

Rosenthal, H. G. (Ed.). (2001). *Favorite counseling and therapy homework assignments.* Philadelphia, PA: Brunner-Routledge.

Rosenvige, J. H. (1990). Group therapy for anorexic and bulimic patients. *Acta Psychiatrica Scandinavica, 82,* 38–43.

Roth, D. M., & Ross, D. R. (1988). Long-term cognitive-interpersonal group therapy for eating disorders. *International Journal of Group Psychotherapy, 38*(4), 491–510.

Rothke, S. (1986). The role of interpersonal feedback in group psychotherapy. *International Journal of Group Psychotherapy, 36*(2), 225–240.

Rowe, J. W., & Kahn, R. L. (1998). *Successful aging.* New York: Pantheon Books.

Ryan, G., & Lane, S. (1997). *Juvenile sexual offending: Causes, consequences, & correction.* San Francisco: Jossey-Bass.

Schmidt, F., & Friedman, A. (1991). *Creative conflict solving for kids.* Miami, FL: Peace Education Foundation.

Schulthesis, G. M. (1998). *Brief therapy homework planner.* New York: Wiley.

Schwartz, B., & Cellini, H. (1995). *The sex offender: Corrections, treatment and legal practice.* New Jersey: Civic Research Institute.

Schwartz, J. P., & Waldo, M. (2004). Group work with men who have committed partner abuse. In J. L. DeLucia-Waack, D. Gerrity, C. R. Kalodner, & M. T. Riva (Eds.), *Handbook of group counseling and psychotherapy* (pp. 576–592). Thousand Oaks, CA: Sage.

Shapiro, J. L., Peltz, L. S., & Bernadett-Shapiro, S. (1998). *Brief group treatment: Practical training for therapists and counselors.* Pacific Grove, CA: Brooks/Cole.

Shechtman, Z. (2004). Group counseling and psychotherapy with children and adolescents: Current practice and research. In J. L. DeLucia-Waack, D. Gerrity, C. R. Kalodner, & M. T. Riva (Eds.), *Handbook of group counseling and psychotherapy* (pp. 429–444). Thousand Oaks, CA: Sage.

Sheffield, A. (1998). *How you can survive when they're depressed.* New York: Three Rivers Press.

Shelton, J. L., & Levy, R. L. (1981). *Behavioral assignments and treatment compliance: A handbook of clinical strategies.* Champaign, IL: Research Press.

Sinberg, J. (1978). *Divorce is a grown-up problem.* New York: Avon.

Singer, V. I., Tracz, S. M., & Dworkin, S. H. (1991). Reminiscence group therapy: A treatment modality for older adults. *Journal for Specialists in Group Work, 16*(3), 167–171.

Sklare, G., Keener, R., & Mas, C. (1990). Preparing members for here-and-now group counseling. *Journal for Specialists in Group Work, 15*(3), 141–148.

Sklare, G., Petrosko, J., & Howell, S. (1993). The effect of pregroup training on members' level of anxiety. *Journal for Specialists in Group Work, 18*(3), 109–114.

Smead, R. (1995). *Skills and techniques for group work with children and adolescents.* Champaign, IL: Research Press.

Smead Morganett, R. (1994). *Skills for living: Group counseling activities for elementary students.* Champaign, IL: Research Press.

Smokowski, P. R. (2003). Beyond role-playing: Using technology to enhance modeling and behavioral rehearsal in group work practice. *Journal for Specialists in Group Work, 28*(1), 9–22.

Sonstegard, M. A., & Bitter, J. R., with Pelonis, P. (2004). *Adlerian group counseling and therapy: Step-by-step.* New York: Brunner-Routledge (Tayler & Francis).

Spinal-Robinson, P., & Wickham, R. E. (1992a). *Flips flops: A workbook for children who have been sexually abused.* Notre Dame, IN: Jalice Publishers.

Spinal-Robinson, P., & Wickham, R. E. (1992b). *Cartwheels: A workbook for children who have been sexually abused.* Notre Dame, IN: Jalice Publishers.

Spinal-Robinson, P., & Wickham, R. E. (1993). *High tops: A workbook for teens who have been sexually abused.* Notre Dame, IN: Jalice Publishers.

Stewart, G. M., & Gregory, B. C. (1996). Themes of a long-term AIDS support group for gay men. *The Counseling Psychologist, 24,* 285–303.

Stockton, R., & Hulse, D. (1981). Developing cohesion in small groups: Theory and research. *Journal for Specialists in Group Work, 6*(4), 188–194.

Stockton, R., & Morran, D. K. (1982). Review and perspective of critical dimensions in therapeutic small group research. In G. M. Gazda (Ed.), *Basic approaches to group psychotherapy and group counseling* (3rd ed., pp. 37–85). Springfield, IL: Charles C Thomas.

Stockton, R., Morran, D. K., & Harris, M. (1991). Factors influencing group member acceptance of corrective feedback. *Journal for Specialists in Group Work, 16*(4), 246–254.

Stockton, R., Morran, D. K., & Krieger, K. M. (2004). An overview of current research and best practices for training beginning group leaders. In J. L. DeLucia-Waack, D. Gerrity, C. R. Kalodner, & M. T. Riva (Eds.), *Handbook of group counseling and psychotherapy* (pp. 65–75). Thousand Oaks, CA: Sage.

Stockton, R., & Toth, P. L. (1997). Applying a general research training model to group work. *Journal for Specialists in Group Work, 22*(4), 241–252.

Sue, D. W. (1990). Culture-specific strategies in counseling: A conceptual framework. *Professional Psychology: Research and Practice, 21*(6), 424–433.

Sue, D. W., Arredondo, P., & McDavis, R. J. (1992). Multicultural counseling competencies and standards: A call to the profession. *Journal of Counseling and Development, 70*(4), 477–486.

Sue, D. W., Ivey, A. E., & Pedersen, P. (1996). *Multicultural counseling and therapy.* Pacific Grove, CA: Brooks/Cole.

Sue, D. W., & Sue, D. (2003). *Counseling the culturally diverse: Theory and practice* (4th ed.). New York: Wiley.

Surrey, J. (1997). What do we mean by mutuality in therapy? In J. Jordan (Ed.), *Women's growth in diversity: More writings from the Stone Center* (pp. 42–49). New York: Guilford.

Sweeney, D. S., & Homeyer, L. E. (Eds.). (1999). *The handbook of group play therapy.* San Francisco: Jossey-Bass.

Tedeschi, R. G., & Calhoun, L. G. (1993). Using the support group to respond to the isolation of bereavement. *Journal of Mental Health Counseling, 15*(1), 47.

Thompson, C. L., Rudolph, L. B., & Henderson, D. A. (2004). *Counseling children* (6th ed.). Belmont, CA: Brooks/Cole.

Thompson, E. H., & Doll, W. (1982). The burden of families coping with the mentally ill: An invisible crisis. *Family Relations, 31,* 379–388.

Thompson, N., & Renninger, S. (1995). Short-term group treatment for survivors of sexual abuse: A psychoeducational approach. *Directions in Mental Health Counseling, 5*(6), 4–11.

Thorngren, J. M., Christensen, T. M., & Kleist, D. M. (1998). Multiple-family group treatment: The under-explored therapy. *The Family Journal: Counseling and Therapy for Couples and Families,* 125–131.

Thorngren, J. M., & Kleist, D. M. (2002). Multiple family group therapy: An interpersonal/postmodern approach. *The Family Journal: Counseling and Therapy for Couples and Families, 10*(2), 167–176.

Torres-Rivera, E., Garrett, M. T., & Crutchfield, L. B. (2004). Multicultural interventions in groups: The use of indigenous methods. In J. L. DeLucia-Waack, D. Gerrity, C. R. Kalodner, & M. T. Riva (Eds.), *Handbook of group counseling and psychotherapy* (pp. 295–306). Thousand Oaks, CA: Sage.

Torres-Rivera, E., Wilbur, M. P., Roberts-Wilbur, J., & Phan, L. (1999). Group work with Latino clients: A psychoeducational model. *Journal for Specialists in Group Work, 24*(4), 383–404.

Toseland, R. W., & Rivas, R. F. (2001). *An introduction to group work practice* (4th ed.). Boston: Allyn & Bacon.

Tyson, L. E., Whitledge, J., & Perusse, R. (2004). *Critical incidents in group counseling.* Alexandria, VA: American Counseling Association.

Ullman, M. (1996). *Appreciating dreams: A group approach.* Thousand Oaks, CA: Sage.

U. S. Bureau of the Census. (1996). *Population projections of the United States by age, sex, race, and Hispanic origin: 1995 to 2050* (Current Population Reports, P25-1130). Washington, DC: U.S. Government Printing Office.

Vacha-Haase, T., Ness, C. M., Dannison, L., & Smith, A. (2000). Grandparents raising grandchildren: A psychoeducational group approach. *Journal for Specialists in Group Work, 25*(1), 67–78.

Van Velsor, P. (2004). Training for successful group work with children. *What* and *how* to teach. *Journal for Specialists in Group Work, 29*(1), 137–147.

Vergeer, G. W. (1995). Therapeutic applications of humor. *Directions in Mental Health Counseling, 5*(3), 1–11.

Villa, V. (1999). The demography, health and economic status of minority elderly populations: Implications for aging programs and services. *Journal of Geriatric Case Management, 18*(2), 5–8.

Wexler, D. B. (2000). *Domestic violence: Group leader's manual.* New York: Norton.

Whisman, M. A., & Bruce, M. L. (1999). Marital dissatisfaction and incidence of major depressive episode in a community sample. *Journal of Abnormal Psychology, 108,* 674–678.

Williams, C. B., Frame, M. W., & Green, E. (1999). Counseling groups for African American women: A focus on spirituality. *Journal for Specialists in Group Work, 24*(3), 260–273.

Williamson, L. R. (1990). *I survived the divorce monster.* Doylestown, PA: Marco Products.

Wilson, F. R., Rapin, L. S., & Haley-Banez, L. (2004). How teaching group work can be guided by foundational documents: Best practice guidelines, diversity principles, training standards. *Journal for Specialists in Group Work, 29*(1), 19–29.

Winslade, J., Crocket, K., & Monk, G. (1997). The therapeutic relationship. In G. Monk, J. Winslade, K. Crocket, & D. Epston (Eds.), *Narrative therapy in practice: The archaeology of hope* (pp. 53–81). San Francisco: Jossey-Bass.

Worden, J. W. (2002). *Grief counseling and grief therapy: A handbook for the mental health practitioner* (3rd ed.). New York: Springer.

Wyatt, G., & Powell, G. (1988). *Lasting effects of child sexual abuse.* Newbury Park: Sage.

Yalom, I. D. (1980). *Existential psychotherapy.* New York: Basic Books.

Yalom, I. D. (1983). *Inpatient group psychotherapy.* New York: Basic Books.

Yalom, I. D. (1995). *The theory and practice of group psychotherapy* (4th ed.). New York: Basic Books.

Yalom, I. D., & Vinogradov, S. (1988). Bereavement groups: Techniques and themes. *International Journal of Group Psychotherapy, 38*(4), 419–446.

Yu, A., & Gregg, C. H. (1993). Asians in groups: More than a matter of cultural awareness. *Journal for Specialists in Group Work, 18*(2), 86–93.

Zimpfer, D. G. (1991). Groups for grief and survivorship after bereavement: A review. *Journal for Specialists in Group Work, 16*(1), 46–55.

Names Index

Subject Index

TO THE OWNER OF THIS BOOK:

I hope that you have found *Groups: Process and Practice, Seventh Edition*, useful. So that this book can be improved in a future edition, would you take the time to complete this sheet and return it? Thank you.

School and address:_____

Department:_____

Instructor's name:_____

1. What I like most about this book is:_____

_____

_____

2. What I like least about this book is: _____

_____

_____

3. My general reaction to this book is: _____

_____

_____

4. The name of the course in which I used this book is: _____

_____

5. Were all of the chapters of the book assigned for you to read?_____

   If not, which ones weren't?_____

6. In the space below, or on a separate sheet of paper, please write specific suggestions for improving this book and anything else you'd care to share about your experience in using this book.

_____

_____

_____

THOMSON

BROOKS/COLE

BUSINESS REPLY MAIL
FIRST-CLASS MAIL   PERMIT NO. 34   BELMONT CA

POSTAGE WILL BE PAID BY ADDRESSEE

Attn: *Counseling/Marquita Flemming*

BrooksCole/Thomson Learning
10 Davis Drive
Belmont, CA   94002-9801

OPTIONAL:

Your name: _____ Date: _____

May we quote you, either in promotion for *Groups: Process and Practice, Seventh Edition*, or in future publishing ventures?

Yes: _____ No: _____

Sincerely yours,

Marianne Schneider Corey

Gerald Corey